Democratization and Authoritarianism
in the Arab World

A *Journal of Democracy* Book

•

SELECTED BOOKS IN THE SERIES

Edited by Larry Diamond and Marc F. Plattner

Will China Democratize? (2013)
(with Andrew J. Nathan)

Democracy in East Asia: A New Century (2013)
(with Yun-han Chu)

Liberation Technology: Social Media and the Struggle for Democracy (2012)

Poverty, Inequality, and Democracy (2012)
(with Francis Fukuyama)

Debates on Democratization (2010)

Democratization in Africa: Progress and Retreat (2010)

Democracy: A Reader (2009)

How People View Democracy (2008)

Latin America's Struggle for Democracy (2008)
(with Diego Abente Brun)

The State of India's Democracy (2007)
(with Sumit Ganguly)

Electoral Systems and Democracy (2006)

Assessing the Quality of Democracy (2005)
(Edited by Larry Diamond and Leonardo Morlino)

World Religions and Democracy (2005)
(with Philip J. Costopoulos)

Islam and Democracy in the Middle East (2003)
(with Daniel Brumberg)

Emerging Market Democracies: East Asia & Latin America (2002)
(Edited by Laurence Whitehead)

Democracy after Communism (2002)

Published under the auspices of
the International Forum for Democratic Studies

Democratization and Authoritarianism in the Arab World

Edited by Larry Diamond and Marc F. Plattner

Johns Hopkins University Press

Baltimore

9 8 7 6 5 4 3 2 1

Chapters in this volume appeared in the following issues of the *Journal of Democracy*: chapters 1 and 17, April 2012; chapter 2, July 2012; chapters 3,4, and 20, January 2013; chapters 5 and 8, April 2013; chapters 6 and 10, October 2012; chapter 7, January 2011; chapters 9, 25, 26, and 28, July 2013; chapters 11, 21–24, October 2013; chapters 12, 13, 14, 15, and 29, October 2011.

For all reproduction rights, please contact the Johns Hopkins University Press.

Johns Hopkins University Press
2715 North Charles Street
Baltimore, Maryland 21218-4363
www.press.jhu.edu

Library of Congress Cataloging-in-Publication Data

Democratization and authoritarianism in the Arab world / edited by Larry Diamond and Marc F. Plattner.
    pages cm
  Includes bibliographical references and index.
   ISBN 978-1-4214-1416-4 (pbk. : alk. paper) — ISBN 978-1-4214-1417-1 (electronic) — ISBN 1-4214-1416-3 (pbk. : alk. paper) — ISBN 1-4214-1417-1 (electronic) 1. Democratization—Arab countries—History—21st century. 2. Authoritarianism—Arab countries—History—21st century. 3. Arab Spring, 2010– 4. Islam and politics—21st century. I. Diamond, Larry Jay. II. Plattner, Marc F., 1945–

  JQ1850.A91D466 2013
  320.917'4927—dc23

                                  2013043027

The photograph on the cover depicts street art by Egyptian artist Adham Bakry calling for the arrest of Safwat El-Sherif, the former head of Egypt's ruling National Democratic Party (NDP). Following President Hosni Mubarak's ouster, Egyptian protesters pushed for the arrest of Sherif and other associates of Mubarak. Sherif was arrested several months after Egypt's uprising on corruption charges but was later released on bail. Further angering his opponents, he and a number of other high-level NDP operatives were acquitted of charges of ordering attacks on protesters during the 2 February 2011 "Battle of the Camel." (The text to the right of El-Sherif's image is an unrelated warning about nearby electrical wiring.)

Bakry's work can be viewed at his website, *http://abakry.com*.

CONTENTS

Acknowledgments   vii

Introduction
Larry Diamond, Marc F. Plattner, and Nate Grubman   xi

I. Thematic Essays

1. The Languages of the Arab Revolutions
Abdou Filali-Ansary   3

2. The Transformation of the Arab World
Olivier Roy   15

3. Arab Democracy or Islamist Revolution?
Hillel Fradkin   29

4. There Will Be No Islamist Revolution
Olivier Roy   38

5. Islamists and Democracy: Cautions from Pakistan
Husain Haqqani   44

6. New Findings on Arabs and Democracy
Mark Tessler, Amaney Jamal, and Michael Robbins   54

7. The Split in Arab Culture
Hicham Ben Abdallah El Alaoui   69

8. Democratization Theory and the "Arab Spring"
Alfred Stepan and Juan J. Linz   81

9. Transforming the Arab World's Protection-Racket Politics
Daniel Brumberg   96

10. Resilient Royals: How Arab Monarchies Hang On
Sean L. Yom and F. Gregory Gause III   112

11. Why the Modest Harvest?
Jason Brownlee, Tarek Masoud, and Andrew Reynolds   127

12. The Global Context
Marc F. Plattner   143

13. The Lessons of 1989
Lucan Way   151

14. The Role of the Military
Zoltan Barany   162

15. The Impact of Election Systems
John M. Carey and Andrew Reynolds   174

16. The Role of Digital Media
Philip N. Howard and Muzammil M. Hussain   186

II. Country Studies

17. Ben Ali's Fall
Peter J. Schraeder and Hamadi Redissi   203

18. Tunisia's Transition and the "Twin Tolerations"
Alfred Stepan   218

19. The Road to (and from) Liberation Square
Tarek Masoud   233

20. Egypt: Why Liberalism Still Matters
Michele Dunne and Tarek Radwan   248

21. Egypt's Failed Transition
Nathan J. Brown   263

22. Yemen Changes Everything . . . and Nothing
April Longley Alley   277

23. Libya Starts from Scratch
Mieczysław P. Boduszyński and Duncan Pickard   289

24. Syria and the Future of Authoritarianism
Steven Heydemann   300

25. Bahrain's Decade of Discontent
Frederic Wehrey   315

26. Algeria versus the Arab Spring
Frédéric Volpi   326

27. Morocco: Outfoxing the Opposition
Ahmed Benchemsi   338

28. Jordan: The Ruse of Reform
Sean L. Yom   351

29. Is Saudi Arabia Immune?
Stéphane Lacroix   364

Index   377

ACKNOWLEDGMENTS

A decade has elapsed since the publication in 2003 of *Islam and Democracy in the Middle East,* the last *Journal of Democracy* book to focus on this region. Many of the essays in that earlier volume had sought to address the pressing question of why the Middle East had proven to be such inhospitable soil for democracy. In subsequent years, the *Journal* published several new articles exploring why the Arab world, in particular, had been so resistant to democratization.

Then suddenly in 2011, a tidal wave of protest emerged that quickly engulfed much of the Arab world. In a number of key countries, long-standing autocratic rulers were toppled, though thus far progress in building democratic regimes to replace them has been disappointing. Yet the impressive scale of the demands for democratization has cast a wholly new light on the region's prospects. The *Journal* has covered developments in the Arab world extensively since the protests began, and the volume that you hold in your hands gathers an entirely new selection of essays to explore the dramatically reshaped political landscape.

We first wish to thank the *Journal of Democracy* staff, who began work on *Democratization and Authoritarianism in the Arab World* while they were still completing our previous volume for Johns Hopkins University Press (*Will China Democratize?*); they did a remarkable job of carrying out both these book projects despite the simultaneous demands of the quarterly publication schedule of the *Journal* itself.

The lucid and readable prose in the chapters that follow owes much to the efforts of Executive Editor Phil Costopoulos and Senior Editor Tracy Brown. As always, Managing Editor Brent Kallmer handled the layout and production of this (and concurrent projects) with great flexibility and skill. Assistant Editor Nate Grubman made an especially important contribution to the preparation of this volume, as has been recognized by his listing as a coauthor of the Introduction. Finally, Dorothy Warner assembled the Index—perhaps the most comprehensive ever to appear in a *Journal of Democracy* book—with character-istic precision.

We are also indebted to our colleagues at the Johns Hopkins University Press—our book editor Suzanne Flinchbaugh, as well as Bill Breichner and Carol Hamblen of the Journals Division. Suzanne deserves special credit for conceiving the new cover-design concept that has enlivened the last few volumes in the *Journal of Democracy* book series.

We cannot conclude without again thanking the Lynde and Harry Bradley Foundation for their longstanding support for the *Journal of Democracy*. And it is a pleasure to express once more our appreciation to President Carl Gershman and the Board of Directors of the National Endowment for Democracy for the steadfast support that they have provided over many years to the International Forum for Democratic Studies and the *Journal of Democracy*.

—Marc F. Plattner and Larry Diamond

INTRODUCTION

Larry Diamond, Marc F. Plattner, and Nate Grubman

It had become commonplace to remark that the Arab countries constituted the only major world region largely impervious to the "third
wave" of democratization, which began in 1974 and over the following
decades brought down scores of authoritarian rulers throughout most of
the world. This impression of "Arab exceptionalism" seemed to change
dramatically, however, when the self-immolation of a fruit vendor in the
city of Sidi Bouzid in December 2010 sparked a series of popular uprisings within Tunisia that quickly spilled over into other countries in the
region. Strikingly, the protesters mostly invoked not religious, sectarian, or anti-Western themes, but universal principles of human dignity,
freedom, and democracy.

Within a month, longtime Tunisian dictator Zine al-Abidine Ben Ali
was ousted from power. Less than a month after that, Egyptian dictator Hosni Mubarak was forced to step down after almost thirty years at
the helm. And following a civil war and NATO intervention in Libya,
strongman Muammar Qadhafi was toppled as well.

Large popular protests also broke out in other Arab countries: Yemen, where longtime president Ali Abdallah Saleh finally agreed to
resign in accordance with a plan negotiated by the Gulf Cooperation
Council (GCC), and a national-dialogue conference is under way; Bahrain, where a GCC military intervention helped to preserve the status
quo in the face of massive protests; Syria, where Bashar al-Assad's regime still survives as a brutal civil war rages; Morocco, where reforms
put forward by the king and approved by a popular referendum helped
to quiet protests at least for a while; Algeria, where a combination of repression and financial inducements preserved the regime in power; and,
on a smaller scale, even Saudi Arabia and some of its Gulf neighbors,
where generous new government-funded benefits helped to forestall the
growth of unrest.

This chain of events, which became widely referred to as the "Arab
Spring," occurred with extraordinary rapidity, and its ramifications are
far from over. Efforts to build democracy continue in those states—
Tunisia, Egypt, Libya, and Yemen—that succeeded in bringing down

their authoritarian rulers, but these transitions have been encountering not only surprising twists and turns but some massive bumps in the road. We are still in the middle of the story, or quite possibly even in its early chapters. So it is a somewhat rash undertaking to offer an edited volume on this topic when so much is still in flux.

The articles gathered here originally appeared in the *Journal of Democracy,* all but one in July 2011 or later—that is, after the Arab Spring had begun.[1] The *Journal* has devoted many of its pages to the region during these past three years, and within the limits of a quarterly publication, we have tried to make our coverage as timely as possible. But that also means that some of the essays in this collection, which were published at earlier stages of the Arab Spring, may now appear in some respects outdated. (The issue of the *Journal* in which a chapter originally appeared is noted at the outset of each essay.) Nonetheless, we believe not only that the slightly older essays contain much analysis that is still valuable, but also that their inclusion here will help readers to see how various developments during the Arab Spring were regarded at the time they occurred. In spite of the difficulties of dealing with a moving target, we concluded that it was important to make available a book on this subject at a time when readers (and teachers) are eager for materials offering serious analysis of these remarkable changes in the Arab world.

The Legacies of Authoritarian Rule

As the essays in this volume demonstrate, the Arab Spring both reflected and accelerated a significant shift in the political culture of the Arab world. Evidence of this shift had been gathering for many years in advance of the eruption of prodemocracy protests in Tunisia in December 2010. Intellectually, a variety of justifications for authoritarian rule—anticolonial, developmental, socialist, Marxist, and Arab-nationalist, among others—had gradually fallen by the wayside. So had the willingness to excuse or legitimate authoritarian rule on the basis of the charismatic leadership of an individual such as Qadhafi. In place of a lot of failed "isms," there emerged a new explanation for stagnation in the Arab world—namely, that the absence of freedom and the dearth of genuine means for holding political leaders accountable had led Arab societies to a profound developmental cul-de-sac. Arab scholars, thinkers, and civil society activists from diverse ideological orientations (aside from extreme Islamists who rejected the legitimacy of any political authority not strictly based on the word and will of Allah) became increasingly outspoken about the need for democratic reform. In the first *Arab Human Development Report* in 2002, a team of Arab scholars identified the "freedom deficit" as a barrier to "human development." [2] They observed:

> There can be no real prospects for reforming the system of governance, or for truly liberating human capabilities, in the absence of comprehensive political representation in effective legislatures based on free, honest, efficient, and regular elections. If the people's preferences are to be properly expressed and their interests properly protected, governance must become truly representative and fully accountable.[3]

Well before the Arab Spring, exhaustion with authoritarian rule was also spreading, particularly in the largest Arab country, Egypt. Six years before the January 25 Revolution (marking the date on which Egypt's 2011 uprising began), there had emerged a protest movement—Kifaya (Enough)—that demanded an end to the indefinite reelection of President Hosni Mubarak and a cessation of the apparent campaign to smooth the path for his son Gamal to succeed him. By mid-2005, many Egyptians were openly calling for Mubarak's ouster, and a combination of societal mobilization and U.S. pressure forced the dictator to allow a multicandidate (though still not free and fair) presidential election that September. Two and a half years later, a new generation of Internet-savvy youth activists rallied behind aggrieved Egyptian workers to organize a general strike on 6 April 2008, stunning the regime and badly denting its legitimacy and self-confidence.

While Egypt led the way in protests, it was not alone. Shortly after the assassination by car bomb of Lebanese prime minister Rafik Hariri in February 2005, tens and later hundreds of thousands of demonstrators took to the streets of Beirut to demand the withdrawal of Syrian forces. Rallying under the banner of "Freedom, Sovereignty, Independence," the protestors compelled the withdrawal of Syrian troops and then in midyear elections helped Hariri allies win control of government. Shortly after this "Cedar Revolution" in Lebanon, about fifty-thousand demonstrators in tiny Bahrain (population 1.2 million) turned out to demand constitutional reform of the country's authoritarian monarchy, and protests continued to erupt repeatedly thereafter.

These stirrings of popular mobilization for democratic change were beaten back by intensified repression in Egypt and elsewhere. But they were also deflated by sobering demonstration effects from other Arab experiments with "democracy." In Iraq, the overthrow of the region's most ruthless dictatorship by a U.S. invasion was seen as bringing not greater political freedom and choice but rather sectarian polarization, economic chaos, and civil war (which was claiming the lives of a hundred Iraqis a day by early 2007). In Egypt, Jordan, Algeria, and Yemen, autocracies that had cautiously granted more political space to the opposition as a periodic gesture of what Daniel Brumberg has called "tactical liberalization"[4] now eagerly seized back that recently opened real estate, pointing to the chaos in Iraq. Arab autocrats warned the West and key constituencies in their own societies that the big beneficiaries of any further political opening would be Islamist political parties. Apparently bolstering this argument were the strong showing of the Muslim Brotherhood in Egypt's November 2005 parliamentary elections, the victory (albeit with less than 45 percent of the vote) of the militant Islamist movement Hamas in the January 2006 elections for the Palestinian Legislative Council, and the electoral strength of both Sunni and Shia Islamists in Iraq, Kuwait, and Bahrain.

These setbacks, however, do not appear to have altered the deeper currents of cultural change in the Arab world. What evidence we have of mass public opinion indicates a surprisingly widespread general aspiration for democracy, first measured systematically in the Arab Barometer surveys of 2006–2007 and confirmed by the second-round surveys four years later. As Mark Tessler, Amaney Jamal, and Michael Robbins note in chapter 6, not only has public support for "a democratic system of government" been remarkably high (between 83 and 96 percent) across a number of countries in North Africa and the Middle East, but these high levels have been sustained between the earlier stirrings of protest in 2006–2007 and the onset of the Arab Spring in 2010–11. Of course, this is not the whole story. The Arab Barometer also found persistent and broad (even overwhelming) agreement that "reform should proceed gradually," as well as limited (and between the two rounds of surveys, declining) support for basic premises of political Islam. It also revealed other aspects of Arab political culture, such as generally low trust and civic engagement, that are unfavorable for democracy.

We thus should not underestimate how hard it will be to overcome the legacies of authoritarian rule. In fact, the more extreme the tyranny, the more difficult it proves for society to establish key cultural foundations of democracy such as trust, tolerance, broad participation, and a strong inclination to keep politics peaceful. The more extreme the tyranny, the more difficult it is to topple it without violence, and the more likely the state is to shatter completely when the dictatorship falls. Iraq and Libya both confront the fundamental dilemma of all postconflict transitions: No country can have a democratic state unless it first has a state that commands a monopoly over the means of organized violence. Should Syria's civil war end with the toppling of the Assad regime or its negotiated exit, the new regime in Syria will face this same existential challenge.

More generally, democratic change following decades of authoritarian rule is rarely swift and certain. Where there is little experience with democracy and an absence of other facilitating conditions—a large middle class, moderate levels of inequality, high levels of education, and a

TABLE—REGIME CLASSIFICATION AND FREEDOM HOUSE SCORES OF 16 ARAB COUNTRIES, 2010–12

Regime Type (2012)	Countries	FH Score for 2010		FH Score for 2012	
		PR	CL	PR	CL
Electoral Democracy	Tunisia	7	5	3 ▲	4 ▲
Electoral Authoritarian	Lebanon	5	3	5	4 ▼
	Iraq	5	6	6 ▼	6
	Libya	7	7	4 ▲	5
	Egypt	6	5	5 ▲	5
	Yemen	6	5	6	6 ▼
Competitive Monarchy	Kuwait	4	5 ▼	5 ▼	5
	Morocco	5	4	5	4
Authoritarian Monarchy	Bahrain	6	5	6	6 ▼
	UAE	6	5	6	6
	Oman	6	5	6	5
	Qatar	6	5	6	5
	Jordan	6	5	6	5
	Saudi Arabia	7	6	7	7 ▼
Civil-War State	Syria	7	6	7	7 ▼

Note: Regime classifications are our own. PR and CL stand for Political Rights and Civil Liberties, respectively; 1 represents the most-free and 7 the least-free rating.

▲ ▼ indicate a change in PR or CL ratings since the last survey.

democratic neighborhood—the struggle to build democracy is likely to be difficult and protracted. In two-thirds of the Arab states, heavy dependence on oil and gas revenues adds another severe handicap, swelling the state, distorting the economy, and stunting the emergence of citizenship. Given these hurdles, there are various ways in which a country in transition may fall short of attaining democracy: It may experience a messy period of "competitive authoritarianism"; it may fall victim to a restoration of the old regime; it may suffer a military coup; and violent conflict is yet another possibility. As we see in the Table above, according to Freedom House a few Arab countries improved their levels of political rights and civil liberties during the first two years of the Arab Spring, but seven countries saw a decline in freedom during this period versus just three that realized a gain.

Tunisia stands out for having achieved the most successful transition of any Arab country thus far. Freedom House, in its 2012 and 2013 year-end surveys of *Freedom in the World*, has classified it as a democracy.[5] Yet as we completed work on this volume in late 2013, Tunisians still had not forged an agreement on their constitutional future, and even this most promising of all the Arab transitions remained stuck in a period of tension and uncertainty. The other case of success in peacefully toppling autocracy, Egypt, flipped backward into failure as a result of the authoritarian excesses of both elected Islamist president Mohamed Morsi and the military, which on 3 July 2013 removed the president and suspended the constitution in response to massive anti-Morsi public protests. While some kind of constitutional veneer may soon be restored in Egypt, the effort to build democracy there appears to have been set back by many years.

Several other regimes in the region hold competitive multiparty elections with some degree of uncertainty as to the results. But in each case the system falls well short of democracy. Libya has political pluralism, but the Libyan state lacks sufficient authority. Lebanon may come closest, but its political landscape is distorted by coercion, regional interference, and entrenched sectarianism. Iraq might have moved toward greater democracy, but under Prime Minister Nuri al-Maliki it has instead sunk deeper into authoritarian and sectarian patterns. Of the monarchies, Morocco is the most liberal, but as Ahmed Benchemsi maintains in chapter 27, recent political reforms have not altered the fundamental logic of kingly rule, which remains ultimately unaccountable to the people or the rule of law. Yemen could reach democracy if its national dialogue proves able to broker a viable constitutional agreement regarding the country's political structure and the division of power among geographic regions and groups. But as April Longley Alley argues in chapter 22, this imperative faces formidable challenges.

If there is one thing that the Arab Spring has taught us, however, it is to allow for the element of surprise. Despite the rising frequency of prodemocracy protests in the Arab world in the first decade of this century, few analysts foresaw that popular revolutions would topple four Arab autocrats at the start of its second decade. In the wake of the Arab Spring, many authoritarian regimes may endure for some time to come, but they seem unlikely to enjoy the levels of stability and acceptance that they once did. The course of democratic protest and change in the Arab world is still in its very early stages.

Islam and Democracy

This volume consists of two parts: The first half contains sixteen chapters that offer a regionwide analysis of what has been transpiring in the Arab world. A number of them focus on the role of Islam and ask what it means if Islamist parties come to power. Others focus on the differences among Arab states and seek causes and patterns that will help to explain why events have unfolded so differently in various countries. Some focus on culture and public opinion in the Arab world. Still others trace the role of particular factors such as digital media, military and security forces, or electoral systems. And several compare the Arab Spring to earlier historical examples of rapidly spreading international revolts such as the revolutions of 1848 and 1989 in Europe.

The second half of this volume takes a case-study approach via thirteen chapters, each of which examines developments in a specific Arab country. As might be expected, multiple chapters are devoted to Tunisia and Egypt, the two countries that launched the Arab Spring, but most of the major Arab states receive a chapter of their own.[6]

Part I opens with a series of chapters analyzing the relationship between Islam and democracy in the context of the Arab Spring. In the opening chapter, Abdou Filali-Ansary writes that the Arabs have begun to speak "a new language of politics." With the diffusion of this language—replete with references to democracy, human rights, civil society, and states bound by the rule of law—democratic legitimacy has become the only type of political authority that Arab peoples now accept. In the context of this new language, the rise of political Islam and the calls for *shari'a* (Islamic law) that have accompanied it may appear incongruous. After all, as Filali-Ansary concedes, some who call for *shari'a* have a very narrow interpretation of the word that contradicts the emergent democratic spirit: They view it as a "catalogue of prescriptions" delineated by "an uncritical and closed-minded brand of traditional religious scholarship." But to others, *shari'a* takes on a far broader meaning in the context of Muslim and Arab history: a system that has protected citizens from arbitrary or despotic rule by binding the hands of the ruler. In this sense, the call for *shari'a* is a cry for "basic decency," and the rise of political Islamists, who suffered great repression under the region's strongmen in the aftermath of what appeared to be secular uprisings, is not so surprising. While Filali-Ansary contends that democratic legitimacy is the only kind that has broad appeal today, he warns that this does not preclude the return of some sort of *Weltanschauung* politics in the future, imposed either by Islamists or by intolerant secularists.

The period that has followed the Arab uprisings has been punctuated by alternating moments of great hope and deep despair. But as Olivier Roy writes in chapter 2, "something irreversible did happen in the Arab Spring" and "democratization is becoming rooted in Arab societies." Demographic and technological changes have allowed young people to acquire greater education, to connect with one another, and to challenge traditional norms of societal organization. According to Roy, "The new generation calls for debate, freedom, democracy, and good governance," rather than for a charismatic leader claiming exclusive access to the road to utopia. This means that not only would a modern-day Gamal Abdel Nasser have trouble rising to power but an Arab Khomeini as well. Religion has become more of a personal choice, and the realm of Islam has become more pluralistic. To Egypt's Muslim Brotherhood, salafists are not faithful foot soldiers in the political struggle against secularists; rather, they are potential political rivals within the broad tent of political Islam. Given these changes, even Islamists who may see democracy less as a desirable political system than as a vehicle by which an Islamic state may be reached are likely to find themselves constrained and forced to play by democracy's rules. Lacking a security apparatus or, especially in Egypt or Tunisia, the rents to build one powerful enough to impose their agenda on an unwilling society, Islamists have few alternatives to turning their movements into political parties, seeking to broaden their constituencies, eschewing dogma for values-based appeals, and consistently defending democracy as an institution. In Roy's words, "Islamists have changed, or at least they have understood that the world has changed."

In chapter 3, Hillel Fradkin disputes this notion, writing that the factors binding Islamists to democracy may not be as constricting as Roy portrays them. Indeed, as Fradkin argues, Egypt's revolutionary condition ensures that the contours of its political system are still very much under negotiation (Fradkin was writing before the July 2013 coup that unseated Morsi). During its time in power, the Muslim Brotherhood showed an ability to reshape its political environment. In the end, Fradkin argues, the Brotherhood's ability to manipulate the constraints upon it and shape the revolution will depend on "how well [Brotherhood leaders] understand the politically relevant terrain, how intelligent they are in exploiting it, and how much in the way of resources they can bring to bear." Fradkin concedes that Egyptian society might be changing in a way that makes impossible the Brotherhood's goal of establishing an Islamist state. Even at the apex of its power, however, the organization offered no indication that it intended to abandon its strategy, organization, or mission of establishing an Islamic government. Absent these indications, the commitment of Islamists to democracy as a desirable system of government will always be shrouded in doubt.

In chapter 4, Roy responds that the Brotherhood, despite its stated ideology, is more of a conservative organization than a revolutionary movement. As Roy writes, "Seventy years of cautious politics hardly qualify a movement as revolutionary." The Brotherhood at times earned the tacit acceptance of past Egyptian governments partially because it never seemed bent on rocking the boat. Its apparent surprise at the January 25 uprising against President Hosni Mubarak shows that revolution in pursuit of an Islamic state was at most on the backburner. While the Brotherhood displayed a taste for power, it did not, according to Roy, pursue the kinds of revolutionary changes to Egypt's laws and institutions that might establish an Islamic government. Its members continue to refer to the group's historical strategy and mission, but "there is a growing discrepancy between ideological references and real practices." In Roy's view, even a Brotherhood that could hold on to power would have little chance of making Egypt go the way of Iran. The Brotherhood had no charismatic leader to play the role of Khomeini, and it controlled no security apparatus to rival Iran's Revolutionary Guard. Perhaps most important, "all political leaders at the very least pay lip service to democracy." According to Roy, the Muslim Brotherhood had no designs for dramatically altering a society in which it was deeply rooted; as the society moved in a more pluralistic, democracy-friendly direction, so too would the Brotherhood.

In chapter 5, Husain Haqqani draws on Pakistan's experience to shed light on the debate about Islamists and democracy. Haqqani argues that Islamists tend to see democracy simply as majority rule, an especially problematic take on this form of government in societies with sizeable ethnic and religious minorities and high levels of polarization. In Egypt and Tunisia, Islamist leaders may talk as if they harbor an unwavering commitment to democracy, even if in the future democratic institutions might allow popularly elected secularist leaders to pass laws that contradict Islamic law. But as long as Islamists are holding the reins of power, such talk is cheap. For Haqqani, "the real test of the Islamists' commitment to democracy will come not while they are in power for the first time, but when they lose subsequent elections." The historical ambivalence of Islamists toward participating in democratic politics offers little indication as to how they will handle this test. The experience of Pakistan—the only country in which governing Islamists were ousted at the ballot box—offers little reason for optimism. Confined to the opposition by a string of electoral defeats since General Muhammad Zia ul-Haq's Islamist-friendly regime ended in 1988, Pakistan's Islamists have resorted to galvanizing their supporters to apply extralegal pressure—violent protests, assassinations, and coups—to ensure that elected leaders maintain Islamic laws. As Haqqani concludes, "There are legitimate grounds to suspect that what mainstream Islamists actually seek is a dictatorship of the pious."

Public Opinion and Culture

The longer-term prospects of democratization in the Arab world will hinge on the depth and breadth of support for democracy among the region's citizens. In chapter 6, Mark Tessler, Amaney Jamal, and Michael Robbins analyze the results of two recent waves of the Arab Barometer public-opinion survey, the first conducted in 2006–2007 and the second in 2011–12. The authors find that popular support for democracy has been consistently robust, exceeding 80 percent in every country in which the survey was administered. Drilling further down, however, they note that some of the norms critical to a democratic society—trust, political interest, and involvement in political and civil society organizations—enjoy comparatively tepid support. It is unclear whether these attitudes have fostered authoritarianism or whether authoritarian rule has fostered these attitudes. With regard to citizens' views of religion and politics, there exists a broad consensus that laws should be consistent with *shari'a,* but respondents increasingly have expressed an aversion to religious figures intervening in the political system.

In chapter 7, Hicham Ben Abdallah El Alaoui sheds further light on the cultural backdrop against which Arab political development is taking place. El Alaoui holds that culture, as an incubator for ideology, will have a far more profound impact on Arab politics than the laws passed by legislatures. Despite the traditionally hostile attitudes of Islamic scholars toward secular culture, El Alaoui argues that part of "Islam's grandeur has been its ability to absorb myriad cultural influences." Yet this norm of openness has in recent years been challenged by the rise of salafism, which has "become the central signifier of resistance to Westernization and neocolonialism." This norm consists of a set of prescriptions and proscriptions based on strict interpretation of religious texts. Whereas Arab nationalists once fought vigorously against dogmatic religiosity, today's secular voices are far meeker. The rise of salafism occurs at the same time that many Arabs are increasingly consuming "profane and basically secular cultural products via television, videos, the Internet, and popular literature." Rising levels of education along with increasingly powerful media have offered access to these cultural creations to a growing number of Arabs, but this flowering of secular culture has been confined largely to the home. In public, the salafist norm is winning the day.

El Alaoui finds the roots of salafism entangled with those of authoritarianism. By confining culture to the realm of private distraction and paying homage to public conservatism, Arab autocrats have sought to decrease the probability of challenges to their rule. By quietly allowing the rise of a conservative, anti-Western religious movement, Arab autocrats have been able to portray themselves to the West as bulwarks against Islamist bogeymen. Even intellectuals opposed to authoritarianism could be induced to align with the lesser evil of secular autocrats. Other intellectuals have seemingly chosen political withdrawal, treating cultural production as a substitute for political activity. If Arab intellectuals and artists are to leave their mark on their countries' political systems, they will have to launch a challenge against the salafist paradigm.

Explaining Divergent Outcomes

The centrality of religion in the Arab world presents new questions for scholars of democracy because, as Alfred Stepan and Juan J. Linz point out in chapter 8, conflicts over religion played little role in the third wave of democratization. Nonetheless, the early progress of Tunisia's democratic transition and the examples of Muslim democracy in other parts of the world give Stepan and Linz reasons to believe that Islam will not hinder democratization. As they emphasize, democracy does not require a strict separation of mosque and state but rather the embrace of the "twin tolerations," an understanding that "religious authorities do not control democratic officials who are acting constitutionally, while democratic officials do not control religion so long as religious actors respect other citizens' rights." Stepan and Linz argue that the relative success of democracy in Albania, India, Indonesia, Senegal, and Turkey—together home to half a billion Muslims—provides strong evidence against Muslim exceptionalism. In each, state and religious officials have together forged consensus on policy.

But Stepan and Linz find a different barrier: Some of the new regimes emerging in the Arab world are "authoritarian-democratic hybrids." In such regimes, political leaders feel constrained by popular opinion to make room for certain features of democracy, including elections. Yet leading actors also are prepared to resort to authoritarian approaches when they feel that these are critical to pursuing their goals. In Egypt, the military, the Muslim Brothers, and liberal secularists all at some point have advocated nondemocratic means of ensuring that their competitors do not grow too powerful. Tunisia, by contrast, has largely avoided this brand of politics, thanks to the moderate leadership of the Ennahda party, the agreements reached between Tunisian Islamists and secularists, and the relative maturity of Tunisian political society. Stepan and Linz also examine the varieties of "sultanism" that have prevailed in Arab countries, and argue that the more sultanistic the prerevolutionary regime, the greater are the obstacles to democratization—a finding that bodes ill for Libya and Syria. Despite the challenges, Stepan and Linz conclude that "the events of the Arab Spring at the very least have made Arab 'presidents for life' increasingly unacceptable, and the dignity of citizens increasingly desired."

In chapter 9, Daniel Brumberg examines the persistence of authoritarian governing arrangements and the problems that they pose for transitions to democracy. In Egypt, Libya, Tunisia, and Yemen, elites are trying to renegotiate the agreements that held authoritarian systems together. As Brumberg puts it, "The challenge is to make sure that these compromises help rather than hinder democratization." Part of the difficulty in constructing a new pact is that those who benefited from the old one now lack the support to win elections, and thus are fearful of relinquishing power to the voters; at the same time, those who were disadvantaged by the old pact see no need to compromise because they are now in a position to win elections. Brumberg predicts that "the difficulties of shifting from an autocratic to a democratic model for protecting different societal interests will preoccupy the Arab world for the coming decade and beyond." Arab autocrats have long stoked the fears of minority groups—including Sunnis in Saddam Hussein's Iraq, Alawites and Christians in Bashar al-Assad's Syria, and secular elites in Algeria, Morocco, and Tunisia—warning that democracy would unleash a harsh form of majority rule guaranteed to render them second-class citizens or worse. The government-citizen pacts built on these fears took different shapes in various corners of the Arab world.

In Egypt, leaders carefully sought to maintain an equilibrium among many interest groups. Elsewhere, as in Syria, leaders sought to repress a majority identity group.

These arrangements began breaking down in 2011, as broad swaths of society, organized by a generation of youth activists and enraged by the increasingly repressive security tactics of insecure regimes, began to turn on their former protectors. But the logic and organizing principles of what Brumberg calls "protection-racket politics" could not easily be abandoned. In Egypt, the military continued to be a key arbiter, the judiciary remained politicized, and neocorporatist structures persisted. Two months after Mubarak stepped down, as Egyptians headed to the polls to vote on a set of constitutional amendments, a major fault line began to appear between the secular and Islamist Egyptians who had not long before stood together in Tahrir Square. As the rift widened into a chasm, nondemocratic actors found themselves with plenty of room to operate. In Tunisia, meanwhile, fear-mongering about a coming Islamist revolution proved less of an obstacle to pact-making. The lack of a military or judicial arbiter forced Tunisian parties to talk directly to one another about their disagreements. The negotiations have been arduous and at times have seemed doomed to fail, but a democratic political accommodation remains within reach. Overall, the difficulty experienced by the new regimes in forging political consensus has given the region's remaining autocracies a boost of confidence.

In chapter 10, Sean L. Yom and F. Gregory Gause III explain why the recent upheavals have shaken the region's republics more deeply than its monarchies. Of the republics, only Algeria, Iraq, and Lebanon passed through the period without seeing the top leader unseated or slipping into civil war. In contrast, although Bahrain experienced sustained mass mobilization, the seven other monarchies enjoyed relative quiet. This observation is puzzling, because in other regions of the world monarchy is an endangered species. Some have theorized that the survival of monarchies in the Arab world is guaranteed by some special cultural affinity for kingship; others have argued that monarchy is well positioned to survive mass uprisings because its leader sits far enough above the political fray to appear as a fair arbiter. Yom and Gause reject these theories. Arab monarchies have been overthrown in the past, and those that remain are not organic extensions of traditional rule but rather a result of installations by foreign powers. Little evidence supports the idea that Arabs prefer dynastic succession. Rather, Yom and Gause argue that political strategy and ample resource endowments saved the Arab monarchies from this round of uprisings. Unlike the overwhelmingly Sunni-supported Bahraini monarchy, most of the monarchies that survived the Arab Spring unchallenged had built coalitions spanning various identity groups. In each country, the work of building such a coalition was eased by oil wealth, foreign aid, or both. One implication of this analysis is that these regimes are not as secure as they seemed while weathering the storm of the Arab uprisings in 2011 and 2012. An exogenous shock, such as a sharp drop in oil prices or in foreign aid, could upend their apparent stability.

In chapter 11, Jason Brownlee, Tarek Masoud, and Andrew Reynolds also seek to explain the variation in regime outcomes—why dictators fell in only four of the fourteen authoritarian regimes of the region (their analysis excludes Lebanon and Iraq). They conclude that while the emergence of uprisings seemed randomly determined, their success or failure depended in each case on whether the government enjoyed enough "money and loyalty" to defeat its opponents. Regimes endowed with vast oil wealth have a greater capacity to employ the carrots and sticks necessary to stave off popular mobilization. Though "loyalty" is more difficult to measure than wealth, the authors identify the successful establishment of hereditary succession as a proxy variable for the cohesiveness that contributes to the capacity of a regime to survive an uprising. In each of the oil-poor, nonhereditary regimes that experienced large-scale protests—Egypt, Tunisia, and Yemen—the leader of the regime was toppled. In those countries that experienced an uprising but also had oil wealth, a hereditary regime, or both—Bahrain, Libya, and Syria—the regime's security forces backed their leader and carried out a violent crackdown. In Libya, the authors argue, the regime's failure to crush its opponents stemmed not from a lack of cohesiveness, but rather from an inability to withstand NATO military intervention. Their conclusion suggests that those Arab regimes which escaped unscathed from the Arab Spring—all of which feature hereditary succession, vast oil or gas wealth, or both—will not easily give way before popular unrest.

Comparing the Arab Revolts

Next follows a series of five chapters based on articles originally written in 2011. Two of these explore the historical precedents for the kind of revolutionary "contagion" that spread so rapidly during the Arab Spring; each of the remaining three assesses a key factor influencing the success or failure of the uprisings. In chapter 12, Marc F. Plattner focuses on the international context of the Arab revolts, which erupted with great suddenness during a period of global democratic decline. Beginning around 2006, the number of countries around the world that qualified as democracies had begun to shrink, while nondemocratic countries had begun to exhibit new dynamism and to increase their cooperation with one another. As unrest rocked many Arab regimes in 2011, however, autocrats elsewhere were jolted from their growing self-confidence. It remains unclear whether the Arab upheavals will usher in a new era of democratic expansion or add up to no more than a short-lived deviation from an underlying trend of authoritarian revival. Plattner notes that the challenges to democracy in places such as Bahrain, Egypt, Libya, Syria, and Yemen are formidable, and that their progress toward democracy is far from assured. Yet even if the revolts of 2011 fail to culminate in functioning democracies, they may one day be remembered, like the failed revolutions of 1848 in Europe, as milestones on the road to a more democratic future.

In Chapter 13, Lucan Way focuses on the lessons that may be gleaned from the revolutions of 1989 in Europe. Like the upheavals in the Arab world in 2011, these revolutions surprised many observers, who had been confusing surface stability with basic sustainability. Both sets of events showed that uprisings against authoritarian systems can prove contagious by demonstrating to nearby nations the vulnerability of their own leaders and suggesting ways to remove them. Yet democracy cannot happen through diffusion alone. As Way argues, structural factors, including the regional balance of power, are often decisive. The degree of international support that an aspiring democratic regime receives can be a critical determinant of the success of a transition. In 1989, the precipitous decline of the Soviet Union stripped Central and East European autocrats of their chief external support. Arab authoritarians today face no comparable challenge.

Moreover, the Arab uprisings were not as unforgiving to autocrats as those of 1989, when Nicolae Ceauşescu, the only ruler to hold out against reform, paid for his resistance with his life. In contrast, Zine al-Abidine Ben Ali, Hosni Mubarak, and Ali Abdallah Saleh avoided such a brutal fate, perhaps suggesting to other Arab leaders that failure to reform need not be a deadly mistake. Even for those polities that succeed in toppling their dictators, the prospect of a Russia-like regression to authoritarianism looms. As Way writes, "people have short memories," and intractable problems such as corruption, inflation, and unemployment make it almost inevitable that eventually "the old regime will look a lot better to a lot of people." In the long run, the lessons of 1989 make it clear that key structural factors, especially levels of economic development and ties to the West, will go a long way toward determining the success or failure of the Arab uprisings. With the global economy sputtering and with political Islam perceived as a threat by Western leaders, Way concludes that "some form of authoritarianism is likely to dominate the Middle East and North Africa for a long time to come."

Throughout the Arab world, militaries have been critical actors in postindependence politics. Indeed, for former military officers Ben Ali, Mubarak, Qadhafi, and Saleh, the path to power passed through the armed forces. Perhaps surprisingly, only two of these commanders enjoyed the widespread loyalty of their officers during their countries' mass uprisings. In Chapter 14, Zoltan Barany examines why this was the case. Generally, Barany writes, a military's decision about how to respond to an uprising is shaped by the regime's track record of addressing citizens' grievances, its past treatment of the military, the degree of cohesion among the various security services, and the extent to which military leaders have perpetrated human-rights abuses. The probability of foreign intervention, the pressures of revolutionary diffusion, and the exposure of officers to Western education can also play a role in determining the military's stance. In Tunisia, Ben Ali had long treated his internal-security forces better than the military. Furthermore, Tunisia's army had a high level of professionalism, no tradition of mixing in politics, and a sizeable cadre of Western-trained officers. In Egypt, military leaders had long enjoyed tremendous economic privileges, but they felt threatened by the rise of Mubarak's son Gamal and by the swelling of the Interior Ministry, which came to employ as many as 1.4 million Egyptians. In Yemen and Libya, respectively, schisms in the armed forces sprang from fragmented societies themselves. Meanwhile, the Bahraini army—a Sunni force formed to protect a Sunni monarchy—loyally cracked down on mostly Shia protestors. And in Syria, the sectarian makeup of the officer corps, which is dominated by members of President Assad's minority Alawite sect, along with the copious opportunities for economic enrichment offered to officers, similarly engendered fealty. It remains to be seen how civil-military relations will evolve in the Arab world, especially as pressures grow to move away from statist economies, but absent greater civilian control of the armed forces, the prospects for democracy may be dim.

In chapter 15, John M. Carey and Andrew Reynolds examine the region's electoral systems as well as efforts made to reform them. Historically, Arab legislatures have been "dubiously representative, fecklessly indecisive, and weak in the face of powerful hereditary monarchs or strongman presidents." In Egypt and Tunisia prior to the uprisings, complex legal webs of quotas, classifications, and regulations ensured commanding majorities for Mubarak's and Ben Ali's ruling parties. In trying to build more democratic electoral systems, reformers must look to five key goals even while navigating the tensions and tradeoffs that will surely arise among them. The goals are 1) promoting inclusiveness that brings representation to new and previously marginalized groups; 2) avoiding distortions that give the leading party an outsized "winner's bonus"; 3) creating incentives for coalition-building; 4) encouraging accountability of individual legislators to voters; and 5) giving voters options in as straightforward a way as possible. Carey and Reynolds argue that the new electoral law adopted by Egypt in 2011 failed with regard to inclusiveness, minimization of distortions, and especially intelligibility to voters. They offer a much more positive assessment of the electoral law chosen by Tunisia for its constituent assembly, which measures up well on all criteria except that of strengthening the accountability of individual representatives to voters.

In chapter 16, Philip N. Howard and Muzammil M. Hussain consider

the role played by digital media in fostering the Arab Spring. They argue that the rise of social media is critical in explaining how a group of
"twenty-somethings with little experience in social-movement organizing" toppled regimes that had stood the tests of decades. The spread of
these media preceded the Arab Spring. For years, Egyptian, Tunisian,
and other Arab dissidents had been disseminating their opinions over
the Internet. In both Tunisia and Egypt, social media allowed citizens
to share the news of a martyred dissident crushed by the state (Mohamed Bouazizi in Tunisia and Khaled Said in Egypt) and generated a
collective sense of outrage. In addition to galvanizing citizens, social
media helped them to organize. When authorities tried to control or direct digital media, activists responded creatively: In Libya, some used
dating websites to communicate; in Syria, they used Google Maps to
distinguish authentic protests from regime-laid traps. Howard and Hussain note that these new tools may be employed in support of authoritarianism as well as democracy, and they caution that social media are
still very much contested terrain. Yet, emphasizing how the Internet has
changed the ways in which Arabs communicate with one another, they
conclude that "social media have become the scaffolding upon which
civil society can build."

Tunisia and Egypt

The second part of our volume, which focuses on individual Arab
countries, begins with two chapters on Tunisia and three on Egypt. In
chapter 17, Peter J. Schraeder and Hamadi Redissi describe the stunning chain of events set in motion in December 2010 in Tunisia—
"case zero" of the "Arab Spring"—when Bouazizi lit himself on fire
after helplessly watching a police officer confiscate his meager capital.
While Ben Ali's fall after nearly a quarter-century in power surprised
many, in retrospect his regime's weaknesses appear painfully clear.
Tunisia faced a number of structural challenges: Its economy struggled
to meet the aspirations of those Tunisians—about two of every five—
aged 25 years or less. Unemployment among educated young people
perversely exceeded that of their less educated counterparts. In the
wake of the global economic slowdown, making ends meet became
even harder as food prices soared. Ben Ali had made the country a
police state: With a population only a sixth the size of France's, it had
the same number of police officers. Elections, the constitution, and the
legislature all bent to Ben Ali's will, while his family crassly exploited
a raft of privileges that enraged citizens at large. Yet despite the growing authoritarianism of Ben Ali's regime, Tunisian civil society had
become surprisingly strong. The number of civil society organizations
had increased nearly fivefold under Ben Ali, and the rise of new media had helped them to grow stronger. The General Union of Tunisian

Workers had become an especially formidable organization. When Ben Ali tried to meet popular protests with force, the many frailties of his regime and the underlying strength of the society confronting it became apparent.

In chapter 18, Alfred Stepan examines Tunisia's early success in moving along a path of democratization. For Stepan, Tunisia's democratic progress stems in large measure from its embrace of the "twin tolerations." In Stepan's view, hard-line secularism on the model of France's *laïcité* or Turkey's Kemalism is not a prerequisite for democracy but in fact a hindrance to it. Stepan reports that Tunisia's embrace of the twin tolerations dated from well before the uprising against Ben Ali. As early as 2003, Tunisian dissidents from across the political spectrum began meeting and issuing declarations affirming democratic values. In tracing Tunisia's history, Stepan finds fertile soil for these values in a legacy of toleration that was suppressed by Ben Ali and his predecessor Habib Bourguiba (1957–87), who found intolerance toward religion useful for maintaining secular authoritarian rule. In charting a path beyond Ben Ali, Tunisian dissidents of many political stripes saw tolerance as a critical value binding them together. Challenges abound in Tunisia, but its more welcoming attitude toward the twin tolerations contrasts with the intolerance that is crippling Egypt's transition, and positions Tunisia as the Arab world's best bet for achieving the status of consolidated democracy.

In chapter 19, Tarek Masoud reconsiders the popular academic view of the Arab world as a bastion of "durable authoritarianism" in light of this view's failure to anticipate the Egyptian uprising. A stream of scholarly studies developed a theory of durable Arab authoritarianism in order to explain the survival and seeming resilience of a host of aging authoritarian systems in the region. In the process, the obvious shortcomings of these regimes were underrated. In the case of Egypt, Masoud notes that many identified Mubarak's ruling National Democratic Party (NDP) and the rubber-stamp parliament that it dominated as pressure valves to let the steam out of the elite-level conflicts that often topple authoritarian regimes. While these institutions may have helped to prolong Mubarak's rule, once confronted with enough popular resentment they proved "far flimsier than previously thought" and quickly melted away. Sham elections may have served to reward regime elites, but they also fed frustration with the regime, and "parliament came to be seen as an abode of swindlers."

Similarly, building up the NDP may have allowed the regime to coopt more of the country's elites, but it also alienated the generals, who in the end were unwilling to fire their guns in defense of Mubarak. This reluctance was driven by the desire to eliminate civilian political competitors to military power in a country where Mubarak's son Gamal had seemed poised to become the first Egyptian president who had not served in the military. Masoud cautions that while some of the remnants of the Mubarak regime were washed away, the power of the military might be more difficult to dislodge. In the end, he concludes that Egypt's ability to build a democracy will hinge in large part on its ability to reform its economy. "Nothing tests democratic commitments like an empty stomach," he writes. While recognizing Egypt's myriad challenges, Masoud calls for humility on the part of political analysts. After all, many who now read doom in Egypt's tarot cards once missed the one depicting the strongman falling from his throne.

Mubarak's tumble from power unleashed a contest between Egypt's Islamists and secularists. In chapter 20, Michele Dunne and Tarek Radwan, writing during the presidency of the Muslim Brotherhood's Mohamed Morsi, argue that despite the Islamists' initial electoral triumph, Egypt's liberals will continue to play a formidable role. "The long-smoldering tinder that set alight the Egyptian revolution" was Egyptian society's mounting consensus that all citizens have unalienable rights, including the right to select their political leaders, to enjoy the rule of law, and to remove from power leaders who have violated these rights. The rise of liberal groups such as Kifaya, the April 6th Movement, and the National Association for Change and their instrumental role in the uprising are well documented. Their ideas increasingly gained currency in the wider society, including among members of Hosni Mubarak's NDP and the Muslim Brotherhood. Even after crushing the liberals in elections, Islamists were constrained from repudiating the liberal message that had become an almost universal aspiration of Egyptians over the past decade. When President Morsi, backed into a corner by the military, the judiciary, and a host of political opponents, sought to immunize the Islamist-dominated constituent assembly from a possible judicial challenge, his decision was met by widespread protest. Dunne and Radwan conclude that "Egypt's liberals . . . remain the vanguard of change in the country."

While the future remains unknown, Egypt's initial attempt at a transition to democracy ended in failure with the military takeover that ousted President Mohamed Morsi in July 2013. In chapter 21, Nathan J. Brown traces Egypt's transformation from a possible model of Arab democracy to a cautionary tale. Brown contends that Egypt's descent into polarization, acrimony, and bloodshed was not inevitable. If a few events had turned out differently, Egyptians might have achieved the level of consensus required to keep the country's democratic hopes afloat. The original sin of the Egyptian uprising, according to Brown, was allowing the military to seize control of the transition. At no point could Egyptian political leaders agree on the rules of the game. In place of the negotiations needed to fashion a broad consensus, political leaders pursued their interests by "pressuring, nagging, and bargaining with the generals." The transition was filled with elections, but rather than imbuing

Egyptians with confidence, each resort to the ballot box seemed to pull political forces further apart. In the end, Egypt's political rift became a canyon: "Islamists plausibly charged non-Islamists with refusing to accept adverse election results, while non-Islamists plausibly charged Islamists with using those same election results to undermine the development of healthy democratic life."

The inadequacy of Egypt's political leadership is only part of the story. Just as important has been the gravitational pull of the country's authoritarian past. The repression perpetrated by Mubarak—and by Gamal Abdel Nasser (1956–70) and Anwar Sadat (1970–81) before him—left behind a political landscape tilted toward the Brotherhood, which for years had worked at building a robust social organization. After the uprising, the key actors in Egypt's authoritarian "republic" continued to recite their lines: Egypt's generals masqueraded as the vanguard of democracy; its police officers continued to prefer their institutional interests to the work of upholding public order; the judiciary used its powers to wage war on the executive and the legislature; and the media continued to amplify the partisan messages of those in power. Years of sham democracy had left Egyptians suspecting that democratic gestures masked insidious intentions. The failure of Egypt's transition will resound for years, Brown writes, and both Islamists and students of democracy everywhere will seek to derive lessons from it. But for Egypt, the tragic conclusion may be that "the very idea of democracy has lost much of its meaning and all of its luster."

Yemen, Libya, Syria, and Bahrain

The next set of chapters covers the four other Arab countries that experienced massive protests during the Arab spring. As April Longley Alley recounts in chapter 22, Ali Abdallah Saleh had been president of Yemen since its unification in 1990, but his regime—challenged by the Huthi insurgency in the north, a separatist movement in the south, and poverty and corruption throughout—was under siege prior to the Arab uprisings. The gravity of Yemen's problems spurred Yemeni leaders and the international community to work out a unique exit from the massive protests triggered by the Arab Spring: Saleh was pressured into relinquishing office, and the country's fractious elites achieved a negotiated settlement, including an agreement to participate in a formal national dialogue. In part, Saleh's downfall can be attributed to his propensity for rankling his allies by hoarding increasing wealth and power for his family at a time when a decline in oil production made rent-distribution more contentious.

In mid-2011, a standoff ensued between Saleh and some of his former allies. The settlement that ended the standoff has so far succeeded in steering Yemen away from the bloody path trodden by Libyans and

Syrians, and it has perhaps saved the country from the intensity of internal strife that Egypt has suffered. Yet because the settlement preserved the influence of key actors in Yemen's corrupt political system, the country runs the risk that its transition will amount to little more than a reshuffling of elites rather than systemic change. Meanwhile, amid the political vacuum that has followed the settlement, the security threats that challenged Saleh during the twilight of his rule have grown more dangerous and the humanitarian issues have become more intractable. Yemen has a potential opening through which greater democracy might be reached, but its path is fraught with challenges. As Alley writes, "At best, a long and tumultuous process of negotiation and change has begun."

Among the countries that deposed longtime rulers, Libya has experienced the most drastic change. Gone is the quixotic and brutal Muammar Qadhafi and his dysfunctional brand of personal rule. For the time being, Libyans are happy to have earned unprecedented freedom. Yet as Mieczysław P. Boduszyński and Duncan Pickard write in chapter 23, the obstacles to democracy are many, and citizens will not forever be content with a free but feckless state. Many of Libya's challenges stem from the legacy left behind by Qadhafi, a military coupmaker who ruled for more than four decades. Qadhafi salted the earth: In an alleged effort to minimize the distance between policy makers and the people, he deliberately undermined the effectiveness of state institutions, fostered discord among potential adversaries, prevented bonds from forming with the West, and presided over an economy consisting of little more than oil extraction and rent distribution.

In trying to address their country's many problems, Libya's new leaders and nascent institutions have achieved little progress, ironically placing them within the tradition of chaotic "governance" established by Qadhafi. Security problems have been the most vexing issue. Militias—many of whom fought in the country's civil war against Qadhafi—have refused to lay down their arms, especially in the absence of an effective national army. Meanwhile, as Libyan leaders try to set the country on a path toward devising a viable constitution, tension has grown among reformers who served in the Qadhafi government, Libyan expatriates who have returned since the revolution, and militia fighters who struggled against Qadhafi. Boduszyński and Pickard speculate that Islamist populism may become the broad basis for a new Libyan national identity, perhaps paving the way for stronger institutions. But they warn that the degree of democratic commitment harbored by Libya's Islamist populists remains the great unknown.

Syria's bloody conflict ranks as one of the world's worst humanitarian disasters in recent decades, and as Steven Heydemann writes in chapter 24, the flames of war have annealed the Assad regime into something even more authoritarian, repressive, and sectarian than it was before 2011. These changes bode ill even for the country's longer-term democratic prospects. In addition to resorting to increasing brutality and leaning even more exclusively on the support of minority groups, Assad's regime has withdrawn from its recent embrace of market-oriented economic reform and has further deepened its strategic relationships with nondemocratic actors such as China, Iran, Russia, and Hezbollah. Of course, the possibility that Assad's regime might be defeated on the battlefield cannot be ruled out. But even if that should occur, some recent changes will not easily be undone. For example, the geographic segregation of the population has grown, reversing a trend of the past few decades in which Syria's various sectarian groups had dispersed throughout the country. Meanwhile, the peaceful protest movement that had emerged during the height of the Arab Spring has mutated into a "thoroughly militarized, militantly Islamist armed movement wracked by internal fissures and frictions, bereft of a coherent and effective political leadership." Like the hardening of the Assad regime, this development further clouds Syria's future prospects for democratization.

While the region's monarchies weathered the 2011 storm far better than its republics, the tiny island kingdom of Bahrain is a notable exception. In Bahrain, early 2011 protests swelled to include a large chunk of the populace. Yet thanks to splits in the opposition and the government's successful repression and countermobilization, the ruling Khalifa family avoided the fate that befell some other Arab leaders. As Frederic Wehrey writes in Chapter 25, the seeds of Bahrain's upheaval were planted far before the Arab Spring. Since taking the throne in 1999, King Hamad al-Khalifa had drained power from the elected parliament. Meanwhile, as a Shia-majority country with a Sunni ruling family, Bahrain saw its political tensions inflamed by the growing sectarianism of a region rent by the war in Iraq. When demonstrations—at first peaceful, largely nonsectarian, and limited in their aims—began in February 2011, the Kingdom responded with force, arresting, torturing, and killing demonstrators.

Since the beginning of the crackdown, Bahrain's key political groupings have been pulled further apart: Al-Wifaq, a moderate Shia formation that withdrew from parliament in protest of the crackdown, has been criticized by more militant Shia factions, and Sunni Islamists have divided into loyalist and oppositionist groups. Even the royal family is split between hard-liners and reformists. Meanwhile, Saudi Arabia, connected to Bahrain Island by a 25-kilometer causeway, continues to wield significant influence. In March 2011, it spearheaded the deployment of the GCC's multinational Peninsula Shield Force to help quell the uprising. More recently, it has sought to steer Bahrain back onto a path of "calibrated reform," trying to craft participatory institutions that can serve as safety valves without packing any real political power. As

Bahrain's elites try to restore a sense of normality, frustration continues to grow in many corners of the island.

Defusing the Protests

This book concludes with four chapters on countries that were able to defuse the protests generated by the Arab Spring. Algeria stands out as one of the few Arab republics to make it through the past few years largely unscathed. In Chapter 26, Frédéric Volpi writes that the Algerian regime outflanked its challengers by "decoupling social unrest from political mobilization." Although Algeria never approached the level of protest seen in neighboring Tunisia, riots did break out there in early January 2011—weeks before the Egyptian uprising began—after the government tried to ease some price controls. Protests continued into February, but they never snowballed into an uprising. In part, this hesitance to push the country to the brink is connected to memories of the country's bloody civil war in the 1990s, which left the Algerian populace deeply wary of conflict. Furthermore, in 2011 leftist and liberal opposition groups generally refused to work with Islamists out of mistrust and a fear that such collaboration would trigger a brutal government crackdown. Also instrumental in the fizzling of antiregime mobilization were the containment strategies of the regime: "pseudodemocratization, redistributive patronage, and an effective use of the security apparatus." Buoyed by its natural-gas wealth, the regime offered many carrots, including a massive increase in social spending. Much of this money flowed to members of the army and other security forces, making the prospect of a Tunisia-style outcome even more remote. The government also was quick to brandish its arms in the hope that it would not be forced to use them. At one rally, security personnel outnumbered protesters by 27,000. Through displays of overwhelming force, the regime avoided having to resort to a violent crackdown that might have generated a severe backlash.

When protests erupted in Morocco in early 2011, King Mohammed VI drew plaudits for his perceived conciliatory approach. The king offered a package of constitutional reforms to be decided by a referendum, and elections were held. Yet in chapter 27, Ahmed Benchemsi writes that the reform process praised by many Western observers was mainly a sleight of hand. Upon closer inspection, the notion that the king had relinquished his sacred status is far less clear than was reported by many in the Western media. Meanwhile, though much was made of the increased responsibility given to the parliament and prime minister, Benchemsi asserts that the new prime minister, Abdelilah Benkirane, will remain "a constitutional hostage of the monarchy." The king retains the ability to legislate by royal decree; the electoral law prevents the rise of a political party with broad support; and the chief of government's newfound ability to dissolve the parliament (after consultation with the king) amounts to little more than a freshly minted means of committing political suicide. Benchemsi credits the king's "clever preemptive move" with sucking the oxygen from the protest movement's balloon. In this respect, Mohammed VI, once hailed as part of a new generation of reform-minded Arab leaders, followed the playbook that his father, King Hassan II (r. 1961–99), had crafted: Curry favor abroad by projecting an image of openness and investing in clever public relations, sow division in opposition ranks, and use repression when necessary. Yet with many of the problems that stirred Moroccan protesters—corruption, unemployment, and political stagnation—remaining intractable, the current king's skill at political legerdemain may not suffice indefinitely. "A strong-enough wind," Benchemsi writes, "will disperse any smokescreen."

Like Morocco, Jordan's monarchy reacted to Arab Spring unrest with its usual response: promises of measured reform. But as Sean L. Yom writes in Chapter 28, this routine response to what was actually a historic swell in discontent may have been a major mistake on the part of the King Abdullah II. Yom argues that "the king has never faced such doubt about his future." Yet despite this unprecedented challenge, the "White Revolution" that King Abdullah has proclaimed merely reprises the old ruse of "controlled liberalization" and is not the more far-reaching democratization that Jordanians are demanding. The parliament that came in via the January 2013 elections still lacks the ability to initiate legislation, control the purse strings, or oversee the activities of the military or security forces.

Like its counterpart in Morocco, the Jordanian monarchy has been careful to craft an image that appeals to Western sensibilities. It has coupled its public-relations campaign with warnings regarding the alternatives to its continued rule: Jordan is constantly depicted as teetering on the brink of destruction, with the forces of Islamic fundamentalism or ethnic conflict ready to erupt should Abdullah lose control. Yet these perils are bogeymen, Yom contends, specters manipulated to suit the monarchy's needs. Democratization is likely to produce neither Islamic theocracy nor Palestinian ethnocracy. Opposition to the Hashemite monarchy transcends both the Islamist-secular and the Palestinian-East Banker divides. The Arab monarchies may have emerged intact from the Arab Spring, but Middle Eastern history suggests that they are far from immortal—such present-day republics as Egypt, Iraq, and Libya were once kingdoms. Thus the king would be wise to move Jordan sooner rather than later toward constitutional monarchy.

The Kingdom of Saudi Arabia is a still relatively closed society dominated by a condominium between the House of Saud and the Wahhabi brand of Islam. Despite its massive petrochemical endowment, the kingdom is beset by soaring youth unemployment, pervasive corruption, and an aging ruling family increasingly out of touch with an enormous co-hort of young people. In short, it suffers from many of the same ailments that brought untold numbers out into the streets in other parts of the Arab world. As Stéphane Lacroix chronicles in chapter 29, there was a period of brief but significant unrest in Saudi Arabia during the early months of the Arab Spring. In February 2011, a group of reformists who over the previous decade had begun issuing calls for a constitutional monarchy published a pair of petitions calling for political reform. In a country that ranks first in the world when it comes to the share of its populace that uses Twitter, an emerging generation of youth activists—including members of the religious Sahwa movement—used social media to call for demonstrations like those that had taken place in Tunisia and Egypt. And in the Eastern Province, home to much of Saudi Arabia's oil and most of its Shia minority, activists began to stage rallies, some calling for Shia rights and others calling for broader political reform.

Yet these rumblings never became an earthquake, as the Saudi re-gime neatly outflanked its opponents. Members of the official religious establishment, drawing upon the state's legitimacy as the guardian of "the two holy places" (the cities of Mecca and Medina), issued a *fatwa* against demonstrations. In late February and March, octogenarian King Abdullah announced a domestic-spending package benefiting youth and the poor, at a price tag that exceeded a fifth of annual GDP. Explicit warnings that the security forces would use force against demonstrators raised the barrier of fear, and those Saudis who might have sympathized with reformists mostly stayed home during what was billed on Facebook as a "Day of Anger." Lacroix concludes that, although Saudi Arabia survived this round of unrest, it would be a mistake to conclude that it is immune to future upheavals. The kingdom's ability to coopt support and dampen unrest hinges on continued high oil prices. Moreover, the regime's monopoly on religious legitimacy is increasingly subject to competition. Perhaps most important is the looming question of suc-cession, as the set of elderly brothers who are sons of the founding king (Ibn Saud, d. 1953) finally passes completely from the scene and the next generation of major royals jockeys for position. The uncertainty that this presages may well present reformists with opportunities such as have never been seen in Saudi history.

As these case studies show, the Arab uprisings have yet to produce a story with a happy ending. As of this writing, Tunisia appears to be the country with the best chance of completing a transition to democ-racy, but it still faces substantial obstacles. Yet the events that we have witnessed during the past three years constitute no more than a single episode in what is likely to be a long and continuing struggle. At the very least, the massively supported popular protests that erupted in 2011 have refuted the notion that Arab culture offers uniquely barren soil for otherwise universal human aspirations for democracy.

NOTES

1. An earlier *Journal of Democracy* book on the region, *Islam and Democracy in the Middle East*, was published in 2003.

2. *The Arab Human Development Report, 2002* (New York: United Nations Development Programme, 2002), 2.

3. *Arab Human Development Report*, 114.

4. Daniel Brumberg, "The Trap of Liberalized Autocracy," *Journal of Democracy* 13 (October 2002): 56–68.

5. Arch Puddington, "The Freedom House Survey for 2012: Breakthroughs in the Balance," *Journal of Democracy* 24 (April 2013): 46–61; "The Freedom House Survey for 2011: The Year of the Arab Uprisings," *Journal of Democracy* 23 (April 2012): 74–88. In 2013, Freedom House also classified Libya as a democracy, but given the weakness of central state authority there, we regard that judgment as premature.

6. We regret the absence of a chapter on Iraq from this volume. Though the *Journal* has extensively covered Iraq in the past, our repeated efforts to recruit a new article on that country did not yield publishable results.

Thematic Essays

1

THE LANGUAGES OF THE ARAB REVOLUTIONS

Abdou Filali-Ansary

Abdou Filali-Ansary *is a professor at the Institute for the Study of Muslim Civilisations of the Aga Khan University in London, where he was founding director from 2002 to 2009. He has served as founding director of the King Abdul-Aziz Foundation for Islamic Studies and Human Sciences in Casablanca, Morocco, and as secretary-general of Mohammed V University in Rabat (1980–84), where he also taught modern philosophy. In 1993, he cofounded the bilingual Arabic-French journal* Prologues: revue maghrébine du livre *and served as its editor until 2005. This essay, based on his 2011 Seymour Martin Lipset Lecture on Democracy in the World, originally appeared in the April 2012 issue of the* Journal of Democracy.

I fully appreciate the honor bestowed upon me by my inclusion in the group of scholars and political leaders who have previously delivered the Seymour Martin Lipset Lecture on Democracy in the World. I am pleased to have this opportunity to engage with Professor Lipset's thought—an opportunity that I had strongly wished for after meeting him briefly during one of my visits to the National Endowment for Democracy, but one that sadly did not materialize during his lifetime.

In preparation for this lecture, I read again several of Lipset's writings that had left a lasting impression on me years ago. These included two of his seminal essays: "Some Social Requisites of Democracy: Economic Development and Political Legitimacy," published in March 1959, and "The Social Requisites of Democracy Revisited," which was based upon an address that he gave as president of the American Sociological Association in 1993.[1] At a time when change seems to be accelerating, and momentous events are happening in quick succession, rereading these essays invites us to step back from the avalanche of everyday events and place them in a larger frame with a deeper perspective. My hope is that this may help us to gain a better understanding of the changes that are taking place around us, as well as give us some useful insights for thinking about the future.

One of the lessons that we learn from Lipset concerns our need to identify categories that will let us study political change—and particularly processes of democratization—from the vantage of the social sciences rather than from a theoretical viewpoint that assumes hidden forces to be at work, be they cultural or material in nature. The polarity of (ideological or cultural) "superstructure" and (material or economic) "base" prevailed in academic circles for decades after Marxists had introduced it. One and only one unambiguous answer was sought to a very large question: What is the ultimate factor that determines the course of history—economics or culture?

Although such formulations may seem to us now to be crude and old-fashioned, in fact they have not really and entirely gone away. The opposition between the material and the cultural is kept alive by, among other things, a kind of inertia reflected in the divisions separating academic disciplines. Most academics studying social and political matters tend to see themselves either as economists (or economic historians) focusing on the material bases of society, or as specialists in cultural expressions in one or another of their multiple forms. As a consequence, these academics wind up lending primacy to this or that "factor"—the one that they have chosen as their main object of study.

Earlier in his life, Lipset had begun at one end of the spectrum,[2] but when his thought matured, he brought the two poles together, as is shown by the subtitle of his 1959 essay. It is significant that he labeled them differently from the common usage of the time, calling one "economic development" and the other "political legitimacy." In doing so, he introduced two categories that could be used to establish clearly bounded objects of inquiry, thus allowing them to be approached through the standard and reproducible methods of the social sciences, including comparisons, tests, and sometimes measurements. At the same time, he spelled out the scope and limits of the type of inquiry upon which he was embarking, stressing the importance of formulating *testable* propositions, of avoiding ideas of mechanical causality in favor of multivariable convergences, and of keeping open the possibility of later adjustment or revision (or "revisitation," as he called it).

In adopting such a perspective, we are no longer in the grip of deep convictions about great turns in history or enduring cultural or civilizational identities, but in the realm of facts and characterizations that can be observed, tested, and interpreted within explicit parameters. When the concept of "material base" or "infrastructure" is replaced by "economic development," it immediately becomes a set of measurable variables. When "superstructure" is defined as "political legitimacy," then questions of history, values, and worldviews can be brought back to the discussion in a "controlled" way, as "variables" that can be studied like other historical matters. The links between the two classes of variables are thus highlighted. The classes cease to be a pair of nonoverlapping sets, each of which comprises objects so completely different from those found in the other that they cannot even be discussed together. Instead, they come to be viewed as collections of variables that can *all* be studied in ways widely accepted and well understood by historians and social scientists alike.

The View from Political Legitimacy

I believe that a Lipsetian (or neo-Lipsetian) approach can help us to understand what is happening in the Arab world today, and may also help us as we strive to peer forward toward what may happen (which is, of course, not the same thing as predicting what *will* happen).

In recent decades, attention directed to developments in the Arab region has focused mostly on its cultural heritage, often assuming a kind of continuity between past and present, a persistence of essential features that can be found in any country or society that belongs to the region. Attempts at Marxist explanations of the region's past, as well as attention to issues of economic development, have been more or less pushed aside or left to fade into the background. Since the upsurge of Islamism, one might say that all eyes have been directed to the region's religious heritage and to the overwhelming effects that this is supposed to have on the present.

Here the approach suggested by Lipset helps us to set aside implicit and unverifiable assumptions that can be neither proven nor falsified, and to focus instead on things that we can observe and interpret. He begins with a telling definition:

> Legitimacy involves the capacity of a political system to engender and maintain the belief that existing political institutions are the most appropriate or proper ones for the society. The extent to which contemporary democratic political systems are legitimate depends in large measure upon the ways in which the key issues which have historically divided the society have been resolved.[3]

Political legitimacy thus understood applies to *all* societies across cultural and historical divides, and it brings their particular histories and value systems into the picture in ways that enable us to study their effects on the present. What should count for us now, in other words, is *not* the past as academics can reconstruct it, but the *memory* of the past as it survives in the consciousness of people and shapes their attitudes regarding present-day challenges.

One must immediately add, however, that memories are not stable, that they vary substantially across different times and places, and that most societies are not bound to a single narrative about their pasts. A clear illustration of this may be found in the recent history of the Arab world, where two different discourses seem to have unfolded at the same time, often interacting and sometimes even becoming intertwined, yet remaining clearly identifiable as two separate strands. One highlights the role of Islam and its religious traditions, and emphasizes the overwhelming influence of the remote past on present-day Arab societies. The other, commonly called the Arab Renaissance or Nahda, emerged in the nineteenth century, bringing together Christians, Muslims, and Jews who spoke the Arabic language and felt that they belonged to one culture and shared common aspirations for the future. The Nahda was secular by definition and converged with the ideals of the European Enlightenment. It included brilliant figures, such as Rifa'a al-Tahtawi, Butros al-Bustani, and Khalil Gibran, who contributed great works in literature, history, and political thought, and whose influence remains substantial.

Today, academics who study the modern history of Muslim societies usually choose to devote their attention either to the Islamic revival or to the Nahda (in fact, more often to the former), although the two of them were unfolding at the same time and engaging in intense mutual debate, highlighting different moments or aspects of the past and providing different reference points on the basis of which societies could choose to shape their respective futures. Quite often, thinkers and activists belonging to one of the two movements adopted and used notions, concepts, and categories from the other. Although the prevailing impression today is that Arab public opinion has settled in favor of the current that has evolved into Islamic fundamentalism or Islamism, there is clear evidence that the ideals of the Nahda also continue to have a powerful influence. In other words, we tend to think nowadays that there are two separate camps, one of fundamentalists and one of secularists. Yet at ground level, things are more nuanced and more complex.

The evidence for this is overwhelming and is clear in the way that people talk, think, and act with regard to politics. Roger Scruton, the author of a popular dictionary of political thought, asks us to consider what we would learn if we were to "extract, both from active debate, and from the theories and intuitions which surround it, the principal ideas through which modern political beliefs find expression."[4] One thing that would immediately draw our attention is the variety and novelty of notions that are being used by Arab populations today to articulate their frustrations and aspirations. Slogans still abound which convey the impression that invoking glorious moments of the past or a return to religion (or traditions linked to religion) is the only real alternative to the ills of the present. Probably the most renowned of these slogans are "a return to *shari'a*" and "Islam is the solution." Alongside them, however, are a number of new terms or phrases—notions that have no apparently traceable origins in the Islamic heritage yet have become common currency, including "human rights" and "democracy." So even though calls for a return to approaches derived from the past or built on religion continue to flourish, their impact may be overestimated, especially by observers who take words at face value and seek their meaning in dictionaries rather than in a grasp of contexts and practices.

As the German historian of the Muslim world Reinhard Schulze has noted, "discourse containing Islamic terms and symbols" may be less about religion than about a certain approach toward the task of coming to terms with the modern world. Religious notions, in other words, are called upon to face the overwhelming challenge of modern concepts. Schulze offers the following description of the situation in the early part of the twentieth century:

> Both kinds of discourse [that is, the Islamic and the European] communicate within Islamic societies and provide a permanent process of cultural translation. This means that Islamic terms and symbols can constantly be translated into "European" ones and vice versa. This in turn allows for *code switching,* that is, the use of one or the other cultural languages of modernism, depending on the context. Islamist parties thus interpreted the leading themes of the "European" political public with a vocabulary of their own, which gave the outside observer the impression that these parties were religious groups. But in fact, the Islamic and the European discourse became widely assimilated to one another, and it was only with the emphasis of new reference points that they were torn apart. This again gave a dynamic impetus to politics in Islamic countries. The common recourse to an Islamic language also enhanced the awareness of belonging to one and the same "cultural community."[5]

The seemingly irreducible opposition between Islamic and modern discourses today, therefore, reflects a recent turn—the outcome of a polarization that, one may add, has never been complete or final. Those who were attentive to Arab discourse in an earlier period saw in it a manner of accommodating modern ideals by grounding them or encapsulating them within a framework of familiar Islamic landmarks.

What the "Arab Spring" shows is that, while this form of appropriation had proven unsuccessful and had receded in the face of intense polarization, an unsuspected wave was gathering strength and producing a *new political language*. This can be seen in the coinage and dissemination of new concepts that capture the aspirations and hopes of the new generations in the Arab world in ways that are aligned with modern political ideals and, at the same time, adjusted to the particular conditions of local populations.

In some cases, there is total equivalence between terms that originated elsewhere, such as "democracy," "human rights," or "civil society," and the corresponding Arabic terms (*dimukratiya, huquq al-insan,* and *mujtama' madani,* respectively) that have now become part of the common language. In other cases, there are "adjustments" or outright creations, as with "rule of law," which becomes *dawlat al-haq wa al-qanun* (a state bound by law and respectful of rights) or *dawlat al-mu'assassat* (literally, a "state made of institutions," as contradistinguished from a state made by and for individual rulers).

Here one should stress the crucial impact of the written press, which has been amplified by satellite TV stations such as al-Jazeera. Attention has rightly been paid to the role of the Internet and social media in stimulating and supporting the protest movements of 2011, but with respect to the long process that led to the emergence of a new political language, it was the written press that played the decisive role.

It remains true, however, that many languages are spoken at the same time. Concepts such as *shari'a, jihad,* and *ijtihad* have even made their way into European languages, where they tend to carry with them specific connotations. Within Muslim contexts, these terms do refer to perspectives well entrenched in the collective memory; in some circles, they are meant to express concrete expectations, as when *shari'a* is used to refer to particular sets of prescriptions in family law and penal matters. The alarm that such terms arouse in the minds of Westerners may, in some cases, be justified. This calls for a renewed attention to the ways in which collective memories (or historical consciousness, as we are proposing to call it) are sustained and shaped by modern education and the media.

But the most significant development may be precisely what is neglected in most studies of the region: the emergence of a new set of notions, phrases, and expressions that are modern, local, and expressive of popular aspirations. These new phrases and expressions will influence the ways in which the older ones are understood, and will expand the discourse concerning the norms and ideals that should guide public policies.

There is now across the Arab world a new language of politics. It includes not only translations of notions familiar to English speakers, but also other formulations of views about popular rights and aspirations that are clearly modern. The remarkable fact is that this new language is now the common speech of *all* parties, Islamists included. Its terms have thus acquired the status of universal yardsticks by which all matters are assessed or measured, including notions rooted in tradition or religion. One might even say that today religious views are being vindicated and justified through the medium of modern norms.

I would assert that, due in large part to the influence of this new political language, democratic legitimacy is becoming the only form of political legitimacy acceptable in Arab societies. But if this analysis is correct, how can we understand the persistence of calls for a return to *shari'a,* and the endorsement that such calls seem to receive when Arabs are allowed to exercise their democratic right to vote in free elections?

Shari'a in the Context of the Arab Revolutions

Wael Hallaq, one of the most prominent contemporary scholars working on Islamic law, states:

> There is no doubt that Islamic law is today a significant cornerstone in the reaffirmation of Islamic identity, not only as a matter of positive law but also, and more importantly, as the foundation of a cultural uniqueness.

> Indeed, for many of today's Muslims, to live by Islamic law is not merely a legal issue, but one that is distinctly psychological.[6]

The scope of this assertion needs to be tempered in light of our earlier observations about the advent of newer modes of expression of public pinion. It is also reductionist in treating personal piety, which is clearly at work among those seeking obedience to *shari'a* in their own daily lives and is a powerful inclination for many individuals in all societies, as a purely psychological phenomenon. Yet while Hallaq's statement is exaggerated, it does capture the impressions that prevail nowadays among many of those who study the Arab world.

To understand how memories of the past shape present-day attitudes regarding *shari'a,* we must look back at the way in which the history of Muslims unfolded. After the early divisions following Muhammad's death in 632 C.E., the political order that stabilized and persisted for centuries in most Muslim contexts was far from unbounded despotism. At the same time, however, it was equally remote from the notions of collective, shared, or distributed power that early generations of Muslims had aspired to and that had been sanctified by widely accepted religious authority. Once it became clear that the latter, the fully legitimate Islamic system of power, could not be maintained or restored, most Muslims settled on a less ambitious goal—namely, the acceptance of de facto rulers provided that they committed themselves to obeying and enforcing the law, understood as the corpus of prescriptions elaborated from the sacred scriptures by scholars independent of the state. In the words of Noah Feldman:

> In its essence, the *shari'a* aspires to be Law that applies equally to every human, great or small, ruler or ruled. No one is above it, and everyone at all times is bound by it. Though the constitutional structure that historically developed to implement the *shari'a* afforded the flexibility necessary for practical innovation and effective government, that structure also maintained the ideal of legality. Judges who are devoted to the *shari'a* in this sense are therefore devoted to the rule of law, and not the rule of the state. The legitimacy of a state in which officials adhere to this structure of beliefs would depend upon the state's faithfulness to implementing the law.[7]

Such an arrangement did provide people with some protection from the arbitrariness of rulers and enabled them to live their lives within the framework of regulations understood to be in conformity with the will of God. This has left lasting consequences, notably a deeply entrenched ethical consciousness among Muslims that extends well beyond the ranks of those who are driven by feelings of personal piety or by a commitment to what has come to be seen as an "Islamic" order.

That being said, one must also stress that calls for a return to *shari'a* do not mean the same thing in every situation. In some cases, they clearly convey an aspiration for the *moralization* of public life. In popular circles, where illiteracy often still prevails, as well as among those whose education conveyed scientific and technical skills with little opening to the humanities, traditional religious formulations remain the way of expressing a wish for what in the West would be described as "basic decency" (the absence of gross abuses of power, widespread corruption, or general cynicism). It is this that lends slogans such as "Islam is the solution" their meaning and their strength, and that explains the success of Islamists in so many places. Having been in the opposition for so long, repressed and rejected by the ruling elites, they have found words to articulate widespread disgust at the gross misbehavior of those in power, words that resonate with popular longings for a return to basic rules of decency. The Islamists are now reaping the fruits of speaking to and for the people in a language that they understand.

At the same time, however, this can foster a number of misunderstandings, as may be observed from some recent trends and turns of events. *Shari'a* is venerated among the popular strata because it refers to the idea of a moral order, and because it still has the prestige of a system that long helped to protect communities from the arbitrariness and abuse of despots. *Shari'a* provided ways to restrain the despot, because it invoked a divine, absolute rule of law (a law given by God, which lies beyond the reach of men, including the rich and powerful).

Yet the absoluteness of *shari'a* is sometimes transferred from its principles to its prescriptions, from the general framework that supports a rule of law to particular rulings that were formulated and implemented through particular interpretations in specific contexts. These rulings are then extracted from their social and historical contexts and used as elements of a modern legal system. This kind of "codification" of *shari'a* began to take place in the nineteenth century, and it often included specific provisions of family law that discriminate against women or harsh punishments that are totally unacceptable in the light of modern ethical principles. Such punishments generally had been implemented rarely, except when despots wanted to deliver strong messages to restive populations. But today they have come to be seen by narrow-minded secularists as an essential feature of *shari'a*.

As indicated earlier, I believe that modern conceptions of political legitimacy, formulated in what I have called the new political language of Muslims, are likely to prevail in future political debates. It is too soon, however, to discount the risk posed by more rigid views that see *shari'a* as a "catalogue of prescriptions," many of which are incompatible with the moral sense acquired by human beings across different cultures. These views derive their continuing resilience from an uncritical and closed-minded brand of traditional religious scholarship.

Will "*Weltanschauung* Politics" Return?

We should not forget that processes of democratization are facilitated by combinations of factors (or prerequisites), and that they remain under threat from adverse conditions even when these prerequisites are present. Extremism comes in various forms, and some of them have more easily gained acceptance than others. As Lipset says:

> *Weltanschauung* politics have also weakened the possibilities for a stable democracy, since parties characterized by such total ideologies have often attempted to create what Sigmund Neumann has called an "integrated" environment, one in which as much as possible of the lives of their members is encapsulated within ideologically linked activities. These actions are based on the assumption that it is important to isolate their followers from contact with "falsehood" expressed by the non-believers.[8]

What prevented most European countries in the early twentieth century from joining the ranks of democracies? One may point with little risk of error to what Lipset called *"Weltanschauung* politics" (hereafter WP), which in Europe took the forms of fascism, communism, and various nationalisms. Movements belonging to this category kept a firm grip on power in some countries for decades, and would not be totally overcome until 1989, the year when the Berlin Wall was torn down, opening the way for the real and perhaps final end of WP in Europe.

In the Arab world, WP emerged shortly after the creation of modern states. It took the form of nationalist regimes (of which the Baathist variants were the most virulent), which prevailed in many Arab countries, often in combination with a proclaimed commitment to socialism.[9] The region's remaining monarchies were spared this particular fate, but in many cases they suffered from another form of extremism, arising from the unleashing of tribal or ultratraditionalist forces. Now, however, WP is receding in the region, and people are starting to have their say in politics, using different "languages" simultaneously: One of them is that of *shari'a* understood as an ethical framework, a language of moral references comprehensible to a majority of the population; another is a new modern language that, as we have already described, has made its mark on the political scene.

Should we push for a sharp contrast and a clear distinction between these two ways of debating about political ideals and policies, in order to avoid ambiguity and the risks that it brings? Theoretically, and from a purely intellectual point of view, nothing short of full clarity should be accepted. On a practical level, however, when the majority of the population chooses, through a democratic process, to keep in its constitution a reference to *shari'a* or Islam, should we not accept the popular will? We know that, for the traditionally educated, the concept of the rule of law is equated with the supremacy of *shari'a,* understood not as a catalogue of specific prescriptions but as a framework for implementing moral norms in the social and political order.

As long as *shari'a* is a kind of flag—a symbol of identity and a way of expressing moral values and the need to uphold them in political practice—more or less in the way that the British monarchy is kept as a symbol of a specific identity and of attachment to cherished traditions, there is no reason to oppose the will of the majority. No democracy can thrive by turning its back on "the ways in which the key issues which have historically divided the society have been resolved." A purely secularist approach, following the French model of *laïcité,* itself may become a form of WP, if it is imposed on people as an external ideology. This is in fact what happened in Syria under the Baathist regime, which today is revealing its true face in all its ugliness.

At the same time, we must remain vigilant against a return of WP from the other end of the ideological spectrum, taking the form of an insistence on restoring an Islamic system as it is imagined to have been in the past, and on implementing *shari'a* viewed as a "catalogue of pre-scriptions." We know that these kinds of conceptions derive from ignorance disguised in the garb of traditional Islamic religious scholarship, and that today they are sustained principally by backward monarchies. The danger here comes from a genre of "pseudo-learning," a range of approaches that employ apologetics as a way of glorifying one's own heritage instead of exploring it in an honest, scholarly way.

Here we must stress that, in the short term, the best way to face the rise of such attitudes may include the acceptance of political leaders who are able to reach the moral sensibilities of their citizens by addressing their concerns in a language that they understand. In the medium and long term, however, the emphasis must be put on fostering an education that helps people to learn about their religious heritage in ways that respect their intelligence rather than take advantage of their lack of sound knowledge.

In conclusion, we now seem to be at a moment when large strata in Arab societies (and in developing countries more broadly) have reached a state of real disenchantment with utopias, and seem to be ready for other forms of political participation. This is the great good news of the Arab Spring, and perhaps its most important lesson. The conviction that there *are* alternatives to the kinds of regimes that have for so long imposed themselves on Arab societies—that life under this or that brand of dictatorship and unaccountable rule emphatically does *not* have to be the Arabs' fate—seems to have taken hold of the collective imagination. An opening-up of the historical awareness of Arab peoples to the democratic ideas, models, and experiences that have emerged in modern times has now become a distinct possibility. This is clear to anyone who *listens* carefully to what people are saying and what they are calling for.

But the news of this favorable turn of events should not lead us to lower our guard. The debate is continuing, and supporters of democracy must still overcome serious challenges. Utopian slogans calling for the restoration of *shari'a* as a list of harsh prescriptions in use many centuries ago still attract followers—especially among large numbers of people who do not clearly see the distinction between *shari'a* as a general injunction to cherish the rule of law and *shari'a* as the enactment of specific legal provisions.

Here we find ourselves confronted by gross misinterpretations of the Islamic heritage that find no support in a careful historical assessment of the development of Muslim societies. These misinterpretations are lent some authority by the support that they receive from a traditional scholarship that refuses to accept any kind of self-criticism. The other aspect of their appeal comes from the feeling, still entrenched in some social strata, that only a full return to the religious heritage can help to moralize the public order. Clarification will be needed in order to disseminate a good understanding of the past and find appropriate ways to learn lessons from it. This process can benefit from the indisputable fact that society has become well aware of the weakness of despotism and of the possibility of finding and implementing workable alternatives that provide dignity and hope to the masses.

In these pages in 1996, commenting on an article by Robin Wright that discussed two visions of Islamic reformation, those of Rachid Ghannouchi (now leader of the Ennahda [or al-Nahda] party in Tunisia) and of exiled Iranian thinker Abdul Karim Soroush, I came to the following conclusion:

> There are voices, like Ghannouchi's, calling for a return to the "implicit constitution" that Islam is supposed to have provided (and which may not be opposed to democracy, or may even find in it a good expression of some of Islam's requirements). These are typically calls to resist "Westernization" and to return to the original (and never fully implemented) Islamic constitution via a course of general reform that usually involves the moralization of public affairs and of political and social relationships. Appeals like these are reminiscent of the "natural and cyclical reflex" to seek a purified and more forceful version of Islam that the fourteenth century Arab historian Ibn Khaldun observed in Muslim societies whenever rulers exceeded the limits of the tolerable. For all their sincerity and effectiveness in terms of influence on the masses, such appeals grow out of attitudes that are trapped in the past. They can in no way lead to a real democratization of society.[10]

Today I would alter that judgment. Having chosen Seymour Martin Lipset as a guide, I recognize the need for "revisiting" old conclusions. I would still insist that thinkers such as Soroush, Fazlur Rahman, Abdelmajid Charfi, and a host of others are needed to offer the education required for Muslims to recover a healthy historical consciousness and, with it, a religiosity fully centered on the individual and his or her ethical outlook. But now I would also accept that figures like Ghannouchi are needed to facilitate the transition from despotism to constitutional ule. Given that the government of Tunisia, well before the Arab Spring, had already put in place reforms that bar any recourse to narrow interpretations of *shari'a,* Ghannouchi will have to find ways to accommodate his "Islamism" to the laws, regulations, and procedures of a modern state—all under the vigilant eyes of well-educated elites and citizens who have shown that they know how to rid themselves of despots.

As Lipset reminds us, "Democracy is not achieved by acts of will alone; but men's wills, through action, can shape institutions and events in directions that reduce or increase the chance for the development and survival of democracy."[11] The challenges confronting Arab societies that aspire to achieve democratic self-government and the rule of law (including respect for human rights) should be addressed in a positive fashion at the level of institution-building and policymaking—not by pursuing quixotic fights against slogans and utopias.

Even the upcoming struggles over the role of *shari'a* can and should be waged in the arenas of mass education and democratic politics. Yet as these day-to-day struggles continue, it is also essential that serious thinkers and scholars strive to clarify the various meanings that *shari'a* has had in the past and to explore how it can be interpreted in ways that meet the needs and aspirations of modern citizens.

NOTES

1. Seymour Martin Lipset, "Some Social Requisites of Democracy: Economic Development and Political Legitimacy," *American Political Science Review* 53 (March 1959): 69–105; and "The Social Requisites of Democracy Revisited," *American Sociological Review* 59 (February 1994): 1–22.

2. In "Steady Work: An Academic Memoir," Lipset says: "Intellectually, I moved a considerable distance, from believing in Marxism-Leninism-Trotskyism to a moderate form of democratic socialism and finally to a middle-of-the-road position, as a centrist, or as some would say, a conservative Democrat." *Annual Review of Sociology* 22 (August 1996): 1.

3. Lipset, "Some Social Requisites of Democracy," 86.

4. Roger Scruton, "Preface to the Third Edition," *Palgrave Macmillan Dictionary of Political Thought,* 3rd ed. (London: Palgrave Macmillan, 2007), xii.

5. Reinhard Schulze, *A Modern History of the Islamic World* (London: I.B. Tauris, 2002), 10.

6. Wael B. Hallaq, *The Origins and Evolution of Islamic Law* (Cambridge: Cambridge University Press, 2005), 1.

7. Noah Feldman, *The Fall and Rise of the Islamic State* (Princeton: Princeton University Press, 2008), 149.

8. Lipset, "Some Social Requisites of Democracy," 94.

9. Lebanon is probably the only exception here, since it has been designed to be and to remain a mosaic of closed communities.

10. Abdou Filali-Ansary, "Islam and Liberal Democracy: The Challenge of Secularization," *Journal of Democracy* 7 (April 1996): 79–80.

11. Lipset, "Some Social Requisites of Democracy," 103.

2

THE TRANSFORMATION OF THE ARAB WORLD

Olivier Roy

Olivier Roy *is a professor at the European University Institute in Florence, where he directs the ReligioWest project. The present essay, which originally appeared in the July 2012 issue of the* Journal of Democracy, *is based on a Raymond Aron Lecture given at the Brookings Institution in December 2011, and includes material from his "The Paradoxes of the Re-Islamization of Muslim Societies," published on the Social Science Research Council's blog,* The Immanent Frame, *and "The Islamic Counter-Revolt," which appeared in the 23 January 2012 issue of the* New Statesman.

The "Arab Spring" at first had nothing about it that was specifically "Arab" or "Muslim." The demonstrators were calling for dignity, elections, democracy, good governance, and human rights. Unlike any Arab revolutionary movements of the past sixty years, they were concerned with individual citizenship and not with some holistic entity such as "the people," the Muslim *umma,* or the Arab nation. The demonstrators referred to no Middle Eastern geopolitical conflicts, burned no U.S. or Israeli flags, offered no chants in favor of the main (that is to say, Islamist) opposition parties, and expressed no wish for the establishment of an Islamic state or the implementation of *shari'a.* Moreover, despite the Western media's frantic quest to put a face on events by talking up some of the protests' astonishingly young and modern spokespersons, the demonstrators produced no charismatic leaders. In short, the Arab Spring belied the "Arab predicament": It simply would not follow the script which holds that the centrality of the Arab-Israeli conflict is fostering an ever-growing Islamization within Arab societies, a search for charismatic leaders, and an identification with supranational causes.

But the demonstrators did not take power—indeed, they did not even try. Instead, they merely wanted to establish a new political scene. Predictably, the Egyptian and Tunisian elections brought ballot-box triumphs for Islamist parties. With deep roots in society, enjoying a legitimacy conferred by decades of political opposition, and defending conservative and religious values shared by most of the populace, Egypt's Muslim Brotherhood and Tunisia's Ennahda party were able to attract votes from well beyond their respective hardcore bases because they looked like credible parties of government. More surprising was the strong showing of the salafist Nour Party in Egypt. Even allowing for salafism's rise in that country, the sudden transformation of an apolitical and informal school of thought into a successful political movement shows that no single Islamist party can claim a monopoly over the expression of Islam in the political sphere.

In any case, the actors who have taken to the electoral stage and benefited from the Arab Spring, whether familiar like the Islamists of the Muslim Brotherhood or newcomers like the salafists, are not known for their attachment to democracy. Even if they have given up talk of the "Islamic revolution," they still put religion at the heart of their agenda. Islamists and salafists alike deplore secularization, the influence of Western values, and the excesses of individualism. Everywhere, they seek to affirm the centrality of religion to national identity, and they are conservative in all areas except the economy. And in Egypt, as commonly happens with parties that are swept into power by landslide margins, they are tempted to think that they can dispense with the grubby business of having to form alliances and hand out government posts equitably. And why should Islamists, with no democratic culture to speak of, behave like good democrats who believe in pluralism?

Once the election results came in, the Western media's enthusiasm faded, and headlines celebrating a democracy-friendly Arab Spring gave way to coverage worrying about the onset of a neoauthoritarian "Arab Winter." Iran, Saudi Arabia, and the Taliban were casting long shadows over Tunis and Cairo. Was there any obstacle to Islamization in the last other than the Egyptian army, whose aversion to democracy is well known? Was the Arab Middle East hopelessly trapped, with no better choices than "secular" dictatorship or "Islamic" totalitarianism?

The answer to that last question is no. Something irreversible did happen in the Arab Spring. Whatever ups and downs may follow, we are witnessing the beginning of a process by which democratization is becoming rooted in Arab societies. Democratization is very much a process in this case—not a program of government implemented by deep-dyed democrats. Comparisons with other world regions (such as Latin America) are difficult, since the Middle East is the only place where the dominant opposition consists of strongly centralized and ideological parties with a religious agenda. A possible comparison might be with the Spanish and Portuguese communist parties of the late 1970s: Like the Islamists of Egypt and Tunisia, they too benefited from a democratization process that they did not trigger. Yet the Iberian communists never achieved the control over elected parliaments that Islamists now enjoy in Cairo and Tunis. Whatever their own agendas, the communist parties had no choice but to negotiate.

The Islamist parties may have more power and freedom to maneuver, but they too will find themselves being pushed to adjust to the democratization process. The pushing will be done by the constraints and dynamics characteristic of the social, religious, political, and geostrategic fields in which these parties must operate. They may accept the demands of the democratization process more willingly (Ennahda) or less willingly (the Egyptian Muslim Brotherhood), but accept them they will, or they will find themselves sidelined. This is not a question of who has or does not have a hidden agenda, or of whether Islam and democracy can or cannot be reconciled.

In order to grasp what is happening in the Middle East, we must set aside a number of deep-rooted prejudices. First among them is the assumption that democracy presupposes secularization: The democratization movement in the Arab world came precisely after thirty years of what has been called the "return of the sacred," an obvious process of re-Islamization of everyday life, coupled with the rise of Islamist parties. The second is the idea that a democrat must also, by definition, be a liberal. There was no flowering of "liberal Islam" preceding the spread of democratic ideas in the Middle East. There are a few reformist religious thinkers who are lauded here and there in the West, but none has ever had much popular appeal in any Arab country. Conversely, many staunch secularists, in Tunisia for instance, are not democrats. They would like to repress Islamists much as the Algerian secularist intellectuals known as *les éradicateurs* did during their own country's civil war in the 1990s. Moreover, fundamentalist religious actors such as the Islamists of Tunisia or even the salafists of Egypt, could become reluctant agents of a form of specifically *political* secularization that should in no way be confused with a secularization of society.

The history of the West does not contradict these theses. Religious tolerance was not the fruit of liberalism and the Enlightenment. Rather, it was the product of grudging truces in savage wars of religion, from the Peace of Augsburg in 1555 to the Treaty of Westphalia in 1648. Politics played a bigger role than philosophy or theology. The greatest Western religious reformer, Martin Luther, was far from a model of democracy, tolerance, or liberalism (to say nothing of his anti-Semitism). The link between Protestantism and democratization is not a matter of theological propositions, but of complex political and social processes. The Founding Fathers of the United States were not secularists; for them, the separation of church and state was a way of protecting religion from government, not the reverse. The French Third Republic was established in 1871 by a predominantly conservative, Catholic, and monarchist parliament that had just crushed the Paris Commune. Christian democracy developed in Europe not because the Catholic Church wanted to promote secular values, but because that was the only way for it to maintain political influence. Finally, let us not forget that populist movements in Europe today align themselves with Christian democracy in calling for the continent's Christian identity to be inscribed in the EU constitution, but few would see this expression of "identity politics" as an omen of Europe's re-Christianization. All the talk of "Islamic identity" in the wake of the Arab Spring does not mean that mosques will henceforth become more crowded. Religious identity and faith are two different (and possibly opposed) concepts in politics. Identity might be a way to bury faith beneath secular politics.

The Islamists as well as the salafists are entering into a political space formatted by certain constraints. These constraints will not only limit their supposed "hidden agenda" of establishing an Islamic state, but will push them toward a more open and democratic way of governance, because therein lies their only chance to remain at the center of political life. Thus the Islamists, and even the salafists, will become reluctant agents of democratization.

A World of Change

The first of these constraints has to do with demographics. As Philippe Fargues has shown, there has been a dramatic decline in fertility across the Arab world.[1] In Tunisia, it has been below the French rate since the year 2000. Women have entered universities and the job market. Young people obtain more schooling than their parents did and marry later. Husbands and wives are more often closer to each other in age and level of education. They have fewer children, with nuclear families replacing extended households. Mobile phones, satellite television, and the Internet have allowed the newer generations to associate, connect, and debate on a "peer-to-peer" basis rather than through a top-down, authoritarian system of knowledge transmission. The young feel less strongly bound to patriarchal customs and institutions that have been unable to cope with the challenges facing contemporary Middle Eastern societies.

Flowing from these changes in demographics have been changes in political culture. The young are more individualistic and less prone to feel the pull of holistic ideologies, whether Islamist or nationalist. Along with the decline of the patriarchal model has gone a drop in the appeal of charismatic leaders. The failure of political Islam that I pointed to twenty years ago is now obvious.[2] This does not mean that Islamist parties are absent from the political playing field—quite the contrary. But their utopian conception of an "Islamic state" has lost credibility. Islamist ideology is now finding itself challenged both by calls for democracy that reject any monopoly claim on power by a single party or ideology, and by neofundamentalist salafists who declare that only a strict personal return to the true tenets of religious practice can serve as the basis of an "Islamic society." Even among the Muslim Brothers, young members reject blind obedience to the leadership. The new generation calls for debate, freedom, democracy, and good governance.

The appeal of democracy is not a consequence of the export of the concept of Western democracy, as fancied by supporters of the U.S. military intervention in Iraq. It is the political consequence of social and cultural changes in Arab societies (though these changes, of course, are part of the globalization process). It is precisely because the Arab Spring is a succession of indigenous upheavals, centered on particular nation-states and delinked from Western encroachments, that democracy is seen as both acceptable and desirable. This is why the ritual denunciations of imperialism—including the usual condemnations decrying Zionism as the source of all the Arab world's troubles—were so remarkably absent from the demonstrations. This also explains why al-Qaeda is out of the picture: The uprooted global jihadist is no longer a model for young activists and fails to find many takers when he seeks to enlist local militants for the global cause (al-Qaeda has been expelled from Iraq by local fighters). The only exceptions are places on the geographic fringes of the Arab world such as Somalia, Yemen, and the Sahel. Al-Qaeda, in short, is yesterday's news, part and parcel of the old anti-imperialist political culture that the Arab Middle East is now leaving behind.

Of course, the social changes are not completely linear and are not necessarily giving rise to a "democratic mind." Their effect is felt earliest, most widely, and most intensely in the big cities and among educated young people with access to the Internet. Others may feel excluded, including villagers in the Egyptian countryside, jobless urbanites in southern Tunisia, shopkeepers and merchants who fear that political tumult will hurt business, conservative milieus upset by what they see as sexual promiscuity among the demonstrators, and so on.

In a word, the Arab Spring masked large reservoirs of underlying conservatism in Arab societies. But even some of the more conservative corners of society are becoming part of the process of individualization. A remarkable field study shows how villagers in Egypt ignored the Muslim Brothers during recent elections because the Brotherhood came across as too monolithic and centralized.[3] These conservative religious voters preferred the salafists on the grounds of what was seen as their greater *political* openness. The salafist Nour Party's recent (albeit passing) endorsement of the presidential candidacy of former Muslim Brother Abdel Moneim Abul Futuh (who counts as a liberal in the Egyptian context) suggests that these villagers may have been onto something.

Change is affecting religion, too. The salafists, like neofundamentalists the world over, are recasting religion as a code and a set of clear-cut norms disconnected from tradition and culture. They are thus best understood not as part of a traditionalist backlash, but as bearers of an attempt to adapt Islam to modernity and globalization.[4] Of course, this adaptation should not be thought of in terms of theology (the propositional content of this or that religion), but rather in terms of religiosity (the way the adherent experiences his or her faith). The wave of re-Islamization hides a very important fact: It has contributed to the diversification and the individualization of the religious field.

Islam as a theological corpus has not changed, but *religiosity* has. And this religiosity, liberal or not, is compatible with democratization because it delinks personal faith from traditions, collective identity, and external authority. The usual religious authorities (*ulama* and Islamist leaders) have largely lost their legitimacy amid the rise of self-appointed and often self-taught religious entrepreneurs. Young "born-again" Muslims have found their own way by surfing the Internet or joining local peer groups. They have criticized the cultural Islam of their parents and have tried to construct their own brand of Islam, one that feels more like a matter of conviction and less like an inherited habit. Religion has become more and more a matter of personal choice, whether that choice be the strict salafist approach to Islam or some sort of syncretism, to say nothing of conversion to another religion.[5]

Fundamentalism and Secularism: The Secret Sharers

This individualization and diversification have had the unexpected consequence of disconnecting religion from daily politics, of bringing religion back into the private sphere and excluding it from that of government management. Fundamentalism, by disconnecting religion from culture and by defining a faith community through believing and not just belonging, is in fact contributing to the secularization of society.[6]

One of the things this means is that an apparent rejection of secularization and democracy may nevertheless express "democracy-compatible" patterns: individualization, refusal of blind obedience, separation of faith from collective identity, and a certain distance from day-to-day politics. In such a context, any endeavor to restore traditional norms through laws and regulations will fail. After all, you cannot change a society by decree. In Saudi Arabia, the official imposition of *shari'a* on the rapidly increasing number of "emancipated" women among the middle and upper classes is leading to unbearable tensions. In Iran, all indicators suggest that society has become more modern and secular under the mullahs. Although a law adopted after 1979 allows girls as young as nine to be taken as brides, the average age at which Iranian women marry has continued to rise and now stands at about 25. In short, even when *shari'a* is theoretically implemented, we are not seeing a return to a traditional society.

As we have seen, the Islamists enjoy no religious monopoly in the public sphere. There are other movements, such as the Sufis and the salafists. This diversification is the consequence of thirty years of "re-Islamization." Religion's centrality in everyday life, coupled with the individualization of religiosity, has given birth to a variety of religious movements. Some have had the encouragement of regimes eager to dilute the Muslim Brotherhood's appeal. Together, their presence contributes to a willy-nilly democratization of the religious field. An unexpected result of the Arab Spring has been that Cairo's al-Azhar Mosque, one of Egypt's most important religious institutions, has found a new legitimacy. The imam there, Sheikh Ahmed el-Tayeb, a conformist appointee of former president Hosni Mubarak, has suddenly become an advocate of human rights, liberty, and the separation of religious institutions from the state. In Tunisia, Ennahda reached power only to discover that it does not control and indeed does not even know the hundreds of young imams who have taken over mosques abandoned by discredited clerics who had held their jobs courtesy of the old Ben Ali regime.

In Egypt, the Muslim Brothers have been upset to learn that their six decades of steady religious and social activism have not been enough to stop salafist newcomers from successfully challenging the Brotherhood's primacy. As a further twist, the Egyptian salafists have been challenging the Brothers from the left by allying themselves with Brotherhood dissidents. (In Tunisia, the salafists have lined up on Ennahda's right by opposing democracy and demanding immediate implementation of *shari'a*.) Among other things, this is a sign that 2011 was not 1979 all over again—unlike the Ayatollah Khomeini's Islamic Republic of Iran, Egypt and Tunisia are not places where some single source (the Muslim Brotherhood or Ennahda) can assert a right "to say what Islam says." The religious arena, too, has become pluralistic and open to democratic pressure, even if, for the faithful, there are some elements that remain nonnegotiable.

That said, there is no agreement among religious political actors over what is and is not negotiable beyond the centrality of Islam. Should there be a body that determines whether laws are sufficiently conformable to Islam? If so, who ought to be nominated to it and by whom? Should *hudud* (corporal punishment) be applied in cases where religious laws have been violated? Is conversion to Christianity possible for a Muslim? It is on the question of the definition of religious liberty that we can expect the most vigorous debates. If the Muslim Brotherhood presents itself as the protector of the rights of the minority Coptic Christians in Egypt to practice their religion, is it ready to make religious freedom an *individual* human right (abandoning the concept of apostasy in the process) rather than merely the collective right of a particular historic minority? The debate has already started. Abdel Moneim Abul Futuh, the Brotherhood dissident turned presidential candidate and surprising recipient of salafist support, has declared that "nobody should interfere if a Christian decides to convert to Islam or a Muslim decides to leave Islam and become a Christian."[7]

Whenever the implementation of Islamic religious norms comes up for discussion, there is an internal debate in the institutions concerned. Democratization has affected the community of believers, too. The salafists will certainly try to raise the stakes over *shari'a* and make the Muslim Brotherhood face up to the contradictions of its position. But they have also leapt into the political realm, forming parties of their own despite having previously challenged the very idea of political parties in the name of Islam. In their case, this is the compliment that vice pays to virtue: The salafists know that without a parliamentary presence, they would lose their influence.

All the same, the salafists have no program other than imposing *shari'a,* and thus are anything but a party of government, as the most realistic among them well know. The Muslim Brotherhood and the salafists are fated to be rivals, and so one cannot rule out the possibility of their entering into unexpected alliances with other political forces.

The Failure of Political Islam

Islamists have changed, or at least they have understood that the world has changed. Even where they have taken control, as in Iran or Gaza, they have been unable to establish a successful model of an Islamic state. The gains that they have made in the wake of the Arab political openings are premised upon previous successes won by "others" (in Egypt and Tunisia, democratic secularists). In earlier cases, the "others" have been nationalists. In Gaza, it was Palestinian nationalism, not political Islam, that brought Hamas (the local wing of the Muslim Brotherhood) to power. Much the same is true for Lebanon's Hezbollah, which has built its success on its opposition to Israel and its ability to position itself as the champion of the country's large but traditionally underprivileged Shia community.

When Islamists went to jail, they rubbed elbows with secularists and human-rights advocates (such as Egypt's Saad Eddin Ibrahim). When they went into exile, it was more often to Europe than to Mecca. The Islamists came to understand the need to make alliances and to take into account other views. They tried to engage the West, but were too often rebuked. Calls for holy war and violent confrontation are the trademarks of countries or groups that are not friendly to these Islamists, and even consider them to be traitors: Iran or al-Qaeda. Implementation of *shari'a* is the official policy of regimes and movements with which they cannot identify, such as Saudi Arabia or the Taliban. Charitable work aside, the Islamists social agenda has slowly faded away as their constituents have become ever more bourgeois and entrepreneurial. The aging of their leadership has put them at odds with the new generation of believers. There is a cultural gap between the Islamists and the younger generation that is less about Islam per se than about what it means for a person to be a believer.

All these changes are pointing toward the rise of what Asef Bayat calls "post-Islamism."[8] This does not mean that the Islamists have disappeared, but that their utopian ambitions have proved to be no match for existing social, political, and even geostrategic realities. There is, for instance, no blueprint of an "Islamic economy." Islamists are fairly status quo–friendly when it comes to economic affairs, content to run charities in poor neighborhoods but opposing strikes and approving the rescinding of land reform in Egypt. The wave of religious revival that has swept the Muslim world did not swell their ranks, but contributed on the contrary to the diversification of the religious field, transforming the Islamists into one set of religious actors among others.

Have the Islamists become "democrats"? They have long favored elections, recognizing that support for armed struggle serves jihadists like al-Qaeda on the one hand and repressive secular governments on the other, especially when the latter are eager to curry Western favor by posturing as the only bulwark against the "Islamist threat." Ennahda's leader Rachid Ghannouchi has explicitly rejected the concept of an "Islamic state," and cites Turkey's Justice and Development Party (AKP) as a model of a post-Islamist religious-minded and conservative party.

Still, most Islamists are uneasy about sharing power with non-Islamic parties and turning their "brotherhood" organizations into modern political parties. They may, as in Morocco and Tunisia, give up formal support for *shari'a,* but they cannot define a concrete ruling program that goes beyond banning alcohol, promoting the veil, or pursuing other petty forms of "*shari'a*-fication." After the Arab Spring, which began outside Islamist ranks and took Islamist leaders by surprise, the Islamists must choose among options. Option 1 is the Turkish model as represented by the AKP. This would mean turning the "brotherhood" into a true modern political party; trying to attract voters from beyond a hard core of devout Muslims; recasting religious norms into vaguer conservative values (family, property, honesty, the work ethic); adopting a neoliberal approach to the economy; and endorsing the constitution, parliament, and regular elections.

Option 2 would be to ally themselves with "counterrevolutionary" forces (as in Egypt, for instance) out of fear that real democracy will prove too unpredictable and too hard to control. This choice would have large downsides, as Islamists would find themselves losing their remaining legitimacy, and might wind up becoming tools of the army. A modified form of this option would see Islamists siding with salafists in a focus on certain high-profile issues (the veil and family law) while leaving other social and economic matters aside. Rather than ideological debate, it will most likely be the course of events itself that shapes what the Islamists do.

They are certainly neither secularists nor liberals, but they can be democrats. The convictions of political actors often play less of a role in shaping their policies than the constraints to which they are subject. The

Islamists are entering an entirely new political space. Egypt and Tunisia did not have revolutions that replaced dictatorships with regimes that resembled their predecessors. There have been elections and there is a parliament. Political parties have been formed and, whatever the disappointments and fears of the secular left, it will be difficult simply to close down this new space, because what brought it into being in the first place—a savvy, connected young generation and a spirit of protest—is still there. And experience has shown that in the Middle East, when people are offered the opportunity to take part in free elections, they show up, even if threatened (as in Afghanistan and Iraq). Islamist movements throughout the region are constrained to operate in a democratic arena that they did not create and that has legitimacy in the eyes of the people.

Wary Voters

The Islamists must also listen to their voters, who will not follow them blindly. The "Islamic" electorate in Egypt or Tunisia today is not revolutionary; it is conservative. It wants order. It wants leaders who will kick-start the economy and affirm conventional religious values. It is not ready to plunge into reviving the caliphate or creating an Islamic republic. Ennahda and the Muslim Brotherhood know all this. They know that they need to attract voters because they have neither the desire nor the means to seize power by force. What is more, the protest movements in Egypt and Tunisia were not shaped by an all-encompassing ideology (as was the case in Iran in 1979) but by the ideals of democracy, pluralism, and good governance.

Iran's November 1979 election was held in the name of the Islamic Republic. The message was clear: This was an ideological revolution (even if there was disagreement about its complexion between the red of the Marxist-Leninists and the green of the Islamists). There is nothing of the kind in either Egypt or Tunisia. There is no revolutionary or ideological dynamic. It is significant, in this regard, that nowhere has the cult of the charismatic strongman reappeared. Instead, there are political parties and a new culture of debate that has influenced even the Islamists.

To impose an Islamist form of authoritarianism, the Islamists would need either control of the police and army or their own paramilitary forces, none of which they have. In Egypt and Tunisia, the army remains outside Islamist control (in Egypt, it may be outside anyone's control), and is not identified with the former regime the way the Imperial Iranian Army was in 1979. Then too, neither Egypt nor Tunisia enjoys oil rents large enough to pay for placating the poor and sustaining loyal militias.[9] Elections will really matter, and their results can be expected to swing back and forth for the next decade or more. Although Islamists tend to adopt a populist profile (talking a lot about matters of "national identity," blaming Westernized elites), they may find themselves being outbid along these lines by demagogues who, if not "holier than thou," are nonetheless "more populist than thou" and better at making populist appeals.

There is one further set of constraints on both the Islamists and the salafists, and these are geostrategic. Neither group has reached office on a platform of *jihad* or special support for the Palestinians. Unlike the Nasserite and Baathist revolutions or even Anwar Sadat's 1974 counter-revolution (when he opened Egypt's economy and swapped the Soviet for the U.S. embrace), the Arab Spring and Winter have not turned on international questions. Neither the Brotherhood nor the salafists have ever articulated a coherent supranational agenda of mobilizing the *umma,* instead leaving attempts to politicize the concept of a transnational Islamic community in the bloody hands of al-Qaeda. The various branches of the Muslim Brothers (whether in Egypt, Jordan, Kuwait, or Syria) as well as the Islamists of the Maghreb have always had their own national agendas and organizations; despite their ideological proximity, they have never been able to devise a regional common strategy. And recent events show how differently they may react: The Jordanian and Tunisian Islamists are far more open in their alliances and in their embrace of democracy than the Egyptians. The national and domestic scene is where the real action is. If supranational dynamics do make themselves felt, moreover, they will only push the Islamists to change their domestic agenda in the direction of more democracy and moderation.

The Israeli-Palestinian conflict surely retains emotional significance, but no one is ready to endanger geopolitical stability and economic development for the sake of the Palestinian cause. The Islamists dislike Israel, and in this respect they are in step with Arab public opinion, but they are not willing to go to war. They have accepted the existing geostrategic constraints. The invitation that Tunisia's new and democratically elected government extended to Hamas leader Ismail Haniyeh in January 2012 is in line with the one that Tunisia extended to the Palestine Liberation Organization after the Israelis took Beirut in 1982, and is evidence of continuity rather than rupture. The care that Egypt's Muslim Brotherhood has taken to open a dialogue with Western diplomats is another sign that it is accepting strategic realities. The Brotherhood wants to remodel the relationship between Egypt and Israel, but through negotiations, not confrontation. Economic constraints such as the lack of oil rents and the need to maintain tourism also drive the new governments to want at least to appear moderate. There are projects to make tourism *halal* with gender-segregated beaches and alcohol-free resorts, but these seem like pipe dreams: Why should wealthy Saudis abandon Marbella or Beirut for a *halal* Sharm el-Sheikh that is just miles away from their own puritanically run five-star hotels?

The major conflict that is taking shape is not a clash between an Islamist-led Muslim world and the West. Rather, it is the one that pits the conservative Sunni Arab world (whether secular, Islamist, Wahhabi, or salafist) against the "Shia crescent" of which Iran is the keystone. In the background is Saudi Arabia's discreet de facto alliance with Israel against the common Iranian threat. The crisis and fighting now raging in Syria are forcing regional actors to make unappetizing choices. Hezbollah is siding with Tehran and its client, the Assad regime in Syria. Hamas, though allied with Syria and Hezbollah, has reluctantly left Damascus for Cairo, returning to the fold of its old family, the Sunni Muslim Brothers. Turkey, having been evicted from the European dream, has turned from its dashed hopes of full EU membership to the task of carving out a new regional role for itself at the head of a Sunni alliance. The AKP leaders are well acquainted with the Arab Islamist leaders, and a new axis is taking shape, bringing together similar conservative Sunni parties. The Turkish connection is also a factor of moderation for the Islamist parties.

Of course this emerging Sunni axis antagonizes local minorities (Alevis in Turkey, Alawites in Syria), and accentuates tensions with the Shias in the Gulf (no support for the Bahraini demonstrators), in Saudi Arabia, Lebanon, and Iraq. Yet the isolation of Iran is also a step in favor of stabilization and moderation. An Israeli military strike against Iran's nuclear facilities will certainly trigger demonstrations in Casablanca, Cairo, and Tunis. But the Arab street will probably not mobilize against newly elected Arab governments, which will keep a lower profile than expected. Saudi Arabia, which cannot stand the concept of an Arab Spring, grows ever more estranged from the Islamist parties. The Saudis have played the salafists against the Brothers, at least indirectly, but Saudis will not be able to find staunch and lasting allies among either Tunisia's hard-line salafists or Egypt's milder variety.

The bottom line is that, for the first time since the early 1950s, the geostrategic situation of the Middle East neither dictates domestic agendas nor spurs the radicalization of domestic politics—both good omens for the process of democratization.

And What of Islam?

Whatever political ups and down lie ahead, whatever the diversity of national cases, and however intricate becomes the predictable fragmentation of both "democrats" and "Islamists" into various trends and parties, the main issue will be to redefine the role of Islam in politics. The growing de facto autonomy of the religious arena from political and ideological control does not mean that secularism is necessarily gaining ground in terms of culture and society. Yet certainly a new form of *political* secularism is emerging. Once it takes hold, religion will not dictate what politics should be, but will itself be reduced to politics.

What is at stake is the reformulation of religion's place in the public sphere. There is broad agreement that constitutions should announce the

"Muslim" identity of society and the state. Yet there is similar agreement on the proposition that *shari'a* is not an autonomous and complete system of law that can replace "secular" law. Instead, *shari'a* is becoming a loose and somewhat hazily defined "reference point" (except in the realm of personal law, which means that issues of women's rights will be at the core of the debate). As we saw, modern forms of religiosity tend to stress individual faith and choices over any sense of conformity to institutional Islam. Whatever descriptive truth was left in the old saying "Islam admits no separation between *din* and *dunya*" (that is, between religion and the world) has been definitively emptied out by the Arab Spring.

What we are seeing is not so much a secularization as a deconstruction of Islam. Is Islam a matter of cultural identity, meaning that one might even be an "atheist Muslim"? Is it a faith that can be shared only by born-again believers (salafists) in the confines of self-conscious faith communities? Or is it a "horizon of meaning," where references to *shari'a* are more virtual than real? The recasting of religious norms into "values" helps also to promote an interfaith coalition of religious conservatives that could unite around some specific causes: opposition to same-sex marriage, for instance. It is interesting to see how, in Western Europe, secular populists stress the continent's Christian identity, while many Muslim conservatives try to forge an alliance with believers of other faiths to defend shared values. In doing so, many of them tend to adopt Protestant evangelical concerns, fighting abortion and Darwinism even though these issues have never been prominent in traditional Islamic debates.[10]

In this sense, the modern neofundamentalists are trying to recast Islam into a Western-compatible kind of religious conservatism. This has become obvious in Turkey. In 2004, when the AKP's Prime Minister Recep Tayyip Erdoğan unsuccessfully tried to promote a legal ban on adultery, the crime was defined not in terms of *shari'a,* but rather by reference to the modern Western family (a monogamous marriage of a man and a woman with equal rights and duties). Interestingly, this made the traditional practice of polygamy, not infrequent among old-line AKP local cadres, a crime. As episodes such as these reveal, Islam is becoming part of the recasting of a religious global marketplace disconnected from local cultures.[11]

Instead of the secularization of society, we might do better to speak of the "autonomization" of politics from religion and of religion from politics, due to the diversification of the religious field and the inability to reconstruct religion as a political ideology. When religion is everywhere, it is nowhere. That was the underlying meaning that I took away from what Egyptian parliament speaker and Muslim Brother Saad al-Katatni said to a salafist deputy who wanted to perform the Muslim prayer call while the house was in session: "We are all Muslims; if you want to pray there is a mosque in parliament, but parliament is not a mosque."[12] The paradox of re-Islamization is that it leads to political secularization and opens the door to debate about what Islam means. This could lead to the reopening of theological debate, but that would be a consequence and not a cause of the democratization of Muslim societies.

NOTES

1. Philippe Fargues, *Générations arabes: L'Alchimie du nombre* (Paris: Fayard, 2000).

2. Olivier Roy, *The Failure of Political Islam,* trans. Carol Volk (Cambridge: Harvard University Press, 1994).

3. Yasmine Moataz Ahmed, "Who Do Egypt's Villagers Vote For? And Why?" *Egypt Independent,* 10 April 2012.

4. Olivier Roy, *Globalized Islam: The Search for a New Ummah* (New York: Columbia University Press, 2004).

5. In Morocco and Algeria, there have been enough Christian conversions for a Protestant evangelical church to have sprung up among former Muslims. See Nadia Marzouki, "Conversion as Statelessness: A Study of Contemporary Algerian Conversions to Evangelical Christianity," *Middle East Law and Governance* 4, no. 1 (2012): 69–105.

6. Olivier Roy, *Holy Ignorance: When Religion and Culture Part Ways,* trans. Ros Schwartz (New York: Columbia University Press, 2010).

7. Noha El-Hennawy, "Islamist Presidential Candidate Declares Conversion Permissible," *Egypt Independent,* 16 May 2011.

8. Asef Bayat, "The Coming of a Post-Islamist Society," *Critique: Critical Middle East Studies* 9 (Fall 1996): 43–52.

9. There is a clear negative connection between the Arab Spring and oil rents. Governments without piles of petrodollars to spend must earn support the old-fashioned way—at the voting booth.

10. The works of the Turkish anti-Darwinist Adnan Oktar, who writes under the pen name Harun Yahya, have been widely distributed in the West since 2007. His *Atlas of Creation,* which he sent unsolicited to thousands of Western scholars and institutions, presents all the arguments and some iconography familiar from anti-Darwinist literature in the United States.

11. Olivier Roy, *Holy Ignorance.*

12. Ed Husain, "Egypt's Piety Contest," *The Arab Street,* 7 February 2012, *http://blogs.cfr.org/husain/2012/02/07/egypts-piety-contest.*

3

ARAB DEMOCRACY OR ISLAMIST REVOLUTION?

Hillel Fradkin

Hillel Fradkin is senior fellow at the Hudson Institute and director of its Center on Islam, Democracy, and the Future of the Muslim World. He is also the founder and coeditor of the Hudson Institute's periodical review Current Trends in Islamist Ideology. This essay originally appeared in the January 2013 issue of the Journal of Democracy.

In his essay on "The Transformation of the Arab World" in the July 2012 issue of the *Journal of Democracy*, Olivier Roy offers a comprehensive interpretation of the "Arab Spring" and its potential for leading to democracy. On the whole, he presents a benign view of where things will wind up, though with some caveats from the perspective of Western liberal democracy. The new Arab regimes, he suggests, will indeed be democratic but not necessarily secular or liberal. Nevertheless, he argues that there will be a trend toward a kind of secularization—a "political secularization" of the role of religion. Though this will not yield a simply liberal order, its effects might be regarded as quasi-liberal insofar as the political agenda will not be driven by a monolithic religious one: "Religion will not dictate what politics should be, but will itself be reduced to politics."

This, obviously, is a crucial assertion. Although the Arab revolts were launched by demonstrators "calling for dignity, elections, democracy, good governance, and human rights"—what one might reasonably call a secular, liberal, democratic agenda—the protesters were not the primary beneficiaries of the elections that ensued. Indeed, as Roy fairly observes, they did not even try to win these elections: "They merely wanted to establish a new political scene." Instead, the electoral beneficiaries, especially in Egypt, were Islamist parties. But these parties are bearers of the tradition of Islamism and its core project of building an Islamic state in which religion will indeed, to use Roy's words, "dictate what politics should be." Hence it seems fair to ask whether the future may hold not democratization, but rather a process in which the Islamists pursue "their supposed

'hidden agenda' of establishing an Islamic state" and achieve their
goal.

Roy's answer to this question is an emphatic no. Islamists have been
"unable to establish a successful model of an Islamic state." Moreover,
"their utopian ambitions have proved to be no match for existing social, political, and even geostrategic realities." As Roy reminds us, he
first pointed out "the failure of political Islam" some twenty years ago.
But such consistency masks a difference and even a contradiction. Two
decades ago, his grounds for proclaiming political Islam a failure were
its inability to take power anywhere and an expectation that it never
would. But now it emphatically has taken power—at least formally—in
the largest and most consequential Arab state.

The paradox is apparently resolved by the view that the Islamists'
"utopian conception of an 'Islamic state' has lost credibility." As "utopian," it was doomed anyway. But questions arise: In the eyes of whom,
precisely, has the Islamic state lost credibility—in those of the Muslim
Brothers, whose political success has now reached its highest point ever
since their founding in 1928? Have the Brothers abandoned the historic
vision of their founder Hassan al-Banna? Or, if they still cling to that vision, will they indeed be compelled to forsake it by constraints built into
the new political scene brought about by the Arab upheavals? What will
be the result of the interaction between their ambitions and necessity?

Roy's view can be summed up in his conclusion that "something irreversible" occurred amid those upheavals: "We are witnessing the beginning of a process by which democratization is becoming rooted in Arab
societies." In defense of this thesis, Roy offers a number of arguments,
both political and sociological. Both sets of arguments are interesting,
but both are also exposed to grave doubts and difficulties.

The Political Argument

Though Roy relies somewhat more heavily on sociological arguments, it is appropriate here to begin with the political side and to focus
on the case of Egypt and its Muslim Brotherhood. There are a number
of reasons for this: The controversy over the character and prospects of
"Arab democracy" remains primarily a political question; the Islamist
project, with its goal of an "Islamic state," has always displayed an overarching concern with politics; and Egypt will provide the most immediate and crucial test of whether that project can be realized.

Roy's argument is threefold. First, the circumstances in which the
Brotherhood and other Islamist groups such as the salafists have reached
power have also put them "into a political space formatted by certain
constraints." Second, the Islamists are aware of this situation and they
have bent or will bend to it: "Islamists have changed, or at least they
have understood that the world has changed." They know that in be-

having accordingly "lies their only chance to remain at the center of political life." Third and finally, if they do not "accept the demands of the democratization process . . . they will find themselves sidelined." So whether the Islamists cooperate or not, democratization will triumph.

All this may eventually prove true. At the moment, however, the political evidence tends strongly in a different direction. Certainly the Brotherhood has found obstacles in its way and encountered constraints upon the effectuation of its will. But so far it has also shown remarkable skill in overcoming them and in achieving political success.

Like many others, Roy expected one of the strongest constraints to be the army; another was supposed to be discontent with the leadership among younger Brothers; yet another constraint would be imposed by actual Brotherhood defectors who, by forming alliances with other political forces (both Islamist and secularist), might obstruct the Brotherhood in the presidential elections.

For months, things seemed to be tending that way. The Brotherhood won the parliamentary elections in late 2011 and early 2012 and was thereby enabled to dominate the constituent assembly tasked with writing a new constitution. But Egypt's courts overturned these achievements, dissolving both the parliament and the constituent assembly. On the eve of the June 2012 presidential election won by the Brotherhood's Mohamed Morsi, the Supreme Council of the Armed Forces (SCAF) drained the presidency of its powers through "supplementary constitutional decrees," and assigned to itself not only executive powers but full legislative ones as well.

Earlier in the presidential campaign, the Brotherhood's most charismatic presidential candidate, Khairat al-Shater, had been blocked from running. His replacement Morsi—an engineering professor whom many dismissed as the "spare tire"—faced a tough campaign. Morsi won, but only narrowly. Many thought that his popular support was thin, and he appeared to confirm this by weak and solicitous gestures on the morrow of his victory. According to a common view, the military had succeeded in effecting a de facto "coup." Field Marshal Mohamed Hussein Tantawi, the head of the SCAF, boasted that "Egypt will never fall. It belongs to all Egyptians and not to a certain group . . . the armed forces will not allow it . . . . The armed forces will not allow anyone, especially those pushed from the outside, to distract it from its role as the protector of Egypt."

The Muslim Brotherhood seemed to have little power in the new "political scene." Moreover, it seemed as if it was being set up to bear the blame for all of Egypt's many problems. Down the road, then, its power might fade still further.

Yet within six weeks, Morsi managed to decapitate the SCAF and to bring the army to heel by the wholesale appointments of new senior officers. At the same time, the SCAF decrees that had been meant to cripple Morsi and the Brotherhood were turned around in their favor. In the absence of parliament, Morsi acquired all legislative power. Since then, he has used it and other powers of the presidency to fill offices in crucial ministries largely with appointees allied to his own views. The Brotherhood thus seems to have staged its own coup.

Roy's analysis of how the Egyptian political dynamic would unfold was written before the Brotherhood's defeat of the army, so it would be unjust to complain that he had failed to take it into account. Moreover, the end of this political story is far from being written.

But it is not unfair to ask whether the general view that Roy takes of the "political scene" or "political space" was on the face of it suspect. Roy asserts that "the convictions of political actors often play less of a role in shaping their policies than the constraints to which they are subject." This may well be true of a normal political environment in which well-established constitutional and other factors place limits on political action. But it is frequently *not* true of revolutionary situations (although of course some constraints operate there too). According to Roy, however, this is an irrelevant consideration, for "there is no revolutionary or ideological dynamic" in Egypt (as there was, for example, in Iran in 1979), other than perhaps the revolutionary dynamic that created the new "political space." "It will be difficult simply to close down this new space, because what brought it into being in the first place—a savvy, connected young generation and a spirit of protest—is still there." These are the real revolutionaries, and the Brotherhood folk, who anyway have abandoned their utopian ambitions, will be forced to operate within the democratic parameters established by the youthful protestors.

It now appears, however, that there is indeed a "revolutionary dynamic" beyond that inaugurated by the earliest demonstrations, and for the moment at least, the Brotherhood is driving it. If that was not simply predictable, it is surely not unprecedented in the record of modern revolutions since the French Revolution, where moderate beginnings yielded to the success of more radical forces. Nor was it ever simply true, as Roy suggests, that the Brotherhood did not play a large and perhaps even decisive role in the anti-Mubarak revolution. It is true that the Muslim Brothers were largely absent from the streets in the first week, perhaps due to habits of caution bred by long years of government suppression. But the Brotherhood rather quickly brought its large cadres to bear in the February 2011 protests that led to Mubarak's fall. It is unlikely that Mubarak would have been ousted without them.

In all events, the Brothers, like other revolutionaries, do not seem to have felt obliged simply to accept the new "political space" along with whatever constraints it might impose. Instead, the Brotherhood has sought to reshape this new space to its own advantage. As with past revolutionary shot-callers, the success of the Brotherhood's leaders will hinge on how well they understand the politically relevant terrain, how intelligent they are in exploiting it, and how much in the way of resources they can bring to bear. Thus far, they appear to be succeeding.

Top Brotherhood officials understood, as others did not, how weak the army actually was. At the time of the "army coup," the Brotherhood indicated that it was not accepting defeat. Jihad al-Haddad, a close advisor and spokesman for Khairat al-Shater, declared that the existing situation was a "chessboard." Haddad also told a reporter that the Brotherhood had "always expected a long struggle to achieve power" and had been "planning for a 7- or 10-year process."[1] Of course, the Brotherhood needed an appropriate occasion to act against the army. As it happened, it found that relatively quickly, in the form of a terrorist attack on a military base in Sinai. By that time, the Brotherhood had also taken the measure of the country's other political forces, including secular ones, and understood that these too would have to support the Brothers' countercoup.

But if Egypt is still in the midst of a revolutionary situation, it then becomes very important to give attention to "the convictions of political actors" (their ideological and revolutionary outlooks), and not just to "the constraints to which they are subject." If Roy does not do so, it is because of his analytic premise, and certainly not because the Brotherhood's agenda (as he somewhat snidely suggests) is merely "supposed" or "hidden." It is neither, and Roy knows that.

Shater Speaks

While the Brotherhood may try to keep hidden its tactics, we are quite well informed about its convictions. In addition to being able to study the movement's long ideological tradition, we can directly consult the views of Khairat al-Shater, who is widely credited with being the mastermind of current Brotherhood strategy and operations. He offered them in a long April 2011 speech.[2] In this address, he made it clear that, for him at least, what Roy calls the "utopian conception of an 'Islamic state'" had not lost its "credibility." Moreover, Shater responded clearly if implicitly to the doubts, raised by Roy and others, about the abiding relevance of the Brotherhood's vision and strategy. Due to the Brotherhood's success to date, his remarks deserve very close attention.

Shater rejected root and branch any notion of seeking a new vision, spirit, or path. Rather, he insisted that the Brotherhood's approach had been vindicated and undertook to restate and elaborate it for the present circumstances. He emphatically and explicitly reaffirmed Banna's goal, which he described as

> restoring Islam in its all-encompassing conception; subjugating people to God; instituting the religion of God; the Islamization of life, empowering of God's religion; establishing the Nahda [Renaissance] of the Ummah [the global Muslim community] and its civilization on the basis of Islam.

With equal emphasis, he reaffirmed the wisdom of Banna's "method" and its success—a success that Shater thought recent events had revealed rather than contradicted. Banna's method was to "build" in progressive order, beginning from the "Muslim individual" and proceeding through the "Muslim family, the Muslim society, the Islamic government, the global Islamic State and [eventually] reaching the status of Ustathiya [preeminence or mastership] with that State." Shater saw that process, which had already done so much to transform Muslim society, as self-evidently entering its next phase, that of Islamic government, just as Banna had foreseen.

Similarly, the current success also vindicated the instrument that Banna had created to apply this method—namely, the Society of the Muslim Brothers—and its mode of organization and operation. This instrument was distinguished by the careful hierarchical organization of its various subgroups and the strict discipline exercised by its highest authorities, the Supreme Guide and the Guidance Bureau. As a result, the Brotherhood had been able to pursue its mission productively through many years of extreme oppression. No other group of Muslims was like it or had enjoyed similar success, no matter how pious or how devoted to the general goals of the Brotherhood these other groups might have been. This was why the Brotherhood was well prepared for the present opportunity.

All these things—mission, method, and organization—were "constants" and not "variables," as Shater was at pains to insist. The constants were not subject to change. Nor did they ever need to be, since they were derived from the highest and most successful model ever, "the Prophet's method" (as Shater called it) offered by Muhammad and his companions and early successors. By following this model, the Brotherhood had created individual members who were "a walking Quran; whose faith, worship, manners, relationships, behavior, thoughts and emotions were identical to the Islam that Muhammad received from God Almighty." So too had it adhered to the guidance of Umar ibn Al-Khattab, the second caliph, who had stated, said Shater, that "there is no religion without a [Society], no [Society] without an Imam, and no Imam without obedience." On this basis, Shater observed, Umar had been the architect of the greatest of the early Muslim conquests and of the global Islamic state that had endured for a thousand years. The Brotherhood's organization as a society—as *the* Society—and its discipline had followed Umar's model and, it was implied, might thus duplicate his success.

But what of the "variables" that Shater acknowledged? Were there new circumstances that might require new methods and policies in pursuit of what he termed "Brotherhood work," and that might introduce the element of "moderation" anticipated by Roy and others? Indeed there were, said Shater. The Brotherhood was responding to new circumstances, for instance by setting up a political party, the Freedom and Justice Party. The Brotherhood had never had a party before, and indeed Banna himself had opposed such a step on principle. But Shater emphasized that this and other possible innovations were entirely secondary. Political parties as such were of alien, Western origin and enjoyed no particular sanctity. Indeed, as instruments of political conflict, Western-style parties violate the unity and harmony that are the goal of Muslim politics. If they turned out to be useful in present circumstances, fine; if not, they could and would be dispensed with.

But what of possible "dissent in the ranks," especially among the younger Brothers? In his speech, Shater acknowledged the young and professed to understand their concerns and temptations. He cautioned them, however, to remember that they were inexperienced and that they were coming of age without benefit of the harsh experiences endured by men such as himself, who had spent much time in prison and suffered other great injustices. It was important for the Brotherhood youth to take the long view and in any event necessary in light of the principle of Brotherhood discipline. The Brotherhood could and did entertain debate about the "variables." But such debate was resolved through its highest organs, and once decisions were taken, they were obligatory. That was a "constant." And in fact, there have been very few defections among the young Brothers, despite the predictions of Roy and others.

Shater's vision, as Roy says, is utopian and thus likely to fail sooner or later. But it surely makes a difference whether it is sooner or later, as we know from the histories of European utopian movements such as Communism and Nazism, or of Khomeini's Islamic Republic of Iran. Roy sees the Iranian regime as on shaky ground, and indeed it is. The Islamic Republic now confronts internal ideological contradictions as well as public discontent, and it may be on the road to collapse. But it is still standing after more than thirty years. How long might the Egyptian revolution take to run its course, and with what consequences?

The Sociological Argument

Roy's sociological analysis may be taken in part as a response to these issues. He appears confident that democratization will put an end to revolution sooner rather than later. According to him, new forces are at work in Arab society that were presumptively lacking in Iran (a rather doubtful assertion) and that will be a more powerful barrier to the Is-lamist project than the political obstacles. In part, these are the result of the effects of modernization on Arab society (in this context, Roy cites the impact of modern university education on the young). But in part they are also the paradoxical result of the influence over the last thirty years of the Islamist project itself: the rebellion against modernity, the "return of the sacred," and the "re-Islamization of everyday life."

Modernization has undermined the "patriarchal model" and weak-ened the "top-down, authoritarian system of knowledge transmission," especially for the young. As a result, the young are more individualistic and less susceptible to "the pull of holistic ideologies, whether Islamist or nationalist" and to "the appeal of charismatic leaders."

The modernization story may appear to be contradicted by the "return of the sacred," but the contradiction is only apparent. For the sacred has returned in the form not of a restoration of authoritative tradition but of a smorgasbord of religious movements competing for the adherence of the young. The result is an upsurge not of religion but of "religiosity." The attachments that it generates are fundamentally an expression of individual preference, a kind of approximation of the individual conscience that led Christians and others to embrace religion within liberal societies. Young Arab Muslims are coming to resemble modern individuals, even if they are not aware of it. Politically speaking, this means that no uniform religious project can prevail: "Religion will not dictate what politics should be, but will itself be reduced to politics."

The evidence for this conclusion is necessarily preliminary, but even as such, it is highly dubious. It has long been rightly observed that the Islamist movement tends to undermine much Muslim and "patriarchal" tradition: In this and in other ways it is "modern." But it is also true that this break with tradition was from the beginning the intention and proud boast of the Islamist movement, with its appeal to the model of the Salaf as-Salah (the virtuous ancestors)—that is, the truly ancestral. Sociologically speaking, moreover, it has been clear over the past thirty years that many young people from the Muslim world (and often especially the educated among them) have embraced the Islamist movement as a refuge from the burdens of the modern individual rather than as a path to individual expression. Perhaps the Egyptian college students who are drawn to the Brotherhood and feel blessed by the services that it provides are suffering from what the Marxists used to call "false consciousness," and a further unfolding of the sociological dialectic will yield the results that Roy predicts. But that remains to be seen.

Roy also appeals to the older and longer European experience in arriving at a settlement of the question of religion and politics, and in particular the emergence of religious tolerance as a principle of political life. According to Roy, "Religious tolerance was not the fruit of liberalism and the Enlightenment. Rather, it was the product of grudging truces in savage wars of religion. . . . Politics played a bigger role than philosophy or theology." In this context, he invokes the Thirty Years' War, the U.S. Founding, and other episodes in modern Western history, and suggests that there is an analogy between this experience and current trends in the Arab world.

But Roy's account of the Western experience neglects certain crucial factors. It is of course true that the modern Western settlement of the question of religion and politics did not proceed directly from the realm of ideas to politics, but was mediated by grievous and bloody experience. But it is also true that, when this suffering produced openness to new views, the latter were available, precisely because the ground had been prepared by works of philosophy and theology. Moreover, the new doctrines of religious tolerance made extensive use (perhaps disingenuously, but nonetheless successfully) of notions of "individual conscience" arising from Christian thought, an approach that is less readily available in a Muslim context. In any event, the only prominent protagonists of "theology" or political thought in the Arab Muslim world today are the Brotherhood and other Islamists. As Roy notes, "there are a few reformist religious thinkers who are lauded here and there in the West, but none has ever had much popular appeal in any Arab country." Roy seems to think that this deficit will be made up by the absorption of modern notions that have gained global currency. Perhaps, but as in the past, this will require overcoming the objection—a very grave one in the Arab and Muslim worlds—that these notions are of alien origin.

Nor does Roy's analogy with the history of the West have benign implications for Arab society in the short term. For if that analogy is accurate, it suggests that Arab society must first undergo an especially grievous period of religiopolitical conflict. The Islamist revolution, as it goes forward, may very well provide such conflict in ample measure. Roy apparently discounts this on the grounds that political Islam is a failure, that it can never establish the Islamic state, and that the impossibility of its aims will be speedily realized. But that is to take a rather serene view of revolutionary utopian politics. When Trotskyites and others attacked Soviet Communists for failing to meet the "communist ideal," the Soviets offered "really existing communism" as their justification and carried on with their bloody seventy-year run in power. As Roy notes, the salafists and other more extreme Islamists may attack the Brothers for not moving full speed ahead to create the "ideal" Islamic state. Yet the Brotherhood will certainly be able to respond that its project is a "work in progress." Whether it can make that argument stick will depend on its political skill.

Of course, Arab society may well get a dose of religious politics so grievous and protracted that Arabs will eventually recoil toward the "democratization" that Roy forecasts. But that is hardly an appealing prospect for those currently living in Arab countries, or for peoples elsewhere who must deal with the international consequences of prolonged religious warfare in the Middle East.

—31 October 2012

NOTES

1. Haddad's "chessboard" quote is from David Kirkpatrick, "Egypt's Military Softens Tone as Vote Count Favors Islamist," *New York Times,* 18 June 2012. Haddad's references to a "long struggle" taking seven to ten years are reported in David Kirkpatrick, "On Eve of Vote, Egypt's Military Extends Its Power," *New York Times,* 15 June 2012.

2. All Shater quotes are from "Translation: Khairat al-Shater on the Rise of the Muslim Brotherhood," *Current Trends in Islamist Ideology* 13 (2012): 127–57. Available at *www.currenttrends.org/research/detail/khairat-al-shater-on-the-nahda-project-complete-translation.*

4

THERE WILL BE NO ISLAMIST REVOLUTION

Olivier Roy

Olivier Roy *is a professor at the European University Institute in Florence, where he directs the ReligioWest project. This essay originally appeared in the January 2013 issue of the* Journal of Democracy.

Hillel Fradkin has quite correctly summarized my analysis before criticizing it. Therefore, apart from the rather crucial detail of what the "failure of political Islam" means, there is no misunderstanding between us, but rather a decisive difference in approach and perspective. Fradkin is concerned about what constitutes the essence of the Muslim Brotherhood (MB) as an ideological movement, whereas I concentrate on how the Muslim Brothers, as political and social actors, are shaped by the political, social, and religious context in which they now find themselves.

Fradkin's main argument is that my thesis on the reluctant entry of Islamists into the democratic process is belied by a "revolutionary dynamic" that is unfolding after some months of moderation and cautiousness; he stresses the fact that the MB has a clear-cut ideological blueprint that it is seeking to implement despite its tactical restraint. My view is that there is no such "revolutionary dynamic" and that the MB is no longer a revolutionary movement, but rather a conservative one. The Muslim Brothers are certainly not liberal, and they are thrilled by their sudden empowerment after many decades of longing in vain for access to power. They may try to establish an authoritarian state, but it would be conservative and rather pro-Western, more in Mubarak's style than Khomeini's, and would confront a strong democratic opposition. I maintain that 1) their "ideology" is more an emotional and vague narrative than a blueprint for ruling, and will mainly affect censorship and gender issues; 2) no dynamic of "Islamic revolution" is at work in either Egypt or Tunisia; and 3) because society itself has changed along with the geostrategic context, the Islamists are shaped more by the new landscape than vice versa.

The first point is about the nature of the Muslim Brothers and their counterparts in other countries, such as Tunisia's Ennahda Party. Fradkin calls the Brotherhood a "revolutionary" ideological movement, like Nazism or Communism. Certainly, the MB has constructed Islam as a political ideology, in contrast to the purely legal approach of the *ulamas*, who see the implementation of *shari'a* as the sole criterion for an Islamic state. Certainly, too, the MB has also always believed state power to be the best tool for "re-Islamizing" society and thus has been striving to arrive at the helm of the state. But the MB is more than that. It is also a religious brotherhood and a social movement deeply rooted in society. If Egypt's old regime tolerated the Brotherhood for so long, it is precisely because its members were not involved in revolutionary activities such as planning an armed coup, an obsession of both the Nazis and communists in the 1930s (the Nazis surely would have seized power had they not won elections so quickly).

The MB, by contrast, always tried to negotiate with the ruling power and always strove to engage politically instead of relying on armed uprisings: If splinter groups like Gama'at Islamiyya and Jihad Islami resorted to violence, it was in opposition to the MB's moderation; seventy years of cautious politics hardly qualify a movement as revolutionary. Like the mid-twentieth-century French Communist Party, the Brotherhood focused on building a kind of "counter-society." But as the Brothers grew closer to the new middle class that benefited from the economic opening led by President Anwar Sadat (1970–81), they became more "gentrified" and grew distant from the new generation. Their charity networks were molded by a paternalistic attitude, and they lagged behind as other groups (from salafists to labor unions) experienced a resurgence of militancy. The Arab Spring took the Brothers by surprise—a clear indication that they had given up any hope of a popular uprising against the regime. In the aftermath of the demonstrations, their actions were confused and clumsy before they determined their political line, which I expect to remain rather flexible and opportunistic, without a "revolutionary" or heavily ideological dimension, though we should not expect them to turn into whole-hearted democrats. They may use traditional, not revolutionary, authoritarian tools in order to stay in power: That is why during the November 2012 protests Morsi's opponents have called him the "new Pharaoh" and not the "new Khomeini."

The fact that the MB is not a "revolutionary" movement but a religious-conservative one reflects the rather conservative society to which it belongs: The Brotherhood's electoral constituency is certainly not revolutionary and will not flood the streets to demand the implementation of an Islamic state. The MB has put forward no blueprint for a "new society" (to say nothing of a new economy) beyond the imposition of outward religious markers such as the veil and the ban on alcohol. In other words, the MB has no great geostrategic design beyond its general rhetoric about the solidarity of the Muslim *umma*: This was made clear by its moderation during the November 2012 crisis between Hamas and Israel.

Of course, decades of repression and opposition have made the MB both cautious and vindictive, and it will do its best to hold on to its newfound power. The Brothers will appoint their militants and cronies to government posts, support censorship on grounds of "morality," and balk at a free and independent press. In this sense, they are not liberal at all. They believe that their time is now, and they do not intend to miss it or to spoil it.

The Failure of Political Islam

The Brotherhood's ideology provides neither a roadmap to the perfect Islamic society nor a guidebook for good governance. This is what I called the "failure of political Islam"—*not* the Islamists' inability to come to power. I never claimed that the Islamists would not come to power, an assertion that Fradkin wrongly attributes to me. Rather, I said that the revolutionary dynamic in the Sunni countries had been exhausted, and that the ideological electoral constituency of the Islamists (except in extraordinary situations like Algeria in 1992) is only about 20 percent. When Islamist groups such as Turkey's Justice and Development Party (AKP) manage to exceed this level during so-called normal times, it is because they have managed to appeal to different and more diverse constituencies—mainly conservative or nationalist voters, as well as the poor and the rising nonsecular middle class. Thus while the Muslim Brotherhood may finally have come to power, it is at the expense of its own ideology: The "failure of political Islam" is not the political failure of the Islamists; it is the collapse of Islamism as a political ideology.

In *The Failure of Political Islam* (1992), I predicted that the collapse of Islamism's revolutionary momentum would be followed by two trends: 1) There would be a wave of "neofundamentalism" that stressed a strict return to purely religious norms (the call to implement *shari'a*), replacing Islamism's ideological-political agenda (building an Islamic state and institutions, setting up an "Islamic economy," striving to build a transnational *umma,* and so on). 2) There would be a move toward a "Muslim democracy" (along the lines of an assertive Christian democracy) that endorses nationalism and recasts Islamic norms as moral and cultural values with appeal to a larger conservative constituency. This is exactly where we are today, and the Brotherhood itself is torn between these two trends.

Nevertheless, it is true that the Brotherhood cannot abandon the centrality of religion in its discourse without losing its trademark, its identity, and its legitimacy—especially in a context rife with other contenders who make religious claims (salafists, Sufis, and traditional religious institutions such as al-Azhar). To prove that the MB's ideology has remained unchanged, Fradkin extensively quotes Khairat al-Shater (the Brotherhood's original candidate for the 2012 presidential election), who hews to the group's traditional discourse, including the tenet that "Islam is the solution." Of course, there is an Islamic "political imaginary" haunted by nostalgia for the times of the Prophet, and this sentiment will fuel many more inflammatory speeches. It is important to note, however, that Shater is not in charge: He is neither Egypt's president nor the MB's Supreme Guide.

In any case, such a narrative cannot serve as a blueprint for governing a complex society. Thus there is a growing discrepancy between ideological references and real practices. This gap will be unsustainable unless the Brotherhood manages to recast its ideology in nontheological terms (that is, as a matter of ethics and identity). In fact, its "religious reference" has been turning into a conservative sociocultural agenda that has nothing to do with either "revolution" or an "Islamic state." The MB faces far greater domestic constraints and possesses far fewer means than revolutionary movements of the past. As a result, it must compromise.

Fradkin offers Iran's 1979 Islamic Revolution as proof that revolutionary Islamists can ride a wave of revolt against dictatorship to establish a true Islamic state. But Iran's experience does not provide an apt comparison with the current upheavals in the Middle East. The Iranian revolution was a real revolution, characterized by the replacement of existing elites with members of other social groups; the use of armed violence; executions and massacres of opponents; the bloody settlement of accounts inside the new regime; the reshaping of the economy; and forced transformations in the daily lives of ordinary people. In Iran, there were no significant democratic movements involved in the revolt—the leftists, Islamo-leftists, and Khomeinists all rejected democracy. Demonstrators were not calling for liberal democracy, but rather for a revolutionary state (some for a "People's" state, others for an "Islamic" state).

Ayatollah Khomeini did not steal the revolutionary movement from liberals. On the contrary, he embodied the revolution. In Egypt today, there is no such charismatic leader, and all political leaders at the very least pay lip service to democracy, because it is the basis of their legitimacy. In Iran, the new regime established its monopoly on religion through a strong and politicized Shia clergy that existed prior to the revolution. There is no equally powerful clerical group in the Sunni countries, where religious diversity within Islam is flourishing. In Iran, the new regime quickly set up the Revolutionary Guard, which became the country's dominant military force. In Egypt, the army went back to the barracks (a prerequisite for any democracy), but it is not under the direct control of the Brotherhood. In Iran, the regime immediately embarked on implementing a revolutionary foreign policy with the storming of the U.S. embassy, whereas in Egypt the new regime not only protected the U.S. embassy but did not close the Israeli embassy or give it to the Palestinians (who, incidentally, would have refused it).

The Illusion of Islamic Exceptionalism

To repeat, my disagreement with Fradkin is not about isolated facts but about his ideological and ahistorical approach. He sees the MB as a closed monadic party that operates in isolation from time and society: For seventy years it has maintained the same agenda, the same ideology, and the same organizational discipline, playing long-term politics on an abstract chessboard where its flexibility is solely tactical. In Fradkin's view, the MB has not changed and has no reason to change, and everything it does must be understood within the paradigm of "Islamic revolution." In this sense, Fradkin's approach is in line with the essentialist school of thought that considers politics among Muslims to be governed by some unchanging Koranic software implanted in their brains.

In fact, Islamists are products of modern history and society. The twentieth century was marked by revolution from 1917 to 1979—from the Bolshevik revolution to the Iranian revolution. But times have changed. In the 1980s, a process of democratization took hold in Latin America, communism imploded, and the Iranian revolution turned into a nightmarish fraud. (Who today would travel to Iran to learn how to build Islamism in the way that earlier generations flocked to Russia, China, and Cuba to learn how to "build socialism"?) In countries all over the world, former extremists and militants have become democratic leaders—examples include former Portuguese prime minister José Manuel Barroso (now president of the European Commission), Brazilian president Dilma Rousseff, and Northern Ireland's Deputy First Minister Martin McGuinness, to name only three. This, of course, does not mean that real democracy is firmly rooted in these countries; just as radicals can turn into democrats, newly minted democrats can turn into dictators. Today, however, dictatorships such as China's flourish by attenuating their ideology. Authoritarianism and ideology are two separate questions: If Morsi turns into a dictator, it will be at the expense of the Brotherhood's ideology and legitimacy. In a word, Fradkin's vision of revolution and ideology is largely anachronistic.

Moreover, the argument that the Arab world cannot democratize because the concept of democracy is a product of centuries of Western Christianity is rather biased. While it is true that a complex chain of events in European history first gave birth to modern democracy, capitalism, and human rights, the notion that they were the offspring of Christian theology is highly questionable. For two centuries, Arab countries have been struggling to cope with challenges from the West. Different countries have tried different models—from enlightened despotism to revolutionary movements driven by charismatic leaders (and even including some short-lived democratic experiences). Over time, Arab societies have changed as a result of mass education and globalization, both of which have altered their social fabric and their political culture.

It is steadily becoming clearer that "Islamic exceptionalism" is an illusion: Both the political and the religious changes in Muslim societies are in tune with global trends. And as I tried to show in *Globalized Islam* (2004), what is perceived in the West as a *return* to a traditional and nostalgic Islam is, on the contrary, a profound *alteration* of traditional Islam, which is now giving way to a more open and diverse religious field. Just as the Protestant Reformation, despite aiming at a return to the scriptures, unwillingly opened the door to modern forms of religiosity, Islamism is opening the door to new forms of religiosity through its passage into politics. Moreover, fundamentalism, as both a tool and a consequence of the deculturation of Islam, has helped to introduce Islam to the global religious market.

The belief that young Muslims turn to religion only out of frustration and disenfranchisement reveals a negative and narrow conception of the "return of the sacred": From San Francisco to Jerusalem and Paris to Cairo, the phenomena of religious conversion and becoming "born again" are more than just a response to social discontent. Indeed, after studying these trends for my book *Holy Ignorance* (2010), I concluded that the social sciences, not to mention politicians and journalists, have a problem with religion and tend to see it only as a source of trouble.

This is reflected in Fradkin's conclusion, which warns of the "international consequences of prolonged religious warfare in the Middle East" that might result from the MB's access to power. To what is he referring? If "religious warfare" is a euphemism for the Israeli-Arab conflict, the role of the MB can only be secondary, because that conflict is above all a national, not a religious, one. No sustainable peace between Israel and the Arab states will be achieved in the absence of elected governments—in other words, there can be no peace without democracy, and in Egypt there can be no democracy without the Muslim Brothers.

Fradkin seems tacitly to refer to Samuel P. Huntington's "clash of civilizations" thesis, yet the MB is not pretending to unite the *umma* against the West. The Brotherhood needs the West for economic development and fears the threat of a nuclear Iran. Egypt's Muslim Brotherhood did not incite the civil war in Syria, but it joined the West in rejecting Bashar al-Assad's bloody dictatorship.

Finally, Fradkin's essay lacks a conclusion. He advocates no particular policy and offers no advice for the international community beyond caution, circumspection, and suspicion. Wariness, however, is not a policy. Pragmatic engagement, on the other hand, at least has the potential to help support democratization in the Arab world.

—30 November 2012

5

ISLAMISTS AND DEMOCRACY: CAUTIONS FROM PAKISTAN

Husain Haqqani

Husain Haqqani, *senior fellow at the Hudson Institute and professor of international relations at Boston University, is the author of* Magnificent Delusions: Pakistan, the United States and an Epic History of Misunderstanding *(2013) and* Pakistan: Between Mosque and Military *(2005). He served as Pakistan's ambassador to the United States between 2008 and 2011. This essay originally appeared in the April 2013 issue of the* Journal of Democracy.

Success in free elections held after the "Arab Spring" protests in Tunisia and Egypt has brought Islamists to power through democratic means, and Islamist influence is on the rise throughout the Arab world. Much of the debate about liberal democracy's future in Arab countries focuses on the extent to which the Islamists might be moderated by their inclusion in the democratic process. There is no doubt that the prospect of gaining a share of power through elections is a strong incentive that favors the tempering of extremist positions. But until the major Islamist movements give up their core ideology, their pursuit of an Islamic state is likely to impede their ability to be full and permanent participants in democratization. The real test of the Islamists' commitment to democracy will come not while they are in power for the first time, but when they lose subsequent elections.

Islamists have been a constant feature of the Muslim world's political landscape for almost a century. They have proven themselves to be resilient under even the most repressive political orders because of their ability to organize through mosques. Secular-nationalist leaders in countries such as Egypt and Jordan have alternately used and crushed Islamists to avoid losing power. Secular autocrats and their apologists have often cited the threat of Islamists taking power as a reason why democracy might be hard to practice in Muslim societies. Such societies, it has been argued, may have either secularism or democracy but not both, as the latter could lead to the erosion of the former under the influence of Islamist ideology.

The opposing argument was that the absence of democracy and free-dom strengthened the Islamists since they were the only dissenting force that could covertly organize—by dint of their access to places of wor-ship—at times when political opposition was banned. According to this argument, the absence of democracy made it difficult for Muslim societies to embrace secular pluralism and thus handed the Islamists a political advantage. Islamists have cashed in that advantage during most of the elections held after the overthrow of authoritarian secular regimes. The question now is whether the Islamists will accept pluralism and give up power in the event of an electoral defeat or will insist on pursuing their notion of an Islamic utopia at all costs, thereby preventing the emergence of secular democratic alternatives.

Even if Islamists play by democratic rules while in power, there is reason to doubt that they—or at least their more fervent followers—will give up their power if they lose an election. The world still has not seen any examples of governing Islamists being voted out of power, but Pakistan does present an example of what can happen when an Islamist (or at least partially Islamist) government is succeeded by a non-Islamist democratic party. Pakistan has never elected an Islamist party. In fact, Islamist parties have never won more than 5 percent of the vote in Pakistan in any year except 2002, when a coalition of Islamist parties won 11 percent.

Yet the country did have a partly Islamist regime under the military rule of General Muhammad Zia ul-Haq. Zia amended Pakistan's constitution and decreed that some provisions of *shari‘a* would be included in Pakistan's penal code. He also made blasphemy punishable by death and made it possible for police to arrest individuals accused of blasphemy immediately upon the filing of a complaint. After Zia's death in a mysterious 1988 plane crash, new elections brought to power the secular Pakistan People's Party (PPP), but a quarter-century later the country continues to be plagued by the extreme Islamist policies introduced under Zia—policies that have proven very difficult to reverse. The Pakistani experience, to which we shall return later in this essay, suggests that there is reason to fear that legislation passed under Islamist influence may be similarly hard to undo in the Arab countries where Islamists have been elected to power. For now, the Islamists are not averse to acquiring power through the democratic method of free elections even if they remain hostile to Western ideas of individual liberty and pluralism.

The Islamists' idea of democracy usually consists of majority rule, which is easy for them to accept when they are in the majority. Elected Islamist leaders in Egypt and Tunisia have said that they are willing to embrace what Alfred Stepan terms "the twin tolerations,"[1] including the notion that elected officials can legislate freely without having to cede to claims that all human laws can be trumped by laws that God has directly revealed. Full acceptance of the twin-tolerations concept would allow future elected governments to change laws rooted in Islamic theology that might be introduced by Islamist-controlled legislatures during their current tenure. If the experience of countries such as Pakistan is any guide, however, Islamists who lose elections nonetheless tend to resist the secularization of laws, with this resistance often taking the form of violence or threats of violence.

The current willingness of Arab Islamists to moderate their stance while taking part in the democratic process appears to be directly tied to the sheer tentativeness of the Arab democratic experiment. The emergence of democratic governance in the Middle East is undoubtedly a positive development, as is the inclusion of Islamists in the process. It would be unrealistic to suppress the Islamists forever, as the fossilized Arab dictatorships had sought to do, and still hope for secular democratic values to evolve. But it is equally important to guard against the prospect of Islamist dictatorships replacing the secular ones, even if Islamists have initially come to power through free and fair elections.

Suspicion of Democracy and Secularism

Most Islamist movements, including the Arab Muslim Brotherhood and its South Asian analog the Jamaat-e-Islami (Islamic Assembly), have a history of questioning Western democracy as well as the basic principles of secularism. Radical groups such as the pan-Islamist Hizbut Tahrir and the British group al-Muhajiroun have gone so far as to describe Western democracy as sinful and against the will of God. Several jihadist movements have taken a similarly extreme position. Other Islamist groups, however, have offered their own versions of democracy that allow for the election of officials but limit the authority of legislators. Disagreements also exist over whether non-Muslims and women are entitled to exercise the franchise or to hold public office on the same terms as practicing Muslim men.

The views of various Islamist factions are important because they provide the context for anticipating the path of Islamist politicians. Many Western observers want to project the future trajectory of Islamist political parties solely on the basis of recent pronouncements by Islamist political leaders. This approach is flawed because Islamists have a strong sense of history; their political behavior cannot be easily comprehended or predicted without taking history into account. The group most relevant to the contemporary Arab political scene is the Muslim Brotherhood. Most Islamist groups in the Middle East, ranging from political parties hastily assembled after the Arab Spring to the terrorists of al-Qaeda, trace their roots to the Brotherhood and its ideology.

At its founding in Egypt in 1928, the Muslim Brotherhood described itself as an organization dedicated to Islamic revival. Two years later, it registered under Egyptian law as a welfare organization, a legal status that (formally at least) precluded its direct involvement in politics. Its founder Hassan al-Banna (1906–49) gradually unveiled a strategy of political participation and even mounted an abortive run as a parliamentary candidate in 1942. To this day, however, the Brotherhood sees itself as an ideological movement dedicated to the cause of Islamic revival rather than as a political party.

Banna declared that the Brotherhood's aim was the "Islamization" of Egyptian society through an Islamic revolution that would begin with the individual and extend throughout the community. He identified four stages of this process: first, to make every individual a true Muslim; second, to develop Muslim families; third, to Islamize the community; and finally, to establish an Islamic state in Egypt. In some ways, Banna's view of this historical progression is reminiscent of Marx's stages of history. It is based on the belief that events will move in one direction and that Islamization will eventually be attained. But implicit in this revolutionary expectation is the notion that different historical stages require different kinds of strategies. Once a critical mass of Islamized individuals is present, a more directly political strategy—including but not limited to contesting and winning elections—can be adopted.

Unlike Marx, Banna did not lay out the details of the historic progression called for by his theory of inevitable Islamization. This has led Islamists into incessant internal debates regarding the stage that their organization (or society at large) has reached, and which strategy is best suited to it. For this reason, the Brotherhood's position on democracy and party politics has not been consistent. At one time, Banna opposed the very idea of political parties and advocated a political system that would eschew them. But since Egyptian president Hosni Mubarak opened parliamentary elections to multiple parties in 1984, the Brotherhood has taken part in polls save for two occasions on which it chose to boycott the voting. Although it was not allowed to form a party, it participated as one in all but the most formal sense (its candidates would run as nominal independents, with everyone knowing their real affiliation). After Mubarak fell in early 2011, the Brotherhood formed the Freedom and Justice Party, which dominates Egypt's parliament and whose chairman Mohamed Morsi won election to the presidency in June 2012.

Like other ideological movements that seek to change the entire sociopolitical order, the Brotherhood has often debated and shifted its strategies. Its objectives of Islamizing society and establishing an Islamic state, however, have remained constant. The question for those trying to gauge the prospects of democracy in the Arab world is whether the Muslim Brotherhood's acceptance of democratic norms is permanent or is just another strategic shift meant to serve the higher ideological goal of establishing an Islamic state. In this connection, it is worth noting that the Brotherhood's decision to contest elections by setting up a party—avowedly separate and distinct from the main movement—allows the Brotherhood to maintain a stance of ideological purity while placing some of its members in a position to undertake political compromises.

Banna's speeches and writings about Islamic revival were exhortatory rather than descriptive. For example, he declared that the Muslim Brotherhood wanted "the foundations of modern Eastern resurgence" to be built "on the basic principles of Islam, in every aspect of life." The task of describing "the precepts of Islam" on which this revival was to be built would fall to others.[2]

Mawdudi, Qutb, and the Islamic State

One of the most detailed accounts of an Islamic political theory was offered by Sayyid Abu'l-A'la Mawdudi (1903–79), the founder of the Jamaat-e-Islami in the Indian subcontinent, who is considered the seminal ideologist of global Islamism. Mawdudi elaborated the idea that in an Islamic state sovereignty belongs explicitly to Allah (God), and thus that the principal function of an Islamic polity must be to enforce the rules laid down in the Koran and early Islamic traditions.

"A more apt name for the Islamic polity would be the 'kingdom of God' which is described in English as a 'theocracy,'" Mawdudi said in a 1948 lecture. But he clarified that Islamic theocracy is "something altogether different from the theocracy of which Europe had a bitter experience." The theocracy that Islam would build, said Mawdudi,

[Is] not ruled by any particular religious class but by the whole community of Muslims including the rank and file. The entire Muslim population runs the state in accordance with the Book of God and the practice of His Prophet. If I were permitted to coin a new term, I would describe this system of government as 'theo-democracy,' that is to say a divine democratic government, because under it the Muslims have been given a limited popular sovereignty under the suzerainty of God. The executive under this system of government is constituted by the general will of the Muslims who have also the right to depose it.[3]

According to Mawdudi's theory, "every Muslim who is capable and qualified to give a sound opinion on matters of Islamic law, is entitled to interpret the law of God when such interpretation becomes necessary. In this sense the Islamic polity is a democracy."[4] But it is a limited democracy, as not even the entire Muslim community has the authority to change an explicit command of God. Sayyid Qutb (1906–66), the Egyptian writer and radical Brotherhood ideologist, claimed that *jahiliya* (the state of human ignorance that preceded the Koran) continues to exist in all times. Qutb further asserted that all those who resist the notion of the Islamic state, or who seek to dilute it with contemporary ideologies, are in a state of *jahiliya*. The Qutbists would be willing to denounce as unbelievers (*takfir*) any who refuse to acknowledge the sovereignty of God as embodied in a state ruled by Islam.[5]

These ideological roots of the Muslim Brotherhood and its allied movements have not disappeared and could resurge if their dominance within fledgling Arab democracies falters. Even now, Islamists serving in the governments of various countries are divided over the extent to which they should push what they consider to be Islamic laws. Some Western commentators have expressed the hope that Islamists might be content with dispensing patronage to their supporters and providing relatively just and decent governance. But this optimism is misplaced. It is unlikely that Islamists can avoid pressure from their ideological core to push for a greater role for Islam in the public sphere.

The brunt of Islamization in contemporary times has been borne by women and religious minorities, and debates over what Islam does and does not allow have been endemic in all countries that have attempted even partial Islamization. Cultural issues such as bans on alcohol, changes to school curricula, requirements for women to wear head coverings, and restrictions on certain images or even on music have always been major Islamist rallying points. There is no way that Islamists in government can completely ignore their movement's promises regarding all these matters, even though the implementation of Islamist measures is sure to divide society and create a backlash. The problem would become especially acute when Islamists, after partially legislating *shari'a* while in office, lose their majority.

If "the law of God" is reversed after being implemented for a few years, violent opposition is inevitable. Such a situation began in Pakistan after General Zia, who came to power in a 1977 military coup and remained as president till his death eleven years later, partially enforced *shari'a*. The winner of the first election following Zia's death was the secular PPP. The Islamists had only a few seats in the new parliament. Yet by using Islamist "street power," issuing *fatwas*, and pronouncing condemnations from the pulpits of mosques, they refused to allow any new legislation that they viewed as contravening *shari'a*, which they said can never be reversed once it has been written into the legal code. To this day, secular legislators trying to amend Pakistan's blasphemy laws, for example, do so at the risk of death threats and assassination.

Upon gaining independence from the British Raj in 1947, Pakistan's secular founders had spoken vaguely of creating a state inspired by Islamic principles. But Islamist agitation forced Pakistan's early leaders to expand the relationship between religion and the country's legal structure. Unlike neighboring India, which was able to agree on a constitution less than thirty months after independence, Pakistan's Constituent Assembly remained bogged down with working out the details of its country's fundamental law for nine long years. In an effort to placate Islamists, the Assembly in 1949 adopted an Objectives Resolution that outlined the underlying principles of the constitution. This resolution declared that "sovereignty over the entire universe belongs to Allah Almighty" and that "principles of democracy, freedom, equality, tolerance and social justice as enunciated by Islam shall be fully observed." Moreover, it pledged the Pakistani state to ensuring that "Muslims shall be enabled to order their lives in the individual and collective spheres in accordance with the teachings and requirements of Islam as set out in the Holy Quran and the Sunnah."

These principles were incorporated into the Pakistani constitutions of 1956, 1962, and 1973, but secular Pakistanis expected them to amount to nothing more than lip service to the religious sentiments of the country's vast majority. The Islamists, however, had other ideas. They invoked what they termed the nation's foundational principles to seek changes in laws based on their beliefs—and they did this *without* winning elections. In 1974, for instance, Prime Minister Zulfikar Ali Bhutto's elected secular government (1973–77) found itself forced by violent street protests to amend the constitution to declare members of the Ahmadiyya sect non-Muslims. Three years later, more protests— this time under the pretext of disputed elections—resulted in legal bans on alcohol and nightclubs, plus the shift of the weekly holiday from Sunday to Friday. These Islamic measures did not suffice to keep Bhutto in office. Zia's coup, which made him Pakistan's third military ruler, had the support of Islamists and may have been planned as the culmination of the anti-Bhutto protests.

Zia was personally religious and deeply influenced by Mawdudi's writings. He spoke publicly of the need to implement fully what had hitherto been a vague promise of government based on Islamic principles. This led to the deepening of Islamist influence in education, academia, the bureaucracy, the media, the military, and the law. The state became an instrument for trying to achieve the Muslim Brotherhood's version of good Muslim individuals and families within a fully Muslim society. In a 2 December 1978 speech, Zia spoke of the need to create a Nizam-i-Islam or Islamic system, which he described as "a code of life revealed by Allah to his last Prophet (Peace be upon him) 1400 years ago, and the record of which is with us in the form of the Holy Quran and the Sunnah."[6]

This announcement was followed by the establishment of *shari'a* courts and the passage of several drastic laws. Among these was the Hudood Ordinance of 1979, which banned alcohol, forbade theft with punishments that could include the amputation of a hand, and forbade all sexual contact outside marriage with penalties that could include death by stoning. Also controversial were the blasphemy laws of 1980, 1982, and 1986. The state took it upon itself as well to mandate the timing of prayers, the observance of the Ramadan fast, and the collection directly from citizens of *zakat,* the annual charitable contribution that all Muslims who have the means to do so are required to make as one of the "five pillars" of Islam.

With respect to the blasphemy laws, Pakistan's Penal Code and Criminal Procedure Code were amended so that various religious offenses would be punishable at a minimum with imprisonment and at a maximum with death. The "use of derogatory remarks in respect of holy personages" is an offense punishable by three years' imprisonment and a fine. Defiling a Koran is an offense that results in life imprisonment, and the "use of derogatory remarks against the Prophet" is punishable by death. Between 1986 and 2010, more than 1,200 people—over half of them non-Muslims—were charged under the blasphemy laws. In 2010, the case of Asia Bibi, a Christian woman sentenced to death for blasphemy, gained international attention (she remains in prison as of this writing in March 2013).

In early 2011, at the height of the controversy over the Bibi case, Governor Salmaan Taseer of Punjab (Pakistan's largest province) and Federal Minister for Minority Affairs Shahbaz Bhatti were assassinated (Taseer by one of his own bodyguards) for requesting leniency for Bibi and publicly supporting a review of these harsh laws. The murder of secular reformers democratically trying to reverse previously decreed Islamization measures in Pakistan makes one wonder whether something similar might happen in Arab countries if Islamists lose an election after having been in power.[7]

Until recently, fears that radicals and jihadist groups would gain influence were cited as a reason for excluding Islamists from the political process, especially in the Arab world. Now that the Islamists are dominant participants in fledgling democracies, it remains to be seen whether they will seek to marginalize the radicals or to maintain them as insurance against future attempts to reverse Islamist ideological gains.

Hard Secularism and Soft Islamism?

Optimists often cite the example of Turkey's Justice and Development Party (AKP), which has Islamist roots yet has ruled Turkey since 2002 without imposing a theocracy. But the AKP emerged in the context of Kemal Atatürk's hard secularism, which since 1924 had imposed upon Turkey *laïcité* in the French Jacobin tradition. The Turkish Republic was not just secular in the U.S. sense, according to which the state must not impose a religion; rather, the Kemalist state actively opposed any public manifestations of religiosity, which it saw as preventing Muslims from attaining full modernity. The AKP presented itself as a conservative party, Islamic only in the sense that the Christian Democratic parties of Europe are Christian.[8] Even its Turkish forerunners, the National Salvation Party and the Welfare Party, which were disbanded by the Kemalist army and judiciary, were hardly comparable to ideological movements like the Muslim Brotherhood or the Jamaat-e-Islami.

Turkey's Islamists were circumscribed in their ability to demand Islamization by the strong secular foundations of Atatürk's republic. The AKP has never described itself as a movement to establish an Islamic state. It has focused instead on rolling back the restrictions on public manifestations of Islam that Atatürk and his successors imposed. There are many Turkish citizens, however, who remain worried that after the rollback of some of the harshest aspects of *laïcité,* an Islamist movement resembling the Muslim Brotherhood might yet emerge in their country.[9] The constraints of living under hard secularism in the past may also help to explain why the Ennahda (Renaissance) party in Tunisia stands out among the post–Arab Spring Islamist groups in being able to claim closer kinship with Turkey's AKP than with Egypt's Muslim Brotherhood. The Tunisian party's ideologist, Rachid Ghannouchi, has made what can be understood as an argument against the concept of rule by a vanguard Islamist movement claiming to exercise God's sovereignty. As Ghannouchi said in a widely publicized speech:

> Throughout Islamic history, the state has always been influenced by Islam in one way or another in its practices, and its laws were legislated for in light of the Islamic values as understood at that particular time and place. Despite this, states remained Islamic not in the sense that their laws and procedures were divinely revealed, but that they were human endeavors open to challenge and criticism. . . . The primary orbit for religion is not the state's apparatuses, but rather personal/individual convictions.[10]

According to Ghannouchi, the state's duty above all is to provide services to people—to create job opportunities, provide education, and promote good health—and not to control the hearts and minds of its citizens.

But the mainstream of the Islamist movement—including the Muslim Brotherhood and the Jamaat-e-Islami—has yet to revise its ideology as drastically as Ghannouchi appears to have revised that of Ennahda. And it remains to be seen what Ghannouchi and his "soft" Islamists will actually do in practice. Most Islamists continue to view the authoritarian experiments undertaken to Islamize Afghanistan, Iran, Pakistan, and Sudan as legitimate. Mawdudi's concept of "theo-democracy" and the Islamic Republic of Iran's doctrine of *velayat-e faqih* (guardianship by the supreme Islamic jurisprudent) are examples of the truncated view of democracy held by Islamists. Just as communists advocated a "dictatorship of the proletariat" that in practice meant domination by communist parties in the name of the proletariat, there are legitimate grounds to suspect that what mainstream Islamists actually seek is a dictatorship of the pious.

NOTES

1. Alfred Stepan, "Tunisia's Transition and the Twin Tolerations," *Journal of Democracy* 23 (April 2012): 89–103.

2. The quoted words are from Banna's essay "To What Do We Invite Humanity," available at *www.ikhwanweb.com/article.php?id=804.*

3. Sayyid Abul A'la Maududi, *The Islamic Law and Constitution,* 7th ed., trans. and ed. Khurshid Ahmad (Lahore: Islamic Publications Ltd., 1980): 139–40.

4. Maududi, *Islamic Law and Constitution,* 140.

5. On Banna, Mawdudi, and Qutb, see Ladan Boroumand and Roya Boroumand, "Terror, Islam, and Democracy," *Journal of Democracy* 13 (April 2002): 5–20.

6. The English text of Zia's speech may be found in *Pakistan Horizon* 32, 1–2 (First and Second Quarters 1979): 277–280. On the Nizam-i-Islam, see John L. Esposito, *Islam and Politics,* 4th ed. (Syracuse, N.Y.: Syracuse University Press, 1998), 175–76.

7. The problem of "blasphemy" in Pakistan is much more than just a juridical matter of excessive prosecutions or even a matter of lethal attacks on a few high-profile ministers. Mere informal allegations of insults against Islam can trigger mass violence, as occurred when numerous homes in a Christian quarter of Lahore were burned in March 2013 after two local men, one a Muslim and one from Pakistan's Christian minority (which forms about 1.6 percent of the population), fell into a personal quarrel and the former accused the latter of saying something—reports did not specify precisely what—that was disrespectful of Islam. See Andrew Buncombe, "Muslim Mob Burns 150 Homes over Christian 'Blasphemy,'" *Independent,* 10 March 2013, available at *www.independent.co.uk/news/world/ asia/muslim-mob-burns-150-homes-over-christian-blasphemy-8528231.html.*

8. Vali Nasr, "The Rise of 'Muslim Democracy,'" *Journal of Democracy* 16 (April 2005): 20.

9. On the AKP's behavior so far, see Berna Turam, "Turkey Under the AKP: Are Rights and Liberties Safe?" *Journal of Democracy* 23 (January 2012): 109–18.

10. Rachid Ghannouchi, "Secularism and Relation between Religion and the State from the Perspective of the Nahdha Party," trans. Brahim Rouabah, Center for the Study of Islam and Democracy–Tunisia, 2 March 2012, available at *http://archive.constantcontact. com/fs093/1102084408196/archive/1109480512119.html.*

6

NEW FINDINGS ON ARABS AND DEMOCRACY

Mark Tessler, Amaney Jamal, and Michael Robbins

Mark Tessler is Samuel J. Eldersveld Collegiate Professor in the Department of Political Science at the University of Michigan and codirector of the Arab Barometer Survey. Amaney Jamal is associate professor of politics at Princeton University and codirector of the Arab Barometer Survey. Michael Robbins is a political scientist and was project manager for the Second Wave of the Arab Barometer Survey. This essay originally appeared in the October 2012 issue of the Journal of Democracy.

Throughout 2011, a wave of protests swept the Arab world. Although multifaceted, with causes and implications specific to each country, these protests shared a number of themes, including frustration over poor economic performance, anger at corruption and the existing political system, and the demand for a government that cares about ordinary citizens and treats them with dignity. These uprisings have dramatically altered the balance between the state and society in many cases, leading to the fall of dictators and a reversal of the deliberalization process that had been going on in many countries for well over a decade.

Against this backdrop, we examine public-opinion data pertaining to governance and politics from the first and second waves of the Arab Barometer survey project, which were carried out in 2006–2007 and 2010–2011, respectively. One constant between the first and second waves is the overwhelming support for democracy in the region. At the same time, support for the role of religion in politics and government declined between the two waves while new questions in the second round revealed that large majorities believe in racial tolerance, support having women in the workplace, and prefer having a range of politicians who espouse diverse political ideas.

The first wave of Arab Barometer surveys was administered via face-to-face interviews to nationally representative samples of men and women aged 18 and older in seven countries: Algeria, Jordan, Kuwait, Lebanon, Morocco, Palestine, and Yemen.[1] Findings based on these surveys were reported in the *Journal of Democracy* in 2008.[2] The second wave of the Arab Barometer employed similar methods and was carried out in all these counties except Kuwait, as well as in Egypt and Tunisia (where political conditions had prevented the conduct of surveys during the first wave), Iraq, Saudi Arabia, and Sudan. This essay focuses mainly on the five countries that were surveyed in both waves, plus Egypt and Tunisia.[3]

As a result of the mass uprisings in the region, the political context in which the second wave of interviews was carried out varied from country to country, depending on when they were taken. Four surveys—in Jordan, Lebanon, Palestine, and Sudan—were conducted just weeks before the 17 December 2010 self-immolation of Mohamed Bouazizi in Tunisia and the subsequent protests that sparked the "Arab Spring."[4] A second battery of surveys was completed in early 2011 as revolutions were sweeping Tunisia and Egypt: In Saudi Arabia, the survey began before the 14 January 2011 ouster of Tunisian dictator Zine al-Abidine Ben Ali but ended before Egyptian ruler Hosni Mubarak stepped down on February 11;[5] in Yemen, the survey was conducted in the first half of February—thus after Ben Ali's fall, though some interviews were conducted before Mubarak's deposal and others after; in Iraq, the survey was completed soon after the overthrow of Mubarak. The surveys in the four remaining countries—Algeria, Egypt, Morocco, and Tunisia—were conducted months after these events took place, in the late spring, summer, and fall of 2011.

According to Freedom House's annual Freedom in the World report for 2010, no Arab country was a democracy at the time of either the first or the second wave of surveys, yet support for democracy is extremely high by a range of measures (see the Figure on page 56). In fact, support for democracy in these countries is higher than in many longstanding democracies.[6] The level of support for a "democratic political system" remained fairly consistent between the two waves, ranging between 83 and 96 percent in all countries.[7] The biggest change was in Algeria, where public support for democracy increased by 6 percentage points.[8] In Jordan, Lebanon, Palestine, and Yemen, support for democracy remained essentially unchanged (within the margin of error of the survey).

As Juan J. Linz and Alfred Stepan as well as others have argued, democracy is most likely to be fully consolidated when it is perceived not only as a desirable political option but also as "the only game in town."[9] The Arab Barometer therefore gauges not only general support for democracy but also ordinary citizens' commitment to the democratization process. After priming respondents with three questions about potential problems associated with democratic governance—the economy runs poorly in democracies, democracies are indecisive, and democracies are not good at maintaining order—investigators asked survey partici-

FIGURE—SUPPORT FOR DEMOCRACY (SECOND-WAVE RESULTS)

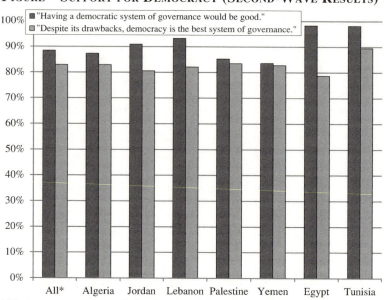

*"All" represents an average calculated on a pooled sample of respondents from Algeria, Jordan, Lebanon, Palestine, and Yemen (the five countries included in both waves). It should be noted that the number of respondents differs among these five countries.

Note: Sample sizes vary by country as follows: All = 6,191, Algeria = 1,220, Jordan = 1,188, Lebanon = 1,392, Palestine = 1,200, Yemen = 1,200, Egypt = 1,219, Tunisia = 1,196.

pants if they still believed democracy to be the best political system despite these possible drawbacks. Not surprisingly, a smaller share of respondents indicated support for democracy in this context, yet levels remained very high, ranging between 81 percent and 92 percent in all the countries surveyed.

There was a shift on this measure between the first and second waves in Lebanon and Jordan, with support in the former dropping by almost ten percentage points and in the latter by five, though overall support remained high in both countries. The other three countries saw no significant change. In sum, both waves demonstrated that most people in these Arab countries believe that democracy, whatever its problems, is the best political system.

Understandings of Democracy

How do Arabs understand the word "democracy"? By asking respondents which characteristic they most associate with democratic governance, the Arab Barometer found important differences in ordinary citizens' understanding of democracy.[10] Survey participants were given four response options: free elections, freedom of speech, low economic inequality, and basic necessities for all. In the first-wave surveys, none is identified by more than a third of respondents in any country as the primary characteristic of democracy. The second-wave surveys yielded a similar result, although there were two additional response options in this round—political equality and eliminating corruption.

In both waves, understandings about democracy form along two dimensions: economic and political. When examined in these broader categories, the data reveal that citizens are divided on what they understand democracy to mean. In the first wave, citizens in Algeria and Lebanon were more or less equally divided, with just over half stating that economic characteristics are more essential to democracy. By contrast, in Palestine a sizeable majority (58 percent) stated that political characteristics are more important, while in Jordan an even larger majority (62 percent) stated that economic characteristics are most essential in defining democracy.

In the second wave, most Lebanese respondents (56 percent) chose economic characteristics—a moderate increase from the first wave (51 percent). Likewise, more Palestinians chose economic characteristics in the second wave than in the first, although a majority in Palestine still chose political characteristics. In Algeria, however, there was a sizeable increase (11 percentage points) in the selection of political characteristics between the two surveys, with just over 60 percent of respondents citing political characteristics in the second wave.

Although this item was not asked in Yemen in the first wave, 61 percent of second-wave respondents identified a political characteristic as being the most critical aspect—a level similar to that found in Algeria in the second wave. Unlike in Jordan, Lebanon, and Palestine, the surveys in Yemen and Algeria were conducted *after* the Arab uprisings began. Thus one effect of the Arab Spring may have been to increase the understanding of democracy in political terms throughout the region.

All the countries surveyed by the Arab Barometer have multiple institutions typically associated with democracy, such as elections and parliaments. Yet at the time of the survey, political power remained concentrated in the hands of either nonelected elites or those whose election had been all but guaranteed, with elected legislatures generally lacking significant power. In other words, these were (and most still are) hybrid regimes—neither fully autocratic nor clearly democratic. As Ellen Lust has noted, elections in these societies are competitive and can have significant implications even though they rarely include any debate over actual policies.[11] To what degree, then, do ordinary citizens consider their regimes to be democratic or authoritarian?

The first wave of Arab Barometer surveys found important differences in the responses to this question (see Table 1 on page 106). Nearly two-thirds of Jordanian respondents believed that their country was closer to being fully democratic than fully authoritarian on a ten-point scale. In Palestine, the survey took place only months after the largely free and fair January 2006 parliamentary elections, which resulted in

TABLE 1—POLITICAL SYSTEM EVALUATIONS AND PREFERENCES

	All*	Algeria	Jordan	Lebanon	Palestine	Yemen	Egypt	Tunisia
"Closer to Democracy than Dictatorship" (Percent)								
1st Wave	44.0	37.8	64.6	24.2	46.9	28.5	-	-
2nd Wave	37.3	34.8	55.7	35.6	32.3	27.7	47.9	28.0
Mean Democratic Rating (10-point scale)								
1st Wave	5.3	4.8	6.6	4.1	5.4	4.3	-	-
2nd Wave	4.8	4.8	6.0	4.6	4.3	4.2	5.6	4.5
"Reform Should Proceed Gradually" (Percent)								
1st Wave	89.5	91.4	90.4	85.2	92.5	87.0	-	-
2nd Wave	77.7	63.3	85.1	82.8	86.6	69.2	88.9	92.0

*"All" represents an average calculated on a pooled sample of respondents from Algeria, Jordan, Lebanon, Palestine, and Yemen (the five countries included in both waves). It should be noted that the number of respondents differs among these five countries.

an opposition victory, yet slightly fewer than half of respondents saw Palestine as more democratic than authoritarian. In Algeria, and particularly Yemen and Lebanon, the proportions believing their countries to be more democratic were much lower.

In the second wave, the percentage of respondents (except in Jordan) indicating that their country was closer to a democracy had converged to about 33 percent. Respondents' belief that Palestine was democratic decreased dramatically during this period, dropping by nearly 15 percentage points, while in Lebanon this figure increased by 11 percentage points. The results from Algeria and Yemen remained more or less constant. In Jordan, a majority still believed that their system was more democratic than authoritarian, but this share fell by nearly 9 points.[12]

Overall, support for democracy is consistently high, and a majority of respondents surveyed in both waves of the Arab Barometer believe that their countries fall short. Nevertheless, Arab citizens generally have a cautious attitude toward the pace of reform. In the first wave of surveys, over 77 percent of respondents in all five countries agreed that reform should proceed gradually rather than all at once. This preference for gradualism declined in each of the five countries surveyed in both rounds, with an especially steep drop in Algeria (from 91 to 63 percent). Yet, as Table 1 shows, there remained a broad consensus in all the countries that reform should proceed gradually.

Democratic Political Culture

Scholars have long recognized that stable democracy depends upon having not only the proper political institutions but also a democratic political culture. This includes, for example, high levels of interpersonal trust, political interest, involvement in community and civic organizations, and tolerance of others. These characteristics tend to be low among Arab citizens in the five societies that were surveyed twice and generally decreased between the first and second waves.[13]

Levels of interpersonal trust varied among societies in the first wave, but in no society did more than half of respondents agree with the statement that "most people can be trusted." Only in Lebanon did trust remain essentially constant between waves, hovering just above 16 percent. In Yemen, the level of trust fell only 1.6 points to 37 percent in the second wave, but in the remaining three societies, the level of trust decreased dramatically, dropping more than 10 percentage points in each. Levels of political interest also exhibited significant variation across both time and space. In the first wave, a slight majority of respondents in Lebanon (59 percent) and Palestine (54 percent) were interested or very interested in politics. Political interest was significantly lower in the other three countries, ranging from 29 percent in Jordan to 36 percent in Yemen. In the second wave, levels of political interest converged to between 33 and 40 percent in all cases except Algeria. This was the result of sharp declines in political interest in Lebanon (19 percentage points) and Palestine (14 percentage points), offering further evidence that the high levels found in both societies in the first wave were probably the result of specific political events.

Rates of civic engagement tend to be relatively low across the region, although there is significant variation from country to country. In the first wave of the Arab Barometer, this rate varied from a low of 6 percent in Jordan to a high of 26 percent in Yemen, with rates of organizational membership falling between 17 percent and 22 percent in the remaining cases. In all countries except Algeria, rates of civic engagement were significantly higher in the second wave, although different items were employed in the two waves to determine this variable.[14] The most dramatic increase was in Yemen, where civic participation rose by 23 percent. Beyond differences in question wording, it is unclear why participation rates would increase so dramatically in this case. Increases in Jordan, Lebanon, and Palestine were all a little less than 9 percentage points, while the participation rate declined by 7 points in Algeria.

Results for a number of measures show variation in levels of tolerance across the countries.[15] Respondents were asked if they would mind having certain types of people as neighbors, including members of a different race or religion. In both waves, the country most tolerant in terms of both race and religion was Lebanon. In other cases, levels of tolerance varied over space and time. In the first wave, Algerian society was the least tolerant. Tolerance was somewhat higher in Yemen and significantly higher in Jordan. Somewhat surprisingly, a number of noteworthy changes took place between the two waves. In Algeria, religious tolerance rose 21.5 percentage points to 70 percent, and racial tolerance rose 12 percentage points to 80 percent. Levels of tolerance in Yemen were only slightly higher than in Algeria in the first wave and were essentially unchanged in the second wave. In Jordan, levels of tolerance increased by about 10 percentage points between the two waves.

Overall, despite a strong desire for democracy and fairly high levels of tolerance, other key elements of democratic political culture are still underdeveloped in these five societies. Broadly speaking, trust is low, political interest is low, and involvement in political and civil society organizations is low to moderate. But these patterns may owe more to the political context than to deeply rooted cultural values that will necessarily persist in the future. Low levels of political interest probably reflect the limited extent of political openings in these still fairly authoritarian regimes. Similarly, the widespread presence of secret police (*mukhabarat*) and periodic crackdowns on civil society probably suppress both interpersonal trust and membership in organizations. As noted by a number of scholars, living in a more democratic system can foster the emergence of democratic values among the population, and thus these patterns are probably open to change.

Islam and Politics

There is a strong desire for democracy among Arab publics, but to what degree do citizens also desire religion to play a role in government and politics? Past research has demonstrated that Arab publics are largely divided about the role that religion should play in the political system, and this trend continues.

When asked in the first wave of the Arab Barometer if the government should implement only the laws of the *shari‘a*, a majority of respondents in each country agreed, except in Lebanon, where only 11 percent agreed. In Algeria, Jordan, and Yemen, an overwhelming majority of respondents (more than 85 percent) agreed. In Palestine, only 56 percent agreed, perhaps reflecting deep divisions over Hamas's victory in the 2006 legislative polls and the party's call for basing all aspects of the law on the *shari' a.*

The second-wave results in Jordan and Yemen changed little (less than 3 percentage points) from the first wave, while in Algeria there was a decline of nearly 8 percentage points. In Lebanon, support for the *shari‘a* jumped sharply to 26 percent in the second wave, but this remained by far the lowest level of any society surveyed. In Palestine, support increased dramatically between the two surveys from 56 to 83 percent. This level of support is similar to that of most of the other societies, further suggesting that the dramatic change is most likely the result of the first survey having been conducted soon after Hamas's electoral win.

TABLE 2—SUPPORT FOR POLITICAL ISLAM (PERCENT)

	All*	Algeria	Jordan	Lebanon	Palestine	Yemen	Egypt	Tunisia
Men of Religion Should *Not* Influence How People Vote in Elections								
1st Wave	67.8	67.9	75.2	77.2	54.8	67.0	-	-
2nd Wave	81.2	83.3	78.0	91.0	79.1	75.1	86.7	78.4
It Would Be Better If More Religious People Held Public Office								
1st Wave	44.6	57.8	49.8	12.4	60.3	40.7	-	-
2nd Wave	35.6	21.6	47.8	12.7	46.2	51.6	46.9	30.7
Men of Religion *Should* Influence Decisions of Government								
1st Wave	49.1	61.0	52.0	17.6	55.6	56.8	-	-
2nd Wave	38.5	27.6	45.8	14.3	43.8	61.1	36.8	25.6
Religion Is a Private Matter and Should Be Separated from Sociopolitical Life								
1st Wave	53.7	35.9	58.3	83.0	48.1	47.5	-	-
2nd Wave	65.1	73.6	56.0	87.8	49.9	50.7	79.7	78.4
Laws Should Be Made in Accordance to the Will of the People								
1st Wave	62.9	66.5	65.8	73.1	60.0	50.3	-	-
2nd Wave	64.5	74.2	64.4	75.4	53.4	56.7	72.8	86.4
Laws Should Be Made in Accordance with the *Shari'a*								
1st Wave	67.3	89.4	86.9	11.4	56.1	93.2	-	-
2nd Wave	73.4	81.8	88.4	26.3	83.3	94.6	79.7	65.1
Democracy and Islam Are Incompatible								
1st Wave	30.2	30.7	29.6	31.0	33.3	27.7	-	-
2nd Wave	30.2	19.2	37.7	31.1	35.9	26.6	17.1	22.1

*"All" represents an average calculated on a pooled sample of respondents from Algeria, Jordan, Lebanon, Palestine, and Yemen (the five countries included in both waves). It should be noted that the number of respondents differs among these five countries.

At the same time, a majority of citizens in both waves also stated that laws should be informed by the people's wishes—perhaps an indicator of ambivalence or tension in popular views about the appropriate sources of legislation. It is possible that the "will of the people" and *shari'a* align in many instances, but these remain two distinct sources of law. In the first wave, in each country except for Yemen (50 percent), a solid majority of respondents (ranging from 60 percent in Palestine to 73 percent in Lebanon) agreed with the statement that "laws should be made in accordance to the will of the people." In the second wave, levels of support were generally similar to the first wave or even higher.

Alternative measures provide a somewhat different understanding of the desired relationship between religion and politics among Arab publics. In response to a number of questions asking about the preferred role of religion in the political system, in nearly all cases a majority preferred a system without a strong role for Islam or religious actors. Moreover, in most cases the proportion of individuals desiring a role for religion in politics declined between the two surveys, suggesting that

Arab publics generally oppose having religious actors affect the political behavior of ordinary citizens. When asked in the first wave if they believed that men of religion *should not* influence voters, for example, a majority of respondents in all five societies agreed. Indeed, in all cases but Palestine (55 percent), nearly two-thirds or more of respondents agreed or strongly agreed. Support for this statement was even higher in the second wave.

There was less of a consensus over the role that men of religion should play in government decision making.[16] In the first wave, slight majorities (ranging from 52 percent in Jordan to 61 percent in Algeria) in all cases except for Lebanon (18 percent) agreed that men of religion *should* have influence over government decisions. In the second wave, however, except in Yemen (61 percent), only minorities held this view, ranging from 46 percent in Jordan to a low of 14 percent in Lebanon.

Another question in this battery asked respondents if they consider religion to be "a private matter" that "should be separated from sociopolitical life." In three countries—Jordan, Palestine, and Yemen—responses were split fairly evenly. In the first wave, support for this statement ranged from 48 to 58 percent in these three societies, and results were similar in the second wave. In Lebanon, in the first wave the vast majority of respondents (83 percent) were in agreement, and this share rose more than 5 percentage points in the second wave. In Algeria, agreement increased from just over a third of respondents in the first wave to nearly three-fourths in the second.

Overall, except in Lebanon, support for religion in public life remains an issue on which ordinary citizens are divided. In Lebanon, a general consensus has emerged that religion should have very little influence on politics, which may be a reflection of the country's confessional diversity as well as fears of returning to the devastation of its sectarian civil war. In the remaining cases, there are important similarities but also clear divisions. First, it is clear that the concept of law under the *shari'a* is popular, which highlights the positive connotation that *shari'a* has in many communities. Although other response patterns demonstrate that most individuals do not desire a harsh Taliban-style legal system and that the law should also be guided by the will of the people, there remains broad agreement that laws should be consistent with people's understanding of the *shari'a*.

Second, there is an emerging consensus in most countries that men of religion should not seek to affect the political behavior of ordinary citizens. At the same time, there is significant disagreement on the role that religious officials should have in government decision making. Some individuals believe that government officials should consider the opinions of religious actors but that these actors should have only limited influence on citizens' political activities.

In addition to these general patterns, the two rounds of surveys have

TABLE 3—DEMOCRATIC VALUES AMONG
SUPPORTERS AND OPPONENTS OF POLITICAL ISLAM (PERCENT)

	Openness to Diverse Political Ideas		Racial Tolerance		Equal Job Opportunities for Women	
	Supporters	Opponents	Supporters	Opponents	Supporters	Opponents
Algeria	37.9	51.8	88.8	85.3	69.7	85.9
Jordan	32.7	44.8	81.6	80.0	60.1	89.6
Lebanon	55.9	63.2	94.6	92.6	78.5	89.6
Palestine	31.1	35.6	80.0	84.4	61.9	76.6
Yemen	34.1	46.4	78.8	90.1	66.2	74.3
Egypt	28.8	32.4	83.3	80.4	67.1	95.9
Tunisia	44.5	43.9	95.4	95.9	81.4	86.6
All*	**35.4**	**47.8**	**84.2**	**87.9**	**68.0**	**79.7**

*"All" represents an average calculated on a pooled sample of respondents from Algeria, Jordan, Lebanon, Palestine and Yemen (the five countries included in both waves). It should be noted that the number of respondents differs among these five countries.

revealed several interesting country-specific changes. In Algeria, support for political Islam dropped significantly between the two waves, perhaps a sign of the Arab Spring's impact on public opinion. In Palestine, the belief that laws should be made in accordance with the *shari'a* increased, but the view that religion should play a significant role in the political process declined. The changes in Palestine may be due, at least in part, to the postelection timing of the first-wave survey. Fears over the imposition of Saudi-style *shari'a* law may have been higher in the immediate aftermath of Hamas's victory but later diminished, whereas frustration over the party's performance may have simultaneously contributed to the decline in support for giving religious officials a significant political role.[17]

A number of Islamist leaders have stated that they support democracy but seek a form of "Islamic democracy," as opposed to a political formula that equates democracy and secularism. This raises the possibility that individuals who profess to support both democracy and political Islam might hold different attitudes and values than those who support democracy but prefer the separation of religion and politics. Assessing the degree to which this is true is particularly important in light of Islamist-party wins in several post–Arab Spring elections.

Accordingly, Table 3 presents data from the second-wave surveys in Algeria, Jordan, Lebanon, Palestine, and Yemen, as well as Egypt and Tunisia, and compares the political values of individuals who support democracy but have different views about Islam's political role.[18] The three categories evaluate elements of democratic culture that some fear are less likely to be found under democratic systems in Islamic societies: the desirability of openness to diverse ideas and opinions among political candidates;[19] the acceptability of having a neighbor of a different race; and the belief that men and women should have equal job opportunities.

The comparisons presented in Table 3 show that, among individuals who support democracy (the vast majority), there are some differences between the attitudes of those who favor political Islam and the attitudes of those who oppose it. For the most part, however, these differences are modest. In regard to openness to diverse ideas as a qualification for political leadership, the greatest difference occurs in Algeria, with secular democrats being 14 points more likely than religious democrats to value this trait in a candidate for political office. Similar gaps are found in Jordan and Yemen, while smaller differences are observed in Lebanon and Palestine. In the cases of Egypt and Tunisia, the two groups hold similar beliefs.

Differences regarding racial tolerance are, with the exception of Yemen (11 percent), extremely small. Moreover, tolerance is relatively high in every society, with more than three-quarters of respondents in each group across all seven countries indicating that they would not mind having a neighbor of a different race. There are larger differences between the two groups with respect to equality of opportunity for men and women. Save for Egypt, secular democrats are more supportive of equal rights for women. The difference is greatest in Algeria, where 86 percent of secular democrats support equality in job opportunities for men and women compared to only 70 percent of religious democrats. In Palestine, the difference between these two groups is 15 points, and in Lebanon and Yemen, 11 and 8 points, respectively.

Overall, it appears that those who support both democracy and political Islam are somewhat less likely to hold democratic values than are supporters of secular democracy. Yet in only eight of the 21 comparisons in Table 3 does the difference exceed 10 percentage points (and it never exceeds 16 points). Moreover, Yemen and Algeria account for five of these eight instances, showing them to be the two countries where differences between religious democrats and secular democrats, although still modest, are most notable and frequent. Thus, both in general and in Egypt and Tunisia in particular, it does not appear that electoral victories by Islamist parties reflect the support of citizens who are significantly less likely than others to embrace democratic values.

Egypt and Tunisia in 2011–2012

Conducted in Egypt in June–July 2011, the Arab Barometer survey found broad support for the Supreme Council of the Armed Forces, which held authority at that time, perhaps because the military had refrained from suppressing the demonstrations earlier in the year. Somewhat surprisingly, support for democracy in Egypt was not quite as high as elsewhere, with only 80 percent of respondents stating that democracy, despite its problems, is the best form of government. The vast majority of Egyptians understood democracy in economic terms, with 77 percent offering an instrumental definition and citing such factors as the provision of basic necessities for all, low levels of economic inequality, and the elimination of corruption. Only 6 percent of Egyptian respondents thought that free and fair elections were the most essential characteristic of democracy.

The Barometer also demonstrated that Egyptians are far more concerned about economic outcomes than political issues—84 percent cited the economy as Egypt's greatest challenge. Egyptians were extremely confident (with over 95 percent agreeing), however, that the revolution would bring an improvement in economic conditions. This confidence also extended to a range of other issues, such as achieving a democratic transition and improving respect for human rights. Still, the vast majority of respondents were cautious about the speed of reform, with 89 percent preferring that it happen gradually rather than all at once.

As in other countries surveyed during and after the Arab Spring, support for political Islam in Egypt was relatively low. Only 37 percent stated that men of religion *should* influence government decisions, whereas 87 percent stated that they *should not* influence how citizens vote in elections. Nearly half (47 percent) felt it would be better for Egypt if more religious figures held public office, but the overwhelming majority (80 percent) agreed that religion is a private matter that should be separate from sociopolitical life.

The poll was taken more than four months before Egypt's parliamentary elections began in late November 2011. In other words, campaigning had not yet begun for the first postrevolution elections. Party affiliation was extremely low, and few respondents reported strong attachment to a political party. When asked which party best represented their personal political, economic, and social views, only 3 percent named the Muslim Brotherhood–affiliated Freedom and Justice Party (and only 47 percent said that they trusted the Muslim Brotherhood). At the same time, in part because of decades of grassroots activity and a history of opposition to the Mubarak regime, the Brotherhood had earned the loyalty of a substantial number of Egyptians. Aided also by a superior mobilization effort, funds from wealthy Arab Gulf states (some of which also went to the salafist Nour Party), and the limited time available for new parties to organize, the Islamist formations were able to score a decisive victory in the parliamentary elections.

These findings shed some light on the complicated reactions of many Egyptians to the developments of mid-2012, when the Supreme Constitutional Court dissolved parliament and approved the presidential candidacy of Mubarak's last prime minister, Ahmed Shafiq. Many felt that the Court, backed by the military, had hijacked the country's revolution. Even those opposing a political role for Islam—a large majority according to the Arab Barometer Survey—saw an impossible choice: Support the Brotherhood candidate in the name of change, or support the military candidate and accept the status quo. In the end, Mohammed Morsi, the Brotherhood candidate, narrowly won the election. The military announced in June 2012 that it would retain key executive powers and would itself name the constitution-drafting commission, thus setting up an ongoing contest between the Brotherhood and the military in which neither side represents the future desired by a majority of ordinary citizens. Two months later, in the next important development in the continuing struggle for political primacy, President Morsi announced the forced retirement of Egypt's top military leader, Mohamed Hussein Tantawi, as part of an effort to reverse the military's power grab.

In Tunisia, the Arab Barometer survey was conducted in September–October 2011, just prior to elections for the Constituent Assembly. At this time, support for democracy remained high, with nearly 90 percent of respondents stating that despite its problems democracy is the best form of government. Like citizens of other Arab countries, Tunisians are divided in how they understand democracy, with a slight majority (52 percent) choosing as the primary characteristic a political element, such as free elections, freedom of speech, or political equality.

As in Egypt, the majority (68 percent) of Tunisians believed that the primary challenges facing their country were economic issues such as unemployment and inflation. The next most commonly cited challenge was corruption (13 percent). By comparison, only 2 percent cited consolidating the democratic transition as the most important challenge. Similarly, a solid majority of Tunisians (63 percent) saw the underlying cause of the Jasmine Revolution as being economic in nature. Again, corruption was the next most frequently cited cause, selected by 17 percent of respondents. Only 14 percent saw political factors as the primary cause of the revolution.

While only half of the respondents felt that they themselves had benefited from the changes so far, Tunisians overall were confident that the Jasmine Revolution would be successful in a number of key ways. More than 90 percent believed that it would result in democracy, better economic opportunities, an improvement in human rights, the establishment of the rule of law, and greater social justice.

Despite the success of the Islamist Ennahda party in the country's October 2011 elections for the Constituent Assembly, a large majority of Tunisians are not supportive of political Islam. For example, 79 percent of respondents stated that men of religion should not influence how people vote in elections; only 30 percent said it would be better for Tunisia if more religious leaders held public office; and only a quarter wanted men of religion to influence government decisions. Additionally, 79 percent affirmed that religion is a private matter that should be separate from public life.

Although political Islam in general received relatively low support, nearly half of respondents had a favorable view of Ennahda, with 49 percent expressing a great deal of trust in the party. This level was higher than for other political and civil society organizations, but significantly lower than support for the transitional government (66 percent) and the armed forces (93 percent). Only 12 percent considered Ennahda to be the party that best represented their aspirations for political, social, and economic development, but 20 percent indicated that they would vote for the party. Considering the 50 percent turnout rate, this finding closely matches Ennahda's actual vote share of 40 percent. As was the case with Islamist electoral victories in Egypt, superior mobilization and a history of grassroots activity and opposition to the regime, as well as the absence of a well-organized alternative, were prominent among the reasons for Ennahda's success at the polls. Thus, following the pattern in Egypt, perhaps as many as half of Ennahda's votes came from Tunisians who wanted to signal a desire for change but do not support an Islamist platform.

Few Tunisians want Ennahda to pursue a strongly Islamist agenda, and the party promised that it would not do so, but there are competing tendencies within it. Further, salafist militants have become increasingly confrontational and are pressuring the party to pursue a more religiously inspired agenda. Since many voters did not cast their ballots for Ennahda, and since the Arab Barometer survey demonstrates that among those who did many do not support an Islamist platform, Tunisians are waiting to see whether the changes brought about by their revolution are indeed the changes desired by the majority. Many in other Arab counties will be watching as well. With debates continuing about the role that Islam should play in political affairs, and also about the reasons for and against voting for an Islamist party, Tunisia's postelection experience will be instructive.

NOTES

1. An additional first-wave Arab Barometer survey was carried out in Bahrain in 2009.

2. Amaney Jamal and Mark Tessler, "The Democracy Barometers (Part II): Attitudes in the Arab World," *Journal of Democracy* 19 (January 2008): 97–110.

3. Morocco was included in both waves, but due to delays in completing the second-wave survey, the results are not available at this time.

4. Additional surveys were conducted in Lebanon and Sudan in March and April 2011.

5. Additional surveys were conducted in March and April 2011 in Saudi Arabia.

6. Ronald Inglehart, "How Solid Is Mass Support for Democracy—And How Do We Measure It?" *PS: Political Science and Politics* 36 (January 2003): 51–57.

7. For a comparison of the first- and second-wave results, see the Table "Support for Democracy" on the *Journal of Democacy* website at *www.journalofdemocracy.org/articles/supplemental-material*. For a discussion of how support for democracy varied by country in the first wave, see Jamal and Tessler, "The Democracy Barometers (Part II): Attitudes in the Arab World."

8. It should be noted that Algeria was sampled after the political transitions in Egypt and Tunisia had already taken place, whereas the majority of respondents in the other cases were surveyed earlier.

9. Juan J. Linz and Alfred Stepan, *Problems of Democratic Transition and Consolidation: Southern Europe, South America, and Post-Communist Europe* (Baltimore: Johns Hopkins University Press, 1996), 5.

10. See the table "Understandings of Democracy" on the *Journal's* website.

11. Ellen Lust-Okar, "Elections Under Authoritarianism: Preliminary Lessons from Jordan," *Democratization* 13 (July 2006): 456–71.

12. Interestingly, this finding represents a reversal of a long-term trend of increasing belief that Jordan was becoming more democratic; see Center for Strategic Studies, 2010 Annual Democracy Poll, available at *www.jcss.org*.

13. See the table "Political and Civic Engagement" on the *Journal's* website.

14. In the first wave, respondents were asked if they were members of any organization and, if so, which two were most important to them. In the second wave, respondents were asked specifically if they were members of six different types of organization: political parties, charities, unions, youth clubs, tribal or village organizations, or an association for local development.

15. This item was not asked in Palestine in either wave.

16. Additional exploratory-factor analysis revealed that this item and the following item (which asks if it would be beneficial to have more religious people hold public office) are the survey's two most reliable indicators of support for political Islam.

17. Surveys conducted by the Palestinian Center for Policy and Survey Research have shown a decline in support for Hamas since the 2007 civil conflict.

18. The figures presented in Table 3 compare, among respondents who support democracy, the views of those who agree or agree strongly and those who disagree or disagree strongly that men of religion should have influence over government decisions.

19. Respondents were asked to rank six characteristics, including personal integrity, piety, and previous political experience, and Table 3 reports the percentages selecting openness to diverse political ideas as one of the three most important.

7

THE SPLIT IN ARAB CULTURE

Hicham Ben Abdallah El Alaoui

Hicham Ben Abdallah El Alaoui, *a visiting researcher at the Center on Democracy, Development, and the Rule of Law at Stanford University, is the founder of the Institute for the Transregional Study of the Contemporary Middle East, North Africa, and Central Asia at Princeton University and the Moulay Hicham Foundation for Social Science Research on North Africa and the Middle East in Geneva. He has published widely on political and social issues in the Arab and Muslim world. A shorter version of this essay (from the January 2011 issue of the* Journal of Democracy) *appeared in* Le Monde diplomatique *in August 2010.*

Amid our constant, understandable worrying about the *political* problem of the Arab and Muslim world, we must be careful not to ignore the equally important and related matter of the *cultural* sphere. Underlying regime politics, geopolitical issues, and even the national and global issues of law and rights, there is a simmering cultural ferment that forms the ideological basis of what is possible in the "higher" spheres of law and politics. Ideology is, after all, more powerful than law: A law can dictate whether a woman must, or even can, wear a *burqa* on the streets; but an ideology can motivate masses of people to fill the streets, voluntarily and militantly, to demand changes to the law. And culture is the realm of discourses and practices in which ideologies are formed.

The *ulama* (Islamic scholars)—the official, state-sanctioned guardians of Islam—have always been suspicious of modern forms of cultural production and expression, because these carve out spaces that allow people to understand their lives and the world in ways which are implicitly autonomous from religion. For the most part, however, and regardless of whatever the *ulama* may have said, artistic and cultural practices have operated on a generally tolerated parallel social track, even if certain activities (modern art and painting, for example) have been relatively Westernized and consumed mainly in *effendi* (Westernized bourgeois) ghettos.

Underlying this wary tolerance has been a theological mode of thought
(kalam) in which religion encompasses more than *shari'a* and accom-
modates a certain pluralist notion of society as a vast ensemble where
culture develops alongside religion. In this conception, a wide array of
casually profane literary and artistic activity—including poetry, callig-
raphy, plastic arts, and music—can be understood as being compatible
with religion, even if certain examples are also understood as being on
the fringe of propriety. In this way, the widest range of diversity and the
most advanced forms of creativity have remained integral and treasured
parts of our Arab and Muslim history.

Indeed, an aspect of Islam's grandeur has been its ability to absorb
myriad cultural influences. The Muslim world protected, studied, and
developed the great traditions of classical literature and philosophy. It
was not a milieu for burning books, but rather one in which libraries
were built to preserve them. The Muslim world was, for some time, the
guardian of the founding documents of what became known as "Western civilization"—it recognized that they were a part of the intellectual legacy of all mankind. This capacity for intellectual openness and
engagement is one of the most treasured aspects of our history and
legacy.

With the rise of Islamist movements, however, a new public norm
has taken root. This norm is often characterized as "salafist," since it
is based on the narrow version of a "return" to religious orthodoxy that
this word has come to imply. (The Arabic noun *salaf* means forefather
or predecessor; salafists are those who favor a return to what they
think of as the ways of their "pious forefathers" from the early generations of Islam.) This new salafist social norm is for the most part
implicit, an unofficial ethos or ideology that is only rarely enforced
with legal or administrative penalties. But it is no less powerful as a
result—in fact, it is even more so. The authority and centrality of this
new public religious norm derive not from the power of a regime but
from the installation of an unapologetic Islam, vaguely salafist, at the
heart of Arab identity; it has become the central signifier of resistance
to Westernization and neocolonialism, creating a "more-Muslim-than-
thou" discursive context.

In earlier decades, a triumphant Arab nationalism fought off any such
overbearing religiosity; today, "moderate," secular voices refrain from
challenging it. They are caught in an identity trap, constantly limiting
their discourse due to fear that religious conservatives or regimes will
charge them with undermining Arab authenticity and independence—
even Arab nationalism itself.

We saw an example of this last year, when a group of young Moroccans decided to break the Ramadan fast with a picnic in a public park.
Along with the predictable reactions from religious quarters, the Socialist Union of Popular Forces (or USFP, Morocco's social-democratic

party), including members of its youth branch, joined in demanding punishment for the fast breakers. This obeisance by the "left" to a religious norm was couched in nationalist terms—the USFP criticized the picnickers' act as an insult to Moroccan national culture and a disruption of the ideological consensus regarding Moroccan identity. The government ended up charging the youngsters with an offense against "public order," using an ostensibly secular statute in a way it had never been used before. This simple, direct challenge to the salafist public norm turned out to be too radical for everyone in the political class.

The New Public Norms

The public space, then, is increasingly dominated by a cultural norm based on the elaboration of a set of strict rules, a series of dos and don'ts taken from religious texts strictly construed. As religion becomes an ever more dominant element of public ideology, it is itself contracting around salafism, creating a normative context in which the cultural is now more easily characterized and perceived by believers as not just profane, but pagan. A capacious understanding of Islam as a partner with culture has shrunk into a narrow version of *shari'a* that excludes the cultural. The pathways between the sacred spaces of religion and the casually secular discourses of profane culture—elaborate and delicate bridges that have long been part of Islamic societies—are being rudely and insistently barricaded.

This dynamic of salafization occurs even as the population continues to live among, experience, and consume a proliferation of profane and basically secular cultural products via television, videos, the Internet, and popular literature. It is easy—too easy—to identify the Western and global forces driving the proliferation of secular and profane culture and therefore to denounce them as "foreign." Yet this would be to ignore the creativity and ingenuity with which Arabs have appropriated and transformed the entire gamut of contemporary means of cultural production. At the level of elite culture, there is a burgeoning patronage system for artistic modernization, financed by Western foundations and transnational NGOs, but also by the Gulf monarchies. This process was accelerated by the 2003 UN Development Programme report that cited the paucity of literary publications in the Arab world, and by doing so helped to encourage transnational organizations and wealthy Arab patrons to remedy this perceived deficit. With its focus on traditional indices, however, this report failed to capture the real flowering of popular cultural creativity in the Arab world.

At the level of popular culture, of course, products of Western media conglomerates are ubiquitous. But there is also an undeniable, and growing, presence of indigenous media outlets—from news sources such as Al-Jazeera and Al-Arabiya, to soap operas, to the popular literature of self-help and romantic advice, to the explosion of musical and artistic creativity that the Internet has made possible and that young Arabs have seized upon enthusiastically. In the Arab world, as everywhere else, the result is a prodigious cultural mash-up—the commercialized version of which is the "festivalization" of modern Arabic culture, a phenomenon in which Arab businesses, promoters, and middlemen are entirely complicit.

Most of these cultural practices are without religious content or intent, are thoroughly saturated with global—not just Western—influences, and are, for all intents and purposes, completely secular. Despite the growth of political Islam, attempts to Islamicize art and culture in the Arab world have been relatively weak and ineffective. Still, caught between the pressure for modernization from secularized global culture and the pressure for solidarity and authenticity from the salafized indigenous public norm, artists and cultural producers in the Arab world now prefer to call themselves "Muslim" (but not "Islamic"), even though their artistic practice has nothing to do with religion and may be implicitly contributing to the secularization of Arab societies. By referring to themselves as Muslims, they are affirming an identity, not a religious practice; but they are doing so in a way that avoids challenging the salafist norm and avoids identifying themselves as secular or even "non-practicing."

What is occurring in the Arab and Muslim world, then, is a kind of schizophrenic lived experience: In private, one regularly consumes the culturally profane—via television, videos, the Internet, and popular literature, or in carefully segmented and reserved semipublic spaces—while in public, one is careful to proclaim his or her Muslim identity, avoids going to a movie theater, and perhaps makes a show of religiosity by attending the mosque, sporting a beard, or wearing the veil. The two forms of cultural experience unfold in parallel, kept at a safe and discreet distance from each other. Yet it is the religious norm that maintains hegemony in the public space, while profane cultural consumption remains private—in the closet, as it were—with all the lesser legitimacy which that implies. In the Arab and Muslim world today, cultural practices produce, and cultural subjects experience, a process of secularization, but no one is allowed to acknowledge or accept it.

It would be a mistake to see this problem simply as an expression of the social division between elites and masses. It is true that, well into the twentieth century, there was a simple working compromise: Westernized elites could partake of profane culture while ordinary people stayed in the cultural sphere dominated by Islam. This traditional sociocultural divergence is by no means irrelevant. Over the last few decades, however, education, literacy, and the exponential growth in the means of communication—particularly television and the Internet—have brought profound changes, and contact with other languages and cultures has begun to spread beyond the elite.

The Diversification of Mass Culture

Today, we have an increasingly diverse set of cultural practices throughout the Arab world. Young Arabs read novels, watch movies and videos, listen to music, read blogs—and also *create* all of these things—in many different languages. They are not just consuming but mastering modern cultural practices that are irreversibly influenced by and inextricably intertwined with linguistic and cultural influences from the East, North, South—and, yes, the West. To pretend that this is not so, to disbelieve that it could be so, or to insist that it should not be so would be folly. It is time to recognize that the days of linguistic and cultural "purity" never really existed and never will. And it is time to recognize the severe shortcomings of any paradigm, whether nationalist or religious, that sees such "purity" as not only possible but necessary.

At the same time, it would be naïve to presume that this diversification of mass culture will inevitably lead to movements for secularization or democratization. Although the growth of mass culture may entail an implicitly secular and democratic dynamic, on an explicitly political level it has often been conjoined with a consensual identity politics that includes the public norms of resurgent religiosity. The mechanism for managing this phenomenon of cultural empowerment combined with cultural confusion is not censorship, but segmentation. While this includes the division of society into isolated cultural sectors, perhaps even more important is the segmentation of cultural practices within the same person, who will read romance novels or astrology books one day and mass-produced religious tracts (bought in the same bookstore) the next, or who watches Iqraa (a religious television channel) at lunch and Rotana (the MTV of the Arab world) after dinner.

Thus within the individual as well as the society, the extension of mass profane cultural production and consumption unfolds in parallel with the propagation of the salafist public norm, which has adapted well to the new means of mass cultural diffusion. Paperback devotional and inspirational tracts and Internet blogs increasingly replace theological texts, and a kind of collective autodidacticism reinforces social and cultural segmentation and alienation from elitist "intellectualism."

It is important for both the salafists and those who rule Arab regimes that mass profane cultural consumption be experienced by the people as a distraction only—something understood to be not entirely respectable and to have no implications for a movement of social or political change. One must show respect for the salafist norm, even if one does not practice it. Indeed, the common and commonplace personal transgressions— with the accompanying *frissons* of slightly shameful pleasure (understood as diversionary, unserious "entertainments")—only reinforce the importance and social respectability of the salafist norm.

The norm may even intrude directly into more profane forms of mass culture—for example, television shows whose stories of romance or adventure are couched in the form of moralizing tales. This trend is particularly evident during Ramadan, a favorite time for televising historical miniseries with Islamic backdrops. A similar kind of superficial Islamicization characterizes the growing genre of self-help and personal-development literature, in which a nod to the power of prayer or devotional ritual is often folded into an individualist and escapist—if not hedonistic—program of personal improvement.

All this has helped to make an ill-defined salafism the reigning explicit norm of the common public sphere while leaving open the possibility of multiple and complex forms of cultural consumption on an individual and private level. Transgression is individual; the public norm is salafist. This is a form of ideological "soft power" that is far more effective than any bureaucratically enforced censorship.

The same schizophrenia is also found in the Arab attitude toward language, the foundation of culture. Historically, the *ulama* have always considered scholarly writing to have the highest intellectual and social importance. Ironically, this belief has led to a constriction of Arab writing today. An Arab intellectual does not write in the language that he or she speaks. On this point, pan-Arab nationalism and Islamism converge. Both insist that classical Arabic (Fus'ha), the language of the Koran, is the only legitimate language for cultural expression: For pan-Arabists, Fus'ha is the glue that holds the Arab nation together; for Islamists, it is the bond of the *umma* (community of believers). This, of course, ignores the profound divergences between everyday spoken and even Modern Standard Arabic (the language of journalism, television, academic discourse, and popular and literary fiction) and Fus'ha, which is rarely used outside religious schools. This paradigm also makes the novel a particularly suspicious genre, since it explores the "existential" questions of life and its meaning in ways that are doubly transgressive—the novel is not only relatively autonomous with respect to religion, but also reinvents the Arabic language in ways that go far beyond the putative limits of Fus'ha.

Yet just as one cannot question salafism as a public religious norm, one cannot question Fus'ha as the public linguistic norm. Although transgressions in linguistic practice are inevitable in real social and cultural life and thus are tolerated, one can never openly recognize them as constituting a new legitimate norm or sets of norms. Even though strict adherence to an ancient univocal linguistic norm is clearly not possible, everyone must nonetheless pretend that it is, upholding it as the ideal. As a result, none of the multitude of dialects in use throughout the Arab world is ever recognized, respected, or codified *in Arabic*. In fact, the grammars of these modern Arabic dialects are always published in other languages. One could hardly imagine a more extreme example of how a religious norm can hobble our language—preventing it from understanding itself and modern Arabic culture as a whole.

A similar ambivalence marks the realm of law. Each Arab state has its own legal code and defines its own version of legality and "Islamicity"—for the most part, by incorporating some modern secular principles of rights and justice. Yet almost all refer to *shari'a* as the ultimate source of law, and none will explicitly refuse to concede supremacy to *shari'a*. This obligatory primacy of the Islamic norm delineates the impassable horizon of the Arab polity at the present moment. Once again, however, this norm can easily become an element of an identity paradigm rather than a rigid religious prescription. It maintains itself as the public standard of judgment, but does not always define or determine the real practices of courts and the law.

Policing Piety

To be sure, today's Arab regimes have found many ways to profit from the increasing salafization of the public norm. This is true even among regimes that do not identify with or claim to represent an "Islamist" project. Authoritarian regimes find numerous ways to take advantage of the social and cultural tensions that arise from such a situation, playing leading roles as mediators and consensus-builders in ways that steer conflictive and potentially contestatory discourses and practices in a nonthreatening direction.

In accepting the salafization of public norms related to everyday mores and behaviors (for example, requiring the veil or suppressing the cinema), the modern authoritarian state can renew its alliance with the *ulama*, who are more interested in exchanging favors with regimes than reforming them. An authoritarian regime can tolerate, while officially keeping at arm's length, politically "quietist" Islamist currents whose program of *shari'a* consists mainly of mobilizing religious ideologues—not agents of the state—to obsessively police piety within local communities. In order to appear to local moderates and Western observers as the only rampart against complete Islamicization, a regime only has to act against a few of the most shocking *shari'a* penalties (such as the stoning of women who have been raped), while leaving unchallenged the ultimate primacy of salafism as a public norm.

At the same time, secular intellectuals who might otherwise pursue democratic reforms often end up relying on the protection of the authoritarian state against the *ulama* or fundamentalists and find themselves having to defend it in return. The state, by protecting some spaces of cultural autonomy and offering the possibility of future liberalization, can sell itself to these intellectuals as the lesser evil when weighed against Islamism. Many secular intellectuals, for example, gave reluctant support to the Algerian state during its struggle against the Islamists in the 1990s, and today the Egyptian state has protected writer Sayyid al-Qimni since a *fatwa* was launched against him. Meanwhile, rural and socially conservative people who fear the intrusion of Western mores find these kinds of tensions and détentes between the regimes and Westernized elites remote from their own concerns.

States may even enter into implicit covenants with certain rhetorically militant but actually quietist Islamist currents considered less politically threatening than salafists of the Muslim Brotherhood stripe—sometimes going so far as to grant such groups minority status within the electoral system as part of the tolerated opposition. This enables the regime to crack down more harshly on those politically militant Islamists and other dissidents who are seriously contesting state power.

The net result, amid all the cultural confusion, is that the regimes reap political benefits from maintaining a precarious equilibrium among these contending social actors. The state has redrawn its contract with the various social forces, freeing itself from too much insistence on democratization and maintaining a program of harsh (but now more finely targeted) repression, while reinforcing the fundamentally undemocratic notion that the salafist public norm is beyond challenge.

Among cultural intellectuals, this frustrating situation can produce various forms of politically debilitating withdrawal. On the one hand, there is both a real and a virtual "brain drain." Many Arab intellectuals and artists actually live and work abroad or direct their intellectual energies outside their home countries. They might, for example, identify themselves as Arab and Muslim rather than Egyptian or Tunisian, in the process asserting an identity whose founding elements are very close to those of salafism: The Arabic language is Fusʻha and to be Arab is inseparable from being Muslim. Intellectuals in the diaspora, whether geographic or ideological, lose touch with their specific national and social bases and become generic "Arab" intellectuals. It is to the benefit of authoritarian regimes that such an identity can make intellectuals more comfortable with an abstract unanimity in support of global causes such as Palestine and Iraq, and less engaged with local political tensions.

The intellectual withdrawal from complex and divisive local struggles into the abstract unity of a virtual international community is exacerbated by the lack of national financial support for cultural activities. State assistance for artists and intellectuals is in free fall, while alternative means of professionalization remain underdeveloped: Many authors and publishers, for example, have little experience with the new competitive realities of international copyright conventions, contract laws, and marketing. The lack of supportive public policy has led to a cultural milieu that is individualistic and depoliticized, forcing cultural producers to seek foreign audiences and sources of support. This external patronage has been forthcoming from Western organizations such as the Ford Foundation, as well as from Gulf princes. As a result, we now see an increasing number of cultural artifacts representing an abstract Arab-Muslim identity, produced for and appearing in Western galleries and Gulf showcases. In the realm of fiction alone, for example, there are now multiple competitions for the best examples of "Arab" culture: the Emirates Foundation International Prize for Arabic Fiction (known as the "Arabic Booker"), Lebanon's Blue Metropolis Al Majidi Ibn Dhaher Arab Literary Prize, and the International Prize for Arabic Fiction (managed with the Booker Foundation in London).

Certainly, the artists, musicians, writers, and thinkers of the Arab world have every right to accept much-needed support from Arab and external patrons. There is nothing wrong with artists from the Arab world becoming more thoroughly integrated with cultural developments globally; in fact, this holds progressive potential. The risk, however, is that, as the status of "Arab" artists is elevated among international audiences, they may become even more disconnected from, and therefore less valuable to, their own compatriots.

Is the Web a Game-Changer?

The Internet has certainly fostered new spaces of cultural production and consumption that have interesting political potential. Yet while the Internet can contribute to the growth and tactical efficacy of an existing political-protest movement with a strong base of support, it cannot create one. As we have seen in Egypt and Iran, it can be an effective tool for mobilizing people, but it cannot substitute for the kind of ground-level organizing in local communities needed to sustain the sort of persistent movement that can pose a serious political challenge.

We should also be aware that old regimes, too, can learn new "e-tricks": After the famous June 2010 "Facebook protest" in Egypt, the security services used the electronic-networking trail to track down and arrest the protesters and organizers. While video-upload and social-networking sites are convenient for organizing flash mobs, it would be naïve not to recognize that these sites are also ideal tools of state surveillance. We must also not forget that jihadis are among the most inventive and effective users of the Internet as an organizing tool and means of disseminating propaganda. Their salafism has no problem with the *technological* aspects of modern culture—a function, perhaps, of the distinction they make between the praiseworthy "thinker" *(mufakkir)* and the reviled "intellectual" *(muthaqqaf)*.

It can be argued, in fact, that while Internet culture encourages the formation of a wider and stronger discourse of community—a potentially powerful political phenomenon, to be sure—it also contributes to isolation and segmentation. Internet users tend to form discrete groups of social subjects who communicate exclusively—and often anonymously—online, continually reinforcing a closed sociopolitical discursive loop. Within each of these closed loops, the preferred mode of discourse becomes permanent irony directed at all the others. Anonymity allows dissenters to ratchet up their radicalism without risking open confrontation and any harsh consequences. Using the Internet, it is easy to mock power while avoiding the real-world organizing that would be necessary to challenge or to seize it.

Too often, then, artists and intellectuals achieve their independence apart from the national public sphere. And even when they completely eschew religion, contemporary artists and intellectuals do not necessarily become part of a secularizing movement. They do not, as they once did (and still do, in such places as Iran and Turkey), form an avant-garde within movements spearheading social, political, and cultural change. Rather, they become a kind of "court" faction, working in spaces protected and tolerated by the state or by wealthy and powerful patrons (both national and international). The figure of the artist with a message of political contestation, such as Egyptian writer Son'allah Ibrahim or the Moroccan musical group Nas El Ghiouan, has largely disappeared. For example, avant-garde painter Farouk Hosni is presently serving as Egypt's minister of culture. In 2008, the prime minister of Syria selected Hannan Qassab Hasan, translator of the often-licentious Jean Genet, to direct the UNESCO-sponsored program "Damascus, Arab Capital of Culture." Other artists, such as Wael Shawqi (featured in the Alexandria Biennial) and Hala El Koussy (winner of the Abraaj Capital Prize from the Gulf), are not engaged in political contestation at all, no matter how modern their cultural and social views may be.

Thus there is a confluence of new cultural forces that, on the one hand, promote an implicit dynamic of secularization and democratization and, on the other, have the immediate effect of further compartmentalizing society. Societies become divided into multiple segments, each of which has greater access to potentially progressive cultural influences. At the same time, however, each of the segments becomes reinforced in its particular subidentity, making it difficult for them to coalesce into something "social" in the large sense of the word. These segmented subidentities prevent rather than encourage the effective socialization of demands for political and cultural reform. They perpetuate the divide between the secular and the religious, between the enlightened artist and the vulgar philistine, between the "in" and the "out." The artist's secularizing and democratizing potential is, in many cases, sealed within an escapist identity that adopts a posture of mental exile from concrete social reality.

The flip side of this segmentation is a process of internationalization, culminating in the already mentioned "festivalization" of Arab culture. This process is a commercialized, middlebrow corollary to the financing of elite cultural projects that focus on Arab identity and the Arab world while encouraging the promotion of secular, modern, Western-friendly sentiments. Festivalization is not just a Western intrusion. In today's globalized reality, it has been enthusiastically embraced by local entrepreneurs and promoters and has inevitably resulted in the proliferation of commercialized Arab-themed cultural celebrations and festivals—some traditional, some contemporary—that provide new outlets for artists and new vehicles for profiting from the cultural tastes of modernized Arab middle classes. This is also the culmination of a process by which states have "privatized" art, just as they have the economy, abandoning it to private-sector guardians (even while preserving the prerogative to police it).

As culture budgets are cut, funds are redirected toward tourism promotion, which is coordinated with privately sponsored galas that present a modern, secular, and festive country. Festivals such as those of Baalbek in Lebanon and Mawazine and Fez in Morocco are at the zenith of this phenomenon. They showcase a wide range of musical and artistic talent far outside any recognizable salafist norm. For example, despite publicizing its program as "sacred music," the Fez Festival features such un-Islamic genres as American gospel music.

No mere picnics, these elaborate celebrations typically span several days and draw international audiences (primarily from Europe and the Arab world). To some extent, then, such festivals are a means of building bridges from the sacred to the profane, but in a way that is highly commodified and controlled, and carefully prevented from leaking into the everyday cultural sphere. They are amply supported by a panoply of sponsors—corporate (banks, airlines, hotels, and media outlets), private (including princely and royal foundations, as well as private individuals), and governmental (especially tourism ministries). There is no public disorder here.

With the creation throughout the region of these protected spaces of imaginary liberalization, culture becomes a substitute for dissent, the accomplice of a state's efforts to contain opposition and to ensure stability through diversification. The "culturalization" of secular and democratic tendencies—a process that both segments and internationalizes progressive elements of society—brings a semblance of freedom (nonpolitical freedom, to be sure) without putting into question the hegemony of the regime or the dominance of salafist ideology. When the audience goes home, however, the salafist norm continues to extend its influence in the public sphere, unchallenged (and even reinforced) by traditionally progressive cultural and political currents—all to the satisfaction of the state.

To be clear, modernizing cultural movements in the Arab world do have real progressive potential. The participants gain a kind of symbolic transnational capital and become global cultural actors. As such, they can either exile themselves from their own society by self-identifying as part of either a global culture or an abstract Arab *umma,* or they can try to influence local trends, using their transnational cultural capital as an asset. Most cultural actors will negotiate this tension with ambivalence, alternately emphasizing the different dimensions of their respective cultural personalities. The manipulations worked by regimes are not perfect, and in their ceding of new spaces to cultural autonomy and experimentation, they may be setting in motion a process that could, over the long term, foster a new type of opposition to authoritarian rule in the Arab world.

One thing is certain, however. If artistic and intellectual practice is to have any effect on democratization, it will be necessary to confront the salafist paradigm on its home ground, armed with a credible and consistent alternative. We must, openly and without fear, take up the challenge of secularism, something that has been done throughout the non-Islamic world—not just in "the West." Of course, this is not a matter of adopting any other region's prefabricated model. Rather, we must first reconnect with the Arab and Islamic tradition that built spaces for cultural autonomy over centuries. A new cultural paradigm, a new public norm—appropriate to the contemporary world as well as to our own traditions—cannot be built by either ignoring the salafist paradigm or merely paying lip service to it. Instead, we must engage it with respect and courage in seeking a transition from religious closure to political openness. This will require carefully negotiating all the intricate passages of our religion and our traditions, as well as our relationship to the world culture in which we are now inextricably entwined. It will not be easy, but we must take bold steps to craft a new paradigm of cultural modernity that will celebrate the diversity and creativity of the Arab world.

8

DEMOCRATIZATION THEORY AND THE "ARAB SPRING"

Alfred Stepan and Juan J. Linz

Alfred Stepan *is Wallace Sayre Professor of Government and found-ing director of the Center for the Study of Democracy, Toleration, and Religion at Columbia University. The late* **Juan J. Linz** *(1926–2013) was Sterling Professor Emeritus of Political and Social Science at Yale University. This essay, based on their 2012 Seymour Martin Lipset Lecture on Democracy in the World, originally appeared in the April 2013 issue of the* Journal of Democracy.

More than twenty-five years have passed since the publication of *Transitions from Authoritarian Rule: Prospects for Democracy,* the four pioneering volumes edited by Guillermo O'Donnell, Philippe C. Schmitter, and Laurence Whitehead that inaugurated third-wave democ-ratization theory. More than fifteen years have passed since the 1996 publication of our own *Problems of Democratic Transition and Consoli-dation: Southern Europe, South America, and Post-Communist Europe.* Looking back, what do we find useable or applicable from works on democratization from this earlier period, and what concepts need to be modified? In particular, what new perspectives are needed in light of the recent upheavals in the Arab world?

Here we focus on three topics that have been illuminated by the events of the Arab Spring: 1) the relationship between democracy and religion, especially in the world's Muslim-majority countries; 2) the character of hybrid regimes that mix authoritarian and democratic elements; and 3) the nature of "sultanism" and its implications for transitions to democ-racy.

Conflicts concerning religion, or between religions, did not figure prominently in either the success or failure of third-wave attempts at democratic transition. The Roman Catholic Church of course played an important and positive role in the democratic transitions in Poland, Chile, and Brazil. But conflicts over religion, which were so crucial in Europe in earlier historical periods, were not prominent. For this and other reasons, religion was undertheorized in scholarly writing about the third wave. Yet the hegemony, perceived or actual, of religious forces over much of civil society in the Arab world, especially in the country-side, had no parallel in the third wave. Thus the central role that Islam has played in the Arab Spring presents students of democratization with a novel phenomenon, and prompts them accordingly to come up with new concepts and fresh data to shed light upon it.

Samuel P. Huntington argued controversially that religion, especially Islam, would set major limits to further democratization. That suggested to one of us (Alfred Stepan) the idea of exploring what democracy and religion need, and do not need, from each other in order that each may flourish.[1] Stepan argued that neither *laïcité* of the French sort (generally recognized not merely as secularist but as positively antireligious), nor a type of secularism that decrees a complete separation between religion and the state, was empirically necessary for democracy to emerge.

What was needed for both democracy and religion to flourish? The answer was a significant degree of institutional differentiation between religion and the state. This situation of differentiation Stepan summed up as the "twin tolerations." In a country that lives by these two tol-erations, religious authorities do not control democratic officials who are acting constitutionally, while democratic officials do not control re-ligion so long as religious actors respect other citizens' rights. Many different patterns of relations among the state, religion, and society are compatible with the twin tolerations. There are, in other words, "mul-tiple secularisms."

This term fits even the EU democracies. France retains a highly sep-aratist, somewhat religion-unfriendly pattern of secularism with roots in the French Revolution. Germany, like Austria, Belgium, the Nether-lands, and Switzerland, displays a very different pattern of state-religion relations that in German law is called "positive accommodation." In the German case, this includes a state role in collecting taxes for the Roman Catholic and Lutheran churches. The twin-tolerations model, of course, can incorporate countries with established churches—overall, a third of the EU's 27 member states have established churches, with the Lutheran Church filling this role in Denmark, Finland, and Sweden, as well as the non-EU states of Iceland and Norway. All the varieties of secularism in Europe are consistent with religious toleration and democracy.[2]

The crucial point is that multiple forms of secularism can be friendly to democracy and the twin tolerations. It should be better known than it is—particularly in most Arab countries—that close to 300 million Mus-lims have been living under democracy for each of the past ten years in the Muslim-majority countries of Albania, Indonesia, Senegal, and Turkey. If one adds the roughly 178 million Muslims who are natives of Hindu-majority India, the total number of Muslims living in democracies outside the West begins to approach half a billion. The Indian experience may be of particular interest, for it means that India had to be histori-cally imagined—not to mention governed for the last six decades—as a democracy that incorporates a huge number of Muslim citizens.

India provides strong evidence against the presumption that there is something "exceptionalist" about Muslim attitudes toward democracy. In a recent survey with 27,000 respondents, India's Hindus and Muslims alike reported themselves as supporters of democracy at an equally high 71 percent.[3] Nearby in overwhelmingly Muslim Pakistan, the cognate figure was a mere 34 percent. That Indian Muslims should back de-mocracy at more than twice the rate of their coreligionists who live just across the border—in a country with a far more checkered democratic history—underlines the great political contextuality of religion.

With that in mind, we should look at the Muslim world's newly emer-gent democracies (Indonesia and Senegal, for example) and ask first if there have been any new conceptual emphases in Islamic political theol-ogy that have aided democratization in these places. Next, we should ask whether any new public policies regarding religion have been friendly to the twin tolerations while assisting democracy's rise.

On the conceptual and theological front, we note a growing emphasis on the importance of the Koranic verse (2:256) that categorically asserts, "There shall be no compulsion in religion." And as the Indonesian civil society leader, politician, and political scientist Amien Rais points out: "The Koran does not say anything about the formation of an Islamic state, or about the necessity and obligations on the part of Muslims to establish a Sharia or Islamic State."[4] Indonesian Muslim leaders say things like this often in order to argue against the imposition of *shari'a* in their country. To date, none of the Muslim-majority democracies has established *shari'a* as its legal code, and none has made Islam its established religion.[5]

We can draw similar examples from Tunisia, which in 2012 became the first Arab country in more than three decades to receive a ranking of 3 or better for political rights on the 7-point Freedom House scale (in which 1 is most free and 7 is least free). Many pan-Arabists or pan-Islamists, not to mention backers of a global Islamic caliphate, often voice doubts about the legitimacy of individual states and the value of democracy in them. Yet in Tunisia as in Indonesia, some influential Islamic advocates of democracy have used the key Koranic concepts of consensus, consultation, and justice to argue that democracy will be most effective and most legitimate if it relates to the *specificities* of its citizens' histories in a particular state. For example, Rachid Ghannouchi of Ennahda, Tunisia's governing Islamist party since 2011, frequently says that his party should embrace the historic specificity that Tunisia for more than sixty years has had the Arab world's most progressive and women-friendly family code.[6]

Another concept that is becoming important in Tunisia is not "secu-larism" as such (in Arabic the word for secularism, *almaniyah,* carries antireligious overtones), but rather the concept of a civil state (*dawla madaniyah*) instead of a religious state. In a civil state, religion (in keeping with the twin tolerations) respects democratic prerogatives—the people are sovereign, and they make the laws. Yet a civil state also respects some prerogatives of religion and its legitimate role in the public sphere. In a May 2011 interview, both Ghannouchi and Tunisia's future prime minister, Hamadi Jebali of Ennahda, spoke extensively of the political imperative of a "civil state."[7]

What are some of the public policies and practices that have encouraged mutual respect between religion and democracy in Indonesia, Senegal, and also India?

First, all three actively contribute to the celebration of more religions than does Western Europe. For example, Denmark, France, Germany, the Netherlands, Sweden, and Switzerland decree a combined total of 76 religious holidays on which workers, by law, enjoy a paid day off. Every such holiday comes from the Christian calendar; none are for minority religions. Indonesia, by contrast, has six such official Islamic holidays, and seven additional holidays to cover days sacred to such minority religions as Buddhism, Christianity, Confucianism, and Hinduism. Senegal has seven public Islamic holidays, and six for the less than one-tenth of the population that is Roman Catholic. Senegal also subsidizes pilgrimages to Rome for Catholic citizens. India has five official Hindu holidays, and ten to accommodate its many minority religions. All three countries also offer state funding to different religions, especially for religious schools and hospitals.

India, Indonesia, and Senegal also embrace greater degrees of policy cooperation between the state and religion than would be found under French-style *laïcité* or even U.S. doctrines of church-state accommodation. In all three countries, discussions between religious authorities and representatives of the democratic state have often led to policy consensus. In both Indonesia and Senegal, education-ministry specialists have worked with Islamic authorities to agree on mutually acceptable curricula, accreditation standards, and texts on the history of religion and Islam. One happy result has been that more parents than ever are choosing to send their daughters to school. Among Indonesians aged 11 to 14 today, 96 percent of boys and 95 percent of girls are literate.

In Senegal, the state asked the secretary-general of the National Association of Imams to inquire whether there is a Koranic basis for female genital mutilation (FGM). After study, the secretary-general sent all the Sufi orders a 43-page report saying that nothing in the Koran or early Islamic sources commands this custom or even indicates that it was ever practiced in the families of Muhammad and his companions. The imam concluded by asserting that a proper understanding of Islam required all imams to cooperate with state officials in a joint campaign—its effectiveness later certified by the UN—to combat FGM.[8]

Such examples put in question the political wisdom of John Rawls's injunction to take religion "off the political agenda" lest it interfere with the "overlapping moral consensus" that democracy requires. If democracy-inhibiting religious arguments are already on the political agenda, should Muslim leaders and activists who favor democracy not vigorously enter the public arena to show, from *within* their own tradition, that Islam and democracy are in fact compatible? Moreover, would it not be a good thing if more people in Arab countries—where "secularism" is too often seen as intrinsically hostile to religion—knew of the progress that Indonesia and Senegal have made toward relating religion, state, and society in ways that are friendly to both Islam and democracy?

Hybrids: The Case of Egypt

In our earlier work we listed five regime types: democratic, authoritarian, totalitarian, posttotalitarian, and sultanistic.[9] To this roster we now propose adding a sixth type, the "authoritarian-democratic hybrid" regime. Like totalitarianism and posttotalitarianism, this is a "historically constructed" category devised to take into account a newly emergent phenomenon seen today in the Arab world and beyond.

No Arab country—not even Syria, and still less Egypt, Libya, or Tunisia under the dictatorships of Mubarak, Qadhafi, and Ben Ali—has ever had a fully institutionalized totalitarian regime as we define it. Therefore, the term "posttotalitarian" does not apply to Arab countries where dictatorships have fallen.[10]

Such countries can no longer be adequately characterized as authoritarian or sultanistic, either, and they are not (or not yet) democracies—hence the "authoritarian-democratic hybrid" label. This concept is obviously a close relation to regime types that other scholars have called "competitive authoritarian" or simply "hybrid."[11] We prefer the lengthier term "authoritarian-democratic hybrid" because it calls attention to the unusual condition of the countries so labeled: They are places where most major actors believe that they will lose legitimacy and their followers' support should they fail to embrace certain core features of democracy (such as elections to produce the leaders of government), while believing at the same time that they must also retain (or at least allow) some authoritarian controls on key aspects of the emerging polity if they hope to further their goals and (again) retain their supporters.

It is possible that we will eventually stop calling this a "regime type" because it fails to last or become institutionalized. In that case, "situation" would be a better word. In the early 1970s, Juan Linz called military rule in Brazil (a rule that began in 1964 and mixed authoritarian with democratic features) a "situation" and predicted that it would never manage to institutionalize itself. In a rare case of political science directly influencing political practice, it appears that the military regime's chief strategist,

General Golbery do Couto e Silva, saw an advance copy of Linz's article and was influenced by it to persuade his colleagues that they should begin slowly to extricate themselves from government while they were still able to control the pace and circumstances of their withdrawal.[12]

It is highly possible that many of the Arab world's current "hybrids" will also turn out to be passing "situations" rather than entrenched "regimes." The evolutionary possibilities include, as in Brazil from 1974 to 1989, a transition toward democracy. Yet should the coercive apparatus find it too difficult and distasteful to coexist with democratic elements (as happened in Algeria in 1991), there could also be a transition, via a military coup or some other means, toward full-fledged authoritarianism.

Why do hybrid situations (if not hybrid regimes) come into being? Recent historical events such as the fall of communism, the entry of ten former communist countries into the EU, the demise of military governments in Latin America, and the aspirations raised by Tahrir Square do not mean the "end of history" and the reign of full democracy. Yet in countries such as Egypt, they have fueled a growing sense of the dignity of the individual, of people as citizens rather than mere subjects, and of democratic practices as things that are normally expected. In this new world, passively accepting for sixty years in a row one military officer after another as Egypt's ruler is no longer possible. The three major players left standing after the last of those three officers (former Air Force general Mubarak) fell—the Supreme Council of the Armed Forces (SCAF), the Muslim Brotherhood (MB), and secular liberals— would have lost much of their legitimacy, and many of their followers, had they failed to embrace central democratic tenets such as reasonably competitive elections for the key offices of state. (Without relatively free elections, of course, a regime would not even qualify as hybrid, but would simply be authoritarian.)

Yet the generals, the Brotherhood, and the liberals all wanted to protect themselves in certain areas by placing limits on the right of democratic institutions to make public policy. Soon after Mubarak's fall, many of the young secular liberals who had filled Tahrir Square began to argue that the MB was so strong and so fundamentally undemocratic that core liberal-democratic values could only be saved if secular liberals cut a deal with a nondemocratic source of power—the military. Many liberals argued that the military should help structure, or even write, the constitution *before* elections for the Constituent Assembly, or at the very least appoint a committee of experts to draft the constitution so that the Brotherhood could not constitute a majority.[13]

For its part, the SCAF supported the holding of elections and implicitly agreed, at a price, to maintain some controls on any Islamist majority that elections might produce. Only weeks before the 26 November 2011 parliamentary elections, the SCAF released the infamous "Silmi Document" asserting a variety of military prerogatives not found in any democracy. For instance, the document's ninth article flatly asserted that the SCAF "is solely responsible for all matters concerning the armed forces, and for discussing its budget. . . . [the SCAF] is also exclusively competent to approve all bills relating to the armed forces before they come into effect."

The Muslim Brothers, meanwhile, partly because they felt under attack from secular liberals, began early on to enter into understandings with the military. In keeping with these, the MB backed the generals' unilateral decision to hold a constitutional referendum on the heels of Mubarak's resignation, and kept silent about several incidents during the last three months of 2011 in which soldiers and police killed protesters, including at least 28 Coptic Christians. In return, the Brothers were allowed to take a historic step by assuming *partial* leadership of a controlled democracy.

More than is commonly understood, the cost of the Brotherhood's gains (which included the elected presidency of Egypt) included a special position for the military in the new constitutional order, the economy, and regional government. The new constitution, largely written by the MB, stipulates a number of arrangements not normally found in democratic constitutions. For example, the document decrees that the defense minister must be a serving military officer (Article 195); provides for a National Defense Council comprising eight uniformed officers and seven civilians that votes on the military budget (Article 197); and gives the armed forces the right to try civilians in military courts for crimes that "harm the Armed Forces" (Article 198).

Much has been made of President Mohamed Morsi's decision to sack certain key generals. Less has been made of his decision to name many of these cashiered officers to influential economic posts—overseeing the Suez Canal, civil aviation, and the extensive network of military-run factories—from which they can work to secure the armed forces' already huge influence over the Egyptian economy. Moreover, instead of following Indonesia's example and making regional executives elected, Egypt has adopted a constitution that is silent on regional elections. Retired military officers continue to fill many powerful regional posts. Such are the ways of an authoritarian-democratic hybrid state.

What Was Different in Tunisia?

Unlike Egypt, postdictatorial Tunisia, despite a destablizing assassination in February 2013, has so far managed to avoid the strong admixture of authoritarianism that makes a hybrid situation or regime. The initial reasons for this were three. First, the leaders of the Ennahda party, which was at one time close to the Muslim Brotherhood, since the early 1980s increasingly came to resemble Indonesia's major Islamic groups in arguing that democracy was not only acceptable, but necessary. This eventually facilitated collaboration between Ennahda's Islamists and secular liberals from other parties in joint efforts against Ben Ali.

Second, due to highly innovative "pacts" formed between secularists and Islamists before the transition started, there was a kind of inoculation against the intense fear of democracy's consequences that drives hybrid authoritarianism. Each of Tunisia's two secular authoritarian presidents, Habib Bourguiba and later Ben Ali, deliberately mobilized fear. Each claimed repeatedly that allowing competitive elections would bring to power Islamists who would be at best overly tradition-bound and at worst "terrorists." Domestic peace, women's rights, and secular liberals would suffer. Tunisians heard a great deal of this, but despite it, leading secular liberals began to ask whether they might have more in common with at least some Islamists than with Ben Ali, and the two groups considered (with some success) whether they could work together. Suspicions remain, of course, but most secular liberals do not fear Ennahda badly enough to want to use authoritarianism as a shield against it.

Third, in Tunisia by contrast to Egypt, not only civil society but *political society* began to develop. Civil society can play a vital role in the destruction of an authoritarian regime, but for the construction of a democracy, one needs a political society. In other words, there must be organized groups of political activists who can not only rally resistance to dictatorship, but also talk among themselves about how they can overcome their mutual fear and craft the "rules of the game" for a democratic alternative.

Although Egypt arguably had a more creative civil society than did Tunisia, the former's specifically political society was and is woefully underdeveloped. As late as four months after Mubarak's February 2011 ouster, the two key social groups that had opposed him—secular liberals and the Muslim Brotherhood—still had not held a single joint meeting to discuss democratic governing alternatives. The Brotherhood's website was still displaying its 2007 draft party platform, complete with nondemocratic features such as a rejection of the idea that a woman or a non-Muslim (two groups comprising more than half the populace) could ever be president of Egypt, and a recommendation that a high court composed of and appointed by imams should be empowered to review all new legislation to ensure its compliance with *shari'a*. Small wonder, then, that a sense of growing distrust has continued to dominate the political atmosphere in Egypt.

In Tunisia, secular liberals and Islamists began meeting regularly eight years *before* Ben Ali's fall to see whether they could reduce mutual fears and agree upon rules for democratic governance. That is, they began to create a political society. As described recently in these pages, such efforts helped to lay the basis for the near-unanimity with which the roughly 155 consensually selected members of the country's key post–Ben Ali reform commission voted for six major rules and principles to govern the selection and proceedings of a constituent assembly.[14] Nothing like this happened in Egypt. There, the SCAF shaped all significant political dialogue with one unilateral communiqué after another (more than 150 all told) over the ten months following Mubarak's fall.

Following a free election in October 2011, Tunisia's democratic political society eased the formation of a three-party governing coalition. The heads of the two largest parties, Ennahda's Rachid Ghannouchi and human-rights activist Moncef Marzouki of the secular Congress for the Republic, knew each other well, having met about twenty times in London over the eight years preceding Ben Ali's fall.[15] Tunisia's post–Ben Ali political society has had to struggle with numerous problems, of course, but initially did so ably enough so that in 2012 Tunisia became the first Arab-majority country in 37 years to receive a political-rights score as good as 3 from Freedom House.

Hopeful Trends and Disturbing Realities

Transitions toward democracy are always filled with uncertainty. Tunisia's is no exception. There are worrisome as well as reassuring trends. During Alfred Stepan's November 2012 research visit there (his fourth since 2011) some of the reassuring trends were as follows:

1. In separate personal interviews, most of the presidents of the largest parties in the Constituent Assembly affirmed their expectation that, after numerous compromises, they would be able to gather a two-thirds majority of the Assembly behind the constitution they were writing.

2. Every major political leader expressed the belief that within eight months of the approval of the constitution, elections would be held, and that if the state could contain the increasing occurences of political violence the voting would be free and fair.

3. Both governing-coalition members and oppositionists in the Constituent Assembly implied that if Ennahda proved unable to command another coalitional majority after these elections (there is a good chance that it will not be able to), Ennadha would, as in any democracy, peacefully step down, perhaps with a view to participating as a junior partner in some new ruling coalition.

4. The draft constitution had one major issue still unresolved: the powers of the executive. But there was growing confidence in November 2012 that an innovative and consensual solution could be found. Ennahda preferred a British-style parliamentary system but with proportional representation. Most of the other parties in the Constituent Assembly argued that, since Tunisia had just had a popular revolution, the people should have the right to play a role in choosing a president. But these parties were painfully aware that from 1956 to 2011, Tunisia

was ruled by presidents so strong they doubled as dictators. There was a growing trend within the Constituent Assembly in favor of a new model that we call "parliamentarized semipresidentialism" of the Portuguese sort—that is, with a weaker president and a stronger parliament than in France, and also with a significant role for a Constitutional Court in adjudicating any potential conflicts between parliament and the president.[16]

But there were also some disturbing realities in Tunisia that have now contributed, as of this writing in March 2013, to what many observers feel is the greatest challenge to confront democracy since Ben Ali's fall:

1. Ennahda became legal only after the transition had begun. Prodemocratic rethinking had occurred within Ennahda, but mostly among its leaders in exile in London and Paris. Also, the hard-line secularist dictators Bourguiba and Ben Ali had nearly destroyed Islamic education within Tunisia, leaving a vacuum that Gulf-financed theocratic extremists rushed to fill amid the new conditions of greater religious liberty. Unfortunately, to date, Ennadha has not yet been able to effectively create alternative spaces and discourses in many key mosques and neighborhoods.

2. Aided by the incompetence or complicity of the police, on 14 September 2012 about a thousand lightly armed salafists radicals occupied the outer courtyard of the U.S. embassy in Tunis for about three hours, before reinforced security forces drove them back. More than a hundred arrests were made. Rioters looted and burned the American Cooperative School of Tunis on the same day. These, and other incidents intensified criticism of the Ennadha ministers of the Interior and Justice by liberals and secularists for what they saw as underzealous control of the Islamist paramilitary Leagues for the Defense of the Revolution combined with overzealous attacks on secular antigovernment protestors.

3. In a display of what Juan Linz calls "semi-loyal opposition," the new Nidaa Tounes party, led by Béji Caïd Essebsi—an elderly but charismatic politician supported by wealthy former Ben Ali loyalists and anticoalition secularists—staged a 23 October 2012 rally declaring that the government had lost its legitimacy because it had failed to finish the constitution within the promised one year following the elections of 23 October 2011. Essebsi called for a fresh mandate to govern, to be reached by roundtable talks held outside parliamentary channels, albeit with discussion and ratification by the Constituent Assembly.

4. The growing crisis intensified on 6 February 2013, when a leading critic of the government, Chokri Belaid, became the first political activist in democratizing Tunisia to be assassinated. The killing triggered a move by Prime Minister Hamadi Jebali of Ennahda to form a government made up solely of nonpartisan technocrats, but his own party would not go along with this and he resigned on February 19. In March, however, Ennahda ceded the cabinet portfolios for Defense, Justice, Foreign Affairs, and the Interior—the so-called sovereignty min-

istries—to nonpartisan technocrats. The new cabinet received a vote of confidence on March 13.

Varieties of Sultanism

Our third set of comments concerns the concept of sultanism. According to Max Weber, "*Patrimonialism* and, in the extreme case, *sultanism* tend to arise . . . when domination develops an administration and a military force which are purely personal instruments of the master." Weber went on to emphasize the importance of the complete discretion of the ruler in a sultanistic system and indeed built it into his definition: Where domination "operates primarily on the basis of discretion, it will be called *sultanism.*"[17] This means that in extreme cases of sultanism there is no autonomy of state careers. All officials, even generals and admirals, are best seen as being on the "household staff" of the sultan.

The ruler's near-complete personal discretion is a hallmark of sultanism and one of the reasons why, in our original typology, we insisted upon a distinction between sultanistic and authoritarian regimes. Rafael Trujillo, the dictator of the Dominican Republic from 1930 to 1961, made his son a brigadier general when the boy was nine.[18] That is sultanism. General Augusto Pinochet, the military strongman who ruled Chile from 1973 to 1990, could never have done such a thing—the Chilean military had a degree of established autonomy as an institution and would not have allowed it. Pinochet might have headed the "military as government," but the "military as institution" retained some of its own ideas and organizational autonomy.[19]

Regimes can be almost entirely sultanistic in their characteristics or have some, but not many, sultanistic characteristics. It is useful to view sultanism as a continuum, for whether a regime is more or less sultanistic will affect the potential range of transitions away from sultanism that are open to it.

When a regime is close to pure sultanism, a relatively peaceful and domestically generated regime change via the classic "four-player game" of democratization theory (in which soft-liners from the regime and opposition work together to sideline the regime and opposition hard-liners) is virtually impossible. Once the two soft-liner camps reveal themselves, the sultan will destroy them. Seeing this, the hard-line oppositionists will grow even harder, vowing never to give up their arms to such a feared and hated foe. There will either be a violent transition or no transition at all.[20]

Yet a regime that is less fully sultanistic might permit some autonomy to certain business and religious groups. Such a regime also might run into pushback from the "military as institution" if officers come to believe that continued support for the sultan will harm their core interests. If powerful forces from abroad (say a large neighbor or an international body) weigh in on the side of democracy, then a fairly peaceful four-player game might ensue and lead to a reasonably rapid democratic transition. The end of the Ferdinand Marcos regime in the Philippines in 1986 is a rare example of this.[21] In general, however, a sultanistic regime is far less likely than an authoritarian regime to give way to a peaceful, "pacted" transition, or one that leads to democracy. The presence of a sultan makes negotiation too difficult.

The Arab world remains predominantly nondemocratic, but none of its nondemocratic regimes is as sultanistic as was that of Trujillo. He treated much of the Dominican economy as his personal property, made no distinction between his personal regime and the state, decreed dynastic succession, and faced no coherent opposition from the military.

Before the Arab upheavals of 2011, the regimes in Libya, Syria, Yemen, Egypt and Tunisia all displayed (to one degree or another) some features of sultanism. Yet if we place them on a continuum and focus on the key variable of the "military as institution," we can see crucial differences that contributed to five quite distinctive outcomes.

Qadhafi's Libya was the most sultanistic, and saw no four-player game. Qadhafi created, dismantled, and re-created chains of commands and security structures at will. His sons were emerging as possible dynastic successors, and core security posts were in the hands of relatives. Few business groups could assume any politically relevant autonomy. It took a civil war—and massive help for the rebels in the form of a UN-backed NATO bombing campaign—to topple the "Brother Leader."

Weber correctly asserted that a "state is a human community that (successfully) claims *the monopoly of the legitimate use of force within a given territory.*"[22] It will be a long time before such a successful monopoly claim can be made in Libya and a useable democratic state comes into existence throughout its territory. A reporter who had traveled widely in the country's interior just two months before the 7 July 2012 parliamentary elections concluded:

> Libya has no army. It has no government. These things exist on paper, but in practice Libya has yet to recover from the long maelstrom of Qadhafi's rule. . . . What Libya does have is militias, more than 60 of them. . . . Each brigade exercises unfettered authority over its own turf. . . . There are no rules.[23]

Rebuilding (or simply building) a useable state and a coherent security apparatus should have been the highest priority for both the interim Libyan government and the international democracy promoters who came to its aid. As it was, elections went forward rapidly and reasonably smoothly. But on 11 September 2012, one or more of the militias (it may have been Ansar al-Shari'a) assaulted the U.S. consulate in Benghazi and killed the ambassador as well as three other U.S. citizens. It took the Libyan government, with some U.S. support, hours to retake possession of the area. The Benghazi attack reveals in the harshest terms that without a useable state there can be no safeguards for human rights, law and order, consolidated democracy, or effective governance. In Libya after sultanism, all these are in desperately short supply.[24]

Syria under Bashar al-Assad clearly has strong sultanistic features, such as the "dynastic" element. He "inherited" the presidency from his father even though he was working in England as an ophthalmologist before being summoned home for grooming as his father's successor after his brother, the heir apparent, died in a car crash. Still, Syria was not quite as sultanistic as Qadhafi's Libya. Parts of the business community and state apparatus enjoyed at least some internal autonomy. The security apparatus, however, has remained tightly controlled. Assad has no important security official in whom he does not have full personal trust, which means that nearly all must come from his own Alawite religious minority. The Alawite dominance within the coercive apparatus signals that we are not in Marcos or Mubarak territory here, where the organized military might unseat the ruler. The Alawite officers who do Assad's bidding know that should he fall, they and their families will face mortal danger. In Syria, there are no influential regime and opposition soft-liners to carry out semi-public negotiations over the terms of the sultan's exit. A civil war prevails, with numerous fronts and competing factions fed by external supply lines. We know of no situations where a long, complicated, and brutal civil war has led to a cohesive state and a rapidly emerging democracy.

Mubarak's Egypt was beginning to display sultanistic features including extreme corruption, "crony capitalism," and the "dynastic" grooming of Gamal Mubarak as his father's successor. Yet the Egyptian military retained a good deal of institutional autonomy (far more than its counterparts in Libya, Syria, or Yemen), and it was easily able to protect its interests quickly and peacefully by pushing the octogenarian Mubarak out of power and into internal exile. The military thus forestalled the threat it feared from Gamal Mubarak, who was known for pushing economic changes that would have threatened the military's vast industrial and commercial holdings. That the elder Mubarak, an air force general himself, in some sense represented the "military as government" made little difference when the interests of the "military as institution" were involved. By getting rid of him, the top generals at least temporarily enhanced their own popular prestige, as the crowds in Cairo's Tahrir Square chanted "The people and the army are one hand!" Yet as we have seen, the next target of the military as institution turned out to be full democracy, as the generals decided that slapping limits on it was what their interests dictated in the new post-Mubarak world.

In Tunisia, the most sultanistic feature of Ben Ali's regime was his habit of letting his wife and her family treat the Tunisian economy as their personal property. Yet Ben Ali's repressive apparatus could not prevent an underground (or exiled) political society involving all the major opposition forces from coming into being and holding talks about what a post–Ben Ali Tunisia should look like. Hence, when he fell, a relatively coherent and democratic alternative was on hand. Just as important, Ben Ali had relied on the police to do his dirty work and had allowed the small Tunisian army to remain professional. This enabled the "military as institution" to play a crucial role in bringing the dictatorship to a quick and nonviolent end. The army stopped the police from using lethal force to protect Ben Ali, and then it let the sultan know that troops would not shield him from protestors, but would assure him safe passage to Saudi Arabia if he left immediately. Wisely, Ben Ali took the deal. Then the army—a modest institution with few special privileges to protect—pivoted to supporting the democratic transition rather than indulging Egyptian-style worries about how to safeguard its own power and perquisites.

Neither the Hungarian Revolution of 1956, the Prague Spring of 1968, nor Poland's Solidarity in 1981 succeeded in immediately creating a democracy. Yet each of these historic movements eroded forever the legitimacy of the dictatorial regime that it challenged. We think that the events of the Arab Spring at the very least have made Arab "presidents for life" increasingly unacceptable, and the dignity of citizens increasingly desired.[25]

NOTES

1. Alfred Stepan, "Religion, Democracy, and the 'Twin Tolerations,'" *Journal of Democracy* 11 (October 2000): 37–57. For a longer version, see Alfred Stepan, "The World's Religious Systems and Democracy: Crafting the 'Twin Tolerations,'" *Arguing Comparative Politics* (Oxford: Oxford University Press, 2001), 213–54.

2. Alfred Stepan, "The Multiple Secularisms of Modern Democratic and Non-Democratic Regimes," in Craig Calhoun, Mark Juergensmeyer, and Jonathan VanAntwerpen, eds., *Rethinking Secularism* (New York: Oxford University Press, 2011), 114–44.

3. See Alfred Stepan, Juan J. Linz, and Yogendra Yadav, *Crafting State Nations: India and Other Multinational Democracies* (Baltimore: Johns Hopkins University Press, 2011), 70–71.

4. Mirjam Künkler and Alfred Stepan, "An Interview with Amien Rais," *Journal of International Affairs* 61 (Fall–Winter 2007): 205–18.

5. Stepan, "The Multiple Secularisms of Modern Democratic and Non-Democratic Regimes," 117.

6. Alfred Stepan, "Tunisia's Transition and the Twin Tolerations," *Journal of Democracy* 23 (April 2012): 94–97.

7. Stepan, "Tunisia's Transition."

8. For more detail on these and other examples of policy cooperation between religious and state officials in Indonesia and Senegal, see Alfred Stepan, "Rituals of Respect: Sufis and Secularists in Senegal in Comparative Perspective," *Comparative Politics* 44 (July 2012): 379–401.

9. Juan J. Linz and Alfred Stepan, *Problems of Democratic Transition and Consolidation: Southern Europe, South America, and Post-Communist Europe* (Baltimore: Johns Hopkins University Press, 1996), 38–65.

10. Although Qadhafi and Saddam Hussein at times had totalitarian ambitions and installed some totalitarian features in their respective regimes, neither boasted the institutional or ideological resources that sustained the totalitarian regimes of Hitler, Stalin, or Mao.

11. For valuable reviews of this literature, see Nicolas van de Walle, "Between Authoritarianism and Democracy," *Journal of Democracy* 23 (January 2012): 169–73; and Leonardo Morlino, "Are There Hybrid Regimes?" in his *Changes for Democracy: Actors, Structures, Processes* (Oxford: Oxford University Press, 2011), 48–76.

12. Juan. J. Linz, "The Future of an Authoritarian Situation or the Institutionalization of an Authoritarian Regime: The Case of Brazil," in Alfred Stepan, ed., *Authoritarian Brazil: Origins, Policies, and Future* (New Haven: Yale University Press, 1973), 233–54.

13. The Carnegie Endowment's "Guide the Egypt's Transition" blog highlighted the persistence of this hybridity by noting on 4 October 2011 that "In general, liberal parties would like the constitution to be written before elections take place, fearing that a post-election constitution-making process will be dominated by Islamists." See *http://egypt-elections.carnegieendowment.org/2011/10/04/constitutional-principles*.

14. Stepan, "Tunisia's Transition," 91–97.

15. Alfred Stepan, personal interview with President Moncef Marzouki, Tunis, 1 November 2012.

16. For a more extensive theoretical and comparative discussion of "parliamentarized semi-presidentialism," see Alfred Stepan, ed., *Democracies in Danger* (Baltimore: Johns Hopkins University Press, 2009), 11–14.

17. Max Weber, *Economy and Society: An Outline of Interpretive Sociology*, ed. Guenther Roth and Claus Wittich (Berkeley: University of California Press, 1978), 231–32. Emphasis in original.

18. Jonathan Hartlyn, "The Trujillo Regime in the Dominican Republic," in H.E. Chehabi and Juan J. Linz, eds., *Sultanistic Regimes* (Baltimore: Johns Hopkins University Press, 1998), 97.

19. For the political importance of this distinction, see "The Military as Institution Versus the Military as Government," in Alfred Stepan, *The Military in Politics: Changing Patterns in Brazil* (Princeton: Princeton University Press, 1971), 253–66.

20. The best comparative analysis of the obstacles to achieving peaceful, negotiated, democratic exits from sultanism is Richard Snyder, "Paths Out of Sultanistic Regimes: Combining Structural and Voluntarist Perspectives," in Chehabi and Linz, eds., *Sultanistic Regimes*, 49–81.

21. See Mark R. Thompson, "The Marcos Regime in the Philippines," in *Sultanistic Regimes*, 206–30.

22. See his "Politics as Vocation" in H.H. Gerth and C. Wright Mills, eds., *From Max Weber: Essays in Sociology* (New York: Oxford University Press, 1946), 78. Emphasis in original.

23. Robert F. Worth, "In Libya, the Captors Have Become the Captive," *New York Times Magazine*, 9 May 2012.

24. On the requirement of "stateness" for all these values, see Linz and Stepan, *Problems of Democratic Transition and Consolidation,* chs. 1 and 2.

25. Roger Owen, *The Rise and Fall of Arab Presidents for Life* (Cambridge: Harvard University Press, 2012).

9

TRANSFORMING THE ARAB WORLD'S PROTECTION-RACKET POLITICS

Daniel Brumberg

Daniel Brumberg *is codirector of the Democracy and Governance Studies program at Georgetown University and senior program officer at the Center for Conflict Management of the U.S. Institute of Peace. This essay originally appeared in the July 2013 issue of the* Journal of Democracy.

Despite the setbacks, conflicts, and violence that the Arab world has endured since the mass rebellions of early 2011, we can at least thank Egyptian heart surgeon turned television satirist Bassem Youssef for giving beleaguered democrats everywhere reason to smile. Even as prosecutors accused him of a host of "crimes"—including insulting the president and Islam itself—Youssef continued to lampoon the government. Taking a page from the previous regime's playbook, prosecutors insisted that the courts were acting independently and that citizens rather than state officials had brought the charges. Invoking this ridiculous rationale, the police compelled Youssef to review tapes of his show in order to explain his jokes to his unamused interrogators.[1]

Does this Kafkaesque tale leave any room for optimism? Watching an unchecked security apparatus regularly operate beyond the reach of a problematic legal system to harass journalists, some Egyptian writers argue that the very idea of transition is a hoax.[2] Still, Youssef's bizarre story does point to some hopeful changes. That he could broadcast for months before the police could question him highlights a constellation of twenty-first-century media forces that will be hard to rein in. Moreover, the controversy drew the public concern of activists in Tunisia, revealing the existence of an expanding regional democratic ethos that no Arab government can wish away or ignore.[3] Clearly, both Egypt and the entire region are experiencing profound change as well as striking continuity. Although local conditions and forces give each case of political revolt a unique cast, one dynamic that can be found throughout the Arab world is a complex three-way contest among those who wish to reimpose the old order, those who wish to overthrow it completely, and those who would accommodate it, at least in part.

If the ultimate outcome of these contests cannot be predicted two years into the Arab revolts, there is a sufficient record to begin charting their multiple trajectories. Indeed, because early steps shape so much of what comes after, the moment for taking stock has arrived. Among these steps, the most crucial is the forging of an implicit or explicit pact that can be accepted by groups that once enjoyed the old regime's protection (or by regime holdovers such as the security apparat). Persuading such elements to agree to such a pact will of course mean making compromises with them. The challenge is to make sure that these compromises help rather than hinder democratization.

In the Arab world, pact-making has proven painful and sometimes politically (if not literally) fatal. There are many reasons for this. Two particularly worth mentioning are the persistence of sharp identity conflicts in Arab societies, and the skill with which the Arab world's "protection-racket" autocracies have played upon these tensions for so long.[4] Where they have fallen, these autocracies have left behind a tricky dilemma: Groups that they once shielded remain significant but cannot win elections, while their rivals (who *can* win elections) wonder why they should make concessions to sure losers. In Tunisia, efforts to address this dilemma have hindered—but not blocked—political accommodation. In Egypt, similar efforts have produced an accommodation between the military and the Muslim Brotherhood that bodes ill for democracy. In Bahrain, Libya, Syria, and Yemen, meanwhile, escalating identity, regional, and social disputes are fueling protracted civil conflict and in some cases state collapse. The difficulties of shifting from an autocratic to a democratic model for protecting different societal interests will preoccupy the Arab world for the coming decade and beyond.

Why have the pacts that budding transitions to democracy need proven so hard to make and sustain in the Arab world? Scholars have cited the strength of Arab security states, the role of oil money and foreign aid in propping up old orders, and the fear that Islamists provoke within key domestic constituencies as well as Western capitals. But all these drivers of authoritarian persistence were part and parcel of a much larger reality: protection-racket systems that fed on regimes' manipulation of multiple identity conflicts. These conflicts encompassed the tensions around political Islam, but also much more. Indeed, a salient feature of Arab autocracies has been their uncanny knack for manipulating a wide array of ethnic, religious, and sociocultural groups by playing upon their fears of political exclusion (or worse) under majority rule and offering them *Godfather*-style "protection" in return for political support.

This protection-racket logic may be most readily seen in such minority-dominated regimes as the Assad family's Syria, where Alawite rulers shield their own community plus other vulnerable groups such as Christians; or Saddam Hussein's Iraq, where before the 2003 invasion a Sunni minority relied on an autocrat to block a Shia majority from real political participation (a similar situation obtains today in Bahrain). Domination by a specific ethnic or religious minority is not among the racket's requirements, however. Egypt is mostly Sunni, but its sizeable numbers of Coptic Christians (about a tenth of the populace) and secular Sunnis were groups that autocrats could offer to protect from Sunni Islamists. In Algeria, Morocco, and Tunisia (to name three more heavily Sunni countries), the split between Islamists and non-Islamists coincides with and has often been magnified by a cultural and ideological gap between those who identify with the French language and Western Europe and those who identify with Arabic and the Arab-Muslim world. In all three countries, many secular elites have seen autocracy as a necessary evil sheltering them from the prospect of uneven democratic contests with Islamists.

The mass uprisings of 2011 suggested that fear-mongering by autocrats was no longer the winning tactic that it once had been. Although no one could have foreseen the exact chain of events by means of which a single Tunisian's desperate self-immolation led to two dictators being toppled and other autocracies being shaken to their roots, it is clear that deep structural changes had paved the way. Two in particular merit comment. The first was the emergence of a new generation of activists who had no patience for the game of protection-racket politics. Their disaffection with autocratic "business as usual"—coupled with their disdain for corrupt, cronyism-riddled forms of neocapitalist development—gave rise to bridge-building efforts between young Islamists and secularists in Egypt, Jordan, Morocco, Tunisia, and Yemen. Seeing the obvious threat that such cooperation posed to the protection racket, regimes reinforced and unleashed their security agencies. But this gave rise to a backlash that was the second major change. Ever more intrusive and aggressive actions by the *mukhabarat* (secret police) caused pain to tens of thousands of law-abiding citizens and generated a terror that made the autocratic arrangement seem a more bitter bargain than before.

Couched in a universal language of dignity, freedom, and economic justice, the heady slogans of rebellion that rang out in Cairo's Tahrir Square and elsewhere across the region were a genuine and fitting response to the humiliation, repression, and twisted economic policies that many Arab regimes had imposed on their societies. Below the surface, however, dynamics were at work that cannot be grasped without careful attention to the varying types of authoritarian legacies with which different Arab societies have had to contend. The main distinction to keep in mind is the one between "liberalized" autocracies and "full" autocracies.

In liberalized autocracies, the protection racket relies on a distorted form of state-controlled pluralism or "neocorporatism." Rulers permit (or even encourage) a wide range of groups to mobilize through parliaments and state-managed electoral systems, professional syndicates, religious institutions, NGOs, universities, media outlets, and even the courts. Amid the fragmentation that this breeds, rulers play one group against another, helped by the patronage ties that they maintain with various groups.[5] The resulting jostle of interests leads to an equilibrium that can endure so long as no one group gains enough power to threaten the vital interests of state actors or rival regime-protected groups. To escape this game, opposition leaders must mobilize constituencies across identity divides. The regimes and their minions know this, of course, so they work to stymie such alliances by playing up whatever religious, tribal, or ethnic themes they can in order to *reemphasize* the divides and make rival groups feel as if they must look to the state to save them. This divide-and-rule strategy is enforced by "reserved domains of power"—that is, by powerful militaries that maintain links to rival identity groups; by vast internal-security services allied with the military; and often by judiciaries that furnish the protection racket with vital legal and institutional tools.

In a full autocracy, by contrast, a powerful executive and its security-sector allies repress a single dominant identity group in return for the tacit or explicit loyalty of other, weaker groups. This is simpler to run, as it does not require constantly adjusting relations among many players. But it is also less resilient, for it leaves the autocracy dependent on at most a few key allies and often makes the permanently repressed group irreconcilable, determined to overthrow the regime rather than negotiate with it. Alarmed by the costly precariousness of hegemonic "success" under this system, new leaders posing as "reformists" have now and then turned to the majority community in search of new allies, be they Sunni businessmen in Syria or "moderate" Shias in Bahrain. But such efforts have tended to alienate oppositionists and to harden the ruling minority against any further shifts toward liberalization.

From and to Autocracy in Egypt?

In large societies, liberalized protection-racket systems allow rulers to contain and use pluralism rather than simply repress it. In Egypt, whose current population is about 80 million, three-and-a-half decades of liberalized autocracy created the political topography on which the "revolution" of early 2011 was fought. The structural legacies that proved most critical were: 1) the military's role as arbiter; 2) the neo-corporatist arrangements by which the regime coopts and fragments the opposition; and 3) the politicization of the judiciary.

The central role played by the military and its allies in the Interior Ministry's security forces loomed large from the start. Having forced President Hosni Mubarak to resign and thereby having sidestepped most of the blame for the violence used against protesters, the military wielded its nationalist credentials—as well as its vast institutional and economic resources—to cement its role as chief arbiter. Mubarak had barely left Cairo for house arrest at Sharm el-Sheikh before the Supreme Council of the Armed Forces (SCAF) began its own partial reinvention of his old protection racket. The generals held talks with Islamists and non-Islamists alike: Both Egypt's secular middle class and its Muslim Brothers have histories of seeking the patronage of the military and its allies within the state bureaucracy and ruling party.[6]

This neocorporatist legacy created the second structural impediment to democracy-friendly pacting. Under liberalized autocracy, the ruling elite had honed patronage networks and (arbitrarily enforced) laws that gave a vast array of organizations different degrees of autonomy to represent competing social and identity-based interests.[7] Whether it was meant to or not, this arrangement worked to the advantage of Islamists. Their charitable organizations supported the Muslim Brotherhood (which technically was banned but in practice was tolerated), and the Brotherhood in turn was able to act as both a social movement and a quasi-legal political party. In a weak party system dominated by Mubarak's patronage-dispending National Democratic Party (NDP), only the Brothers could mobilize a mass constituency. Thanks to it, they would from time to time make gains (usually while running their candidates as nominal independents) in elections for the national legislature or within Egypt's various trade and professional syndicates, and the state would then push back to contain Brotherhood influence.

Running the Table

The upheaval of early 2011 imposed new realities on the old political terrain. Although periodic crackdowns were still possible, henceforth Egypt's security sector could no longer preclude genuine democratic competition or the election of a truly authoritative parliament. Indeed, SCAF's plan to have such a parliament appoint a hundred-member constituent assembly to write a permanent constitution created the real prospect that an Islamist-dominated legislature would be able to handpick an Islamist-controlled constitution-drafting body. Whereas a *democratizing* pact requires a consensus respecting the vital interests of *all* key players, what was looming in Egypt was a situation in which *one* player was about to run the table and be in a position to dictate terms to all the rest.

In the run-up to the 19 March 2011 referendum on the SCAF's proposal, non-Islamist groups mobilized for a "no" vote. If their campaign had merit, it also inadvertently invited Islamists to portray non-Islamists as "anti-Islam." Amplified by growing salafist activism, this scare tactic seems to have swayed many rural Muslims, who made up about two-fifths of those eligible to vote. The lopsided result, with its 77 percent majority for the "yes" side, set the stage for a year of living dangerously.

With a parliamentary-election period scheduled to span late 2011 and early 2012, rival opposition forces proceeded to read from what sounded like a script written by the SCAF. Youth activists from the April 6 Movement and other leftist groups were for rejecting any compromise with the military while many veteran activists favored trying to talk to the generals. Muslim Brotherhood leaders played both sides, sometimes endorsing (if not always joining) protests in Tahrir Square in order to press the SCAF, but placating the generals when they took decisions that helped Brotherhood political fortunes. When the SCAF floated basic-law provisions such as one giving the military the role of guarding "constitutional legitimacy," the Brotherhood quickly condemned the idea, thereby seeming to suggest a closing of ranks with non-Islamists. But when the military then announced that the presidential elections would be pushed back to late 2012 or early 2013—a sign that the generals meant to stay involved in the constitution-drafting process—the Brothers chose to avoid a confrontaton with the men in uniform. Thus when SCAF's actions provoked protests in Tahrir Square in November 2011, Muslim Brotherhood members avoided them.

The Brothers' opportunism may have burned whatever bridges were left between Islamists and non-Islamists, but it had a clear logic: With parliamentary elections on the horizon, and with Field Marshal Mohamed Hussein Tantawi (the defense minister and head of SCAF) pledging that an elected president would take power by 30 June 2012, the Brotherhood chose to focus on keeping its leaders together and mobilizing its base. Some younger members tried to break ranks, but the leadership frustrated their efforts. The quest for party discipline paid off. From the lower-house balloting that took place between November 2011 and January 2012, the Brotherhood's Freedom and Justice Party (FJP) and its allies emerged with almost 38 percent of the vote and 235 of the 498 elected seats (ten additional lower-house seats are appointed). The salafist Nour Party, meanwhile, won a surprising near-quarter of the seats, leaving non-Islamists with about 30 percent of the seats in the lower house. With Islamists showing no sudden readiness to offer "credible assurances" to their non-Islamist rivals, the chances for a consensus-based draft constitution—and indeed for accommodation in general—appeared slim.

The mid-2012 presidential election may have provided one last chance for Egypt to escape the gravitational pull of protection-racket identity politics. The first need was for a consensus candidate supported by all opposition factions. But the closest thing to one who appeared, ejected Brotherhood member Abdel Moneim Abul Futuh, could not muster that kind of support and ended up coming in fourth among the first-round candidates. The mid-June runoff was between the Brotherhood's Mohamed Morsi and Ahmed Shafiq, a former general and Mubarak's last prime minister, who championed a security-oriented platform. Facing this unappetizing choice, many non-Islamists stayed home and Morsi benefited, winning the runoff by a nonresounding 51.7 to 48.3 percent.

The military's response to the changed landscape wrought by Morsi's victory made accommodation between Islamists and non-Islamists even less likely. Shortly after the runoff, the SCAF issued a set of additional constitutional "principles" that limited the president's authority but gave the generals new powers, including what amounted to a veto on decisions by the constituent assembly.[8] Although this step seemed aimed at checking the Brothers, they readily accepted a new cabinet in which the leading internal and external security portfolios remained in military hands, thereby hinting at a power-sharing deal between Islamists and generals that would leave non-Islamists even farther out in the cold.

The non-Islamists still had one institution left over from the *ancien régime* with which they could hope to deflect Islamist challenges. Egypt has a complex judicial system featuring a multiplicity of institutions and actors equipped with varying degrees of autonomy. This state-tolerated quasi-pluralism had been essential in the days of divide and rule, creating courts that could favor Islamists one day and non-Islamists the next. Moreover, liberal judges could occasionally even defy state dictates, while the state could use its judicial-appointment powers to blunt such challenges.

After the parliamentary elections, several NGOs and human-rights organizations—upset that non-Islamists accounted for only 15 of the 100 people whom parliament had named to write the new constitution—had asked an administrative court to suspend the constituent assembly. As the presidential runoff loomed, a mixture of liberal groups and former regime apparatchiks appealed to the High Constitutional Court and its Mubarak-appointed chief justice. In a decision with a questionable legal rationale issued just two days before the presidential second round, this court declared that the procedures used to elect parliament had been unconstitutional. The legal basis for the constituent assembly's very existence was now in doubt, since there is no way that an unconstitutionally chosen legislature could name a body with legally valid powers.

Morsi could not remain idle in the face of this ruling and keep his followers' backing. He struck back on 12 August 2012, forcing Tantawi to retire and overruling the military's previous decree limiting presidential powers. A hundred days later, on November 22, Morsi issued decrees that assigned his office unprecedented powers, including the right to override the judiciary. Thus within six months of his election, he had opened the door for the Islamist-controlled constituent assembly to complete a draft constitution with no interference by the military and the judiciary—and no input from non-Islamist groups. The new constitution passed with 64 percent of the vote in a low-turnout December 2012 referendum, coming into force shortly before the end of the year.

Despite the Islamists' control of the writing process, the new constitution *does not* create an Islamist state per se. True, Articles 4 and 219 contain provisions that could enhance the capacity of al-Azhar's religious authorities to influence legislation. But these articles are not the document's center of gravity. Instead, other provisions suggest a power-sharing formula, with Islamists and the military retaining key areas of authority. On the positive side, the new constitution provides an elected lower house with real authority and sets out the civil and political rights that should support a multiparty system. Moreover, Articles 126, 127, and 152 ensure that a strong president will be cheked by a powerful judiciary. Yet given the constitution's vague language regarding the procedures for appointing the High Constitutional Court (Article 177), in the very likely event that the same party controls both the executive and legislature there could very well be fewer checks on the joined power of both institutions. What is more, the constitution reintroduces an institution—the upper legislative house known as the Shura Council—that all former Egyptian presidents used to manipulate and divide the opposition. With a third of its 264 members appointed by the president, the Shura Council could in theory give the executive a means to check the authority of a lower house, but it could also provide yet another ally for a hegemonic policial party.[9]

The abuse of power by such a party is made more likely by a series of troublesome articles that sustain and even enhance the state's authoritarian toolkit. For example, Articles 10, 11, 38, 43, 44, and 81 set out vague criteria that could give the police and judiciary power to arbitrarily limit freedoms whenever the state purports to detect a violation of communally defined norms of national, Islamic, family, or cultural "unity." Finally, the new constitution *expands* the military's institutional autonomy by providing for a National Defense Council (NDC) that will probably have more room for maneuver than the SCAF.[10] Although the president is to chair the fifteen-member NDC, serving military officers will have eight permanent seats, thus ensuring their control. The military also now has special courts in which it can try civilians arrested for crimes involving military or police personnel.[11] In sum, the new constitution provides the basis for a pact that protects both newly empowered players and holdovers from the old regime. Given the failure to reform the security sector and the total absence of any plans for serious efforts at transitional justice or judicial reform, key groups that once received at least some sort of protection under autocracy—secular professionals, intellectuals, businessmen, the Coptic Christian minority, and labor—will face an uphill struggle or worse.

Democratization in Tunisia: *Too Much* Consensus?

Tunisia's transition has run into many obstacles, but the pact-making process there has enjoyed advantages that are lacking in Egypt. First and foremost, the authoritarian protection-racket system in this small North African country (population 10.6 million) was much simpler and more centralized than its sprawling Egyptian counterpart. The Tunisian military was and is small and politically neutral, and does not run a business empire. The authoritarian regime's praetorian guard consisted not of soldiers but of police and intelligence personnel who were kept split into separate institutional silos in order to prevent them from turning as one against the regime. The security apparat's main task was to repress Islamists. Non-Islamists such as secularly oriented Sunni Muslim businessmen, professionals, and students relied on the regime's protection, but the regime relied at least in part on their tacit support as well. Bolstering this entente was the corporatist relationship between the state and the Tunisian General Labor Union (UGTT). Although friction between labor and business was not unknown, the hostility that many rank-and-file unionists felt toward Islamists helped to glue the protection racket together for decades.

The racket's center of gravity lay in the cities. This helped the regime to keep the underdeveloped rural interior—exploited for its crops and mines and potentially restive—safely cut off. Or so it seemed: The upheavals that would sweep like wildfire far beyond Tunisia began in December 2010 in the dusty hinterland town of Sidi Bouzid. In Tunisia itself, the sheer speed with which demonstrations spread to Tunis and coastal areas kept the focus on the cities. With protestors pouring into the capital's streets and soldiers refusing to shoot, middle-class professionals and a newly emerged vanguard of civil society groups made known their rejection of the old protection racket. As in Egypt, the early and heady days of revolt fed a giddy notion that all political horizons lay open. But such excitement could not long hide the truth that the advent of competitive politics would open the door to Islamists, many of whom might well want to seek a settling of scores in a democratic Tunisia.

The Political *Tabula Rasa*

How then to explain the relative lack of fear—and even more remarkable, the efforts of Islamists and non-Islamists to find common ground—during Tunisia's first postauthoritarian year? Perhaps it was because the old regime left behind neither an arbitrating mechanism nor the courts and security apparatus to support it. Without these things, Islamists and non-Islamists had little choice but to talk. Then too, many leaders of Ennahda (the foremost Islamist group) had enjoyed much time for new thought and reflection while in West European exile. Their "sheikh," Rachid Ghannouchi, had lived abroad for decades and returned promoting a current of pluralism that may also reflect deeper historical legacies, including Tunisia's Sufi heritage and the influence of a certain strain of reform-oriented Islamism associated with Zeytouna University in Tunis. More recently, efforts at reaching a political accommodation between Islamist and secular opposition parties had begun with meetings held in Europe starting in 2003, thus offering a useful precedent for the pact-making that followed the toppling of Ben Ali.

That said, the rocky path of political bargaining that Tunisia found itself inching painfully along in 2012 and early 2013 shows how unrealistic it is to expect some cultural or ideological legacy or exchange of "mutual assurances" to smooth every rough spot. To romanticize a "useable past" is to underrate two challenges. The first is the persistent nature of identity conflicts. Tunisia's experience shows how hard it is for Islamist leaders to sideline a distinctly Islamist agenda without stripping their movement of its symbolic force. The second comes from open political competition itself. As the focus shifts from elite pact-making to public election campaigning, Islamists inevitably make identity-based appeals to their followers that rouse non-Islamists' fears.

With the return of Ghannouchi and other London-based exiles, many in Ennahda began hoping for a new dawn of political consensus and inclusion that would somehow win over non-Islamists. But in truth, Ennahda's sudden reemergence unnerved the secular intellectuals and activists who held most of the places on the special commission that had been set up in March 2011 to oversee the transition. With a mere handful of seats on this body, Ennahda staged repeated boycotts of its meetings and had to be coaxed back. As plans for electing a constituent assembly were debated, secular activists insisted that it should have only constitution-drafting powers and no authority to pass laws. Ennahda sharply disagreed on this and related points, and came to suspect that secular groups were bent on sabotaging the transition. Eventually the problem was finessed by means of a vaguely worded joint declaration that skirted some of the hottest hot-button issues, including the central question of a legislative mandate for the constituent assembly.

This agreement to disagree set the stage for two years of escalating struggles around the wording of a new constitution. The October 2011 elections for the constituent assembly made things harder by producing an outcome that no one had anticipated: Ennahda won 89 of 217 seats, putting it in a position to dominate the majority-coalition "troika" that it formed with a pair of smaller secular parties that had 28 seats between them. The choice of veteran opposition leader and human-rights activist Moncef Marzouki as assembly president was not enough to allay the fears of non-Islamists, who dismissed Ennahda leaders' avowals of readiness to compromise as "double speak" that would stop once the Islamists got their hands on power.

Although this perception of Ennahda's leaders is understandable, it does not capture the full complexity of their motives or how changing circumstances affected their decisions. Like other Islamist intellectuals who had lived in the West or grappled with Western political thought, Ghannouchi and many of his allies had not clearly thought out how the quest for a more democratic and pluralistic politics could be hitched to an Islamic agenda. Such dissonance left them vulnerable to the sudden proliferation of diverse forms of Islamist activism, not merely by jihadi groups that were often placed under the blurry "salafist" rubric, but also by a wide range of Islamist actors who came from within Ennahda itself.

If decades of oppression had invited this surge of exuberant public activity by Islamists, there is no denying that it left many non-Islamists feeling terrified. Radical Islamists viewed settings that many Tunisians had long assumed would (or should) protect secularism—public universities, the media, theaters, and even in some ways the family—as providing venues for Islamists to vent their rage and shout their agenda. Amid the polarization that ensued, the conversation regarding a new constitution became a hostage to the wider Islamist-secular conflict. The 1959 Constitution opened by declaring, among other things, that Tunisia's "religion is Islam," but some veteran Ennahda leaders (contradicting an earlier assurance by Ghannouchi) insisted that the new constitution's preamble would have to include language making Islamic law a source (or even the sole source) of legislation.[12]

Likewise on women's issues, including the explosive topic of the *hijab,* Ghannouchi had pledged in October 2011 that Ennahda would "not change the way of life. It will leave that up to Tunisian women."[13] The Family Code—the Arab world's most liberal and egalitarian—seemed invulnerable to direct assault, but some sought to bypass it by proposing a constitutional article that would declare women "complementary" to men. Finally, alarms went off over proposals to revise Article 3 to state that its provision guaranteeing "freedom of speech and practice" would be conditioned by the government's obligation to "criminalize all attacks on that which is sacred." In this proposal lay the groundwork for replicating the blasphemy laws that autocrats in the Arab world and elsewhere (Pakistan, for instance) had long used to cow secularists and curry favor with Islamists.[14]

Non-Islamists responded with intensified political action. In April 2012, former premier Béji Caïd Essebsi tied a number of small secular parties (plus elements of the outlawed former ruling party) into the Nidaa Tounes party. Fearing an old-regime comeback, Ennahda called for a ten-year ban on political involvement by former ruling-party politicians. Later in the year, the rising public profile of the League for the Defense of the Revolution (LDR) and its local committees provided the context for an escalation of violent attacks on secular activists and Sufi shrines. The September 2012 burning of the U.S. embassy and nearby American Cooperative School in Tunis while security forces failed to quickly respond (the LDR denied any involvement) was a disaster with near-fatal implications for the transition. It fed non-Islamists' fears that they could not depend on the police and courts for protection. Worse yet, Ennahda's leaders were slow to condemn the violence, while Ghannouchi's behind-the-scenes talks with salafists—widely reported by the secular media—reinforced non-Islamists' suspicions that his conciliatory rhetoric was duplicitous.

While (again) understandable, this familiar concern risked caricaturing a far more complex reality. As Monica Marks noted, Ghannouchi seems to have genuinely believed that through dialogue, education, and political participation in electoral politics, some salafist parties could be integrated into a pluralist democracy. But this was too much for secular leaders. They pointed out that the government was putting intellectuals and journalists on trial for alledgedly insulting religious values even as those who had carried out violent antisecular assaults were walking around free.[15] Many asked whether a share of blame for the 6 February 2013 assassination of veteran liberal activist Chokri Belaïd should not be laid at the feet of government inaction.

A Consitutional Balancing Act

The 22 April 2013 Tunisian draft constitution may be understood as the product of a renewed search for the center after the painful shock of these events. But what has inevitably (and perhaps necessarily) resulted is a pragmatic compromise that tries to take account of Islamist and secular sensibilities and thus includes fundamental agreements on rights and democratic protections as well as several "agreements to disagree." Striving to forge this difficult consenus, Ennahda renounced previous (and highly controversial) language on Islamic law, the status of women, and blasphemy. It also endorsed many articles that protected individual rights and, created a mixed system that provides for both legislative and executive powers (while favoring the former). Moreover, in sharp contrast to Egypt's constitution, Tunisia's basic law sets out clear provisions that reinforce the political neutrality of the military and the independence of the judiciary. The provision, for the first time in Tunisia's history, of a Supreme Court with the right of judicial review, is especially encouraging.

Still, in a bid to pacify its base, Ennahda added to the preamble "conditional" language that promises to respect "universal human rights that are in harmony with the Tunisian people's cultural specitivity (*al-khasysiyaat*), and retained Article 148, which provides that "no constitutional amendment shall harm Islam in so far as it is the religion of the state." This latter provision sharply contradicts Article 2's provision that "Tunisia is a civil state," and thus could be used to water down other democratic freedoms or to remove Article 2 itself.[16] In the coming weeks and perhaps months, these and other potentially conflicting articles will provoke heated debate both within and outside the assembly. Indeed, sharp disagreements over both content and procedure have been emerging ever since the most recent constitutional draft appeared on 1 June 2013. But so long as the domestic-security situation remains stable, Tunisia's leaders will probably reach one final compromise, thus paving the way for passing the constitution by a two-thirds majority of the assembly itself. Such an event would mark a huge step forward, even if, in the long haul, democratizaton will depend far less on a paper political consensus, and far more on creating a wider balance of social, political, and civil forces whose collective voice can impel Tunisia's Islamist and secular leaders to jointly focus on the country's pressing social, economic, and environmental challenges.

The Challenges Ahead

Whatever its shortcomings, the pre-2011 scholarly literature on authoritarian persistence in the Arab world did illuminate structural similarities that linked together a wide range of hybrid regimes and semi-autocracies.[17] Although this literature could not have possibly predicted the upheavals that began in late 2010, it remains valuable for the light that it sheds on the deeply embedded character of authoritarian mechanisms and their ability to endure even after the formal institutions of democracy have been installed. Still, an emphasis on path dependency is risky, threatening to trick us into "reading history backward" as we trace any particular turn of events during a transition to its apparently sufficient causation in some historical legacy or point of origin. Thus a transition that seems to be succeeding must be feeding off a "useable past," but if things begin to go sour then that past shrinks back into irrelevance or insignificance amid a complex welter of more immediate circumstances. In point of fact, transitions are always affected by rapidly changing internal and external conditions—by a "useable present" that can produce positive or negative consequences that loom far larger than even the nearest and clearest historical legacy.

One key illustration of such present challenges is the striking degree of convergence that we can detect between the Egyptian and Tunisian cases, particularly as regards the conflict between Islamists and non-Islamists. This conflict has an intrinsic psychological and symbolic dimension that resists—although it does *not* necessarily exclude—the pragmatism required for democratic pact-making. In both countries, the rise of salafists has confronted mainstream Islamists with a choice between watering down long-held principles or mobilizing support for those principles and frightening non-Islamists. What, after all, is an Islamist party if it distances itself from the very symbols and ideals that gave it force and authenticity in the first place? In this sense, if political Islam is not *the* problem, as I have argued elsewhere, it is surely one difficult challenge.[18]

In Tunisia this challenge complicated but did not prevent accommodation, even if firming up what is still a highly fragile consensus will take years of effort. Paradoxically, persistent economic crisis might help, if only because it may spur the UGTT to mobilize in ways that cross the identity divide or promote a more level playing field. But economic crisis would also intensify the suffering of the same poor areas whose protests ignited the revolution. These places remain vulnerable to the allure of radical Islam in a region where jihadi groups can and do move easily across porous borders, a dynamic that has produced violent confrontations with the Tunisian military. If this threat fuels the rise of beefed-up and more intrusive security agencies, obvious political dangers could ensue. Thus Tunisia's democratic-consolidation prospects could hinge as much on regional as on domestic factors.

In Egypt, both the near- and medium-term prospects are grim. Class divisions within the non-Islamist camp will impede the opposition unity that will be essential if non-Islamists are to make major gains in the next parliamentary election. In the meantime, the only remaining barrier (other than the military) to Islamist hegemony is the judiciary. If the Muslim Brotherhood and its FJP take control of courts and judges, this check will disappear, and Egypt could move from liberalized autocracy to electoral authoritarianism and a version of the "Turkish model." If this happens, some semblance of stability may emerge, but at a high cost. And if a superficial political stability gives way under the weight of fear and popular resistance, or if economic conditions worsen, the resulting domestic strife could provoke the military to jump directly back into politics, even if the generals loathe the prospect.

Although the comparative trajectories of Tunisia and Egypt illustrate the difficulties of bridging identity divides, this challenge is even greater where such cleavages fall along sectarian, tribal, or regional lines, with disparities in numbers or access to natural resources acting as further irritants. In Bahrain and Syria, rulers and their constituents lash out with violence—in Syria's case, to the point of prolonged mass bloodletting—for fear that they could never survive any real democratic opening. Regional and global dynamics add fuel to the fires of internal strife in both states as Gulf money backs radical Sunni Islamist forces in Syria and the Saudis and their regional and global allies stand behind the Sunni king of Bahrain. As Sunni-Shia tensions worsen across the region—Iraq included—and the U.S.-Iran cold war continues, internal reconciliation in Bahrain or Syria comes to seem an ever more distant prospect.

In Libya and Yemen, things do not look quite so gloomy. Yemen's fragmentation along tribal, religious, sectarian, and geographic lines is so multifaceted that it might even act as an incentive for compromise as the current "national dialogue" goes forward—no one player can really dream of dominating the place. As for Libya, the growth of militias has compounded tribal and geographic splits between east and west and left competing leaders viewing negotiations over creating a new constitution as nothing more than a chance to outfox rivals. This only feeds the militias while undermining the prospects for uniting a weak state

The "stateness" problem, of course, is hardly unique to Libya. With the possible exception of Bahrain (a small island), state collapse looks to be a real threat across all these countries. Yemen may escape via the dialogue route, but then again, the Arab world has a long tradition of state-managed dialogues that lead nowhere. Bahrain has a dialogue going on as well, but in contrast to the more earnest efforts of Yemen's leaders to discuss their future, so far nothing has induced the ruling

Khalifa family to offer concessions that might meet the opposition's minimal requirements. Indeed, given the widespread sense among Bahraini Shia that the power-sharing arrangement (dating to 2004) which preceded the February 2011 uprising was a failure, prospects for meaningful and durable compromise are slim.

Viewing the above developments, the leaders of the region's remaining autocracies have not ventured beyond cosmetic reforms. Thus versions of liberalized autocracy will probably endure in the Middle East for some time to come. While there is room to debate why some monarchies have so far weathered rising discontent better than one-party-dominant presidential systems, I remain convinced that the arbitrating capacity of many monarchies enhances their capacity to sustain the divide-and-rule protection racket. Liberalized autocracy is indeed a trap, and one that is likely to become more painful as the constant alliance-shuffling that is central to it saps regimes of credibility and legitimacy.[19] But unless oppositions can join forces to create an organized alternative to this trap—one that ensures democratic protections—many potential oppositionists will likely choose to endure the status quo rather than attempt to overthrow it.

NOTES

1. Youssef's encounter with the police is described in Robert Mackey and Kareem Fahim, "Egypt and U.S. Argue over Jon Stewart, 'America's Bassem Youssef,'" 2 April 2013, http://thelede.blogs.nytimes.com/2013/04/02/egypt-and-u-s-argue-over-jon-stewart-americas-bassem-youssef.

2. See Reem Abou-El-Fadl, "Mohamed Morsi Mubarak: The Myth of Egypt's Democratic Transition," Jadaliyya, 11 February 2013, available at www.jadaliyya.com/pages/index/10119/mohamed-morsi-mubarak_the-myth-of-egypts-democrati.

3. Farah Samti, "Tunisians Show Solidarity with Egyptian Satirist Bassem Youssef," Tunisia Live, 3 April 2013, www.tunisia-live.net/2013/04/03/tunisians-show-solidarity with-egyptian-satirist-bassem-youssef/.

4. See Charles Tilly, "War Making and State Making as Organized Crime," in Peter Evans, Dietrich Rueschemeyer, and Theda Skocpol, eds., Bringing the State Back In (Cambridge: Cambridge University Press, 1985), 169–86. Tilly used the term "protection racket" in reference to the dynamic by which rulers tried to establish state authority. This involved raising armies to defeat external threats, a goal pursued by providing protection to local populations from those threats in return for their raising revenue for the state. This was a "racket" because to varying degrees it involved producing "both the danger and, at a price, the shield against it" (171). I use the term to refer to domestic dynamics between regimes and oppositions, but warmaking also fed such domestic rackets. See Steven Heydemann, ed., War, Institutions, and Social Change in the Middle East (Berkeley: University of California Press, 2000).

5. Thus as is the case in all protection-racket systems, one dancer may be much stronger than the other, but it still takes two to tango. See Holger Albrecht, "How Can Opposition Support Authoritarianism? Lessons from Egypt," Democratization 12 (June 2005): 378–97; and Albrecht, Raging Against the Machine: Political Opposition Under Authoritarianism in Egypt (Syracuse: Syracuse University Press, 2013).

6. See Wael Eskandar, "Brothers and Officers: A History of Pacts," *Jadaliyya,* 25 January 2013, available at *www.jadaliyya.com/pages/index/9765/brothers-and-officers_a-history-of-pacts.*

7. See Sarah Elisabeth Yerkes, "Pluralism, Co-optation and Capture: Navigating the Civil Society Arena in the Arab World," PhD diss., Georgetown University, 2012.

8. Evan Hill, "SCAF's Last-Minute Power Grab: The New Decree from Egypt's Military Rulers Means the Incoming Civilian President Will Have Very Limited Powers," *Al Jazeera,* 18 June 2012, available at *www.aljazeera.com/indepth/spotlight/egy pt/2012/06/201261812449990250.html.* The text of the declaration may be found at *www. jadaliyya.com/pages/index/6061/english-text-of-scaf-amended-egypt-constitutional-.*

9. The current situation illustrates this point. The Shura Council was reconstituted in early 2012 through national elections in which less than a fifth of all voters took part. Having won 105 of the 180 elected seats, and having obtained nearly all the appointed seats, the Muslim Brotherhood was in a position to start passing laws unilaterally so long as the lower house was not convened.

10. The previous constitution also provided for an NDC, but that institution had a neglible role given that the president himself was closely tied to the military. Now that the presidency and the military have been more clearly separated, the NDC will have a more formal, corporate role.

11. See Yezid Sayigh, "Morsi and Egypt's Military," *Al-Monitor,* 8 January 2013, available at *www.al-monitor.com/pulse/originals/2013/01/morsi-army-egypt-revolution.html.*

12. Duncan Pickard, "The Current Status of Constitution Making in Tunisia," Carnegie Endowment for International Peace, 19 April 2012, available at *http://carnegieendowment.org/2012/04/19/current-status-of-constitution-making-in-tunisia/ah1s.*

13. Heba Saleh, "Tunisia Victors Seek to Calm Women's Fears," *Financial Times,* 28 October 2011.

14. Monica Marks, "Speaking on the Unspeakable: Blasphemy and the Tunisian Constitution," *Sada,* 4 September 2012, *http://carnegieendowment.org/2012/09/04/speaking-on-unspeakable-blasphemy-tunisian-constitution/drca.*

15. See Monica Marks, "Ennahda's Rule of Engagement," *Sada,* 18 October 2012, available at *http://carnegieendowment.org/sada/index.cfm?fa=show&article=49728&solr_hilite=.*

16. Article 34 also provides reasons for concern because it states that the "right of access to information shall be guaranteed within limits that do not prejudice national security, public interest, or the personal information of others." If by *maloumat* (information) is meant *governmental* information, as some have argued, this will have to be clarified. Even so, the vague language contravenes other protections and rights afforded to Tunisians by their basic law.

17. See the May 2011 report prepared by the Stimson Center, "Seismic Shift: Understanding Change in the Middle East," available at *www.stimson.org/images/uploads/research-pdfs/Full_Pub_-_Seismic_Shift.pdf.*

18. Daniel Brumberg, "Islam Is Not the Solution (or the Problem)," *Washington Quarterly* 29 (Winter 2005–2006): 97–116.

19. Daniel Brumberg, "Democratization in the Arab World? The Trap of Liberalized Autocracy," *Journal of Democracy* 13 (October 2002): 56–68.

10

RESILIENT ROYALS: HOW ARAB MONARCHIES HANG ON

Sean L. Yom and F. Gregory Gause III

Sean L. Yom, assistant professor of political science at Temple University, is the author of "Jordan: Ten More Years of Autocracy" in the October 2009 issue of the Journal of Democracy. *F. Gregory Gause III, professor of political science at the University of Vermont and nonresident senior fellow at the Brookings Doha Center, is the author, most recently, of* The International Relations of the Persian Gulf *(2010). This essay originally appeared in the October 2012 issue of the* Journal of Democracy.

The Arab Spring might just as well be called the Arab *Republics'* Spring. Since December 2010, the wave of uprisings and protests across the Middle East has produced spectacular changes in the region's authoritarian republics but has largely bypassed its autocratic monarchies. Tunisia's President Zine al-Abidine Ben Ali fled the country, Egypt's President Hosni Mubarak effectively transferred power to the military, and Yemen's President Ali Abdullah Saleh acceded to a transitional framework. Revolts in other countries triggered more violent reactions. In Libya, "Brother Leader" Muammar Qadhafi perished in an insurrection, while in Syria, President Bashar al-Assad's single-party dictatorship teeters on the brink of collapse.

The eight Arab monarchies, by contrast, stand firm. Saudi Arabia and Oman saw only isolated protests, while in Qatar and the United Arab Emirates (UAE) virtually no dissent mobilized. In Jordan and Morocco, youth-driven oppositionists filled some streets but failed to rouse the masses. In Kuwait, popular protest stemmed from long-running tensions between parliamentary factions and the ruling family rather than any new political demands. Only Bahrain has seen large-scale unrest, but the ruling al-Khalifa clan has weathered it, aided by the armed intervention of the Saudi-led Gulf Cooperation Council (GCC).

In short, the scorecard of the Arab Spring neatly divides by regime type. Monarchies fared far better than republics. The popular belief has been that Arab kings and princes are "sitting on their thrones fairly comfortably," secure against the winds of change.[1] To explain this striking correlation between regime type and regime persistence, many analysts have pointed to culture and institutions. The cultural approach holds that Arab kingships enjoy traditional religious and tribal legitimacy, which induces exceptionally loyal support from citizens. Meanwhile, the institutional approach contends that because kings organizationally stand above everyday politics, they can skillfully intervene in the system to spearhead controlled reforms that defuse public discontent. Dynasticism, wherein royal blood relatives monopolize key state offices, further helps to keep the regime intact.

Yet such explanations do not hold up under scrutiny. For one, in March 2011 a social revolution nearly *did* succeed in Bahrain—a crucial counterexample that we shall revisit later. More generally, the postcolonial record reveals that royalism has hardly guaranteed authoritarian perpetuity; since the 1950s, just as many Arab monarchies have fallen as have survived. Cultural arguments recycle old Orientalist logic, are patently unfalsifiable, and ignore the historical reality that powerful ruling monarchies owe much of their modern power to colonial machinations rather than indigenous forces.

The institutional approach carries more credibility, in that monarchs in liberalized kingdoms such as Morocco and Jordan often outmaneuver opposition by offering limited democratic openings. Yet this functionalist argument restates the unobjectionable adage that autocrats pursue policies to maximize their survival. Royalism presents different institutional options than republicanism, but not all kings adopt them; if they did, no ruling monarchy would collapse. Furthermore, in the Gulf monarchies, dynastic strategies of familial rule prevent royal leaders from making the limited democratic reforms seen in Morocco and Jordan.

Of course, culture and institutions are seminal forces that shape politics in every state. Many autocracies regardless of type appeal to cultural values in order to establish their authenticity. Institutional structures determine access to power and modes of policy making. Yet distanced from such truisms, in an explanatory sense structures have little to do with why eight monarchies have held on to power since the outbreak of the Arab Spring. There is no cultural or institutional DNA that renders royal regimes in states as disparate as Morocco, Oman, and Saudi Arabia impervious to overthrow.

Here, we instead offer a *strategic* explanation for monarchical exceptionalism, one that links the historical legacy of domestic choices with a permissive international environment. First, many of these royal houses have historically mobilized cross-cutting coalitions of popular support, coalitions that have helped to forestall mass opposition and to bolster the ruling family against whatever opposition has emerged. Second, most have also reaped ample rents from oil or foreign aid, allowing them to pay for welfare and development programs meant to alleviate public discord. Finally, when all else fails, these kingdoms have enjoyed the backing of foreign patrons who assist them through diplomatic assurances, economic grants, and military interventions. For a long time, the United States played this role. The Arab Spring marked new Saudi prominence as guarantor of monarchical order in the Arab world, as Saudi cash aided poorer kingdoms and Saudi troops spearheaded the intervention in Bahrain.

Exploring the persistence of the Arab monarchies provides a stern reminder about comparative analysis: Explanations for regimes of an exceptional type need not abide by essentialist logic suggesting that some innate feature such as cultural inheritance or institutional destiny predetermines long-term outcomes. The prospects for popular revolution in the Arab kingdoms will remain slim so long as their leaders continue to maintain broad-based coalitions, secure access to hydrocarbon rents, and enjoy bountiful support from foreign patrons.

The New Monarchical Exceptionalism

A monarchy is a regime led by a hereditary sovereign who may hold varying degrees of power. Royal houses in the eight Arab monarchies—Jordan, Morocco, Saudi Arabia, and the Persian Gulf littoral states of Bahrain, Kuwait, Oman, Qatar, and the UAE—all wield near-absolute power.[2] None qualifies as a constitutional kingship in which the enthroned incumbent exercises only ceremonial influence while an elected parliamentary government makes policy. Instead, the region's various kings and emirs not only reign but *rule*: They name cabinets, dictate major domestic and foreign policies, control the state's coercive apparatus, and allow parliaments (where these exist) and judiciaries only limited authority.

The persistence of these monarchies runs against the dominant analytical tradition in political science, where such regimes are considered "an anachronism in the modern world of nations."[3] The longstanding assumption held ruling monarchies—given their inability to overcome what Samuel Huntington deemed the "King's Dilemma"[4]—to be incompatible with modern political order. In newly independent Arab countries, the thinking went, the centralization of power required for state-building would ironically undercut absolute monarchy by requiring kings to share authority with crucial new groups such as the urban middle class. Kings could yield to the logic of this process and become constitutional monarchs, or they could face violent revolution. Either way, continued absolutism would not be an option.

Outside the Middle East, political development since 1945 seems to have confirmed this prediction. As recently as 2008, the last king of Bhutan gave up his supremacy in favor of parliamentary democracy. Only a handful of absolutist kingships remain outside the Arab world, such as those in Swaziland and Brunei. Mirroring this development, theorists of authoritarianism have largely neglected to study monarchies. Many studies either fail to include ruling monarchism or else subsume it under broader concepts such as "personalism" or "sultanism." By the 1990s, specialists of the Persian Gulf region were among the few scholars left who still studied monarchism.

The stability of monarchies during the Arab Spring has so strikingly defied theoretical expectations that many analysts have reversed the decades-long consensus and now contend that inherent cultural and institutional forces make such regimes *more* durable than their republican peers.[5] The cultural argument holds that Arab monarchs enjoy exceptional legitimacy. Whereas presidents for life, such as Mubarak or Ben Ali, need constantly to manipulate elections and inflate national-security imperatives in order to govern indefinitely, Arab kings, emirs, and sultans command natural authority thanks to Islamic values, tribal mores, and hereditary principles that resonate with their societies.[6] The Alaouite Crown of Morocco and the Hashemite House of Jordan claim descent from Muhammad himself. The dynastic families ruling Bahrain, Kuwait, Oman, Qatar, Saudi Arabia, and the UAE command respect among the tribal confederations in their societies. As Saudi sociologist Khalid al-Dakhil contends, this makes monarchies "closer to the society they govern" than republics, for their traditions produce reverence and support from Arab subjects wooed by such powerful cultural appeals.[7]

Resilient royalism also stems from institutional structure. Monarchism deliberately positions Arab kings and emirs above the fray of everyday politics, since their power cannot be contested through elections. Thus, say some scholars, monarchs can initiate economic and political reforms in response to popular pressure with fewer constraints than republican dictators encumbered by the interests of ruling parties, military councils, and other auxiliary organizations.[8] By appealing directly to the masses, kings can calm opposition and prevent further unrest with promises of change. Further, the Gulf royals' practice of putting kin in key posts[9] enhances regime unity by preventing elite defections and surrounding the ruler with loyal cousins, brothers, and uncles.

These arguments do not hold up under close examination. History shows that the "inherent" qualities of Arab monarchism are hardly safeguards against deposition. In the postcolonial era, monarchies have been overthrown in Egypt (1952), Tunisia (1957), Iraq (1958), North Yemen (1962), South Arabia (1967),[10] and Libya (1969). If we include Muslim (albeit non-Arab) countries in Southwest Asia, then Afghanistan (1973) and Iran (1979) join the list. If royal authoritarianism has intrinsic cultural legitimacy, how could so many Arab kings have lost their thrones? If kings by nature wisely handle opposition with visionary reforms through institutional manipulation, then why did so many fail to do so?

These explanations are also vulnerable to more precise critiques. Cultural-legitimacy arguments repeat the longstanding stereotype that Arabs, due to Islamic identity or tribal heritage, are predisposed to embrace despotism. Even disregarding that many Arabs are neither Muslim nor of tribal descent, this presumption ignores the transition of Muslim and tribal societies elsewhere—in sub-Saharan Africa and Southeast Asia, for example—from ruling monarchism to more democratic forms of government.

Likewise, no evidence suggests that Arab citizens see hereditary succession as the key to authenticity. Of the five presidents challenged by large-scale uprisings recently, three (Mubarak in Egypt, Qadhafi in Libya, and Saleh in Yemen) had drawn widespread condemnation for trying to groom their sons to rule, while a fourth (Syria's Bashar al-Assad) is deprecated by many in his country for having received his office from his late father.[11] Moreover, few in any of these states now demand a return to monarchy of any kind.

We cannot reason from the absence of revolution to the presence of legitimacy, for by this measure *any and every* regime must be legitimate unless overthrown. Even if we take legitimacy broadly to mean the absence of regime-threatening revolt, many of today's Arab monarchies have already failed the test. Sultan Said bin Taimur of Oman suffered regional rebellions during the 1960s; King Hussein of Jordan endured civil war in 1970; and King Hassan II of Morocco escaped a military coup in 1972. These regimes persist because they survived close calls with destruction—not because they never faced such threats in the first place.

Finally, the near-absolute power wielded by Arab royals originates not from some ancient cultural essence but from modern colonialism, which turned weak and fragmented claims of dynastic authority into centralized autocracies.[12] Most of the Gulf region's royal families, including the al-Khalifas of Bahrain and the al-Sabahs of Kuwait, indeed have tribal origins. But they could not impose their will on rival tribes and clans until Britain formalized their respective claims to rule through defense treaties in the late nineteenth century, and later helped to put down internal resistance. Likewise, the Hashemites arrived in Jordan from the Arabian Peninsula at the behest of the British Colonial Office after World War I. Only after a decade of social conflict and British support did local Bedouin confederations begin grudgingly to obey their foreign king. The Alaouites may have claimed Morocco's throne in the seventeenth century, but regional revolts challenged them till French-colonial troops crushed all rivals in the early twentieth century.

Capacity and Will

Similarly, the institutional explanation for monarchical stability runs into empirical roadblocks. First, it is true that ruling monarchs are not elected politicians like presidents or prime ministers, and their uncontested authority allows them to impose economic and political reforms from above to assuage opposition groups and the wider public.[13] Yet the institutional *capacity* to reform does not always result in the *will* to reform. Kings pursue policies that they hope will keep them in power, but so do all authoritarians. Whether royal rulers facing popular discontent choose reform and dialogue over coercion and closure hinges on contingencies such as leaders' inclinations, historical circumstances, and economic conditions.

King Mohammed VI of Morocco and King Abdullah II of Jordan have reacted to growing unrest with political-liberalization initiatives that have satisfied some opposition demands and helped to stanch protests. While in no rush to democratize, by mid-2011 these monarchs had offered their respective peoples constitutional amendments, new cabinets, and at least the promise of fresh parliamentary elections. King Hamad of Bahrain might have chosen such a path, but instead he reacted more harshly. After briefly tolerating demonstrations in early 2011, he violently quashed them with help from GCC military forces that came rumbling over the 25-kilometer King Fahd Causeway linking Bahrain to Saudi Arabia.

This Bahraini example introduces a final critique regarding institutions: The practice of dynasticism can have serious destabilizing consequences. In the Gulf, because these ruling houses have many branches, monarchs are flanked by relatives who fill top spots in the bureaucracy, the security forces, and the economy. Meant to seal regime unity, this strategy diminishes prospects for political reform by trapping the monarch between the interests of relatives and popular pressures for change.

Bahrain demonstrates how dynasticism can reduce the monarch's freedom of action. Among the major opposition petitions in early 2011 was a call for King Hamad to appoint a new cabinet. Yet powerful hardline relatives such as his prime minister and military chief rejected such concessions. Their resistance escalated tensions with the burgeoning opposition and convinced some protesters to target the monarchy itself.

Kuwait's al-Sabah dynasty has also struggled with this problem. Since 2006, an unruly legislature and contentious civil society have compelled the emir to dissolve his appointed government (dominated by his al-Sabah relations) no fewer than ten times and to hold new legislative elections five times—a stop-and-start cycle of street protests and royal concessions that continued during the Arab Spring. Allowing parliament to name a commoner as prime minister, instead of the current practice of the emir appointing a relative, would satisfy a wide swath of democratic activists. But the emir cannot overcome fierce opposition to such a step within the royal family. Even lesser moves, such as enhancing public transparency, would financially harm untold numbers of al-Sabah relatives. Here, as elsewhere in the Gulf, the same blood ties that unite a regime around a monarch now form a serious obstacle to reform.

If not culture and institutions, then what explains the exceptional persistence of monarchism during the Arab Spring? The hallmark image of the turbulent period from December 2010 through late 2012 has

TABLE 1—UNREST IN THE ARAB WORLD
(DECEMBER 2010–AUGUST 2012)

	Little or no protest mobilization	Significant protests but moderate demands	Mass protests and radical demands
Monarchical states	Qatar United Arab Emirates Saudi Arabia Oman	Morocco Jordan Kuwait	Bahrain
Republican states	Palestine	Algeria Iraq Lebanon Sudan	Tunisia Egypt Libya Yemen Syria

been the popular protests, demonstrations, and other contentious acts by everyday citizens that defy state authority and symbolize demands for political change. The Arab kingdoms experienced remarkable variation in the size and scope of opposition, which underscores a crucial point: The persistence of eight royal autocracies through the Arab Spring says little about *how* each managed to survive.

Table 1 reveals the extent of this variation. Four of the eight kingdoms experienced only negligible levels of protest mobilization. Dissent remained mild in Qatar and the UAE, though a handful of writers, bloggers, and thinkers criticized royal governance. In Saudi Arabia, Shias rioted while youth activists and advocates of women's rights became more vocal. Likewise, Oman saw unexpected demonstrations by frustrated workers. Yet these were small-scale events that did not seriously threaten these regimes.

In Morocco, Jordan, and Kuwait, larger numbers took to the streets in favor of economic and political change. In the former two, youth-led grassroots movements hit a ceiling within months of the first demonstrations. They failed to attract a critical mass of public support, and, more important, they moderated their demands, focusing on *how* their kings should govern rather than *whether* they should rule in the first place. Kuwait also saw boisterous rallies, but these reflected a vibrant tradition of civic dissent that pre-dates the Arab Spring. These protests did not break new ground and quickly pivoted to old issues such as tribal rivalries, citizenship rights, and political corruption—longstanding problems that did not threaten the al-Sabah dynasty.

By contrast, Bahrain experienced near-revolution. Its opposition trend was massive in size, cross-sectarian (at least at its outset), and existentially threatening to the regime. At the height of the unrest in February 2011, well over a hundred-thousand Bahrainis marched in protest, an astonishing number given the tiny island country's citizen population of less than 570,000.[14] If Charles Kurzman's estimate that modern revolutions seldom involve more than 1 percent of the population is true, then what transpired was proportionally one of the greatest shows of "people power" in modern history.[15] Although most Bahrainis desired constitutional reforms, a vocal and growing faction called for the overthrow of the staunchly Sunni monarchy as repression intensified. Furthermore, to the surprise of many observers, protesters came not only from the long-suffering Shia majority but also from the stereotypically loyal Sunni minority. The perceived threat was so dire that in March 2011 the GCC, led by Saudi Arabia, sent about 1,500 soldiers and police officers to the island. Thus reinforced, the monarchy launched a full-scale crackdown.

Comparing these patterns of protest mobilization suggests a comprehensive new explanation for monarchical exceptionalism. First, most of the monarchies rested upon *cross-cutting coalitions*—that is, historical alliances linking different social constituencies to the ruling family. Broad-based coalitions are the hallmark of successful autocracies regardless of institutional structure. Whether they rule upon a throne, command a mass political party, or sit amongst military generals, dictators cannot rule through repression alone; they need supporters who will not only validate regime policies but also counter opponents during crises. Because regime supporters' prosperity and status typically depend on the regime's survival, the payoff of authoritarian continuity remains significantly higher than the "payoff" of revolutionary turnover. This helps to explain why antiregime protests failed to spread in many parts of the Gulf and also why popular movements in Morocco and Jordan failed to secure allies. While these publics desire reform, key elements within them have little faith that any new order can provide the same benefits and protections as their imperfect ruling families.

In the 1960s, Morocco's monarchy began using economic payments, policy guarantees, and nationalist appeals to secure the interests of the business class, agricultural elites, and religious authorities. Such partnerships helped the Alaouites to weather this period of postcolonial unrest. In Jordan, the Hashemites expanded the public sector in order to marginalize the Palestinian majority while incorporating tribal communities, the Christian minority, and other settled groups into the state after the politically tumultuous 1950s. Palestinian businessmen later became part of this authoritarian contract, receiving economic largesse in return for political acquiescence.

Similar balancing acts abound in the Gulf, with the distinction that the large ruling families of these kingdoms, due to their monopoly over oil money and state power, assume a leading social role with other partners.[16] For example, Saudi autocracy revolves around an alliance between the al-Saud family, the conservative Wahhabi Islamic establishment, and regional business captains. These partnerships created the modern Saudi state by unifying disparate regions. In Kuwait, the al-Sabahs gave political voice to wealthier Sunni merchant clans, the settled Shia minority, and tribal communities after the 1930s. Having nearly lost power against a concerted legislative revolt in 1938, it sought to protect itself from future domestic unrest by striking popular compromises that today still characterize the social foundations of the modern Kuwaiti state.

If rallying diverse coalitions of support is the winning strategy, then why do all authoritarians not do it? One answer lies in the historical circumstance of state-building. In historical perspective, many state-builders in the developing world mobilized cross-cutting coalitions when they faced intense widespread opposition but lacked the coercive resources needed to consolidate power.[17] Unable to conquer resistance from below, they were forced to compromise with social forces instead—nascent bargains that helped guarantee future support in return for economic or political sacrifices. In Southeast Asia, for instance, the Suharto dictatorship of Indonesia lasted for decades, and the UMNO-dominated regime of Malaysia still persists today, partly because they struck early alliances with key constituencies like student movements, urban businessmen, and ethnic elites that years later helped them weather periods of unrest.[18]

Most of the monarchies in the Arab world today confronted social conflict early in the postcolonial era and thus rallied the coalitional pillars for their royal autocracies to survive. By contrast, overthrown kingships like those in Egypt, Iraq, and Libya could have mobilized broad social bases to anchor their absolutism but felt little need to do so— either because they did not face those early struggles or because they thought that they enjoyed enough external support to suppress them. As a result, they lacked defenders when challenged by left-wing oppositionists and restive military officers.

The same pattern can be seen in Bahrain today. The Sunni-Shia sectarian division runs deep, but it does not predestine conflict. A quarter of Kuwait's national population is Shia, yet they remain among the staunchest supporters of that Sunni regime. The al-Khalifa dynasty, however, never felt *threatened* enough to reach beyond its Sunni-minority base and forge new alliances with the Shia majority, the same demographic that authored uprisings in the 1990s and most recently during the Arab Spring. The al-Khalifas faced severe worker riots and Shia protests in the 1950s, but British intervention squashed the unrest and restored their authority. Exposing the regime to potential overthrow might have encouraged it to reach across the sectarian aisle merely in order to survive; instead, it felt secure enough without such coalitional sacrifices.

The Cost of Coalitions

Coalitions do not maintain themselves. Autocrats must constantly nurture their alliances with material patronage. Ben Ali and Mubarak, for instance, both inherited dominant ruling parties that housed broad coalitions. That mass support that they enjoyed in the 1980s when they assumed power dwindled over the years, yet they did not realize how few groups still backed their rule in 2011. In these cases, the social foundations of authoritarianism withered from cronyism and were compounded by economic neglect and scarce resources. Libya, Syria, and Yemen all suffered from inadequate development and widespread poverty; even Egypt and Tunisia, both middle-income countries, suffered from high unemployment, particularly among young university graduates.

By contrast, most of the Arab monarchies have access to *hydrocarbon rents* and thus material inducements for their supporters. Most of the Gulf kingdoms possess enormous proven oil and gas reserves that provide revenue for public-payroll jobs, welfare payouts, and state contracts that have long made social forces dependent upon the regime.[19] More important, after watching oil-rich monarchies such as Iran's fall to revolutions in the past, today's kings and emirs grasp that, rather than hoarding wealth (as Qadhafi did), they must strategically disperse their hydrocarbon windfalls in order to satisfy social allies. Corruption may run rampant in these states, but so too do coalitional payments: Loyalty has a price, and everyone knows this.[20]

Hence, when grassroots protests began spreading across the region in early 2011, the wealthiest monarchies reacted quickly. Kuwait announced a US$5 billion domestic program that provided $3,500 in cash to every citizen along with free foodstuffs for a year; the Saudi monarchy committed $130 billion to job creation, salary increases, and development projects; and Qatar announced massive pay and benefit hikes for public servants and military personnel. This *rentier* logic is not confined to royal autocracies. Oil-rich Algeria, too, ramped up spending on salaries, housing, and other public services, and succeeded in stemming strife with targeted social spending borrowed from the Gulf-state playbook.[21] Thus, while hydrocarbon rents remain crucial to political stability in many monarchies, regime type has little to do with this endowment: The Arabian Peninsula happens to sit atop massive hydrocarbon reserves, and on that landmass reside six Arab monarchies today. Put another way, had Hosni Mubarak suddenly discovered $100 billion in oil wealth when underemployed Egyptians began congregating in Tahrir Square, he may well have weathered the storm.[22]

Of course, not every Arab monarchy floats on a sea of petrochemical riches. Bahrain, for instance, is fast depleting its oil reservoirs, and Jordan and Morocco have virtually no oil or gas resources while laboring under sizeable foreign debts. Yet oil rents easily recirculate across borders in the form of aid. By the end of the first quarter of 2011, Saudi Arabia, Kuwait, Qatar, and the UAE—the four wealthiest kingdoms— had announced generous new economic-assistance packages for poorer monarchies. Transforming the GCC from an alliance organized around external security into one focused on domestic stability, these states pledged $20 billion to a fund to help stabilize fellow GCC members Bahrain and Oman, and then offered Jordan and Morocco access to a $5 billion pot of aid should they choose to join the organization.

In effect, these external bounties will allow these regimes to behave *as if* they had oil wealth, even in an era of global downturn and financial austerity. Jordan and Oman, for instance, reacted to demonstrations by expanding public employment and costly price subsidies, policies made possible by the promise of oil-fueled GCC assistance. Had Saudi Arabia not delivered its first $1.4 billion to Jordan in August 2011, the latter would have had to declare a record budget deficit.

Finally, when all else fails, the Arab monarchies can call upon powerful *foreign patrons* to furnish diplomatic, economic, and military support during crises. Washington has consistently championed the Jordanian monarchy since early in the Cold War, when the Hashemite regime adopted pro-Western foreign-policy positions, and still regards the kingdom as one of its closest Middle Eastern allies. The Alaouite autocracy in Morocco has received support from both the United States and France, the latter of which has longstanding linguistic, cultural, and trade ties with the country. Following the British withdrawal from the Gulf in 1971, Washington gradually assumed the mantle of guarantor for Saudi Arabia and the oil-rich littoral. In return, the Gulf kingdoms have cooperated with U.S. strategic interests while keeping energy production high. Bahrain hosts the U.S. Navy's Fifth Fleet while major U.S. bases sit in Qatar, Oman, the UAE, and Kuwait. Saudi forces also cooperate with the U.S. military. More recently, and especially during the Arab Spring, Saudi Arabia has emerged as a regional patron of its smaller neighboring kingdoms.

The Consequences of Unwavering Support

Unwavering support from abroad exerts two major effects. First, it lowers the cost of repression by diminishing any international backlash it might arouse. For example, the United States barely criticized Bahrain's brutal crackdown, noting human-rights protests but ultimately accepting the al-Khalifa monarchy's hard-line stance against opposition forces. Absent external pressure, the al-Khalifa regime chose to eviscerate its opposition because it could *afford* to do so—unlike, say, Qadhafi, whose actions drew international intervention, and arguably Mubarak, who received inconsistent U.S. support throughout the crisis that toppled him. The surety of U.S. diplomatic backing holds true for Saudi Arabia and the other kingdoms: Regardless of the scale of protest, the U.S. position during the Arab Spring was to favor incremental reform over revolutionary transition. Likewise, at the height of the Moroccan protests, France pushed for no political change in its former protectorate, particularly after watching the end of the Ben Ali regime in Francophone Tunisia.

Second, foreign patrons can arm local regimes with additional economic and coercive resources. The well-documented U.S.-Jordanian relationship provides an exemplary case, as Amman has reaped close to

$12 billion in fiscal payments and military subsidies from Washington over the past several decades, making this kingdom one of the highest per capita recipients of U.S. aid in the world.[23] Although Egypt under Mubarak received nearly five times more U.S. aid than did Jordan, that country received more aid per capita. Aid to Egypt, moreover, mostly took the form of military assistance that satisfied generals hungry for the latest weaponry but did not offset domestic expenditures.

By contrast, more than half of Jordan's annual $660 million aid package consists of cash grants and other economic support designed to stave off fiscal collapse. In addition, Jordan's aid usually grows thanks to Congressional supplemental funding; in 2011, Congress affirmed that, given Jordan's strategic value, such support will remain steady despite domestic pressure to slash foreign aid. In turn, the Hashemite regime continues to integrate this patronage into its domestic coalitional formula by underwriting public-sector employment and state investments that satisfy its mostly non-Palestinian base. Recently, U.S. assistance has been dwarfed by new GCC aid pledges, which have padded the treasuries of Jordan and other poorer kingdoms during the Arab Spring. The $20 billion Gulf "Marshall Plan," for instance, is three times the size of Bahrain's entire budget last year. As both Bahrain and Oman are running deficits, such external patronage will support the strategies of coalitional maintenance that have kept fellow monarchies afloat.

When all else fails, foreign patrons can intervene by force. Two formal military interventions punctuated the Arab Spring: In Libya, Western firepower (mostly delivered from the air) helped to destroy the Qadhafi regime, while GCC troops helped to restore the al-Khalifas' sway over the streets of Bahrain. Fearing unrest in its own Shia communities near Bahrain as well as the possibility that sectarian turmoil might undermine fellow Sunni Arab monarchies, Saudi Arabia headed the armed GCC force that rolled into Manama in March 2011, just weeks after nearly a fifth of Bahrain's citizens had joined protest marches. The presence of these troops not only deterred new protests but also enabled Bahraini security forces to focus on targeted raids and arrests of leading dissidents. Today the regime believes itself well guarded against future strife, which helps to explain its continuing resistance to major political reform.

Table 2 below details the cross-cutting coalitions, hydrocarbon wealth, and foreign patrons that distinguish the Arab monarchies. These are the real roots of their exceptionalism—not inherent qualities of royalism, Arab culture, or Islam, but deliberate regime strategies pursued amid fortuitous geographic and other circumstances. Not all kingdoms possess all three factors, but each possesses at least two—and that is analytically sufficient to account for their persistence up to and through the Arab Spring. Possessing only one would make any of these monarchies far more vulnerable to unrest and instability.

For instance, Qatar's al-Thani dynasty never needed to marshal a

TABLE 2—COALITIONS, OIL, AND GEOPOLITICS

	Cross-cutting Coalition	Hydrocarbon Rents	Foreign Patron
Morocco	Yes (business class, religious authorities, agricultural elites)	None (but offered GCC economic aid)	Yes (U.S., France)
Jordan	Yes (East Bank minorities, Palestinian business, tribal communities)	None (but offered GCC economic aid)	Yes (U.S., Saudi Arabia)
Saudi Arabia	Yes (ruling family, regional business elites, religious establishment)	High	Yes (U.S.)
Kuwait	Yes (ruling family, Sunni merchants, Shi'a minority, tribal communities)	High	Yes (U.S.)
Bahrain	No (ruling family, Sunni minority)	Moderate (but offered GCC economic aid)	Yes (Saudi Arabia)
Qatar	No (not necessary due to small homogenous population)	High	Yes (U.S.)
UAE	Yes (seven ruling families)	High	Yes (U.S., Saudi Arabia)
Oman	Yes (ruling family, regional elites from Muscat, Inner Oman, and Dhufar; tribal communities)	Moderate (but offered GCC economic aid)	Yes (U.S., Saudi Arabia)

cross-cutting coalition because it seldom faced threatening conflicts within its small homogeneous community. Even so, well-distributed oil wealth effectively negates material grievances for many Qataris. Further, U.S. support for the regime's authoritarian orientation remains steady for geopolitical reasons: Qatar hosts a large U.S. airbase and adopts foreign-policy positions that enhance U.S. interests, such as backing the Western intervention in Libya. An energy-poor Qatar would be unpredictable because it would expose the al-Thani regime to something that it has not faced for half a century—a disgruntled citizenry that lacks political rights *as well as* viable jobs, living wages, and adequate services. Similarly, Jordan lacks hydrocarbon riches, but the Hashemite House has a social base and resolute U.S. and Saudi promises of support. Without that external patronage, the regime would have to face the reality that it cannot afford to maintain its coalition alone.

The monarchical exceptionalism that characterized the Arab Spring surprised many observers who had long assumed that the era of absolute monarchy had passed. Yet what makes these regimes persist, especially in a climate of regional tumult and political contention, is not cultural traditions and institutional structures but rather a set of three overlapping factors—cross-cutting coalitions, hydrocarbon rents, and foreign patronage. Collectively, these realities explain why half these royal autocracies never confronted widespread protests, why many popular protests ultimately moderated and dissipated, and finally why in the one case where the masses did mobilize for change, the regime nonetheless survived.

Several implications flow from this. First, these kingdoms remain highly vulnerable to exogenous shocks, such as fluctuations in global energy prices and the geopolitical preferences of outside powers. While most retain domestic support from a diverse array of social forces, that coalitional backing will weaken if these regimes no longer have vast sums of oil or aid money to funnel to these internal allies. Likewise, should Saudi Arabia ever decide to abandon its patronage of Bahrain—an admittedly unlikely scenario—the al-Khalifa regime may struggle to suppress its next uprising.

Second, on an analytical level, students of democracy and authoritarianism must exercise caution when addressing outcomes for regimes of an uncommon type. Ruling monarchism flourishes in the Arab world, but the reasons for this do not stem from any mysterious essence of kingship. They stem, rather, from historical choices and physical resources amenable to matter-of-fact analysis. To be sure, culture and institutions are central forces in the politics of any state. Yet they do not constitute convincing explanations for the resilience of royalism in the Arab world.

NOTES

The authors wish to thank Hicham Ben Abdallah El Alaoui and fellow participants at the May 2011 Arab Spring Exploratory Conference for their comments.

1. See, for example, Brian Whitaker, "God Save the Arab Kings?" *Guardian*, 27 April 2011.

2. If we disaggregate the federal UAE into its seven constituent parts, then effectively there are *fourteen* royal families in the Arab world with legally recognized claims over some territory.

3. Michael Hudson, *Arab Politics: The Search for Legitimacy* (New Haven: Yale University Press, 1977), 166; and Manfred Halpern, *The Politics of Social Change in the Middle East and North Africa* (Princeton: Princeton University Press, 1963), 42.

4. Samuel Huntington, *Political Order in Changing Societies* (New Haven: Yale University Press, 1968), 177–91.

5. Jean-Pierre Filiu, *The Arab Revolution: Ten Lessons from the Democratic Uprising* (New York: Oxford University Press, 2011), and Marina Ottaway and Marwan Muasher, *Arab Monarchies: Chance for Reform, Yet Unmet* (Washington, D.C.: Carnegie Endowment for International Peace, 2011).

6. Bernard Lewis, "Monarchy in the Middle East," in Joseph Kostiner, ed., *Middle East Monarchies: The Challenge of Modernity* (Boulder: Lynne Rienner, 2000).

7. Khalid al-Dakhil, "Mawqi' al-malakiyyat wa al-jumhuriyyat fi al-mashhad" [The situation of the kingdom and the republic in perspective], *Al-Hayat*, 26 June 2011.

8. Russell Lucas, "Monarchical Authoritarianism: Survival and Political Liberalization in a Middle Eastern Regime Type," *International Journal of Middle East Studies* 36 (February 2004): 103–19; Michael Herb, "Princes and Parliaments in the Arab World," *Middle East Journal* 58 (July 2004): 367–84.

9. Michael Herb, *All in the Family: Revolution, Absolutism and Democracy in Middle East Monarchies* (Albany: SUNY Press, 1999).

10. The Federation of South Arabia, now the southern part of Yemen, was a British-constructed collection of sheikhdoms and sultanates surrounding the Crown colony of Aden. It resembled the UAE but without oil. It did not survive Britain's withdrawal from its territory in 1967.

11. Dina Shehata, "The Fall of the Pharaoh: How Hosni Mubarak's Regime Came to an End," *Foreign Affairs* 90 (May–June 2011): 26–32.

12. Lisa Anderson, "Absolutism and the Resilience of Monarchy in the Middle East," *Political Science Quarterly* 106 (Spring 1991): 1–15.

13. Ottaway and Muasher, *Arab Monarchies,* 21.

14. The 2010 Bahraini census reported a citizen population of 568,399 out of a total population of 1,234,571, but the remainder consisted of foreign residents who did not participate in the 2011 protests. Sharon Otterman and J. David Goodman, "Hundreds of Thousands Protest Across the Middle East," *New York Times*, 25 February 2011.

15. Charles Kurzman, *The Unthinkable Revolution in Iran* (Cambridge: Harvard University Press, 2004), 121.

16. J.E. Peterson, *The Arab Gulf States: Steps Towards Political Participation* (New York: Praeger, 1988), 16–21.

17. Though applicable to the developing world, the best exposition of this argument comes from American political development. See Martin Shefter, *Political Parties and the State: The American Historical Experience* (Princeton: Princeton University Press, 1994), 6–7.

18. For more on the bargained nature of durable autocracies in Indonesia and Malaysia, see Benjamin Smith, *Hard Times in the Lands of Plenty: Oil Politics in Iran and Indonesia* (Ithaca: Cornell University Press, 2007), and Dan Slater, *Ordering Power: Contentious Politics and Authoritarian Leviathans in Southeast Asia* (New York: Cambridge University Press, 2010).

19. F. Gregory Gause III, *Oil Monarchies: Domestic and Security Challenges in the Arab Gulf States* (New York: Council on Foreign Relations, 1994).

20. Whereas early work on oil politics suggested that *rentier* dependence undermined regime stability, more recent work reveals the opposite: *How* rulers redistribute their fiscal rents matters just as much as *whether* they have access to those rents in the first place. See Smith, *Hard Times in the Land of Plenty*, and Sean L. Yom, "Oil, Coalitions, and Regime Durability: The Origins and Persistence of Popular Rentierism in Kuwait," *Studies in Comparative International Development* 46 (June 2011): 217–41.

21. Lahcen Achy, "Why Did Protests in Algeria Fail To Gain Momentum?" *Foreign Policy*, 31 March 2011.

22. We are grateful to Marc Lynch for this telling counterfactual.

23. For more on this tight relationship, see Sean L. Yom, "Jordan: Ten More Years of Autocracy," *Journal of Democracy* 20 (October 2009): 151–66.

11

WHY THE MODEST HARVEST?

Jason Brownlee, Tarek Masoud, and Andrew Reynolds

Jason Brownlee *is associate professor of government and Middle Eastern studies at the University of Texas–Austin.* ***Tarek Masoud*** *is associate professor of public policy at Harvard's John F. Kennedy School of Government.* ***Andrew Reynolds*** *is associate professor of political science at the University of North Carolina–Chapel Hill. This essay originally appeared in the October 2013 issue of the* Journal of Democracy.

Nearly three years after the Arab uprisings began, democracy remains elusive in the Middle East. Tunisians, who lit the torch of revolution in December 2010, now walk a precarious line between institutional reform and social violence. In Egypt, a fitful transition to democracy, marked by intense polarization between Islamists and their opponents, seems to have been stopped in its tracks by a military coup and follow-on strife. More than a year after the overthrow of Yemen's dictator, that country has yet to hold multiparty elections for a new government. Meanwhile, violent militias and endemic state weakness threaten Libya's democratic experiment. And those are the "success stories." Elsewhere in the Arab world, uprisings have subsided or never materialized. The Bahraini monarchy literally beat its opponents into submission. In Syria, President Bashar al-Assad's war on his own country has killed or rendered homeless tens of thousands. In eight more Arab-majority countries, autocrats have yet to face any concerted challenge.

The Arab Spring that resides in the popular imagination is one in which a wave of mass mobilization swept the broader Middle East, toppled dictators, and cleared the way for democracy. The reality is that few Arab countries have experienced anything of the sort. The Arab Spring's modest harvest—a record far less inspiring than those of the East European revolutions of 1989 or sub-Saharan Africa's political transitions in the early 1990s—cries out for explanation. Why did regime change, which we conservatively define as merely the replacement of a dictator rather than the installation of a democracy, take place in only four of fourteen Arab countries?

This essay attempts to answer that question. It develops what we believe to be the first *regional* explanation of regime outcomes from the Arab uprisings of 2010 to 2012. Our explanatory framework owes a tremendous intellectual debt to the leading initial studies of the Arab Spring, but differs from its precursors in empirical breadth and causal depth. First, we seek to account for the full range of variance: from the absence or failure of uprisings in places such as Algeria and Saudi Arabia at one end to Tunisia's rocky but still hopeful transition at the other. Second, we broaden our temporal aperture, shifting from the proximate variables that have hitherto commanded the most attention, such as the diffusion of social-networking tools and the posture of the army, to examine the historical and structural factors that determined the balance of power between incumbents and oppositionists. By rooting our explanation in structural variables whose values could have been observed and measured prior to the Arab Spring, we avoid the risk of generating a post hoc "just-so story" that retrospectively reads causes from outcomes.

Surveying the region, we find that there were no structural preconditions for the *emergence* of uprisings: The fundamentally random manner in which protests spread meant that a wide variety of regimes faced popular challenges. We find, however, that the *success* of a domestic campaign to oust the ruler was structurally preconditioned by two variables: oil wealth (which endows the ruler with enough material resources to forestall or contain challenges) and the precedent of hereditary succession (which indicates the heightened loyalty of coercive agents to the executive). We find that *only* regimes that lacked major oil revenue *and* had not established hereditary succession succumbed relatively quickly and nonviolently to domestic uprisings. By contrast, where dictators had inherited rule (whether through traditional monarchism or corrupted republicanism) or commanded vast oil rents, their repressive forces remained sufficiently loyal and cohesive to conduct brutal crackdowns, often reaching the level of outright warfare.

In the discussion below, we strive to put forward a framework that builds theoretically and conceptually on previous approaches to this subject and sheds light on the future of the Arab world and its current season of tumult. An important implication of the theory presented here is that the Arab Spring's low-hanging fruit have already been picked. Those hoping that some new wave of popular protest in a Saudi Arabia or a Jordan will trigger a Tunisian-style flight of the dictator and the ushering in of a new constitutional order will find those hopes to be forlorn.

Social scientists studying the Arab Spring have made significant contributions to our understandings of the dynamics of protest, the breakdown of autocracy, and the establishment of democracy. Like their predecessors who analyzed transitions away from authoritarianism in

Southern Europe and Latin America, scholars of the Arab uprisings have focused on proximate causes, emphasizing the agency of activists and officers. Activist-centered explanations of the uprisings made particular sense, at first. The grievances of protesters captured attention because the demonstrations of the Arab Spring were the most potent expressions of mass discontent that those countries had witnessed in decades. Activists spoke powerfully of both the old regimes' failings and of popular aspirations for "dignity," so it was natural for observers to locate in these the drivers of citizen activism. Similarly, the speed with which previously disparate social groups managed to organize collectively to challenge regimes naturally caused scholars to home in on the new information technologies that supposedly made such collective action possible. But the narrative of youthful pluck and technological savvy goes only so far. Activists from Rabat to Riyadh had access to Twitter, Facebook, and YouTube, and yet the story of most democratic activists in the Arab world remains one of disappointment and defeat.

In order to explain the fall or survival of autocracies during the Arab Spring, scholars shifted their attention from activists to the central elites of the regimes themselves, placing military leaders center stage. In both Egypt and Tunisia, the dictator's position became untenable when the armed forces refused to use force, whereas in Syria the military flew swiftly and savagely to the regime's defense. In one of the most influential attempts to explain this variation, Eva Bellin argued that the likelihood that a military will resist calls for a brutal crackdown on behalf of the dictator is a function of its bureaucratization and professionalization.[1] Yet while it is easy to argue in hindsight that the Egyptian military was more professionalized—and less loyal to the president—than Syria's, it is much harder to identify variables that in 2010 or earlier would have forecast the defections of militaries in Tunisia and Egypt and the military's loyalty in Syria. In fact, few would have predicted that Egypt's military would follow the Tunisian army's lead and break from the incumbent. For though Tunisia has boasted a long tradition of civilian control over the military that might explain the army's reluctance to back Ben Ali, the scholarly wisdom on Egypt had long held that the army and the regime were one. Thus, most accounts of military behavior during the uprisings have been exercises in post hoc reasoning that read the generals' preferences from their actions.

Other scholars have looked toward structural and historical explanations. For example, some have pointed to the importance of monarchism in staving off regime change, while others have noted the stasis-enhancing effects of oil.[2] Though these accounts are valuable (as we shall see below), they nonetheless fail to explain the entire range of outcomes. After all, Syria is neither a monarchy nor a major oil exporter, and yet its regime has managed to hang on in the face of one of the most concerted challenges to authoritarian rule in modern Middle Eastern history.

This essay builds upon competing theories. Noting the decision calculus of generals, the political effects of oil revenues, and the peculiar qualities of monarchism, we offer a parsimonious theory that predicts outcomes in fourteen Arab-majority states of the Middle East and North Africa. (Iraq and Lebanon lie outside our scope conditions because they exhibit a high degree of multiparty competition, unlike the authoritarian situations of the remaining cases.) In the following sections, we present our theory, and then illustrate how the dynamics that we identify operated in the fourteen cases of regime continuity and change during the Arab Spring.

Cash, Commitment, and Control

To stay in power, an autocrat needs two things: money and loyalty. Cash can be used to buy off foes—and to buy the means of crushing them in case they turn out not to be for sale. Rulers also need the loyalty of the agents who wreak state violence. The fealty of the men with guns imbues an autocrat with extraordinary despotic power, enabling him to act *upon* the population rather than in dialogue with it.

The notion that despots with enough resources and repressive forces will stay in power is true by definition. Going from tautology to causality means rooting these proximate variables in factors that pre-dated the Arab Spring by years, if not decades. Specifically, we trace the command of money to the massive inflows of oil rents that began after October 1973, and we tie loyalty—and hence, despotic power—to the inception of dynastic rule through hereditary succession.

Oil wealth. Though all autocrats possess material resources, we argue that only oil wealth endows the dictator with sufficient means to stave off mass challenges. Thus, we sort the fourteen Arab countries under consideration based on whether they are major oil exporters. We code as oil-rich the seven Arab OPEC members (Algeria, Kuwait, Libya, Oman, Qatar, Saudi Arabia, and the United Arab Emirates) plus Bahrain, a tiny country that has fairly small reserves by regional standards, but which still enjoys petrochemical rents that in real terms are three times what Venezuela took in from oil in 1958, the year of that country's democratic transition.[3]

Why equate oil with regime-stabilizing revenue? Scholars of the Middle East have long maintained that the oil-rich regimes of the region have a distinctive form of politics based on vast resource rents that obviate the need to tax the citizenry.[4] There are many ways in which oil wealth is thought to hold back democracy. For example, the flow of hydrocarbon rents can weaken civil society and stunt the growth of a modern workforce, diminishing the capacity of populations to mount serious challenges to their regimes.[5] We focus on two more direct mechanisms by which oil hinders democracy: by enabling an autocrat to buy the quiescence of his citizens, and, failing that, to purchase the means to silence them by force.

Anyone seeking examples of how Middle Eastern rulers use oil wealth to keep popular discontents at bay need not look far. On 18 January 2011—just days after Ben Ali's flight and a week before the onset of Egypt's revolution—Kuwait's government announced a grant of US$3,500 to every man, woman, and child, as well as a year's worth of free staples such as sugar, cooking oil, and milk. The following month, the Saudi government followed suit, announcing a $80-billion package of public-sector wage hikes, unemployment payments, increased college stipends, and investments in low-income housing. In September 2011, the government of Qatar—not usually thought to be at risk of a popular uprising—declared that it would raise public-sector salaries and pensions by 60 percent, at a cost of more than $8 billion.

Rentier states are good not only at handing out carrots, but also at piling up sticks. Michael Ross finds that "oil-poor Tunisia . . . spent $53 per capita on its armed forces in 2008 [while] its oil-rich neighbor, Algeria, spent $141 per capita and had far fewer protests."[6] From 2006 to 2009, Saudi Arabia spent close to $30 billion on arms imports. Over the same period, Bahrain spent more than $14 billion and Algeria nearly $7 billion for the same purpose. Saudi Arabia ranks among the top ten arms procurers worldwide, neck-and-neck with such major powers as India and Germany.[7]

Dynasticism. Buying guns is easy, however. Much harder is retaining the loyalty of those who are trained, organized, and paid to wield them on the state's behalf. A truly predictive sign that such loyalty exists is the autocratic regime's ability to transfer power smoothly from one member of the ruling family to another. Such a trouble-free transfer is the best *a priori* evidence that the coercive apparatus has pledged its fealty to the top family, and will thus likely go to serious lengths to guard it.

Why is hereditary succession such a strong sign of regime cohesion? In authoritarian regimes, successions are inherently perilous. Former allies plot against one another, and palace intrigues often mean that things end in ways that the departing autocrat neither expected nor desired. In the decades since the Second World War ended, transfers of executive power from fathers to sons have been rare.[8] Whether occuring by convention in monarchies or appearing as innovations in autocratic republics, such transfers signal that the state's repressive agents have rallied around the executive (whether king or president) to an extraordinary degree.

Since Max Weber, social scientists have argued that rulers who concentrate power in their families—scholars of comparative politics call the resulting regimes "personalistic" or "sultanistic"—are less resilient than those who adhere to a more rational-legal tradition.[9] As Jack Goldstone recently put it:

> Although such [sultanistic] regimes often appear unshakable, they are actually highly vulnerable, because the very strategies they use to stay in power make them brittle, not resilient. It is no coincidence that although

popular protests have shaken much of the Middle East, the only revolutions to succeed so far—those in Tunisia and Egypt—have been against
modern sultans.[10]

We argue the opposite—the regimes of presidents Ben Ali and
Mubarak fell *not* because they were too sultanistic, but rather because
they were not sultanistic enough. Though Ben Ali and Mubarak were
corrupt and nepotistic, their excesses were typical of conventional authoritarianism and did not rise (or sink) to the level of sultanism. What
then separates a "sultan" from a run-of-the-mill autocrat? We argue that
hereditary succession is the distinguishing mark. With this important
conceptual refinement, it then becomes clear that there is a *positive* relationship between the intense personalism that characterizes true sultanistic regimes and the durability of those regimes.

To see the difference between a genuinely sultanistic regime and a
merely authoritarian one, compare Mubarak's Egypt and the Assads'
Syria. A pre–Arab Spring visitor to both countries would have been
struck by how differently the executive's family and his regime inter-
acted. A study of high-level army officers in Syria would have turned
up dozens of Assad relatives, including Maher, the younger brother of
President Bashar al-Assad and the commander of the Republican Guard
as well as of the army's Fourth Armored Division. In Egypt, by contrast,
one would have looked in vain for Mubarak's kin among the ranks of
the country's top officers. These dissimilarities can be traced back to
the 1990s, when Bashar and Maher's father, President Hafiz al-Assad,
was establishing familial rule with the consent of the Syrian military.
The elder Assad made no attempt to hide his dynastic plans, putting forward his oldest son Basil as first choice. When Basil died in a 1994 car
crash, Bashar began to appear with his father and dead brother in official
iconography.[11] When Hafiz died in 2000, the security state's notables
backed Bashar and power stayed in Assad hands.[12]

Like Hafiz al-Assad, Mubarak also seems to have wanted his son to
succeed him, but the topic in Egypt was far more fraught and the regime
was far more coy about it. In 2005, Gamal Mubarak felt compelled to
publicly dismiss the notion that he would ascend to the presidency.[13] By
2009, the elder Mubarak was deemed to have left the succession question in the hands of the security state, whose movers and shakers were
widely thought to dislike the idea of Gamal ever taking power.[14] While
the Mubaraks hesitated to enact dynasticism, the Assads plowed ahead,
thanks to much stronger bonds between the executive and the repressive
apparatus.

Hereditary handoffs are easily observed and measured. Thus we favor replacing the general notion of sultanism with the more precise and
replicable indicator of "dynasticism," defined simply as an instance of
executive authority being inherited.[15] Where a dynasty exists, despotic

TABLE—THE STRUCTURE OF ARAB REGIME CHANGE, 2010–12

	Major Oil Exporters	Minor or Non-Oil Exporters
Non-Hereditary Regimes	Algeria *Libya**	*Egypt* *Tunisia* *Yemen*
Hereditary Regimes	**Bahrain** Kuwait Oman Qatar Saudi Arabia UAE	Jordan Morocco **Syria**

power will follow. Far from being brittle, highly personalized regimes are actually stronger than their depersonalized counterparts. Whereas the latter may fracture in the face of protest, personalized regimes close ranks and fight.

We coded the fourteen Arab countries into two groups: those with and without an instance of hereditary succession *in the postcolonial period* (or in other words, since the early 1970s). Our periodization matters. Were one surveying Arab states in the 1950s and 1960s, one would have observed the dissolution of dynastic regimes in Egypt (1954), Iraq (1958), Libya (1969), Tunisia (1957), and Yemen (1968). Those regimes all differed crucially from present-day dynasties, however, for they were sustained not by purely domestic pacts between a family and the state apparatus, but by colonial powers as well. Today's hereditary Arab regimes are the six Gulf Cooperation Council (GCC) states plus Jordan, Morocco, and Syria (the only republic among them).

Explaining Outcomes

Based on our two explanatory variables, we sort the regimes of the Arab world into four families (see Table). We also identify the countries that experienced uprisings and regime change, the principal outcomes we seek to explain. A country's name in boldface type indicates the presence of an "uprising." Countries in italics experienced "regime change." An asterisk (*) indicates "foreign-imposed regime change" (FIRC). In the following sections, we discuss the relationship that our variables have to both the occurrence of uprisings, and the unseating of autocrats.

Uprisings. We define an uprising as a major type of contentious collective action marked by 1) the eruption of nonviolent mass protest over multiple days, 2) the spread of that protest across multiple geographical locations, and 3) the control by protesters of public places such as Cairo's Tahrir Square, Manama's Pearl Roundabout, or Tunis's Bourguiba Avenue.[16] Uprisings depart from conventional demonstrations in their size, national resonance, and persistence. They differ from armed insurgencies in the methods used by their organizers. In Libya, Syria, and, to a lesser extent, Yemen, peaceful protest gave way to violent rebellion,

but the two phenomena are distinct. Militias can emerge without uprisings, and uprisings do not have to produce militias.

As our Table shows, uprisings occurred in every regime combination,
hereditary or not, oil-rich or not. Tunisia's uprising began on 17 December 2010, and by early 2011 the ferment had spread to Egypt (January
25), Yemen (February 3), Bahrain (February 14), Libya (February 15),
and Syria (March 15).

Strikingly, the protest wave touched various corners of the region
almost without regard to structural preconditions. This suggests that
new technologies and activist tactics enabled unprecedented challenges
to authoritarian rule in unexpected places. Because the role of human
agency and chance looms large, seeking a parsimonious theory of where
uprisings will occur may be a fool's errand. That said, although there
was no hard prerequisite, it does appear that uprisings were most likely
to appear under nonhereditary authoritarian regimes without much oil
wealth. Still, the massive uprisings in Libya, Bahrain, and Syria should
caution against overinterpreting this pattern. Considering the full scope
of cases, the biggest lesson is that agents, not structures, drove the uprisings. To invert Theda Skocpol's dictum about social revolutions, the
Arab uprisings did not come, they were made.[17]

Domestic Regime Change and Continuity. While the relationship
between the main explanatory variables and the outbreak of uprisings
is indeterminate, stronger correlations appear when we look at regime
change. Though activists emerged everywhere, their aspirations were
not self-fulfilling. Many who took to the streets in countries other than
Egypt, Tunisia, and Yemen underestimated the staying power of local
regimes.[18]

We define regime change as the ousting of an authoritarian ruler and
his inner circle (an assassination that leaves the top echelon in place
does not count). For some, this may be too low a threshold, as it is possible for a leader and his coterie to depart without altering the underlying
authoritarian infrastructure. But requiring Arab cases to clear a higher
bar of substantive democratization might leave us with no cases of regime change at all. Among the countries that we cover, only Tunisia currently meets the minimal standards of electoral democracy. (Freedom
House counted Libya as an electoral democracy in 2012, but that judgment appears premature given Libya's unresolved constitutional and institutional questions.) Still, the rupture of authoritarian regimes—even
in the absence of democratization—is a rare and consequential enough
outcome to warrant explanation.

In comparing instances of regime change with periods of regime continuity, we focus on *domestically driven* political transformations. These
happen when a mass movement impels a leadership change. Although
that change may be carried out by military figures, the element of social pressure is sufficient that the regime change is not a simple coup.

Tunisia (2010–11), Egypt (2011), and Yemen (2011–12) all underwent such domestically driven regime changes. In each case, the armed forces were instrumental in ushering a dictator from power, yet they were responding to a popular groundswell and moving without active foreign military assistance.

A second type of turnover is a FIRC. This involves one or more outside powers (hence the "foreign-imposed" part) and differs fundamentally from a purely internal overthrow.[19] The U.S.-led Operation Iraqi Freedom in 2003, which ousted Saddam Hussein, and the NATO-directed Operation Unified Protector of 2011, which enabled rebels to topple Muammar Qadhafi's regime in Libya, are the most recent FIRCs in the region.

Cases where there was no regime change during the years 2010 through 2012 are Algeria, Bahrain, Jordan, Kuwait, Morocco, Oman, Qatar, Saudi Arabia, Syria, and the United Arab Emirates. Lack of regime change does not mean that these countries were politically stagnant. Even aside from the dramatic events in Bahrain and Syria, a number of Arab rulers flirted with reforms and allowed limited elections. Yet such initiatives, while *potentially* momentous, did not remove incumbents and may even have left them stronger.[20]

How does our explanatory framework account for the variation in outcomes? As the Table shows, oil exporters were able to withstand the shocks of domestic protest—the one exception was Qadhafi's Libyan dictatorship, which fell only after the world's strongest military alliance launched a sustained aerial-bombing campaign against it. There is more variation, though, among oil-poor regimes. Civilian dissidents and disgruntled generals replaced dictators in Egypt, Tunisia, and Yemen. The hereditary regimes of Jordan, Morocco, and Syria, on the other hand, remain in place (the last at a terrible and mounting cost in human life). The pattern of regime stability during 2010–12 was that *either* oil wealth *or* hereditary rule was enough to preserve authoritarian continuity unless outside powers intervened.

Pathways of Causation

There were two paths through which regime traits determined whether mass protests would deliver political change. The first was when the state's coercive apparatus shifted in favor of toppling the executive. The second was when that apparatus remained loyal and cracked down on the opposition. The former path entailed the breakdown of despotic power; the latter entailed its use to devastating effect. We now trace these paths in the six cases of regime-challenging protest movements: Bahrain, Egypt, Libya, Syria, Tunisia, and Yemen.

Opposition success in the nonhereditary, oil-poor regimes. Prior to December 2010, few would have deemed the Tunisian, Egyptian, or Yemeni regimes vulnerable to revolt. Yet each of these security states

FIGURE—CAUSAL PATHWAYS OF THE ARAB SPRING

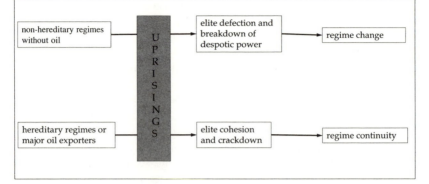

depended on a coalition that proved susceptible to fissuring when the people arose. In none of the three had the coercive apparatus previously united behind the ruler in a hereditary succession. In addition, presidents Ben Ali, Mubarak, and Saleh had limited rents with which they could buy military loyalty or social quiescence.

In Tunisia, Ben Ali used as much despotic power as he could muster, but the backstop of the coercive apparatus, the uniformed military, soon abandoned him. A week into the uprising, Interior Ministry forces began firing live bullets. Two demonstrators were shot dead on December 24; in the weeks that followed, more than two hundred would die.[21] On January 9, regime forces fired on demonstrators in the city of Kasserine, and three days later Ben Ali ordered the army to move into the city.[22] The order backfired. The top general, Rachid Ammar, not only refused Ben Ali's order but deployed soldiers to shield protesters from further Interior Ministry assaults. The president fled to Saudi Arabia on January 14, and the military let him go.

General Ammar's counterpart in Egypt, Field Marshal Mohamed Hussein Tantawi, also bowed to popular pressure and forced out a long-ruling president.[23] After demonstrators in Cairo overran police vehicles and security men on January 29, Mubarak's interior minister told him that events had spun out of control. Mubarak ordered a nationwide military deployment, only to have protesters and the army defy him with a mutual embrace. On January 31, Tantawi declared that the army backed the revolution and would not shoot. The next evening, Mubarak tried to mollify his angry people by vowing that neither he nor his son would run in the next election, but the crowds did not abate. The Supreme Council of the Armed Forces (SCAF), comprising Egypt's twenty highest-ranking uniformed officers, met on February 10 and declared that it would work to protect what the protesters had achieved. On February 11, it announced that it would oversee a transition to a new constitution, free elections, and an eventual end to the hated state of emergency. Later that day, Vice-President Omar Suleiman revealed that Mubarak had stepped down.

Compared to his counterparts in Tunis and Cairo, Yemen's President Ali Abdallah Saleh had gone much farther toward establishing familial rule. He had seen to it that most military officers were members of his own tribe, and had placed a nephew and a son, respectively, atop the Central Security Service and the Republican Guard. Yet Saleh had not managed to forge an Assad-like coalition behind his offspring. On the contrary, power players such as the country's leading business family had made clear their opposition to any dynastic project. Saleh might have wielded significant despotic power, but he could not command the kind of loyalty that Hafiz al-Assad had known.

Demonstrations began in Sana'a on January 15, the day after Tunisians ousted Ben Ali. Protests spread into February, prompting Saleh to pledge that he would not seek reelection in 2013.[24] This worked no better on Yemenis than it had on Egyptians. Activists insisted that Saleh should go immediately and mobilized twenty-thousand people for a "Day of Rage" on February 3. In general, Saleh retained the overall support of the armed forces, which are 138,000-strong (in a country of 23 million). The main exception to military loyalty was General Ali Mohsen al-Ahmar, a tribal confederate of Saleh's who commanded a division of the army used against protesters in Sana'a.[25] In March, Ahmar joined the call for Saleh to resign.

After a failed assassination attempt in early June, the president was rushed to Saudi Arabia for medical care. Despite U.S. urgings that he step down and accept a transition plan put forward by Saudi Arabia and the GCC—which offered him and his family immunity from prosecution—it was not until November 23 that he finally acquiesced. On 21 February 2012, Vice-President Abdu Rabu Mansour Hadi was elected (unopposed) to the presidency as a "consensus candidate" of the regime and opposition. This was enough to put Yemen in the regime-change category, though the country cannot be considered promising ground for democracy.

Crackdowns in hereditary or oil-rich regimes. In the remaining cases where protest occurred, regimes benefited from firm coalitions backing the dynasty (Syria), oil largesse (Libya), or both (Bahrain). These traits enabled them to hold the repressive apparatus together during major uprisings and to lash out violently against the opposition. The record so far is that such repression has been enough to keep rulers in power unless foreign military forces intervene, as happened in Libya.

Hafiz al-Assad maintained one of the most active and politically loyal militaries in the Middle East, using it to wage war against Israel in 1973, to crush the Muslim Brotherhood in the city of Hama in 1982 (killing as many as thirty-thousand people), and to establish Syrian hegemony in Lebanon. By 2010, Syria had a larger military per capita than any of our other core cases: more than 400,000 troops for a population of 22 million. As a result of France's colonial policy, the country's senior officers had long been disproportionately drawn from the Alawite religious minority. Hafiz al-Assad, an Alawite and an air force general, carefully maintained this custom.[26] It proved a good investment for the regime, creating a reservoir of determined support for despotism that smoothed Bashar's succession to the presidency and supported his continued rule after protest and then armed resistance broke out in 2011.

The major demonstrations began on 15 March 2011, as another of the Arab world's by now familiar "Days of Rage." The regime's response was draconian. Five people were killed in the southwestern town of De-raa, which was then sealed off. After laying siege to Deraa in April, tanks moved against towns around the country in subsequent months. While opposition movements inside the country and abroad were push-ing reforms or seeking ways to usher Bashar al-Assad from power, the Syrian president was unleashing heavy weapons to keep his seat.

Aside from a few isolated military defections, the armed forces con-tinued to back the regime. Further, the core of the repressive machine— the Republican Guards and the intelligence services—stood behind Bashar, as did his foreign enablers Iran, Hezbollah, and Russia. As 2013 wore on, things seemed unlikely to tip in the opposition's favor, despite aid from Saudi Arabia and Qatar, among others. It seemed that absent something like a major foreign air campaign on the order of the one seen in Libya, the Assads would stay.

Whether or not Assad and his entourage survive the current war is as much a question of military as of political science, but here too the comparative evidence underscores the resilience, not the fragility, of the regime. The armed Syrian opposition has failed so far to hold ma-jor swaths of territory, while the regime has succeeded in keeping its military cohesive and active. This outcome of regime durability during crisis merits attention. The regime's dynastic nature and the dynamics this implies go far toward explaining it.

In Bahrain, the Sunni Khalifa family epitomizes dynasticism. Princ-es hold all top government posts. Unlike Syria, however, the Bahraini regime also benefits from significant oil wealth that enables it to hire foreign mercenaries for domestic repression (Pakistan is a popular re-cruiting spot). Bahrain had its own "Day of Rage" on 14 February 2011. Tens of thousands called for reform—including the replacement of hard-line prime minister Khalifa bin Salman al-Khalifa—rather than regime change. The government responded with violence; seven protesters lost their lives during the uprising's first four days. Yet the movement pressed on, soon drawing Shia parliamentarians and members of the judiciary to its cause. Demonstrators occupied the Pearl Roundabout, Manama's ver-sion of Tahrir Square. The regime made no major concessions.[27]

In mid-March, soldiers from the Bahraini Defense Forces began clearing the roundabout by force while a thousand Saudi troops crossed the King Fahd Causeway and took up posts guarding key government sites. They were joined by five-hundred UAE soldiers and a small Qatari contingent, with Kuwait providing naval support. Within days, the roundabout was empty, hundreds of activists were under arrest, and several leading regime opponents were facing military trials.[28]

Explaining Libya. If we are right that oil wealth is enough to stave off regime change, then the outcome of the Libyan revolution requires explanation. Since seizing power in 1969, Qadhafi had used oil wealth and his own unique brand of populism to keep Libyans atomized while building up a vast coercive apparatus.[29] The country should thus have gone the way of Bahrain rather than Egypt or Tunisia. Instead, the Libyan revolution ended with Qadhafi dead by the side of a road. Why?

We argue that, without NATO's intervention, Qadhafi and his regime would have survived. The armed resistance that he faced was mainly limited to eastern Libya, and unable to topple the regime on its own. Some of Qadhafi's armed units in the east did defect in February 2011, but much of the coercive apparatus was bound to him by regional and tribal ties and stayed loyal. By mid-March, Qadhafi was poised to regain control of the east by attacking Benghazi. It was this prospect—and the threat of subsequent massacres—that finally spurred the United States to support the imposition of a UN-backed no-fly zone, forcing Libya into the regime-change category.

Are Structural Factors Key?

This essay has offered a theory of regime change and continuity based on two preexisting regime traits: oil wealth and hereditary rule. These structural characteristics do not account for the emergence of popular protest—that seems to depend on local activists. These factors do, however, help to explain the wide array of outcomes among the six Arab countries that experienced uprisings. In particular, they offer new insights regarding how and why Arab militaries and security forces—under pressure from the streets—either obeyed their rulers, or ousted them.

The Arab Spring produced such a modest harvest because regimes continued to benefit from reservoirs of rents and repressive capacity, the same characteristics that many scholars cited to explain the prevalence of authoritarianism in the region *before* the uprisings began. In this sense, the limited scope of regime change requires us to take a second look at the historic sources of autocratic resilience.

While striving for parsimony, we are able to reconcile anomalies raised by prior arguments and to make progress toward a more integrated theoretical approach to regime change. If oil exports scotched uprisings, why has the Syrian regime lasted so long against its domestic opponents? If Arab republics were more vulnerable, why, again, have Syria *and* Algeria avoided regime change? The answer, we find, comes from considering hereditary rule—whether in its monarchic *or* its "republican" permutations—as a sign of unusually strong ties between the ruler and the repressive apparatus. Further, dynasticism and oil rents operate as complementary, rather than competing, variables. *Either* characteristic is enough to ensure that the regime will retain power, while a regime without either will fall quickly once popular pressure and military defections begin to mount.

In terms of revising prior expectations, our theory yields two major lessons. The first is about personal rule, while the second concerns the importance of foreign interventions. By homing in on dynasticism, instead of sultanism, comparativists can more readily distinguish polities with "normal" levels of authoritarian corruption from those where the ruler fuses his family into the regime. Further, the fragility of the most personalistic of dictatorships may have been exaggerated. Dynasticism bonds autocrats and agents of repression. Such regimes may eventually fall, but they will only go down violently.

Regarding FIRCs, it appears that foreign interventions in the Middle East and North Africa serve as the *deus ex machina* for embattled oppositionists. Whether in Iraq in 2003 or Libya in 2011, military campaigns spearheaded (or, in the latter case, at least supported) by the United States effectively overrode the domestic factors that had produced a severe imbalance between oil-fed security states and long-repressed dissidents. The premise of the Obama administration's decision to back a no-fly zone in Libya was that the Libyan uprising would have been crushed without foreign military help. Our analytical framework supports that claim. By extension, one may reach a similar conclusion about the Syrian rebellion in 2013.

Here one may ask whether the Bahraini case, with its Saudi-led intervention, defies our logic: Was not foreign intervention needed to *rescue* a major oil exporter from domestically driven change? A comparison of the NATO intervention in Libya and the GCC intervention in Bahrain offers an explanation. In Libya, foreign militaries took the lead in bringing the regime to heel, whereas in Bahrain, it was domestic police and soldiers who were out front bludgeoning the regime's critics. The GCC troops were mere auxiliaries. This account does not ignore the GCC's support for a bloody crackdown, but it assigns the dominant causal role to the local regime.

As Egypt, Libya, Tunisia, and Yemen attempt to move forward, all ears are listening for the dogs that have not yet barked. Many think that it is only a matter of time before the doleful dynastic stability of Jordan, Morocco, and Saudi Arabia gives way to popular demands for dignity and freedom. This may be so. But our theory predicts that these regimes will not respond to such challenges by turning in on themselves, packing the autocrat off to exile, and negotiating the dismantling of the old order. Monarchies that have ruled for the better part of 250 years in Saudi Arabia, 400 in Morocco, or 100 in Jordan, and gathered into their hands all the threads of power and privilege, will not go quietly.

These sobering predictions are a useful corrective to the sunny optimism that the Arab Spring initially inspired. The breathtaking spectacle of peaceful young crowds triumphing over long-entrenched dictators suggested—misleadingly—that an inexorable march toward democracy had begun. The Arab Spring's meager yield—a bitter litany of failed uprisings, halting or reversed "transitions," and autocratic continuity—suggests that a less teleological process is at work, and that inherited political structures remain critically important.

NOTES

The authors wish to thank Jack Goldstone, Dan Slater, Joshua Stacher, Nicolas van de Walle, and participants at workshops at the University of North Carolina–Chapel Hill and the University of Texas–Austin for constructive comments on earlier versions of this essay.

1. Eva Bellin, "Reconsidering the Robustness of Authoritarianism in the Middle East: Lessons from the Arab Spring," *Comparative Politics* 44 (January 2012): 127–49.

2. Sean L. Yom and F. Gregory Gause III, "Resilient Royals: How Arab Monarchies Hang On," *Journal of Democracy* 23 (October 2012): 74–88; Michael L. Ross, "Will Oil Drown the Arab Spring? Democracy and the Resource Curse," *Foreign Affairs* 90 (September–October 2011): 2–7.

3. Ross, "Will Oil Drown the Arab Spring?" 5.

4. Hossein Mahdavy, "The Patterns and Problems of Economic Development in Rentier States: The Case of Iran," in M.A. Cook, ed., *Studies in the Economic History of the Middle East from the Rise of Islam to the Present Day* (Oxford: Oxford University Press, 1970), 428–67; Lisa Anderson, "The State in the Middle East and North Africa," *Comparative Politics* 20 (October 1987): 1–18.

5. Michael L. Ross, "Does Oil Hinder Democracy?" *World Politics* 53 (April 2001): 325–61.

6. Ross, "Will Oil Drown the Arab Spring?" 4.

7. Richard F. Grimmett, *Conventional Arms Transfers to Developing Nations, 2002–2009* (Washington, D.C.: Congressional Research Service, 2010), 44. For Saudi Arabia's global ranking as an arms buyer, see *www.sipri.org/research/armaments/milex/resultoutput/milex_15/the-15-countries-with-the-highest-military-expenditure-in-2011-table/view*.

8. Jason Brownlee, "Hereditary Succession in Modern Autocracies," *World Politics* 59 (July 2007): 595–628.

9. Juan J. Linz, "Totalitarian and Authoritarian Regimes," in Fred I. Greenstein and Nelson W. Polsby, eds., *Handbook of Political Science, Volume 3: Macropolitical Theory* (Reading, Mass.: Addison-Wesley, 1975), 175–357.

10. Jack A. Goldstone, "Understanding the Revolutions of 2011: Weakness and Resilience in Middle Eastern Autocracies," *Foreign Affairs* 90 (May–June 2011): 8.

11. Lisa Wedeen, *Ambiguities of Domination: Politics, Rhetoric, and Symbols in Contemporary Syria* (Chicago: University of Chicago Press, 1999).

12. Joshua Stacher, "Reinterpreting Authoritarian Power: Syria's Hereditary Succession," *Middle East Journal* 65 (Spring 2011): 197–212.

13. Summer Said, "Mubarak to Name Vice-President After September Elections," *Arab News,* 16 June 2005, available at *www.arabnews.com/node/268587.*

14. Available at *www.cablegatesearch.net/cable.php?id=09CAIRO874&q=gamal%20 mubarak.*

15. We thank Alfred Stepan for encouraging us to narrow the range of what we mean by "sultanism." Note that our sense of the term leaves out such corrupt but nonhereditary regimes as the Philippines under Ferdinand Marcos and the Dominican Republic under Rafael Trujillo while still including the Somozas' Nicaragua and the Duvaliers' Haiti.

16. Doug McAdam, Sidney Tarrow, and Charles Tilly, "Dynamics of Contention," *Social Movement Studies* 2 (April 2003): 99–102.

17. Theda Skocpol, *States and Social Revolutions: A Comparative Analysis of France, Russia, and China* (New York: Cambridge University Press, 1979).

18. Kurt Weyland, "The Arab Spring: Why the Surprising Similarities with the Revolutionary Wave of 1848?" *Perspectives on Politics* 10 (December 2012): 917–34; Doug McAdam, *Political Process and the Development of Black Insurgency, 1930–1970* (Chicago: University of Chicago Press, 1982).

19. Suzanne Werner, "Absolute and Limited War: The Possibility of Foreign-Imposed Regime Change," *International Interactions* 22 (July 1996): 67–88; Alexander B. Downes and Jonathan Monten, "Forced to Be Free? Why Foreign-Imposed Regime Change Rarely Leads to Democratization," *International Security* 37 (Spring 2013): 90–131.

20. Daniel Brumberg, "Survival Strategies vs. Democratic Bargains: The Politics of Economic Reform in Contemporary Egypt," in Henri Barkey, ed., *The Politics of Economic Reform in the Middle East* (New York: St. Martin's, 1992), 73–104.

21. Peter J. Schraeder and Hamadi Redissi, "The Upheavals in Egypt and Tunisia: Ben Ali's Fall," *Journal of Democracy* 22 (July 2011): 5–19.

22. Joel Beinin and Frédéric Vairel, eds., *Social Movements, Mobilization, and Contestation in the Middle East and North Africa* (Stanford: Stanford University Press, 2011).

23. Tarek Masoud, "The Upheavals in Egypt and Tunisia: The Road to (and from) Liberation Square," *Journal of Democracy* 22 (July 2011): 20–34.

24. International Crisis Group, "Popular Protests in North Africa and the Middle East (III): The Bahrain Revolt," *ICG Middle East Report,* No. 105, 6 April 2011.

25. Zoltan Barany, "Comparing the Arab Revolts: The Role of the Military," *Journal of Democracy* 22 (October 2011): 24–35.

26. Ayse Tekdal Fildis, "Roots of Alawite-Sunni Rivalry in Syria," *Middle East Policy* 19 (Summer 2012): 148–56; Daniel Pipes, "The Alawi Capture of Power in Syria," *Middle Eastern Studies* 25 (October 1989): 429–50.

27. International Crisis Group, "Popular Protests in the North Africa and the Middle East (III): The Bahrain Revolt."

28. Scheherezade Faramarzi, "Clampdown in Bahrain: When Protesters Called for a Republic, the U.S. Position Changed, Allowing a Saudi Invasion," *Nation,* 12 September 2011, 41–42.

29. Dirk Vandewalle, *Libya Since Independence: Oil and State-Building* (Ithaca: Cornell University Press, 1998).

12

THE GLOBAL CONTEXT

Marc F. Plattner

Marc F. Plattner *is coeditor of the* Journal of Democracy *and vice-president for research and studies at the National Endowment for Democracy. This essay is a revised version of a paper first presented at the annual International Meeting in Political Studies in Estoril, Portugal in June 2011. It originally appeared in the October 2011 issue of the* Journal of Democracy.

The ultimate outcome of the revolts that have been sweeping the Arab world during 2011 remains almost impossible to predict, yet they have already had a dramatic impact on global perceptions of the fortunes of democracy. These uprisings broke out at a moment when democracy seemed to be mired in a period of decline. After the extraordinary progress that democracy had achieved during the last quarter of the twentieth century—what Samuel P. Huntington had famously labeled the "third wave" of democratization—it was perhaps inevitable that its global advance would falter.

That is what finally happened during the first decade of our current century. There was no reverse wave on the scale that Huntington had identified in earlier epochs, but signs of democratic decline did begin to appear in the annual Freedom House survey *Freedom in the World* for 2006.[1] Discouraging evidence mounted over the succeeding years, and the survey for 2010 reported a fifth straight year of decline, with the number of electoral democracies in the world having shrunk to 115 (from a high of 123) and the number of countries designated as Free having shrunk to 87 (from a high of 90).[2]

Moreover, nondemocratic countries had increasingly begun cooperating with one another and displaying a new level of confidence and assertiveness. The final months of 2010 alone, as the narrative accompanying the Freedom House survey pointed out, witnessed China's efforts to counter the awarding of the Nobel Peace Prize to dissident intellectual Liu Xiaobo through diplomatic intimidation and crackdowns on domestic critics; blatantly rigged parliamentary elections in Hosni Mubarak's Egypt; similarly rigged elections in Belarus followed by brutal repression of protesters and arrests of opposition candidates; a second prison sentence for Russian dissident entrepreneur Mikhail Khodorkovsky based on charges widely seen as fraudulent; and a move by Venezuelan president Hugo Chávez to assume decree powers before a newly elected legislature came into office.[3]

Amid this bleak landscape, however, a seemingly minor event occurred in the small and impoverished town of Sidi Bouzid in central Tunisia. It was there, on 17 December 2010, that a 26-year-old fruit vendor, Mohamed Bouazizi, set himself on fire in order to protest his ill treatment by local officials. This desperate act touched off demonstrations that quickly spread to other parts of the country. In less than a month, the decades-old dictatorship of Tunisian president Zine al-Abidine Ben Ali, generally regarded as one of the Arab world's stablest regimes, came tumbling down in what came to be called the Jasmine Revolution. The spark set off in Tunisia ignited a series of protests across the Arab Middle East. By February 11, persistent and massive demonstrations in Cairo's Tahrir Square—watched on television across the world—had forced Mubarak to step down from the presidency of Egypt. The wave of unrest soon touched virtually every Arab country. In several of them the conflicts to which it gave rise are still raging (and in Libya, Tripoli has just fallen to the rebels). Moreover, the events in Tunisia and Egypt resonated in places as far away as Uganda and even China, where frightened officials clamped down in reaction to nothing more than a few Facebook messages urging the Chinese to start a Jasmine Revolution of their own.

Suddenly, authoritarians around the world, who had been riding high, became newly fearful about maintaining their hold on power and lost much of their previous self-confidence. Many analysts compared the Arab uprisings to the revolutions of 1989–91 in the Soviet bloc, and some went so far as to speak of the beginning of a new "fourth wave" of democratization that might sweep away many of the world's remaining nondemocratic regimes. Subsequently, however, as the transitions in Tunisia and especially in Egypt began to experience setbacks and encounter difficult challenges, and as authoritarians in other Arab countries continued to cling to power, this early enthusiasm became somewhat tempered, and today a more cautious mood prevails.

Some Preliminary Conclusions

Have the events in the Arab world been a "game-changer," reversing what had merely been a short-lived downturn in the fortunes of democracy and prefiguring a new period of global democratic progress? Or did the growing strength of authoritarian regimes prior to 2011 reveal the real underlying trend, from which we have been momentarily distracted by the exciting and dramatic developments that we have been watching unfold in the Middle East? Undoubtedly, the wisest answer is the one that Chinese premier Zhou Enlai supposedly gave in 1972 when asked for his assessment of the French Revolution: "It's too soon to tell."[4] Still, even at this early stage, it is worth trying to draw some preliminary conclusions.

The first is that the events of 2011 have clearly disproved the view that the Arab world was the one global region essentially impervious to the spread of democracy. This proposition was not implausible. The Arab countries, with the possible and at best partial exceptions of Lebanon and Iraq, had managed to evade the global resurgence of democracy that had touched every other region during the third wave. Unlike in much of the rest of the world, people in Arab countries opposing tyrannical regimes had a discourse and a worldview other than liberal democracy to which they could appeal—namely, Islamism. It has been widely speculated that if existing Arab regimes were exposed to genuinely free elections, their citizens would vote for Islamists rather than democrats. It is still far too soon to be confident that such speculation is misguided—we will have to see how Tunisians and Egyptians actually vote when they are given the opportunity.

It is clear, however, that the Arab protest movements invoked universal principles of human dignity, freedom, and democracy along with nationalist notions of citizenship rather than any specifically religious or sectarian slogans (or anti-Western ones, for that matter). While this hardly guarantees that Islamism and sectarian strife have no future in the Arab countries, it does prove that the discourse of liberal democracy can appeal to a considerable segment of Arab public opinion, and especially to the young. This suggests that proponents of democracy have at least a fighting chance in the struggle to shape the future of the region.

Although Tunisians and Egyptians have explicitly set out on a course meant to culminate in a transition to democracy, there are many obstacles in their path. As of now, prospects look brightest in Tunisia, which scholars have long seen as having the Arab world's most promising social and economic "preconditions" for democracy—a relatively advanced economy, an educated populace, little in the way of sectarian or ethnic divides, and a fairly moderate brand of Islam. The decision by the Tunisian transitional authorities to postpone elections for a constituent assembly from July until October 2011, and the acceptance of this change by the country's principal political forces, constitute a positive sign, as the postponement will give liberal forces more time to build new parties. Indeed, one may detect among some supporters of democracy a tinge of regret that the protests spread so quickly beyond Tunisia, making it impossible for providers of democracy assistance to focus their energies and resources on trying to help make Tunisia a model for Arab democracy.

But the events in Tunisia were soon overshadowed by those in Egypt, the largest and most influential country in the Arab region, and one whose geopolitical importance far exceeds that of Tunisia. Egypt faces far greater challenges in achieving a successful transition to democracy than does Tunisia. Egypt is not only a much more populous country, with more than eighty-million inhabitants, but also a much poorer one. It has strong Islamist movements—not only the Muslim Brotherhood, whose democratic commitment remains in doubt, but also even more radical salafist groups—as well as a significant minority of Coptic Christians that has been the target of discrimination and sectarian violence. Egypt's interim rulers during the transition are not a civilian body, as in Tunisia, but the Supreme Council of the Armed Forces, representing a military that had been a key pillar of the Hosni Mubarak regime, who himself had once been commander of the air force. Some analysts deny that Egypt has experienced a genuine revolution at all, claiming that the military still holds power and is likely to try to continue wielding it behind the scenes, Pakistan-style, even after a transition to an elected government. Only an optimist would predict a successful democratic outcome for the Egyptian transition that is now in process—but the dedication and energy of the forces that sparked Egypt's uprising against Mubarak may yet prove the optimists correct.

A Monumental Task

In the other Arab countries that have experienced large-scale protests and violent conflict, the prospects for a transition to stable democracy are even less favorable. In Bahrain the protestors were crushed, at least for the time being, with the aid of Saudi military forces. In Syria, the regime continues to slaughter its citizens, and despite the incredible courage displayed by the resistance, it has been unable to unite politically. Yemen has descended into multisided civil strife, and it is hard to forecast how the crisis there can be resolved. Even if Assad or Saleh were to fall, building democracy atop the rubble generated by so much violence and loss of life would be a monumental task.

A comparable challenge confronts Libya, where the opposition now appears to have driven the Qadhafi regime from power. The rebels' political leadership, the Transitional National Council (TNC), has now been recognized by most key countries, and for the most part its official actions and pronouncements have been hearteningly democratic. Yet doubts persist about the democratic bona fides of some elements within rebel ranks, and it is far from clear whether the TNC will be able to exercise control over the military commanders who defeated Qadhafi's forces on the battlefields. The "revolutionary legitimacy" of the fighters may trump the democratic goals proclaimed by the political leadership. So there are really only two cases—Tunisia and

Egypt—where democratic transitions can plausibly be said to be already under way.

Of course, in October 1989 it might have been said that Poland and Hungary were the only two East European countries that had embarked on a democratic transition. Yet at that time, there also had not been any outbreaks of armed conflict elsewhere in the region. As Lucan Way argues later in this volume,[5] the analogy between the Arab revolutions and those of 1989 breaks down in a number of respects, even if the events in both regions involved a cascading series of challenges to dictatorial rulers in countries that were geographically and culturally related. The regimes in Eastern Europe and the Soviet Union were all of the same type, belonged to the same ideological and geopolitical camp, and were sustained by Moscow. In the Middle East, by contrast, there was a wide variety of different types of nondemocratic regimes—civil and military, religious and secular, monarchical and republican. In addition, the region was split between pro-Western and anti-Western governments, as well as being divided by the other fault lines that run through the Arab world—Shia versus Sunni and anti-Iranian versus pro-Iranian. Thus, even if the pattern of the protests in the various Arab countries displayed significant similarities and unmistakably reflected a process of "contagion," there is every reason to expect that subsequent political developments will take different courses in different countries.

Some have likened the Arab uprisings to the so-called color revolutions in postcommunist countries, but here the differences are even more clear-cut. Although the color revolutions in Georgia in 2003, Ukraine in 2004, and Kyrgyzstan in 2005 obviously were each influenced by their predecessors, as well as by earlier instances in which authoritarian leaders were ousted in Serbia, Slovakia, Romania, and Bulgaria, these cases all followed an "electoral model" based on contesting elections and protesting against falsified results, and they were largely peaceful. The connection linking the color revolutions was a much slower process of diffusion over a period of years, with democratic oppositions in one country learning from the techniques and experiences used elsewhere—not the kind of rapid contagion that quickly infected almost the entire Arab world.

Others, including Anne Applebaum, have more convincingly compared the recent Arab events to the European revolutions of 1848.[6] These were uprisings that spread very rapidly from country to country but took quite different forms in different places. Most of the 1848 revolutions, even the initially successful ones, were soon overturned. Yet it is generally acknowledged that, over the longer run, many of the ideas and movements that inspired them eventually triumphed. We cannot know at this point whether in the long run democracy will triumph in the Arab world, and it would be rash to ignore the still-potent influence of various strands of Islamism. Yet if democracy does finally prevail, the Arab revolutions of 2011 will no doubt be seen as a key milestone along the way.

A Two-Sided Struggle

But have the Arab revolutions altered the global balance between democratic and authoritarian forces in the contemporary world? Based on what we know so far, they certainly represent at least a temporary boost for the democrats. First, they have once again demonstrated the universal appeal of democracy. This does not mean that it is attractive to every individual. Antiliberal and antidemocratic worldviews have always had their adherents and no doubt will continue to do so. But it does mean that there are substantial numbers of people in every contemporary society who would prefer that their country be governed democratically and that their individual rights be protected.

At the same time, the Arab revolutions have proven that authoritarian regimes are not as formidable as they may appear. During the crest of the third wave, as dictatorships kept falling around the world, there had been a tendency to see them all as doomed by the inexorable advance of democracy. But by the time that the fall of the Berlin Wall had become a distant memory, and authoritarian regimes in such places as China, Burma, Cuba, Iran, much of the former Soviet Union, and most of the Arab Middle East had proved their ability to survive, the pendulum in scholarly thinking had begun to swing to the other side. An entire political science literature grew up to explain what China scholar Andrew Nathan labeled "authoritarian resilience."[7] A significant subset of this literature focused on the Middle East, explaining how Arab autocrats had successfully adapted superficially democratic-looking institutions such as parliamentary elections to shore up authoritarian rule. Partly as a result, political scientists studying the Middle East were taken completely by surprise when popular revolutions brought down the Ben Ali and Mubarak regimes with such remarkable swiftness.

Of course, not all Arab authoritarians would go so easily. Rulers in Bahrain, Libya, Syria, Yemen, and elsewhere have fought for power tenaciously and have been able to rely upon the support of substantial elements within their societies. A key factor in these struggles has been the role of the armed forces, which is the subject of an article by Zoltan Barany in this volume.[8] Barany points out that the quick success of the Tunisian and Egyptian revolutions owed much to the relatively independent standing of each country's military, which could look forward to a decent institutional future if it facilitated a change of regime.

In Bahrain and Syria, by contrast, the armed forces (or at least their leaderships) belonged to sectarian minorities—Sunnis in Bahrain and Alawites in Syria—whose fate would be endangered by democratic change, and thus far they have continued to support the regime (though there have been some reports of defections in the Syrian armed forces). In Libya and Yemen, the armed forces suffered internal splits, leading to civil wars whose final results are still in doubt. The importance of the armed forces in these cases reminds us that efforts at democratic change usually involve a two-sided struggle. To evaluate such efforts properly, therefore, we must consider not only the strategies and demands of opposition groups, but also the strategies and the resolve of authoritarian rulers.

Another factor that came to the fore during the Arab revolutions is the capacity of new communications technologies to promote democratic change. On this subject as well, the pendulum of scholarly thinking had swung quickly. After an outburst of euphoria reflecting the notion that Twitter and Facebook were tools with an inherently democratic character that would keep dictators permanently on the defensive, other scholars began to examine how "networked authoritarianism" could use these same tools to counter and even to get the better of the democratic opposition.[9] The Arab revolutions suggest that, at least for the time being, these tools seem more dangerous than helpful to authoritarians, especially in their remarkable ability to help mobilize large numbers of people in a very short time.

One problem with using the new technologies to achieve rapid mobilization, however, is that the young people at the forefront of these efforts usually are very skilled at communications strategies but have little experience in devising political strategies. This partly accounts for the often-noted fact that the Arab uprisings were "leaderless revolutions," which may be fine at the popular-mobilization stage but is not a terribly helpful circumstance when it comes to navigating the potentially treacherous currents of democratic transition.

The new communications technologies are likely to be a key battleground in future struggles between authoritarians and democrats, in some ways resembling a classic arms race, with one side making offensive advances and the other coming up with defensive capabilities to thwart them.

An arms race is not a bad metaphor for the overall struggle that lies ahead. Although a number of Arab authoritarian regimes have been deposed or shaken, authoritarians elsewhere still seem firmly in the saddle—especially in China, the most successful and by far the most important of all nondemocratic regimes in the world today. Popular demands for individual rights and democracy will continue to be voiced in autocratic states, but the rulers of those states will continue to respond with brutal repression when they deem it necessary in order to maintain their power. In some cases—particularly in China—they will also respond with cunning and efficiency. In those countries, democratic oppositions may seem overmatched, but over the long run there is one critical factor in their favor—namely, democracy's superior legitimacy.

Andrew Nathan, who coined the term "authoritarian resilience" in a 2003 article in the *Journal of Democracy,* wrote a new article in 2009 that he titled "Authoritarian Impermanence." Though his estimate of the capabilities of the Chinese government had not diminished, he emphasized its potentially fatal flaw. I close by quoting him at length:

> [L]ike all contemporary nondemocratic systems, the Chinese system suffers from a birth defect that it cannot cure: the fact that an alternative form of government is by common consent more legitimate. Even though the regime claims to be a Chinese form of democracy on the grounds that it serves the people and rules in their interest, and even though a majority of Chinese citizens today accept that claim, the regime admits, and everyone knows, that its authority has never been subject to popular review and is never intended to be. In that sense, the regime is branded as an expedient, something temporary and transitional needed to meet the exigencies of the time. Democratic regimes, by contrast, often elicit disappointment and frustration, but they confront no rival form that outshines them in prestige. Authoritarian regimes in this sense are not forever. For all their diversity and longevity, they live under the shadow of the future, vulnerable to existential challenges that mature democratic systems do not face.[10]

—1 September 2011

NOTES

1. Arch Puddington, "The 2006 Freedom House Survey: The Pushback Against Democracy," *Journal of Democracy* 18 (April 2007): 125–37.

2. Arch Puddington, "The Freedom House Survey for 2010: Democracy Under Duress," *Journal of Democracy* 22 (April 2011): 18.

3. Puddington, "The Freedom House Survey for 2010," 17–31.

4. Chas Freeman, a retired U.S. foreign-service officer who was present when Zhou Enlai supposedly gave this response to U.S. president Richard Nixon, has recently stated that it was based on a misunderstanding, and that Zhou thought he was responding to a question about the French events of 1968. But as Freeman aptly remarked, this misunderstanding was "too delicious to invite correction." Richard McGregor, "Zhou's Cryptic Caution Lost in Translation," *Financial Times,* 10 June 2011.

5. See chapter 12 in this volume.

6. Anne Applebaum, "In the Arab World, It's 1848—Not 1989," *Washington Post,* 21 February 2011.

7. Andrew J. Nathan, "China's Changing of the Guard: Authoritarian Resilience," *Journal of Democracy* 14 (January 2003): 6–17.

8. See chapter 13 in this volume.

9. Rebecca MacKinnon, "Liberation Technology: China's 'Networked Authoritarianism,'" *Journal of Democracy* 22 (April 2011): 32–46; and Evgeny Morozov, "Liberation Technology: Whither Internet Control?" *Journal of Democracy* 22 (April 2011): 62–74.

10. Andrew J. Nathan, "China Since Tiananmen: Authoritarian Impermanence," *Journal of Democracy* 20 (July 2009): 37–40.

13

THE LESSONS OF 1989

Lucan Way

Lucan Way is associate professor of political science at the University of Toronto and coauthor (with Steven Levitsky) of Competitive Authoritarianism: Hybrid Regimes After the Cold War *(2010). This essay originally appeared in the October 2011 issue of the* Journal of Democracy.

Since it began, the "Arab Spring" has been subject to a proliferation of comparisons with 1989, and rightly so.[1] Two decades after the collapse of communism in Eastern Europe, we have learned a great deal about regime transitions—lessons that can improve our understanding of events in the Middle East and North Africa (MENA) today. Unfortunately, the comparison does not make one optimistic about democracy's near-term prospects there. The similarities and differences with 1989 suggest that more autocrats will hang on in 2011, and that those countries which do witness authoritarian collapse will be less likely to democratize than their European counterparts were.

Both 1989 and 2011 caught regional experts completely off guard, as protest and crisis spread across regimes that almost all observers had seen as exceptionally stable. In 1989, Mikhail Gorbachev's liberalization in the USSR and the fall of communism in Poland inspired previously quiescent populations and moribund oppositions to take to the streets and demand change in Hungary, Czechoslovakia, East Germany, Bulgaria, and finally Romania. Such unprecedented mobilizations in turn terrified incumbents into making extraordinary concessions. Change in the MENA region came even more suddenly after the self-immolation of a lone Tunisian street vendor, Mohamed Bouazizi, in late 2010 sparked nationwide protests that eventually affected almost all countries from Morocco to Iran.

The events of 1989 and 2011 provide stark examples of how the mere sight of change in one country can have an explosive impact on seemingly stable autocracies nearby. Since the inner workings of nondemocratic regimes are hidden, it is often difficult for outsiders to assess their real strength. Dramatic examples of regime change next door may (rightly or wrongly) convince activists that regimes they once thought invincible are in fact quite vulnerable and motivate people to take to the streets.

The demonstration effect of transitions nearby also offers oppositions new strategies and symbols for mobilizing support.[2] Thus, Bouazizi's extreme expression of discontent in Tunisia inspired self-immolations in nearby Algeria, Egypt, and Mauritania. As a result, the contagion of regime crisis can spread to countries where populations have long been quiescent and where domestic conditions may not have been conducive to protest.

Comparison of these two sets of cases, however, also suggests the limits of diffusion alone as a force for regime change. The changes in Europe in 1989 proved so deep and long-lasting because diffusion was backed up by a basic transformation in the regional balance of power and the sudden elimination of a key source of communist stability. Gorbachev's decision to end the Soviet Union's extensive backing of communist regimes in Central and Eastern Europe created qualitatively new challenges to authoritarian survival in the region. Like their Central and East European counterparts in 1989, many Arab autocrats now face unprecedented unrest at home. Yet many if not most Middle Eastern autocracies retain the coercive and diplomatic resources that have kept their regimes in place for so long. Elements of the external environment that have bolstered these regimes for generations (for example, U.S. financial support and the Arab-Israeli conflict) have changed little.

The upshot is that 2011 in the Middle East is not 1989 in Eastern Europe. The Arab autocracies of today enjoy better survival prospects than did the communist autocracies of yesterday. Indeed, the contradictory results of the Arab Spring so far—including authoritarian retrenchment in Bahrain, massive repression in Syria, and instability in Libya and Yemen—illustrate the paradoxical influence of diffusion in the absence of other structural changes. As long as the structural underpinnings of authoritarianism remain, diffusion is unlikely to result in democratization.

At the same time, the character of diffusion in the Arab world may ultimately be more conducive to authoritarian retrenchment than was the case in Europe two decades ago. In 1989, demonstration effects all pointed to the dangers of hard-line repression. It was lost on no one that the sole East European autocrat to hold out against any reform, Romania's Nicolae Ceauşescu, fell to a military coup, was shot on Christmas Day, and had his body displayed on television—a very public lesson to other heads of one-party regimes trying to decide whether to liberalize or hang onto power at all costs. Indeed, after witnessing these events during a visit to Romania, Julius Nyerere, the leader of Tanzania's single-party regime, decided to initiate a transition to multiparty rule. As he told a journalist, "When you see your neighbour being shaved, you should wet your beard. Otherwise you could get a rough shave."[3] In contrast to Eastern Europe, the MENA region so far has been host to a larger number of autocrats who have shown that popular demands for regime change can be put down with force. At the same time, the trial of former Egyptian president Hosni Mubarak may convince other autocrats that yielding power is more likely to result in a "rough shave" than holding on at all costs.

Why Autocrats Fall

Yet as Ceauşescu's example shows, authoritarian survival is determined by more than just the desire of autocrats to hold on. More often than not, autocrats let go of power not because they want to, but because key political, economic, and military allies force them to give up after deciding that the regime is no longer worth supporting. The readiness of elites to back the regime in a crisis is generally more decisive to authoritarian survival than the number of protesters in the streets. Thus Tunisia's President Zine al-Abidine Ben Ali was forced out of the country by angry crowds of thousands which, though sizeable by Tunisian standards, were hardly large enough to overwhelm the military and police. By contrast, the rulers of the Islamic Republic of Iran withstood protests by hundreds of thousands over six months following a fraudulent election in June 2009. Indeed, leaders who can keep the support of crucial elites are likely to survive even severe crises. From 1989 through 1991, communist regimes whose elites remained cohesive were able to survive significant mass protests (China) and severe economic downturns (Cuba and North Korea).

What makes regime elites in some countries willing to hold on in the face of crisis while in other cases they quickly run for the exits? Today, students of authoritarian durability focus largely on the importance of institutionalized elite access to power and patronage.[4] Those authoritarian regimes that provide stable mechanisms to regulate leaders' access to material goods—especially through political parties—lengthen time horizons and create incentives for long-term loyalty to the existing regime. According to this argument, allies will remain loyal as long as the regime has the capacity to pay them off.

Yet the sudden communist collapse of 1989, like the fall of Ben Ali and Mubarak more recently, shows that even the most extensive and well-established patronage-based regimes are vulnerable to sudden collapse and mass defections. In Tunisia and Egypt, high unemployment and exorbitant food prices fed mass-level discontent; yet the regimes benefited from positive economic growth in 2010, had plenty of money to pay their police personnel and soldiers, and felt no shortage of patronage to hand out to top civilian and security officials.

Indeed, strictly material incentives offer a weak source of cohesion for regimes in crisis.[5] If the crisis makes those near the top of the regime doubt that it will still exist in a year, they may calculate that they will have less to lose and more to gain by joining the opposition. As Steven Levitsky and I have argued, the most robust authoritarian regimes are those that augment patronage with nonmaterial ties. These ties bolster trust within the elite during times of crisis and make it more costly for high-level allies to defect. Nonmaterial connections include shared ethnicity or ideology in a context of deep ethnic or ideological cleavage.

The strongest and most enduring bonds, however, may be the ones forged amid armed revolutionary struggle. As Samuel P. Huntington noted a generation ago, revolutions are "history's most expeditious means of producing fraternity."[6] Further, revolutionary struggle is often accompanied by strong partisan ties and the sense of a "higher cause" that may motivate leaders to hold on even if the regime looks vulnerable and patronage is threatened.

Finally, and perhaps most important, revolutionary struggle frequently creates strong ties between the political rulers and the security forces. Having emerged out of the revolutionary struggle, security forces are often deeply committed to the survival of the regime and infused with the ruling ideology—all of which enhances discipline. Violent revolutionary struggle tends to produce a generation of leaders with the "stomach" for violent repression.

The existence or absence of a recent revolutionary struggle largely explains which communist regimes survived 1989 and which did not. The ones that outlasted the end of the Cold War—China, Cuba, Laos, North Korea, Vietnam—were all led by veterans of revolutionary struggles.[7] Regime survival was particularly striking in China, which faced massive protests in 1989, and Cuba and North Korea, which suffered severe economic decline in the early 1990s when Soviet aid disappeared. By contrast, most East European communist regimes did not emerge out of a prolonged violent struggle and collapsed despite maintaining the kind of institutionalized ruling-party structures that are said to foster authoritarian stability. Similarly, in Yugoslavia and the USSR, where the revolutionary generation had mostly died off by 1989, rulers lacked an *esprit de corps* strong enough to withstand serious challenges. As in Tunisia and Egypt, there was little to hold these regimes together in the event of a crisis.

Iran, grounded in revolutionary struggle, is perhaps the MENA region's most robust regime. Among other legacies, the 1979 Islamic Revolution and the Iran-Iraq War of 1980–88 helped to generate ideologically motivated and effective security forces including the Islamic Revolutionary Guard Corps and its paramilitary auxiliary, the Basij, which is considered "one of the Islamic regime's primary guarantors of domestic security."[8] The strength and motivation of these forces may explain why the Iranian regime has survived years of international isolation as well as the massive 2009 protests, which were about as large and sustained as those we have seen more recently in Egypt, and much more extensive than those in Tunisia.

Other countries in the Middle East lack such a revolutionary tradition but possess other nonmaterial ties that bolster cohesion during crisis. In Bahrain and Syria, the regimes rely on the intense support of minority groups. In Bahrain, many in the Sunni minority view the Sunni monarchy as key to defending their interests from the Shia majority. In Syria, President Bashar al-Assad's chief weapon against dissent has been a military and intelligence establishment controlled by his fellow Alawites, members of a religious minority that forms about a tenth of the population. Minority backing is not an absolute guarantee against collapse: Protests may grow too large for even a cohesive military to handle, or things may get so bad that minorities abandon their former patrons. On the whole, however, minority backing provides a potentially critical source of high-level cohesion that other regimes lack.

In still other cases, such as that of Libya, autocrats have relied on family ties. In such "sultanistic" regimes,[9] the ruler's sons, brothers, and in-laws control the country's main economic and administrative resources. Autocrats in these cases consciously weaken the state, both by filling it with cronies picked more for loyalty than competence and by starving those parts of it not controlled by close allies. Thus in Libya, Muammar Qadhafi severely underfunded the military while ensuring that his sons commanded the most highly trained and best-equipped militias.[10] Such family ties gave the regime a reliable, if small, base of support in the security forces. In contrast to Tunisia and Egypt, where professionalized militaries drove Ben Ali and Mubarak out, the army in Libya was too poor and weak to force Qadhafi from power. Qadhafi was able to rely on the unswerving support of his militias in the face of international isolation and five months of NATO bombing. At the same time, gutting the state and relying on cronies created its own problems. By weakening the state, Qadhafi made his regime vulnerable to the kind of sudden breakdown in social order that left eastern Libya under the control of an inchoate opposition in early 2011. Such weakness, together with NATO attacks, forced the regime to its knees in August.

Why Democratization Succeeds

But even when opposition does succeed in ousting dictators, democracy is far from guaranteed. In mid-2011, autocrats in much of the Middle East were on the defensive, promising reforms that eight months ago would have seemed unimaginable. After Mubarak fell, for instance, the ruling Supreme Council of the Armed Forces (SCAF) made significant concessions that included putting Egypt's former president on trial. "[T] he generals," one report notes, "seem anxious to please the crowd, fearful, perhaps, that they may become the next target."[11] In a similar fashion, ex-communists throughout the former Soviet Union reacted to the failure of the August 1991 hard-liners' coup by abolishing the Communist Party and proclaiming their support for democratic change. Russia's President Boris Yeltsin promised to fundamentally reform the KGB. Yet in the absence of a well-entrenched civil society, social pressures that had stimulated political reform proved unsustainable over the medium term. Unchecked by any well-organized liberal opposition, autocrats throughout the former Soviet Union rapidly regrouped after the initial shock of transition. Yeltsin changed his mind and kept many of the old KGB structures in place. Today, free media and competitive elections that had once seemed irreversible are no more than a distant memory.

Such rapid retrenchment is made easier by the fact the most people have short memories. In the early 1990s, public opinion throughout the former Soviet Union was seized by hatred of communism, which citizens associated with empty shelves, shoddy products, and geriatric leaders. A few years of economic collapse and hyperinflation changed all that, turning the communist era into something remembered much more fondly as a time of stable expectations, guaranteed benefits, and global power. Such nostalgia has been one source of support for Vladimir Putin in Russia. In Moldova, such feelings helped to bring the Communist Party back to power in 2001. In Poland and Hungary, ex-communists were able to win elections just a few years after communism's fall.

In countries such as Tunisia and Egypt, it is almost inevitable that within a few years—if not sooner—the old regime will look a lot better to a lot of people. There is scant reason to think that new leaders will have an easier time solving the problems of corruption, inflation, and unemployment that helped to spark the protests. Further, Egypt's transition has already brought renewed sectarian strife and increased crime that may be blamed on regime change. As in much of the former Soviet Union, democracy is likely to be seen by many as synonymous with chaos.

None of this means, however, that democratization is doomed to fail. Since 1989, all the countries of Central Europe and even most of those in the Balkans have become democratic. The resurgence of ex-communists in Hungary and Poland did not kill democracy there. What made the difference in these countries?

Based on the postcommunist experience, there are a few things that we now know are *less* important. First, constitutional design matters little. Many scholars have argued that emerging democracies with stronger legislatures were more likely to survive than those with powerful presidencies.[12] Yet the postcommunist experience suggests that a strong presidency was as much the result of authoritarianism as its cause.[13] Russia and Belarus acquired their "superpresidential" regimes in 1993 and 1996, respectively—*after* autocrats had already violently disbanded each country's parliament. Generally, the degree of presidentialism correlated very highly with a country's distance from Western Europe—the farther away, the greater the likelihood of authoritarianism and strong presidents rather than democracy and weaker presidents. Finally, there is little evidence that the formal powers of legislatures played a role in East European democratization.[14] Constitutional rules were widely ignored throughout the region. For example, both Serbia's Slobodan Milošević and Slovakia's Vladimír Mečiar were far more powerful than their countries' laws dictated; and their ousters by democratic forces had almost nothing to do with any formal legislative powers.

Next, the postcommunist experience suggests that we should pay less attention to proximate factors such as the mode of transition. Initially, many thought that democracy's success would hinge on whether opposition and incumbents made transitional "pacts" to ensure long-term democratic stability. Indeed, pacts played an important role in facilitating stable transitions in a few cases in Latin America such as those of Venezuela and Colombia in 1958. Yet the postcommunist experience reminds us that—more often than not—agreements made amid the chaos of the transition have little staying power. When Poland's Solidarity, for instance, won virtually all competitively elected parliamentary seats in the June 1989 elections, an agreement that guaranteed the Communist Party a legislative majority suddenly went out the window. Indeed, democratization occurred both in East European countries that experienced pacted transitions (Hungary and Poland) and in those that did not (the Czech Republic and Romania).

With the passage of twenty years, it has become clear that democratization prevailed across Central and Eastern Europe thanks mainly to long-range structural factors. First, the level of economic development seems to have been important. Of the ten richest postcommunist countries in 1990,[15] Russia is the only one where democracy failed to take root—an exception explained in part by Russia's heavy dependence on natural-resource wealth, a dependence that is widely considered to promote authoritarianism. But the single most important factor facilitating democratization was the strength of ties to the West. While relatively developed countries like the Czech Republic and Hungary would likely have democratized even absent the European Union, the EU played a central role in other parts of Europe such as Albania, Romania, and Serbia, where domestic conditions (underdevelopment or severe ethnic tensions) were unfavorable to democratic development.

Indeed, with the possible exception of Mongolia, the only stable democracies that emerged after 1989 were those that were offered full membership in the European Union. The EU is unique among regional organizations in its long-term commitment to democracy as a condition of membership. In the 1990s, EU membership came to be seen as synonymous with prosperity, and enlargement became "one of the most important variables of political life."[16] In countries such as Macedonia, Romania, and Slovakia, extensive engagement by European and U.S. actors was key to discouraging authoritarian abuses and promoting a vibrant independent media as well as prodemocratic nongovernmental organizations.

An Unfavorable Environment

It hardly needs stating that the external environment in the Middle East and North Africa is not conducive to democracy. There is obviously no equivalent to the European Union and the region's relations to the West are, to put it mildly, rather fraught. Further, both the threat of radical Islamism and key Western energy interests in the area will continue to make it tempting for Western actors to support non-Islamist authoritarian forces for some time to come. Such factors by themselves do not doom democratic development, but they do suggest that, in stark contrast to Central and Eastern Europe, democratization in the Middle East and North Africa will hinge almost entirely on each country's domestic balance of power between pro- and anti-democratic forces.

In both Tunisia and Egypt, there are reasons for optimism. In proportion to its size, Tunisia has the Arab world's largest middle class and, historically, its strongest labor movement. Egypt also possesses a relatively well-organized opposition, albeit in the form of the Muslim Brotherhood. In both cases, leaders of the revolutions included many relatively young and secular democratic forces that were in many ways similar to the forces that emerged during the "color revolutions" of the early 2000s in Serbia, Georgia, and Ukraine.

Nevertheless, the democratic forces in both Tunisia and Egypt are remarkably weak. Early in 2011, secular and democratic leaders benefited from pent-up frustration with the status quo but were never unified. They also lack well-established organizations capable of penetrating society and mobilizing consistent political support. In many cases, leaders command organizations that have existed for just months or weeks. As a result, secular oppositionists in Egypt and Tunisia pushed to delay elections.

Most critically, as of mid-2011 power in each country remained in the hands of holdovers from the old regime. In Tunisia, veterans of the old order continued to dominate the transitional government. In Egypt, the military was still very much in charge. As Jason Brownlee notes, after Mubarak fell, "the country's generals . . . did not return to the barracks, repeal the Emergency Law (a core aim of January 25th organizers), or transfer executive power to a civilian-led transitional committee."[17] Indeed, the SCAF, its occasional responsiveness to opposition criticism notwithstanding, continued to censor the media and put severe restrictions on protest. The fact that democratic prospects hinge on the magnanimity of longtime authoritarians is troubling to say the least.

At the same time, in both Tunisia and Egypt the best-organized social forces are rooted in traditions of radical Islam and have an uncertain commitment to liberal democracy. In Tunisia, the recently legalized Islamist party known as Ennahda (Renaissance) is by far the most highly organized, extensive, and experienced political force in the country. Although Ennahda bills itself as a moderate Islamic grouping in the mold of Turkey's Justice and Development Party, some fear that its victory in elections might lead to the birth of an undemocratic Islamist government.[18] Still others argue that intransigent secular reactions to al-Nahda promote polarization that will undermine the establishment of a stable democratic order.

In Egypt, the Muslim Brotherhood, which at first did not support protests in January, has now replaced the secular youth as the driving force of change in the country. The young people who filled Cairo's Tahrir Square may know how to use Facebook, but the Brotherhood has a branch in every neighborhood and town. In March, it used religious appeals to urge voters to approve a referendum on early elections that passed overwhelmingly despite strong opposition from newer democratic forces. The Brotherhood is itself facing internal divisions and has so far refrained from seeking executive power. Nevertheless, its dominance—as well as the emergence of more radical Islamic forces such as the salafists—could threaten democratic development. This is especially true if Islamists secure an alliance with the military—an outcome that some fear has already occurred.[19]

Finally, the prospects for democracy are dimmest in Libya. Here, the central challenge is not just the potential dominance of old-regime elites or a civil society weakened by 42 years of quasi-totalitarian rule, but the difficulties that leaders will have in establishing *any* kind of political order—democratic or authoritarian.

In both 1989 and 2011, the world witnessed the surprising vulnerability of many ostensibly stable and entrenched authoritarian regimes. These events have taught us that, just because an autocracy has persisted for many years, we cannot assume that it will remain stable in the face of serious opposition. In order to better understand the potential for authoritarian instability, we must look at what forces hold authoritarian elites together. Those regimes rooted in recent revolutionary struggle often survive even the most severe economic crises or opposition challenges, as did China's rulers in 1989 and Cuba's and North Korea's in the early 1990s. For this reason, Iran may be the most robust authoritarian regime in the MENA region today. By contrast, regimes that lack nonmaterial sources of cohesion are likely to be vulnerable if a strong opposition challenge emerges. At the same time, as we saw in the former Soviet Union, authoritarian collapse hardly guarantees democracy. Given the continued dominance of old-regime actors, the weakness of democratic forces, and the current international environment, some form of authoritarianism is likely to dominate the Middle East and North Africa for a long time to come.

NOTES

The author wishes to thank Jason Brownlee and Jean Lachapelle for their comments on an earlier draft of this essay.

1. Marc Morjé Howard, "Similarities and Differences between Eastern Europe in 1989 and the Middle East in 2011," available at *http://themonkeycage.org/blog/2011/05/30/similarities-and-differences-between-eastern-europe-in-1989-and-the-middle-east-in-2011*.

2. Valerie Bunce and Sharon Wolchik, *Defeating Authoritarian Leaders in Postcommunist Countries* (New York: Cambridge University Press, 2011).

3. Quoted in Colleen Lowe Morna, "Tanzania: Nyerere's Turnabout," *Africa Report*, September–October 1990, 24.

4. See especially Barbara Geddes, "What Do We Know About Democratization after Twenty Years?" *Annual Review of Political Science* 2 (1999): 115–44; Beatriz Magaloni, "Credible Power-Sharing and the Longevity of Authoritarian Rule," *Comparative Political Studies* 41 (April 2008): 715–41; and Bruce Bueno de Mesquita and Alastair Smith, "How Tyrants Endure," *New York Times*, 9 June 2011.

5. Steven Levitsky and Lucan A. Way, *Competitive Authoritarianism: Hybrid Regimes After the Cold War* (New York: Cambridge University Press, 2010).

6. Samuel P. Huntington, *Political Order in Changing Societies* (New Haven: Yale University Press, 1968), 311.

7. The one exception to this pattern is Albania, where—despite continued dominance by veterans of armed struggle—the regime collapsed in 1991, largely due to extreme state weakness.

8. Hossein Aryan, "Iran's Basij Force: The Mainstay of Domestic Security," *Radio Free Europe/Radio Liberty*, 7 December 2008.

9. For the classic analysis and description of sultanistic regimes, see H.E. Chehabi and Juan J. Linz, eds., *Sultanistic Regimes* (Baltimore: Johns Hopkins University Press, 1998).

10. Tony Capaccio, "Coalition Aircraft Watching Qaddafi Son's Elite Unit, U.S. Commander Says," Bloomberg News, 23 March 2011.

11. Richard F. Worth, "Egypt's Next Crisis," *New York Times*, 27 May 2011.

12. The classic statement of this argument was made by Juan J. Linz in these pages more than twenty years ago in "The Perils of Presidentialism," *Journal of Democracy* 1 (Winter 1990): 51–69. See also M. Steven Fish, "Stronger Legislatures, Stronger Democracies," *Journal of Democracy* 17 (January 2006): 5–20.

13. Gerald M. Easter, "Preference for Presidentialism: Postcommunist Regime Change in Russia and the NIS," *World Politics* 49 (January 1997): 184–211.

14. Levitsky and Way, *Competitive Authoritarianism,* ch. 6.

15. Measured in GDP per capita current dollars. Data from World Bank World Development Indicators at *www.worldbank.org.* Includes countries that were not independent as of 1990.

16. Jan Zielonka, "Introduction: Enlargement and the Study of European Integration," in Jacques Rupnik and Jan Zielonka, eds., *The Road to the European Union. Vol. 1, The Czech and Slovak Republics* (Manchester: Manchester University Press, 2003), 1.

17. Jason Brownlee "Egypt's Incomplete Revolution: The Challenge of Post-Mubarak Authoritarianism," 5 July 2011, available at *www.jadaliyya.com/pages/index/2059/egypts-incomplete-revolution_the-challenge-of-post.*

18. Scott Sayare, "Tunisia Is Uneasy Over Party of Islamists" *New York Times,* 15 May 2011.

19. "Muslim Brotherhood Gains Power in Egypt," United Press International, 25 March 2011.

14

THE ROLE OF THE MILITARY

Zoltan Barany

Zoltan Barany *is Frank C. Erwin, Jr. Centennial Professor of Govern-ment at the University of Texas. He is the author of* Building Demo-cratic Armies: Lessons from Africa, Asia, Europe, and the Americas *(forthcoming) and the coeditor of* Is Democracy Exportable? *(2009), which is to be published in Arabic next year. This essay originally ap-peared in the October 2011 issue of the* Journal of Democracy.

No institution matters more to a state's survival than its military, and no revolution within a state can succeed without the support or at least the acquiescence of its armed forces. This is not to say that the army's backing is *sufficient* to make a successful revolution; indeed, revolu-tions require so many political, social, and economic forces to line up just right, and at just the right moment, that revolutions rarely succeed. But support from a preponderance of the armed forces is surely a *neces-sary* condition for revolutionary success. Thus, close scrutiny of what determines that support (or its lack) is in order. Like any other large organization, a military and security establishment has institutional in-terests to safeguard and advance. Its decision—whether to back the re-gime, support its foes, or stay neutral until the dust settles—will depend on several factors.

My goals here are to explore how the armed forces of the Arab world have responded to the recent uprisings there, and why each national military has acted as it has. Questions about the uprisings' causes, the reasons for their failure or success, the power dynamics within opposition forces, or the directions that these polities might take going forward are outside the scope of my inquiry. My focus is limited to the military's role in the six Arab-majority states where considerable bloodshed took place: Bahrain, Egypt, Libya, Syria, Tu-nisia, and Yemen. Aside from the tiny island kingdom of Bahrain in the Persian Gulf, each of these countries was or is ruled by a sultanistic regime under the sway of a despot bound by no apparent term limits:

Hosni Mubarak, Muammar Qadhafi, Bashar al-Assad, Zine al-Abidine Ben Ali, and Ali Abdallah Saleh, respectively.

If all regimes depend on the loyalty of their soldiers and police, sultanistic regimes do so with a particular immediacy born of their rigid authoritarianism and the constant need for naked coercion or its threat. The "sultans," who often come from a military or security background themselves, usually divide the armed forces into separate entities that must compete for resources and influence; they often command them personally or through trusted family members. Notwithstanding these commonalities, the six regimes' experiences ran the gamut from rapid collapse to robust survival. The roles played by the military likewise varied widely.

A large number of internal and external factors shape how an army responds to a revolution. How legitimate is the regime, in the eyes of the soldiers and top security officials as well as those of the general public? How do the armed forces relate to the state and civil society? Does each of the state's various armed organizations get along smoothly with the others and enjoy unity within its own ranks, or are "the guys with guns" divided against themselves by differences of ethnicity and religion or rivalries between ordinary and elite units, soldiers and police, and so on? Do the military and security services have civilian blood (whether recent or even decades old) on their hands?

In general, the stronger a regime's record of satisfying political and socioeconomic demands, the more likely the armed forces will be to prop it up. A state that pays its soldiers generously and otherwise treats them well will be better placed to receive their enthusiastic protection. Services that cooperate with rather than distrust one another, and that are free from internal cleavages (over regime performance, for instance), should likewise be more steadfast in defending the established order. An officer corps that has a record of extensive human-rights abuses is more likely to stick with the regime than to throw its lot in with the demonstrators.

The key external variables are the threat of foreign intervention, the impact of revolutionary diffusion, and the type and degree of education or training that officers may have received abroad. Clearly, the generals' decision to support or suppress an uprising will be affected by their calculations about whether foreign powers might intervene to save the regime or back the rebels. Waves of revolutionary fervor rolling in from abroad may affect not only the protesters but also those who are supposed to face them down. And officers who have participated in training or schooling abroad will probably view a potential invasion from overseas differently than those who have not had such exposure.

Naturally, the relative significance of these variables can and will vary from case to case. One country's generals may view the prospect of foreign intervention, for example, quite differently from the way in which their counterparts elsewhere would. Similarly, ethnoreligious differences within the armed forces may mean much in one country and little or nothing in another. Moreover, these factors may be reinforced or weakened by circumstances that have a bearing on revolutionary outcomes in some contexts but not in others. The point is that to be able to form an educated guess regarding an army's response to an uprising, one must be familiar with the given context. There is no substitute for detailed, particular knowledge of a country and its armed forces.

One of the main reasons why recent Middle Eastern and North African events took so many observers by surprise was the sheer opacity of these countries, especially their military establishments, to outsiders. Gathering reliable information about our six states is extraordinarily difficult. In just a three-page span within her latest book, Sarah Phillips, one of the few Western academics who can claim to be an authority on Yemen, qualifies her assertions about Yemeni military affairs with phrases such as "a point of great contention," "shrouded in secrecy," "notoriously inaccurate self-reported statistics," "extremely vague," "an unknown quantity," "casting further doubt on the reliability of any figures presented," and "accurate figures are still impossible to obtain."[1] Analysts from the U.S. intelligence community who study Tunisia, the most open of these states, were nonetheless baffled by the unexpected course of events there. It is hard not to be sympathetic to the researchers; until recently these regimes seemed so well entrenched and their armed forces so dedicated that, as one expert put it slightly over a decade ago, "even the most professional militaries of the region would not hesitate to intervene in politics to try to maintain the status quo."[2]

Some commentators seeking to find patterns among the Arab uprisings suggested that they failed in countries where rulers told the military to open fire, but triumphed in places where rulers could not stomach killing citizens.[3] That suggestion is incorrect. In our six cases, *every* ruler ordered his military and security agencies to suppress protests by force (including lethal force). In some cases, the generals said yes; in others, they said no because they calculated that their own and their country's interests would be best served by regime change. Our six states can be grouped into three categories defined by how the regular military—as distinct from special elite units and security detachments—responded to the revolt. In Tunisia and Egypt, the soldiers backed the revolution; in Libya and Yemen, they split; and in Syria and Bahrain, they turned their guns against the demonstrators. What explains the disparities?

Siding with the Rebels: Tunisia and Egypt

Tunisia was the country where the wave of unrest began, in mid-December 2010. When it became apparent that the police and security forces would not be able to stop the quickly spreading street demonstrations, President Ben Ali unleashed gangs of thugs and his elite Presidential Guard against the protesters. He also ordered General Rachid Ammar, the army chief of staff, to deploy troops in support of the regime's security detachments. General Ammar rejected this order and was soon placing his men between the security units and the protesters, thereby effectively saving the revolution and forcing Ben Ali into exile. Why did Ammar act this way?

Ben Ali's predecessor, Habib Bourguiba, had deliberately kept soldiers out of politics during his three decades as president (1957–87), even banning them from joining the ruling party. Although in 1978 and 1984, the army answered the government's call to restore order following civil disturbances, the generals resented being told to assume police functions and were happy to have their men return to barracks as soon as the crises had passed.[4] Ben Ali, a police-state apparatchik who overthrew Bourguiba bloodlessly in 1987, continued the policy of keeping the armed forces on the political sidelines. Unlike most other North African armies, Tunisia's had never even attempted a coup, had never taken part in making political decisions, had never been a "nation-building" instrument, and had never joined in economic-development schemes. Ben Ali kept it a small and modestly funded force focused on border defense.[5]

Ben Ali's Tunisia was a police state. As in many other sultanistic regimes, it was a place where the regular military found itself overshadowed by far larger, more amply funded, and more politically influential security agencies run by the Interior Ministry. In order to counterbalance the close professional ties that had developed between Tunisian security agencies and their French counterparts, Ben Ali sent many of his military officers for training in the United States, where some were exposed to programs on the principles of civil-military relations under democracy. Undistracted by politics and despite its meager budget and equipment, the Tunisian military in time came to rank among the Arab world's most professional forces. With its comparatively disadvantaged status and its officers' disdain for the notorious corruption of the presidential clique, the military had no special stake in the regime's survival and no strong reason to shoot fellow Tunisians on the regime's behalf. As soon as Ben Ali found himself forced to turn to the soldiers as his last resort, he was doomed.

Although Egypt's generals also opted to back the uprising, their road to that decision was by no means as clear and straightforward as the path that Tunisia's senior soldiers trod. For the first two-and-a-half weeks of the uprising in Egypt, the country's military elites hedged their bets. The top brass worked quietly to advance its position in the government while some army units were actually detaining and abusing protesters or enabling the police to assault

them. Troops themselves never actually fired on the people, however, nor did the army prevent demonstrators from filling Cairo's
Tahrir Square.[6] When security agents and President Mubarak's loyalists unleashed extensive violence on February 2, whatever credit
his regime still had with the people was shattered, and the soldiers
went over to the side of the rebels. The generals concluded that
Mubarak's mix of concessions (agreeing not to seek reelection or
have his son succeed him) and repression (the February 2 attacks)
had failed, and that rising violence and disorder would only hurt the
military's legitimacy and influence. Thus, on February 10, the Supreme Council of the Armed Forces (SCAF) assumed control of the
country and, the next day, persuaded a reluctant Mubarak to resign
and head for internal exile.

This was a less predictable outcome than the one in Tunisia, for
several reasons. To begin with, Egypt's armed forces have long been
privileged in a way that Tunisia's never were. Although Cairo's Interior Ministry security *apparat* began bulking larger in the 1970s, much
as did Tunis's,[7] the Egyptian military remained a key part of the support base for Mubarak (himself an air force general) and never came
under opposition or media criticism.

The generals were able to make up for their waning political clout,
moreover, with growing economic involvement in everything from
housewares and military-gear production to farming and tourism. The
revenue from these enterprises goes straight to the military's coffers
and is disbursed without state oversight. We can sense the importance
of these business endeavors by noting that Field Marshal Mohamed
Hussein Tantawi, who chairs the SCAF and heads the Defense Ministry, also runs the Ministry of Military Production. Military officers
directly profit from the army's business endeavors through relatively
high salaries plus preferential treatment in medical care, housing, and
transport. And, of course, the armed forces also reap US$1.3 billion
every year in military aid from the United States.

So why did the Egyptian army decline to save Mubarak's regime?
First, military elites despised Gamal Mubarak, the president's son and
putative successor. A businessman, Gamal headed a faction of what
might be called "state entrepreneurs" who, like him, were dedicated to
exploiting his family's status and his ruling-party post in order to profit
from the liberal economic reforms of the past decade.[8] Second, the top
brass were growing anxious about youth alienation and spreading Islamist radicalism, as well as economic malaise and stagnation. Third,
Egypt's soldiers, like Tunisia's, were not pleased to see the regime leaning on—and sluicing ever more privileges to—a large police and security apparatus that in Egypt is thought to have employed as many as
1.4 million people. Finally, Egypt's conscript army has so many ties to
society at large that, even had the generals been willing to shoot dem-

onstrators, many officers and enlisted men would probably have refused to obey such an order.

Divided Loyalties: Libya and Yemen

Although Yemen is far poorer than oil-rich Libya, the two states share many similarities, including low levels of institutional development and towering corruption. Independent public institutions are not to be found. Libya has not had a constitution since 1951. It has no formal head of state (Qadhafi was nominally the "supreme guide" of what he saw as a large clan), its parliament was symbolic, and Qadhafi had decades to sap its governmental institutions (the military included) in order to bolster his highly personalized brand of rule.[9] Corruption is rampant in both countries, but the government in Sana'a "makes even the Karzai regime, in Afghanistan, seem like a model of propriety."[10]

Tribal affiliations, of relatively little consequence in Tunisia and Egypt, are of foremost importance in Yemen and Libya. Saleh and Qadhafi gave most positions of trust, including key military and security commands, to their own tribesmen and close relatives: Both named sons and nephews to head various security agencies and choice military units. In each country, but particularly in Libya, the military and security establishment was divided into numerous organizations that had little contact with one another. The regular military was ostensibly charged with the external defense of the country while the security forces were supposed to protect the regime, though in practice ensuring regime survival was the main mission of *all* these forces.

Soon after protests began, President Saleh cut taxes, hiked food subsidies, and vowed to raise civil-service pay. More important, he promised not to extend his rule beyond 2013 and not to permit his son Ahmed—the commander of the elite Republican Guard—to succeed him. The crowds, initially dominated by students, were not satisfied with these concessions and demanded that Saleh immediately resign. The ensuing violence, and particularly the killing of 52 protesters by security forces on March 18, galvanized the opposition and divided the armed forces.

The biggest loss for the regime was the defection of General Ali Mohsen al-Ahmar, Saleh's tribesman and longtime ally who had distinguished himself over the past decade by fighting Huthi separatists in the north. A dozen generals joined Ahmar. They included the southerner Abdallah al-Qahdi, who had recently been cashiered for refusing to use force against peaceful demonstrators.[11] Although the defense minister insisted that the military was still faithful to Saleh, many ordinary soldiers either went over to General Ahmar and the opposition or simply deserted. To keep his hold on power, Saleh relied on the better-equipped and -trained Republican Guard, Central Security Forces, and elite army units, whose loyalty he retained.

Qadhafi's response to the revolt against him in Libya was to unleash his half-dozen or so paramilitary organizations against his opponents.[12] The security units rather than the regular military were the regime's first line of defense for good reasons. After Lieutenant-Colonel Qadhafi seized power in a bloodless 1969 coup, his fellow army officers attempted to remove him from power four times (most recently in October 1993). Not surprisingly, Qadhafi deliberately neglected the military and gave priority treatment to parallel elite and paramilitary forces, most of them newly established and commanded by his relatives.

Once the uprising broke out, the regime tried to guarantee the regular military's obedience by giving out cash and making threats, by purging commanders who hesitated to use their guns against the rebels, and by holding the families of unit commanders as hostages. Suspecting disloyalty, Qadhafi dismissed his brother-in-law Abdallah Senoussi from his post at the head of the secret service, and kept top army general Abu Bakr Yunis Jabr under house arrest from the beginning of the revolt.[13] Even so, the army and air force units based in and near Benghazi and Tobruk in eastern Libya defected more or less in their entirety, while large segments of units stationed in Kufra, Misrata, the Western Mountains, and Zawiya deserted as well.[14] In order to compensate for the resulting shortage of loyal troops, Qadhafi allegedly brought in mercenaries from sub-Saharan Africa, Europe, and Latin America.[15] Soldiers who continued to fight against the rebels reported that their officers lied by telling them that they were being sent to put down not domestic rebels, but foreign-inspired terrorists.[16]

The divisions in the Yemeni and Libyan armed forces reflected the many and deep-seated divisions in their respective societies. Although the bonds of tribe and kinship do not override every discord, as General Ahmar's example shows, they are tremendously important in determining military attitudes. In addition, coercion and bribery played a role in persuading some segments of the Libyan and Yemeni armed forces to stay with the regime. The threats and bribes were necessary because, as the many defections and desertions show, major segments of the armed forces entertained doubts about the legitimacy of these regimes. Significant external factors included NATO's bombing campaign against Qadhafi, Tripoli's isolation by the international community in general, and the efforts of the Gulf Cooperation Council (a group that Yemen has long been eager to join) to ease Saleh out of power.

By mid-2011, both countries were in a state of civil war, with their militaries still split and the outcome of the fighting uncertain. After months of fighting, the poorly organized rebels were still unable to take Tripoli and other Qadhafi strongholds in western Libya, despite continuing combat support from NATO. On 15 July 2011, the United States joined more than thirty countries in officially recognizing the rebel leadership, the Transitional National Council, as Libya's legitimate government. Nevertheless, Qadhafi appeared as determined as ever to fight on, and held out till late August.[17] The situation in Yemen, meanwhile, remained inconclusive. In June, President Saleh was flown to Saudi Arabia to receive medical treatment after being severely wounded in a rocket attack during clashes between his troops and tribal fighters. In Saleh's absence, the combat between government and opposition forces—the latter made up not only of army defectors and tribal soldiers but also, most worryingly, al-Qaeda fighters—has continued unabated, and an end to the hostilities seems remote.

Sticking with the Status Quo: Bahrain and Syria

Although Bahrain and Syria are widely differing countries with widely differing military establishments, the regime in each reacted similarly to large-scale demonstrations. Sheikh Hamad bin Isa al-Khalifa, Bahrain's monarch, and President Bashar al-Assad, Syria's dictator, both offered a mix of financial concessions and reform vows. When these "soft" measures failed to diminish the size and intensity of the protests, both rulers turned to a "hard" strategy based on force. Their militaries backed them strongly—albeit for different reasons in each country. In Bahrain, moreover, that backing took on a regional quality when Sheikh Hamad's appeal to the Gulf Cooperation Council resulted in the arrival of five-hundred policemen from the United Arab Emirates plus a thousand Saudi troops who came rumbling over the 25-kilometer King Fahd Causeway in armored vehicles.[18]

The Bahraini military is of modest size (the island kingdom has only 1.2 million people) and must contend with several institutional rivals. Many oil monarchies keep their armies small and build up competing security agencies in part out of mistrust, but also in order to satisfy the ambitions of various ruling-family members and to keep different family factions in balance.[19] Bahrain's soldiers are well taken care of: They enjoy good pay, up-to-date weapons, and top-notch training. Still, given the more lucrative career alternatives available, military service is not especially prestigious in Bahrain, and the monarchy has resorted to hiring qualified officers and sergeants from abroad to keep the forces adequately staffed.

The key thing to grasp about the Bahraini military, however, is that it is *not* a national army. Rather, it is a fighting force of Sunni Muslims who are charged with protecting a Sunni ruling family and Sunni political and business elites in a country that majority-Shia Iran has officially claimed as a province since 1957, and where about three of every four or five people are Shia. Bahrain's Sunnis dwell in constant fear of Iranian influence among local Shias, who are barred from sensitive jobs and live under suspicion of wanting to seize power at the first opportunity. Bahrain has no conscription precisely because its ruling elites do not want

Shias bearing arms and receiving military training. It is hardly surprising, then, that Bahrain's Sunni army speedily confirmed its allegiance to Bahrain's Sunni monarchy by suppressing the overwhelmingly Shia revolt that began on 14 February 2011.

The conditions of the armed forces are somewhat different in Syria, although there too sectarian identity has figured in the military's decision to stand firm behind Assad's Baath Party dictatorship and to inflict massive violence in its defense. The Syrian officer corps has been dominated by members of the minority Alawite sect[20] at least since 1955, when Alawites began to control the military section of the Baath Party.[21] The Assad family—Bashar succeeded his father Hafiz as president after the latter's death from natural causes in 2000—also hails from the Alawite community. Tensions between majority Sunnis and Alawites, a traditionally disadvantaged group of hill-country origin that makes up about 15 percent of Syria's population of 23 million, are of long standing. To the extent that there is sectarian peace, it is uneasy, and the threat of coercion is never far from the surface. In February 1982, the Assad regime met the establishment of a Muslim Brotherhood stronghold among Sunnis in the city of Hama with a fierce heavy-weapons assault that lasted for more than three weeks and is believed to have killed tens of thousands.[22]

The Syrian military has some combat experience and is, by regional standards, a capable fighting force. It has done well by the regime and, unlike the Libyan and Tunisian armies, has not had to accept de facto second-place status behind other security formations. To help keep soldiers loyal, the Assad regime permits them a degree of economic involvement. As is common among armies of authoritarian states, the Syrian military is heavily politicized; loyalty to the regime often outweighs skill or professional merit in determining who gets promoted.

Since March 2011, the army has been using tanks and other heavy weapons against largely unarmed protesters, slaughtering hundreds as unrest continues. Although there have been isolated reports of desertions and even fighting among the troops, the military is highly unlikely to turn against the regime, for several reasons.[23] The mostly Alawite top brass considers the rule of Assad and the Baath Party to be legitimate, officers enjoy a privileged position in Syrian politics and society, and the opposition—disorganized and fragmented as it is—would be highly unlikely to improve the military's lot. Moreover, the army's involvement in past episodes of brutality such as the Hama massacre counsels against trying to switch sides. Hence Syria's soldiers, regrettably, have continued to do the dictatorship's dirty work.

Events in the Arab world during 2011 have been consistent with the contention that how a military responds to a revolution is the most reliable predictor of that revolution's outcome. When the army decides not to back the regime (Tunisia, Egypt), the regime is most likely doomed.

Where the soldiers opt to stick with the status quo (Bahrain, Syria), the regime survives. Where the armed forces are divided (Libya, Yemen), the result is determined by other factors such as foreign intervention, the strength of the opposition forces, and the old regime's resolve to persevere.

"Successful" regime change—whether it leads to democracy, an Islamic republic, or socialism—needs, at the very least, the acquiescence of the armed forces. In what direction can we expect future civil-military relations to shift in the Arab states? The evolution of civil-military relations is likely to mirror developments in the overall political sphere. Just as a genuine transition to democracy is somewhat likely only in Tunisia, there is reason to feel the most optimistic about the place which that country's armed forces will find in its emerging, post–Ben Ali polity. After the dictator fled, General Ammar found himself easily the most popular figure in the land and could have expected widespread support had he seized a political role.[24] His clear decision to stand back and let a civilian government assume genuine control and responsibility should earn him lasting respect and will (one hopes) serve as a beneficent example for the future.

It is harder to feel sanguine about democracy's prospects in Egypt, not least because of the prominent political and economic roles that the armed forces have traditionally played there. The military's full withdrawal from politics is hard to imagine given the weight of tradition, the interests that the army feels it has at stake, and the absence from the scene of any cluster of political forces capable of both preventing disorder and governing in a manner acceptable to the high command. The likelihood of the military's departure from the economic sphere is even more remote—too many officers have too much to lose in an immediate material sense.[25]

Some analysts have suggested that Turkey can provide a model for Egypt to emulate, but I disagree.[26] Mustafa Kemal Atatürk's staunchly secular vision of a modern state is unlikely to take root in contemporary Egypt. For realistic Egyptians, it seems to me, post-Suharto Indonesia is the example to aspire to.[27] Over the past twelve years, Indonesia's traditionally powerful military has gradually withdrawn from politics and has been successfully subordinated to democratic civilian control by mostly skillful political elites. The one major flaw in Indonesian civil-military relations is the armed forces' continued economic participation. This problem has been difficult to solve—and, under the circumstances, would be politically unwise to press—given the lack of state resources to compensate the military for the revenue they would lose. In any case, Indonesian generals use a large part of the proceeds from their enterprises to pay for operational expenses that the state's meager defense budget fails to cover.

The prospects of anything resembling democracy arising in Bahrain,

Libya, Syria, and Yemen appear dim, as does the outlook for democratizing their civil-military relations. In fact, I expect the nexus between the governments of Bahrain and Syria and their armed forces to become even closer, because events in those two countries have reminded the political elites there of just how much they rely on the loyalty of their troops. What sorts of polities (and militaries) will eventually emerge from the civil wars in Libya and Yemen is difficult to foretell, although the intensive political and military involvement of Western democracies on behalf of the rebels holds out some hope for Libya's future. Yemen, an enigmatic place at the best of times, has already descended into quasi-anarchy. The solution to Yemen's puzzle, once again, is going to be in the hands of those who carry the guns.

NOTES

1. Sarah Phillips, *Yemen's Democracy Experiment in Regional Perspective: Patronage and Pluralized Authoritarianism* (New York: Palgrave Macmillan, 2008), 69–71.

2. Mehran Kamrava, "Military Professionalization and Civil-Military Relations in the Middle East," *Political Science Quarterly* 115 (Spring 2000): 92.

3. See, for instance, Simon Sebag Montefiore, "Every Revolution Is Revolutionary in Its Own Way," *New York Times,* 26 March 2011.

4. See L.B. Ware, "The Role of the Tunisian Military in the Post-Bourguiba Era," *Middle East Journal* 39 (Winter 1985): 27–47.

5. Ware, "Role of the Tunisian Military," 39.

6. Elisabeth Bumiller, "Egypt Stability Hinges on a Divided Military," *New York Times,* 5 February 2011; and Scott Shane and David D. Kirkpatrick, "Military Caught Between Mubarak and Protesters," *New York Times,* 11 February 2011.

7. Imad Harb, "The Egyptian Military in Politics: Disengagement or Accommodation?" *Middle East Journal* 57 (Spring 2003): 269–90.

8. Wendell Steavenson, "On the Square: Were the Egyptian Protesters Right to Trust the Military?" *New Yorker,* 28 February 2011, 43.

9. Wolfram Lacher, "Libya after Qadhafi: State Formation or State Collapse?" *SWP Comments* 9, March 2011; available at *www.swp-berlin.org/fileadmin/contents/products/comments/2011C09_lac_ks.pdf.*

10. Dexter Filkins, "After the Uprising: Can the Protestors Find a Path Between Dictatorship and Anarchy?" *New Yorker,* 11 April 2011, 42.

11. Tom Finn, "Yemen Showdown Looms as Army Loyalties Divide," *Guardian,* 21 March 2011.

12. See Hanspeter Mattes, "Challenges to Security Sector Governance in the Middle East: The Libyan Case," paper delivered at the Geneva Center for the Democratic Control of the Armed Forces, 12–13 July 2004, 11–17.

13. Lacher, "Libya after Qadhafi," 4.

14. E-mail message to author from Wolfram Lacher, North Africa expert at the German Institute for International and Security Affairs, Berlin, 25 May 2011.

15. Ashish Kumar Sen, "Libyan Rebels: Colombian Female Snipers Fighting for Gadhafi," *Washington Times,* 12 April 2011.

16. C.J. Chivers, "Captive Soldiers Tell of Discord in Libyan Army," *New York Times,* 13 May 2011.

17. Sebnem Arsu and Steven Erlanger, "Libya Rebels Get Formal Backing, and $30 Billion," *New York Times,* 15 July 2011.

18. Kenneth Katzman, "Bahrain: Reform, Security, and U.S. Policy," Congressional Research Service, 95-1013, 21 March 2011, 7.

19. Steffen Hertog, "Rentier Militaries in the Gulf: The Price of Coup-Proofing," *International Journal of Middle East Studies* 43 (August 2011): 400–402.

20. Alawites are often described as a branch of Shia Islam, though the question of their religious categorization is a complicated and somewhat fraught one. For background, see Martin Kramer, "Syria's Alawis and Shi'ism," in idem, ed., *Shi'ism, Resistance, and Revolution* (Boulder, Colo.: Westview, 1987), 237–54.

21. Hanna Batatu, "Some Observations on the Social Roots of Syria's Ruling Military Group and the Causes for Its Dominance," *Middle East Journal* 35 (Summer 1981): 331–44.

22. See Thomas L. Friedman, "Hama Rules," ch. 4 in *From Beirut to Jerusalem* (New York: Farrar, Straus and Giroux, 1989), esp. 77–87.

23. Anthony Shadid, "Syrian Forces Shoot at Protesters Trying to Break Siege of Town in 'Friday of Rage,'" *New York Times,* 30 April 2011, A8.

24. See "No One Is Really in Charge," *Economist,* 27 January 2011.

25. See, for instance, David D. Kirkpatrick, "Egypt Military Aims to Cement Muscular Role in Government," *New York Times*, 16 July 2011.

26. See, for instance, "Egyptians Choose Order over Further Political Upheaval," *IISS Strategic Comments* 17, Comment 13 (March 2011).

27. Harold A. Crouch, *Political Reform in Indonesia after Soeharto* (Singapore: Institute of Southeast Asian Studies, 2010), 127–90.

15

THE IMPACT OF ELECTION SYSTEMS

John M. Carey and Andrew Reynolds

John M. Carey *is John Wentworth Professor in the Social Sciences at Dartmouth College.* **Andrew Reynolds** *is associate professor of political science at the University of North Carolina–Chapel Hill. The present essay is based on the authors' experiences studying and offering advice regarding electoral systems in Egypt, Jordan, Lebanon, the Palestinian Authority, Tunisia, and Yemen. This essay originally appeared in the October 2011 issue of the* Journal of Democracy.

Among their other effects, the seismic political events of late 2010 and early 2011 have set off a wave of actual and proposed electoral reforms throughout the Middle East and North Africa (MENA). This wave has touched countries where long-ruling authoritarian regimes have collapsed as well as those where existing regimes have (so far) managed to retain power. In the first two MENA countries to experience unrest, Tunisia and Egypt, the most pressing electoral issue has been how to choose representative and deliberative bodies—in Tunisia a constituent assembly to rewrite the basic law and in Egypt a new parliament whose tasks will include the naming of a hundred-member constitution-drafting panel. Throughout the region, even in places not at the center of the recent upheavals—Iraq, Israel, Lebanon, and the Palestinian Authority, for instance—the rules for deciding who will sit in parliament are the topic of intense debate.

There is nothing surprising about this: The question of how to elect representative assemblies is a basic issue with which any democratic or would-be democratic society has to contend. Assemblies must reflect and represent the diversity of interests and views within society, deliver majorities that can support legitimate governments and ratify their key decisions, and provide checks on the exercise of executive authority. The track record of parliaments has not been promising on any of these scores in the Arab world, where legislatures are all too often dubiously representative, fecklessly indecisive, and weak in the face of powerful hereditary monarchs or strongman presidents. The pressing question confronting reformers is whether changing the way assemblies are elected can improve their performance.

What are the key criteria by which democrats should evaluate the design of election systems? No single method of elections can be best for all countries and moments. Demographic and historical particularities must weigh in the choice. That said, electoral reformers should pursue certain general goals. These include:

Inclusiveness. Elections should provide a means for new groups— even relatively small ones—to win a measure of representation, and for the assembly to reflect the diversity of society. One element of inclusiveness is the adaptability of electoral systems to rules that provide representation for previously marginalized groups—particularly women, but sometimes specific ethnic and religious groups too.

Minimal distortions. Elections should avoid the danger of a large "winner's bonus" whereby the biggest party or coalition receives a share of seats that far outstrips its share of the popular vote.

Incentives to build coalitions. The rules should encourage likeminded candidates and groups to band together under a single banner. Distrust of parties is deep-seated across much of the MENA region, yet whatever the label (list, movement, alliance, house) they travel under, such formations give voters clearer and more coherent choices than would be available were all politicians lone operators bound solely by personal loyalties.

Individual accountability. Elections should allow voters to reward or punish the performance of individual legislators, not just this or that party or coalition as a whole.

Simplicity. The options that voters face, the decisions that they are expected to make, and the connection between those decisions and who governs should all be as straightforward as possible.

It is, of course, impossible to pursue all these goals or principles to their fullest extent simultaneously. Yet some sets of trade-offs may be better than others. Viewed in light of the broad principles laid out above, the debates and initiatives that the Arab world has seen over the last several months offer a mixture of the promising and the troubling.

Egypt

At the end of President Hosni Mubarak's three decades in power, his ruling National Democratic Party (NDP) dominated a 518-member lower house in which 444 seats were contested in two-member districts by means of a two-round system. An additional 64 seats, elected from the country's 27 governorates, were reserved for women. The final 10 seats were filled by direct presidential appointment and went mainly to Coptic Christians, a religious minority comprising perhaps a tenth of Egypt's total population of 83 million. Article 87 of the 1971 Constitution, reflecting the 1950s-era nationalist and socialist ideology of President Gamal Abdel Nasser (d. 1970), required that within each two-member district at least one winning candidate had to be a worker or a farmer. Voters were *required* to cast two votes, and casting both for the same candidate was not allowed. The occupational quota and the nest of rules for distributing votes that went with it vastly complicated the process of determining winners. The quota had the upshot of giving any candidate whom election administrators listed as a worker or a farmer a significant edge, and opened the door to manipulation—a door that the Mubarak regime used often.[1]

Since Mubarak's February 2011 ouster, the electoral system has been subject to a series of changes at the hands of an opaque military junta. In early February, the panel of senior officers known as the Supreme Council of the Armed Forces (SCAF) dissolved the old parliament. In May, the SCAF released its draft of a new elections law. The generals judged the worker-farmer quota too much of a constitutional fixture to be done away with. Their draft retained it along with the system of two-member districts, but limited that system to two-thirds of the seats. The draft law, which also abolished the set-aside of 64 seats for women (seats which had been seen as levers of NDP manipulation in the old parliament), called for the remaining third of the seats to be contested under the rules of closed-list proportional representation (PR) in governorate-based districts.

After considerable criticism, most of it to the effect that the new law would not open sufficient electoral space for the embryonic movements that had fueled the Tahrir Square uprising, the cabinet produced a new law in July. In the new system, 252 legislators are to be elected from 126 two-member districts, another 252 are to be chosen by closed-list PR in 58 districts (an average of just over four seats per district), and ten members are to be appointed by the president, for a total of 514. The threshold for representation, presumably in the PR districts, is 0.5 percent of the nationwide vote.

This new law has dramatic consequences for the shape of the party system and the balance of power within the polity. Within the district races, one would expect that Egypt's fragmented new political reality will make it easier for stronger, more experienced, or better-organized groups such as the Muslim Brotherhood (MB) and the holdovers from Mubarak's old NDP to win sizeable seat bonuses. The new and still inchoate groups clustering on the more liberal and secular end of the spectrum (including the Free Egyptians, the Social Democrats, and the Democratic Front Party) will be at a disadvantage. The older secular-liberal movements such as the Wafd and al-Ghad seem like little more than elite shells without members or momentum, and the moderate Islamists of al-Adl and al-Wasat look as if they will find themselves swamped by the MB and the salafist parties. The PR districts open greater space for the newer parties but most districts will be too small to offer voice to fledgling parties outside the dominant players. Only in the largest districts will a party be able to win representation with 5 to 10 percent of the vote. The disproportionality generated by the two-member districts will be huge, but the disproportionality of the PR races may also be significant, with many small parties failing to reach the threshold.

Coptic Christians, lacking significant geographical concentration, are likely to be overwhelmed, and women's representation will suffer not only from the abandonment of the old quota but also because the thinly spread PR seats will not yield the usual advantages that they otherwise might to female candidates. If most parties win only one of two PR seats in any given district, then a woman must occupy one of those top positions on the party list—something that is unlikely to happen without a legal requirement.

The need for the outnumbered secular liberals to form alliances is obvious. Yet the first significant coalition announcement, in mid-June, featured two such parties (al-Ghad and the Wafd) signing on as decidedly junior partners in a supercoalition spearheaded by the MB and also comprising two moderate-Islamist formations (al-Adl and al-Wasat), a salafist party (al-Nour), and six additional parties. If this disparate assemblage holds together (the devil will be in the details of seat allocation), it will form an electoral juggernaut comprising nearly all significant parties aside from the reorganized former ruling party.

The logistical challenges facing Egypt's elections are formidable. New electoral-district boundaries will have to be drawn for both the two-member districts and the PR districts. As with some previous elections, the country will be divided into thirds, with multiple ballotings held in subsets of districts in order to allow judges and domestic observation groups to oversee the polls. Given the fragmented party landscape and the quota requirements, moreover, most races will take two rounds to resolve. Results will trickle out week by week, possibly heightening tensions. The potential for fraud, mismanagement, and a catastrophically botched electoral process will remain.

While the new Egyptian system may perform adequately in promoting coalition formation and a degree of individual accountability on the part of legislators, it appears headed for failure on the scores of inclusiveness, distortion minimization, and simplicity. There are too many moving parts. The multistage electoral process and its complex, too-easily-manipulated criteria for determining winners in districts could breed confusion, tension, and suspicion among voters, parties, and electoral officials alike. Neither the exclusion of smaller groups nor the seat bonuses set to go to the larger ones bode well for the future of democratic hopes along the banks of the Nile.

Tunisia

The electoral system that Tunisia had before President Zine al-Abidine Ben Ali was toppled in January 2011 was meant to reinforce the dominance of his party. The inclusion of token parliamentary opposition furnished a democratic veneer. The Chamber of Deputies had 214 members, 161 of whom were elected from multimember districts of varying sizes (ranging from 2 to 11 seats), while the remaining 53 legislators were elected on a nationwide basis. In the districts, bloc voting was the rule—voters could choose only among slates, and the slate with the most votes would receive each of that district's seats in parliament. The nationwide at-large seats were distributed on the basis of proportionality to "district-level losers," but that only slightly mitigated the huge winner's bonus that bloc voting delivered to the ruling party—which, at the time Ben Ali fled into exile, controlled every single one of the 161 district-based seats. The task of choosing a new constituent assembly would clearly require a different system.

In April 2011, the political council of the High Commission for the Fulfillment of Revolutionary Goals—one of the special bodies that interim authorities created to navigate the post–Ben Ali changeover—approved a legal decree on elections to choose a constituent assembly.[2] The law stipulates that elections will be by closed-list PR using Tunisia's existing governorates as districts. Seats are allocated according to population, with less-populous governorates moderately overrepresented. The law includes provisions, however, to maintain the number of seats awarded in each district within a limited range: Governorates with fewer than four seats are combined, and the largest governorates are subdivided, such that district magnitude ranges from four to twelve. Finally, the law includes a gender quota stipulating that women and men must be represented equally on candidate lists.

What do these details imply with regard to realizing the general principles outlined above? Tunisia's new system scores high on almost all key markers: inclusiveness, minimizing distortions between voter support and assembly representation, encouraging coalitions, and simplicity. With list-PR voting in districts with four to twelve seats, it is unlikely that any alliance will be able to secure an assembly majority on the basis of less than a majority of the popular vote, and coalitions that can secure anywhere from 5 to 20 percent of the vote within a governorate will be assured representation in the constituent assembly. These effective thresholds for representation are low enough that any movement with substantial support can get a seat at the table, but high enough to encourage splinter groups and vanity candidates to seek coalition partners—with the compromises that process entails—or risk being left out.

Tunisia's closed electoral lists also allow for gender inclusiveness via the exercise of effective quotas, with male and female candidates alternating on lists. The proportion of women in the constituent assembly will almost certainly surpass the 23 percent included in Tunisia's last parliament under Ben Ali. And the closed-list ballot is simple to use, demanding only that voters identify their first-choice list. What closed lists mainly sacrifice is the accountability of individual representatives. Voters will be casting ballots for slates only, with no option to indicate a preference for any individual on the preferred list. With regard to each list, the members who receive seats will be those chosen by party or coalition leaders—not voters—before the election.

Tunisia's shortcoming on individual accountability is less damning in elections for a constituent assembly than such a defect would be in a permanent system for electing a legislative assembly. At the constitution-making moment, the inclusiveness of electoral rules must be a top priority. The body charged with drafting a new basic law should reflect the diversity of society, providing representation to a wide array of groups so there are voices that can speak to the importance of protecting minority rights. It should not dramatically overrepresent the largest groups and thus run the risk that short-term winners will write a charter for government that entrenches their advantage. The rules under which this body is elected should be clear and readily understandable even by voters who may lack experience with genuinely competitive elections. When elections shift from the constitutional moment to the ongoing business of legislating, of distributing benefits and burdens among citizens, and of monitoring the executive, there will be an increased premium on giving citizens the ability to reward or punish individual legislators with the ballot.

Tunisia's constituent assembly will look beyond the constitutional moment to the governing moments to follow, and so it may wish to consider electoral reforms to increase accountability to voters, while seeking to preserve inclusiveness and simplicity as much as possible. If the assembly's agenda includes such reforms, it will be starting from a relatively propitious position. The constituent-assembly elections' district structure, in particular, should be able to accommodate a shift from closed to open lists so as to give voters leeway to prefer some candidates over others while at the same time maintaining proportionality across party and alliance lists.

Jordan

Throughout the 1990s and up to 2010, the Hashemite Kingdom of Jordan was one of the few countries in the world to use the single nontransferable vote (SNTV) system for its parliamentary elections. This system uses a simple plurality rule in multimember districts, with each voter allowed to indicate a single preferred candidate. In Jordan's case, district sizes could range up to seven seats (in such a district, the top seven candidates would each win a seat). SNTV is mechanically simple, but strategically complex, both for voters and candidates. Strong individual candidates may win many votes beyond the number needed to win a seat, yet efforts to coordinate alliances among candidates and distribute votes so as to translate electoral support more efficiently into party representation are risky for the top voter-getters. As a result, SNTV elections tend to be contests among individuals, with party labels and platforms counting for little.[3]

A second key characteristic of Jordanian parliamentary elections has been the malapportionment of the districts. The number of voters per seat currently ranges from about 16,000 to more than 80,000, with rural districts dominated by East Bank Jordanian tribes vastly overrepresented at the expense of the urban districts where Jordanians of Palestinian extraction tend to live. A third key element is the reservation of 9 seats in the 120-member lower house for Christians, 3 for Chechens and Circassians, and 3 more for Bedouins, awarded by quotas within the SNTV contests, plus 12 additional seats for women, awarded separately.

In March 2011, as political turmoil rocked the Arab world, King Abdullah II and his government announced the formation of a National Dialogue Committee (NDC) to reform the Kingdom's party and election laws. In June, the NDC proposed changes meant to remedy some of the main distortions associated with the existing rules, and to encourage the formation of electoral alliances with more substantive policy content. The proposal awaits ratification, and possibly amendment, by the cabinet and parliament. At its core is a move from purely candidate-centered elections to open-list PR in districts based on Jordan's twelve governorates. In addition, the proposal includes an upper tier of fifteen seats that would be contested nationwide by open-list PR.

Open lists represent a middle ground between purely individualistic SNTV competition and closed lists. The system maintains the vote for specific candidates, and hence an element of individual accountability, but pools the votes from candidates allied on a given list for the proportional distribution of seats within the relevant governorate. Relative to SNTV, this generates a much stronger incentive to form electoral coalitions, whether in the form of political parties or looser alliances, that could advocate competing national policy platforms.

Jordan's new system will ask more of voters than will Tunisia's. Open lists, with their opportunities to prefer some candidates over others, present a larger number of choices than do closed lists, and Jordanian voters will also cast a second vote for the national-tier contest. Moreover, the candidate-preference vote in open-list elections will complicate the implementation of Jordan's religious, ethnic, and gender quotas, since who wins a seat under the quotas will be decided by who is the "top loser" with a preference-vote total closest to the cutoff for nonquota candidates.

As in Tunisia, the Jordanian proposal divides the largest governorate-based districts, effectively placing an upper limit on district magnitudes at ten seats per district. This means that lists, and with them the number of candidates that voters must consider, will remain of manageable size.

But when it comes to one of the biggest and potentially most explosive problems with the Jordanian electoral system, the reform proposal is timid. The proposed apportionment of seats across districts would only slightly mitigate the dramatic underrepresentation of the cities and their Palestinian residents that characterized the prior system.

The Palestinian Authority

Although the Palestinian Authority has not so far played a central role in the so-called Arab Spring, the continuing controversy that swirls around the Palestinians' legislative-elections system directly informs the likely systemic consequences in Egypt and Syria and gives evidence to system designers beyond. The elections conducted to choose members of the Palestinian Legislative Council (PLC)—the first was held in 1996 and the second in 2006—have come to symbolize the pernicious consequences of the Block Vote (BV) system.[4] Under this arrangement, voters are allowed as many votes as there are seats to be filled in multi-member districts, but prohibited from according more than one vote to any single candidate. In 1996, the Palestinians used a pure BV system to elect all 88 of their legislators. Fatah, Yasser Arafat's party, won 55 seats. This asymmetrical result reinforced evidence from Lebanon, Syria, and Tunisia that BV systems yield large seat bonuses for dominant parties while starving opposition groups of the oxygen needed to compete in the electoral arena.

Success in the Block Vote requires restraint. It requires that a party should field no more candidates in a district than can be realistically expected to win, and that the party's supporters must shun all ticket-splitting and stick exclusively with their "own" candidates. Reforms in 2006 established a parallel system that featured 66 list-PR seats alongside 66 BV seats. This time, Fatah faced a much more serious challenge from the Islamic Resistance Movement (Hamas), which had developed powerful grassroots networks and proved to be much more adept in the BV contests. Hamas won 44 percent of the overall vote but took 68 percent of all BV seats, enough to give it a 57 percent majority on the PLC. Fatah, by contrast, ran far too many BV candidates in Gaza, Hebron, Nablus, and Ramallah, diluting its own vote and paying a steep price. Fatah finished with 41 percent of the overall vote, only three points behind Hamas, but Fatah's indiscipline in the BV races left it with barely a third of the seats on the PLC.

Since 2006, which system to use in future legislative elections has been a major subject of dispute between Hamas and Fatah. Hamas went into Egyptian-facilitated negotiations with a proposal to have 60 percent of the seats elected by PR and 40 percent by BV, arguing also for a 3 percent threshold for PR seats that would likely eliminate such moderate and prodemocratic formations as Prime Minister Salam Fayyad's Third

Way party and Mustafa Barghouti's Palestinian National Initiative. Fatah wanted 80 percent PR and 20 percent BV with a 2.5 percent threshold and fewer but larger districts. No final agreement has been struck, but the "Egyptian paper" accord of 2011 suggests 75 percent PR and 25 percent BV with a 2.5 percent threshold plus retention of the current districts. All these proposals would reduce the expected winner's bonus and with it the element of distortion in the Palestinian electoral system.

Yemen

Yemen has not held a parliamentary election since 2003. Its people have been barred from regular recourse to the ballot by insurgent violence, separatist movements, and bouts of emergency rule that have now given way to de facto state collapse. The lower house has 301 single-member districts, each of which can be carried by simple plurality. In 2009, the ruling General Popular Congress (GPC) party of President Ali Abdallah Saleh agreed in principle with the Joint Meeting Parties (JMP), an opposition umbrella group headed by the Islamists of the Islah Party, to replace the single-member-district plurality (SMDP) system with some form of proportional system, or at least one that mixed proportionalism with the plurality principle.

Elections under Saleh tilted sharply in favor of his GPC when it came to candidate registration, campaign finance, matters of speech and assembly, and vote counting. The huge winner's bonuses that SMDP gave the GPC—62 percent of the seats on 42 percent of the official vote in 1997, and 80 percent of the seats on 58 percent of the vote in 2003—were icing on the cake. A move toward proportionality, or even a mixed system combining SMDs with some list competition in multimember districts, could mitigate such distortions. Yet in January 2011, before protests against Saleh had begun but when he could see other Arab regimes in trouble, his government proposed constitutional changes that appeared to renege on earlier vows regarding electoral reform. The proposal included the creation of 44 reserved seats for women, but was silent on PR, and included a relaxation of the 5 percent maximum deviation in constituency size currently stipulated in the Yemeni Constitution.[5] This latter provision implies that the government envisioned no departure from SMD-based elections, and would allow elections to go forward based on the 2003 district boundaries despite population shifts since that time. Saleh and his lieutenants, in short, were dug in behind SMDP.

The violent events that have shaken Yemen since January 2011 now overshadow any discussion of electoral-reform particulars. Saleh, who was wounded in a bombing and went to Saudi Arabia for medical treatment, remains nominally president as of this writing in July, but his control is tenuous at best. If and when the time for electoral reform ever comes, the Islamists will still likely be strongly in favor of PR. The demands of the tribal leaders and student-led groups that are at the center of the anti-Saleh revolt will also likely figure into any reform equation, but what those demands might be is at present hard to say.

As the Table on page 184 shows, virtually all the Arab states where the strongest antiregime rebellions took place had either a majoritarian electoral system underpinning executive authoritarianism (Bahrain, Egypt, Syria, and Yemen), or else a parallel system heavily weighted toward majoritarian outcomes favoring the strongman president's ruling party (Tunisia). The sole exception, Muammar Qadhafi's Libya, did not even bother with legislative elections. Although one cannot trace the more muted character of the protests in Algeria, Jordan, Lebanon, Morocco, and the Palestinian Authority to the design of their respective electoral systems, it is true that all those systems included either proportional elements or significant guarantees of ethnic representation (this last being particularly the case in Lebanon).

Along with quotas or set-aside seats for ethnic and religious minorities, some polities featured quotas guaranteeing parliamentary seats to women. Here the picture is mixed and inauspicious. Seats were (or are to be) reserved for women in Jordan, Morocco, Tunisia, and Egypt, the last of which has now dropped its gender quota. Given the powerlessness of Arab legislatures before the upheavals began, it is far from clear whether any of these quotas actually promoted the political influence of women or merely served as "progressive-looking" camouflage for kings and dictatorial presidents.

The electoral-reform picture that is emerging in the Arab world is checkered. There are encouraging signs, particularly in Tunisia and Jordan. The former's new system promises much greater inclusivity than before, thus distributing bargaining power broadly within the constituent assembly. Voters will find it relatively easy to navigate, and it is amenable to future reforms aimed at making individual lawmakers more accountable to their constituents. Jordan's leading reform proposal strengthens incentives for the rise of electoral alliances offering meaningful policy platforms, while maintaining voters' ability to reward or punish individual candidates at the polls, and without increasing the complexity of the process for ordinary voters. Its great flaw may be that it does little to redress the apportionment imbalance that favors rural East Bank Jordanians over urban Palestinian Jordanians.

The picture in Egypt, which is by far the largest and most important of these countries, remains unclear. There, the sheer complexity of the electoral arrangements will pose a problem. Elections in two-member districts under a two-round system, with voting for individual candidates plus the occupational quota, add up to a formidable obstacle to achieving the basic goals outlined at the beginning of this essay. A complicated process is difficult to administer and creates openings for manipulation and corruption. The majority requirement makes it hard

TABLE—PRE– AND POST–ARAB REVOLT ELECTION SYSTEMS

	Pre-2011			Post–Arab Revolt		
Case	System	Parl. Size	Reserved Seats	System	Parl. Size	Reserved Seats
Egypt	Two-Round System/ Two Members	518	• 64 Women • 222 Workers/ Farmers	**Proposed**: Parallel TRS(50%)/ PR (50%)	514	226 Workers/ Farmers
Tunisia	Parallel-Block (75%) PR (25%)	214	-	List PR	191	50% Women Quota
Jordan	Single Non-Transferable Vote*	120	• 12 Women • 9 Christian • 3 Chechen/ Circassian • 3 Bedouin	**Proposed**: 115 seats Open-List PR in governor-ates. Three largest governorates sub-divided.	130	• 15 Women • 9 Christian • 3 Chechen/ Circassian • 3 Bedouin
Yemen	First Past the Post	301	-	Unknown	-	-
P.A.	Parallel-Block (50%) PR (50%)	132	6 Christian	**Proposed**: Parallel-Block (25%)/ PR (75%)	132	-
Bahrain	Two-Round System	40	-	Two-Round System	40	-
Syria	Block Vote	250	51% Farmers	Block Vote	250	51% Farmers
Lebanon	Block Vote	128	128 Confessional	Block Vote	128	128 Confessional
Algeria	List PR	389	-	List PR	389	-
Morocco	List PR	325	30 Women	List PR	325	30 Women
Libya	-	-	-	Unknown	-	-

*For 2010 election only, SMD contests in "virtual" districts embedded within existing multimember SNTV districts.

for new groups and new faces to win seats, favoring instead those who already have name recognition and other resources. As currently conceived, Egypt's post-Mubarak electoral system is going to produce large seat bonuses for the top one or two parties or coalitions.

In Yemen, the breakdown in transition negotiations and the rise of widespread political violence have pushed electoral reform off center stage. If momentum toward elections in a post-Saleh Yemen is ever restored, it will be essential to replace the country's pure SMDP system with one that is more open to a wide range of movements and groups. Yemen's regional divisions will continue to demand that representation include a strong geographical component, but there is plenty of room within the family of proportional systems to maintain regional representation.

When it comes to matters of institutional design and reform, we can see patterns emerging in the Arab world. The one country that has seen a relatively clean removal of the old regime (Tunisia) has gone for full PR. Where the old regime has been ousted but the military has retained the last word (Egypt), electoral reforms have been more piecemeal, and PR is being mixed into the old rules. In Jordan, liberalization that stops short of fully remedying prior seat imbalances across regions and the rural-urban divide appears to be the result of negotiations within the regime between reformers, who seek to empower parties and the parliament more generally, and an "old guard" that is more skeptical of representative institutions. Reforms (or the lack of them) in Lebanon and the Palestinian Authority reflect the balance of power between competing camps within those polities. In Bahrain, Libya, and Syria, where dictators have been holding on to power by violence, electoral laws number among the pillars of regime dominance, and are not likely to be altered unless a change of regime comes first.

In all these cases, we find the same core challenge for reformers and democratizers: How to open space for new parties and movements to challenge the old ones and gain a voice in the making of laws? From Amman to Sana'a and Cairo to Rabat, progressives, liberals, and young people are all struggling to build coherent and effective political organizations after having been shut out of politics for so long. Their need to find electoral space is particularly crucial in transitional elections that are supposed to mark a fault line between authoritarianism and hoped-for democracy. Elections to determine who will write a new basic law—whether in a constituent assembly or a parliament acting as a constitution-drafting body—must place a premium on inclusivity, as the experiences of Nepal and South Africa teach. Sadly, only Tunisia seems to have taken this lesson thoroughly to heart so far. Without electoral systems leading to fully inclusive constitutional-design processes and parliaments, many of the hopes for democracy in the Arab world may falter at the first hurdle.

NOTES

1. Tarek Masoud, "Why Islam Wins: Electoral Ecologies and Economies of Political Islam in Contemporary Egypt," PhD diss., Yale University, 2009. Masoud explains that under Mubarak, the process of certifying candidates as workers or farmers was thoroughly corrupt. Many, if not most, "worker" or "farmer" candidates were in fact neither.

2. The date for elections was initially set for July, but in June was moved back to October. The reason given for the delay was administrative: The electoral commission needed more time to compile accurate voter rolls and provide all citizens with valid voter-identification cards.

3. For its 2010 parliamentary election, Jordan adapted its system so that candidates self-selected into what were, effectively, SMD-plurality contests in "virtual" subdistricts embedded within its existing SNTV districts. The virtual-subdistrict experiment was widely dismissed as inscrutable and untenable, even by the winning parliamentary candidates, and the point of greatest consensus among Jordanian reformers is that the virtual-subdistrict system will not survive.

4. The authors wish to thank Vladimir Pran for providing details regarding elections in the Palestinian Authority.

5. Authors' communication with Manuel Wally, EU and UN electoral-mission advisor, and "Transition in Yemen: An Overview of Constitutional and Electoral Provisions," International Foundation for Electoral Systems briefing paper, 7 June 2011.

16

THE ROLE OF DIGITAL MEDIA

Philip N. Howard and Muzammil M. Hussain

Philip N. Howard *is professor of communication, information, and international studies at the University of Washington and a professor in the School of Public Policy at Central European University.* **Muzammil M. Hussain** *is assistant professor in the Department of Communication Studies and faculty associate at the Center for Political Studies at the University of Michigan, and research fellow at the Qatar Computing Research Institute. They are coauthors of* Democracy's Fourth Wave? Digital Media and the Arab Spring. *This essay originally appeared in the July 2011 issue of the* Journal of Democracy.

As has often been noted in these pages, one world region has been practically untouched by the third wave of democratization: North Africa and the Middle East. The Arab world has lacked not only democracy, but even large popular movements pressing for it. In December 2010 and the first months of 2011, however, this situation changed with stunning speed. Massive and sustained public demonstrations demanding political reform cascaded from Tunis to Cairo, Sana'a, Amman, and Manama. This inspired people in Casablanca, Damascus, Tripoli, and dozens of other cities to take to the streets to call for change.

By May, major political casualties littered the ground: Tunisia's Zine al-Abidine Ben Ali and Egypt's Hosni Mubarak, two of the region's oldest dictators, were gone; the Libyan regime of Muammar Qadhafi was battling an armed rebellion that had taken over half the country and attracted NATO help; and several monarchs had sacked their cabinets and committed to constitutional reforms. Governments around the region had sued for peace by promising their citizens hundreds of billions of dollars in new spending of various kinds. Morocco and Saudi Arabia appeared to be fending off serious domestic uprisings, but as of this writing in May 2011, the outcomes for regimes in Bahrain, Jordan, Syria, and Yemen remain far from certain.

There are many ways to tell the story of political change. But one of

the most consistent narratives from civil society leaders in Arab countries has been that the Internet, mobile phones, and social media such
as Facebook and Twitter made the difference this time. Using these
technologies, people interested in democracy could build extensive networks, create social capital, and organize political action with a speed
and on a scale never seen before. Thanks to these technologies, virtual
networks materialized in the streets. Digital media became the tool that
allowed social movements to reach once-unachievable goals, even as
authoritarian forces moved with a dismaying speed of their own to devise both high- and low-tech countermeasures. Looking back over the
last few months of the "Arab Spring," what have we learned about the
role of digital media in political uprisings and democratization? What
are the implications of the events that we have witnessed for our understanding of how democratization actually works today?

On 17 December 2010, Mohamed Bouazizi set himself on fire. The
young street vendor in the small Tunisian city of Sidi Bouzid had tried
in vain to fight an inspector's small fine, appealing first to the police,
then to town officials, and then to the regional governor. Each time he
dared to press his case, security officials beat him. Bruised, humiliated, and frustrated by this cruel treatment, Bouazizi set himself alight
in front of the governor's office. By the time he died in a hospital on
January 4, his plight had sparked nationwide protests. The news had
traveled fast, even though the state-run media had ignored the tragedy
and the seething discontent in Sidi Bouzid. During the angry second
half of December, it was through blogs and text messages that Tunisians
experienced what the sociologist Doug McAdam calls "cognitive liberation."[1] In their shared sympathy for the dying man, networks of family
and friends came to realize that they shared common grievances too.
The realization hit home as people watched YouTube videos about the
abusive state, read foreign news coverage of political corruption online,
and shared jokes about their aging dictator over SMS. Communicating
in ways that the state could not control, people also used digital media
to arrive at strategies for action and a collective goal: the deposition of
a despot.

For years, the most direct accusations of political corruption had
come from the blogosphere. Investigative journalism was almost solely the work of average citizens using the Internet in creative ways.
Most famous is the YouTube video showing Tunisia's presidential jet
on runways near exclusive European shopping destinations, with on-
screen graphics specifying dates and places and asking who was using
the aircraft (the suggestion being that it was Ben Ali's high-living
wife). Once this video appeared online, the regime cracked down on
YouTube, Facebook, and other applications. But bloggers and activists pushed on, producing alternative online newscasts, creating virtual spaces for anonymous political discussions, and commiserating

with fellow citizens about state persecution. With Bouazizi's death, Ben Ali's critics moved from virtual to actual public spaces. Shamseddine Abidi, a 29-year-old interior designer, posted regular videos and updates to Facebook. Al Jazeera used the content to carry news of the events to the world. Images of a hospitalized Bouazizi spread via networks of family and friends. An online campaign called on citizens and unions to support the uprising in Sidi Bouzid. Lawyers and students were among the first to take to the streets in an organized way.

The government tried to ban Facebook, Twitter, and video sites such as DailyMotion and YouTube. Within a few days, however, people found a workaround as SMS networks became the organizing tool of choice. Less than 20 percent of the population actively used social media, but almost everyone had access to a mobile phone. Outside the country, the hacker communities of Anonymous and Telecomix helped to cripple the government by carrying out denial-of-service attacks and by building new software to help activists get around state firewalls. The government responded by jailing a group of bloggers in early January. For the most part, however, the political uprising was leaderless in the classic sense—there was no longstanding revolutionary figurehead, traditional opposition leader, or charismatic speechmaker to radicalize the public. But there were prominent nodes in the digital networks, people whose contributions held sway and mobilized turnout. Slim Amamou, a member of the copyright-focused Pirate Party, blogged the revolution (and later briefly took a post in the national-unity government). Sami ben Gharbia, a Tunisian exile, monitored online censorship attempts and advertised workarounds. The middle-class Tunisian rapper who calls himself El Général streamed digital "soundtracks for the revolution."

By early January, urgent appeals for help and mobile-phone videos of police repression were streaming across North Africa. Ben Ali's position seemed precarious. There were major protests in Algeria, along with several self-immolations. Again, the state-run news media covered little about events in neighboring Tunisia. The Algerian government tried to block Internet access and Facebook use as traffic about public outrage next door increased. But with all the privately owned submarine cables running to Europe, Algerian authorities lacked an effective chokepoint to squeeze. When the government also became a target for Anonymous, the state's own information infrastructure suffered.

By the time Ben Ali fled Tunisia for Saudi Arabian exile on January 14, civil-disobedience campaigns against authoritarian rule were growing in Jordan, Oman, and Yemen. In other countries, such as Lebanon, Mauritania, Saudi Arabia, and Sudan, minor protests erupted on a range of issues and triggered quick concessions or had little impact. But even in these countries, opposition leaders drew inspiration from what they were tracking in Tunisia. Moreover, opposition leaders across the region were learning digital tricks for catching a ruling elite off guard. Compared to Tunisia, only Egypt had a more wired civil society, and the stories of success in Tunisia helped to inspire the largest protests that Cairo had seen in thirty years.

Egypt, Inspired

In Egypt, almost everyone has access to a mobile phone. The country also has the region's second-largest Internet-using population (only Iran's is bigger). News of Ben Ali's departure spread rapidly in Egypt, where the state-run media gave his exit grudging coverage even while continuing to move slowly on reporting the larger story of regionwide protests, including the demonstrations that were breaking out in Cairo.

Like Tunisia, Egypt has long had a large and active online public sphere frequented by banned political parties, radical fundamentalists, investigative journalists, and disaffected citizens. The state could not shut it down entirely: When the online news service of the Muslim Brotherhood (MB) was banned, for instance, servers were found in London and the organization continued to convey its views across the ether. But more than any established group, what turned anti-Mubarak vitriol into civil disobedience was a campaign to memorialize a murdered blogger.

Local Google executive Wael Ghonim started the Facebook group "We are All Khaled Said" to keep alive the memory of the 28-year-old blogger, whom police had beaten to death on 6 June 2010 for exposing their corruption. Just as digital images of Bouazizi in the hospital passed over networks of family and friends in Egypt, an image of Said's grotesquely battered face, taken by his brother as Khaled's body lay in the Alexandria city morgue, passed from one mobile-phone camera to thousands. And just as the 26-year-old Iranian woman Neda Agha-Soltan became a protest icon after her death at the hands of a regime sniper during postelection demonstrations in Tehran was caught on camera in June 2009, so did Said and his memorial Facebook page become a focus for collective dissent and commiseration. But more than being a digital tribute to someone from a group long tormented by Egyptian police, the Said Facebook page became a logistical tool, and at least temporarily, a strong source of community. Ghonim quickly emerged as Egypt's leading voice on Twitter, linking a massive Arabic-speaking social network with networks of mostly English-speaking observers and well-wishers overseas.

The first demonstrators to venture into Cairo's Tahrir (Liberation) Square on 25 January 2011 shared many hopes and aspirations with their counterparts in Tunis. They were a similar community of like-minded individuals, educated but underemployed (in a "youth-bulge" society chronically unable to create enough jobs for its legions of young people), eager for change but committed neither to religious fervor nor political ideology. They found solidarity through digital media, and then used their mobile phones to call their social networks into the streets. Protests scaled up quickly, leaving regime officials and outside observers alike surprised that such a large network of relatively liberal, peaceful, middle-class citizens would mobilize against Mubarak with such speed. Islamists, opposition-party supporters, and union members were there too, but liberal and civil society voices dominated the digital conversation. News about and speeches by Mubarak, U.S. president Barack Obama, and regional leaders were streamed live to the phones and laptops in the square.

In the last week of January, an increasingly desperate Mubarak tried to unplug his country. His attempt to cut Egyptians off from the global information infrastructure met with mixed success. Anticipating the maneuver, tech-savvy students and civil society leaders had put in place backup satellite phones and dial-up connections to Israel and Europe, and were able to maintain strong links to the rest of the world. It appears, moreover, that some of the telecommunications engineers charged with choking off Internet access were slow to move. The first large Internet service provider (ISP) received the shutdown order on Friday, January 28, but took no action until Saturday. Others responded promptly, but restored normal service on Monday. For four days, the amount of bandwidth going into Egypt dropped, but it was far short of the information blackout that Mubarak had been seeking. The regime had to deal with costs and perverse effects, too. Government agencies were crippled by being knocked off the grid. And middle-class Egyptians, denied home Internet access, took to the streets in larger numbers than ever, many driven by an urge simply to find out what was going on.

A few days later, the Egyptian security services began using Facebook and Twitter to anticipate the movements of individual activists. They abducted Ghonim once his Facebook group topped three-hundred thousand members (it now has four times that many). Digital media technologies not only set off a cascade of civil disobedience across Egypt, but made for a unique means of civic organizing that was replicated around the region.

Digital media spread the details of successful social mobilizations against the strongmen of Tunisia and Egypt across the region. As had happened in Tunisia and Egypt, authorities in Algeria, Bahrain, Libya, Saudi Arabia, and Syria tried to stifle digital conversation about domestic political change. These governments also targeted bloggers with arrests, beatings, and harassment. It is clear that digital media have played an important role. Images of jubilant protesters in Tunisia inspired others across the region. Facebook provided an invaluable logistical infrastructure for the initial stages of protest in each country. Text-messaging systems fed people within and outside these countries with information about where the action was, where the abuses were, and what the next step would be.

Within a few weeks, there were widely circulating PDFs of tip sheets on how to pull off a successful protest. The *Atlantic Monthly* translated and hosted an "Activist Action Plan," *boingboing.net* provided tips for protecting anonymity online, and Telecomix circulated the ways of using landlines to circumvent state blockages of broadband networks. Through Google Earth, the Shias of Bahrain—many of whom live in one-room houses with large families—could map and aggregate photographs of the ruling Sunni minority's opulent palaces. Digital media provided both an awareness of shared grievances, and transportable strategies for action.

The prominent Bahraini human-rights blogger Mahmood al-Yousif tweeted during his arrest, instantly linking up the existing networks of local democratization activists such as @OnlineBahrain with international observers through @BahrainRights. In Libya, the first assertion of a competing political authority to that of Muammar Qadhafi came online, on a website declaring an alternative government in the form of an interim national council. One of Qadhafi's senior advisors defected by tweeting his resignation and urging Qadhafi to leave Libya.

Algerians, goaded by the same sense of economic despair and dissatisfaction that drove Tunisians and Egyptians, broke out in similar demonstrations. Salima Ghezali, a leading Algerian activist, told Al Jazeera that the protests were "both very local and very global." Union-led strikes had been common in Algeria for decades, but nothing like the unrest of 2011 had been seen since 1991. Algerian protesters were not among the region's most tech-savvy, but before the country's state-run media reported on local protests or Mubarak's resignation, many residents of Algiers received the inspirational news via SMS.

Digital Contexts, Political Consequences

Ben Ali had ruled for almost 25 years, and Mubarak for nearly thirty. Each was tossed out of power by a network of activists whose core members were twenty-somethings with little experience in social-movement organizing or open political discourse. Seeing this, other governments scrambled to make concessions that they hoped would head off explosions. Algeria's rulers lifted an almost two-decade-old state of emergency. Oman's sultan gave its elected legislature the authority to pass laws. Sudan's war-criminal president promised not to seek reelection. All the oil-rich states committed to wealth redistribution or the extension of welfare services.

Real-world politics, of course, is about much more than what happens online. A classically trained social scientist trying to explain the upheavals would point to the youth bulge, declining economic productivity, rising wealth concentration, high unemployment, and low quality of life as common circumstances across the region. These explanatory factors are typically part of the story of social change, and it does not diminish digital media's causal contribution to note their presence. Such media were singularly powerful in spreading protest messages, driving coverage by mainstream broadcasters, connecting frustrated citizens with one another, and helping them to realize that they could take shared action regarding shared grievances. For years, discontent had been stirring, but somehow the drivers of protest never proved sufficient until mobile phones and the Web began pervading the region. It never makes sense to look for simple, solitary causes of a revolution, to say nothing of a string of revolutions, and the precise grievances have varied significantly from country to country. Yet the use of digital media to rouse and organize opposition has furnished a common thread.[2]

It is true that journalists have focused on the visible technological tactics that seemed to bring so much success, rather than looking at the root causes of social discontent. Yet this does not mean that analysts should overcorrect and exclude information technologies from the list of causes altogether. Indeed, social discontent is not something ready-made, but must gestate as people come to agree on the exact nature and goals of their discontent. In the last few years, this gestation process has gone forward via new media, particularly in Tunisia, Egypt, and Bahrain. Social discontent can assume organizational form online, and can be translated into workable strategies and goals there as well. Over the last few months, this translation process has occurred via mobile phones and social-networking applications even in countries whose governments are very good at coopting or brutally suppressing opposition, such as Saudi Arabia, Syria, and Yemen.

In the Middle East and North Africa, dissent existed long before the Internet. Yet digital media helped to turn individualized, localized, and community-specific dissent into a structured movement with a collective consciousness about both shared plights and opportunities for action. It may make more sense to think of conjoined causal combinations: the strength of existing opposition movements, the ability (or inability) of the regime to buy off opposition leaders, and the use of digital media to build opposition networks. The precise mixture of causes may have varied from country to country, but the one consistent component has been digital media.

It is premature to call these events a "wave" of democratization—their outcomes are still far too uncertain for that—yet we can say that opposition to authoritarian rule has been the consistent collective-action goal across the region. Arab social-movement leaders actively sought training and advice from the leaders of democratization movements in other countries, and rhetorical appeals for civil liberty appeared consistently from protest to protest.

As we look back over the first quarter of 2011, the story of digital media and the Arab Spring seems to have unfolded in five or perhaps six parts or phases. The first was a *preparation* phase that involved activists using digital media in creative ways to find each other, build solidarity around shared grievances, and identify collective political goals. The second was an *ignition* phase involving an incident that the state-run media ignored, but which came to wide notice online and enraged the public. Then came the third phase, a period of *street protests* made possible, in part, by online networking and coordination. As these went on, there came the *international buy-in,* during which digital-media coverage (much of it locally generated) drew in foreign governments, international organizations, global diasporas, and overseas news agencies. Matters then built toward a *climax* as regimes, maneuvering via some mixture of concession and repression, either got the protesters off the street; failed to mollify or frighten them and began to crumble before their demands; or ended up in a bloody stalemate or even civil war as we are seeing in Bahrain, Libya, Syria, and Yemen. In some cases, such as those of Tunisia and Egypt, we are seeing an additional phase of *follow-on information warfare* as the various players left standing compete to shape the future course of events by gaining control over the revolutionary narrative.

Across the region, the process of building up to political change involved "building down" the credibility of authoritarian regimes by investigating their corrupt practices. The best and perhaps the only place that critics could find for getting their message across was the Internet. Blogs, news websites, Twitter feeds, and political listservs offered spaces where women could debate on an equal footing with men, where policy alternatives could be discussed, and where regime secrets could be exposed. What set the scene for a dramatic event such as the occupation of a central square was the undramatic process of people buying cheap mobile phones or time online at cybercafés. The arrival of new digital technologies became an occasion for individuals to restructure the ways in which they produced and consumed content. When a political crisis flared, the new habits of technology use were already in place.

After 2000, new communications technologies spread rapidly across the Arab world. For many Arabs, especially in cities, reading foreign news online and communicating with friends and relatives abroad became habits. Digital media could become a near-term cause of political upheaval in 2011 precisely because they were already so popular. It may seem that digital-media use in times of political crisis is novel. But for residents of Tunis, Cairo, and other capitals, it was the sheer everydayness and familiarity of mobile phones that made them a proximate cause of political change. The revolution may be televised, and it is surely online.

What ignites popular protest is not merely an act of regime violence such as the police beating Mohamed Bouazizi or Khaled Said, but the diffusion of news about the outrage by networks of family, friends, and then strangers who step in when the state-run media ignore the story. When Al Jazeera failed at first to cover digital activism in Syria, civic

leaders there lobbied the influential network into producing a long doc-
umentary and featuring Syrian-activist content on its website. Consequently, interest in homegrown opposition to dictator Bashar al-Assad
grew rapidly both within the country and across the region.

Interestingly, the recent protest ignitions seem to have occurred without recognizable leaders. Charismatic ideologues, labor-union officials,
and religious spokespeople have been noticeably absent (or at least they
were at first). In Tunisia, the igniting event was Bouazizi's suicide. In
Egypt, it was the Tunisian example. The rest of the region followed as
scenes of demonstrators and fleeing dictators went out over Al Jazeera
and social-media networks.

After ignition, the street battles of political upheaval began, albeit
in a unique manner. Most of the protests in most of the countries were
organized in unexpected ways that made it difficult for states to respond.
The lack of individual leaders made it hard for authorities to know whom
to arrest. Activists used Facebook, Twitter, and other sites to communicate plans for civic action, at times playing cat-and-mouse games with
regime officials who were monitoring these very applications. In Libya,
foes of the Qadhafi dictatorship took to Muslim online-dating sites in
order to hide the arrangements for meetings and protest rallies. In Syria,
the Assad regime had blocked Facebook and Twitter intermittently since
2007, but reopened access as protests mounted, possibly as a way of
entrapping activists. When state officials began spreading misinforma-
tion over Twitter, activists used Google Maps to self-monitor and verify
trusted sources. Then, too, authorities often flubbed their information-
control efforts. Mubarak disabled Egypt's broadband infrastructure yet
left satellite and landline links alone. Qadhafi tried to shut down his
country's mobile-phone networks, but they proved too decentralized.

News coverage of events in the region regularly revealed citizens using their mobile-phone cameras to document events, and especially their
own participation in them. In Tahrir Square, both the crowds and the
crewmen of the tanks that were sent to watch them took pictures of one
another for instant distribution to their various social networks. When
army vehicles were abandoned, people clambered aboard and posed for
pictures to post to their Facebook pages. Arrestees took pictures of themselves in custody. Some Egyptians speculated that the army did not act
systematically against protesters because soldiers were made suddenly
aware of their socially proximate connection to the square's occupants,
and also because the troops knew that they were constantly on camera.
In countries where the armed forces did act with aggression, including
Bahrain and Syria, the resulting carnage was still documented. YouTube
had to add a special waiver to its usual no-gore policy in order to allow
shocking user content such as a mobile-phone video of unarmed Syrian
civilians—including children—being shot by Assad's troops.

Sooner or later, regime opponents must seek some form of international support, and this, too, has become a digitally mediated process. Domestic turmoil can eventually capture international attention. Of course, the degree to which a popular uprising finds an international audience depends on strategic relations with the West, but also on the proximity of social-media networks. Most technology users in most countries do not have the sophistication to work around state firewalls or keep up anonymous and confidential communications online. But in each country a handful of tech-savvy students and civil society leaders do have these skills, and they used them well during the first months of 2011. Learning from democracy activists in other countries, these information brokers used satellite phones, direct landline connections to ISPs in Israel and Europe, and software tools for protecting user anonymity in order to supply the international media with pictures of events on the ground—even when desperate dictators attempted to shut down national ISPs.

Desperate Tactics

When conflicts between a regime and its domestic opposition come to a head, one or the other may give in, or else a stalemate (often punctuated by violent clashes) may ensue. Mounting tensions led several governments to make clumsy attempts at disconnecting citizens from the global digital "grid." Banning access to social-media websites, powering down cell towers, or disconnecting Internet switching points in major cities were among the desperate tactics to which authoritarian regimes resorted as they strove to maintain control. Even short disruptions of connectivity were costly. Egypt lost at least US$90 million to Mubarak's only partly successful efforts to cut off digital communications. Perhaps even more damaging in the long run, this episode harmed the country's reputation among technology firms as a safe place to invest. In Tunisia, the situation was reversed: It was not the government but rather activist hackers—or "hacktivists," as many call themselves—who did the most economic damage by shutting down the national stock exchange.

When regimes struck back, their counterblows had digital components. Bahrain, Morocco, and Syria saw cyber-struggles to dominate Twitter traffic. Every country that experienced turmoil witnessed delays or disruptions in mobile-phone and Internet service, but it is hard to say whether this was due to regime-driven shutdowns or overwhelming traffic volumes at moments of maximal uncertainty. Quite likely it was both. The zenith of crisis tended to mark the nadir of connectivity as regimes cracked down on large telecommunications providers while skyrocketing traffic was rerouted to a few small available digital switches.

The information wars that followed the protests of the Arab Spring began with the efforts of regimes to hide their tracks. In Egypt, the State Security Investigations Service—Mubarak's political police—did all it could to destroy its archives, though some records leaked online. The websites of activists, meanwhile, became portals for criticisms of the interim government and its leaders.

The victors in a popular uprising generate ever more digital content, while the supporters of failed dictators produce less and less. Deposed dictators find only a small audience online, while the entrepreneurial activists who served as important nodes in the social-movement network find themselves with newfound leadership roles. By the time the protests are over, a few of the "digerati" such as Wael Ghonim find that they have become newly prominent public figures. And the public expectation of being able to use information technology to access political figures remains. When U.S. secretary of state Hillary Clinton was booked for a Web chat with a popular Egyptian website, around 6,500 questions were submitted in just two days.

Traditional media sources also played an important role in the Arab Spring. Satellite television forged a strong sense of transnational identity across the region, and everyone recognized the importance of coverage in this medium: Both Mubarak and his information minister called television anchors personally to berate them for unflattering stories. Of the existing news organizations, Al Jazeera certainly enjoyed the highest profile and the most influence regionally. The network's Dima Khatib, a native of Syria, was the most prominent commentator on Tunisia when that country erupted, and she served as a key information broker for the revolution through her postings on Twitter. Al Jazeera had an exceptionally innovative new-media team that converted its traditional news product for use on social-media sites and made good use of the existing social networks of its online users. But a key aspect of its success was its use of digital media to collect information and images from countries in which its journalists had been harassed or banned. These digital networks gave Al Jazeera's journalists access to more sources, and gave a second life to their news products. Indeed, the use of social media itself has become a news peg, with analysts eager to play with the meme of technology-induced political change.

Regime responses varied in sophistication, but often seemed several technological paces behind the behavior of civil society. In February, during one of his televised speeches, Qadhafi interrupted his train of thought when an aide drew his attention to real-time coverage of his rant. Qadhafi had simply never encountered such instant feedback from a source that could not easily be silenced or punished. In Bahrain, the successful suppression of protest by the country's Sunni-dominated monarchy gave it an opportunity to plug the security holes in its telecommunications network. Though never as severely challenged by demonstrators, Saudi Arabia's rulers have reorganized the server infrastructure of the Kingdom so that all Internet traffic there flows through exchange points that are physically located in Riyadh.

It is a mistake to build a theory of democratization around a particular kind of software, a single website, or a piece of hardware, or to label these social upheavals "Twitter Revolutions" or "WikiLeaks Revolutions."[3] Nor does it make sense to argue that digital media can *cause* either dictators or their opponents to achieve or fall short of their goals. Technological tools and the people who use them must together make or break a political uprising.

The Digital Scaffolding for Civil Society

Digital media changed the tactics of democratization movements, and new information and communication technologies played a major role in the Arab Spring. We do not know, at the time of this writing in May 2011, where events in the various countries will lead, and whether or not change will come to the remaining, more recalcitrant authoritarian governments. But the consistent narrative arc of the uprisings involves digital media. The countries that experienced the most dramatic protests were among the region's most thoroughly wired, and their societies boasted large numbers of people with the technical knowledge to use these new media to strong effect.

In times of political crisis, technology firms may "lean forward" with new tools or applications introduced to serve an eager public (and in doing so, capture market share). In late January, for example, Google sped up its launch of its speak-to-tweet service, an application designed to translate voicemails into tweets as a means of bypassing Mubarak's Twitter blockade. Several tech firms built dedicated portals to allow in-country users to share content. But as Evgeny Morozov has pointed out, information technologies—and the businesses that design them— do not always end up supporting democratization movements.[4] Opposition leaders in countries where political parties are illegal sometimes use pseudonyms to avoid government harassment. But doing so on Facebook is a violation of the company's user agreement, and so the company actually shut down one of the protest-group pages in December. Supporters eventually persuaded Facebook to reinstate the page, but the incident showed how businesses such as Facebook, YouTube, and Twitter may not fully appreciate the way in which their users treat these tools as public-information infrastructure, and not just as cool new applications in the service of personal amusement. Whereas Google has signed the Global Network Initiative—a compact for preventing web censorship by authoritarian governments—Facebook has refused to do so. It might be technically possible to require Facebook users in Western countries to use real identities while allowing people living under dictatorships to enjoy anonymity, but no such feature currently exists.

Absent digital media, would the Arab Spring still have occurred? It is hard to say. The Arab world has long had democratic activists, but never before had any toppled a dictator. Radio and television have long reached most Arabs, but only 10 to 20 percent of those living in a typical Middle Eastern or North African country can easily gain access to the Internet. Yet this minority is a strategic one, typically comprising an elite made up of educated professionals, young entrepreneurs, urban dwellers, and government workers. These are the people who formed the networks that initiated, coordinated, and sustained successful campaigns of civil disobedience against authoritarian rule. Looking at the other side of the coin, the countries with the lowest levels of technology proliferation have also tended to have the weakest democratization movements. As fascinating as it can be to think of counterfactual scenarios, it would be a mistake to see these as belonging on an equal footing with actual events in concrete cases concerning which we have ample empirical evidence. Counterfactuals and thought experiments can be fun, but in the search for patterns that is the social scientist's task, prominence should always be given to real cases and the real evidence they yield.

As we have noted, it is premature to assert that we are witnessing a wave of democratization. Several states are still in crisis. In countries where authoritarian governments have collapsed or made major concessions, it is hard to know whether stable democracies will emerge. Democratization waves are measured in years, not months. In 1998, Indonesia's Suharto fell when students using mobile phones successfully mobilized and caught his regime off guard, but it took a decade of difficult political conversations for democratic practices to become entrenched. The Arab Spring had a unique narrative arc, involved a particular community of nations, and caught most autocrats and analysts alike by surprise. Digital media are important precisely because they had a role in popular mobilizations against authoritarian rule that were unlike anything seen before in the region.

It is also noteworthy that a remarkable amount of political change has occurred in a surprisingly nonlethal manner. In Algeria, Egypt, Jordan, Morocco, and Tunisia, civil society leaders found that the security services showed a remarkable reluctance to move aggressively against protesters (and the Tunisian and Egyptian militaries did not want to move against them at all). Could this hesitancy have had anything to do with the large numbers of mobile-phone cameras that demonstrators were carrying? Sadly, a distaste for the use of deadly violence by regime forces has not been evident in Bahrain, Libya, Saudi Arabia, Syria, and Yemen. Yet even in those cases, it can at least be said that solid documentation of regime abuses or even atrocities has reached the international community, in no small part thanks to mobile phones.

Scholars of social movements, collective action, and revolution must admit that several aspects of the Arab Spring challenge our theories about how such protests work. These movements had an unusually wide or "distributed" leadership. The first days of protest in each country were organized by a core group of literate, middle-class young people who had no particular affinities with any existing political parties or any ideologies stressing class struggle, religious fundamentalism, or pan-Arab nationalism. Broadcast and print media—long associated with the mobilization phase of democratization waves—took a decided backseat to communication via social networks. This communication, moreover, itself had a strongly distributed or lateral character and did not consist of one or a few relatively simple ideological messages beamed by an elite at a less-educated mass public, but had more the character of a many-sided conversation among more or less equal individuals.

Seeing what has unfolded so far in the Middle East and North Africa, we can say more than simply that the Internet has changed the way in which political actors communicate with one another. Since the beginning of 2011, social protests in the Arab world have cascaded from country to country, largely because digital media have allowed communities to unite around shared grievances and nurture transportable strategies for mobilizing against dictators. In each country, people have used digital media to build a political response to a local experience of unjust rule. They were not inspired by Facebook; they were inspired by the real tragedies *documented* on Facebook. Social media have become the scaffolding upon which civil society can build, and new information technologies give activists things that they did not have before: information networks not easily controlled by the state and coordination tools that are already embedded in trusted networks of family and friends.

NOTES

1. Doug McAdam, *Political Process and the Development of Black Insurgency, 1930–1970* (Chicago: University of Chicago Press, 1982).

2. Philip N. Howard, *The Digital Origins of Dictatorship and Democracy: Information Technology and Political Islam* (New York: Oxford University Press, 2010).

3. Elizabeth Dickinson, "The First WikiLeaks Revolution?" Foreign Policy Online, available at *http://wikileaks.foreignpolicy.com/posts/2011/01/13/wikileaks_and_the_tunisia_protests*. See also Andrew Sullivan, "Tunisia's Wikileaks Revolution," Atlantic Online, available at *www.theatlantic.com/daily-dish/archive/2011/01/tunisias-wikileaks-revolution/177242*.

4. Evgeny Morozov, *The Net Delusion: The Dark Side of Internet Freedom* (New York: PublicAffairs, 2011).

Country Studies

17

BEN ALI'S FALL

Peter J. Schraeder and Hamadi Redissi

Peter J. Schraeder *is professor and chair of the Department of Political Science at Loyola University in Chicago. He has been a Fulbright lecturer at the University of Tunis, teaches every January at the University of Carthage, and each May leads U.S. students to Tunisia.* **Hamadi Redissi** *is professor of political science at the Tunisian Faculty of Law, Tunis, and has been a visiting scholar at Yale University.* This essay originally appeared in the July 2011 issue of the Journal of Democracy.

On 14 January 2011, what has become known as the Jasmine Revolution forced Tunisia's dictator of 23 years, President Zine al-Abidine Ben Ali, to give up power and leave the country. After just 28 days of protests that even lethal police repression could not quell, senior Tunisian military officers resolved that Ben Ali would have to go because they found themselves asked to turn their guns on the Tunisian people—which they refused to do. As the winter evening fell, he found himself boarding a plane bound for exile in Saudi Arabia.

A spontaneous and secular popular uprising, driven by young Tunisians using social media such as Facebook and Twitter, had revealed a civil society intent on securing the Arab world's first democracy. The uprising also prompted a regionwide domino effect, as prodemocracy demonstrators began to confront dictators across the Middle East and North Africa. In the "Arab Spring" of 2011, Tunisia is "case zero." Understanding how that case unfolded—and where it might lead—should be of interest to all students and friends of democracy in this so far most democracy-resistant of all world regions.

To say that Ben Ali's sudden fall caught specialists by surprise would be an understatement. His *mukhabarat* (intelligence-based) police state had turned back an outbreak of popular unrest as recently as 2008, and at age 74 he remained, if not youthful, at least aware and seemingly in charge. Ben Ali was only the second president that Tunisia has had since it won independence from France in the mid-1950s. He gained that office by means of a 1987 constitutional coup against 84-year-old Habib Bourguiba, whose erratic behavior during his later years had damaged his revered status as one of the founding fathers of modern Tunisia.

Defying early hopes that he would prove a liberalizer after packing Bourguiba off into involuntary retirement, Ben Ali had instead built an authoritarian regime that some considered impervious to change owing to the creation of a "strong neo-corporatist state" or the "force of obedience" or an "authoritarian syndrome" in Tunisian society.[1] The new regime adopted "le changement" (change) as its mantra, and marked the November 7 anniversary of Ben Ali's putsch every year with much fanfare celebrating Tunisia's "democratic transition." As Mark Gasiorowski concluded in these pages just five years after Ben Ali seized power, the "failure of reform" in Tunisia meant that the "opportunity" to establish a democratic regime there had been missed, and would "not appear again for quite some time."[2]

Aside from a military establishment totaling 35,000 troops, the key to the state's control was a set of security forces commonly assumed to number as high as 130,000—enough to saddle Tunisia and its 10.5 million people with a police presence as large as that of France, a country with almost six times Tunisia's population.[3] Security formations included the Presidential Guard (roughly 8,000 members) with its headquarters in Carthage, the National Guard (roughly 20,000) with its main base next to Tunis-Carthage International Airport, and a variety of other forces such as the political police, the tourism police, and the university police.

Reinforcing this *mukhabarat* state was a neopatrimonial form of governance that exalted Ben Ali's personal rule. The key to personal success was not achievement in a given field, but links to the extended family of the ubiquitously photographed president. Regional specialists like to joke that you can tell how bad a dictatorship is by the number of presidential portraits on display everywhere. Ben Ali was known for posting large and ostentatious images of himself—sporting suspiciously jet-black hair for a man in his seventies—on countless billboards and buildings. One multistory portrait loomed over the busy port of La Goulette, where the smiling strongman seemed to be reminding cruise-ship passengers and other travelers that he and his *mukhabarat* were always watching and listening. Another consisted of a massive and supremely tacky mosaic that Ben Ali had positioned within the ruins of the magnificent Roman amphitheater at El Djem.

Before December 2010, the last major manifestation of discontent amid the dictatorial kitsch had come in 2008 in the southwestern region of Gafsa. The immediate target had been the state-owned Gafsa Phosphate Company, the main employer in a poverty-stricken area with few jobs.[4] After two decades of shedding posts, the company had announced plans to add 350 workers. When results of the formal employment competition became public, the vast bulk of the new hires turned out to be people with no ties to the region but strong political links to Ben Ali and his regime. Infuriated locals launched demonstrations in a string of mining towns. Massive police cordons, including riot squads brought in from Tunis, surrounded the towns, and the protests were quashed. Hundreds were arrested and prosecuted, with some receiving prison sentences of up to eight years. Although in retrospect it seems clear that the Gafsa protests were a harbinger of deepening socioeconomic crisis, at the time the regime was able to portray them as the isolated problem of a single region and industry.

The event that undid the ability of Ben Ali's *mukhabarat* to maintain control happened in the small and impoverished central Tunisian town of Sidi Bouzid. It was there, on Friday, 17 December 2010, that a 26-year-old fruit vendor, Mohamed Bouazizi, set himself on fire in order to protest the harassment he was suffering at the hands of local officials. This act of desperation touched off demonstrations in Sidi Bouzid that focused at first on deteriorating socioeconomic conditions, the lack of jobs, and unfair treatment at the hands of local administrators and police. Unlike the Gafsa protests of two years earlier, however, the unrest soon began to spread throughout the country and gave rise to demands for Ben Ali's departure and the creation of a government more responsive to the people.

The endgame for Ben Ali began as demonstrators filled the streets of Tunis, the capital. On December 28, he gave a nationally televised speech in which he charged the protesters with hurting the economy and threatened to deal with them severely. When this did not work, he gave a second address on January 10 in which he tried to paint the demonstrators as "terrorists" serving foreign masters, but also vowed to create 300,000 new jobs. As protestors scoffed, Ben Ali made a third and final television appearance on January 13, assuring demonstrators that he had "heard" and "understood" them, and promising not to run for a sixth term in October 2014. This was too little, too late, as swelling numbers of emboldened Tunisians carried signs reading "Game Over!" and chanting "Ben Ali, dégage!" ("Get out!"). Confronted two days later with the largest antigovernment demonstration that Tunis had ever seen, Ben Ali fled.

Sowing the Wind

Although the speed with which the Ben Ali regime folded was stunning, several socioeconomic and political-military indicators suggested that Tunisia was ripe for change. Unemployment had risen to 14 percent in 2010, with the figure for those aged 15 to 24 years—a huge chunk of the populace in a typically "youth-predominant" developing-world society—exceeding 30 percent. Strikingly, the well-educated were especially affected. More than 45 percent of college graduates could not find work in a country that offered its citizens higher learning but no job prospects to go with it.

Another sign of socioeconomic stress could be read in rising food costs. As of 2008, the average Tunisian household was devoting nearly 36 percent of its domestic budget to the purchase of basic foodstuffs for home consumption. A comparable figure for the United States at that time would be less than 7 percent. Between 2008 and 2010, not surprisingly, the proportion of Tunisians who rated themselves as "thriving" dropped from 24 to 14 percent, meaning that at least a million citizens had witnessed a reversal in their economic fortunes. Tom DeGeorges, director of the Tunis-based Center for Maghreb Studies (CEMAT), argues that this was due at least in part to the global economic crisis that began in 2008. Austerity measures in Europe, he notes, caused a drop in remittances from Tunisians working abroad and thereby pinched a major source of national income.[5]

A second factor was the intensifying authoritarianism of the Ben Ali regime.[6] Since taking power in 1987, Ben Ali had "won" five consecutive presidential elections, most recently in October 2009 with 89.6 percent of the vote. In a 2002 bid to make himself president for life, Ben Ali arranged a constitutional referendum to remove the three-term limit on incumbency in his post. His ruling party, the Democratic Constitutional Assembly (RCD), and the rubber-stamp Chamber of Deputies that it dominated were increasingly brought under presidential control. With each passing term, the regime became more authoritarian and less in touch with local socioeconomic and political realities.

Tunisia's annual Freedom House (FH) ratings capture the trend. The New York–based nonprofit assigns countries scores for Political Rights and Civil Liberties that range from 1 (most free) to 7 (least free), with the worst-possible combined score being 14. Tunisia had been an 11 during Bourguiba's last year in power, but improved to an 8 within two years of Ben Ali's takeover. This reflected Ben Ali's early decisions to grant amnesty to Bourguiba-era political prisoners and to open up civil liberties generally. No improvement was seen beyond this point, however, and by 1994 Tunisia was back to being an 11, on its way to a 12 and an abysmal Not Free rating in more recent FH surveys.

As Ben Ali hung on to power year after year, his regime began to arouse special resentment by dint of its worsening capriciousness. One typical example involved a young graduate student named Ali Khlifi. His "crime" was having a friend who, unbeknownst to Ali himself, was also friendly with two young men who had mentioned within earshot of the wrong person their desire to see an Islamist regime replace Ben Ali. Anything that smacked of an Islamist threat had long been a "red-line" matter for the president,[7] especially after al-Qaeda bombed the el-Ghriba synagogue on the island of Djerba in 2002. When an informant went to the authorities claiming knowledge of the problematic discussion, Ali found himself caught up in the resulting police sweep and sentenced to a year in prison—all for an incident of which he had never even heard. During his first nights behind bars, he cried out to his jailers that he was not guilty and should be set free. After several nights of this, one of the guards told Ali that they of course knew he was innocent, which was why he had received such a short sentence. When Ali asked why he was in jail at all, he was told: "Because you should know who the friends of your friends are." The effect of policing like this on the climate surrounding political discussions can easily be imagined. "If I don't know you, I don't speak freely," explained Ali after his release. After he left prison, Ali found himself ostracized even by friends and family. "Why should someone run the risk of losing a job, not getting a place at the university, or worst of all, being sent to prison, simply because of their association with me?"

A third cause making Tunisia ripe for upheaval was public disenchantment with the growing corruption of the president's extended family of more than 140 persons. This trend shows up in the annual Corruption Perception Index maintained by Transparency International, in which Tunisia's ranking declined from 43rd in 2005 to 59th in 2010, out of a total of 178 countries monitored. Tunisians reserved special disdain for Leila Trabelsi, Ben Ali's second wife. A former hair stylist more than two decades younger than her husband, she became known as the "regent of Carthage," a reference to her growing assertiveness in matters political.[8] She was particularly despised for having enabled her ten rapacious siblings to sink their teeth into businesses throughout Tunisia. Her brother Belhassen, called *le parrain* (the godfather), illegally assumed control over an array of enterprises that the U.S. embassy in Tunis listed as including "an airline, several hotels, one of Tunisia's two private radio stations, car assembly plants, Ford distribution, a real estate development company, and [more]."[9] According to the Central Bank of Tunisia, relatives of the former president and his wife owned at least 180 major companies.

Nor did the presidential kinfolk limit their avidity to major corporations and business initiatives. In 2009, a Tunis-area clock repairman named Moncef Ben Rhouma found himself in a land-ownership dispute with Slim Ben Mansour and Habib Mzabi, the presidentially connected owners of a development company called La Renaissance (Mzabi is married to Leila Trabelsi's niece). The real estate in question was a walled garden, attached to an existing residence, that the Trabelsis coveted for a planned housing complex in the Tunis suburb of La Marsa. In a case typical of hundreds, members of the powerful family sent bulldozers to breach the wall and start construction, ignoring all prior claims by current residents. Moncef and fourteen other inhabitants (all of them women), bravely but futilely confronted the "land developers"—with Moncef physically blocking the bulldozer's path—while the first lady's niece looked on. Police made arrests, a local court declared La Renaissance the lawful owner, and the expropriation went forward under cover of this legal fig leaf.

From Tinderbox to Funeral Pyre

Declining socioeconomic conditions and rising authoritarian caprice provided ample fuel for the conflagration that consumed Ben Ali's rule, but the combustion was not spontaneous. Several other factors were important. First was the literal and figurative spark of Bouazizi's fatal self-immolation (he would succumb to his severe burns on 4 January 2011). The desperation implicit in this horrifying act caught Tunisians' imagination, in no small part because Bouazizi's story was so typical. With his fruit cart, he had been eking out a living not only for himself but for his mother, uncle, and five siblings. Harassed and hit up for bribes for years by brutal police, he had snapped when they overturned his cart, confiscated the scale without which he could not work, and subjected him to a final humiliation in the form of a public slap in the face from a 45-year-old female officer.[10]

When Bouazizi followed the well-worn path of approaching the local governor's office for redress, he was refused an audience even after vowing to set himself alight. Incredibly, Ben Ali sought political gain from this situation by visiting Bouazizi in the burn unit at a hospital outside Tunis on December 28, after reportedly having greeted news of the self-immolation with the words "Let him die." The hospital visit backfired badly, further enraging Bouazizi's supporters and spurring intensified calls for Ben Ali's ouster.

A still more costly presidential blunder came in the form of Ben Ali's decision to authorize deadly force against the protestors. The *mukhabarat* had in the past used tear gas, clubs, rubber bullets, and torture to cow protestors and political prisoners. On December 24, it fired real bullets at protesters in Manzel Bouzayane, killing 18-year-old Mohamed Ammari and 44-year-old Chaouki Belhoussine El Hadri, according to a report published by Amnesty International.[11] In Tala from the last week of December through the first two weeks of January, hundreds of security officers repeatedly and brutally assaulted demonstrators. The French magazine *Paris Match* carried poignant coverage, with a picture of Sauhi Wajhi, 28 years old, who was shot in the back on January 10.[12] Kasserine, known as the site of a major tank battle between Allied and Axis forces in early 1943, saw a particularly gruesome attack on protesters. One eyewitness saw snipers, firing from rooftops, kill as many as fifty citizens. Yet instead of retreating when faced with deadly force, protesters became more willing to confront the regime in the streets.

According to the transitional government's most recent estimate, at least three hundred were killed and more than seven hundred were wounded between December 17 and the end of January.

The widespread use of cellphones and social media, most notably Facebook and Twitter, was critical to the protests' rapid spread throughout the country. The initial protests in Sidi Bouzid following Bouazizi's self-immolation were recorded on cellphone video cameras, posted on the Internet, and shared on Facebook, capturing the attention of Al Jazeera, which became the first international news outlet to run the story. As protests spread and the regime responded with deadly force, clinic and hospital staffers as well as family members and activists began going online to share cellphone pictures and videos of protesters killed by the government. Since about one out of every three Tunisians is an Internet user, awareness of what was happening was soon pervasive in what has been widely called "the first Facebook revolution" (about one of every five Tunisians maintains a profile on the social-networking site). According to a March 2011 survey that Peter Schraeder conducted in Tunis, 91 percent of university students visit Facebook at least once a day, and on average spend 105 minutes there daily. Nearly two-thirds (64 percent) of student respondents said that Facebook had been their primary source of information about demonstrations between December 17 and January 14. Almost a third (32 percent) of all students indicated that they had first learned of Bouazizi's self-immolation via Facebook.

Grasping the importance of the Internet, the Ben Ali regime employed a virtual army of censors to block or filter YouTube, DailyMotion, and other sites. Joe Sullivan, Facebook's chief security officer, confirmed that in December 2010 the Tunisian government tried to hack into Facebook and steal user passwords, but was stopped from doing so.[13] On the antiregime side, Web-savvy young Tunisians downloaded proxy software for use in evading government controls. Among those from the Internet generation who rose to prominence during the protests are Azyz Amami and Slim Amamou, the latter of whom joined the transitional government for a time as its youth minister. They networked not only with each other, having met in 2010, but with external groups, such as Anonymous (the confederation of hackers), that coordinated attacks against Tunisian-government websites. As protestor Habib Redissi explains:

> The sheer volume of shared information across a network of more than three-million Internet-connected Tunisans reached a tipping point where it became virtually impossible for the Tunisian government to suppress information short of completely shutting down the Internet, which was not an option because the Tunisian economy—[which promotes] tourism and [welcomes] the annual arrival of five-million tourists—depends on it.

In January 2011, Hicham Ben Abdallah El Alaoui reflected in these pages on the political and media culture of the Arab world, asking "Is the Web a Game Changer?"[14] Looking at how events unfolded in Tunisia, we would answer his question with a resounding yes. Social media are mightier than the sword.

In what now appears an ironic twist, Ben Ali had declared 2010 to be the "Year of Youth," little dreaming that so many of those whom he "honored" would take to the streets to topple his regime. A few statistics tell the story of youth and its impact: Slightly more than two of every five Tunisians are under 25 years old; almost 35 percent of those between 19 and 24 are students; and one of three young people is unemployed. It is thus no surprise that a large portion of the Tunisian protesters were under 30, with students or jobless recent graduates swelling their ranks.

"History Was on Our Side"

One of the most fascinating developments was the emergence of a generational split between the younger protesters and older, more established opponents of Ben Ali. When the president went on television on January 13 to vow that he would step down at the end of his term in 2014, many of his old foes welcomed the move as an amazing victory for prodemocracy forces. Young people, meanwhile, scoffed and wondered what was to be gained by giving Ben Ali and his family four more years to pillage and work on arranging an authoritarian succession. Students and other under-30 Tunisians embraced the giant protests planned for January 14 in downtown Tunis as their generation's "moment." Despite their fear of regime violence, they set out to demonstrate that day with resolution and a hope that, as protester Sinda Redissi said, "history was on our side."

As important as their drive and uncompromising attitude proved to be, the young people were but one part of a larger civil society coalition that filled the streets. According to a recent report by Syrine Ayadi, a Tunisian lawyer working with NGOs, the number of civil society organizations had increased nearly fivefold from 1,976 in 1988 to 9,592 at the beginning of 2011.[15] A legacy of the Bourguiba era is that women's organizations such as the Tunisian Association of Democratic Women are strong and well organized, ensuring that women were amply represented in demonstrations throughout the country. One of the classic pictures from the January 14 demonstration that provoked Ben Ali's departure shows attorney Leila Ben Debba holding the Tunisian flag above her head and exhorting her compatriots to stand firm.[16] Uncowed by government persecution, human-rights organizations such as the Tunisian League for Human Rights were equally vocal in their denunciations of the Ben Ali regime. Tunisia also has a highly organized labor movement, represented by the nationwide General Union of Tunisian Workers (UGTT), which includes thousands of affiliates, 24 regional unions, 19 labor federations, and 21 general unions. It is unsurprising that regional unions, which are closer to conditions on the ground, were earlier and more intense critics of the Ben Ali regime.

What was surprising was that Islamist parties and organizations were left largely on the sidelines by the success of the essentially secular antiregime movement. It is true that Ben Ali had long repressed the Islamists, forcing a number of their leaders into exile. Yet one should not underrate the strength of secular beliefs—especially the need to keep mosque and state separate—within a general populace that in many ways is tied more closely to Europe than to the wider regional environment of the Middle East and North Africa. While religious Muslims could certainly be found among the demonstrators, the larger scene was more notable for its diversity of faces: secular folk as well as the old and young, men and women, urbanites and rural dwellers, and professionals along with blue-collar workers.

As events moved toward a climax, the Tunisian army and its chief of staff, General Rachid Ammar, became critical players. Tunisians now hail the army as the "hero" of the revolution because Ammar refused to follow Ben Ali's order to have the Tunisian military fire on the demonstrators.[17] Had the general decided differently, the outcome would have been much bloodier, and might have included an outright military coup. According to one widely believed account, Ali Seriati, the head of Ben Ali's Presidential Guard, persuaded the president to leave by convincing him that Seriati—who was actually planning to seize power for himself—would set the stage for the dictator's return "to restore calm and stability." Upon learning of this plot, Ammar reportedly ordered the arrest of Seriati and his associates, while at the same time securing the airport so that Ben Ali could have safe passage out of the country.

The general subsequently ordered troops to secure the major cities and crossroads, but made it clear that neither he nor the military had any intention of playing any political role beyond protecting the demonstrators and the Tunisian public more generally and ensuring the formation of a civilian-led democracy. Peter Schraeder looked on as tanks and their crews stood post at the main "round point" (intersection) in downtown La Marsa in front of the Zephyr shopping complex. Throughout the day, in a tableau played out again and again all over the country, smiling civilian families would walk up and eagerly pose for cellphone photos in front of the tanks, with beaming soldiers joining them. The young troopers' pride over the role that they had played in defending the Tunisian people was obvious.

A final element in the Jasmine Revolution was the role of foreign powers, most notably France and the United States. Revolutions are always driven from within, with outside powers at best playing a facilitating role. In the case of the United States, statements by Secretary of State Hillary Clinton and President Barack Obama, who mentioned Tunisia in his State of the Union Address on January 25, ensured that Washington was on the right side of history. The current U.S. ambassador to Tunis, Gordon Gray, is credited with informing Ben Ali that he had to leave power, and that he could not count on exile in the United States. The French government of Nicolas Sarkozy cannot claim to have been on the right side of history. Michèle Alliot-Marie, the French foreign minister, not only vacationed in Tunisia during the week after Christmas 2010, as demonstrations were intensifying, but flew there on the private jet of a Tunisian businessman tied to Ben Ali. Even worse, two days before Ben Ali fled the country and more than two weeks after the Tunisian police started using live ammunition against the protesters, Alliot-Marie offered to send French police to help the Tunisian police "restore calm," because the French were skilled in "security situations of this type."[18] On February 27, Alliot-Marie was forced to resign as a result of her actions regarding Tunisia.

The United States had been inadvertently involved in setting the stage for Ben Ali's ouster via the November 2010 WikiLeaks release of a trove of U.S. State Department cables. Particularly damaging to the dictator were those written by Robert F. Godec, the U.S. ambassador from 2007 to 2009. In damaging detail, Godec described Ben Ali's authoritarianism and the rampant corruption of his in-laws and extended family. Ironically, both the U.S. and Tunisian governments had sought to prevent these cables from appearing, each for its own reasons: Washington wanted to avoid diplomatic embarrassment, whereas Ben Ali sought to stifle revelations that might fuel antiregime sentiment. Tunisian bloggers rendered such calculations moot by creating an alternate "TuniLeaks" site that tens of thousands of Tunisians visited. The WikiLeaks cables undoubtedly fueled the events of December and January. "It was one thing to hear rumors about the extensive corruption of the Ben Ali regime," Syrine Ayadi told us. "It was quite another to actually see a great amount of detail in print, written by the U.S. ambassador, which everyone was talking about."

Toward a Democratic Second Republic

The first few days after Ben Ali left were a time of heightened danger, as remnants of the Presidential Guard and other state-security forces tried to sow terror.[19] It took the army to blunt these threats—whether by arresting Seriati's confederates as they fled toward the Libyan border or by fighting pitched battles at the presidential mansion in Carthage and the Interior Ministry headquarters in downtown Tunis. The army also called on citizens to form neighborhood-watch groups that could take responsibility for keeping order as the once-formidable police presence melted away.

There was political instability too, as the first transitional government headed by interim president Fouad Mebazaa (former president of the Chamber of Deputies) and Prime Minister Mohamed Ghannouchi (who had been premier under Ben Ali) confronted demonstrators who opposed continuing leadership roles for Ben Ali holdovers. Asserting that Tunisians had not braved police bullets so that Ben Ali's henchmen could keep running things, foes of the interim government organized themselves into a Council for the Protection of the Revolution comprising no fewer than 28 organizations from civil society, most notably the UGTT, the Islamist party known as Ennahda (Renaissance), and several leftist groups. They mounted a "caravan of liberation" to bring protesters to Tunis from the rural areas, organized a sit-in at Kasbah Square (the seat of government), and precipitated bloody clashes with riot police who were now serving the interim government.

The demonstrations finally ended on February 27, when Ghannouchi and all other former ministers of the Ben Ali regime resigned their posts, and a new interim government took power under the leadership of Prime Minister Béji Caïd Essebsi. The 84-year-old Essebsi was a brilliant choice, in that he both hailed from and had been a critic of the Bourguiba era, had been a prominent critic of the Ben Ali regime (despite having served as the president of the Chamber of Deputies between 1990 and 1992), and remained a charismatic leader with strong interpersonal and diplomatic skills. Among his first acts were publicly embracing the court ruling that banned Ben Ali's RCD party, ordering the public arrest and arraignment of high-ranking regime hard-liners, and dismantling the political police—all steps that the vast majority of Tunisians greeted with enthusiasm. Essebsi's government also confiscated the properties, assets and businesses of 110 members of Ben Ali's family, including the ex-president and his wife.

Several early signs suggest that Tunisia's Second Republic will be marked by strong prospects for democratic transition and consolidation. First, the scope of political debate has increased as prominent exiles have returned home. These include the Islamist Rachid Ghannouchi, and also human-rights activists Kamel Jendoubi and Moncef Marzouki. Second, in preparation for the elections (scheduled for October 23) that will choose the members of a constituent assembly, political parties are forming at a quick pace. As of this writing in early June 2011, 63 parties have been legalized, and that number is sure to grow before the October elections. Equally impressive is the complete freedom of speech that is now evident throughout Tunisian media, including newspapers, radio, television, and social media. Tunisians today can and do freely voice their political beliefs and opinions, regardless of who is listening. This stands in stark contrast to both the government-imposed censorship and the self-censorship that were the hallmarks of the Ben Ali era.

It is also heartening to see that the interim government has created three commissions of experts to expose past wrongs and move the country forward. The National Fact-Finding Commission on Abuse is dedicated to uncovering and documenting physical violations such as the killings of protesters that took place in December and January. The Fact-Finding Commission on Corruption and Embezzlement is focusing on the financial misdeeds of the Ben Ali era, including the Trabelsi family's land grabs. The High Commission for the Realization of Revolutionary Goals, Political Reforms, and Democratic Transition (known as the Commission for Political Reform or the Ben Achour Commission for short) is a broadly consultative body that brings together most political forces for the purpose of fostering a democratic transition, most notably via the electoral code and a new set of core constitutional principles. The drafting of this document will be a primary responsibility of the new constituent assembly to be popularly elected in July. Once ratified by that body and perhaps submitted to a popular referendum, the new constitution will pave the way for either presidential or parliamentary elections (depending on the choices that the assembly makes). It is striking to note that more than five-thousand dossiers have been submitted to the three commissions, with 762 seeking redress for past abuses, 42 dealing with political reform, and the vast majority (4,239) focusing on specific acts of embezzlement and corruption.[20]

Several recent institutional developments are also important for understanding Tunisia's transition. First, the interim government issued a legal decree on March 23 dissolving institutions strongly influenced by the old regime, including the Chamber of Deputies, the upper house, and the Constitutional Court, while maintaining other institutions needed for the state to function. Second, interim-government leaders have repeatedly noted that they have two main tasks: resuscitating an economy damaged by strikes and revolutionary turmoil, and reestablishing security throughout the country. This latter end was greatly served by replacing Interior Minister Farhat Rajhi with Habib Essid, who is well regarded by the police. The police, smarting under public obloquy and eager to stress that they were not all brutal Ben Ali enforcers, have undertaken the extraordinary action of creating a police officers' union. On April 19, it called on its members to wear red armbands in protest against what the union called a "campaign of unjustified denunciations." In an attempt to meet public demands for justice, the interim government continues to arrest former RCD members and to publicly confiscate the property of individuals associated with Ben Ali–era corruption.

With the return of calm, the army—traditionally a small and professional body—has mostly returned to base while maintaining a discreet presence at key urban intersections. Once again, the police are doing the main work of keeping order. Although the army has welcomed the interim government's plan to create several thousand new officer billets, it remains sensitive to criticism. Defense Minister Abdelkarim Zebidi, a civilian, has reminded critics that the army "refuses to enter into the political game" and remains "vigilant to protect the achievements of the revolution." General Ammar, who has stayed out of the public eye since Essebsi became premier, has been promoted to armed-forces chief of staff and remains the ground forces' commander, which would give him extra authority in a crisis.

Whither the Electoral System?

The real issue remains the electoral system. In April, the Commission for Political Reform approved two important legal decrees regarding it. The first mandates proportional representation (PR), which is typical of parliamentary systems. The PR method favors smaller parties while by the same token risking splits and fractiousness. Two provisions of this decree have sparked controversy. Article 16, which was approved by a large show of hands (including the Islamists) on April 17, seeks to guarantee female representation in parliament by requiring that all electoral lists must consist of male and female candidates ranked alternately (that is, with a man heading the list and a female in the second spot and so on, or vice-versa). The even more controversial Article 15 excludes from participation in the upcoming elections all former leading members of the RCD, of the late government, and "all people having assumed any responsibilities during the last 23 years." This ban will have the effect of penalizing both the Watan (Homeland) and the Wifeq (Concord) parties, each of which is the creation of a former Ben Ali cabinet official. Former RCD members, not surprisingly, have strongly protested Article 15.

A second decree concerns the election of the Electoral Commission. This body is to comprise fifteen members who are to be independent of both the state (including the interim government) and any political party, and who are to be elected by the Commission for Political Reform. The Electoral Commission is to bear responsibility for all operations relating to elections, ranging from voter registration to vote counting. Despite these decrees, the exact contours of Tunisia's electoral system remain somewhat indefinite, and there is a chance that the elections set for July may be delayed.

Finally, although the Jasmine Revolution was a largely secular affair, Islamists are not remaining on the political sidelines. On the contrary, Islamist forces and especially Ennahda have been speaking out frequently in the media and the newly free public square. The veil is no longer illegal, and may be worn even in the photographs on national identity cards. Seemingly contradictory declarations by Islamist leaders have aroused their middle-class critics. For example, Ennahda says that it accepts the Personal Status Code (which forbids polygamy), but also calls for "traditional" values—and many wonder what this means. Islamists' statements on the applicability of *shari'a,* and their avowals of a desire to ban alcohol and tourism (a major source of national income) have led to turbulent countercampaigns by secular groups. In coming months, the debate between Islamists and secularists will attract much attention both foreign and domestic. That said, the signs as of this writing—including the vigorous response that the Islamists have aroused—suggest that Tunisia is on the right path, and will emerge as the Arab world's first democracy.

—9 June 2011

NOTES

The authors wish to thank Jessica Mecellem, doctoral candidate in the Department of Political Science at Loyola University of Chicago, for her research assistance.

1. See Hamadi Redissi, "Etat fort, société faible en Tunisie," *Maghreb-Machrek*, Summer 2007, 89–117; Beatrice Hibou, *La force de l'obéissance: Economie politique de la répression en tunisie* (Paris: La Decouverte, 2006); and Michael Camau and Stephen Geisser, *Syndrome autoritaire: Politique en Tunisie de Bourguiba à Ben Ali* (Paris: Presses de Sciences Po, 2003).

2. Mark J. Gasiorowski, "The Islamist Challenge: The Failure of Reform in Tunisia," *Journal of Democracy* 3 (October 1992): 97.

3. John P. Entelis, "The Democratic Imperative vs. the Authoritarian Impulse: The Maghrib State Between Transition and Terrorism," *Middle East Journal* 59 (Autumn 2005): 537–58. According to Farhat Rajhi, a judge who was appointed minister of interior in the interim government, the police force under Ben Ali did not number more than 50,000.

4. Amin Allal, "Réformes néolibérales, clientélismes et protestations en situation autoritaire: Les mouvements contestaires dans le bassin minier de Gafsa en Tunisie (2008)," *Politique Africaine* 117 (March 2010): 109.

5. Personal correspondence, undated.

6. Nicolas Beau and Jean-Pierre Tuquoi, *Notre ami Ben Ali* (Paris: La Decouverte, 1999).

7. Abdelwahab Sdiri, *Dans cinq ans il n'y aura plus de Coran: Un prisonnier tunisien témoigne* (Paris: Editions Paris-Méditerranée, 2003).

8. Nicolas Beau and Catherine Graciet, *La régente de Carthage: Main basse sur la Tunisie* (Paris: La Decouverte, 2009).

9. See Robert F. Godec, "Tunisian Corruption and President Zine el-Abidine Ben Ali," cable dated 23 June 2008, and published by WikiLeaks.

10. The officer has denied slapping Bouazizi, but few believe her. "She humiliated him," the vendor's half-sister Samia Bouazizi told a reporter. "Everyone was watching." See Kareem Fahim, "Slap to a Man's Pride Set Off Tumult in Tunisia," *New York Times,* 21 January 2011.

11. Amnesty International, "Tunisia in Revolt: State Violence during Anti-Government Protests," 1 March 2011. Available at *www.amnestyusa.org.*

12. "Tunisie: Le souffle de la liberté. Le récit des jours où le peuple a brisé ses chaînes," *Paris Match*, 20–26 January 2011.

13. Alexis Madrigal, "The Inside Story of How Facebook Responded to Tunisian Hacks," *www.theatlantic.com*, 24 January 2011.

14. Hicham Ben Abdallah El Alaoui, "The Split in Arab Culture," *Journal of Democracy* 22 (January 2011): 13.

15. Syrine Ayadi, "Civil Society in Tunisia: Legal, Political and Judicial Panorama During the Post-Revolutionary Period," unpubl. report, 20 March 2011.

16. See the cover of *Paris Match*, 20–26 January 2011.

17. Abdelaziz Barrouhi, "L'Homme qui a dit non," *Jeune Afrique*, 30 January–5 February 2011, 44–48.

18. Steven Erlanger, "French Foreign Minister Rebuked for Tunisian Trip," *New York Times*, 4 February 2011.

19. See the excellent description written by the Tunisian novelist Kamel Riahi, "A Night in Tunisia," *New York Times*, 19 January 2011, A23.

20. See "4,239 dossiers, au 7 mars," *Le Quotidien*, 10 March 2011, 4.

18

TUNISIA'S TRANSITION AND THE "TWIN TOLERATIONS"

Alfred Stepan

Alfred Stepan *is Wallace S. Sayre Professor of Government at Colum-bia University and director of Columbia's Center for the Study of De-mocracy, Toleration, and Religion. This essay originally appeared in the April 2012 issue of the* Journal of Democracy.

For many of the most influential theorists of secularism and modern-ization, religion was seen as something "traditional and irrational"—a force for authoritarianism and an obstacle to the quest for "modernity and rationality" that alone could lead to democracy.[1] Was their percep-tion correct? My study of actual democratization efforts in countries ranging from Brazil, Chile, India, and Indonesia to Senegal, Spain, Tur-key, and now Tunisia tells a different story. The experiences of these countries over the last several decades suggest that "hard" secularism of the kind associated with France's Third Republic or Mustafa Kemal Atatürk's post-Ottoman Turkey is not necessary for democratization, and may even create problems for it.

An examination of the transition in Tunisia helps to illustrate the point. Over the past year, I have made three research trips to this small, predominantly Sunni Muslim country in North Africa where the Arab Spring began. Tunisia's recent story is complex, and here I have room to cover only part of it—but it is an important part that observers, particu-larly in the West, should take care not to overlook or underappreciate.

In 2011, Tunisia achieved a successful democratic transition, albeit not yet a consolidation of democracy. It did so while adhering to a re-lationship between religion and politics that follows the pattern of what I have called in these pages and elsewhere the "twin tolerations." What are the twin tolerations? The first toleration is that of religious citizens toward the state. It requires that they accord democratically elected of-ficials the freedom to legislate and govern without having to confront denials of their authority based on religious claims—such as the claim that "Only God, not man, can make laws."

The second toleration is that of the state toward religious citizens. This type of toleration requires that laws and officials must permit religious citizens, as a matter of right, to freely express their views and values within civil society, and to freely take part in politics, as long as religious activists and organizations respect other citizens' constitutional rights and the law. In a democracy, religion need not be "off the agenda," and indeed, to force it off would violate the second toleration.[2] Embracing the twin tolerations is a move that is friendly toward liberal democracy because the embrace involves a rejection not only of theocracy, but also of the illiberalism that is inseparable from aggressive, "top-down," religion-controlling versions of secularism such as Turkish Kemalism or the religion-unfriendly *laïcité* associated with the French Third Republic and its 1905 "Law Concerning the Separation of Churches and the State."

Before exploring how the twin tolerations gained a purchase in Tunisia, contributing to that country's promising start as a democracy, it will be helpful to review the Tunisian transition itself. On 23 October 2011, following the Jasmine Revolution that ousted longtime dictator Zine al-Abidine Ben Ali in January, Tunisia held its first free election since gaining independence from France in 1956. Voters chose a 217-member Constituent Assembly, whose largest single party (with 41 percent of the seats) is the Islamist movement known as Ennahda (sometimes also called al-Nahda). The Assembly has since elected a prime minister, Ennahda's former secretary-general Hamadi Jebali, and a president, human-rights activist Moncef Marzouki. They and the rest of the government's members were sworn in and began their duties on 23 December 2011, marking Tunisia's achievement of a successful transition. In an estimated twelve to fifteen months, after the constitution is completed, there will be new elections for all these posts.

In my view, Tunisia can be said to have accomplished this transition—and now turns to face the more protracted challenge of democratic consolidation—because it has met all four of the requirements that Juan J. Linz and I have argued, based upon our study of numerous cases, are crucial for such a shift.[3] The first of these requirements is "sufficient agreement" on "procedures to produce an elected government." The second is a government that comes to power as "the direct result of a free and popular vote." The third is this government's de facto possession of "the authority to generate new policies," and the fourth is that "the executive, legislative and judicial power generated by the new democracy does not have to share power with other bodies de jure" (such as military or religious leaders).

Nothing is certain, of course. Democracy is always only "government pro tem," and always faces dangers that must be guarded against by a constitution with protections against majority tyranny, a vigilant independent judiciary, a robust and critical civil society, and a free press. Although Tunisia needs many reforms and much institution-building, it already has in place a reasonable number of credible con-straints that should help to make democracy more secure and give it a fair chance to deepen and consolidate.

One key constraint is that Ennahda fell short of a majority in the Constituent Assembly. It won its 89 seats based on 37 percent of the popular vote. Thus it had to form a coalition with two secular parties, Marzouki's Congress for the Republic (CPR), which won 29 seats, and Ettakatol, which won 20 seats. Should Ennahda succumb to pressure from militant Islamists in its base, its secular partners could withdraw—a total of 109 seats is needed to form and sustain a government—in or-der to threaten Ennahda's control over the Assembly. Indeed, under the Assembly's parliamentary procedures, Ennahda could even find itself subjected to a vote of no confidence that could lead to the accession of a new ruling majority in that body.

Another constraint is suggested by the agreement on the free and fair nature of the October 2011 voting on the part of virtually all the opposition-party and government leaders with whom I spoke—notably including Ahmed Nejib El Chebbi of the Progressive Democrats (PDP), the top secular opposition party, which did worse than expected. While affirming the integrity of the balloting, Chebbi went on to express his certainty that another competitive election will be held within a year to eighteen months after the Constituent Assembly has completed its work. When I asked him why his party had done so poorly, he said that he had erred in heeding the advice of U.S. election consultants who urged him to focus on televised campaign advertising. He told me that next time, the Progressive Democrats will do more grassroots or-ganizing and predicted that, given the problems of the world economy and the pressure on Ennahda to deliver on material expectations and promises, a broader coalition of opposition parties will have a serious chance to govern.

Chebbi, like virtually all the party leaders I talked to, sees elections as "the only game in town" when it comes to gaining political pow-er. He and others praised the work done by the Independent Electoral Commission and international observers, and want and expect them to play a major role in the next election. Attitudes such as these, as Linz and I have argued, are key if democracy is to take root.

Preparing the Way for Transition

How did Tunisia, late in 2011, carry out a transition process that won the approval of even those parties who came out (for the time being, at least) on its short end? The answer lies in the events of early 2011, when a process of consensual national decision making laid down the ground rules for what would unfold later in the year. Within days of Ben Ali's flight into Saudi Arabian exile on January 14, an interim government filled with his appointees decreed a new organization to craft procedures for a rapid presidential election, presumably aimed at allowing Ben Ali's longtime premier, Mohamed Ghannouchi, to become the new chief executive.

Soon, however, a strong, nonviolent civil society protest outside the prime minister's office, as well as demands for full participation in decision making by newly emergent and solidly united groups within political society, secured a change of course. There would be a fresh entity comprising not Ben Ali holdovers but representatives from all parties as well as civil society. Generally known as the Ben Achour Commission after its chairman, attorney Yadh Ben Achour, this turned out to be one of the most effective consensus-building bodies in the history of "crafted" democratic transitions. It stands in particularly stark contrast with the situation in neighboring Egypt, where dictator Hosni Mubarak fell shortly after Ben Ali but was replaced not by an open civilian body, but rather by the Supreme Council of the Armed Forces (SCAF), with its penchant for attempting to manage fundamental political change by means of unilateral communiqués (more than 150 of which have been issued so far).

In November 2011, I talked at length with Ben Achour himself, two of his expert (but nonvoting) legal advisors, and various Commission members from political parties as well as civil society. I also received copies of many of the key documents upon which the Commission had voted. Here are the main points they discussed at length and the decisions they made:

1. The Commission members recognized that many changes were important for improving Tunisia and consolidating democracy. Yet they wisely took a "process-first" view and agreed to concentrate as a body only on decisions that were *indispensable* to the creation of a democratic government capable of carrying out reforms legitimately and with public consent. Key decisions thus concerned matters such as voting rules and guarantees of electoral freedom and fairness.

2. The Commission decided that the first popular vote to be held would be to choose the members of a constituent assembly. As the name implies, this body's central task would be to draft for voters' approval a new constitution that would set up a presidential, a semipresidential, or a parliamentary system. This "decision to defer the decision" was important because an alternative course, such as early direct election of a president, would have lowered incentives for party-building as prominent national figures lined up to run as nonparty candidates for president (as happened in Egypt), and would

have given whomever was the directly elected president great capacity to shape the still not fully formed constitution.

3. The Commission agreed that the Constituent Assembly, as a legitimately elected body, should possess powers like those of a parliament in that it would select a government that would be responsible to the Assembly and be subject (as in the Indian and Spanish transitions) to its vote of no confidence.

4. The Commission agreed that the electoral system would be one of pure proportional representation (PR). This decision was correctly understood to have crucial antimajoritarian, democracy-facilitating, and coalition-encouraging implications. Had a Westminster-style "first-past-the-post" system of plurality elections in single-member districts been chosen, Ennadha would have swept almost nine of every ten seats, instead of the slightly more than four in ten it was able to win under PR.

5. To help ensure strong participation of women in the constitution-drafting process, it was agreed to aim for male-female parity in candidates by having every other name on the candidate lists be a woman's.[4] By all accounts, the first party to accept this gender-parity provision was the Islam-inspired Ennahda.

6. To ensure that all the contesting parties would have confidence in the fairness of the electoral results, it was decided to create Tunisia's first independent electoral commission, and to invite many international electoral observers and give them extensive monitoring prerogatives. In Egypt, by contrast, the SCAF initially barred international observers with the claim that they would be violating Egypt's sovereignty. Eventually, the SCAF allowed entry to "election followers" (authorities insisted that they not be called observers) in smaller numbers and with weaker prerogatives than observers in Tunisia had enjoyed.

7. On the issue of what to do with Ben Ali's official party, the Commission decided to ban the party and some of its most important leaders from being candidates for the first election. However, in order not to exclude a large group of citizens from participating in the first free elections, the Assembly declared that former Ben Ali party members or supporters were free to form new parties.

On 11 April 2011, approximately 155 members of the Ben Achour Commission voted on this package of measures to create a democratic transition. Two members walked out and two more abstained, but all the others voted for the package. The formal basis of a successful tran-

sition to democracy had been laid, providing a foundation for the October 2011 election.

The Egypt Comparison

The scholarly literature on democratic transitions normally makes
a distinction between the tasks of resistance within "civil society" that
help to deconstruct authoritarianism, and the tasks of "political society"
that help to construct democracy. Among political society's constructive tasks is to bring opposition leaders into agreement on plans for an
interim government as well as elections capable of generating constitution-making authorities with democratic legitimacy. When to hold such
elections and under what rules often figure among the most important
questions that postauthoritarian leaders must resolve.

In my judgment, the civil societies of Tunisia and Egypt produced
some of the most creative and effective civic-resistance movements in
the history of democratization struggles. Yet as of this writing in March
2012, Egypt has done remarkably little to create an effective political
society, while Tunisia has made reasonable strides toward endowing
itself with one that is relatively autonomous, democratic, and effective.
Much of Tunisia's superior record in this regard can be credited to Islamic and secular leaders, who have worked to overcome their mutual
fears and distrust by crafting agreements and credible guarantees in
political society. In the process, they have begun to build (or rebuild)
a type of religion-state-society arrangement friendly to the twin tolerations that had been foreclosed for many years by the aggressive top-
down secularism of modernizing autocrats.

Drawing on the contrasting experiences of Egypt and Tunisia, I
would suggest that in countries where religious conflict is likely to be
salient, the sooner the major secular and religious parties accept both
of the "twin tolerations," the better. In practice, this means that parties
with religious roots must refrain from asserting special claims, based
on access to the divine, to wield an authority capable of nullifying or
superseding human laws. It also means that secular parties must not
deny the right of citizens influenced by religion to articulate their values democratically in civil and political society.

A second lesson is that, from the standpoint of democratization, the
critical thing to study is not the military itself, but the nature of civil-
military relations. The less inclined civilians are to abdicate their right
to rule to soldiers—in an "Eighteenth Brumaire"–style exchange for
military protection against perceived threats from class or sectarian
rivals newly empowered by democracy—the better the chances for a
successful democratic transition not constrained by excessive influence
or privileges in the hands of the military.[5]

A third lesson is that the more political actors do to reach consensual agreement on the rules of democratic contestation by negotiating among themselves, the better.

Over the last year, Tunisia has seemed to be heeding all these lessons, while Egypt has seemed to be doing the reverse. This may go a long way toward explaining why the former had completed all four of the classic requirements for a democratic transition before the end of 2011, while the latter has yet to complete one.[6]

This is not to deny that there have been deep fears and Brumairian temptations in Tunisia. In March 2011, when I interviewed journalists and leading secularists in Tunis, I found many of them extremely frightened by the prospect of free elections and the expected appeal of Islamists. Indeed, some of those I interviewed were, like their counterparts in Egypt, toying with the idea of trading away the prospect of civilian democratic rule for the security that an authoritarian body such as the army could supposedly offer. Yet within a month, the urge to knock on the barracks door, if not the fear behind the urge, had begun to recede in Tunisia. Why?

In 1997, I had interviewed in London and Oxford Ennahda's exiled leader, Rachid Ghannouchi. In March 2011, after Ghannouchi returned to Tunis, we met again immediately following my interviews with three top Muslim Brotherhood (MB) officials in Egypt. I quickly asked Ghannouchi what he thought about the Egyptian Brotherhood's still-unrepudiated 2007 platform plank declaring that no woman or Christian could make an acceptable president of Egypt. He did not hesitate: "Democracy means equality of all citizens. Such a platform excludes 60 percent of all the citizens and is unacceptable."[7] He calls himself an "advocate of absolute equality of men and women."[8]

Ghannouchi said that he had entered into agreements (confirmed in numerous interviews and documents) with a number of political parties as early as 2003, promising that Ennahda would not try to reverse the family code. We also discussed the proposed Shari'a Council that appears in the Egyptian MB's 2007 platform as a forum for reviewing parliamentary legislation to ensure its compliance with Islamic law. Ghannouchi made it clear that he saw this as an unwarranted intrusion of religious authority into the realm of democratically constituted political authority—a violation of the twin tolerations. He insisted to me that neither he nor his party would push for such a body.

In May, I saw Ghannouchi again. This time we were joined by Hamadi Jebali, whom the Constituent Assembly would later elect to the premiership but who was then serving as Ennahda's elected secretary-general. When I asked if Ennahda considered itself closer to the Egyptian MB or to Turkey's ruling Justice and Development Party (AKP), Jebali said:

> We are much closer to the AKP than to the Muslim Brotherhood. We are a civic party emanating from the reality of Tunisia, not a religious party.

> A religious party believes it has legitimacy not from the people but from
> God. A religious party believes it has the truth and no one can oppose it
> because it has the truth.

Ghannouchi concurred and added that the goal was for Tunisia to be "a civic state, not a religious state."[9] As the campaign went on, Ghannouchi and Jebali continued to try to tamp down fears of Islamic fundamentalism. Many, if not most, secularists remained unconvinced, but at least Ennahda did not have an unrepudiated platform (such as the Egyptian MB's) that was clearly hostile to the twin tolerations and open to secularist denunciations.

Unlike Egypt, where military men have held the presidency continuously since the Free Officers took power on 22 July 1952, Tunisia has never had a military strongman. Founding president Habib Bourguiba and then later Ben Ali deliberately kept the military small, and preferred to rule through sprawling and hated police and intelligence services that dwarfed the tiny army. Nonetheless, a senior soldier, General Rachid Ammar, had played a key role in facing down the police and ushering Ben Ali out of the country. There might have been a move to draft him into the presidency somehow, but there was not. Within less than a month of Ben Ali's flight, civilians in political society had demanded, and received, responsibility for crafting the key rules needed to make the democratic transition work.

A Useable Past

If understanding the success of the October election requires understanding the success of the Ben Achour Commission's deliberations earlier in the year, understanding the two together requires widening the optic still further to encompass events that took place nearly a decade ago, in June 2003. In France during that month, representatives from four of Tunisia's major nonregime parties (Ennahda, the CPR, Ettakatol, and the PDP—all of which hold seats in the current Constituent Assembly) met in order to negotiate and sign a "Call from Tunis."[10] This document endorsed the two fundamental principles of the twin tolerations: 1) any future elected government would have to be "founded on the sovereignty of the people as the sole source of legitimacy"; and 2) the state, while showing "respect for the people's identity and its Arab-Muslim values," would provide "the guarantee of liberty of beliefs to all and the political neutralization of places of worship." Ennahda accepted both these fundamental agreements. "The Call" also went on to demand "the full equality of women and men."

From 2005 on, these four main political parties, together with representatives of smaller parties, met to reaffirm and even deepen their commitment to the Call's principles. One document that they produced under the heading of "The 18 October Coalition for Rights and Freedoms in Tunisia" stressed that, after a "three-month dialogue among party leaders," they had reached consensus on a number of crucial issues. All the parties, including Ennadha, supported in great detail the existing, liberal family code.[11] Moreover, the document added, any future democratic state would have to be a "civic state . . . drawing its legitimacy from the will of the people," for "political practice is a human discipline [without] any form of sanctity." Finally, the manifesto asserted that "there can be no compulsion in religion. This includes the right to adopt a religion or doctrine or not."[12]

In building for the future, it often helps to be able to look to the past. There is historical evidence that Tunisia was already becoming what we might call "twin tolerations–friendly" as long ago as the nineteenth century (and perhaps even earlier, if one wants to search back as far as Ottoman and medieval times for cultural roots of tolerance and openness). Recently, Tunisian democrats have explicitly evoked this legacy in order to explain their own thinking and their hopes for their country.

Important aspects of Tunisia's cultural heritage are indeed friendly to both of the twin tolerations. Tunisia has a long intellectual and educational tradition that combines important secular and spiritual elements. Moreover, nineteenth-century Tunisia played a pioneering role in building constitutional and state structures that were religiously neutral and rights-enhancing, and it was home to politically engaged Islamic thinkers who argued for a more rights-based reading of Islam, especially in the area of rights for women.

Perhaps *the* iconic figure in Tunisian cultural history is Ibn Khaldun (1332–1406), the Tunis-born writer who is seen by many as a foundational thinker in the fields of sociology, historiography, and economics due to his rational and systematic methods for studying empires and cultures and comparing them to one another. Today, his statue is the only one that adorns the long plaza running down the Avenue Habib Bourguiba, the center of public, social, and café life in Tunisia's capital city. But what made Ibn Khaldun a great thinker, scholar, and hero of Tunisian culture? Most analysts of his work fail to mention his appreciation of religious contemplation as an end in itself and also as a way of helping rational thought. Indeed, many assert that Khaldun's way of thinking had little connection to Islam. They tend to ignore his great intellectual and spiritual attention not only to rational analysis but also to the study of Sufism, saints, and mystics.

Among the more important aspects of Tunisia's cultural history are the country's links to the old Muslim kingdom of Andalusia in southern Spain and to the Ottoman Empire, of which Tunisia was a de facto autonomous part from 1580 until the imposition of the French Protectorate in 1881.[13] Ibn Khaldun, who himself came from an Andalusian family, makes a point of stressing in his monumental *Muquaddimah* that Tunis in his day had become a preferred destination for Muslim and Jewish emigrants; he estimated that the "bulk of inhabitants of 13th century Tunis were of Andalusian families who had emigrated from the Spanish Levant."[14] These emigrants, Muslims as well as Jews, brought from Spain such extensive high-level experience in governing and administration that many of them, for centuries, filled high posts under the Hafsid Dynasty (1229–1574).[15]

Some of Tunisia's most prestigious institutions were religious, and some were secular. The Islamic-based Zeitouna Mosque University was founded in Tunis in 737, making it more than two centuries older than Cairo's al-Azhar University. Sadiki College was founded as a secular institution in 1875, and rapidly became the most prestigious and competitive school in Tunisia. Sadiki was noted for the religiously mixed character of its students: As late as the 1950s, about a third of its nearly four-thousand students were Tunisian Jews.

An important part of Tunisia's useable past—one to which secular and religious democratic activists alike enjoy appealing—is the middle of the nineteenth century, a time that saw significant constitutional reform and steps toward the building of a religiously neutral state.

The high degree of de facto autonomy that Tunisia and Egypt enjoyed as nominal provinces of the fading Ottoman Empire allowed the two of them—and Tunisia especially—to become arguably the most liberal and rights-friendly polities in the Arab world. In 1846, two years before France banned slavery in its dominions, Tunisia adopted abolition after an effective campaign of pressure and argument driven by both religious and secular groups. This was a first for the Muslim world, and occurred 19 years before abolition in the United States (1865), 42 years before Brazil (1888), and 116 years before abolition in Saudi Arabia (1962).[16]

In 1861, Tunisia adopted the first written constitution in Arab history. The French social scientist Jean-Pierre Filiu, who lived for four years in Tunisia, argues in a recent book that this constitution "enshrined a political power distinct from religion: Islam was barely mentioned, only to stress that the text was not contradicting its principles, and it was not even explicit that the Bey [the ruler] had to be Muslim."[17] Articles 86 to 104 of the 1861 Constitution, drafted under the influence of the statesman and political theorist Khayr al-Din (who later served briefly as grand vizier of the Ottoman Empire), declared that everyone in the kingdom, "whatever their religion have the right[s]" to be judged by tribunals including some of their coreligionists, to enjoy complete physical security, and to engage in all types of commerce. Filiu notes that this basic law had been preceded by a "Covenant of Social Peace" emphasizing "public interest, equality before the law and freedom of religion."[18]

To be sure, neither the covenant nor the constitution was ever fully

enforced, but at least they introduced into Tunisian discourse the idea
that people from *all* religious backgrounds should enjoy equal rights.
As Albert Hourani notes:

> [This Tunisian] experiment in constitutional government . . . left its mark:
> it helped to form a new political consciousness in Tunis, and to bring to
> the front a group of reforming statesman, officials and writers...until they
> were scattered by the French occupation in 1881. This group had two
> origins: one of them was the Zaytuna Mosque [University], where the
> influence of a reforming teacher, Shaykh Muhammad Qabadu, was felt;
> the other was the new School of Military Sciences.[19]

Zeitouna and Sadiki, together with the new School of Military Sciences, produced some major political thinkers who argued, *from within
Islam,* for the expansion of rights, including women's rights. The most
important such work was written by Tahar Haddad (1899–1935), who
in 1924 had cofounded the first major free trade union in Tunisia. Haddad argued in his *Notre femme dans la Législation Musulmane et dans
la Société* that a correct reading of the Koran should lead to women's
equality. The cover of this book, first published in 1930, depicts a sta-
tionary and completely veiled woman in the front, and soaring up behind her, a curly-haired young female basketball player in athletic attire.[20] Haddad was building on the work of Khayr al-Din, who Nathan
J. Brown argues "advances a powerful argument for a constitutionalist
policy, and locates constitutionalism not only in European practice but
also in the Islamic tradition."[21] In the 2003 "Call from Tunis" that signaled the readiness of secular and Islamic oppositionists to cooperate,
al-Din and Haddad are both praised by name as defenders of constitutionalism and the rights of women.

Thus, without following a path toward "exclusive humanism" or
hard, religion-unfriendly *laïcité,* Tunisia at independence in 1956 was a
country where rational and religious reasoning and insights had a place
in public argument in an environment that was relatively friendly to the
"twin tolerations." What happened at independence to set this process
back for a time?

The Lost Decades, 1956–2011

As the independence movement's leader, Bourguiba had appealed
to Muslim sentiments. As president, he followed a bareknuckled policy
of French- and Turkish-style state-led "modernization" peppered with
harsh denunciations of "so-called religious belief."[22] He closed Zeitouna University despite its broadened curriculum and replaced it with the
thoroughly secular and French-inspired University of Tunis. As part of
his aggressive land-reform program, he nationalized the "pious trusts"
(in effect, landholding foundations whose revenues paid for mosques

and some Muslim social programs). He cut the study of religion in public schools to a single hour a week, and required teachers to be able to teach in French as well as Arabic (the vast majority of imams knew only the latter). Private Koranic schools "all but disappeared."[23]

While there were major religious losers under Bourguiba, there were major secular gainers, especially women, who not only enjoyed greater protections under Bourguiba's new family code, but also began to enroll in higher education in larger numbers.

During his 31 years in power, Bourguiba never allowed a free election. Part of the reason why his middle-class urban constituency, female and male, did not demand elections was his implicit raising of the question: "After me, what?" Everyone knew that his modernizing and secularizing reforms had been imposed by the sheer power of the state riding roughshod over the misgivings of traditional Muslims. In free elections, what would happen, and what would be the fate of the changes that Bourguiba had pushed through?

In 1987, Ben Ali ousted Bourguiba in a bloodless "doctors' coup" (it was alleged that Bourguiba had dementia), and a brief thaw ensued. Key dissidents came home from exile, and a slightly more competitive legislative election was held in 1989. In the context of the 1979 Iranian Revolution, the growth of the Islamic Salvation Front in neighboring Algeria, pent-up resentment among Tunisian Muslims angry at their exclusion from politics, and the emergence of Zeitouna and Sadiki graduate Rachid Ghannouchi as the leader of a political group, Ennahda, that could mobilize this opposition, more aggressive Muslims challenged Ben Ali. Ennahda was not legalized and so could not run as a party, but it fielded candidates competing as independents.

In what was certainly not a fair election, even Ben Ali's officials acknowledged that Ennahda's candidates took 15 percent of the nationwide vote (and 30 percent in greater Tunis). In a polarized atmosphere, two people died in explosions. It is still unclear who committed the bombings, but Ben Ali charged Ennahda. According to estimates offered by a Tunisian human-rights group, Amnesty International, and Ennahda, respectively, in the next few years at least twenty-thousand Ennahda members were tried for subversion and sent to jail, and about ten-thousand went into exile, many after passing through Algeria, like Ghannouchi.[24] The thaw had turned to ice.

The new polarization helped Ben Ali to prolong his authoritarian rule for two more decades. To Bourguiba's warning that Islamists would reverse the gains of secularism, Ben Ali, helped by the spectacle of the bloody civil war between Islamists and the military that raged throughout most of the 1990s in neighboring Algeria, added the fear of Islamist violence, which he argued that only he and his regime could prevent.[25]

But, in post–Ben Ali Tunisia no such violence has occurred. Indeed, the country's secular parties and Islamists have a chance to add to the world's repertoire of ways in which religion, society, and the state can relate to one another under democratic conditions. Analysts often downplay the importance of Tunisia, overshadowed as it is by its much larger and strategically weightier neighbor, Egypt. But since Tunisia is so far the only Arab country to have met the four requirements of a democratic transition, analysts and activists alike should pay it more attention, especially for its example of how secular and religious actors can negotiate new rules and form coalitions.

When considering Muslim countries, too many commentators focus on the "missing factors" that they see as necessary for democracy but lacking in these countries. Much of what they see as "missing," however, draws from the repertoire of what these observers think, rightly or wrongly, actually existed in this or that Western country when democracy emerged there. A better and more imaginative approach might be to look for actions and events—whether deliberate or fortuitous—that may aid the emergence of "twin tolerations–friendly" practices. And it is important to be aware that their emergence does not presuppose the need for "exclusive humanism" and aggressive secularism to triumph, or for a decline in religious participation, or for a Muslim-world variant of the Protestant Reformation (and its follow-on wars of religion?) to transpire, or for uniformed authoritarians to come along and impose secularism as in Kemalist Turkey.

In the century or so leading up to independence in 1956, Tunisia showed signs of movement toward the twin tolerations model, but the modernizing autocrat Bourguiba disrupted all that by imposing authoritarian secularism from above. Worse still, he created an objectively pro-authoritarian constituency of frightened secularists that served as a source of support for both his own and his successor's dictatorial rule.

It should be counted as all the more remarkable, then, that as early as 2003, secular and religious opposition activists were agreeing on a common program for "the day after Ben Ali" that to some extent drew upon their shared useable past to imagine a democratic future. With secularists agreeing that Islamists could participate fully in democratic politics, and Islamists agreeing that popular sovereignty is the *only* source of legitimacy, Tunisia was surprisingly well situated to make a good showing at the work of democratic transition when the moment to undertake that work came around.

NOTES

1. Alfred Stepan, "Multiple Secularisms of Modern Democratic and Non-Democratic Regimes," in Craig Calhoun, Mark Juergensmeyer, and Jonathan VanAntwerpen, eds., *Rethinking Secularism* (New York: Oxford University Press, 2011), 114–44. John Rawls once went so far as to assert that, in the name of arriving at an "overlapping consensus," religious arguments should be "taken off the public agenda." See his *Political Liberalism*

(New York: Columbia University Press, 1993), 151–54. Charles Taylor, in his book *A Secular Age* (Cambridge: Harvard University Press, 2007), has explained the complex historical processes that led the North Atlantic world to embrace the idea that a mostly religion-free "exclusive humanism" is the only ground upon which public policies can be designed and defended. See especially 19–21, 26–28, 642, and 674.

2. See Alfred Stepan, "The World's Religious Systems and Democracy: Crafting the 'Twin Tolerations,'" in *Arguing Comparative Politics* (Oxford: Oxford University Press, 2001), 213–53. A shorter and less heavily annotated version of this essay appeared as "Religion, Democracy, and the 'Twin Tolerations,'" *Journal of Democracy* 11 (October 2000): 37–57.

3. Juan J. Linz and Alfred Stepan, *Problems of Democratic Transition and Consolidation: Southern Europe, South America, and Post-Communist Europe* (Baltimore: Johns Hopkins University Press, 1996), 1.

4. The actual outcome of the elections unfortunately did not produce the hoped-for parity. Although all parties ran slates that were 50 percent female, most of them (with the notable exception of Ennahda) failed to place any women's names first. In many constituencies, only a single candidate from the party won, and thus many more men than women won seats. Nevertheless, about a quarter of the members of the Constituent Assembly are women.

5. My use of the "Eighteenth Brumaire"—a term made famous by Karl Marx's 1852 work *The 18ᵗʰ Brumaire of Louis Napoleon*—is a reference to the date on the French Revolutionary calendar (9 November 1799) when Napoleon Bonaparte staged a coup against the Directory and made himself a military dictator. Tensions between different Revolutionary factions had led some of them to make deals with Napoleon (in hopes of using him for their own ends) that created the opening for him to seize power.

6. For reasons of length, this essay focuses on Tunisia, but I present substantial evidence for my assertion about Egypt in my "The Recurrent Temptation to Abdicate to the Military in Egypt," 13 January 2012, at *http://blog.freedomhouse.org/weblog/2012/01/two-perspectives-on-egypts-transition.html.*

7. Author's interview with Rachid Ghannouchi, Tunis, 26 March 2011.

8. Since about 1980, Ghannouchi (who was born in 1941) has stressed the need for much greater equality of men and women within Islam. See Azzam S. Tamimi, *Rachid Ghannouchi: A Democrat Within Islamism* (Oxford: Oxford University Press, 2001).

9. Author's interview with Rachid Ghannouchi and Hamadi Jebali, Tunis, 30 May 2011.

10. I received a copy of the "Appel de Tunis de 17 juin 2003," with signers' names and affiliations listed, from several of those who took part in the meetings that produced it. A version in French is now available at *www.cprtunisie.net/spip.php?article30.* Participants included the current presidents of the CPR, Ettakatol, and the PDP. Ennahda's two top leaders were, respectively, in jail and unable to obtain a French visa, so the Islamist movement was represented by the head of its Political Bureau.

11. Tunisia's family code, widely agreed to be the Arab world's most progressive, was decreed by President Habib Bourguiba in 1956. It abolishes polygamy; requires mutual consent before marriage; entitles women to start divorce proceedings and to enjoy an equal division of goods after divorce; forbids husbands from unilaterally ending their marriages; and raises the minimum marriage age for girls. In 1966, Bourguiba's government launched a family-planning program that included free birth-control pills and legal abortion.

12. I received a copy of this document on 11 November 2011 while visiting the Tunis headquarters of the most secular party in the current ruling coalition, Ettakatol. The person who gave it to me was one of the drafters, Zied Dooulotli. The Arabic-to-English translation is the work of Mostofa Henfy.

13. For example, see Maria Rose Menocal, *The Ornament of the World: How Muslims, Jews, and Christians Created a Culture of Tolerance in Medieval Spain* (New York: Little, Brown, 2002). On religious toleration in the Ottoman Empire, see Karen Barkey, *An Empire of Difference: The Ottomans in Comparative Perspective* (Cambridge: Cambridge University Press, 2008).

14. For this estimate by Khaldun, see John D. Latham, "Towards a Study of Andalusian Immigration and Its Place in Tunisian History," *Les Cahiers de Tunisie* (1957): 203–52.

15. For the names of Jewish high officeholders and the posts that they held in Tunisia, see Latham, "Towards a Study of Andalusian Immigration," 216–20.

16. For the religious and secular reasons behind early abolition in Tunisia, see Roger Botte, *Esclavages et abolitions en terres d'Islam* (Brussels: André Versaille, 2010), 59–92.

17. See Jean-Pierre Filiu, *The Arab Revolution: Ten Lessons from the Democratic Uprising* (London: C. Hurst, 2011), 142.

18. Filiu, *Arab Revolution*.

19. Albert Hourani, *Arabic Thought in the Liberal Age: 1798–1939* (New York: Cambridge University Press, 1983), 65.

20. For a picture of the cover, see *Pensées de Tahar Haddad* (Tunis: Snipe, 1993), 38. As early as 1904, the influential Sheik Thaalibi argued in his *The Liberal Spirit of the Koran* that a true reading of the Koran would lead to overdue political and social reforms.

21. Nathan J. Brown, *Constitutions in a Nonconstitutional World: Arab Basic Laws and the Prospects for Accountable Government* (Albany: State University of New York Press, 2002), 19.

22. These and other similar speeches are cited in Mark A. Tessler, "Political Change and the Religious Revival in Tunisia," *Maghreb Review* 5 (January–February 1980): 8–19. Also see Lotfi Hajji, *Bourguiba et l'Islam: Le politique et le religieux,* trans. Shiem Bouzgarou Ben Ghachem (Tunis: Sud Editions, 2011).

23. Tessler, "Political Change and the Religious Revival in Tunisia," 10.

24. Author's interview with Samir Ben Amor, defense lawyer and secretary-general of the Ex-Prisoners' Association, Tunis, 29 May 2011. See also Amnesty International, "Tunisia: Prolonged Incommunicado Detention and Torture," March 1992, MDE 30/004/1992.

25. This regime-orchestrated "double fear" served Ben Ali well. As one account noted: "Many secular democrats have been grudgingly complicit in Ben Ali's authoritarianism. . . . [viewing it] as the lesser of two evils." Christopher Alexander, *Tunisia: Stability and Reform in the Modern Maghreb* (London: Routledge, 2010), 66.

19

THE ROAD TO (AND FROM) LIBERATION SQUARE

Tarek Masoud

Tarek Masoud *is assistant professor of public policy at Harvard University's John F. Kennedy School of Government and a Carnegie Scholar. This essay originally appeared in the July 2011 issue of the* Journal of Democracy.

It is easy now to see why Egypt's revolution had to happen, and why President Hosni Mubarak's thirty-year reign had to end in the spectacular manner in which it did. Even the most casual observer of the Egyptian scene can recite from the expansive catalogue of ills that Mubarak had visited upon the land: a large and growing corps of angry young people with no jobs and no prospects; the repeated thwarting of the voters' will; crumbling public infrastructure whose sole purpose seemed to be supplying newspaper headlines about train crashes and ferry sinkings; corruption so brazen that it was often written into law; and daily acts of casually dispensed brutality, culminating in the June 2010 murder of a young man in a seaside town by the very police who were ostensibly charged with protecting him.

And then there was the matter of the dictator's age. In recent years, the octogenarian ruler's health had become a matter of state, and woe betide anyone daring (or foolish) enough to suggest that the president could be anything less than fully fit. In 2008, a court sentenced the journalist Ibrahim Eissa to six months in prison for "damaging the public interest and national stability" by publishing what it called "false information and rumors" about Mubarak's health. Yet despite the regime's attempts to present the leader as immortal, the specter of his eventual demise loomed over the political landscape. The regime never quite managed to convey the impression that it had planned for the day after Mubarak, that the ship of state would sail on undisturbed. There was an attempt—half-hearted and clumsy—to present Mubarak's second son, an international banker named Gamal, as the inevitable successor, but this did not sit well with the Egyptian street or, it seems, with the

Egyptian military. The atmosphere of uncertainty brought with it a sense of possibility—Egypt's prodemocracy activists knew that there would soon be an opening in the country's political fabric and that they would have to prepare themselves to take advantage of it.

And prepare themselves they did. We can locate the beginnings of the Mubarak regime's final act in the 2004 founding of the Egyptian Movement for Change. This organization—whose unofficial moniker of Kifaya (Enough!) deftly encapsulated the national mood—gathered political activists and thinkers from across the spectrum to declare that Egyptians were fed up with the Mubarak regime and would not stand for Gamal's inheritance of the presidency. Although the movement was fractious and its activities fitful, it made two great contributions to Mubarak's eventual overthrow. These, as one Western diplomat described them, were to break the taboo against public criticism of Mubarak and to serve as the training ground for and gateway to political activism for many of the individuals who would lead the protests. Ahmed Maher, the young civil engineer who founded the April 6th Youth Movement, joined Kifaya in 2005 and recently acknowledged it as "the mother of all of the protest movements in Egypt."

Maher's use of the plural when referring to protest "movements" reflects the growing willingness of Egyptians in recent years to take to the streets to demand their rights. Judges have protested election rigging. Tax collectors have protested pay inequities. The poor have protested food-price increases. The scholar Joel Beinin has calculated that the last decade saw more than three-thousand labor protests. It is part of the genius of the April 6th Movement—a group of young Web-based activists who took their name from the date of a 2008 textile-workers' strike in a Nile Delta mill town—that they were able to yoke labor's newfound militant energy to the national drive for democracy.

And then came Mohamed ElBaradei. The Nobel laureate did not make the revolution, but he adopted it and was adopted by it. His refusal to play the regime's games, to participate in its elections, to credit any of its claims of democracy, gave heart to the youth and heartburn to Mubarak and his lieutenants. Documents smuggled out of the now-defunct State Security Investigations arm of the Interior Ministry reveal the extent to which the regime was obsessed with the mild-mannered former UN bureaucrat, which in turn suggests that the president's men knew better than most just how vulnerable they really were.

Given this combustible mix of a failing regime, an aging leader, and a people increasingly willing to confront both, one might conclude that the revolution was not only inevitable, but overdetermined. Yet those of us who study the region not only failed to predict the regime's collapse, we actually saw it as an exemplar of something we called "durable authoritarianism"—a new breed of modern dictatorship that had figured out how to tame the political, economic, and social forces that routinely did in autocracy's lesser variants. So durable was the Mubarak regime thought to be that, even after Tunisia's President Zine al-Abidine Ben Ali was forced to flee in mid-January, the predictions of stability on the banks of the Nile continued to roll in. "Egypt is not Tunisia," became the refrain of the hour.

The Mirage of "Durable" Authoritarianism

At one level, the inability to see the impending revolution was born of human nature: We expect things that have happened in the past to keep happening in the future. A successful autocrat, like a basketball star, can come to be seen as having a "hot hand." But this alone cannot explain the failure. After all, practically every journalist who visited Egypt in the last few years seemed to mark the occasion by filing a piece warning of the regime's impending collapse. But we scholars of the country—none of us blind to the regime's failures and the people's misery—thought that we knew better. The predictions of regime failure had been coming in for so long that we had become inured to them. Mubarak had faced down assassination attempts, an Islamist insurgency, and near-constant economic crisis, and his regime's remarkable durability demanded explanation. But a side effect of our intellectual exertions was that the theories we generated to explain authoritarian survival also tended to predict it.

Beginning from the premise that authoritarian collapses usually begin when there is a rupture in the ruling elite, we began to ask whether the Mubarak regime had developed tools that somehow allowed it to manage such ruptures or avoid them entirely. Once we began looking for such tools, we found them. Scholars identified two pseudodemocratic political institutions in particular as containing the keys to regime longevity: the ruling National Democratic Party (NDP) and the periodic elections to Mubarak's rubber-stamp parliament, the People's Assembly.

Both of these institutions were supposed to forestall elite conflict— the former by providing a forum for dispute resolution among the regime's core supporters, the latter by offering a means for the regime to distribute the fruits of corruption among those supporters without having to pick winners and losers itself.[1] There is much that rang true in these accounts. The ruling party, founded by President Anwar Sadat in 1978, had by the end become an unprincipled collection of political and economic elites, joining neoliberal businessmen with ambitious academics and veteran regime *apparatchiks* under the beneficence of Mubarak and his big tent. The party leaked prominent members from time to time, but the ambitious continued to flock to it. And elections to the People's Assembly, while often rigged, nonetheless saw actual and would-be regime cronies expend vast resources to run for office, secure in the knowledge that those who locked up (or bought up) the most votes would be more than reimbursed in the form of preferential access to state resources.

It is entirely possible, even likely, that the Mubarak regime would not have held on for as long as it did without these mechanisms for securing and maintaining elite loyalty. But these institutional underpinnings of durable authoritarianism were far flimsier than previously thought. Once the demonstrations began, the ruling party collapsed almost immediately. Ahmed Ezz, the steel tycoon whom the government-controlled newspaper *Al-Ahram* had celebrated as "the man behind the sweeping win by the ruling party in the recent parliamentary elections," and the party's whip in parliament, resigned after only four days of protests, with the party's entire executive committee following a week later. Mubarak seemed to forget about his party entirely, preferring to rely on the security apparatus. Party *apparatchiks* complained to me that at the height of the crisis the president and his son were practically incommunicado. When the party finally did manage to muster some anemic counterdemonstrations on February 2 (the revolution's ninth day), they were notable only for having included armed camel drivers whose principal effect was to inflame the youth further. Parliament was similarly useless. Speaker Ahmad Fathi Surur's sole contribution to regime maintenance was to declare weakly on the third day of protests that "matters are in safe hands—the hands of President Hosni Mubarak," before disappearing from the scene.

The marginalization of the NDP and parliament during the regime's death throes should not surprise us. Neither was capable of repelling the tens, then hundreds of thousands of protesters who flooded central Cairo's Liberation (Tahrir) Square and the streets of other Egyptian cities. In the face of so much popular unrest, the mechanisms of regime cohesion mattered little. What counted was the regime's ability to mete out violence, and this was something that no ruling party or rubber-stamp legislature could do.

Much has been and will be written about the military's decision not to bring the full weight of its might to bear against the protesters. Robert Fisk has reported that the top brass gave their field commanders orders to fire, but that these were refused by loyal sons of Egypt who would not shed the blood of their countrymen.[2] (But then, one must explain the military's subsequent willingness to fire on protesters in Tahrir Square on April 12 and in front of the Israeli embassy on May 15.) The military's own explanation for its restraint is that it was born of patriotism and belief in the legitimacy of the revolution. (But then, again, one must explain the armed forces' strangely neutral position between the protesters and the regime's thugs during the particularly bloody confrontations of February 2.)

A more likely possibility is that the military's refusal to back Mubarak was in part a function of its jealousy over the rise of the NDP and the latter's eclipse of the military as the fount of political authority. In this telling, the NDP was less a source of Mubarak's strength than a cause of his downfall. The country's last four presidents may have been military men, but it was a virtual certainty that the next one would be a man of the ruling party. Although military spokesmen now love to trumpet the armed forces' opposition to Gamal Mubarak's rise and to the various corruptions of the regime's cronies, the truth is that this stance may have had little to do with support for democracy and clean government, and much to do with the urge for continued preeminence.

Elections, too, may have hurt as much as they helped. The sweetheart deals that accrued to ruling-party parliamentarians probably made them more loyal to the regime, but at the price of the loyalty and good will of the Egyptian people. Anticorruption, after all, was one of the bywords of the revolution, and the current venom against Surur—who was forced to resign as speaker and as of this writing is under investigation for ill-gotten gains—is an indication of the extent to which parliament came to be seen as an abode of swindlers. And it is not just the graft of parliamentarians that aroused public fury—it was the brazenly corrupt manner in which they were elected. The seven elections of the Mubarak era were all stage-managed to generate victories for the ruling party, and the regime's various electoral manipulations served only to remind the people of the regime's lack of regard for them or their will. The parliamentary contests of late 2010 were particularly egregious—it is worth noting that there was greater opposition representation in Ben Ali's last parliament than in Mubarak's—and sparked the season of protests that ended with Mubarak's downfall. There is no better indication of the extent to which Egyptians had become estranged by elections than the preternaturally low turnout—23 percent in 2005 and 25 percent in 2010, and this according to the regime's own (usually inflated) figures.

But even as elections were alienating the silent majority, they may have been activating the young people who would help to craft the revolution. Egyptian opposition parties were often said to be wasting their time and resources by playing the mug's game of elections, but many of Egypt's young activists got their start in these parties and their political campaigns. The youth of the Muslim Brotherhood (MB), who helped to defend the protesters of Tahrir against the regime's thugs, deployed tactics that they had learned defending MB voters, candidates, and activists against those same thugs during election times. Other, more secular-minded protest leaders had been part of the doomed 2005 presidential campaign of leading liberal and al-Ghad (Tomorrow) Party founder Ayman Nour or members of the Democratic Front Party. Opposition parties may not have brought change directly, but they helped to prepare those who would do so.

These reflections on what the revolution in Egypt teaches us about our understanding of authoritarian regimes and their durability are of more than merely academic interest. They suggest that autocracies are inherently unstable, that their persistence rests primarily on their ability either to mute popular grievances or to suppress collective action spurred by those grievances, and that small events (such as the self-immolation of a fruit seller in a dusty Tunisian town) can upend the seemingly settled order of things and cause a seemingly apathetic population to bring down a seemingly unshakeable regime. They also suggest that academics, like autocrats, court peril when they focus on elites and ignore the people. Moreover, it may be that "limited liberalizations" in autocratic regimes are not as limited as we think. In Myanmar, we rightly view the military's recent "civilianization" and reintroduction of elections as nothing more than a sham. But the lesson of Egypt may be that such shams often contain within them the seeds of their own destruction. Samuel Huntington, it turns out, may have been right to say that "liberalized authoritarianism is not a stable equilibrium; the half-way house does not stand."[3]

Back to the Barracks?

It may, of course, be premature to say that Egypt's autocratic regime has fallen at all. Though many of us have been calling what has happened in Egypt a revolution, it remains a fact that, as of this writing in early June 2011, the country is being governed by a military junta not unlike the one that seized power in 1952 and inaugurated the autocratic era from which Egyptians are now trying to extricate themselves. At the most basic level, then, whether or not Egypt can be said to have undergone a revolution depends on how sincere the Supreme Council of the Armed Forces (SCAF) is being when it promises to midwife a transition to democracy. There are grounds for doubt.

The first ground is political. The military currently enjoys a kind of impunity in Egyptian political life, operating above civilian control. As Michele Dunne notes, the army's budget has been considered a "state secret and therefore not subject to parliamentary oversight."[4] It is possible that the SCAF's enthusiasm for democracy would be dampened if the generals expected it to put an end to this particularly congenial arrangement. In fact, Major-General Mamdouh Shahin, assistant minister of defense for parliamentary affairs, recently called for any new Egyptian constitution to protect the military from the "whims" of elected officials, and declared that military affairs should remain out of bounds in any new parliament.

The second ground is economic. The military is a major manufacturer of everything from foodstuffs to petrochemicals to kitchen supplies. Analysts have pegged the army's share of the Egyptian economy at anywhere from 5 to 40 percent, although hard numbers are hard to come by. It is worth noting that in mid-2010, the Ministry of Military Production announced the total output of its fourteen factories during the previous fiscal year as 4.3 billion Egyptian pounds (approximately US$750 million, or a little more than a tenth of 1 percent of Egypt's GDP). Yet this figure—if it is to be believed—almost certainly fails to capture the entirety of the military's economic portfolio, which also includes land holdings and service-sector enterprises. Whatever the precise size of the military's holdings, it stands to reason that it would want to protect them from grasping politicians who could be tempted to meet popular demands for redistribution by dipping into the army's coffers.

The third ground is geopolitical. The military values its relationship with the United States and the peace with Israel—things about which most potential claimants to Egypt's democratic future are decidedly ambivalent. For example, though none of them advocates war with the Jewish state, politicians from across the political spectrum—from Islamists to secular leftists—appear united in their desire to revise the Egyptian-Israeli relationship. The MB's supreme guide, Muhammad Badi, recently declared that the new Egyptian parliament (once one is elected) should revisit the terms of the Camp David Accords. Hamdin Sabahi, a popular former member of parliament and potential presidential candidate, told an Egyptian newspaper in January 2011 that "people are unhappy. They want better living conditions. They want to say no to the U.S. and Israel." Even Ayman Nour says that the continuation of the treaty must be put to a popular vote. As if to prove that these politicians have their fingers on the pulse of the street, thousands of Egyptians protested outside the Israeli embassy on May 15, provoking the military and riot police to respond with force and mass arrests.

Given its jealously guarded political autonomy, its economic interests, and its relationships with Israel and the United States, it is hard to see the military embracing unfettered democracy. At the same time, it is clear that the generals have little stomach for the business of day-to-day governance. Policing the streets, protecting religious minorities, setting economic policy—these are not the core competencies of the men with guns. Instead, the military prefers to reign but not quite rule—maintaining its economic prerogatives and freedom from civilian oversight while controlling (or at least setting the parameters of) Egyptian foreign and defense policy, but otherwise letting elected politicians run the show. It is a delicate balancing act, and other countries—Pakistan, Sudan—have failed to pull it off. Optimists may hope that Egypt can achieve the so-called Turkish model, but this can easily devolve into stretches of ineffectual civilian government punctuated by numerous "corrective coups."

Crafting the New Republic

In the meantime, the SCAF continues to try to engineer its preferred outcome, to steer Egypt between the Scylla of democracy and the Charybdis of military government. But the project has come perilously close to failing. In fact, Egypt's prodemocracy forces are today embroiled in a season of internecine conflict that can be traced to one of the SCAF's first decisions in power—to suspend the 1971 Constitution. From the SCAF's standpoint, this was a necessary decision. After all, the protesters wanted change. If the constitution's rulebook had been followed after Mubarak's departure, then Speaker Surur would have become president, ruling until the middle of April, when a new presidential election would have been held. The NDP-dominated parliament would have remained in place, and the popular desire for change would have gone unfulfilled. This was clearly a nonstarter. But there was self-interest at play, too. The 1971 Constitution, after all, contained no provisions for military rule.

But the suspension of the constitution also stoked fears that the military was settling in for the long haul. In order to allay them, the SCAF announced the selection of a committee of eight jurists whose task would be to amend the existing constitution so as to facilitate a rapid transfer of power to an elected, civilian government. The committee produced a set of amendments that strengthened judicial oversight of elections, limited presidential terms, opened up competition for the presidency, and eliminated some of the most egregious presidential powers. The most important amendment, however, was one that stipulated that the newly elected parliament would have six months to select a hundred-member constituent assembly that would then have another six months to craft a new constitution and put it to a popular vote.

The amendments were put to a popular referendum on March 19, and passed with 77 percent of the vote, amid record—although still rather low—turnout of 41 percent. Islamists were pleased with the outcome, believing that it offered a clear roadmap out of military rule and to a new parliament and constitution. Others, including every major candidate for Egypt's presidency—from Ayman Nour to Amr Moussa to Mohamed ElBaradei—decried it. They argued that a new constitution should come *before* elections (which, they feared, were poised to bring an Islamist majority). And though the result of the referendum should have settled this debate, it merely intensified it. As of this writing, more than ten weeks after the referendum, liberal politicians continue to call for a constitution first, then elections. On May 27, thousands of Egyptians took to the streets to press this demand. The MB argued that the the protesters' appeal was at odds with the will of the voters expressed during the March referendum. Calls to depart from the timetable set by the referendum, the Brothers said, were undemocratic.

Of course, the MB's exquisite sensitivity to democratic niceties would carry more weight had the group not countenanced an even greater violation of the voters' will immediately following the referendum. One could have been forgiven for expecting that, once the amendments passed, the existing Egyptian constitution would have been reactivated. This, after all, is what the Egyptian people were led to believe. The ballot paper referred specifically to Articles 75, 76, 77, 88, 93, 139, 148, and 189—numbers that only make sense as part of a larger document. Yet the SCAF—perhaps realizing that it could not reanimate the 1971 Constitution without facing the same legitimacy problem that caused it to suspend it in the first place—decided after the referendum to scrap the existing constitution entirely. What has taken its place is an interim "constitutional declaration" that includes not only the referendum-approved amendments, but 55 other articles never put to a vote. Not only was this move of questionable legitimacy, but the interim document—as Nathan Brown and Kristen Stilt have shown—actually contains fewer mechanisms for parliamentary oversight of the executive than did the previous charter.[5] And yet the Muslim Brothers—who today accuse their opponents of trifling with the will of the people—viewed the SCAF's high-handed decision with serenity.

The quarrel among Egyptian opposition forces over the *timing* of the new constitution could be a preview of the conflict that will ensue when they are forced to discuss its actual substance. Constitution-writing processes are inherently turbulent, involving arguments over fundamental values. The nature of the economy, the extent of individual rights, legislative-executive relations, and the role of faith in matters of state all have to be settled. It is not clear that the fragile Egyptian political fabric is ready for this. By making the writing of a new constitution issue number one on Egypt's post-Mubarak political calendar, the SCAF may have bequeathed the country an even greater challenge than the unseating of Mubarak.

The issue of religion will be particularly fraught. The 1971 Constitution (like the interim charter) guarantees that the "principles of the Islamic *shari'a* constitute the main source of legislation." Secularists understandably would prefer no mention of Islamic law, whereas Islamists would prefer a far more robust and specific one. Deputy Prime Minister Yahya al-Gamal recently proposed splitting the difference and declaring Islamic law to be "a major" as opposed to "the main" source of legislation, but was met with calls for his dismissal by Islamist groups including the MB. Christians—who make up 10 percent of Egypt's population—are understandably alienated by the Islam-specific language. Naguib Sawiris, a Christian billionaire and the founder of a new political party, has argued for tempering that language with a provision allowing non-Muslims to be governed by their own religious laws—a proposition that some see as divisive. One of the old constitution's advantages was that it did not resolve these questions to anyone's full satisfaction. Now these issues will have to be refought.

The Islamist Challenge

The SCAF, in an attempt to soothe the liberals, has convened a National Accord of all major Egyptian political and social forces (from political parties to soccer clubs) and tasked them with generating basic principles for the new constitution in advance of the parliamentary elections. This idea has merit—Jamal Benomar, writing in these pages, has argued that if you cannot write a constitution before you have elections, then agreement on basic constitutional principles prior to elections is the next best thing.[6] The MB, however, has refused to take part in what it views as an attempt by secularists to usurp the authority of the parliament that will be elected in September.

Given that the recommendations of the Accord are not binding and that the country's best-organized political force has rejected it out of hand, it is hard to see the Accord achieving anything. It therefore seems—barring another surprise from the SCAF—that the real fight over the constitution will come at the ballot box in September. Liberal and secular Egyptians, fearful of a sweeping victory by well-organized Islamists, are not likely to succeed in their calls for delaying elections. The Brotherhood, for its part, has tried to allay fears of Islamist domination by announcing that it will compete for only a portion of the seats. Yet that portion has been going up. In February, Badi announced that the MB would seek only a third of the seats, but last month the Brotherhood's new political party announced that it would seek half. (At the time of this writing, the Brothers are still standing by their decision not to field a presidential candidate.)

Recent polling data shed some light on the MB's likely electoral fortunes. A telephone poll of 615 Egyptians conducted between March 9 and 20 by the International Peace Institute found that 38 percent of respondents viewed the MB somewhat or very favorably, but only 12 percent said that they would vote for the MB in the upcoming parliamentary election. A Pew Research Center poll of 1,000 Egyptians conducted between March 24 and April 7 found that 75 percent rated the MB somewhat or very favorably, while 17 percent declared that the MB should lead the next government.

These figures are consistent with past MB performance. In the 2005 elections that gave the MB a fifth of the seats in parliament, the Brothers ran only 160 candidates, enough to compete for slightly more than a third of the seats. They won somewhere between 2.5 and 3 million votes out of 8 million cast. The number of eligible voters in that election was approximately 32 million. To put it another way, the Brothers were supported by around 30 percent of actual voters and less than 10 percent of eligible ones. But we should not read too much into these numbers, generated as they were by an electoral process riddled with fraud and voter intimidation, and conducted under a majoritarian, candidate-centric electoral system that magnified the MB's organizational advantages.[7]

In any case, hand-wringing over the MB's electoral fortunes may be beside the point. Islamist representation in the coming parliament will not be restricted to the Brothers, and will include parties and groups whose electoral weight and commitment to democracy remain unknown. There has been a proliferation of Islamist parties and political actors in the post-Mubarak landscape, from the moderately Islamist Wasat Party, to the Renaissance Party founded by breakaway MB members led by Abdel Moneim Abul Futuh, to salafist groups such as the Salafi Preaching Society and the Supporters of Muhammad's Path—the latter of which has declared its intention to form a political party. Secularists must worry about more than just the MB.

How many votes would the broader Islamist bloc get? It has been argued that the 77 percent of Egyptians who voted "yes" in the recent constitutional referendum are a reflection of the Islamists' voting strength, since all Islamist groups supported the amendments and campaigned hard for their passage. Egypt's largest and oldest Islamic charity, the Legitimate Association for the Cooperation of the Adherents of the Book and the Path of Muhammad, ran an ad on the front page of *Al-Ahram* on March 16 declaring it a religious duty for Muslims to vote for the amendments. After the vote, Muhammad Hussein Yaqub, a popular salafist preacher, declared the result a victory for the faith and is reported to have announced, "That's it, the country is ours."[8] But just because Islamists supported the amendments does not mean that everyone who voted yes is an Islamist (the NDP, which would be dissolved by court order in mid-April, called on its members to vote yes). Moreover, as with referenda elsewhere, yes votes are probably best understood as popular endorsements of the current rulers (in this case, the SCAF).[9]

All of which is to say that we do not know how powerful the various Islamist groups are or will prove to be come September. What we do know is that Islamists of all stripes will do their best to convince tradition-minded Egyptians that the coming election is about who gets to draft Egypt's constitution, and thus about whether or not the country will retain its Islamic identity. If a religious cleavage takes hold in Egyptian politics, we may have the SCAF and its insistence on constitutional innovation to thank.

Out with the Old?

Although retaining the 1971 Constitution (at least for a time) may have had its upsides, it is easy to understand why this move would have been unpalatable (even as most Egyptians seemed willing to accept it). The country had undergone a revolution, and revolutions require the elimination of old orders and the erection of new ones. Symbols of the old regime needed to be torn down, whether these were documents, institutions, or people. This yearning for a clean break with the past was behind the protests that on March 3 brought down the cabinet of Mubarak's last prime minister, Ahmed Shafiq; the storming and subsequent dissolution of the Interior Ministry's State Security Investigations Ser-

vice on March 4; and the April 7 "Friday of Cleansing" protests that culminated in the disbanding of the NDP and the military's acquiescence in
the arrest of Mubarak, his wife, and his sons.

Today, a number of NDP leaders and former Mubarak ministers cool
their heels in prison, awaiting trial on charges ranging from corruption
to torture to murder. Former interior minister Habib al-Adli—a man
responsible for gruesome violations of Egyptians' human rights—was
sentenced on May 5 to twelve years in jail for money laundering, and
is currently standing trial for ordering the use of deadly force against
the January 25 protesters. On May 22, a police officer was sentenced to
death *in absentia* for slaughtering twenty Egyptians during the demonstrations. These punishments are not simply emotionally satisfying, they
help to obliterate the culture of impunity with which high government
officials—and the security forces in particular—have operated. They
remind all in the new Egypt that the lives and property of citizens are
sacred.

But the wider the net of justice is cast, the higher the potential political
costs may mount. Military leaders, for example, may worry that handing
over power could subject them to the same treatment that Mubarak is
now receiving. Businessmen, many of whom benefitted from the Mubarak regime's turn toward crony capitalism, may withhold investment
out of fear of prosecution and expropriation. As Adam Przeworski has
noted, one of the challenges of democratic transition and consolidation
is convincing potential spoilers that their chances under democracy are
better than their chances if they try to subvert democracy.[10]

That such subversion is taking place is the conventional wisdom in
Egypt. The months since the revolution have seen multiple clashes between Muslims and Coptic Christians, including church burnings in the
Giza village of Sul on March 5 and the poor Cairo neighborhood of
Imbaba on May 8. On May 4, extortionists touched off a gunfight in
downtown Cairo that wounded more than sixty people. Egyptians at-
tribute recent acts of violence to sinister counterrevolutionary forces
that, according to Deputy Prime Minister Gamal, are drawing on funds
provided by businessmen associated with the old regime and manpower
furnished by veterans of the old state-security forces. It is impossible at
this remove to know how accurate his charges are—but even if there is
no grand conspiracy to foment disorder, the Interior Ministry and the
police have certainly approached the task of restoring order with an unusual degree of hesitancy.

This should not surprise us. The Interior Ministry was for thirty years
both the guardian of public order and the boot of the regime on the necks
of the Egyptian people. Inducing it to take up the former of its two roles
with vigor may require Egyptians to give up the dream of prosecuting
too many people for being part of the latter role. And time is running out.
Without a functioning security apparatus, the September parliamentary

contests can be expected to turn bloody. As unappetizing as it sounds, getting Egypt to democracy may require allowing those whose job was to protect the old system to take on the job of protecting the new one.

Of course, only Egyptians can decide whether they will be best served by seeking justice or by making sure that all players—including elements of the old regime—feel that they have a place in the new system.

Making Democracy Durable

It is not just elements of the old regime that must see benefits in the new system; so too must the average Egyptians whose support for democracy will be critical to its endurance. In 1954, as Gamal Abdel Nasser (then vice-chairman of the military junta that had seized power two years earlier) dueled with the more democratically minded President Muhammad Naguib, the former was able to mobilize workers to march through the streets yelling, "Down with democracy!" Nasser could do this not because the workers were stupid, but because their only experience with so-called democracy, under the constitutional monarchy of King Farouk, had been marked by high unemployment, poor working conditions, and low pay. We may think that democracy enjoys unshakeable legitimacy in the world, but nothing tests democratic commitments like an empty stomach.

And the number of empty stomachs in Egypt is mounting. Economic growth has slowed to around 1 percent (down from more than 5 percent the previous year). On May 16, the SCAF warned darkly of economic calamity, with a 25 percent drop in Egypt's foreign reserves, a complete halt to foreign direct investment, and more than $40 million dollars a day in lost tourism revenue. According to the SCAF, 70 percent of Egyptians now live below the poverty line, inflation hovers around 12 percent, and a quarter of the workforce is unemployed. The SCAF has urged Egyptians to get back to work, but its February decision to outlaw labor strikes failed to do much more than intensify suspicion of the military's sincerity about democracy.

Given this gloomy picture, there are two temptations to which any democratically elected Egyptian government could succumb. The first is to deal with unemployment by padding the state payroll. Since the revolution began, more than half a million temporary government employees have been put on permanent contracts with full benefits, and in May the Finance Ministry announced that it was poised to provide two-million new job opportunities (although not all of these were in the public sector).[11] Today, workers protest to demand the reversal of Mubarak's privatization initiatives, and it is easy to imagine candidates for political office making concessions to such demands.

The second tendency is to return to a kind of old-fashioned but still-popular Nasserist development strategy. This would involve not only reversing Mubarak-era privatization measures, but embarking on new large-scale, state-led development projects—as if to match the dramatic refashioning of Egypt's politics with an equally dramatic reshaping of its economy. Thus, in April 2011 the government of Prime Minister Essam Sharaf announced its plan to undertake a "Desert Development Corridor" megaproject that involves a 2,000-kilometer superhighway in Egypt's western desert running from the border with Sudan to the Mediterranean, with water diverted from the Nile to allow new "urban communities, industrial plants, and agricultural farms" to bloom.[12]

But neither the dole nor grand development schemes are likely to solve Egypt's deep economic problems. Expanding the public sector may make a dent in youth unemployment, but experience has shown that such gains will be hard to sustain. Similarly, massive state-driven projects may stimulate the economy in the short term, but they may also waste scarce resources and generate unforeseen and potentially catastrophic environmental consequences. As James Scott has noted, high-modernist, top-down schemes that emerge fully formed from the brains of individual geniuses (in the superhighway's case, Egyptian geologist and NASA scientist Farouk El-Baz) are almost always inferior to small, incremental experiments built on local knowledge.[13]

The success of democracy in Egypt will ultimately rest on the success of the country's economy. The relationship between democracy and economic development remains a subject of dispute, but we do know that the two are correlated, and that no democracy has ever failed at a per capita GDP above that which Argentina enjoyed on the eve of the bloodless coup that toppled President Isabel Perón in 1976.[14] In constant 2005 dollars, Argentina's 1976 GDP per capita was approximately $11,500. Today Egypt's is just under half that. This is not the place to review theories of democracy and development—although some might argue that Egypt's lack of a sizeable middle class renders it bereft of democracy's civic and cultural underpinnings. A more modest claim is simply that, just as poverty and unemployment were important drivers of the protests that brought down an autocratic government, so too could they drive protests against democratic ones.

Where does all this leave us? It is easy to be pessimistic about Egypt's prospects. But just as we failed to predict revolution in Egypt, so too will we likely fail in our attempts to foresee Egypt's fortunes after the revolution. The Egyptian people, after all, have more than amply demonstrated their ability to confound the predictions of experts. What is clear is that where Egypt leads, other Arab countries will (try to) follow. Egypt has long been the cultural and intellectual center of gravity of the Arab world, and the stakes of the Egyptian transition are high. If the country manages to become a functioning democracy, one could imagine every election there becoming a focal point for fresh protests in Syria or Saudi Arabia, with the people of each yearning for their own version of the democracy that eighty-million of their fellow Arabs enjoy. But if Egypt's transition detours into chaos, Islamist extremism, or economic collapse, its neighbors may consider themselves fortunate to dwell under the lugubrious stability furnished by the strongman.

—8 June 2011

NOTES

I am grateful to David Dapice, Will Dobson, Mohamed Helal, Jill Goldenziel, Amaney Jamal, and Ellen Lust for incisive comments on an earlier draft of this essay.

1. Jason Brownlee, *Authoritarianism in an Age of Democratization* (New York: Cambridge University Press, 2007); Lisa Blaydes, *Elections and Distributive Politics in Mubarak's Egypt* (New York: Cambridge University Press, 2011).

2. Robert Fisk, "As Mubarak Clings on . . . What Now for Egypt?" *Independent,* 11 February 2011.

3. Samuel P. Huntington, *The Third Wave: Democratization in the Late Twentieth Century* (Norman: University of Oklahoma Press, 1991), 174.

4. Michele Dunne, "Evaluating Egyptian Reform," Carnegie Paper No. 66, Middle East Series, January 2006.

5. Nathan Brown and Kristen Stilt, "A Haphazard Constitutional Compromise," Carnegie Endowment for International Peace, Commentary, 11 April 2011.

6. Jamal Benomar, "Constitution-Making After Conflict: Lessons for Iraq," *Journal of Democracy* 15 (April 2004): 86.

7. For a discussion of the Egyptian electoral system and the Brotherhood's adaptation to it, see Tarek Masoud, "Why Islam Wins: Electoral Ecologies and Economies of Political Islam in Contemporary Egypt," PhD diss., Yale University, 2008.

8. See "Prominent Egypt Salafist Proclaims Victory for Religion in Referendum," *Al Masry Alyoum,* English edition, 22 March 2011, *www.almasryalyoum.com.*

9. I am grateful to Jacques Rupnik for alerting me to this point.

10. Adam Przeworski, *Democracy and the Market: Political and Economic Reforms in Eastern Europe and Latin America* (New York: Cambridge University Press, 1992).

11. Alaa Shahine and Maram Mazen, "Egypt Plans Stimulus to Revive 'Sudden Stop' Economy," *Bloomberg Businessweek,* 14 February 2011; and *www.rosaonline.net/Daily/News.asp?id=111271.*

12. On the proposed superhighway, see *http://faroukelbaz.com/index.php?option=com_content&view=article&id=22&Itemid=34.*

13. James C. Scott, *Seeing Like a State: How Certain Schemes to Improve the Human Condition Have Failed* (New Haven: Yale University Press, 1998).

14. Adam Przeworski and Fernando Limongi, "Modernization: Theories and Facts," *World Politics* 49 (January 1997): 155–83.

20

EGYPT: WHY LIBERALISM STILL MATTERS

Michele Dunne and Tarek Radwan

Michele Dunne, director of the Rafik Hariri Center for the Middle East at the Atlantic Council in Washington, D.C., has served in the White House on the National Security Council staff, on the State Department's Policy Planning Staff, and as a diplomat in Cairo and Jerusalem. Tarek Radwan is associate director for research and the chief editor of the MENASource blog at the Atlantic Council's Rafik Hariri Center for the Middle East. He previously reported on the Middle East with Human Rights Watch and served as a human-rights officer for the United Nations–African Union Hybrid Operation in Darfur. This essay originally appeared in the January 2013 issue of the Journal of Democracy.

A recent Egyptian political cartoon depicts a bearded man in traditional Muslim attire stepping on the back of another man labeled "the revolution" in order to ascend to a seat labeled "the dictator's throne."[1] Although those familiar with Egypt will recognize the first man's clothing as the garment of a salafist, many would interpret the meaning of the drawing more broadly: The liberals who in 2011 upended the thirty-year-old Hosni Mubarak dictatorship were duped, and now Islamists with completely different goals—including the country's newly elected president, Mohamed Morsi of the Muslim Brotherhood—are using the liberals as stepping stones to power. As a result, Egypt is becoming increasingly Islamist and is on the road to becoming more of a theocracy than a democracy.

According to conventional Western wisdom, liberal ideas are unpopular among Egyptians, despite what some enthusiastic young people said in Tahrir Square in early 2011. Consequently, liberals fared poorly in the legislative elections that took place in late 2011 and early 2012, in which Islamists won 70 percent of the 498 directly elected seats in the People's Assembly. In the June 2012 presidential election, no liberal was a serious contender. Many Egyptians associate liberal ideas with Western colonialism and hegemony, and hence find these ideas distasteful. In addition, Egyptian liberals tend to be elitist, distraction-prone, and given to squabbling over petty differences.

Threads of truth run through these claims, but the overall pattern that they weave is misleading. While it is true that social mores have become more conservative in Egypt in recent decades, it is not true that core liberal ideas are in retreat. On the contrary, the essentials of political liberalism—citizens' rights, government accountability, the rule of law, limits on state power—have become so popular that the liberal ideological field has become crowded. Liberals have had a hard time gaining public support in part because others—notably, the Brotherhood and, before the revolution, Mubarak's National Democratic Party (NDP)—appropriated liberal ideas, leaving liberals with a smaller portfolio of social issues, such as women's equality and minority rights, with which to distinguish themselves from the others. So we must therefore ask, is there any space or need in Egypt for liberals?

In discussing the progress of liberal ideas in Egypt, we take as our starting point core ideas that have evolved since John Locke set forth the classic formulation of the concepts of natural rights and the social contract. Locke argued that the rights of the individual must be kept free from interference by the state, which exists solely to protect and preserve the individual's welfare. The consent of the governed allows the state to rule over a civil society and justifies the removal of the government by any means if the terms of the social contract are broken.

The idea that individuals have inalienable rights—*karama* (dignity)—which they should be able to enjoy without government harassment—*hurriya* (freedom)—was the long-smoldering tinder that set alight the Egyptian revolution. Explicit in the uprising's calls for democracy and implicit in its demands for Mubarak's removal and a transition to democracy was the notion that citizens should have the right and the ability to choose their government and to change it if it fails to fulfill the social contract.

"Liberal" is not a static concept, of course, and while the basic tenets of a liberal understanding of political life have endured, those related to economic and social matters have expanded over time. What liberal values embody in a social sense has changed in the West, as the notion of equality now includes more and more people, regardless of sex, race, class, religion, or sexual orientation. In Egypt, such economic and social ideas are far more contested than are the core political principles of liberalism.

The fact that the term *librali* (liberal) is fraught in mainstream Egyptian discourse is an additional distraction. In Egypt, the word "liberal" is often considered synonymous with "secular," which in turn implies "atheist" to some—a concept both foreign and offensive to many Egyptians. As an alternative, the less troubled term *madani,* which can mean either "civilian" (not military) or "civil" (not religious), has become common in political parlance. Thus current discourse parallels the dilemma in which Egyptian liberals often find themselves: Should they define themselves primarily as nonmilitary (and hence also nonauthoritarian) or as non-Islamist? This dilemma has effectively divided liberals since the 2011 revolution, with some (often the younger ones) opting to cooperate tactically with Islamists in order to end military rule and others (often older liberals, used to dealing with the Mubarak regime) choosing to cooperate with the military or other elements of the *ancien régime* in order to forestall Islamist dominance.

In this essay, those referred to as "liberals" are political actors who have made democratic governance, the rule of law, equal rights for all citizens (including women and religious minorities), and a free-market economy the main principles of their ideology. Such actors might refer to themselves as "liberal" but, due to the issues mentioned above, rarely use that moniker for their political movements or parties. And as we will see, core tenets of political liberalism such as democratic governance and rule of law have also come to be broadly accepted by Islamists (who might not accept the full equality of all citizens regardless of sex or religion) and leftists (who do not necessarily accept a free-market economy), making the political spectrum increasingly muddled.

Liberalism Before the Revolution

Although a full exploration of liberalism in Egypt would need to begin in the early nineteenth century, here we shall focus on the last twenty years. Over these two decades, ideas such as democratic governance, citizenship, and individual rights came up for wide discussion even though political freedom notably contracted during the 1990s as the ossifying Mubarak regime, pointing to the threat of domestic terrorism in the early part of the decade, put the clamps on.[2] Prominent figures—Mubarak, members of the ruling NDP, opposition politicians, and public intellectuals—often discussed concepts such as democracy, political reform, and civil society, in part to show that they were in touch with the major global developments of the time, including the spread of democracy in Central and Eastern Europe after the fall of the Soviet Union.[3]

The ruling NDP performed poorly in the 2000 parliamentary elections. Showing a lack of party discipline, many prospective candidates deserted the NDP, ran as independents, and then rejoined after winning their (largely corrupt) races. President Mubarak's son Gamal, who was being positioned to succeed his father, took advantage of the party's poor showing at the polls to propose reinventing the NDP. Gamal saw political liberalism as promising turf for his new NDP to occupy and attracted prominent liberals such as intellectuals Aley Eddin Hilal, Abdel Moneim Said, and Hossam Badrawi. Adopting the slogan *tafkir jadid* (new thinking), Gamal's NDP focused on economic reform and concepts such as citizenship, modernization, government efficiency, and women's rights.

Gamal Mubarak's push for liberal economic reform had real vitality, and by 2004 there was an economic-reform dream team in the cabinet led by Prime Minister Ahmad Nazif that made significant macroeconomic changes over the next six years. Gamal's vision for political reform, however, was incoherent and apparently driven by two factors: 1) the need for a certain degree of openness (in terms of the media and Internet freedom) and government efficiency in order to attract foreign direct investment; and 2) the need for at least tacit support from the United States for his eventual succession to the presidency. President George W. Bush had articulated his "forward strategy of freedom" in a November 2003 speech at the National Endowment for Democracy, signaling U.S. backing for democratic reform.

The NDP was not the only group to respond to the growing calls for change from inside and outside Egypt. The Muslim Brotherhood put forward a political-reform program in 2004 after Mahdi Akef became Supreme Guide, partly as an attempt to accommodate younger members who desired more political engagement and partly as a response to the Bush freedom agenda. As Mona El-Ghobashy observed, the program was also a message to other Egyptian opposition groups that "the Muslim Brothers and they are in one camp, speak the same constitutionalist language, agree on the foundational issue of the division and rotation of powers, and can be counted on in any future common initiatives."[4] The 2004 program expressly embraced a constitutional, parliamentary form of government in conformity with Islam—a remarkable step given the movement's prior political thought.[5] By the early 2000s, the debate among Islamists over representative government was nearly over, as support for the key concepts of political, if not social, liberalism had become widely accepted.

Still, it was not the Brotherhood but rather a new opposition group that became the vanguard of political change: the Egyptian Movement for Change, formed by leftist, Nasserite, Islamist, and human-rights activists. Generally known by its slogan "Kifaya" (Enough), the movement captured the Egyptian popular imagination upon its founding in 2004 and tapped public weariness with Mubarak-era stagnation and the prospect of Gamal's succession. Showing the resourcefulness and wit that would become a hallmark of revolutionary groups later on, Kifaya's first public protest in December 2004 featured several hundred activists demonstrating mostly silently before the High Court building, wearing round seals emblazoned with "Kifaya" over their mouths.

Although the Kifaya movement declined in importance within two years, it made several important contributions to political life in Egypt. It broke the taboo against direct criticism of Mubarak and overcame the fear of engaging in antiregime public protests. In addition, the group began to establish a public consensus in favor of liberalizing political life. Kifaya was not the first or only group to bring activists of different political stripes together, but it did so with the explicit call to build "a homeland of democracy and progress" via "breaking the hold of the ruling party on power and all its instruments" and the "cessation of all laws which constrain public and individual freedoms." It called for constitutional reform to provide for the direct and competitive election of the president, limited presidential terms and powers, stronger parliamentary and judicial independence, free media, the establishment of new political parties, and the holding of free and fair parliamentary elections.[6]

Precursors of Change

Kifaya not only addressed the need for political reform but also connected that issue to public anger about economic injustice, corruption, and Egypt's diminished role in regional affairs (which Kifaya attributed to "American and Zionist influence"). While the movement broke new ground by holding a number of joint protests with Brotherhood activists, it still insisted on a certain rigor when it came to liberal political ideas. During one memorable demonstration in May 2005, Kifaya protestors objected to the Brotherhood's habit of waving copies of the Koran in the air and challenged the Islamists on the meaning of the gesture.[7] Did the Brotherhood envision sovereignty in a future Egyptian democracy belonging to the people or to God? After a brief consultation, the Brotherhood protestors reportedly replied, "To the people," and agreed to put their holy books away for the remainder of the protest.[8]

Kifaya's influence declined rapidly after the group failed to prevent Mubarak's election to his fifth six-year presidential term in September 2005. Independent candidates affiliated with the Brotherhood (at the time still an illegal movement with no political party) won a fifth of the seats in parliament, a stunning victory that might well have been larger had the elections been completely fair. The few candidates affiliated directly with Kifaya, lacking a political machine to back them, fared poorly at the polls.

The period between late 2005 and 2010 was difficult for Egyptian activists, bringing waves of arrests and financial repression against the Muslim Brothers as well as regime measures to restrict pro-reform judges and other groups. Along with the Brotherhood, the explicitly liberal al-Ghad (Tomorrow) Party received special punishment, with its leader Ayman Nour, who had run against Mubarak for the presidency, convicted on trumped-up forgery charges in late 2005 and the remaining party leaders harassed into resigning.

The repressive environment forced activists to become more resourceful. The April 6th Youth Movement, a loose grouping of young liberal and leftist activists, was founded in 2008 and attempted to escape repression by doing most of its organizing via Facebook. Its leaders faced intimidation after they succeeded in promoting a nationwide general strike on

April 6 of that year. The strike alarmed the regime by linking youth activists with the large labor protests that had been rocking the country for several years. Although repression and internal struggles took their toll on the movement, it remained at least symbolically important and eventually played a role in the early days of the 2011 revolution.

Throughout this period, dialogue continued between liberal and other secular political groups and Islamists, even amid government crackdowns on the media, exclusion of opposition candidates from many elections, other forms of election rigging, and the systematic use of torture against political opponents of the regime. One of the most remarkable episodes of Islamist-liberal dialogue revolved around the circulation of a draft Brotherhood political program in 2007. The fact that it was shared in draft form with activists outside the Brotherhood was in itself notable, considering the organization's usually opaque decision making.

While the program supported the idea of parliamentary democracy for Egypt and detailed the Brotherhood's vision in more than a hundred pages, it contained two elements that alarmed non-Islamists: the creation of a clerical council to review legislation for conformity with Islamic law, and a ban on both female and non-Muslim candidates for head of state. These positions provoked a firestorm of criticism and were opposed by some of the Brotherhood's more progressive members. The 2007 draft remained unfinished, and the clerical council and presidential exclusion would fail to appear in future Brotherhood platforms.[9] Yet as late as 2012, some figures in the organization continued to say that they personally considered women unsuited for the presidency.

Not all the political activity in the years leading up to the revolution took place behind the scenes. In February 2010, Mohamed ElBaradei, the former head of the International Atomic Energy Agency, returned to his native Egypt to challenge the Mubarak regime. Unlike the April 6th Youth Movement, which was arguably too small to attract much harassment from the regime, ElBaradei was too big. Returning just a year before Mubarak would either attempt to run again or promote his son as successor, the Nobel laureate quickly became Egypt's leading liberal and, in the eyes of many, a possible future president. He adopted an explicitly liberal program that was similar to those of Kifaya and al-Ghad but more focused on free elections as the engine of political change. Like Kifaya, ElBaradei reached out to groups with different ideologies, especially the Brotherhood.

Forming the National Association for Change (NAC), ElBaradei and other prominent figures drafted a seven-point petition and said they planned to gather a million signatures. The petition called for measures specific to the preelectoral context of Egypt in 2010: ending the state of emergency, empowering the judiciary to supervise elections, allowing domestic and international monitoring of elections, providing a level playing field for all presidential candidates, allowing expatriates to vote, limiting the president to two terms in office, and allowing voting with national identity cards rather than requiring registration. Prominent Brotherhood politician Mohamed al-Beltagy actively participated in the NAC, and the petition became one of the most striking instances of liberal-Islamist cooperation. Because the Brotherhood promoted the petition, the NAC managed to obtain hundreds of thousands of signatures by late 2010.

The most prominent protest group to arise in the months ahead of the revolution was We Are All Khaled Said, an assortment of activists drawn together in protest against the June 2010 beating death of a young Alexandrian blogger by police. It mattered not whether the killing was spontaneous brutality or premeditated murder; the death of a middle-class youth at the hands of police in the street outraged Egyptians. As the April 6th Movement had done, We Are All Khaled Said organized via Facebook, bringing four-thousand people into the streets on 25 June 2010 at a time when few protests other than labor strikes attracted more than a meager few hundred. Prominent liberal figures such as ElBaradei and Ayman Nour joined in. While the group's main purpose was to galvanize public outrage against police brutality and other widespread human-rights abuses, it also called for political change, saying that "Egyptians are aspiring to the day when Egypt has its freedom and dignity back, the day when the current thirty-year-long emergency martial law ends and when Egyptians can freely elect their true representatives."[10]

The contribution of We Are All Khaled Said, like that of the April 6th Movement, was more in mobilizing dissent than in spreading political ideas; its Facebook page was the primary organizing venue for the January 25 Day of Rage that spiraled into the eighteen-day revolution. Still, these groups primarily comprised activists who espoused a liberal political agenda and used their ingenuity and social-media skills to knit the various strands of grievance—economic, rights-based, and political—as well as the various political tendencies into a unified call for a transition from authoritarian to democratic rule. Young activists from the April 6th and Khaled Said movements also began to interact intensively with the youth wing of the Brotherhood, a partnership that would prove potent and inspiring to many Egyptians during the revolution.

Liberalism During and After the Uprising

Egyptian demonstrators stunned the world in January 2011 not only with their courage but also with their liberal demands: dignity, freedom, and economic opportunity. This was by no means the Islamic revolution that many had predicted would eventually challenge Mubarak. Not only did the Brotherhood have little to do with starting the uprising—although its website advertised the January 25 Day of Rage, few Brothers showed up at the outset—but the group continued for many months to shift tactics in order to maximize its advantage, cooperating at one moment with the authorities and at the next with the revolutionaries.

After Mubarak's dramatic ouster on 11 February 2011, the assumption of executive power by the Supreme Council of the Armed Forces (SCAF) marked the start of the military's stewardship of the political transition. To create a legal and constitutional framework, the SCAF suspended the 1971 Constitution and summoned a constitutional-review committee, led by the moderate Islamic political intellectual Judge Tarek al-Bishri. Working directly against liberal and revolutionary activists who were calling for the early drafting of an entirely new constitution, the Brotherhood and the ultraconservative salafists spent tremendous energy and resources to persuade the public to vote in the 19 March 2011 referendum for a package of constitutional amendments that would pave the way for early parliamentary elections.

In the months that followed, liberal activists felt betrayed by Islamists, who did not participate in the antimilitary demonstrations that exposed liberal and leftist protesters to grave human-rights abuses including torture and military trials. Assaults by the military on civilian demonstrators in the run-up to the parliamentary elections that began on 28 November 2011 drew severe criticism from local and international activists and politicians. The Brotherhood had been calling for calm and hoping to avoid confrontations with the SCAF in order to maintain a laser-like focus on winning elections. Only when it appeared that the SCAF intended to usurp control of the constitution-drafting process did the Islamists begin to protest in mid-November 2011. Most later withdrew, however, leaving the liberal, secular, and leftist youth to face the tear gas and rubber bullets on downtown Cairo's Mohamed Mahmoud Street in November and December. When asked about the Islamists' absence from the demonstrations, one protester smiled and said, "The Muslim Brotherhood will fight to the very last liberal."[11]

The first parliamentary elections after the revolution were held in three rounds between November 2011 and January 2012 and illustrated the liberals' failure to convert their momentum into a political presence. The evidence suggests, however, that their losses stemmed more from political miscalculations than public antipathy to liberal ideas. In a typical postrevolutionary scenario, multifarious parties (liberal, Islamist, leftist, and nationalist) proliferated once the Mubarak era's draconian limits were lifted. While the Brotherhood's new political arm, the Freedom and Justice Party (FJP), and the several salafist parties (of which the most important was the Nour Party) worked assiduously at their campaigns, liberals and other non-Islamists frequently suspended their activities amid clashes with security forces and flirted till the last moment with the idea of an election boycott.

Nonetheless, the jockeying for parliamentary power produced coalitions in which Islamist factions joined forces with secular, liberal, and leftist parties, if only temporarily. In June 2011, the FJP formed the Democratic Alliance for Egypt as a unified front against former regime politicians contesting parliamentary seats. Notably, Ayman Nour's Ghad al-Thawra Party remained a part of the alliance despite a series of defections, some based on ideological differences and others on administrative ones.[12] The moderating effect of pluralist voices within the alliance led the FJP to agree to drop the slogan "Islam is the answer" and adopt in its place the religiously neutral "We bring good for all of Egypt."[13] Alliance members also committed to the "Fundamental Principles for the Constitution of the Modern Egyptian State," a document that would guide the draft constitution toward upholding the rule of law, free expression, free association, and freedom of belief, while at the same time preserving Islam as the official state religion and *shari'a* as the principal source of legislation.

Campaign Disarray

The Egyptian Bloc, led primarily by the Free Egyptians Party and cast as the vehicle that secular liberals would use to counter Islamist contenders, comprised groups dedicated to a civil democratic state. It too suffered massive defections, mainly due to disagreements over electoral lists, though leftist and revolution-affiliated parties such as the Socialist Popular Alliance Party and Amr Hamzawy's Egypt Freedom Party left the coalition in outrage over the inclusion of former NDP officials as candidates as well as the lack of transparency in candidate selection. The defections left the Bloc with only three formations, forcing it to vie with a multitude of other liberal-leaning parties such as the Adl (Justice) and Wasat (Center) parties as the alternative to the Brotherhood and salafists. The venerable New Wafd Party, a onetime liberal standard-bearer that had become tainted by its cooperation with the Mubarak regime, at first planned to run as part of the FJP coalition but eventually ran on its own.

As an example of the chaos that afflicted many liberal campaigns, candidate George Ishak—a founder of Kifaya and a household name in his hometown of Port Said—lost in the first round to a Brotherhood challenger in what many expected would be a hard-fought race. Ishak's campaign managers confessed that almost none of their volunteers showed up for last-minute pamphleteering and electoral observation because they had all taken buses to Cairo to participate in a massive protest just before the elections and had failed to get back to Port Said on time.[14] In fact, it is possible that some of the volunteers and voters were uncertain on election day whether Ishak was running or boycotting—hardly a recipe for success.

There were exceptions to the trend of liberal failure: Liberal intellectual and media star Amr Hamzawy handily won his Cairo seat in the first round of voting, and several other prominent liberals such as analyst Amr Chobaky and young revolutionary Mostafa Naggar gained seats as well. But the overall result was that the FJP's Democratic Alliance for Egypt won nearly half the seats in the People's Assembly and the salafist parties won another quarter, leaving all non-Islamists combined (liberals, leftists, and Nasserites) with only a quarter of the seats in parliament. Still, this was the liberals' best performance at the polls since the Wafd Party began to decline in the 1930s.

After the elections, the Brotherhood and the salafists, believing the country to be behind them, overplayed their hand by selecting a 100-member constituent assembly that included 66 Islamists, but only five non-Muslims and six women. Walkouts by non-Islamist members, a court freeze on the assembly's activity, and popular disapproval of the extent of Islamist domination forced the Islamists to back down and agree to the assembly's dissolution in April 2012. That same month, parliament agreed on a second, slightly more balanced assembly. Despite another round of walkouts, the new body held together thanks to yet another round of dramatic political shifts: the Supreme Constitutional Court's June 14 order to dissolve the People's Assembly, the SCAF's appropriation of executive and legislative authority by constitutional addendum, and the impending presidential runoff set for June 16–17.

Nearly two-dozen candidates initially entered the presidential race. Yet by the time of the first-round voting on May 23–24, due to a number of disqualifications and withdrawals, only five serious contenders remained: Ahmed Shafiq (secular, ex-military), Amr Moussa (secular, ex-diplomat), Mohamed Morsi (FJP), Abdel Moneim Abul Futuh (liberal Islamist), and Hamdeen Sabahi (Nasserite). To the disappointment of the youth movements and liberal revolutionaries, Mohamed ElBaradei withdrew from the contest in January 2012. He claimed that the lack of a proper democratic structure and the SCAF's mishandling of the post-Mubarak transition forced him to pursue the revolution's goals through unofficial channels. ElBaradei's withdrawal from the race meant that liberals were without any independent alternative candidate.

Abul Futuh and Moussa appeared to be the frontrunners, but both lost public standing after participating in Egypt's first (and so far only) televised presidential debate on May 10. In the first-round voting later that month, Morsi won 25 percent and Shafiq won 24 percent to edge out competitors Sabahi (21 percent), Abul Futuh (18 percent), and Moussa (11 percent). Morsi won the second round with 52 percent of the vote. Yet despite the significance of a Muslim Brother succeeding Mubarak as president and the lack of a truly liberal candidate in the race, liberal values had a strong presence throughout the campaign, and voting results indicated that a non-Islamist president might well have been elected had the leading secular candidate not been a former military officer. Moussa, Abul Futuh, and Sabahi—combining to win roughly half the first round votes—divided the ballots of relatively moderate voters. Thus Morsi and Shafiq actually represented the preferences of only a minority of the

Egyptian public, which is not necessarily polarized between Islamists and secularists; many voters seem to favor some shade of gray.

Moussa and Abul Futuh battled for what was clearly liberal political turf. Although a former member of the Mubarak regime, Moussa publicly supported the uprising early on and railed against religious rule while promoting a reformist agenda and promising to serve only one term if elected.[15] Abul Futuh's campaign team incorporated leftists, liberals, and young Islamists who backed his vision of a civil state, based on Islamic values, that would respond to the demands of the revolution. Abul Futuh gained support from an unlikely source: the salafist Nour Party. Known for its regressive and distrustful stance toward liberal-democratic values, this party surprised many by endorsing Abul Futuh over Morsi. Khalil al-Anani, an analyst of Islamist movements, noted that "politics, not ideology, dictated the salafist's decision," citing Nour spokesperson Nader Bakkar, who said that the party was "looking for a president who can be a mere executive manager, not an Islamic caliph."[16] The Nour Party's decision offers a compelling example of the implicit acceptance of liberal ideas within the democratic process.

Shafiq campaigned on an anti-Islamist, security-oriented platform, while Morsi's platform focused on the "Nahda (Renaissance) Project," which emphasized economic revival and social justice. Morsi and the Brotherhood promoted the project, distributing pamphlets describing its details. Despite its explicitly religious overtones, the document echoed Morsi's rhetoric and used liberal language that stressed "respect [for] citizens' rights and dignity inside the country and abroad," alongside a focus on a "centrist understanding of *shari'a* (Islamic law), without which [Egypt] could not attain progress or justice and equality."[17]

After Morsi won the presidency, the SCAF, supported by Supreme Constitutional Court rulings, blocked his attempt to reinstate parliament, a move that some liberals decried and others hailed as the final bulwark against Islamist domination. Morsi, however, played the winning hand in August by issuing a presidential decree annulling SCAF's June constitutional addendum, ending its formal political role in the transition, and replacing the top generals. The decree, by virtue of its popular acceptance, granted Morsi unprecedented interim constitutional, legislative, and executive authority. Critics accused him of assuming more power than Mubarak ever had. Initially, Morsi only used his legislative power cautiously: to strike down pretrial detention for journalists accused of insulting the president and to release prisoners held on crimes related to supporting the revolution. Nonetheless, Morsi's move to stack state media with Brotherhood members and his failure to pursue internal-security reform raised concerns that he might use the still-extant authoritarian bureaucracy inherited from Mubarak for his own ends.

Liberal and secular politicians refused any association with Morsi's government. In July 2012, Morsi recruited Hisham Qandil, the relatively unknown minister of water and irrigation in Kamal al-Ganzouri's interim government, for the premiership. Qandil, who is not a member of any political party, in turn formed a technocratic government that granted to Brotherhood members only five (out of 35) ministries—information, higher education, housing, labor, and youth. Revolutionary activists praised Morsi's pick for vice-president, Judge Mahmoud Makki, who was best known for challenging Mubarak on judicial independence. Morsi chose the judge's more Islamist-leaning brother, Ahmad Makki, as his justice minister. Liberals pointed out, however, that Morsi reneged on his campaign promise to appoint a woman or a Coptic Christian as vice-president.

Constitutional Contention

The most important debates surrounding liberal principles in 2012 revolved around the draft constitution. Salafists and other Islamists clashed with liberals and other non-Islamists over the wording of Article 2, which in the 1971 Constitution states, "Islam is the religion of the state and the principles of *shari'a* are the main source of legislation." Despite an initial agreement to leave the article unchanged, the draft released on 24 October 2012 surprised secular and liberal members of the constituent assembly with the inclusion of an article defining those principles, in effect producing a more theocratic foundation. The religious institution of al-Azhar was also granted a formal role in reviewing legislation, and blasphemy (already against Egyptian law) was specifically banned in the constitution. Inadequate protections for human rights and women's rights, as well as articles limiting press freedom and allowing military trials of civilians, also drew objections, prompting liberal-minded members (roughly a quarter of the assembly) to withdraw in protest.

In an effort to preserve the transitional roadmap, Morsi issued on November 22 a constitutional decree that protected the assembly from dissolution by the courts, insulated his sweeping powers from judicial oversight, and gave him any authority needed to "protect the revolution." The constituent assembly, fearing that judges might ignore the decree, replaced the members who withdrew in protest with last-minute stand-ins and rushed the passage of a draft in a marathon session that lasted through the night of November 30.

The large public backlash that followed showed how unacceptable it was to Egyptians for Morsi to seize unlimited power, even temporarily; to deprive the judiciary of its role in the system; and to ignore liberals' unhappiness with the draft constitution. Political heavyweights Mohamed ElBaradei, Hamdeen Sabahi, and Amr Moussa pulled together to form the National Salvation Front. Supported by massive popular protests staged in front of the presidential palace in Cairo and in many other cities, as well as by resignations of some of Morsi's advisors, the Front demanded that the president rescind his decree and postpone the constitutional referendum, set for December 15. Morsi insisted on pressing ahead with the referendum but was forced to concede the point about the inviolability of his decisions. The episode has produced some unusual bedfellows—young revolutionaries and members of the old regime on one side and the Muslim Brotherhood together with the military on the other—but also showed that, even two years into a difficult and tiring transition, there were tens of thousands of Egyptians willing once again to take to the streets to protest a constitution they considered not liberal enough.

How Liberal Is Egyptian Liberalism?

The Egyptian uprising's calls for human dignity, freedom, bread, social justice, and equality embodied basic demands in liberal philosophy. If the protesters who took to the streets initially approached the matter from a social perspective, the Islamists who joined them fused it with a religious one. Shortly after the Brotherhood launched the FJP, party vice-chair Essam el-Erian said, "When we talk about the slogans of the revolution—freedom, social justice, equality—these are all in the *shari'a*. This revolution called for what the Islamic *shari'a* calls for."[18]

Islamist and liberal ideology in Egypt have converged over the years around a strongly held recognition of the importance of building democratic institutions and the rule of law. The primary difference between liberals and Islamists lies in the Islamist conception of the state as a moral actor responsible for social transformation. This belief is reflected in the postrevolution policies and behavior of Islamist groups and the Islamist-dominated government that promote and defend checks and balances within government, the right to protest, and political participation, but mostly within an Islamic framework that places limits on free speech and on the equality of women and non-Muslims, as delineated by *shari'a*. The result might be a more intrusive state than what liberals advocate. Nonetheless, having assumed the presidency, Morsi (and, by extension, the Muslim Brotherhood) is under pressure to maintain the terms of fair democratic governance, as domestic liberal actors and the public will measure his performance against the country's authoritarian past.

On the economic front as well, several factors—the vast needs of Egypt's poor, the military's large economic interests, and the association of reform with Mubarak-era cronyism—will continue to lead toward more government involvement in the economy than most liberals think advisable. Thus Egypt might well forge its own brand of liberalism, in which politics is largely liberal, but society remains more conservative and the economy more statist than liberals would like.

The dominant narrative that focuses on Islamist electoral ascendance ignores not only the increasing acceptance and even dominance of liberal political ideas in Egypt, but also the transformative and moderating effect upon the political scene exerted by liberals both before and during the transitional period. Leading political figures such as Mohamed ElBaradei and Amr Hamzawy have done yeoman's work in assembling a public consensus behind liberal political ideas, and groups such as Kifaya have had an unmistakable impact on the changing political views of the Muslim Brotherhood as well as Egyptians generally. Civil society organizations such as the Cairo Institute for Human Rights Studies and the Egyptian Initiative for Personal Rights (among many others) act as checks on the institutionalization of Islamist social conservatism. Liberal journalists such as television host Yosri Foda, newspaper editors Ibrahim Eissa and Hani Shukrallah, and publisher Hisham Kassem are a constant presence in the mass media and help not only to shape public debate but to raise difficult questions for Islamists.

Acceptance of the civil, if not secular, nature of the state by mainstream Egyptian society has forced the Muslim Brotherhood to adopt the language of democracy, equality, and human rights in order to appeal to the public and to promote its political platform in what Abdou Filali-Ansary has called the "new political language" of the Arab Spring. The merging in this new language of religious and modern ideas of governance, Filali-Ansary argues, represents a reconciliation of widely accepted contemporary liberal principles with familiar Islamic concepts that help to establish their democratic legitimacy.[19]

Egypt's liberals, though they do not dominate political life and perhaps never will, remain the vanguard of change in the country. They have helped to make the entire political space more liberal and to defend that space against regressive initiatives, forcing the peaceful (if heated) dialogue and negotiation necessary to resolve differences through a democratic process. From Kifaya to April 6th to the National Association for Change to We Are All Khaled Said, liberals have been the ones to crystallize the growing public desire for political reform and individual rights, and to light the way forward. To dismiss liberals now as hopeless or irrelevant would be to misunderstand the outsized but underappreciated role that they have played and will likely continue to play in shaping Egypt's future.

—11 December 2012

NOTES

1. Ashraf Hamdi, "Kursi al-Diktator" [The dictator's chair], *Mashy.com*, 22 March 2011, *http://bit.ly/QQZOiP*.

2. For a thorough documentation of the decline in political liberties during the 1990s, see Eberhard Kienle, *A Grand Delusion: Democracy and Economic Reform in Egypt* (London: I.B. Tauris, 2001).

3. See Michele Dunne, *Democracy in Contemporary Egyptian Political Discourse* (Philadelphia: John Benjamins, 2003).

4. Mona El-Ghobashy, "The Metamorphosis of the Egyptian Muslim Brothers," *International Journal of Middle East Studies* 37 (August 2005): 390.

5. By contrast, in the early 1990s prominent Islamist intellectual Fahmy Huweidy considered the Muslim Brothers so backward in their thinking about liberal political concepts that he wrote an entire book arguing in detail why democracy was fully consonant with Islamic law and texts. See Fahmy Huwaidy, *al-Islam wal-Dimuqratiyya* [Islam and democracy] (Cairo: Al-Ahram Center for Translation and Publication, 1993).

6. Kifaya manifesto, *www.harakamasria.org/node/2944.*

7. Mahmud Sultan, "Ala hamish daftar mudhaharat al-ikhwan" [On the margins of the record on Brotherhood demonstrations], *al-Asr*, 9 May 2005, *http://alasr.ws/articles/view/6639.*

8. As told to Michele Dunne by participants in the 2005 protest.

9. Amr Hamzawy and Nathan J. Brown, "The Egyptian Muslim Brotherhood: Islamist Participation in a Closing Political Environment," Carnegie Endowment for International Peace, Carnegie Paper No. 19, March 2010.

10. "We are all Khaled Said" Facebook page, *www.facebook.com/elshaheeed.co.uk/info.*

11. Tarek Radwan, conversation with a member of the April 6th Movement, Cairo, 21 November 2011.

12. The Democratic Front (DF), a liberal party, withdrew from the Democratic Alliance over the incompatibility of the DF platform with that of the Islamists. Wafd, a secular party, had similar disagreements, but ultimately withdrew over the relative placement of their candidates' names lower on the electoral lists.

13. "Democratic Alliance (Freedom and Justice)," *Egyptian Elections Watch* (Ahram Online and Jadaliyya staff), 18 November 2011, *http://bit.ly/SFNe6L.*

14. Michele Dunne, conversation with members of Ishak's campaign, Port Said, 29 November 2011.

15. Kareem Fahim, "Candidate in Egypt Makes an Insider's Run for President," *New York Times*, 12 May 2012, *http://nyti.ms/SFNtyx.*

16. Khalil al-Anani, "Egypt's 'Blessed' Salafi Votes," *Foreign Policy*, 2 May 2012, *http://bit.ly/SFNAKA.*

17. *Mashru al-Nahda: Nahda Masriyya bi Marjaiyya Islamiyya* [The Renaissance project: An Egyptian renaissance with an Islamic reference], Muslim Brotherhood pamphlet, Cairo, April 2012, 3–4.

18. "Muslim Brothers See Corruption-Free Egypt Flourishing," *al-Arabiya News*, 23 February 2011, *http://bit.ly/SFOmr2.*

19. Abdou Filali-Ansary, "The Languages of the Arab Revolutions," *Journal of Democracy* 23 (April 2012): 11.

21

EGYPT'S FAILED TRANSITION

Nathan J. Brown

Nathan J. Brown *is professor of political science and international affairs at George Washington University and nonresident senior associate at the Carnegie Endowment for International Peace. This essay originally appeared in the October 2013 issue of the* Journal of Democracy.

The July 2013 military ouster of elected president Mohamed Morsi clearly marked the failure of Egypt's two-year attempt to realize a transition to democracy following 2011's mass uprising against authoritarian rule. That uprising had given birth to tremendous hopes that the region might see the forging of a new politics—a politics in which those wielding power would find themselves held accountable by the people acting through regular free elections; in which official actors would safeguard rather than trample human rights; and in which the long-overdue reform of numerous political institutions could take place in a manner both systematic and in keeping with societal needs and international norms. There were significant differences among Egyptians about what those goals meant in practice, how they were to be aligned with prevailing cultural and especially religious values, and how they should be pursued. But in the heady aftermath of President Hosni Mubarak's overthrow, such strains seemed manageable—and indeed, they seemed to be precisely the sorts of policy differences that democratic mechanisms are designed to handle.

The failure of Egypt's democratic experiment was not inevitable, but there were deep problems that repeatedly summoning voters to the polls could not overcome. Although elections were not the cause of the country's political woes, voting threw the growing fissures in the Egyptian body politic into stark relief and sometimes aggravated them. Those divisions have not only sabotaged Egypt's post-2011 democratic hopes, but have also undermined its prospects for future democratic development.

During the almost thirty months between 11 February 2011, when Mubarak was forced to resign, and 3 July 2013, when the military deposed and detained his elected successor Morsi—with both men targets of widespread popular demonstrations as well as military action—each step along the path of democracy ended with opposing segments of Egyptian society driven farther apart. Egyptians were called to the polls over and over—for a total of five national elections or referenda, some with multiple rounds—but every vote led to differences being redefined and magnified rather than managed or resolved.

Partisan Motives

There was considerable debate in Egypt about the sequence of events and procedures that should follow Mubarak's forced departure. Should elections come first, and if so, for what? Should a constitution be written first instead to clarify such questions, and if so, how should Egypt be governed in the meantime? Most of that debate missed the point. All answers to such questions were partisan. Early elections would benefit civilian actors who were more popular, especially those experienced at translating general support into voters at the polls. But critics who decried the "rush" to elections were predictably enough also those who seemed most likely to lose them; only rarely was a call for delay in voting coupled with a realistic alternative that was recognizably democratic.

Finding the best sequence in the abstract was not the problem. Instead, two things were needed for Egypt's post-2011 democratic development: a broad agreement among elites on the rules of the transition, and a procedure that allowed people to express their will early without having all matters settled by backroom deals. Without general consensus on the rules, spoilers would cover the landscape; without popular participation, there might be a stable outcome but it would not be democratic.

These two ingredients would have been difficult to combine in the best of times, but Egyptians lost much hope of obtaining either when they allowed the military to seize control of the transition process in February 2011 and to start making all the rules on its own. Thus, the problem was not that Egypt rushed to elections but instead that the elections did not always deliver authoritative outcomes that bound those who held real power. Just as ominously, votes went forward under conditions that the eventual losers often ended up rejecting.

It was for these reasons that elections seemed only to deepen rather than ease or resolve differences. The resulting political crisis continued for almost two-and-a-half years until July 2013. At that point, a mass uprising that saw millions of demonstrators cheering the military and even the once-reviled police brought down the president that Egyptians had elected just a year earlier and suspended the constitution that they had approved at the polls barely six months before.

A review of the frequent marches to the voting booth shows the numerous false starts on the democratic path. Egyptians were initially called to the polls in March 2011 by the military to approve a series of constitutional amendments (drafted by a small committee) that spelled out a way to build a new constitutional order. With this very first balloting, the revolutionary coalition began to find itself torn asunder. Islamists embraced the referendum because it promised a quick transition process and, implicitly, the rapid return of an elected parliament and president (to be chosen via elections in which then-popular Islamists would be the most experienced contestants and would no longer have to treat scruffy revolutionary youngsters as equals). Non-Islamists, for their part, rallied around the idea of writing the constitution first, but they were too slow in laying out a coherent alternative plan for a transition. When voters supported what they were told were "amendments," the military decided not to insert the approved language into the old constitution. Instead, hiding behind the cloak of what they called "revolutionary legitimacy," the generals opted to write a new, temporary "constitutional declaration" that inserted the clauses voters had approved into a forest of other articles on how the state would be run during the transition. That document was issued by military fiat, thus setting the dangerous precedent of insisting that the constitution was whatever those in power said it was.

The Islamists' response was to accept the March 2011 constitutional declaration but to push for the elections that it stipulated, hoping to edge the military aside through the establishment of democratic institutions (ones that, not coincidentally, would likely give Islamists much voice and heft). By contrast, many of the groups that had organized the uprising in early 2011 opted instead for renewed street protests, increasingly redirecting their ire from the old regime to military rule.

The next two elections came in late 2011 and early 2012 as Egyptians voted in several rounds first for a lower house of parliament and then for an upper house. Those elections returned a resounding Islamist majority but left few satisfied. Non-Islamists felt their fears of Islamist majoritarianism deepening; Islamists discovered that their parliamentary majority meant little because the military had taken care in the constitutional declaration to ensure that the new parliament would have no power to oversee the cabinet or pass legislation without the generals' approval. Even the military itself suddenly realized that it had engineered a transition plan that gave it an oversight role which was potent but only temporary. Once a new president was sworn in, the military would have no formal role and no clear tools with which to influence the outcome of the constitutional process.

That constitutional process was supposed to begin with an indirect election. The two houses of parliament were jointly to choose a hundred Egyptians who would spend six months drafting a final document, which would then go before the voters within fifteen days. The parliament was given no guidance as to who should serve among the hundred constitution-writers, and talks among various political forces regarding a consensus slate broke down. The result was that Islamists selected a body that was drawn half from parliament (with its heavy Islamist majority) and half from various social groups and official bodies (with Islamists significantly represented there as well). Many non-Islamists boycotted the process, and some turned to the courts in a bid to stop it altogether. An administrative court agreed with them, disbanding the hundred-member committee on the grounds that it was unrepresentative and that parliamentarians could not elect themselves to it. The result could have been as politically healthy as it had been legally implausible if it had led to an agreement among Egypt's rival political groupings, but instead it resulted in parliament once again failing to craft a consensus and the Islamists electing a very similar body to replace the disbanded constitution-writing committee.

As these drafters went to work, voters were summoned back to the polls in May 2012, this time to elect a president. Several leading candidates were disqualified on obscure or questionable grounds (one leading candidate was eliminated when it was revealed that his mother had taken U.S. citizenship, while the Brotherhood's first choice, Khairat al-Shater, was banned from running because he had a criminal record arising from a trumped-up charge that the old regime had lodged against him). After the first round, Egyptians found that they had sent forward to a June runoff a former general who had loyally served the old regime and the 60-year-old Morsi, the Muslim Brotherhood's second choice. After persuading a wide range of groups that he was the lesser of two evils in the runoff, Morsi managed a narrow win.

Once again, however, Egyptians woke up on the morning after an election to find the conflicts tearing at their society deepened rather than assuaged. On the eve of the balloting, the Supreme Constitutional Court had rushed out a ruling that the law under which parliament had been elected was unconstitutional, and that the lower house of parliament should therefore be disbanded. Just as presidential voting was beginning, the military also sprang a new constitutional declaration that robbed the presidency of significant power and carved out a strong role for the military in the constitution-writing process then underway.

Once elected, Morsi tried to reverse these steps. He reconvened the parliament before finally bowing to the courts and acquiescing in its suspension. More successfully, he asserted that the military's claimed authority to issue constitutional declarations now belonged to the presidency, and followed up with a decree nullifying the military's recent actions. The military acquiesced, even allowing Morsi to negotiate personnel changes at the top of the uniformed officer corps. Other political players also went along with Morsi's moves, but fears lingered that the presidency was now unchecked. Most non-Islamists continued to refuse to involve themselves in the constitutional process while growing increasingly shrill in their criticisms of Islamists. Morsi treated these oppositionists as so many annoyances who could safely be overlooked. His supporters met shrill critiques with shrill responses, sometimes resorting to authoritarian speech restrictions that were still very much part of Egypt's legal order.

By November, as the deadline for completing the draft constitution approached, both Morsi and his foes betrayed signs of panic. The president charged that a cabal of opposition politicians, old-regime elements, and judges was scheming to dissolve the constituent assembly, roll back his own moves to tame the military, and even disband the upper house of parliament. Such maneuvers would have amounted to a counterrevolution, leaving the shell of a presidency but returning Egypt to de facto military tutelage. His fears were almost certainly overblown, though they do not seem to have been fully imaginary. Morsi tried to seize the initiative by issuing yet another constitutional declaration, this one removing the issue of the constituent assembly and other matters from judicial review. This was effectively an assertion of absolute presidential power, even if only a temporary one meant to expire with the passage of the new constitution. The effect was to set off a new round of protests, this time not against the old regime or the military but against the Muslim Brotherhood and the president who hailed from that movement.

In the midst of this tumult, the constitutional assembly rushed to finish its task. Completing their work in an all-night session, the assembly members forced Egyptians to trudge back to the polls one more time in a referendum (held between 15 and 22 December 2012) that large parts of the opposition boycotted, contributing to a low turnout of about 33 percent. The constitution passed, but majorities in the largest cities turned out against it.

And according to the newly approved constitution, Egyptians were still not done voting. They were to be summoned before the end of February 2013 to elect a new lower house of parliament to replace the one disbanded in June 2012. (According to a later Supreme Constitutional Court ruling, that step would itself set off a new election: The still-sitting upper house would be dissolved, with new elections scheduled as soon as the lower house finally sat.) But those later elections never came. Under the new constitution, the upper house was required to submit a draft election law to the Supreme Constitutional Court before elections could be scheduled, and the Court sent it back twice after finding constitutional flaws. In late June 2013, one of the upper chamber's last acts was to submit a third draft to the Court; the Court had no opportunity to act before a political crisis brought the entire system down.

On June 30, millions of Egyptians marched in the streets nationwide to demand an immediate end to Morsi's presidency, effectively signaling that they were not willing to wait until the next elections to remove him. The military rewarded them on July 3 by forcibly deposing Morsi, arresting him and his top aides, shutting down Islamist broadcasters, and taking a series of steps (threatening even graver ones) against the Brotherhood's leadership.

But having launched their coup, military leaders quickly proclaimed that Egyptians would still keep voting. The constitution was suspended, it was true, but two small committees, one legal and one political, would work on amending it, and Egyptians would then be summoned to approve their work. The upper house of the parliament was disbanded, but the Supreme Constitutional Court was urged to speed its review of the electoral law so new parliamentary elections could be scheduled. And as soon as a new parliament was seated, a new president would be elected.

Bad Behavior

If democracy failed to develop in Egypt, then, it was not for lack of voting. The problem was not that elections came too early or too often: A revolution that is carried out in the people's name is unlikely to be able to keep them out of the voting booths for long. And better-timed elections might have helped: Had parliamentary elections been successfully scheduled for the second quarter of 2013, it is likely that significant opposition energies would have gone into campaigning rather than street protests, thereby forestalling any mass uprising.

The immediate problems in Egypt can be traced not to voting as such but to the choices of the main political actors. And at a still deeper level, anyone seeking to grasp what went wrong in Egypt must reckon with the persistence of underlying authoritarian patterns as well as a transition process (dating from 2011) that was, in actuality, neither a real process nor anything that provided for a real transition.

First, the actors' bad choices are obvious. The Brotherhood's behavior ranged from high-handed to extremely heavy-handed. Some of its moves were subtle but far-reaching in significance. The problem was not that the Brotherhood was antidemocratic but that its conception of democracy was shallow and often illiberal; further, Egypt had no rules of accepted democratic behavior. For instance, when forming the constituent assembly, the Brotherhood's parliamentary deputies agreed that half the drafters would be nonpartisan representatives of various institutions and organizations in Egyptian society—but then chose numerous formally "nonpartisan" people with Islamist inclinations. The Brotherhood pressured institutions that were supposed to stand outside partisan politics, sending followers to prevent the Supreme Constitutional Court from meeting by surrounding its building, filing legal complaints against critical journalists, and pushing legislation that would have forced all senior judges into retirement. Some of its actions were rough indeed, such as when the Brotherhood called out movement stalwarts to protect the presidential palace in December 2012—and those stalwarts seized, beat, and interrogated demonstrators. As his presidency tottered in June 2013, Morsi decided on a strategy of bluster and threats that merely united and augmented an already implacable opposition.

The opposition could also be blamed for nondemocratic behavior. Major opposition actors not only tried to stave off or boycott several elections; even when they found one they could like (the mid-2012 presidential balloting, for example), they ended up seeking to overturn its results with street protests. Oppositionists complained about the make-up of the constituent assembly but did little to articulate their own constitutional vision, instead simply pressing non-Islamists to withdraw from the body. And virtually every sin with which the opposition charged the Brotherhood—using force against protestors, trying to purge judges, denying and even applauding security-force abuses, harassing media— was a sin that the opposition embraced with unseemly enthusiasm in July 2013.

In short, Islamists plausibly charged non-Islamists with refusing to accept adverse election results, while non-Islamists plausibly charged Islamists with using those same election results to undermine the development of healthy democratic life.

That said, it must also be acknowledged that both charge and countercharge also contained unfairness and exaggeration. It is true, for instance, that the Brotherhood dominated the constitutional process, but it is not clear that non-Islamists would have accepted any process that reflected the Islamists' electoral strength. It is true that non-Islamists struck a petulant pose every time that the Brotherhood made one of its clumsy conciliation efforts, but those attempts offered very little in the way of guarantees, and those participating exposed themselves to charges of breaking opposition ranks. It is true that the Brotherhood used force against protestors in December 2012, but it was also true that Egyptian security forces made no effort to defend the offices of the Brotherhood and its political party from a very real series of attacks, leaving the Brotherhood to fall back on its own devices. It is true that non-Islamists relied on courts and ultimately chose to invite military intervention, but it was also true that they had few ways to affect the rules of the political game as these were being written.

Turning to the deeper reasons for failure, it is impossible to ignore the heavy weight of Egypt's authoritarian past. This legacy—a factor with which key actors have still not come to grips—made itself felt in four ways. First and most obviously, authoritarian actors played a key role in the transition both through what they did and what they did not do. The Egyptian military did not seek to exert direct day-to-day control over public affairs, but it refused to accept civilian oversight and for more than a year monopolized the making of key decisions. That led most other political forces to gear their actions to the military's. The only gestures made toward challenging the officer corps—first by revolutionary youth and later and in a much more limited way by the Brotherhood—were ineffectual.

The general pattern was for civilian political actors to seek an accommodation with the military in order to avoid having to deal with each other. The Morsi presidency did not invent this strategy, though it seemed at first to perfect it—but the gambit ultimately proved fatal. As for the civilian opposition, it prodded the military to depose Morsi but quickly found that it had stirred up a force beyond its control. If the military's role was corrupting, that of the security services was even more pernicious. These services provided a level of public safety that was uneven at best, and they too often stood deliberately idle while violent protests raged, giving a green light to disorder. Egyptian media were fed a steady stream of outlandish information (in 2011, directed primarily against revolutionary youth; in 2012 and especially in 2013, aimed mostly at the country's newly elected leadership) that undermined trust.

Second, decades of authoritarian rule had left behind an unbalanced political scene that tilted elections toward the Islamists and gave non-Islamists a deep mistrust of the ballot. The problem was not that the Mubarak regime had repressed non-Islamists more than Islamists—just the opposite. Islamists were treated far more harshly. But because participation in formal politics was so unpromising under authoritarian rule, non-Islamist parties that had focused their energies in that direction had by 2011 become little more than dried-out husks. With their broader social agenda, Islamists had deeper and more extensive organizations that could be quickly turned to electoral purposes. Non-Islamists had nothing to match these (and mostly were not inclined toward building such organizations).

Third, the infrastructure of authoritarianism remained in place. A virtually permanent official state of emergency may have come to an end in 2012, but authoritarian practices and procedures had become so deeply woven into laws and institutions that it sometimes seemed to political rivals as if their only way to deal with one another was to reach for the very sticks that had been wielded against them in the past. Mubarak had gone, but there were still powerful public prosecutors whom those outraged by press stories could lobby for the filing of criminal charges; military and state-security courts stayed open regarding some cases; and the state-owned press promoted the agenda of those in power with mindless and shameless enthusiasm.

Even where the machinery of state was not clearly authoritarian, it provided imperfect tools (or none at all) for civilian oversight. The judiciary and the religious establishment, for instance, were able to exercise considerable autonomy within their own realms and had some ability to resist the newly elected institutions (the presidency and the parliament). The judiciary in particular went beyond resisting partisan oversight and tried to make itself self-perpetuating to a degree that undermined democratic mechanisms. Judges had the means not merely to defend against encroachments on judicial turf by parliament and the presidency, but to undermine these institutions by striking at their legal basis.

Fourth, Egyptians discovered that authoritarian politics—and perhaps especially the brand to which they had long been exposed, with its meaningless elections and hollow but still formally democratic procedures—is a poor school for democracy. By discrediting democratic promises, leaving a cloud of distrust and suspicion hovering over the rules and conduct of elections, suppressing healthy organizations in both civil and political society, and favoring a divide-and-rule approach to opposition, autocratic politics can reach out from its grave to hobble efforts to move toward democracy.

Thus, each actor went into democratic politics with unrealistic expectations regarding what it could achieve and exaggerated suspicions of the motives of all rivals. It was not so much that Egypt's political actors lacked democratic commitments (though some did), but more that they deeply distrusted their adversaries and regarded real democratic processes as full of potential pitfalls. Here they paid for decades of life under dishonest rulers who mouthed democratic promises and sought to hide behind democracy's form while withholding its substance. After the 2011 uprising, the Egyptian political landscape was filled with actors who had learned always to look for the fine print and to distrust every promise and procedure until its advantages were proven in practice. In short, fear ruled the day: Everyone was suspicious that democratic promises were worth little (they had been made and ignored so often in the past), and that democratic procedures were nothing but traps destined to end up helping only one's rivals.

Bad Choices

If the authoritarian past weighed heavily on Egyptian politics after the uprising, the transition "plan," such as it was, only made things worse—even if more by accident than by intention. Egypt's transition was not badly designed; it was simply not designed at all. Its original failing lay in a series of shortsighted decisions made by generally well-meaning but myopic actors who found themselves thrust into positions of limited authority in February and March 2011. In retrospect, we can see that the extensive debates which at the time swirled around the topics of how to sequence the writing of a constitution and the electing of a president and parliament only obscured the real mistakes that were being made.

The most basic problem was the huge amount of political control that fell into the hands of the military high command for no other reason than that the high command claimed it and no one else could come up with a timely alternative. The soundest idea heard was a call for a presidency council capable of compelling the main political forces (assuming that they could be identified and could manage their differences) to move forward by consensus. But revolutionary groups did not unify around this notion until it was too late.

So the military was free to take the next misstep. It began when the generals charged a tiny ad hoc committee with marking the outlines of a transition by amending parts of the 1971 Constitution. Then the committee's work was folded into the March 2011 constitutional declaration, a document whose authors have never been revealed. Nor did anybody in the military bother to explain why this declaration borrowed some elements from the suspended 1971 Constitution but not others. Among the 2011 declaration's gaps was its silence on the matter of amendment: If a change needed to be made to the constitutional text (and various actors quickly came to feel that some were necessary) first the military and then the president (once elected) would have to assert the constitutional power to do so. Had a process of broad and careful consultation been used to adjust the basic law, the results might have been made palatable. But the generals were predictably bad at consultation, and later the first freely elected president turned out to be even worse. So Egypt's rulers took turns decreeing unilateral changes with ultimately disastrous results.

Suspicions arising from the opacity of the process emerged as early as the March 2011 referendum. Islamists suspected that their revolutionary partners' real agenda was to delay elections for fear of how well Islamists would do. Non-Islamists felt (with similar legitimacy) that Islamists were shoving hard for a vote so they could elbow their way into the most seats at the table.

Such political rivalries were not in themselves bad. The deeper problem was that the only way to settle them was not through negotiation, compromise, and consensus but by pressuring, nagging, and bargaining with the generals. Suspicions of separate deals and secret agreements deepened fears, and Egypt's contending political forces quickly learned that allegations need not be coupled with evidence in order to be taken seriously.

Differences on questions of political machinery were not that vast in early 2011, and a more consensual process could certainly have been devised. Much of the basic framework for making a postrevolutionary political order—a weaker presidency, stronger safeguards for freedoms, more democratic procedures, and judicial independence—united almost the entire political spectrum. But the tiny ad hoc committee, acting in haste, had created a number of procedural time bombs.

The first of these was the stipulation that a new constitution would be drafted by a hundred figures chosen by parliament. This offered no guarantee that everyone would have a voice. The hundred-member assembly's draft was to go before the electorate immediately for an up-or-down, simple-majority vote. No one realized at the time how much these procedures would favor Islamists. Their electoral abilities were not a surprise, but the scale of their eventual parliamentary and presidential victories was. This was a process that could work well only if there was already a deep consensus. It could hardly produce a consensus on its own, nor did it give anyone much incentive to pursue one.

For a brief period in early 2011, it looked as if goodwill could make up for a bad process. But as the revolutionary coalition broke apart, few saw compromise as a paying proposition. Periodic efforts to achieve it—in 2012, when it was time to pick members of the constituent assembly, or in early 2013, when domestic and international mediators tried to bring Morsi and the opposition together—foundered in an atmosphere of mistrust.

The Meaning of Failure

Elections themselves were hardly the cause of Egypt's democratic fiasco. While the mundane realities of democratic politics are not particularly pretty anywhere, they nonetheless offer real possibilities to which Arab societies still strongly aspire. But those who build a democracy for the first time must do so on foundations that autocracy has built. Getting rid of autocrats is easier than getting rid of their structures or erasing the stains on political practice that autocrats have left behind. Egypt's post-2011 politics has not overcome the legacy of the past.

Failure was not inevitable. We have already seen that there were moments when Egypt's course could have taken a very different turn. Had a deal over the constituent assembly been struck in the first half of 2012, a more consensual process might have emerged; had the strong opposition within the Brotherhood to fielding a presidential candidate carried the day or had a few percentage points shifted in the 2012 first-round presidential results, there might have been a different runoff; had President Morsi learned how to reach beyond his narrow base, the showdown of mid-2013 might never have happened. Even as late as June 2013, had the upper house succeeded in passing a Constitutional Court–approved election law, the confrontation might have taken the form of an election campaign rather than massive street protests and a military coup.

Missed opportunities, in short, have abounded, leaving three sets of lessons—for students of democracy, for Islamists, and for Egyptians.

For those interested in transitions from authoritarian rule, Egypt's experience provides a stark lesson: Not only do decisions about timing, sequence, and rules have a large impact on political outcomes, but those decisions themselves are the outcomes of deeply political processes. To put it more paradoxically, the design of a transition matters, but at the same time transitions are *not* designed—instead they are shaped by political contests among confused and confusing actors at a time when the basic rules of political life are unclear, constantly reshaped, and broken. There is no force outside the political process that designs a transition; there is no time-out when politics ceases so that political systems can be designed in a pristine atmosphere; there is no magic moment when political actors put aside their own goals, values, and experiences and stand aloof from day-to-day political struggles.

The generals who were given a free hand to steer the transition in February 2011 did so in a way that guarded their institutional interests but walled off important parts of Egypt's authoritarian state from reform. Their decisions about the timing and sequencing of elections not only affected electoral outcomes but also undermined trust among civilian political actors and aggravated their tendency to shun the hard work of coalition-building. No one, at any rate, should have expected the military to give up its institutional self-interest, the opposition to embrace elections that it knew it would lose, the Brotherhood to ignore its edge in electoral support, or the judiciary to abjure its tools for self-defense.

When the mass uprising of 30 June 2013 culminated in the military coup of July 3, Egypt appeared to reprise the mistakes of 2011—seeing the country's problems as the work of a few individual miscreants, mistaking purges of personnel for the reform of institutions, rushing a transition process, failing to provide for consensual constitutional design, walling off particular institutional interests from discussion, and failing to provide for meaningful public participation. But while it seemed that "Egypt" was making the same mistakes again, that is not quite correct, for it was not the entire nation of Egypt that was acting. Instead, various political actors (the military, some judicial personnel, the security apparatus, and a small number of political movements) were taking decisions in Egypt's name, sincerely believing themselves in each case to be defenders of the nation as a whole. Those decisions, however much they damaged hopes for a democratic transition, were not mistakes for the actors who made them—for by its choices each actor acted on behalf of its particular partisan interests, interests that no actor could see as distinct from Egypt's national interest.

If the lesson for analysts is that transitions are not designed but politically shaped, the lesson for Islamists is far less clear. Islamists will almost surely try to learn from the Morsi presidency, but they will take considerable time to do so. For the past generation, the Arab world's leading Islamist movements have become increasingly politicized—taking part in elections, writing platforms, and seeking public office out of a belief that the political process, even if flawed, was one of the best ways they had to pursue their Islamizing agenda. Egypt's Muslim Brotherhood was the largest movement to try such an approach, and from 2011 until 2013 its investment in politics seemed to be paying off more handsomely and quickly than expected. Islamists swept parliamentary elections, won the presidency, and dominated the constitution-writing process. The Brotherhood's rivals on the Islamist spectrum began racing to follow a similar path.

What Next for the Muslim Brotherhood?

In July 2013, that sudden success came to a sudden end. The Morsi presidency is without a doubt one of the most colossal failures in the Brotherhood's history. What lesson will the movement learn from it?

The Muslim Brothers (as well as Islamists more generally) may conclude that their failure was a result of their own miscalculations. And it seems undeniable that Morsi and the Brotherhood made almost every conceivable mistake—including some (such as reaching too quickly for political power or failing to build coalitions with others) that they had vowed they knew enough to avoid. They alienated potential allies, ignored rising discontent, focused more on consolidating their rule than on using the tools that they did have, and used rhetoric that was tone deaf at best and threatening at worst.

Such introspection might go deeper than tactics and lead to new thought about basic organizational issues. Although the Brotherhood had tried after Mubarak's fall to refashion itself into a national governing party, the movement had been built not for open democratic competition but for resilience under authoritarian pressure. It was tight-knit, inward-looking, and even paranoid. It came to be led by figures, including Morsi himself, who were termed "organization men," little used to dealing with the world beyond Brotherhood confines. A thorough recognition of these limitations might have induced the Brotherhood itself to step aside and leave the political game to its post-Mubarak spinoff, the Freedom and Justice Party (a body that the Brotherhood instead decided to keep on a short leash). Things could have even gone so far as an announcement by the movement that its members were free to join any political party they liked, an idea that a few young Brotherhood activists favored in 2011. Either path (a far more autonomous party or no direct political role at all) would have been very hard for the current leaders—raised as they have been on hierarchy, coordination, and discipline—to follow.

But even if Islamists eventually engage in reflection and self-criticism of this sort, they will likely conclude that whatever mistakes they made in organization, one of their biggest errors was to underestimate their adversaries' resistance to the Brotherhood's political role. In other words, the Brotherhood's mistake lay in ever thinking that it would be allowed not merely to win elections, but to govern. In Islamists' eyes, the Morsi presidency might come to be seen as similar to the experiences of Algeria's Islamic Salvation Front in the early 1990s (when the military halted an electoral process to prevent an Islamist victory) or of Hamas in 2006 (when that Islamist group won the Palestinian elections only to have domestic rivals and international actors sabotage its ability to rule). This diagnosis may well win out over the long term, but where will it point? Will it lead to the movement abandoning political work, to individuals abandoning the Brotherhood, or to the Brotherhood determining that it will play politics but no longer by peaceful rules?

At a minimum, many Islamists will likely find that electoral politics holds far less appeal. The effect may not set in immediately—the feeling of having been cheated, the urge to fight back, and the desire to salvage whatever institutional and constitutional achievements can be preserved may win out for now. Eventually, however, Islamists will have to come to terms with the longer-run factors that they pride themselves on knowing how to reckon with. At that point, the strategies that have won most favor among Islamists for the past generation could give way to some very different approaches. The sudden unexpected success of Islamists in 2011 and 2012 led them to make decisions on the fly; their defeat in 2013 will give them time to ponder how they should face the years ahead.

As for those Egyptians who aspire to a more democratic future, the lessons that they learn may end up being oddly similar to those that the Islamists draw. A leading lesson might be phrased as "Do not let victory take you by surprise." When the decades-old Mubarak regime perished in the sudden and spectacular crash of early 2011, the triumphant revolutionaries found themselves beholding the wreckage of a shattered authoritarian presidency with no shared platform and no authoritative structures to guide them beyond those needed to hammer out communiqués from Tahrir Square. By showing disdain for politics and ceding control to the military, those who pulled off the revolution revealed that they lacked a common understanding of how to overcome authoritarianism's malign legacies. In June 2013, a new Egyptian revolutionary movement made precisely the same mistake, effectively allowing the military to seize the reins once again.

The Egyptian failure to produce a democracy may have been avoidable, but it could still have effects that are highly damaging and long-lasting. Indeed, the failure has discredited democratic mechanisms as a means for managing differences, at least for the present. Islamists have come to feel that even when they win at the ballot box, they will be denied the right to exercise authority. Their opponents, meanwhile, decry "ballotocracy" as mindlessly majoritarian but have shown themselves to be even more ruthlessly majoritarian than the Muslim Brotherhood when they can outmobilize their foes in street demonstrations.

And that might be the greatest cost of the Morsi presidency—that, at least for a time, it has left behind an Egypt in which the very idea of democracy has lost much of its meaning and all of its luster.

22

YEMEN CHANGES EVERYTHING . . . AND NOTHING

April Longley Alley

April Longley Alley is senior Arabian Peninsula analyst for the International Crisis Group. She writes extensively on Yemen and currently resides in Sana'a. This essay originally appeared in the October 2013 issue of the Journal of Democracy.

Yemen is the only country to have exited the Arab world's 2011 uprisings by means of a negotiated settlement and a transition plan that makes provision for a national dialogue to guide the country's political future. There has been nothing like the Syrian bloodbath, and Yemen's transition process has exceeded Egypt's in inclusiveness. Yet many Yemenis increasingly see this process as an empty affair run by a gaggle of reshuffled old-regime elites. What is more, events on the ground, particularly in the far north and south, reveal enduring crises that are pulling the country apart and, in the south, putting its territorial integrity directly at risk.

Since Abdu Rabu Mansour Hadi replaced long-ruling President Ali Abdallah Saleh via an uncontested February 2012 election, everything and nothing has changed. After 33 years in power, Saleh is no longer chief executive and grand patron, nor does his family dominate the upper echelons of the security services. In early 2012, he stepped down under the terms of a transition road map laid out by a Gulf Cooperation Council (GCC) initiative, which offered Saleh immunity from domestic prosecution in return for his resignation. The transitional government now includes the former opposition bloc, the Joint Meeting Parties (JMP), a five-party alliance that includes Islah (the leading Islamist party) as well as the Yemeni Socialist Party (YSP), the Nasirist Popular Unity Party, and two small Zaydi parties.[1] The JMP holds half the cabinet posts and the premiership. In March 2013, Yemenis launched the National Dialogue Conference (NDC) to bring together 565 delegates from across the country to debate longstanding challenges and guide a constitution-writing process.

On the level of political economy, there has been almost no change. Old-regime elites, including many who were nimble enough to join the uprising, now have a role in reforming the very system that they helped to create. These include Saleh's partner-turned-foe General Ali Mohsen al-Ahmar, his allies in Islah, the powerful Ahmar clan (no blood relation to Ali Mohsen), and even the Salehs and their backers in the old ruling party, the General People's Congress (GPC). None has more than a limited interest in reform, and all will likely seek to preserve a corrupt political economy based on the concentration of wealth and power in Sana'a, the capital.

As elites jostle, security, political, and humanitarian challenges dating from well before the 2011 upheaval have multiplied. Al-Qaeda remains active throughout the country, routinely assassinating security officials and forcing the temporary closure of several diplomatic missions in August 2013. In the south, separatist feeling runs high and most citizens are at best deeply skeptical of the NDC. In the north, Zaydi Shia rebels known as the Huthis now control swaths of ground and act as a state within a state. They take part in the dialogue even as they remain armed in case talks fail. Newly empowered regionally based constituencies are demanding more say in governance as well. Such ferment could pull Yemen apart, yet at the same time regionalism could help to guard against any effort to rebuild the overcentralized, corrupt regime under a realigned set of old actors.

In principle, the national dialogue is the place to resolve grievances and negotiate the outlines of a new constitution. Yet the NDC is beset by shortcomings. Its key failing is the lack of broad participation by southern supporters of separation. Their absence undermines the NDC's legitimacy in the south and raises doubts as to whether its decisions will mean anything on the ground. Then too, many Yemenis worry that the time set aside to debate complex institutional options is too short, even as the UN, the EU, the United States, and the United Kingdom push for elections under a new constitution by the February 2014 deadline. Finally, should the NDC stall or fail, there is no backup plan.

As I noted not long before the Arab uprisings, the Yemeni regime faced numerous crises, largely of its own making.[2] Citizens were unhappy about corruption, the concentration of power and wealth in the hands of Saleh and his family, and the lack of jobs.

In the south—a region that was an independent socialist state until 1990—frustration produced widespread popular mobilization in 2007. The southern movement (Hirak) began as a rights-based protest campaign demanding equal citizenship, access to government jobs and services, fairer distribution of resources, and a degree of local autonomy. By 2009, after spotty reforms and regime repression, the Hirak solidly shifted to calls for separation. Just before the 2011 uprising, the separatist trend was gaining traction.[3]

Map—Yemen

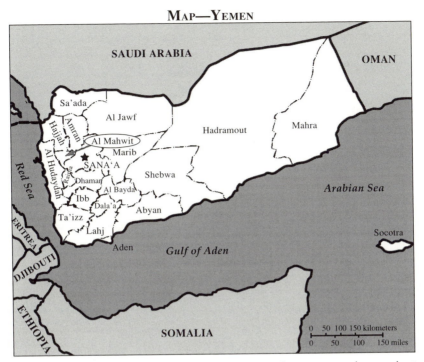

In the far north, the regime waged a stop-and-start campaign against the Huthis.[4] This multilayered conflict began in 2004 and spread. Both sides drew in local tribes; Saudi forces got involved in 2009 only to suffer an embarrassing defeat. The struggle was in many ways a product of the regime's penchant for divide-and-rule tactics and internal rivalries. In the 1980s, the regime had supported Wahabi and salafist[5] expansion into traditionally Zaydi areas in the north. In the 1990s, Saleh switched his support to the Huthis before opposing them again in 2004 when their political and military clout became threatening. As the conflict dragged on, Saleh used the fighting to wear down General Ahmar's troops in hopes of helping a son, Ahmed Saleh, who commanded the rival Republican Guard. On the eve of the 2011 uprising, the Huthis not only ruled territory but also enjoyed support from local tribes and sympathy from a larger subset of Yemenis who were opposed to civilian casualties and harsh military tactics.

Even as these internal conflicts went on, a resurgent al-Qaeda—hardened by experiences in Iraq and Afghanistan—began showing more interest in attacking Yemeni government personnel and interests, and less interest in striking deals. Saleh was growing more isolated too; having ditched his alliance with Islah and marginalized what was left of South Yemen's old ruling party, the YSP.

Yet friction among parties was the least of Saleh's worries. His worst problem was the growing discontent that powerful regime insiders were feeling over his practice of increasingly concentrating wealth and power in his hands and those of his closest relatives. For years, he had ruled Yemen through a complex web of tribal and regional patronage. Broad inclusion had been the key to overall stability. Saleh threw all that away, however, and alienated his own partners (General Ali Mohsen al-Ahmar among them) by resolving to settle the succession upon his son at the expense of longtime allies.

Saleh's timing was bad: He was narrowing patronage networks even as Yemen's old political economy was becoming less viable. Oil wealth paid for about three-quarters of the national budget as well as feeding patronage and corruption, yet oil was sinking into decline. Without new oil finds, the state badly needed a growing economy to keep the patronage tap open and meet the needs of a fast-growing populace. Yet personalized politics had so undermined both the state and the private sector that Yemen could barely utilize the foreign aid that came its way, let alone blaze a trail to economic diversification.

By 2009, the deepening economic and political crisis had spurred calls for a national dialogue to reform the political system. Despite growing frustration with political parties and an increasing number of constituencies (including the Hirak and the Huthis) seeking recourse outside the party system, the dialogue was originally built around the GPC and JMP and was to focus on a narrow set of electoral reforms meant to break the impasse between them. As crises deepened, however, the JMP expanded the agenda to questions of limits on centralized power and the executive. Had it been held before the uprising, the dialogue might have produced enough incremental changes to forestall the popular mobilization of 2011—but we will never know for sure.

Uprising and Transition

The Tunisian protests of early 2011 inspired small groups of Yemeni youth and civil society activists to take to the streets demanding regime change. Hosni Mubarak's fall in Egypt added to the pressure for change. Saleh tried to stay a step ahead, but his promises of reform proved too little, too late. The tipping point came on 18 March 2011 when supporters of the president fired on unarmed demonstrators in Sana'a, killing more than fifty. Of the ensuing regime defections the key one was Ali Mohsen's, which split the army.

As mid-2011 neared, the coalition of unlikely antiregime bedfellows included ex-insiders such as Ali Mohsen, the Ahmars, and the prominent salafist sheikh Abdul Majid al-Zindani. Joining them were the JMP (including its strongest member, Islah), the Huthis, and some Hirak elements. The ex-insiders were driven mainly by their opposition to Saleh's efforts to elevate his son. The most formidable portions of the security services, such as the Republican Guard, remained mostly loyal to Saleh. Soon they (as well as tribes friendly to the president) were involved in armed confrontations with Ali Mohsen's army units, Ahmar tribal forces, and tribal militias associated with Islah. By June 2011, the country was on the brink of civil war. Both sides, however, felt unsure enough of victory that space opened for negotiations.

Alarmed by the prospect of prolonged instability, international and regional actors stepped in to broker a transition. After months of delay, Saleh signed the GCC initiative in November 2011. At heart, it was an elite compromise that gave Saleh and his supporters domestic immunity in return for the transfer of power to his vice-president. A set of UN-backed implementation mechanisms specified a two-year transition period during which a coalition government would restructure the military, address outstanding transitional-justice issues, and administer an inclusive national dialogue with the goal of producing a new constitution in advance of February 2014 elections.[6]

Theoretically, the transition agreement opens space for institutional reforms that could allow for greater political participation and accountability. Yet Yemenis are far from assured of this. Elites have proven adept at checking off boxes: They held an uncontested presidential election, formed a coalition government, gave the security forces an organizational and personnel shakeup, and launched (albeit belatedly) the national dialogue. These are all positive steps that could pave the way for more far-reaching reforms. But no consensus on such reform exists. Instead, the festival of patronage and corruption centered in Sana'a rolls on, with a larger subset of traditional elites taking part.[7]

To a degree, these are problems of success: The GCC agreement spared the country worse bloodshed. But the pact's price was the vast influence over the transition and future rules of the political game that it handed to holdover elites from the Saleh regime and the traditional parties. This situation could limit reform at a time when it should be obvious that a status quo tweaked around the edges is *not* going to work, either politically or economically.

In the political reshuffle so far, the Salehs have lost ground while the loose coalition of Ali Mohsen, the Ahmars, and Islah has gained. A third major player is President Hadi, whose supporters—many of them political and military elites hailing from his home governorate of Abyan—are enjoying newfound influence.

The reshuffle began in 2012. During that year, the coalition in favor of the uprising sensed the Salehs' weakness and claimed new gains in the security services and the bureaucracy at large. At the same time, this coalition tried to settle what its members saw as the uprising's unfinished business by excluding Saleh and his close supporters from politics. Saleh loyalists lost their jobs in JMP-controlled ministries while Hadi made personnel changes in security-service ranks designed to weaken the Saleh camp. Ali Mohsen, the Ahmars, and Islah made modest gains, such as being permitted to add twenty-thousand new recruits to the security services, ostensibly to balance similar numbers that the Salehs had added during the uprising.[8]

The dust began to settle in 2013, revealing no significant redistribution of resources or hard power outside the traditional elite. Despite their losses, the Salehs remain in the game as one of many competing power centers. The former president still heads the GPC and retains not only significant personal wealth but also (it is said) stockpiles of arms. President Hadi, meanwhile, began to move against Ali Mohsen, the Ahmars, and Islah in December 2012 by disbanding Ali Mohsen's military unit, the Firka, and shunting him into an advisory role.

The redistribution of resources among elites is not necessarily bad; it may open room for more inclusive power-sharing in the future. Yet many reform advocates and original uprising participants worry that Ali Mohsen, the Ahmars, and Islah will try to set up their own version of Saleh's arrangement, or that the two sides will realign under some new modus vivendi that leaves the overcentralized and unaccountable political system unchanged in the decisive respects. As the time for making deals and drafting a new constitution draws near, elites will likely work to restrict institutional change by limiting decentralization and power-sharing measures. Reportedly, leaders in both the GPC and JMP are seeking to strike deals with President Hadi in return for supporting his possible term extension or 2014 presidential bid.[9]

While elites in the capital compete for state spoils and prepare for the next round, players ranging from the Hirak and the Huthis to activists from various regions of Yemen including the Red Sea Coast as well as Ta'izz, Marib, Hadramout, Mahra, and Socotra are all demanding greater local autonomy and control over local resources. Significant decentralization will be hard to achieve, but it would likely have the advantage of shifting fights over resources out to the periphery, thereby providing a broader distribution of power and wealth as well as a check on the central government. Support for regional checks and balances has gained broad appeal within the JMP coalition, even among the rank-and-file of Islah and within the GPC, which are both now supporting federalism in the NDC. President Hadi is also supportive of federalism. Yet the centers of hard power—Saleh and his circle, Ali Mohsen, the Ahmars, and some senior Islah leaders—have financial interests that decentralization would harm. Thus they may be expected to do what they can to bound the scope of institutional change or to limit its effects.

Diverse constituencies' growing demands for increased regional authority could lay the basis for a more lasting power-sharing arrangement that will complement Yemen's rich historic, geographic, sectarian, and cultural diversity. As yet, however, there is no consensus about details or how decentralized governance should work. Most Hirak supporters no longer hope for reform within a unified Yemen, and now want separation. Equally important, worsening security and economic conditions are making compromise less likely as they sap confidence in the transition process and boost the forces that are pulling the country apart.

In some ways, life is now worse than it was before 2011. Crime is up in cities such as Sana'a, Ta'izz, and Aden. The kidnapping business is booming and often means holding foreigners for ransom. At the same time, al-Qaeda has been assassinating security personnel with no effective government response. In southern governorates, many officers are afraid to wear their uniforms in public.[10]

The parlous economy continues to pain average citizens. Chronic power outages hamper business and make daily life a trial, especially in the south and along the Red Sea coast, where summers are furnace-hot. More than eighteen months into its tenure, the transitional government still seems helpless to stop tribal saboteurs from attacking not only the nation's electrical grid, but its oil, gas, and Internet infrastructure too. Yemen's humanitarian crisis rages on, with 10 million of its approximately 24 million people needing food aid and a million children facing malnutrition.[11] Left to fester, these ills will strain even the best-crafted political settlement.

The situation is especially precarious in the south, where separatist feeling runs high and many openly reject the GCC initiative and the NDC as northern impositions.[12] A few Hirak activists are open to a federal, two-state (north-south) solution, but their influence is limited. Moreover, the government's inability or unwillingness to take confidence-building steps in matters of security, land, and jobs is not helping. President Hadi took a full year to set up committees to deal with southern grievances regarding land and employment. Results thus far have been negligible even as the crime, terrorism, and power-outage problems continue.[13] Security-service violence against Hirak demonstrators continues, as does unlawful detention, providing fodder to critics who claim that nothing has changed since the transition.

In the far north, the Huthis expanded their territorial control while the Saleh regime spent 2011 preoccupied with regaining its grip on Sana'a. Sa'ada Governorate is in Huthi hands, as are parts of three surrounding governorates. Many observers claim that these areas are relatively well governed, while critics complain of Huthi human-rights violations against political detractors, such as salafists and members of Islah.[14] The Huthis take part in the dialogue, but keep their land and arms. They publicly reject the legitimacy of the GCC agreement and the transitional government on the grounds that each betrays the revolution. Since the uprising, the group seems to have embarked on a campaign to rebrand itself and widen its reach. "Huthis" is a reference to the family name of their founder; they now prefer to call themselves Ansar Allah (Supporters of God). Thanks to their opposition to Islah and the old regime, as well as their reputation for rejecting corruption and transparently administering justice, they have made inroads into traditionally Sunni areas of Yemen.[15]

In sum, the transition period so far has seen a marked reduction in the state's capacity to provide basic services and security. This is eroding confidence in the transition, stirring antigovernment ire, and allowing groups such as the Hirak and Huthis to grow stronger. Theoretically, the erosion of state capacity can be reversed, but this will take time and, most importantly, must be part of a durable political settlement with buy-in from all major stakeholders.

The National Dialogue

When it comes to forging that lasting settlement, the NDC is the only game in town. Comprising 565 delegates from Yemen's main political parties and social groups, it began on 18 March 2013 and is set to end in September 2013. Parties hold a large bloc of seats: the GPC and its allies have 112, Islah 50, the YSP 37, and the Nasirist party 30, with five other small parties holding 4 seats each. The Hirak has 85 delegates and the Huthis have 35. Overall, women comprise about 30 percent of all delegates, while youth account for 20 percent. Half the delegates are from the south,[16] a compromise that was meant to attract Hirak participation. The NDC is divided into nine working groups. The most politically sensitive are those dedicated to, respectively, the southern issue, state-building, and the Sa'ada issue (which addresses grievances surrounding the six rounds of conflict between the government and the Huthis). The nine working groups present recommendations to the full Conference. Any recommendation that passes with a three-quarters vote of that body then goes to the constitution-drafting committee.[17]

The NDC is beset by numerous challenges, the most obvious of which is the difficult work of forging consensus among so many diverse delegates. As arduous as it is, however, this may prove the easiest of the tasks that lie ahead. Many delegates are veteran party cadres who are used to negotiations, or activists who truly believe in dialogue and would like to see a compromise. Yet there are technical issues that could slow things down. For example, as the groups move from talks focused on defining problems to the thornier task of agreeing on solutions, they may require more active mediation from the UN or accepted local arbiters. Delegates also say that as regards complicated issues such as state structure or the electoral system, they badly need expertise to help them identify options and weigh their costs and benefits.[18]

The southern issue is the most hotly contested of all the matters that the NDC is dealing with, yet it is also the one that must be resolved if Yemen is to have a fully articulated, new constitution. In essence, it is a question about the state structure. Most Hirak activists in the south demand independence. A minority that is taking part in the dialogue (this group is largely aligned with President Hadi) is willing to discuss a two-entity federal solution followed by a national-unity referendum to be held after a set time.

The GPC and Islah will not accept either independence or the two-entity federal option. At most, they are willing to consider multiple-entity federalism, but not the kind with just two players, which they view as a big step back toward two Yemens. Sadly, no group is well versed in the likely second- and third-order effects of various decentralization options and how they would affect the political and economic needs of Yemenis. At this time, it seems that some federal option is the most likely compromise, but the devil is in the details and it is unclear how much each side is willing or able to compromise.

Another significant political obstacle could come from an external shock that drives a large constituency out of the NDC. Already, several prominent politicians have resigned, damaging the NDC's credibility and giving the impression that decisions are being made in backrooms rather than working groups. The wholesale withdrawal of a major constituency would deal the dialogue a devastating blow. The Hirak and Huthi delegations are the likeliest to pull out. So far, both have resisted any such impulse even in the face of violence: Security forces killed at least four Hirak demonstrators in Aden on 21 February 2013; there was an assassination attempt against Huthi delegates during the first month of the NDC in Sana'a; and in early June security forces killed ten Huthi supporters during a demonstration in front of the National Security Bureau headquarters. As negotiations enter their final phase, it is unclear how these groups would react if there were a major attack on their supporters or, in the Hirak's case, if other delegates are unwilling to compromise on two-part federalism or the promise of a future referendum on unity.

The timeframe set by the implementation mechanism may also prove an obstacle. The NDC's international supporters are, at least publicly, determined that Yemenis should complete the dialogue, write the constitution, put it to a referendum, and hold elections roughly on schedule. The worry is that if the timeline slips, then all sense of urgency will be lost and negotiations will drag on, giving spoilers an opening to derail the whole thing. Both the UN and the governments supporting the transition are eager to tout Yemen as a success story proving the value of international engagement. Many Yemenis and some internationals, however, are convinced that negotiations will need at least a few more months, if not more, to reach compromises on complex institutional options. For them, the substance of these far outweighs arbitrary deadlines pointing to a hurried and thinly supported result.

Challenges to Implementation

If writing a new constitution for Yemen will be no mean feat, making it a reality on the ground may be thornier still. The first and largest obstacle is the NDC's lack of southern support. The Hirak delegates who are taking part in the dialogue speak for only a minority in their home region, and it is far from certain that they will be able to convince the separation-supporting street there to accept a new political settlement. A wider representation of Hirak leadership in the NDC, along with confidence-building measures to strengthen the moderates' bargaining position, might have eased popular acceptance of the new basic law. But neither happened.

Should things go on as they are now, there can be scant doubt that significant portions of the southern citizenry will resist attempts to implement dialogue decisions. The first test will likely occur if and when the government tries to register new voters and, then, to hold a referendum on the new constitution, followed by new presidential and parliamentary elections in 2014. In the absence of improvements on the ground and political negotiations with a wider subset of Hirak leaders to engender some buy-in, elections are likely to trigger violence.

The south is only the most immediate challenge to implementation. Currently there is no enforcement mechanism to ensure implementation of NDC outcomes writ large. There are no strong state institutions to compel or oversee domestic enforcement. State institutions, including the security services, are divided along tribal, personal, party, and regional lines, with the "master cleavage" within the state being the one that divides Saleh and his GPC supporters on the one hand from Ali Mohsen, the Ahmars, and Islah on the other. And then there is the gulf that separates both of these elite camps from the Huthis, the Hirak, and other emergent groups. None can enforce its will on a national scale.

The implementation of any agreement is therefore deeply contingent on the strength of the domestic consensus behind it and on the willingness of powerful stakeholders to honor their commitments to that consensus. Already, the intentions of some players are suspect. For example, some GPC and Islah members are talking about taking up to ten years to implement financial and administrative decentralization. For skeptics, this is a clear indication of their desire to kill reform with foot-dragging.

In the end, paper reforms mean nothing without concrete implementation. Under Saleh, Yemen had many formal institutions to check the central government and the executive, but none of that mattered—informal practice always trumped such formal arrangements. Implementation of any new agreement will require at the very least a clear timeline and discussion of possible enforcement mechanisms. If old-regime elites are to be barred from perpetuating the corrupt, centralized political economy, implementation will also require cooperation from formerly marginalized groups such as the Huthis, the Hirak, and activists in Ta'izz, Hadramout, and other governorates, as well as reformers within the party system. Opposition to the old system is palpable throughout the country, yet coordination against that system is only nascent. Indeed, groups such as the Hirak have an agenda—separation—that is far removed from national reform.

Yemen is not new to periods of political opening and closure.[19] Unification in 1990 ushered in a short period of genuine liberalization and political competition that was quickly closed by the 1994 civil war, when President Saleh was able to marginalize political competitors and gradually consolidate power.[20] The 2011 uprising has brought another opening that could move the country toward a more democratic, accountable future. Reconsolidating power around the same northern-based, tribal, and Islamist elites will be difficult, if not impossible, largely because newly empowered constituencies will reject this outcome.

But, it is far too early to start cheering Yemen for choosing a more inclusive and accountable future. There is as yet no durable settlement regarding political and economic power-sharing. Even if one is reached, implementation will be fraught with difficulties, especially in the south, where demands for separation are unlikely soon to abate. At best, a long and tumultuous process of negotiation and change has begun. The future is likely to hold bouts of localized violence, along with growing economic and humanitarian challenges.

—13 September 2013

NOTES

1. Zaydism is a form of Shia Islam that is distinct from the more commonly known Twelver Shiism prevalent in contemporary Iran, Iraq, Lebanon, and Bahrain. Zaydis form a majority in the far north of Yemen.

2. April Longley Alley, "Yemen's Multiple Crises," *Journal of Democracy* 21 (October 2010): 72–86.

3. For more on the Hirak's origins, see Stephen Day, "Updating Yemeni National Unity: Could Lingering Regional Divisions Bring Down the Regime?" *Middle East Journal* 62 (Summer 2008): 417–36. For a discussion of the Hirak's origins, component parts, and political evolution, see International Crisis Group, "Breaking Point? Yemen's Southern Question," *ICG Middle East Report,* No. 114, 20 October 2011.

4. For more on the Huthis, see International Crisis Group, "Yemen: Defusing the Sa'ada Time Bomb," *ICG Middle East Report,* No. 86, 27 May 2009; and Barak A. Saloni, Bryce Loidolt, and Madeleine Wells, *Regime and Periphery in Northern Yemen: The Huthi Phenomenon* (Santa Monica: RAND Corporation, 2010).

5. Wahabis follow a strict interpretation of the Hanbali school of Sunni jurisprudence. Salafis seek to revive "original" Islam by following the practices of Muhammad and his companions. Both groups often stigmatize Shiism as a false form of Islam.

6. For more on Yemeni uprising dynamics, see International Crisis Group, "Popular Protest in North Africa and the Middle East (II): Yemen Between Reform and Revolution," *ICG Middle East and North Africa Report,* No. 102, 10 March 2011. For an overview of the GCC initiative and UN-backed implementation mechanisms, see International Crisis Group, "Yemen: Enduring Conflicts, Threatened Transition," *ICG Middle East Report,* No. 25, 3 July 2012.
7. International Crisis Group, "Yemen: Enduring Conflicts, Threatened Transition."

8. On security-sector reform through April 2013, see International Crisis Group, "Ye-

men's Military-Security Reform: Seeds of New Conflict?" *ICG Middle East Report*, No. 39, 4 April 2013.

9. Author's interview with three prominent Yemeni politicians, Sana'a, May 2013.

10. Author's interview with a military officer, Sana'a, May 2013.

11. UN News Centre, "Yemen's Humanitarian Crisis Could Threaten Political Gains, Warns UN Relief Official," 16 May 2013, available at *www.un.org/apps/news/story. asp?NewsID=44924#.UcgNxj5gYkc*.

12. Author's interviews with more than a dozen Hirak activists, Aden, February 2013.

13. In 2011, al-Qaeda affiliates known as Ansar al-Shari'a seized ground in Abyan Governorate. When the government proved unable or unwilling to stop the expansion, locals formed popular committees which, in June 2012, fought alongside government forces to expel Ansar from cities. Today the government backs the committees, albeit with no plan to integrate them into the security services.

14. Author's interviews with a NDC delegate, Sana'a, May 2013 and with an Islah member, March 2013.

15. Author's interview with a tribesman from Al Bayda supportive of the Huthis, Sana'a, March 2013.

16. "National Dialogue Conference's Share Distribution Decided," *Yemen Times*, 29 November 2012.

17. National Dialogue Conference official website, "National Dialogue FAQ," available at *www.ndc.ye/page.aspx?show=73*. Voting procedures are meant to bring maximum buy-in. All recommendations garnering 75 percent in working groups go to the plenary. Yet any recommendation gaining less than 90 percent in a working group goes to the Consensus Committee (charged with reaching a higher level of agreement) before receiving a plenary vote. These rules will likely produce generalities, leaving much interpretive authority to the constitution-drafting committee.

18. Author's interview with NDC delegate, Sana'a, May 2013.

19. On Yemen's political openings and civil society activism, see Sheila Carapico, *Civil Society in Yemen: The Political Economy of Activism in Modern Arabia* (Cambridge: Cambridge University Press, 1998).

20. Jillian Schwedler, "Democratization in the Arab World? Yemen's Aborted Opening," *Journal of Democracy* 13 (October 2002): 48–55.

23

LIBYA STARTS FROM SCRATCH

Mieczysław P. Boduszyński and Duncan Pickard

Mieczysław P. Boduszyński is assistant professor of international relations at Pomona College. A former U.S. Foreign Service officer, he served from 2012 to 2013 as public-affairs officer at the U.S. Embassy in Tripoli. Duncan Pickard is a nonresident fellow at the Atlantic Council's Rafik Hariri Center for the Middle East. The views expressed here are their own. This essay originally appeared in the October 2013 issue of the Journal of Democracy.

The sources of Libya's 2011 revolution—anger and disaffection roused by political repression and economic inequality—are much like the causes of upheaval elsewhere in the Arab world, but in Libya the groundwork for democracy is much weaker. Indeed, the country lacks nearly all the features generally deemed crucial to successful democratization. For 42 years, the regime of Muammar Qadhafi pursued a policy of "statelessness," preventing the development of effective governing institutions.[1] Qadhafi exploited conflicts among Libya's tribes and regions, harming national cohesion. His ideology, along with international sanctions, isolated Libya and precluded most democracy-enhancing linkages with the West.[2] The history of Libya before Qadhafi's 1969 coup features no democratic experience on which to build. Moreover, the country remains heavily dependent on oil revenues and hence under the influence of that well-known crippler of democratic development, the "resource curse."

Two years after the August 2011 liberation of Tripoli and Qadhafi's death at rebel hands in October, Libya boasts the institutional symbols of an emerging democracy. There is an elected government formed around a 200-member unicameral parliament called the General National Congress (GNC). The media are free, and civil society is emerging. Libyans can criticize their government without fear of reprisal. Yet the old regime and its legacy cast a long shadow. The post-Qadhafi state is weak while local and nonstate actors drive the transition.[3] Armed militias operate with impunity throughout the country; smugglers cross borders unimpeded. Extremist groups, some of them armed, are growing. Separatists agitate in the east and south. Courts and police barely function.[4] Since its election in July 2012, the GNC has accomplished little. Many Libyans still feel a postrevolutionary euphoria, but worry that voting and free speech will count for little if security, the rule of law, and a legitimate state remain only dreams.[5]

The Libyan revolution began in mid-February 2011 against a backdrop of regionwide unrest. Strongmen in Tunisia and Egypt had been forced to step down, while protests raged in Algeria, Bahrain, and Yemen. On February 15, residents of Benghazi in eastern Libya took to the streets in opposition to the arrest of a human-rights lawyer. Soon strife flared, Qadhafi lost control of the city, and a chain of events began that would end his rule and his life. In contrast to the less sweeping turnovers that occurred in Egypt, Tunisia, and Yemen, Libya has experienced a nearly complete rejection of all things past. In other "Arab Spring" cases, entrenched institutions such as the Egyptian security establishment, the General Union of Tunisian Workers, and Yemen's political parties survived the end of dictatorship. In Libya, however, Qadhafi left behind few if any institutions.

This is because Qadhafi did not merely run the old system—he *was* the system. Such state institutions as did exist barely functioned and were often undermined in ways that reflected Qadhafi's paranoia and his ideology of Jamahiriya, a neologism that he coined to signal his regime's supposed trumping of republicanism with direct popular rule. The only encompassing "institution" in Libya was the colonel himself and his clutch of advisors. Subordinate institutions were entangled in overlapping and contradictory networks with no common ordering principle or chain of authority beyond Qadhafi's presence at the top of every heap.[6] The resulting confusion served as a deliberate instrument of rule, allowing Qadhafi's directives to cut through the noise and reinforce his authority over the state. Instead of entrusting sovereignty to the people as envisioned in the *Green Book,* Qadhafi's revolutionary manifesto, the state relied on violence and fear.

Paradoxically, then, the postrevolutionary vacuum that has emerged as new leaders try to break with the past represents a strange kind of continuity. Qadhafi's logic of deinstitutionalization both empowered dictatorship and ensured that efforts at democratization would find little to work with once dictatorship collapsed. An overview of the apparatus of the Qadhafi "government" demonstrates the institutional challenge facing transitional policy makers. Formally, Jamahiriya worked through a system of local congresses, elected from within municipalities. These congresses would select working committees charged with running public utilities and services and with representing their respective municipalities in the district congresses.

Each district congress would in turn choose a working group to sit in the General People's Congress (GPC). Nominally, the GPC was the sovereign authority in Libya, though in practice its authority was limited by Qadhafi's Revolutionary Committees, created in 1977, two years after the publication of the first volume of *The Green Book*. These committees, filled with Qadhafi loyalists, had broad powers over state policy and legislation, enforcing unwritten "revolutionary law" through extrajudicial courts and often violence. The power of the Revolutionary Committees proved that, despite the rhetoric of statelessness, state authority was punishingly strong.

Qadhafi coopted or spread patronage among fractious ethnic groups in order to extend his control over Libya's vast borderlands. In the southeastern town of Kufra near the frontier with Chad, for instance, he brokered a fragile peace between the Zuwaya, an Arab tribe, and the Tebu, a group with ethnic ties to Chad and sub-Saharan Africa. Qadhafi paid both groups to keep order despite their quarrels over claims to land and citizenship, selectively tolerating some cross-border smuggling in the process. In other areas, he practiced the politics of divide-and-rule by encouraging rifts within tribes large enough to challenge the state. Over time, he stripped the national army of training and resources, leaving only a few well-equipped brigades whose mission was to protect Qadhafi and his cronies from internal threats.[7]

Qadhafi's fall left a power vacuum. Fights for control of smuggling routes broke out in various cities including Kufra, exacerbating decades-old tensions. Ceasefires have consistently broken down, and the battle in Kufra remains one of the most intractable and bloodiest conflicts in a country that is not lacking in internecine strife. In February 2012 alone, the Kufra fighting claimed more than a hundred lives, with almost fifty more killed in July.

Libya's current security problems, especially the proliferation of militias, are the most visible consequences of underdeveloped institutions. Countless militias—organized along regional, ideological, family, or tribal lines—are the only consistent security forces in Libya, and many of their members receive government salaries. These militias often have their roots in the revolution, when the unelected National Transitional Council (NTC)—the temporary body officially formed in March 2011 in Benghazi that governed the country until August 2012—relied on allied revolutionary brigades and military councils established in liberated towns to fight Qadhafi's forces. The brigades were not loyal to the NTC, however, and the subsequent government has failed to consolidate them despite multiple attempts.

Currently, the government and private companies have militias under contract to protect facilities throughout the country. Militias run checkpoints, patrol borders, defend airports, and administer their own prisons. In April 2013, militias from Misurata and other cities laid siege to several key ministries, including the Ministry of Foreign Affairs, paralyzing

them for nearly two weeks with demands to pass a law on "political isolation," or the removal of individuals associated with the former regime
from public life. The GNC hastily and nearly unanimously passed the
law, compelling GNC head Mohamed Magarief and others to resign, but
its passage under the intimidation of armed groups further accentuated
the state's weakness vis-à-vis the militias and sparked a major political
crisis.

There are many other manifestations of institutional underdevelopment. Many well-intentioned and competent ministers, some with training in Europe and the Americas, preside over hollow organizations with
staffers who, if present at all, lack the skills to plan or carry out policies.
Basic state authority in areas such as tax collection, border control, law
enforcement, strategic planning, and the like is tightly constrained. Libya's past—not only the years of the Qadhafi regime but also decades under brutal Italian colonial rule and then a corrupt monarchy—has made
many Libyans deeply distrustful of *all* central authority. One expert has
portrayed the dearth of institutions as a plus, depicting Libya as a *tabula
rasa* on which there is nothing left over from the old regime to hinder
democracy,[8] but for now there is little doubt that the institutional void
forms a major obstacle to democratization.

The Struggle for Constitutionalism

In August 2011, the NTC passed a Constitutional Declaration that
currently governs Libya's institutional framework. The NTC had originally called for the GNC to appoint a sixty-member body to draft a
more permanent constitution, but amended this plan two days before
GNC elections to call for separate constitutional-commission elections
at a later date. Libya's Supreme Court ruled that amendment unconstitutional, causing confusion about the way forward. In April 2013, the
GNC resolved this murkiness by calling for the sixty-member body to be
popularly elected in a vote expected to be held by year's end.

The constitution-building process is a first attempt at institutionalization, but the lack of institutions itself has hampered the drafting of a new
constitution. Libya lacks the legal and political frameworks that could
support elections and public engagement in the constitution-making
process. Lines of authority are so blurry that it is hard to say just who is
responsible for what.

A postauthoritarian impulse to reject top-down authority in favor of local and nonstate solutions has not helped. Indeed, this impulse is so strong
that one might even say Libyan society is subverting the Libyan state.[9]
Libyans reject the idea that central planners or national processes can adequately represent local demands. Intense localism thwarts national-level
collaboration and with it any hope of building national institutions. National leaders are immobilized, beset by what one observer calls a "lack

of capacity to act."[10] Reluctance to lead goes along with a tendency to deflect responsibility: One arm of the government waits for others to act, or officials throw up their hands and retreat into calls for some new vote or poll "to let the people decide."

The negotiations over the constitution-making process have been telling. Decision makers have had to face basic issues of representation raised by an intricate set of regional, ethnic, and social demands as these weigh on seat shares in the constituent assembly. Qadhafi's development priorities privileged coastal cities in the center and west, mainly Tripoli and Sirte, his hometown. Even in the west, the lion's share of cash payouts and industrial-development spending benefited only the upper classes, contributing to the vast underdevelopment of most of the country despite an oil-fueled GDP per capita (at PPP) that is on par with Turkey's. The disparity in development-fund allocation exacerbated regional tensions that go back to modern Libya's origin in a 1949 UN-mandated fusion of three historic provinces—Cyrenaica in the east, Tripolitania in the northwest, and Fezzan in the arid southwest—that had been ruled by the Ottomans and later by European powers. Questions about how best to represent Libya's array of regions, groups, and interests in the electoral system and the constitution are central to the transition to democracy.

Elected officials are also vying for their *own* claim to represent Libya. The process by which the unelected NTC designed the GNC is revealing in this regard. The NTC's own members were either self-appointed or sent by local councils, themselves often self-appointed. The NTC made laws as it went along. One such law set a specific timeline for naming a new government and electing a sixty-member constituent assembly. That timeline collapsed under the weight of challenges to the NTC's authority to call for election (rather than appointment) of the constituent assembly as well as failed government-formation talks. The NTC's legal framework made no provision for disruptions in the timeline or for the drafting of an election law (with all the thorny representation-related issues such a drafting process must confront). Not having inherited a sturdy legal framework from the NTC, the GNC faces the troubling double task of having to institutionalize itself while trying to manage the democratic transition at the same time.

The call for local-council elections also points to the deficiency of institutions and the challenge of building a national community. Even in the absence of an overarching legal framework, municipalities expect to organize and vote for their own local councils. Indeed, the February 2012 local elections in Misurata came five months before those that chose the GNC. Municipalities are calling for a fresh round of municipal elections to be held independently of those for the constituent assembly. The way in which elections are administered, moreover, reflects the lack of collaboration among Libyan policy makers. Two separate commissions have been established to run local-council and constituent-assembly elections, respectively. Despite the similarity of their mission, these councils have no formal means of sharing facilities, resources, or voter registers. The lack of coordination, fueled by the impulse to seek purely local solutions, resembles the Qadhafi-era system of popular representation through district, regional, and national "popular congresses."

The Trust Deficit

The Libyan transition is in many ways a product of the attempt at reform that began during Qadhafi's last years. This uneasy continuity accounts for the sharp rivalry between late Qadhafi-era reformists, who played key roles in postrevolution governing bodies, and anti-Qadhafi frontline fighters. The former claim legitimacy bestowed by the voters or high-value technical skills, while the latter point to their sacrifices during the revolution. Over time, the revolutionary veterans have asserted themselves and through sustained pressure have succeeded in removing NTC members and, later, government ministers.

Libya's rapprochement with the West, which started in the late 1990s and led to the resumption of U.S. diplomatic relations in 2004, spurred an opening in Qadhafi's highly repressive political and economic system. Libyans got access to mobile phones, pan-Arab satellite channels, and the Internet. They were allowed to travel and study in the West. Many exiles returned with assurances of amnesty. Technocrats took key jobs in institutions such as the National Oil Corporation. Amid this greater openness, Qadhafi's charismatic and Western-educated son Saif al-Islam (b. 1972) began to speak the language of reform.

Saif sponsored new media outlets that criticized corrupt officials and ineffective state bureaucracies. (The outlets were eventually shut down.) He launched a failed push for a new constitution. He invited Western experts and consulting companies to advise the Libyan government. Apart from some symbolic economic-policy reforms, Saif achieved nothing concrete as an antireform old guard pushed back hard. Yet he helped to raise expectations, and he empowered people, groups, and institutions that would play major roles in the revolution and beyond.

A number of quasi–civil society groups emerged in the late 2000s as a result of the regime's more accommodating posture toward its fiercest opponents, many of whom were concentrated in the east. In 2007, Qadhafi attended an Amazigh (Berber) conference and subsequently allowed, at least for a time, limited Berber cultural expressions.[11] In 2008, the regime permitted the creation in Benghazi of a committee to represent families of people who had been political detainees in Tripoli's notorious Abu Selim prison, where thousands of inmates were known to have been summarily executed in 1996. These families were led by Fathi Terbil, the well-known Benghazi lawyer whose February 2011 arrest sparked the revolution. Another group was formed by the families of children who had been infected by HIV-tainted blood at a Benghazi hospital. The lawyer Abdelhafiz Ghoga, who later became the NTC's spokesperson, achieved greater independence for the Libyan Bar Association.

In the end, Qadhafi and reactionaries around him quashed most of this, but opposition groups were left bolder and more organizationally savvy. Perhaps most fatefully, Saif had spearheaded a program to rehabilitate imprisoned Islamists, especially those from the Libyan Islamic Fighting Group (LIFG). Many LIFG cadres went free in 2010 after promising to give up violence and their struggle against the regime. Once the revolution broke out, however, the LIFG and other Islamic groups played a leading role among the revolutionaries and later formed the NTC-affiliated Tripoli Military Council.[12]

Saif's reforms also empowered future leaders of the NTC. In fact, the NTC was able to gather support abroad quickly because Western policy makers had recently come to know many key NTC players as Qadhafi-regime reformists.[13] Mahmoud Jibril, the head of the NTC's executive office and Libya's de facto prime minister, had been one of Saif's prominent reformists as head of the National Economic Development Board. NTC member Fathi Baja had criticized regime corruption in one of Saif's media outlets. As Qadhafi's reform-minded justice minister, NTC chair Mustafa Abdel Jalil had helped to resolve the diplomatic crisis that erupted in 2007 over the case of five Bulgarian nurses whom a Libyan court had accused of knowingly infecting children at a Benghazi hospital with HIV. The defections of Libya's ambassador to Washington and UN ambassador also helped to generate crucial international support for the revolution. Without their lobbying, it is unlikely that the UN Security Council would have passed Resolution 1970, which put the regime under harsh sanctions and referred the situation to the International Criminal Court.

During the reformist interlude, these future leaders of the revolution gained administrative know-how plus an acute understanding of local conditions. Yet their old-regime ties have roused demands—pushed with special fervor by certain militias and their affiliated parties—that they be formally isolated from politics. With NTC leaders such as Jibril unable to build strong ties with the rebels who actually fought Qadhafi's forces, the divide between "holdover" technocrats and soldiers of the revolution remains sharp.

Joining those with old-regime ties in the "circle of mistrust" are the dissidents who returned from exile during the revolution, including former GNC president Mohamed Magarief. Many Libyans view them with suspicion and find their links to the West problematic—a predictable if dismaying circumstance in a society where trust extending beyond immediate circles of friends and kinfolk is a rare commodity. Again we see Qadhafi's malign handiwork: His regime destroyed interpersonal and institutional trust not only with an omnipresent security apparatus that urged Libyans to spy and report on each other, but also by means of capricious policies that discredited the state. Qadhafi wantonly tortured and killed—he liked to show executions on live television—to keep power and punish anyone suspected of plotting against his rule. People learned to shun gatherings for fear that they might look bad to the colonel's hard-eyed security men. During the worst years of repression, interrogators would threaten public torture and hangings to make neighbors, relatives, and friends inform on each other. Libyans turned inward under this onslaught, hewing solely to direct family ties and rarely venturing outside their hometowns and native regions.

Some of Libya's toughest democratization tasks, such as building up the legitimacy of the central state and its institutions, are made even harder by low trust levels. Citizens will not give up their weapons until they can trust the government to protect them. Rogue militias will not integrate into legitimate military units until they trust these structures. Ministers will not make decisions if they cannot trust their subordinates to implement them, especially in an atmosphere in which policy failure may invite corruption charges. Those institutions that have succeeded have been the ones enjoying high levels of trust. The NTC was able to coalesce and act under harrowing circumstances because at its core stood a group of lawyers from the east who knew each other well. Likewise, some of Libya's most effective civil society groups are built on preexisting ties among close family members, friends, colleagues, or classmates.

Islam and Islamists in the Transition

Islam has served as a platform for Libyans to build postrevolutionary, trust-based institutions of various kinds: religious communities, political parties, and armed groups. Yet it would be a mistake to see the Libyan transition as being a matter of long-suppressed Islamists storming through freedom's open doors. Qadhafi was not a secular dictator in the mold of Ben Ali, Mubarak, or Assad. Qadhafi began making Islam a part of his ideology as early as 1975, and at various points his regime coopted some Islamists, including a number of "status quo" salafists who became tools of official propaganda.[14] A rapprochement between the regime and certain Muslim Brotherhood elements, meanwhile, led the latter to shun the Libyan opposition's first conference, held in London in 2005. Other Islamist groups such as the LIFG took an active part in the anti-Qadhafi struggle and now wield great influence in the security sector.

Libya has always been a deeply pious and socially conservative Muslim country, and Islam has long been central to Libyan identity, especially in the absence of trust or a legitimate state. The Sufi Sanussi order played a vital role in the struggle against Italian colonialism, and its leader Mohamed Idris was crowned Libya's king upon independence in 1951. Sanussi revivalism and, in more recent times, salafism continue to influence society. The east is particularly religious and home to thousands of Islamist fighters who fought the Qadhafi regime both before and during the revolution and also fought as *mujahideen* in Afghanistan, Algeria, Bosnia, Chechnya, Iraq, and Syria. Islamist fighters (jihadis among them) can invoke many years of struggle against the regime, and played a decisive role in the 2011 revolution. They have a deep reservoir of revolutionary credibility in the new Libya. Some, including the extremist militia Ansar al-Shari'a (the name means "adherents of Islamic law"), also fill the current institutional void by providing welfare services and security.[15] Painfully aware of its own weakness, the government is reluctant to confront Islamist militias—including those that openly proclaim hostility to elected officials and democracy itself—even when these armed bands attack security organs or other arms of the central state.

While no single group holds a monopoly on Islamism in Libya, religion has become the baseline of political competition. Politicians, militias, and other actors draw on Islam to build support and give Libyans a sense of identity and unity, thereby contributing to the reconstruction of both state and nation. Many in the press and diplomatic corps saw the July 2012 GNC election results, in which former NTC leader Jibril's National Forces Alliance (NFA) won 39 of the 80 seats reserved for political parties, as a victory for "secular" parties, but the truth is that no party or politician in Libya can afford to eschew appeals to Islam and *shari'a*. Of the 120 seats allocated to individual candidates, the preponderance went to figures who were nominally independent but in reality sympathized with the Muslim Brotherhood and salafist movements.

Organized Islamist parties such as the Brotherhood-affiliated Justice and Construction Party fared much worse than their brethren in Tunisia and Egypt, winning just 17 seats. Yet this outcome should not be seen as a "vote for liberal, let alone secular values."[16] Islam is not the metric that Libyans use to distinguish between political parties, as all parties refer to Islam as a source of inspiration. Even the ostensibly "secular" or "liberal" NFA plays the Islamic card. According to interviews with participants, an NFA party gathering in early 2013 featured a parade of speakers extolling the virtues of *shari'a*. There is no truly secular political camp in Libya—a reality that the remainder of the transition process, especially the writing of the constitution, will likely reflect.

The appeal of populist Islamism was evident in the NTC's May 2011 choice of a salafist-oriented cleric, Sadeq al-Gheriani, as Libya's Grand Mufti. The office of Grand Mufti had existed under Qadhafi in toothless form, its sole task being the provision of religious justifications for regime actions. Gheriani had earned popular support by opposing Qadhafi during the revolution. As Grand Mufti, his *fatwas* have become increasingly conservative and political. He has declared that no Muslim may vote for parties promising to restrict the role of *shari'a,* issued a *fatwa* against a UN report on violence against women, condemned teaching about the freedom of religion and the development of democracy in ancient Greece in schools, and called on the government to forbid marriages between Libyan women and foreign men. He has also issued *fatwas* proclaiming it a religious duty for Libyans to demonstrate in support of the political-isolation law. Although many Libyans resent Gheriani for his interference in politics and scoff at politicians who attempt to teach them about "proper" Islam, this brand of Islamist populism promises to play a leading role in the coming years.

Trying to build democracy in a landscape stripped of institutions is like making bricks without straw. Creating democracy and institutions side-by-side is immensely challenging, since fledgling democracy must rely on working institutions that can legitimate it and enable it to deliver the public goods (order, prosperity, and the rest) that any government worthy of the name must provide. The legacy of crushed, shattered, starved, and neglected institutions that Qadhafi left behind has placed a gigantic task on the shoulders of leaders who are not short of good intentions and Western expertise, but are stymied by a lack of institutional capacity to enforce the rule of law and implement reform. A lack of interpersonal trust magnifies these challenges.

The July 2012 elections were an impressive achievement, but the lingering effects of Qadhafi's decades in power still work against stability and the consolidation of such democratic gains. Tensions between the country's regions, made worse by Qadhafi's long neglect, are a defining feature of Libyan politics. The need to balance east, west, and south pervades all decision making. The impulse toward inclusion has a positive side, but the three-part nature of every committee also bespeaks the divisive notion that regional ties must define all interests. Tribal and ethnic tensions further threaten the national unity that is critical to democratic development. A new civil society and free media may yet prove allies of democratization, but they remain inexperienced, underdeveloped, and hampered by security concerns. On top of that, Libya is undergoing a parallel transition from a quasi-socialist economy with a weak private sector, and it is struggling to build a cohesive identity.

In the face of such challenges, Islamist populism may appear an attractive way to construct a new national identity and to promote unity, but the commitment of the protagonists of this worldview to democracy is unclear. The single-minded focus of Islamist groups and their militia allies on a harsh form of "political isolation" could sideline many individuals with the requisite experience and skills to reconstruct the state institutions vital to the legitimization of democracy. These are also the institutions upon which a new conception of Libyan citizenship must ultimately rest.

NOTES

1. Dirk Vandewalle, *A History of Modern Libya,* 2nd ed. (Cambridge: Cambridge University Press, 2012).

2. On the importance to democratization of Western linkages, see Steven Levitsky and Lucan Way, *Competitive Authoritarianism: Hybrid Regimes After the Cold War* (Cambridge: Cambridge University Press, 2010).

3. Wolfram Lacher, "Fault Lines of the Revolution: Political Actors, Camps and Conflicts in the New Libya," German Institute for International and Security Affairs, May 2013.

4. International Crisis Group, "Trial by Error: Justice in Post-Qadhafi Libya," *ICG Middle East/North Africa Report,* No. 140, 17 April 2013.

5. On the concerns of Libyan citizens, see Megan Doherty, "'Give Us Change We Can See': Citizen Views of Libya's Political Process," National Democratic Institute for International Affairs, December 2012.

6. Vandewalle, in *A History of Modern Libya,* argues that deinstitutionalization under Qadhafi continued a legacy from the monarchy. Libya was a new state when the kingdom was created in 1951 and was unable to establish institutions before Qadhafi's 1969 coup.

7. International Crisis Group, "Divided We Stand: Libya's Enduring Conflicts," *ICG Middle East/North Africa Report,* No. 130, 14 September 2012.

8. Dirk Vandewalle, "After Qaddafi: The Surprising Success of the New Libya," *Foreign Affairs* 91 (November–December 2012): 8–15.

9. Joel Migdal, *Strong Societies and Weak States: State-Society Relations and State Capabilities in the Third World* (Princeton: Princeton University Press, 1988).

10. Karim Mezran, quoted in "How Libya Can Earn Back 'Frontier Market' Status," *Vancouver Observer,* 31 January 2013.

11. Ethan Chorin, *Exit the Colonel: The Hidden History of the Libyan Revolution* (New York: PublicAffairs, 2012).

12. Omar Ashour, "Libyan Islamists Unpacked: Rise, Transformation, and Future," Brookings Doha Center, May 2012.

13. Chorin, *Exit the Colonel,* 244–45.

14. John Davis, *Libyan Politics: Tribe and Revolution—An Account of the Zuwaya and Their Government* (Berkeley: University of California Press, 1988), 50; Ashour, "Libyan Islamists Unpacked," 3.

15. Ansar al-Shariʻa is also suspected of playing a central role in the 11 September 2012 attacks on the U.S. Mission to Benghazi.

16. Lacher, "Fault Lines of the Revolution," 10.

24

SYRIA AND THE FUTURE OF AUTHORITARIANISM

Steven Heydemann

Steven Heydemann is vice-president of the Center for Applied Research on Conflict at the U.S. Institute of Peace and adjunct professor of government at Georgetown University. This essay originally appeared in the October 2013 issue of the Journal of Democracy.

As the third anniversary of the Arab uprisings draws nearer, the democratic possibilities that they appeared to create have receded. Among the countries that experienced significant mass protest movements in early 2011 transitions have revealed the difficulty of overcoming the stubborn institutional and social legacies of authoritarian rule, and the extraordinary lengths to which authoritarian regimes will go to survive. In Syria, any possibility that protesters might bring about the breakdown of authoritarianism and initiate a transition to democracy was extinguished early on, first by the Assad regime's ferocious repression and then by the country's descent into a brutal and increasingly sectarian civil war. Grim statistics only hint at the toll: more than a hundred thousand killed, millions more forced to flee, and eight million in need of humanitarian aid. Officials of the United Nations describe Syria as the worst humanitarian disaster since Rwanda in 1994, and instability is rising among Syria's Arab neighbors.

The democratic aspirations of the protesters who filled streets and public squares across Syria in early 2011 were among the conflict's first casualties. If democracy as an outcome of the uprising was always uncertain, democratic prospects have been severely crippled by the devastation of civil war and the deepening fragmentation of Syrian society. Whether ethnosectarian diversity is a cause of conflict remains deeply contested.[1] However, countries emerging from ethnosectarian civil wars are widely understood to be among the least likely to democratize once conflict ends.[2] Postconflict democratization in such cases fails far more often than it succeeds.[3] More than half of all countries that experience civil wars relapse into conflict after a period of interim peace.[4]

In Syria, however, democratic prospects appear bleak for reasons that extend beyond the destructive effects of civil war. Conflict has not only eroded possibilities for democratic reform, but it has also provided the impetus for a process of authoritarian restructuring that has increased the Assad regime's ability to survive mass protests, repress an armed uprising, and resist international sanctions. Even as state institutions have all but collapsed under the weight of armed conflict, war making has compelled the Assad regime to reconfigure its social base, tighten its dependency on global authoritarian networks, adapt its modes of economic governance, and restructure its military and security apparatus. While the outcome of the current conflict cannot be predicted, these adaptations are likely to influence how Syria is governed once fighting ends. Should they become consolidated, they will vastly diminish prospects for a postconflict democratic transition, especially if Syria ends up either formally or informally partitioned.

The role of war as a catalyst for authoritarian restructuring in Syria, and the obstacles that this process poses for political reform, are noteworthy for several reasons. First, research on war and democratization has found little correlation between regime type at the outset of conflict and prospects for democratization once conflict ends. The presence of an authoritarian regime at the start of a civil war has not been found to reduce the chances for a postconflict transition to democracy. According to Leonard Wantchekon, for example, civil war so thoroughly destroys prewar political systems that they exert little influence on the shape of postconflict settlements. Distinguishing between authoritarian breakdown and war as causes of democratization, he argues that

> war itself has such a profound effect on the government that post–civil war democracy is more an institutional response to civil war than to pre–civil war authoritarian rule. In Mozambique and Nicaragua, the civil war almost annihilated the authoritarian political situation that led to war.

In cases of authoritarian breakdown that do not involve civil war, however, "many features of the previous regimes have [persisted]."[5]

Syria's experience challenges these claims, for several reasons. It highlights the possibility that an authoritarian regime might adapt to the demands of an insurgency, increasing the likelihood of regime survival and affecting both the outcome of a conflict and whether a postwar political settlement will be democratic. Syria's civil war is far from over. It is possible that the authoritarian system of rule initiated by the Ba'ath Party in the early 1960s and later captured by the Assad family and its clients will yet be "annihilated" as a result of protracted civil war. Such an outcome would broaden the range of potential postconflict settlements to include a transition to democracy. From the vantage point of the latter half of 2013, however, the process of authoritarian restructuring that the regime has undergone during two years of armed insurgency makes such an outcome far less likely. What seems more plausible is that the repressive and corrupt authoritarian regime that entered civil war in 2011 will emerge from it as an even more brutal, narrowly sectarian, and militarized version of its former self.

Second, the Assad regime's reconfiguration over the past two years stands out as an extreme instance of a broader phenomenon: the adaptation of Middle Eastern authoritarianism to the challenges posed by the renewal of mass politics.[6] As waves of protest spread across the region in early 2011, authoritarian regimes appeared more vulnerable than at any time in the contemporary history of the Middle East. Protest movements gave voice to the failure of Arab autocrats to address deeply held economic, social, and political grievances, challenging notions of authoritarian regimes as adaptive and capable of adjusting their strategies and tactics to changing conditions. These movements would help to topple four longtime rulers—in Tunisia, Egypt, Libya, and Yemen—while threatening the stability of others. As popular struggles continued throughout much of the region, analysts began to reassess longstanding assumptions about the durability and adaptability of authoritarianism in the Arab world.[7]

Since those heady days almost three years ago, however, the limits of mass politics have become clearer. Ruling elites from Morocco to Bahrain have learned to contain popular demands, reassert control over restive societies, and recalibrate ruling formulas to limit the revolutionary potential of protest movements.[8] Attention is thus pivoting back to the dynamics of authoritarian governance and to the strategies that Arab autocrats and militaries have deployed to preserve their hold on power. As the July 2013 coup in Egypt demonstrates, these adaptations have been decidedly authoritarian and are often both repressive and exclusionary, yet they do not follow a uniform template. Their shape has varied from the strategies of contained accommodation seen in Jordan, Kuwait, and Morocco to the more coercive approaches of Algeria, Egypt, Saudi Arabia, and Bahrain. Despite this variation, these experiences all stand as case studies in the recombinant capacity of authoritarian regimes, the dynamics of authoritarian learning, and the conditions under which such learning contributes to regime survival.

Lastly, while Syria may be an extreme case, it is not an outlier as regards the violence that has marked the Assad regime's response to the rise of mass politics. The brutality of the regime's tactics falls at the far end of a spectrum of reactions to antiregime protests. These tactics reflect Syria's distinctive social composition, institutional make-up, and political orientation as a lead member of the "resistance front" facing Israel. In their details, therefore, the adaptations that are reshaping authoritarianism in Syria may not be generalizable to regimes that govern differently configured societies and polities. Yet milder versions of the Assad regime's coercive tactics may be seen on the streets of both Bahrain and Egypt, underscoring the insights that can be gleaned from the Syrian case into how Arab autocrats will react as the dynamics of mass politics continue to unfold in today's Middle East.

The adaptations of the Assad regime can be traced to the earliest months of the Syrian uprising in March 2011, if not earlier. Syrian scholar Hassan Abbas says that in February 2011, President Bashar al-Assad "formed a special committee" which concluded that the Tunisian and Egyptian regimes had failed because they did not crush the protests instantly.[9] Thus, almost as soon as the first major protest broke out in the southern city of Deraa on 18 March 2011, the Assad regime started shooting.[10] As more protestors took up arms to defend themselves, the regime escalated its violence to the level of large-scale military offensives involving armored units and heavy artillery against major urban centers. It also moved to brand a peaceful and cross-sectarian protest movement as a terrorist campaign led by Islamist extremists. Peaceful protests continued across much of the country into 2012, but the uprising gradually transformed into a full-fledged and increasingly sectarian civil war.

The regime's responses to these developments included a set of internal institutional adaptations and policy shifts. They also included modifications to its management of regional and international relations in the face of deepening international isolation and the imposition of a dense web of economic and diplomatic sanctions. Domestically, the Assad regime has promoted exclusionary sectarian mobilization to reinforce defensive solidarity among the regime's core social base in the Alawite community and non-Muslim minorities—benefiting from but also contributing to broader trends toward regional sectarian polarization. It has reconfigured the security sector, including the armed forces, paramilitary criminal networks, and the intelligence and security apparatus to confront forms of resistance (in particular, the decentralized guerrilla tactics of armed insurgents) for which the security sector was unprepared and poorly trained.

Regime officials have reasserted the role of the state as an agent of redistribution and provider of economic security—despite the utter destruction of the country's economy and infrastructure. Officials now blame the limited economic reforms championed by economist and former deputy prime minister Abdullah Dardari as the cause of grievances that moved citizens to rebel. The regime has also continued to make use of state-controlled Internet and telecommunications infrastructure to disrupt communications among regime opponents, identify and target opposition supporters, and disseminate proregime narratives. At the regional and international levels, the Assad regime has exploited its strategic alliance with Iran and Hezbollah both for direct military and financial assistance and also for expertise and training in specific modes of repression, including urban and cyber warfare, in which its own security sector lacked experience.

Leveraging Strategic Relationships

The regime has similarly exploited its strategic and diplomatic relationships with Russia, China, and other authoritarian counterparts. These give the regime sources of direct military and financial support as well as a set of advocates who act on its behalf within international institutions—a role that neither Iran nor Hezbollah is able to play. One of the effects is to insulate the Assad regime from the force of UN-backed sanctions that might otherwise impede the ability of its key authoritarian allies to provide it with essential assistance.

These relationships, especially the regime's ties to Iran and Hezbollah, have implications not only for the survival of the Assad regime but for the shape of an eventual postconflict settlement. First, Iran, with Russian support, seeks a role for itself in the event that negotiations to end Syria's civil war take place. While the United States and its European allies currently oppose such a role, they recognize that for a negotiated settlement to be stable it will need to take Iran's interests into account, decreasing prospects for an eventual transition to democracy. Second, and perhaps more important, as the Assad regime deepens its dependence on authoritarian allies and is increasingly isolated from both Western democracies and international organizations populated by democracies, it becomes further embedded in relationships that diminish opportunities to moderate its authoritarian practices through either of the modes indentified by Steven Levitsky and Lucan Way ("linkage" and "leverage") or through other forms of conditionality.[11]

These adaptations can be seen as extensions of earlier strategies of authoritarian upgrading, but with a more compact, militarized, sectarian, exclusionary, and repressive core.[12] That the Assad regime could accomplish these shifts was by no means certain. For many years, the regime's critics have described it as little more than an inept mafia, sometimes likening Bashar al-Assad to the fictional Fredo Corleone. As recently as mid-2012, the regime's survival seemed very much in doubt. Opposition forces had seized much ground, including most of the Damascus suburbs, and many observers were predicting the regime's imminent collapse.

Mafias, however, do not have sovereignty. They do not control armed forces. They do not have vast state institutions and state resources at their disposal. While its supporters fretted, the Assad regime recalibrated its military tactics and reconfigured its security apparatus. With a capacity for learning that has surprised its detractors, the regime integrated loyalist *shabiha* militias (the word means "ghost" or "thug")—

including a wide array of armed criminal and informal elements—into a formal paramilitary, the National Defense Forces (NDF), under direct regime control. Since mid-2012, hundreds (perhaps thousands) of NDF members have gone through combat training in Iran, a direct form of authoritarian knowledge transfer. Following defections among lower-ranking Sunni conscripts and officers, new methods of monitoring and controlling soldiers' movements were adopted. Iranian and Hezbollah advisors arrived to teach local commanders the fine points of crowd control, urban warfare, and insurgent tactics. The regime expanded its dependence on battle-hardened Hezbollah combat units, enabling it to regain control of strategic sites.

Exploiting its monopoly of air power, the regime has sown chaos and instability in opposition-held areas, driving millions of Syrians out of their homes, eroding popular morale and support for the opposition, and preventing stabilization or reconstruction in opposition-controlled areas. Official media routinely highlight the prominent role of militant Islamists associated with al-Qaeda in opposition ranks to reinforce the uprising-as-Sunni-terrorism narrative, and tout the regime's commitment to minority protection and secularism (its reliance on Iran and Hezbollah notwithstanding) to rally its base. The regime has also restructured key institutions, including the Ba'ath Party, to enhance cohesion and ensure the fealty of senior officials to President Assad and his immediate family.

By mid-2013, this amalgam of ad hoc adaptations permitted the regime to reclaim authority over most of the country's urban "spine" from Homs in the north to Damascus in the south. The adaptations solidified support among the regime's social base, prevented the fracturing of its inner circle, and disrupted attempts to return life to normal in areas outside regime control. The regime now dominates the strategically important Mediterranean coast and every major city except Aleppo. It has secure access to Hezbollah-controlled parts of Lebanon and to the sea. With the partial exception of central Damascus, this zone has suffered massive destruction, economic paralysis, and large-scale population movements. Accurate statistics are not available, but it is safe to say that Homs now has many fewer Sunnis, while Damascus, Tartus, Latakia, Hama, and other areas under regime control have seen large inflows of internally displaced persons—perhaps numbering in the millions—including Christians, Alawites, and Sunnis fleeing the instability and violence of insurgent-held territories.

In the decades before the war, Syria's population of 22 million—which is 65 to 70 percent Sunni Arab, 10 to 12 percent Sunni Kurdish, 10 to 12 percent Alawite, and 10 to 12 percent Druze, Christian, and other non-Sunni minorities—had become increasingly dispersed across the country, shrinking the areas inhabited almost exclusively by one community or another. Urban centers had become increasingly cosmopolitan, benefiting from the inflow of Alawites and Kurds and from processes of urban migration as Syria's economy modernized. The vast population displacement caused by the war is producing fundamental shifts in these trends. It has increased sectarian segregation within cities even as they become more diverse in the aggregate due to internal displacement. It has also led to partial sectarian cleansing in rural areas, destroying longstanding patterns of intersectarian tolerance between Sunni and minority villages in conflict-affected areas.

Whether the regime's changes will be enough to ensure its survival is uncertain. Also uncertain is whether adaptations made to defeat a popular insurrection will last once conflict ends. There is no reason to imagine that the regime will not evolve further as its environment changes. Contrary to notions that civil war wipes the political slate clean, the available evidence suggests that Bashar al-Assad and his regime are determined to remain central to any postwar political order, whether it comes via the military defeat of its adversaries or through internationally supervised negotiations. Even as conflict rages across the country, and with more than half of Syria's territory outside regime control, Bashar al-Assad has signaled his intent to seek reelection when his current term as president expires in 2014—potentially imposing a macabre veneer of faux-democratic legitimacy on a regime that the UN Human Rights Commission has condemned repeatedly for gross and systematic violations of human rights, atrocities against its own people, and crimes against humanity.

Explaining Authoritarian Adaptations

Authoritarian survivors across the Middle East have adapted to the challenges posed by the Arab uprisings. Yet the form that such adaptations have taken is a product of the specific domestic and external resources that define any given regime's "opportunity set." There is a strong path-dependent quality to the adaptive choices of regimes: Existential crises have not been moments of creative innovation among the Arab world's authoritarian survivors. Instead, adaptations have tended to magnify regimes' existing attributes as rulers turn to strategies that have proven their effectiveness in the past.

In the Syrian case, three such resources have been particularly important. The first is how patterns of elite recruitment have strengthened the cohesion of formal institutions, notably the extent to which the regime has populated senior positions in the armed forces and the security apparatus with Alawite loyalists. For Eva Bellin, this makes Syria the example *par excellence* of a coercive apparatus organized along patrimonial lines, with more at risk from reform than its less patrimonial counterparts, and more willing to use coercive means to repress reformers.[13]

Patrimonialism, however, is a broad-spectrum diagnosis. It cannot by itself explain the cohesion of the Syrian officer corps and its continued loyalty to the regime. Contra Bellin's prediction, even large-scale and persistent social mobilization has not eroded the regime's will to repress. Escalating violence did produce cracks in the military. Tens of thousands of rank-and-file conscripts, together with more than fifty non-Alawite generals and other senior officers, defected rather than shoot fellow citizens.

Yet the center held. It did so because patterns of recruitment into the upper ranks of the military and its elite units were not simply patrimonial, but also sectarian and exclusionary in character. Identity-based recruitment was explicitly designed to strengthen bonds between the regime and senior officers, to raise the cost of defection, and to make defending the regime the military's top priority. The result is an almost entirely Alawite officer corps that is stubbornly loyal to the Assads, willing to use every weapon it can (from cluster bombs and ballistic missiles to helicopter gunships and, reportedly, chemical munitions), and annealed against repeated attempts to persuade key figures to defect. Specific patterns of patrimonialism thus produce distinctive forms of cohesion and provide regimes with widely varying organizational, coercive, and adaptive capacities.

At the same time, even if the defection of the military may be fatal for an authoritarian incumbent its cohesion is no guarantee of survival, especially once regime violence propels social mobilization beyond protest to the point of armed insurgency. Throughout 2012, with defections sweeping the rank and file, opposition forces seizing territory, and key units pushed to the point of exhaustion, it was far from clear that the cohesion of the officer corps and security elites would prevent the overthrow of the regime. A second resource played a critical role in stemming opposition advances and stabilizing the regime: informal networks of nonstate actors, organized on the basis of familial ties, sectarian affinity, or simple mercenary arrangements, and cultivated by regime elites over the years to provide a range of (often illegal) functions that could be conducted without any formal scrutiny or accountability.

Prior to the uprising, members of these networks, typically described as *shabiha,* engaged in officially sanctioned criminal activities, served as regime enforcers, and used violence to protect the privileges and status of regime elites. When protests began in March 2011, the regime recruited these loose networks to brutalize demonstrators.[14] As the opposition militarized, these criminal networks were gradually transformed, first into informal and decentralized paramilitary groups and later into more formally structured armed units that have been integrated into the regime's security apparatus. Almost exclusively Alawite in composition, *shabiha* forces are responsible for some of the worst atrocities of the civil war. They serve as shock troops, defend Alawite and minority communities against opposition attacks, terrorize and brutalize Sunni communities, assist the regime in controlling army units to prevent desertions and defections, and fight alongside the armed forces in offensives against opposition-held areas. They provide levels of cohesion and loyalty that sustain the regime's capacity to repress far more effectively than it could with ordinary conscripts. Had it not been possible for the regime to draw on and professionalize these informal sectarian-criminal networks, its prospects for survival would be much more precarious.

A third critical resource grows out of the Assad regime's alliances with Hezbollah and Iran, and the additional military capacity that both have provided. Hezbollah has dispatched thousands of fighters to assist the regime in a major offensive against opposition-held positions in western Syria along the border with Lebanon, in Homs, and in the suburbs ringing Damascus. Iran is alleged to have dispatched its own combat forces as well, and has sent military and security advisors who have produced tangible improvements in regime units' combat effectiveness. Perhaps most important, however, has been an explicit effort to model the newly established NDF after the Iranian Basij, a "volunteer people's militia" created at the urging of Ayatollah Khomeini during the 1980–88 Iran-Iraq War that subsequently became a central component of Iran's internal-security apparatus and played a major role in the suppression of the "Green Movement" protests following Iran's 2009 presidential election.

Authoritarian learning and knowledge transfer have thus produced significant adaptations in the scale and organization of the Assad regime's coercive apparatus, enhancing its capacity to fight a popular armed insurgency. They have also amplified that regime's existing tendencies, boosting sectarian hard-liners and institutionalizing repressive exclusionary practices within what is left of the Syrian state. To be sure, the regime has leveraged its strategic relationships with Iran, Hezbollah, and other authoritarian actors for purposes that go well beyond the upgrading of its coercive apparatus. Iran has provided the regime with billions of dollars in the form of loans and contracts. Russia has provided arms, money, and diplomatic cover, several times voting to prevent the imposition of UN Security Council sanctions. China has followed Russia within the UN, though it has otherwise played a negligible role with respect to Syria thus far. Nonetheless, the reconfiguration of the Assad regime's coercive apparatus, and the consolidation of power within institutions organized along exclusionary sectarian lines, are most consequential for the kind of postwar political arrangements that will emerge, and least conducive to the prospects for an eventual transition to democracy.

Other elements of regime adaptation since March 2011 have been less effective. These include the regime's attempts to distance itself from the economic reforms of the 2000s, to reassert a more active role for the state in managing Syria's war-shattered economy, and to extract resources and support from the business networks that it helped to create over the previous decade. During the 2000s, the Assad regime enriched itself and new coalitions of state-business elites and private businesses by, in effect, corruptly exploiting economic liberalization.[15] In the process, it sidelined and alienated large segments of Syrian society that had benefited from their positions within state institutions and the Ba'ath Party.[16]

These shifts in patterns of patronage and economic governance were intended to strengthen the regime's economic base but have proven problematic since March 2011. On one hand, they fueled the economic grievances and resentments among former regime clients that sparked mass protests in March 2011. On the other hand, they fostered the regime's dependence on business networks whose loyalty to the regime has proven less durable as Syria's conflict has dragged on. While the regime continues to benefit from the loyalty of a shrinking cohort of key business cronies, Syria's private sector more broadly has withdrawn its political and financial support, forcing the regime to become increasingly predatory in its extraction of desperately needed revenues. In response, officials have returned to the populist rhetoric of an earlier era, but with little practical impact thus far. With Syria's economy in a state of complete collapse, economic and social policy have become little more than tools in the regime's fight for survival. Nonetheless, its recent criticism of neoliberal economic reforms as responsible for the grievances that drove Syrians into the streets has echoed a theme often heard since 2011 from Arab governments, including both authoritarian survivors and those undergoing postauthoritarian transitions.

Opposition Responses to Regime Adaptation

The transformations undertaken by the Assad regime are not occurring in a vacuum. Nor is the gradual, bloody reconsolidation of the regime entirely a product of its own actions. It has benefited from an opposition that is divided along many different lines yet increasingly dominated by Islamist extremists. These latter include terrorist groups affiliated with al-Qaeda such as the Islamic State of Iraq and Syria and Ahrar al-Sham, whose vision for Syria's future is no less sectarian, repressive, and exclusionary than that of the Assad regime itself. The opposition leadership that has emerged outside Syria, including the National Coalition for Syrian Revolutionary and Opposition Forces (better known as the Syrian Coalition or SC) and its military wing, the Supreme Military Council (SMC), have repeatedly affirmed their intent to create a "civil democratic Syria."[17] The Syrian Muslim Brotherhood, which holds more seats within the SC than any other party or movement, in March 2012 publicly affirmed its commitment to "a civil and democratic republican state with a parliamentary system, in which all the people are treated equal regardless of faith or ethnicity."[18]

As violence within Syria has escalated, however, the external opposition has largely failed to establish its legitimacy, credibility, or even relevance to Syrians living under the authority of local and foreign armed groups. A significant (if hard to measure) segment of Syria's non-Sunni minorities and Kurdish population have not found the external opposition's commitment to a civil, inclusive democracy sufficiently credible to persuade them to abandon the Assad regime and join the uprising.

Such a commitment is even less evident among the opposition's internal leadership. The Free Syrian Army (FSA), a highly decentralized and loosely coordinated network of hundreds of armed groups, including local civil-defense units, groups of defectors from the Syrian military, and foreign fighters, was formally established in July 2011 to defend peaceful protests from regime attacks. By mid-2013, its numbers had increased, nominally, to some 80,000 fighters, yet less than a third of the battalions identified with the FSA could be said to operate under the leadership of the SMC.[19] Political authority within opposition-held territories has become increasingly concentrated in the hands of those who command local battalions, the largest and most effective of which are affiliated with Jabhat al-Nusra, Ahrar al-Sham, Liwa al-Mujahideen, and other salafist groups that explicitly reject democracy, espouse strict adherence to rigid interpretations of Islamic law, have themselves been accused of atrocities, and have contributed to the intensification of ethnosectarian tensions within the opposition—a trend that the Assad regime has avidly exploited.

The regime has particularly benefited from violent clashes among elements of the armed opposition. These fights have pitted moderate battalions loyal to the SMC against their salafist counterparts, Syrians against foreign fighters, and, most recently, Arab salafists against Kurdish forces in Syria's "liberated" northeastern regions. The Arab-nationalist rhetoric of the secular opposition and the Islamist ideologies of leading armed groups have fortified the ambivalence that Syria's Kurds feel regarding their role in the uprising and their future in a post-Assad Syria. Violent clashes between Kurdish forces and salafist battalions have reinforced the inclination among Kurdish political parties and movements to exploit the uprising on behalf of long-held demands for Kurdish autonomy.

Although Kurds, along with other minorities, are active in the political and military wings of the opposition, Kurdish leaders frequently complain about underrepresentation within opposition structures and preserve their independence from the SC. At times, Arab oppositionists have accused their Kurdish counterparts of cooperating with the Assad regime. These frictions have distracted the opposition while the regime reasserts its control over previously liberated areas. The frictions also increase the likelihood that Syria will end up fragmented into three warring zones: one controlled by the regime, one by the Arab opposition, and a third by Kurdish forces allied with Kurdish counterparts in northern Iraq and southeastern Turkey.

The transformation of Syria's opposition since 2011 has been remarkable. What began as a peaceful protest movement calling for democratic change and defended by moderate armed groups is now a thoroughly militarized, militantly Islamist armed movement wracked by internal fissures and frictions, bereft of a coherent and effective political leadership, and hard-pressed to respond to a reconsolidated regime backed by a stubbornly cohesive security apparatus. These changes have certainly contributed to the renewed momentum of the regime and its supporters. The shifts help to validate the opposition-as-terrorist narrative that the regime has cultivated from the start of the uprising. They sustain the defensive solidarity with the regime that is evident among Alawites and other minorities, many of whom are bound to the Assads more by fear than by loyalty. They have been exploited effectively by Russia and Iran in justifying their support for the Assad regime, and have eroded Western backing for the opposition.

Yet the course that the opposition has taken is not entirely a product of its own intentions or design. The Assad regime itself has helped to mold that course, by resorting immediately and disproportionately to violence when protests first broke out in March 2011, by relentlessly demonizing protesters, by sowing fear among the populace whom it still controls, and by creating disorder in the areas that it has lost to the opposition. In this sense, there are clear and significant interaction effects between how the regime has adapted to the challenges of mass politics—driving peaceful protests toward an armed insurgency—and the transformations experienced within the opposition. Extremism, polarization, and fragmentation are much easier targets for the regime than peaceful protesters seeking constitutional and economic reforms. Its cynical manipulation of the opposition succeeded, but at a terrible price. The regime has also failed to defeat the insurgency despite the concerted military efforts of Assad's forces, Hezbollah, Iran, and Russia. Indeed, even as the regime was regaining lost ground along the coast and in villages near Latakia, it continued to lose new ground to opposition forces in the south, in Aleppo, and on the outskirts of Damascus itself.

A Darker Outlook

The Assad regime's fate remains uncertain. The regime's learning and the adaptations that it has undergone since 2011 may not save it from defeat, and will surely (should it survive) weaken its ability to govern all or part of what remains of prewar Syria when the conflict ends. Yet some tentative conclusions can be drawn about the future of authoritarianism in Syria, and perhaps more broadly, from the ways in which the Assad regime has reconfigured itself since the outbreak of the Syrian uprising. Much of the Assad regime's experience is *sui generis,* driven by the scale of violence that it unleashed and by the distinctive resources at its disposal. Yet its underlying strategies reveal features that are visible to varying degrees among other authoritarian survivors in the Middle East as they struggle to adapt to the revival of mass politics. Few of these features offer a basis for optimism concerning Syria's democratic prospects—or the region's.

In Bahrain, Jordan, and Saudi Arabia, nervous and embattled rulers have turned to ethnosectarian and exclusionary strategies of popular mobilization in order to shore up regime support within divided societies. Regimes across the region have reconfigured and upgraded their coercive capacities to contend with mass protests, uprisings, or insurgencies. Democratization's chances, never strong to begin with, have suffered amid the fallout as dissent and protest have come to be defined as threats to the security of the nation. Syria presents additional disturbing elements: a regime whose social base has been welded into the security apparat; ordinary citizens who now act as agents of regime repression; regime-society relations defined to a disturbing degree by shared participation in repression.

In the Syrian case, this narrowing has been critical for regime survival. Yet it has also enhanced the capacity of an increasingly repressive and sectarian authoritarian regime to define postconflict political arrangements (if indeed the Assad regime survives the war); gives authoritarian allies greater influence over the terms of an eventual political settlement; and diminishes the leverage that Western democracies might bring to bear for the sake of moving Syria toward a more democratic postwar political order. Syria represents an extreme instance of these trends, but it is far from alone: The Arab uprisings have generated a broad increase in the interdependence of authoritarian survivors across the Middle East—tightening connections among the member states of the Gulf Cooperation Council (GCC) as they worked to help repress mass protests that threatened the ruling Khalifa family in Bahrain, for instance, and also strengthening ties between the GCC and the ruling monarchies of Jordan and Morocco

The uprisings of 2011 marked a moment of unprecedented challenge for the authoritarian regimes of the Middle East. The only world region that had experienced neither a single authoritarian breakdown nor a single transition to democracy found itself shocked by a wave of mass protests that led in less than a year to the overthrow of four longstanding autocrats—men who between them had held power for 132 years.

Yet for protesters across much of the rest of the Arab world, including Syria, the response was quite different. The Assad regime brought the full weight of its repressive apparatus down on the heads of peaceful protesters, provoking reactions that led gradually to civil war. Conflict has erased the Syria that existed prior to the civil war, yet it has not "annihilated" the authoritarian regime that drove Syria into the war. When it comes to details, the specific form that authoritarian adaptations have taken in the Syrian case differs from what we see elsewhere in the region. Yet the trends that civil war has amplified and exaggerated are not unique to Syria. Authoritarian survivors throughout the region have moved in directions similar to those evinced by the Assad regime. Even as the aftershocks of the Arab uprisings continue to make themselves felt across the Middle East, it seems that the future of Arab authoritarianism, like that of the Assad regime itself, will be darker, more repressive, more sectarian, and even more deeply resistant to democratization than in the past.

NOTES

1. M. Steven Fish and Matthew Kroenig, "Diversity, Conflict and Democracy: Some Evidence from Eurasia and East Europe," *Democratization* 13 (December 2006): 828–42; James D. Fearon and David D. Laitin, "Ethnicity, Insurgency, and Civil War," *American Political Science Review* 97 (February 2003): 75–90.

2. Virginia Page Fortna and Reyko Huang, "Democratization After Civil War: A Brush-Clearing Exercise," *International Studies Quarterly* 56 (December 2012): 801–808.

3. "Of the eighteen single countries that experienced UN peacekeeping missions with a political institution-building component between 1988 and 2002, thirteen (72 percent) were classified as some form of authoritarian regime as of 2003." Charles T. Call and Susan E. Cook, "On Democratization and Peacebuilding," *Global Governance* 9 (April–June 2003): 233–34.

4. Barbara F. Walter, "Conflict Relapse and the Sustainability of Post-Conflict Peace," Background Paper for the World Development Report, 2011, World Bank, Washington, D.C., 13 September 2010; Paul Collier et al., *Breaking the Conflict Trap: Civil War and Development Policy* (Washington, D.C.: World Bank, 2003).

5. Leonard Wantchekon, "The Paradox of 'Warlord' Democracy: A Theoretical Investigation," *American Political Science Review* 98 (February 2004): 18.

6. Steven Heydemann and Reinoud Leenders, eds., *Middle East Authoritarianisms: Governance, Contestation, and Regime Resilience in Syria and Iran* (Stanford: Stanford University Press, 2013).

7. Ellen Laipson et al., *Seismic Shift: Understanding Change in the Middle East* (Washington, D.C.: Henry L. Stimson Center, 2011). See also Eva Bellin, "Reconsidering the Robustness of Authoritarianism in the Middle East: Lessons from the Arab Spring," *Comparative Politics* 44 (January 2012): 127–49.

8. Steven Heydemann and Reinoud Leenders, "Authoritarian Learning and Authoritarian Resilience: Regime Responses to the 'Arab Awakening,'" *Globalizations* 8 (October 2011): 647–53.

9. Hassan Abbas, "The Dynamics of the Uprising in Syria," Arab Reform Initiative, *Arab Reform Brief,* No. 51, October 2011.
10. Reinoud Leenders and Steven Heydemann, "Popular Mobilization in Syria: Opportunity and Threat, and the Social Networks of the Early Risers," *Mediterranean Politics* 17 (July 2012): 139–59.

11. Steven Levitsky and Lucan A. Way, "International Linkage and Democratization," *Journal of Democracy* 16 (July 2005): 20–34.

12. Steven Heydemann, "Upgrading Authoritarianism in the Arab World," Saban Cen-

ter for Middle East Policy, Analysis Paper No. 13, Brookings Institution, Washington, D.C., 2007, 23.

13. Compare with Bellin, "Reconsidering the Robustness of Authoritarianism in the Middle East," 129.

14. Ariel Ahram, *Proxy Warriors: The Rise and Fall of State-Sponsored Militias* (Stanford: Stanford University Press, 2011).

15. Bassam Haddad, *Business Networks in Syria: The Political Economy of Authoritarian Resilience* (Stanford: Stanford University Press, 2012).

16. Caroline Donati, "The Economics of Authoritarian Upgrading in Syria: Liberalization and the Reconfiguration of Economic Networks," in Heydemann and Leenders, *Middle East Authoritarianisms,* 35–60.

17. See the website of the SC, *www.etilaf.org/en/about/principles.html.*

18. The statement can be found, in Arabic, on the website of the Syrian Muslim Brotherhood, *www.ikhwansyria.com.* See also an English summary of the text, *www.ikhwanweb.com/article.php?id=29851.*

19. Aron Lund, "The Free Syrian Army Doesn't Exist." *Syria Comment* (blog), 16 March 2013, *www.joshualandis.com/blog/the-free-syrian-army-doesnt-exist.* See also analysis conducted by the Syria Project of the Institute for the Study of War, *www.understandingwar.org/project/syria-project.*

25

BAHRAIN'S DECADE OF DISCONTENT

Frederic Wehrey

Frederic Wehrey is senior associate in the Middle East Program at the Carnegie Endowment for International Peace. He is the author of Sectarian Politics in the Gulf: From the Iraq War to the Arab Uprisings *(2014). This essay originally appeared in the July 2013 issue of the* Journal of Democracy.

Sparked by the protests in Tunis and Cairo, the 2011 Pearl Roundabout uprising was a watershed in the political life of Bahrain—an unprecedented challenge to the tiny island kingdom's ruling bargain and, ultimately, its social fabric. At first, the protests of the young activists who sparked the February 14 uprising were peaceful, while their demands were limited and nonsectarian—this last, an especially important point in a country where the Sunni al-Khalifa family rules a populace that is 70 percent Shia.

At their peak, the demonstrations would involve about a fifth of Bahrain's half a million people. Yet the protests' impressive size could not save them from being quickly undone. At the core of their failure lay not only the regime's use of force and political countermobilization, but also fissures in the opposition over goals and strategy. On February 17, government forces advanced on the iconic Pearl Roundabout—a key traffic circle in the capital of Manama—claiming the first lives in strife that has since killed more than a hundred people. On March 14, after protesters failed to respond to the crown prince's offer of public dialogue and blockaded the city's financial district, troops and armored vehicles sent by the Gulf Cooperation Council came rumbling across the King Fahd Causeway from Saudi Arabia. A few days later, authorities destroyed the roundabout with its lofty pearl-topped statue (meant to hail Bahrain's history as a center of pearl cultivation) in a failed bid to quash the uprising.

In July came an abortive stab at reaching a "national consensus" through a dialogue that al-Wifaq, the main Shia political "society" (parties are formally banned), first agreed to join and then quit. In November, a royally appointed but autonomous fact-finding body, the Bahrain Independent Commission of Inquiry (BICI), headed by the widely respected Egyptian international lawyer Cherif Bassiouni, released a report on the unrest that criticized the government's "use of unnecessary and excessive force, terror-inspiring behavior, and unnecessary damage to property." The report went on to denounce the government for arbitrary detentions, denial of medical care, and torture, chiding the opposition at the same time for brushing off the crown prince's dialogue offer.[1] The government has taken steps to act on the BICI's findings, but some observers dismiss these efforts as cosmetic and incomplete.[2]

As the regime and parts of the opposition began fresh talks in February 2013, many onlookers, including the United States, suggested using the BICI's report as a way to measure progress toward lasting reform. But the document is mostly about regime abuses in the security, labor, and judicial areas, and says nothing of the deeper structural deficiencies that fueled such heated dissent in the first place.

The BICI never explored how to fix Bahrain's weak bicameral parliamentary system, whose defects have long been at the heart of opposition discontent. By subordinating an elected 40-member parliament (the National Assembly) to an appointed consultative council (the Majlis al-Shura), the current structure deprives legislators of lawmaking and oversight authority. The opposition, as one of its members told me in Manama in 2006, sees the Assembly as a "toothless debating society" and the loyalist-dominated Majlis as a "buffer" that shields the ruling family from public accountability. For their part, government officials and members of the al-Khalifa family see the appointed Majlis as a critical check against what a Sunni member of the Majlis described to me as an "immature and fractious parliament that is prone to religious extremism." ("Extremism" in this case meaning a Shia challenge to the throne.) Looming over this debate is the domineering role of the al-Khalifa family's principal patron, the Kingdom of Saudi Arabia, which fears that the spectacle of an empowered parliament in Bahrain would spread the democratic contagion throughout the Gulf region.

For Bahrain to achieve lasting social peace, this basic dispute over the place and powers of parliament must be resolved. If that is to happen, each side will have to find a way to move forward despite the mistakes of the past. The opposition must avoid maximalist demands, boycotts, and an excessive focus on social legislation. For its part, the royal family must eschew its policies of gerrymandering electoral districts and "sectarianizing" parliament—coopting Sunni Islamists to balance and neutralize the power of Shia deputies. More important, the monarchy must breathe life into parliament and make it a real political institution through which elected representatives can deliver meaningful results to their constituents. It was al-Wifaq's inability to do anything like this during a five-year stint holding seats in parliament (2006 to 2011) that fueled the youthful rage behind the Pearl Roundabout uprising and now adds impetus to current protests.

Roots of Dissent

To understand why the "Arab Spring" upheavals hit Bahrain with so much force, one must follow the arc of parliamentary politics from the early reformist hopes of 2001 to the disenchantment and paralysis that suffused the atmosphere of late 2010. From 1961 through 1999, Bahrain's political landscape was dominated by a partnership between the late emir (the father of the current king) and his brother, who acted as prime minister. Under the two, whose family had ruled Bahrain since the late eighteenth century, a division of labor emerged. The emir enjoyed greater popularity owing to his accessibility and espousal of reform, while the premier acted as an authoritarian overseer who ran the island's bureaucracy, budget, and security forces.

In 1973, the emir set up a 30-member elected parliament with full legislative power, inaugurating a brief period of participatory politics. Two years later, however, he grew alarmed at a burgeoning alliance between leftist and religious blocs that would have effectively overturned a repressive state-security law, and he abruptly shut the legislature down. As Bahraini scholar Abdulhadi Khalaf has argued, this first parliament was never a truly democratic body, but rather a form of institutionalized tribalism and sectarianism guided by certain rules of conduct. Once a cross-sectarian coalition began to emerge and threatened al-Khalifa absolutism, the experiment was ended.[3] It was a pattern that would repeat itself again in late 2010.

Democratic reforms during the first half of the 1990s were mostly cosmetic. In 1993, the emir created the unelected Majlis, which had no legislative power and did not lead to any significant policy changes. The outbreak of a five-year period of largely Shia-led unrest in 1994 injected an economic urgency into demands for more substantial political reform.[4] Aside from Saudi oil subsidies, Bahrain's economy is largely dependent on financial services, offshore banking, tourism, and some heavy industry—all of which were threatened by the unrest.[5]

It was not until the old emir's death and the 1999 accession of Crown Prince Hamad to the throne that more substantial reform proposals began to take shape. Here again, questions of economics and preemption of trouble appear to have been foremost—the idea was to reassert state control after nearly six years of unrest, but without fundamentally altering the relationship between ruler and ruled.[6] The fresh reforms—the new emir framed them as "concessions"—included the right to form political "associations," the curtailment of state-security laws, the release of 320 political prisoners (including a Shia cleric who had been a major inspiration behind the 1994 dissent), the pardoning of dissidents abroad, and the creation of an elected 40-member parliament. In 2001, the emir introduced the National Action Charter, which called for the creation of a constitutional monarchy, a bicameral legislative structure comprised of an elected lower house and an appointed upper house, an independent judiciary, and women's political participation. It also gave all men and women over the age of twenty the right to vote. On 14 February 2001, voters strongly endorsed the document in a nationwide referendum. Much of Bahrain, and particularly its large numbers of relatively impoverished Shias, worked itself into a state of near-euphoria over these initiatives.[7]

By 2002, however, the reforms had either stalled or evaporated. Cynicism and resentment rose to new levels, particularly among the Shia. In October 2002, the emir, having now begun calling himself king and his son Salman the crown prince, issued restrictive "Press and Publication Laws" that gave the regime widespread censorship power. More gravely still, the king unilaterally changed the 1973 Constitution to make the Majlis superior to the elected parliament, which would no longer have the power to introduce new legislation or subject government ministries to financial oversight.[8] Today, activists and dissidents call these moves a pivotal moment in Bahrain's quick descent into authoritarianism. But the government sees it differently. As a Majlis member told me in 2006, "The parliamentary structure is designed so it couldn't be hijacked by extremists. We don't want a forty-person elected house composed of religious clerics who will ban alcohol, forbid women from driving, take Bahrain backwards, and drive away the foreigners who enjoy our liberal society."

The Parliamentary "Reprieve": 2002 to 2005

The weakening of parliament, along with gerrymandering designed to ensure Sunni dominance, spurred a widespread Shia boycott of the 2002 parliamentary elections. The boycott left parliament under the control of Sunni Islamists organized as a Muslim Brotherood affiliate (al-Minbar) and a salafist group (al-Asala). This gave the regime a chance to strengthen ties between itself and these parliamentary Islamists—an investment in preparedness that would pay crucial dividends when the Shia finally entered parliament in 2006.

By late 2005, the question of whether to join parliament was splitting the Shia opposition, with al-Wifaq in favor of participation and a more militant grassroots movement known as al-Haq opposing it. A year after the split came the November 2006 parliamentary election. Al-Wifaq, backed by senior Shia clerics, ran candidates. Al-Haq stayed on the sidelines, refusing to become involved in what it condemned as a rigged game.

The run-up to the 2006 elections was marred by widespread charges of gerrymandering, "floating" election sites, and voting by recently naturalized Sunnis. Most significantly, the disclosure of a semi-official government study, termed the "Bandar Report," hit the country's political life like a bombshell. The leaked document outlined an elaborate government plan to rig the elections and ensure continued Sunni dominance by coopting salafist and Muslim Brotherhood candidates and—still more outrageously in Shia eyes—by rapidly naturalizing Sunnis from Jordan, Pakistan, Saudi Arabia, Syria, and Yemen.[9]

Despite everything, al-Wifaq managed to win 17 of 40 seats—a significant gain, but still short of the majority needed to pass laws. The Sunni Islamist formations al-Asala and al-Minbar gained 8 and 7 seats respectively. Independent Sunnis won another 8 seats.[10] The final electoral results were a near-even split between Sunni and Shia, suggesting that parliament would be deadlocked. Al-Wifaq, meanwhile, now found itself challenged on one side by the Sunni Islamists in parliament and on the other by the militancy of al-Haq and its rejectionist allies in the "Shia street."

Polarization, Disenchantment, Repression

The years after 2006 saw the rise of three equally deleterious and mutually reinforcing trends: 1) The government and the Sunni Islamists working together to neutralize the Shia; 2) a worsening sectarianism within the weak parliament; and 3) a heightening of regional tensions interwoven with growing Bahraini Shia frustration (especially among the young), as al-Wifaq proved helpless to deliver any real reforms.

During the 2002 campaign, al-Minbar and al-Asala were often at odds, differing especially over the question of loyalty to the Bahraini state and constitution. The Muslim Brothers of al-Minbar swore allegiance to the constitution, whereas the salafists of al-Asala—sticking to their claim that the Koran is the only valid source of law—refused to take such an oath.[11] Aside from their ideological differences, the two groups stand for divergent sectors of Bahraini society: Al-Minbar appeals to a middle-class base, while al-Asala is closer to less-affluent Sunnis and tribal elements.[12]

Four years later, as the 2006 voting neared, the two groups shelved their differences to keep the Sunni Islamist vote together for the sake of countering an emerging coalition between al-Wifaq and a leftist formation known as al-Wa'ad. Numerous observers inside and outside Bahrain alleged that the royal family was deliberately encouraging and even funding the cooperation between al-Minbar and al-Asala, while leaving out a pair of alternative Sunni Islamist societies that it saw as too critical of the existing order. Those Sunnis who tried to remain independent or engaged in outreach to the Shia faced mounting pressure from other

Sunnis, often in social media. The Sunni Islamist MPs from al-Minbar and al-Asala, meanwhile, became even more entrenched supporters of regime policies and the sectarian status quo.

Given Bahrain's Gulf location, its Sunni-Shia tensions and other cleavages, and its lack of truly representative institutions, it is hardly surprising that sectarian strife in nearby Iraq (and to a lesser extent, Lebanon) reverberated strongly. Parliament itself often felt the heaviest shocks. In the wake of the 2006 Lebanon War and Iraq's Sunni-Shia violence, Bahraini MPs adopted increasingly sectarian positions on the dramatic events unfolding around them. Instead of legislating reforms that might improve the lives of their constituents, deputies tried to pass parliamentary expressions of solidarity with the defenders of Fallujah, Najaf, or Beirut. During loud and heated debates, Sunni MPs called their Shia counterparts "Sadrists," and were called "al-Qaeda" in return.

The mounting sectarian discord's ultimate winner was the ruling family. The gridlock and shouting matches confirmed the longstand-ing royal narrative of an "immature" parliament prone to sectarian and tribal passions and badly in need of supervision by the technocratic Ma-jlis. Who but the al-Khalifa family, went the clinching argument, could stand as arbiters shielding the delicate equilibrium of a divided society in a region beset by sectarian furies? "There are two ways," argued an al-Minbar member with whom I spoke in 2006. "Saddam's way or the al-Khalifa way. The al-Khalifas are mediators; without them, Bahrain would go the way of Lebanon or Iraq."

Throughout its time in the legislature, al-Wifaq faced criticism that its parliamentary "experiment" was failing. In its first year, there were signs that al-Wifaq was softening its advocacy with regard to "Shia is-sues" and trying to build cross-sectarian consensus.[13] In October 2007, U.S. diplomatic cables reported that the group's number two in parlia-ment had made a secret coordination deal with his al-Asala counterpart. The two sides, said the cable, "will support each other in the use of par-liamentary tools (investigation committees, hearings, and extraordinary sessions)." They also agreed not to block each other's legislative initia-tives.[14] Much of this cooperation may have stemmed from the belief of al-Wifaq's secretary-general, an official of that group told me in 2006, that Bahrain's Sunni Islamists were mostly moderates who could be-come productive partners if the hard-liners in their camp could be mar-ginalized. For its part, the Bahraini government told U.S. diplomats— concerned about a country that provides an anchorage to the U.S. Fifth Fleet and houses the U.S. Navy's main base in the Gulf region—that it appreciated al-Wifaq's efforts to keep order in the Shia street.[15]

Yet the outreach to the Sunni Islamists was destined to fail. Their limited notion of reform, the royal regime's continued obstructionism, and the region's growing sectarianism were too much to overcome. By 2008, frustration with the parliamentary experiment was simmering within al-Wifaq. Its secretary-general was reportedly telling U.S. diplomats that he was growing tired of enforcing discipline in party ranks and was hinting that he might resign.[16] In parliament, meanwhile, al-Wifaq walkouts were becoming more common.

One of the few areas where al-Wifaq could make some limited progress was the fight against corruption. But even here, the regime was obdurate and eventually lashed back furiously. In August 2010 came dragnet arrests of Shia oppositionists. A prominent Shia cleric lost his citizenship, and a Shia cabinet minister went to jail on charges of funneling money to Iran's Islamic Revolutionary Guard Corps. What triggered the crackdown? It was likely the cross-sectarian cooperation that had begun to appear in recent months around a shared desire to promote public integrity. Sunni and Shia legislators had put aside differences in order to pursue an investigation of the ruling family's appropriation of public lands.[17] In royal eyes, this was crossing a red line. According to what a Bahraini academic told me in early 2012, the government flouted the constitution by stopping the relevant committee of parliament from reviewing land records. "We were in the middle of a war," he said. "It was eight months of siege. The government was trying to break the back of the committee."

Despite this rough handling and the popular disappointment with its performance, al-Wifaq won all 18 seats that it contested in 2010, increasing its share of parliament by one seat. In many respects, its success was born of a realization that, whatever its failings, it was still the strongest option for real opposition. "People were angry with al-Wifaq, but they voted out of protest," a Bahrain observer told me in 2012. "And it had won some applause for its recent anticorruption investigation, which was its only real success." The Sunni Islamist groups, meanwhile, suffered losses. Al-Minbar went from 7 to 2 seats and al-Asala dropped from 8 to 3. Nevertheless, wins by 17 Sunni independents were enough to bar al-Wifaq from a majority.

Whatever potential had existed for the Bahraini parliament to resolve the crisis was undone at the Pearl Roundabout in the early morning hours of 17 February 2011—a day that lives on in the memory of protestors as "Bloody Thursday." In a predawn raid, Bahraini security forces in armored personnel carriers closed in on sleeping protestors, using rubber bullets, birdshot, and tear gas. At least four protestors were killed immediately; others died later. It was the prelude to what would become a systematic campaign of repression that would include arbitrary detentions, torture, denial of medical care, and unlawful killings. In a press statement defending the assault, the foreign minister invoked the specter of Bahrain falling into a "sectarian abyss." In fact, the attack hastened a Sunni-Shia split in what had originally been a populist, cross-sectarian protest.[18] In response, al-Wifaq pulled its 18 members out of parliament, dealing the troubled institution what amounted to a death blow.

Since then, Bahraini politics has largely been a story of widening fissures within the country's three main political camps. Al-Wifaq has found itself confronted by increasingly militant activists who gather under the umbrella of the February 14 Revolutionary Youth Movement. The ruling family is itself divided, with the king and crown prince heading a reform faction while the upper hand belongs to a more hard-line group led by the prime minister, the minister of the royal court, and the commander of the Bahrain Defense Forces. The Sunni Islamists are split between loyalist groups and oppositionist currents represented by the National Unity Gathering, an umbrella group of Sunni societies that emerged during the early days of the uprising.

Critics charge that the Gathering is yet another of the ruling family's ploys—an "opposition to the opposition" meant to stymie the Shia. Yet the Gathering's origins are hardly artificial. Instead, they reflect the growing anger of poorer Sunnis with the corruption and economic mismanagement of the royal family. In many ways, the Gathering's goals are not unlike those of the Shia opposition: As an al-Wifaq official told me in February 2012, the Gathering's agenda aligns with "90 percent of our demands, with the key exception of a fully empowered parliament."

Bereft of Shia representatives, the Bahraini parliament continues to function according to the pattern set as far back as 2002. Importantly, the inclusion of deputies from al-Asala and al-Minbar has served as a way for the ruling family to counterbalance the more activist and dissident strands of the Sunni "opposition" embodied in the National Unity Gathering. More than ever, parliament acts as a rubber stamp for the ruling family's policies. And it has still been susceptible to sectarian partisanship, this time focusing on Syria's escalating civil war.

The Saudi *Deus ex Machina*?

Several observers both inside and outside Bahrain have suggested that the February 2013 resumption of talks that marked the uprising's two-year anniversary sprang from a sea change in Saudi thinking about the country. Given the opaque nature of court politics in both these monarchies, this notion is nearly impossible to substantiate. Yet as the al-Khalifa family's chief economic and political patron, Saudi Arabia obviously has an impact on Bahraini politics that merits attention.

From 2002 to 2011, Saudi influence in Bahraini parliamentary politics loomed large. Conventional wisdom holds that Riyadh remains implacably opposed to any liberalization in the tiny island kingdom next door. It would be more accurate to say that the Saudis see *calibrated* political reform as a means to release pressure and marginalize more hard-line elements of the opposition. In this respect, Riyadh welcomed al-Wifaq's participation in the 2006 parliamentary elections because, at least for a time, it siphoned support away from the more rejectionist Shia currents embodied by al-Haq.

Ultimately, however, Riyadh remains opposed to giving the parliament real power. Typically this opposition is couched in terms of the need to counter Iranian subversion and influence. What the Saudis are really trying to prevent is not an Iranian takeover of the island through elections—Tehran does not want this, whatever its rhetoric, and the Saudis know it—but rather an experiment in truly participatory politics that will set what Riyadh sees as a dangerous precedent for the rest of the Gulf. Most immediately, the Saudi government worries about the effect of any Bahraini liberalization on Sunni liberals and also on the tenth of all Saudis who are Shia—and who mainly live in the kingdom's oil-rich Eastern Province. The rapidly spreading ripple effects and cross-sectarian reach of the Arab Spring taught Saudi authorities a lesson they will not soon forget.

As a result, the Saudis have pursued various strategies to shape the course of parliamentary life in Bahrain. In 2006, their influence took the form of funding for Sunni Islamist actors such as al-Asala, as well as the possible dispatch of tribal voters with dual citizenship to cast ballots in Bahrain. In the wake of the Pearl Roundabout uprising, Saudi efforts have focused on reestablishing order and equilibrium through dialogue—but, again, without any significant changes to the bicameral parliamentary structure. Throughout 2012, there were repeated intimations by Saudi and Bahraini officials that the two countries would form a formal political and military union. Although ostensibly aimed at mutual defense against Iran, the move carries a subtext of profound uncertainty about the durability of U.S. support and a desire to stave off continued domestic unrest. The opposition views the possible union as a ready-made source of excuses for regime hard-liners. They "can simply say, 'See, our hands are tied. The Saudis are calling the shots now,'" a Bahraini observer told me in 2012.

Reflecting the enormous importance of the island's affairs to Saudi Arabia's own security, it is reportedly the Saudi Interior Ministry and not the Foreign Ministry that deals with Bahraini matters. Some observers have argued that the June 2012 death of Saudi Arabia's conservative Prince Nayef, who ran the Interior Ministry, cost the Bahraini prime minister a key ally. Nayef's place has been taken by his 54-year-old son Muhammad, who may be more pragmatic and was reportedly the driver behind the al-Khalifa family's decision to restart negotiations with the opposition. Will the ongoing natural rise of second-generation princes—Nayef was one of the sons of Ibn Saud (d. 1953), the first king—lead to a looser Saudi policy toward Bahrain? It remains to be seen, though it seems likely that institutional changes within Saudi Arabia—an elected Majlis, for example—could be mirrored in Bahrain's own political system. But the Saudis are unlikely to endorse sweeping reforms that might threaten the al-Khalifa family's survival or promote undue Shia power—particularly at a time of unprecedented bilateral tensions with Iran.

The dramatic events unfolding in Tunis and in Tahrir Square may have sparked the Pearl Roundabout uprising, but the seeds of dissent were sown much earlier, as Bahrain's post-2001 parliamentary experiment came undone. Other causes of discontent are many, including corruption, housing shortages, shady land-reclamation deals, discrimination in government hiring, particularly in the police and military, unequal labor practices, and judicial excesses. But it was the failed parliament that became the poster child for the dashed hopes that fueled the youthful rage behind the uprising and continue to bedevil al-Wifaq today. Much of this disappointment sprang from the structural limitations that parliament labored under following the abrogation of the 1973 Constitution, as well as a government strategy of using the legislature to incite sectarianism so that the monarchy could play the role of arbiter. Finally, MPs themselves must share some of the blame owing to their political immaturity, brinksmanship, and failure to seize opportunities.

Behind the tentative steps toward dialogue, the Bahraini parliament continues to loom as the country's most contested institution and also the best-available foundation for lasting peace in the country and even for a political solution that would preserve al-Khalifa rule. Al-Wifaq is negotiating on the basis of its October 2011 Manama Document, which calls for a constitutional monarchy and an empowered parliament. Yet in the poorer Shia villages outside the capital—where currents of rejectionism run strong and al-Wifaq's appeal is limited—tolerance for the participatory option and even monarchy itself is wearing thin. Banners that once demanded an empowered parliament and a return to the 1973 constitution are now replaced by angrily scrawled graffiti that read "Down with [King] Hamad!" and "The people want the fall of the al-Khalifas."

NOTES

1. Report of the Bahrain Independent Commission of Inquiry, presented in Manama, Bahrain, on 23 November 2011 (final revision of 10 December 2011), 416, *www.bici.org.bh/BICIreportENG.pdf*.

2. The regime's steps may be reviewed at *http://houdanonoo.wordpress.com/2012/07/31/my-statement-to-the-tom-lantos-human-rights-commission*. For an example of criticism, see the Project on Middle East Democracy's assessment at *http://pomed.org/wordpress/wp-content/uploads/2012/11/POMED_BahrainReport_web-FINAL.pdf*.

3. Abdulhadi Khalaf, "Contentious Politics in Bahrain: From Ethnic to National and Vice Versa," paper presented at the Fourth Nordic Conference on Middle Eastern Studies, "The Middle East in a Globalizing World," Oslo, 13–16 August 1998, available at *www.smi.uib.no/pao/khalaf.html*.

4. For accounts of the uprising, see Munira Fakhro, "The Uprising in Bahrain: An Assessment," in Gary Sick and Lawrence Potter, eds., *The Persian Gulf at the Millennium: Essays in Politics, Economy, Security, and Religion* (New York: St. Martin's Press, 1997), 167–88; Fred H. Lawson, "Repertoires of Contention in Contemporary Bahrain," in Quintan Wiktorowicz, ed., *Islamic Activism: A Social Movement Theory Approach* (Blooming-

ton: Indiana University Press, 2004), 89–111; Graham Fuller and Rend Rahim Francke, *The Arab Shi'a: The Forgotten Muslims* (New York: St. Martin's Press, 1999), 21–54.

5. Katja Niethammer, "Voices in Parliament, Debates in Majalis, and Banners on Streets: Avenues of Political Participation in Bahrain," European University Institute Robert Schuman Centre for Advanced Studies, *Mediterranean Programme Serie*s, No. 27, 2006, 2.

6. 'Abd al-Nabi al-Ekri, "Bahrain: Reform Project: Prospect and Limitations," paper presented at the Sixth Mediterranean Social and Political Research Meeting, Montecatini, Terme, 16–20 March 2005.

7. International Crisis Group, "Bahrain's Sectarian Challenge" *ICG Middle East Report*, No. 40, Brussels: International Crisis Group, 6 May 2005, 7.

8. Niethammer, "Voices in Parliament," 5. Author's interview with a Shia activist, Manama, 8 November 2006.

9. Author's interview with a Bahraini academic, Manama, 6 November 2006. Also, 'Abd al-Nabi al-Ekri, "Bahrain: Reform Project."

10. See F. Gregory Gause III, "Bahrain Parliamentary Election Results, 25 November and 2 December 2006," *International Journal of Middle East Studie*s 39 (May 2007): 170–71.

11. Katja Niethammer, "Stubborn Salafis and Moderate Shiites: Islamic Political Parties in Bahrain," paper presented at the annual meeting of the International Studies Association, Chicago, 28 February 2007, available at *www.allacademic.com/meta/p181437_index.html*.

12. Muhammad 'Uthman, "Al-Faruq al-Salafiya fi al-Bahrayn," [Salafist groups in Bahrain], *al-Wasat* (Manama), 29 June 2005.

13. An activist for the cause of women's rights noted tacit cooperation between salafists and al-Wifaq over morality issues and social matters, such as inheritance and divorce laws. A prominent al-Haq leader also accused al-Wifaq of "flirting" with salafists. Author's interviews in Manama, November 2006.

14. U.S. Embassy, Manama, "Tactical Alliance Between Sunnis and Shi'a in Bahraini Parliament," 19 November 2007 (Wikileaks), *Telegraph* (London), 18 February 2011, available at *www.telegraph.co.uk/news/wikileaks-files/bahrain-wikileaks-cables/8334448/TACTICAL-ALLIANCE-BETWEEN-SUNNIS-AND-SHIA-IN-BAHRAINI-PARLIAMENT.html*. It is unclear if al-Wifaq's governing board approved the agreement.

15. U.S. Embassy, Manama, "Rivals for Bahrain's Shi'a Street: Wifaq and Haq" 4 September 2008 (Wikileaks), *al-Akhbar*, n.d., available at *www.al-akhbar.com/node/9124*.

16. Jane Kinninmont, "Bahrain: Assessing al-Wefaq's Parliamentary Experiment," *Arab Reform Bulletin*, Washington, D.C.: Carnegie Endowment for International Peace, 18 October 2007.

17. Habib Toumi, "Bahrain Pledges Zero-Tolerance, Arrests Opposition Figure," *Gulf News* (Dubai), 14 August 2010.

18. "Bahrain Pulled Back from 'Sectarian Abyss': Foreign Minister," *Reuters*, 17 February 2011.

26

ALGERIA VERSUS THE ARAB SPRING

Frédéric Volpi

Frédéric Volpi *is senior lecturer in the School of International Rela-tions of the University of Saint Andrews (Scotland). He is the author of* Political Islam Observed: Disciplinary Perspectives *(2010) and editor of* Political Civility in the Middle East *(2011). This essay originally ap-peared in the October 2011 issue of the* Journal of Democracy.

What accounts for continuing authoritarian success in the Arab world today? In light of the "Arab Spring," explanations of "authoritarian re-silience" in the region clearly need to be revised. Yet it is important to remember that many of these authoritarian regimes have weathered the storm well. As Sean Yom and Gregory Gause recently noted in these pages, most of the region's monarchies have so far remained unbowed by the winds of revolutionary change.[1] It is much harder—though not impossible—to identify Arab republics that have not been deeply and adversely affected by the wave of uprisings. In the Republic of Algeria, not only did the regime survive this tumultuous period, but it hardly deviated from its habitual methods of authoritarian governance. Is Al-geria the exception that confirms the rule? Or does it underscore the complexity of the mechanisms underpinning authoritarianism in the re-gion, and the limitations of revolutionary models of regime change of the Arab Spring? In my view, Algeria illustrates a type of authoritarian resistance to popular challenges that is based on pseudodemocratization, redistributive patronage, and an effective use of the security apparatus.

It would be misguided to evaluate the prospects for political change in the Middle East simply in light of the recent uprisings. The patterns of democratic revolutions and authoritarian resilience observed during the Arab Spring indicate that specific combinations of factors can be conducive to regime failure, but they hardly provide a comprehensive map of all the causes that can lead to regime change in the region. For one thing, authoritarian elites do learn from their mistakes and those of others; in that respect, the Algerian regime is no exception.[2] Furthermore, and somewhat counterintuitively, just because a particular regime survived this wave of revolts does not mean that it is strong or stable in the full sense, but only that it was not vulnerable to the particular forms of mobilization that marked those uprisings. Here again, Algeria is a good illustration. Despite its unsteady mode of authoritarian governance, the Algerian regime currently possesses the means to cope with the difficulties presented by popular uprisings. Yet it cannot survive in its current form for long, given its dwindling legitimacy, its lack of truly institutionalized mechanisms for transferring power, and the intrinsic limits of its system of patronage.

How did Algeria reach this pass, and what does that tell us about authoritarian resilience in the region today? Authoritarian stability during the Arab Spring was path-dependent and sprang from the combination of three sets of factors related, respectively, to institutions, the socioeconomic situation, and the security services. If an authoritarian regime survives mass protests, it does so because its mechanisms for decoupling social unrest from political mobilization—namely, pseudodemocratization, state patronage, and robust militarism—are effective. The authoritarian rulers prop themselves up with the help of a pseudodemocratic multiparty system that coopts and divides the opposition while generating a modicum of international recognition. They also entrench a patronage-based rentier economy that, in effect, buys social quiet with financial rewards. Finally, the well-resourced repressive apparatus is both willing and able to put down social unrest and armed rebellions.

What makes the case of Algeria during the Arab Spring all the more puzzling is that, compared to its North African neighbors (Morocco, Tunisia, Libya, and Egypt), it had long been a troubled polity where social order remained elusive. Colonized by France in the nineteenth century, Algeria won independence in 1962 after a deadly eight-year war. The National Liberation Front (FLN) had led the fight for independence, and afterward formed a one-party state. The National Liberation Army would repeatedly impose its choices on the FLN after the military coup of Colonel Houari Boumediene in 1965. After severe rioting and social unrest in 1988, the government introduced a series of political and economic reforms, and the country held multiparty local elections in 1990 and the first round of national parliamentary elections in late 1991.

This first attempt at democratization saw an Islamic constituency mobilize and come close to gaining state power—until the electoral gains of the Islamic Salvation Front (FIS) were wiped out by the military coup of January 1992. The fallout from this ill-fated move was nearly a decade of civil conflict between the military-backed regime and the newly created Armed Islamic Groups. It engulfed ordinary Algerians in a vicious cycle of brutality and retribution that claimed around 150,000 lives. Although the general armistice that marked the end of the Islamist insurrection in 1999 reduced the fighting to a level that was manageable for the government of newly elected President Abdelaziz Bouteflika (b. 1937) of the FLN, residual violence has continued to plague the country—most notably due to the activities of the Salafist Group for Preaching and Combat, an organization that in 2007 rebranded itself al-Qaeda in the Islamic Maghreb.

A principal consequence of the civil conflict was a fragmented political community in which nationalists, secularists, liberals, and Islamists distrusted each other as much as they distrusted the regime. Although the state had reclaimed a degree of legitimacy through the reestablishment of a (rather unrepresentative) parliamentary system, the regime had also been rocked by powerful social and political protests. The Berber "Black Spring" of 2001, in which more than a hundred demonstrators in the Kabylie region were killed while protesting against the regime's policies toward Berbers, showed how continuing failures of political dialogue—this time with Kabyle social movements—and heavy-handed repressive tactics ensured an atmosphere of mutual distrust in the country.

Algeria's electoral system—which lacked credibility despite praise from the international community for the regime's democratic reforms—did little to change these perceptions. Backed by the military, Bouteflika won the presidency unopposed in 1999. The other six candidates had withdrawn from the contest on the eve of the election, claiming that it was rigged. Bouteflika went on to win the 2004 and 2009 elections with 84 percent and 90 percent of the vote, respectively. (He was allowed to run in 2009 only after a constitutional amendment permitted him a third term.) Bouteflika's administration has been careful to include the Islamist Movement for a Peaceful Society (MSP) and the National Democratic Rally (RND; a party founded in 1997 by entrenched elites who backed the then-president, retired general Liamine Zeroual) in the governing coalition in order to widen its support base. Yet the token Islamist participation of the MSP, former competitors of the FIS, is not an indication of a substantive political opening; rather, it shows how the regime uses cooptation and patronage.

During the 2000s, the socioeconomic climate in Algeria remained harsh despite state subsidies and infrastructural investments paid for by oil and gas rents. In a leaked 2008 cable, U.S. ambassador Robert Ford told Washington that Algerians were striking nearly every week and that "almost daily there are isolated demonstrations, with the occasional government office in some distant town attacked."[3] In the year before the Arab Spring, Algerian newspapers regularly reported episodes of rioting in various parts of the country. Yet by the end of 2010, if the Algerian regime was not proving to be as solidly in control as its neighbors seemed to be, neither did it appear to be on the brink of collapse. Crucially, most Algerians did not consider the aging and increasingly incapacitated Bouteflika to be the main driver of the country's predatory regime, and therefore did not think that ousting him would dramatically improve their lives. Moreover, the partial political opening that the regime had orchestrated kept the dissensions within the opposition alive while giving many a stake in the status quo.

Missing the Revolutionary Bandwagon

At the beginning of 2011, Algeria was one of the first countries in the region to be affected by the wave of uprisings that had begun in Tunisia as 2010 ended. In Algeria, a deregulation of the state-subsidized economy triggered price hikes and shortages just as Algerians could see unrest reaching a crisis next door in Tunisia. Protests broke out in several of the poorer suburbs of Algiers and Oran on January 3. By the next day, rioting had spread to other areas near the capital. On January 5, there was major unrest in Algiers, Oran, and many other towns all around the country. Algeria's relatively free press covered the events, and soon riots were reported in twenty regions (*wilayat*). As the rioters—mainly young men—blocked roads, burned tires, and ransacked government buildings and commercial centers, the initial discontent over a decrease in subsidized staple goods gave way to protests over a wide range of socioeconomic grievances.

The shadow of the October 1988 riots loomed over these events, and the connection was explicitly made in the domestic press. While the socioeconomic complaints did resemble those of 1988, the roles of the military and the Islamists were different. Although former FIS leader Ali Belhadj and his supporters turned up at the demonstrations in Algiers, Islamists did not lead the protest or even turn out in large numbers. Likewise, the response of the security forces was nowhere near as brutal or lethal as it had been in 1988, when the army fired live ammunition at the crowds. In January 2011, by contrast, the security forces targeted key urban areas—in central Algiers around the Parliament, the Senate, and other government buildings—and simply abandoned the suburbs to the rioters.

A few days after the riots began, the government announced a reversal of the price increases and put in place new policies designed to lower the cost of food imports. This swift action appeared to meet the protesters' demands. Within a couple of days, most protests had subsided and mass public disobedience was losing momentum. Moreover, the relative restraint of the security forces ensured that state repression itself did not become the cause of further protests (as had happened in Tunisia). In this context of subsiding revolutionary fervor, even radical acts, such as a self-immolation on January 12, failed to reignite the contestation.[4]

During the Arab Spring, popular unrest and regime responses in Algeria ended up following rather predictable patterns and thus strengthened preexisting dynamics of state-society interactions. This does not mean that the Algerian regime used the "correct" combination of repression and cooptation to defuse a revolution, but merely that on this occasion what it did worked well enough. In 2011, popular unrest did not gather enough momentum to deinstitutionalize routine authoritarian practices and induce a reframing of the roles of the regime and the protesters. In the ensuing months, however, "normalcy" in Algeria still included regular protests—clashes with police, road blockades, strikes, ransacking of buildings, and so on—but these were disparate episodes rather than part of a nationwide event.

In the aftermath of the riots, however, a group of social and political organizations started a new and far less spectacular protest movement. On January 20, several opposition parties, nonlegalized unions, and civil society organizations joined forces to articulate the implicit political demands of the protesting crowds. These groups formed the National Coordination for Change and Democracy (NCCD) and issued a call for greater democracy, social justice, an end to the state of emergency, relaxation of media laws, and the release of imprisoned protesters, as well as more job opportunities.

As the movement signaled its intention to organize a demonstration against the regime, its call for public protest was swiftly echoed by the pro-Islamist activist network Rachad. Soon after, Saïd Saadi, the leader of the Rally for Culture and Democracy (RCD), a Berber political party, announced that the RCD was organizing a march for democracy in Algiers on January 22. The demonstration, which gathered a few hundred activists in central Algiers, was quickly broken up by a large police force that also prevented busloads of activists from entering the city to join the protest. In its turn, the NCCD announced that it would organize its own march on February 12. The regime made good use of the lull between the two protests to ease socioeconomic and political tensions. On February 3, the government indicated that the nineteen-year-old state of emergency would soon be lifted, opposition parties would be allowed greater airtime on state-controlled television and radio, and a new job-creation scheme was about to be implemented.

On 12 February 2011—the day after Egyptian president Hosni Mubarak resigned—protestors in Algeria responding to the NCCD's call converged on May First Square in central Algiers. In an event that some viewed as a miniature version of Cairo's Tahrir Square protests, around three-thousand protesters managed to occupy the square for a while after breaking through police lines. Yet in Algiers, unlike in Cairo, security forces outnumbered protesters by ten to one; about thirty-thousand police had been mobilized for the occasion. Riot police blocked would-be protesters from neighboring suburbs and other towns from reaching the center of the capital to participate in the demonstration in May First Square.

One incident in particular illustrated the NCCD's difficulties at unifying the opposition: Former FIS leader Ali Belhadj and several dozen of his supporters were pushed back while trying to join the demonstration.

The expulsion of Belhadj and his cohort was not the work of the police, however, but rather of the demonstrators themselves, who feared that the Islamists might hijack their protest. The impact of the 1992 military coup and the civil conflict on Islamic-secular relations is such that leftist and liberal actors prefer to go it alone against the regime at the risk of failure, rather than seek a potentially more powerful coalition with the Islamists.

The February 12 demonstration illustrated the limited capabilities of the NCCD to unite different opposition forces in the country and to connect with the large number of depoliticized youth who had driven January's social protests. Undaunted, the NCCD called for demonstrations to continue every Saturday in May First Square. The following week, on February 19, a similar protest was duly organized, with the same disappointing turnout. The choice of Saturday for weekly demonstrations—despite earlier calls by Islamic groups such as Rachad to hold the protests on Fridays—further entrenched the divide between liberal secularists and Islamists. The symbolic death knell for the NCCD was probably a March 7 rally in Algiers of tens of thousands of communal guards—local police auxiliaries that the regime had organized in the countryside to hinder the activities of Islamist guerrillas—demanding better pay and greater recognition for their role during the civil conflict. This rally mobilized far more protesters than the NCCD ever had and temporarily disrupted police control of central Algiers. It illustrated that even a well-oiled security apparatus could be outfoxed, as long as protesters had the numbers and surprise on their side.

Patronage and Militarism

Comparing Algeria to Tunisia, Jack Brown observed how counterintuitive it was that Algerian civil society had not done a better job of harnessing the momentum of the January 2011 riots for their February demonstrations, since Algeria under Bouteflika had a freer and livelier civil and political society than Tunisia under Ben Ali.[5] What the February political protests showed, however, is that this greater political space can actually be a hindrance to large-scale mobilization if opposition forces are powerful enough to turn out their core constituencies but too weak to attract support beyond them, not least because of an unwillingness to create cross-ideological alliances. The political unrest in February was far less significant in scope than the social unrest in January, when the motley crew of demonstrators could join in the protest for any reason. In February, protesters had to subscribe to a particular agenda to join the movement, which disempowered the crowds by dividing them into competing factions. This same predicament prevailed throughout the 2000s and was most vividly illustrated by the Berber Black Spring of 2001.

By March 2011, it was clear that the initial wave of Arab uprisings would not affect Algeria in the way that it had its eastern neighbors. In Algeria, the return to normalcy meant the routinization of discontent and disorder through semi-institutional mechanisms designed to render such displays of disaffection nonthreatening to the ruling elite. In March in Algiers, typical instances of social unrest included nearly two-hundred youths throwing stones and Molotov cocktails at the police, a crowd of several hundred protesters similarly attacking the police and contractors headed to bulldoze a shantytown, and the like. That same month, socioeconomic discontent generated at least seventy strikes throughout the country by professional associations and unions—from teachers to rail workers and doctors to court clerks. As Ali Chibani remarked at the time, the regime's position of relative weakness "is well understood by Algerians who recognize that now is the time to obtain promotions and improve their working conditions and their social circumstances."[6] The dynamics of these strikes, which would remain commonplace throughout the year, illustrate the continuing relevance of the traditional social contract proposed by the Algerian regime: The administration provides better socioeconomic conditions in exchange for continuing (albeit grudging) political quiescence.

In May 2011, in an effort to finance the concessions made to various striking sectors, the Algerian government unveiled a revised budget that increased public-sector spending by a massive 25 percent. This spending spree constituted an affordable short-term option for a regime seeking to buy its way out of trouble, Gulf-monarchy style. Yet, with an ever-expanding public sector—and a much larger population than in the Gulf—the Algerian state has burdened itself with a soaring wage bill that can only be paid as long as oil and natural-gas prices keep rising.[7]

As Luis Martinez has noted, the regime's ability to reorient system-challenging unrest into more mundane benefit-seeking protests stems from the economic system, which has been modeled over the years to buttress the patronage structures that ensure dependence of the population and local elites on the state elite's redistribution of oil and gas rents. In 2010, these rents "accounted for 60 percent of [Algeria's] budget revenues, 36 percent of its GDP, and over 97 percent of its export earnings."[8] This patronage system can expand and contract depending on the economic and political circumstances, and as the events of the late 1980s and early 1990s illustrate, periods of contraction are costly for the regime. Tellingly, throughout the 2000s, the Bouteflika administration consistently and deliberately underestimated the price of oil and gas in its budget calculations so as to build large reserves of foreign currency that could be used precisely at times when the regime needed to counter dissent with financial incentives.

In addition to the support that it derives from the patronage system, the regime also owes its resilience to the backing of the security forces, as the 2011 protests illustrated. This is not to be understood simply in terms of the sheer repressive capability of the state, impressive though it is—the police and the gendarmerie were bolstered during the civil conflict of the 1990s, and by the end of the 2000s they numbered more than 200,000 all told. The strength of the security forces stems more from the effectiveness of their response to the unrest. In that respect, the repressive apparatus of January 2011 was far superior to that of October 1988, when the army killed more than five-hundred demonstrators in just over ten days. During the week of rioting in January 2011, only three demonstrators died. In addition, at the end of February 2011, the government lifted the state of emergency that had been in place since the 1992 military coup. This symbolic concession was counterbalanced, however, by the adoption of new "antiterrorism" measures granting the security forces extensive freedom of action with regard to any matter that they deemed "a threat to the nation"—demonstrations in the capital included.

Some analyses of "robust" authoritarianism in the Middle East note that, in addition to the actual repressive capabilities of the security forces, two other aspects of repression are crucial to authoritarian rule: The first is the willingness of the military leadership (and other key security actors) to use force, and the second is the material and ideational interests of the military and other key security forces.[9] For the Algerian military, these material interests have included not only a budget that has increased yearly during the 2000s in order to sustain existing levels of patronage, but also a more direct interest in various public and private-sector ventures. Steven Cook likened the 1980s-era generals to "godfathers" who intervened in the delivery of business licenses and exclusivity contracts.[10] The 2000s, meanwhile, have seen the ongoing involvement of military figures in crony capitalism and corruption scandals—most spectacularly in relation to the national oil company, Sonatrach, in early 2010.[11]

The rank-and-file security personnel have benefited, too. In December 2010, the government announced that the wages of most police forces—totaling 170,000 personnel—were to increase by 50 percent and would include a three-year back-pay deal. Similarly, in December 2011 military personnel saw their salaries go up by 40 percent, also with a three-year back-pay package. Unmistakably, the postcolonial social contract of socioeconomic gratification in exchange for quiescence applied even more to rank-and-file members of the security apparatus than it did to the populace at large.

Over the years, the upper ranks of the Algerian military have repeatedly proved willing and able to use lethal force on a massive scale to secure their preferred system of political governance. This pattern of intervention—and the belief of many junior officers that their oversight of politics is good for the country—has entrenched a neopraetorianism that leaves little chance for a protest-induced regime-change scenario in which the military stands by and lets a revolt run its course.[12] Specialists have been predicting for years that the military would progressively lose influ-

ence—not least due to the dying off of the older generation of leaders—
but this has not yet translated into significant institutional and behavioral
changes. In the current international and sociohistorical context, it seems
unavoidable that the military's influence will wane over time; the Turkish model and some steps taken by the Egyptian military illustrate such
trends. In the short term, however, the neopraetorian dynamics in Algeria
constrain the kinds of political changes that are likely to occur. The vicious circle created between low mobilization and low-cost repression is
self-reinforcing. In addition, the population's weariness of conflict since
the 1990s contributes to the perception that, even if a revolt were to succeed, it could generate more unwanted violence and misery.

Authoritarian Upgrading After the Revolts

In April 2011, President Bouteflika went on national television to tout
his Arab Spring–inspired program of reforms. The president announced
"political reforms to deepen the democratic process and to enable the
citizens to better contribute to the choices that shape their future."[13] In
practice, however, this initiative resulted only in the establishment of a
commission to organize limited constitutional reforms, broader access
to national television and radio for opposition parties, and a revision of
the electoral code to facilitate the creation of new political organizations. The underwhelmed response of the main opposition parties and
civil society organizations to these propositions was reflected in their
decision to boycott the consultation process of the committee charged
with drafting the constitutional amendments the following month.

In an effort to show that the electoral reforms had substance, the Interior
Minister Daho Ould Kablia eagerly announced at the start of October 2011
that all new parties applying for recognition would be legalized before the
end of the year. In practice, however, the proliferation of microparties—
nearly doubling the number of existing political parties from 22 to 40—
merely enabled the expansion of the regime's patronage network via business politics. Most of the new parties were either splinter groups of existing
parties—especially the FLN and the RND—or vehicles for self-promotion
by personalities and businessmen close to the regime.[14]

The electoral victories of Islamist parties in Morocco, Tunisia, and
Egypt raised some international observers' concerns about an Islamist
resurgence in Algeria's 10 May 2012 elections for the National People's
Assembly (the lower house of Parliament). Lending credence to these
fears was the MSP's withdrawal from the ruling coalition in January
2012 in order to join forces with two smaller Islamist opposition groups,
Islah and Ennahda, to form the Green Algeria Alliance. Algerians, however, were skeptical of the credentials of this new Islamist alliance,
which was dominated by political actors with a long history of cooperating with the regime—even during the unrest in 2011—and who only

moved to the opposition during the run-up to the elections. Moreover, the regime reaffirmed its policy of containing the Islamist vote with legislative amendments that prohibited political actors previously associated with the FIS from creating new parties. In this context, as seasoned analysts of Algeria had predicted and as the regime had planned, the parliamentary elections brought few surprises.[15]

Most of the new parties struggled to win just 1 or 2 percent of the vote, and none—not even the vaunted Green Algeria Alliance, which stayed stuck in single digits and won only 49 of 462 seats—emerged as a significant opposition force. If anything, the regime's tinkering with the electoral rules may have been too effective for its own good. Although the country's proportional-representation, largest-remainder system with a 5 percent threshold for earning seats remained intact, having so many opposition parties compete considerably boosted the FLN's electoral performance. The ruling party won 45 percent (208) of the seats in the Assembly—an outcome that was all the more remarkable given that the FLN received only a little over 17 percent of the vote. The RND, also a member of the ruling coalition, was the next-highest seat earner with 69. The Front of Socialist Forces and the Workers' Party won 27 and 24 seats, respectively. The remaining seats were divided among independent candidates and more than twenty other parties.[16]

Internationally, the stability of Algeria's pseudodemocratic system was once again commended. The elections were "a welcome step in Algeria's progress toward democratic reform," said U.S. secretary of state Hillary Clinton.[17] Domestically, the election results generated the usual level of suspicion and incredulity from the Algerian public and political actors, and accusations of vote rigging and manipulation flew. In short, by encouraging an explosion of tiny new parties in an attempt to make the political field appear more pluralistic, the regime in fact (re)produced an ultradominant-party system. Yet in the new post–Arab Spring regional context, such authoritarian maintenance of the status quo suddenly appeared abnormal.[18]

The patron-client economic programs that the regime had devised in the run-up to the 2012 local and parliamentary elections helped to mobilize those voters who would directly benefit from these subsidies. The show of electoral strength by the pro-regime parties (FLN and RND) was akin to the mass demonstrations of public support that the state party organized in the 1960s and the 1970s. Indeed, since the 1992 military intervention, elections have always swung massively (and suspiciously) in favor of candidates and parties representing the incumbent leadership. At the same time, this system of political patronage generates constant infighting in and among regime-aligned parties, as different networks try to maximize their gains and leverage vis-à-vis the central administration. In Algeria, the flurry of political activity leading up to the 2014 presidential election should not obscure the limited political opportunities that the country's electoral model allows. As long as the ruling elite makes sure to keep power within its ranks, it will be able to manage a smooth transition, and the state-party system and its pseudodemocratic successor will remain mere tools for this rotation of power.

Thus, who better to replace the current president in the forthcoming election than someone just like him? Who better to sit at the head of state than a longtime member of the ruling elite who knows how not to upset a system that works (at least for members of the elite)? The presidential election scheduled for April 2014 presents an opportunity for the regime to ease into office someone ostensibly new, but who would not upset the status quo in any significant way. Unsurprisingly, in the first half of 2013 the most touted potential replacements for Bouteflika are all well known to both the regime and the electorate—FLN secretary-general Abdelaziz Belkhadem, current prime minister Abdelmalek Sellal, and former prime ministers Ahmed Ouyahia, Ahmed Benbitour, Mouloud Hamrouche, and Ali Benflis.

As for the Islamists, will they eventually be able to mount a successful, institutionalized political challenge to obtain at least a share of state power, as has happened elsewhere in the region? For now, that seems an unlikely possibility in Algeria, even if we take into consideration the foothold inside ruling circles of former public-works minister Amar Ghoul, formerly of the MSP. Indeed, both Islamist and liberal opposition forces are still searching for a new kind of leadership and organization that will enable them to mount a convincing challenge to the ruling elites, either on their own or as part of a yet-to-be-imagined grand coalition. It is doubtful that will happen in time for the 2014 presidential election, but it is bound to happen at some point. When it finally does, the dynamics of authoritarianism in Algeria—patronage, neopraetorianism, and all—will change significantly.

NOTES

The author wishes to thank Francesco Cavatorta and Yahia Zoubir for their valuable comments on previous versions of this essay.

1. Sean L. Yom and F. Gregory Gause III, "Resilient Royals: How Arab Monarchies Hang On," *Journal of Democracy* 23 (October 2012): 74–88.

2. Steven Heydemann and Reinoud Leenders, "Authoritarian Learning and Authoritarian Resilience: Regime Responses to the 'Arab Awakening'," *Globalizations* 8 (October 2011): 647–53.

3. Ambassador Robert Ford, "Scene Setter for A/S Welch Visit to Algeria," U.S. Embassy in Algiers, 28 February 2008, *http://wikileaks.ch/cable/2008/02/08ALGIERS198.html#*.

4. There would be dozens of attempted or successful self-immolations across the country in the following few weeks. See Chawki Amari, "Je brûle, donc je suis, " *Courrier International* (Paris), 21 January 2011.

5. Jack Brown, "Algeria's Midwinter Uproar," *Middle East Report Online*, 20 January 2011, *www.merip.org/mero/mero012011*.

6. Author's translation; Ali Chibani, "En Algérie, répression et opportunismes," *Le Monde diplomatique*, 8 April 2011.

7. "Economic Health Check: Algeria Should Reduce Reliance on Oil, Create More Jobs, Says IMF," *IMF Survey Magazine*, 26 January 2011, *www.imf.org/external/pubs/ft/survey/so/2011/int012611a.htm*.

8. Luis Martinez, *The Violence of Petrodollar Regimes: Algeria, Iraq and Libya,* trans. Cynthia Schoch (New York: Columbia University Press, 2012); for quote, see the Energy Information Administration, "Country Analysis Briefs: Algeria," 8 March 2012, *www.eia.gov/cabs/Algeria/pdf.pdf*.

9. Eva R. Bellin, "Reconsidering the Robustness of Authoritarianism in the Middle East: Lessons from the Arab Spring," *Comparative Politics* 44 (January 2012): 127–49.

10. Steven A. Cook, *Ruling but Not Governing: The Military and Political Development in Egypt, Algeria, and Turkey* (Baltimore: Johns Hopkins University Press, 2007).

11. John P. Entelis, "Algeria, Revolutionary in Name Only," *Foreign Policy.com*, 7 September 2011, *http://mideast.foreignpolicy.com/posts/2011/09/07/algeria_revolutionary_in_name_only*.

12. See Isabelle Werenfels, *Managing Instability in Algeria: Elites and Political Change Since 1995* (New York: Routledge, 2007).

13. "Discours du Président de la République à la Nation," Algiers, 15 April 2011, *www.elmouradia.dz/francais/president/activites/PresidentActi.htm*.

14. These include the Future Front, led by Abdelaziz Belaid; the Youth Party, led by Hamana Boucharma; the Party of Dignity, led by Mohamed Ben Hammou; the Front of Rightly Guided Governance, led by Aissa Bel-Hadi; the Movement of Free Citizens, led by Mustapha Boudina; and New Dawn, led by Tahar Benbaibeche.

15. See Yahia H. Zoubir and Ahmed Aghrout, "Algeria's Path to Reform: Authentic Change?" *Middle East Policy* 19 (Summer 2012): 66–83.

16. See National Democratic Institutions, "Final Report on Algeria's Legislative Elections, 10 May 2012," *www.ndi.org/files/Algeria-Report-Leg-Elections-ENG.pdf*.

17. Press statement of U.S. secretary of state Hillary Rodham Clinton on Algerian elections, Washington, D.C., 12 May 2012, *www.state.gov/secretary/rm/2012/05/189811.htm*.

18. Steven Heydemann, "Upgrading Authoritarianism in the Arab World," Brookings Institution, *Saban Center Analysis Paper Series,* No.13, October 2007.

27

MOROCCO: OUTFOXING
THE OPPOSITION

Ahmed Benchemsi

Ahmed Benchemsi *is a visiting scholar at Stanford University's Center on Democracy, Development, and the Rule of Law. An award-winning journalist, he founded and was the publisher and editor of* TelQuel *and* Nishan, *Morocco's two best-selling news magazines. This essay originally appeared in the January 2012 issue of the* Journal of Democracy.

On 1 July 2011, voters in Morocco cast ballots in a constitutional-reform referendum that the government claimed drew a turnout of 73 percent and passed with a near-unanimous 98.5 percent majority. That such a turnout was abnormally high by international as well as Moroccan standards,[1] that there is a history of rigged constitutional referendums in Morocco, that such exaggeratedly lopsided results are unknown in open and fair elections, and that holding a referendum a mere two weeks after announcing it is unusual (to say the least) by normal democratic standards seemed to trouble surprisingly few Western observers.

Instead, the favorable press that had begun flowing even before King Mohammed VI gave his June 17 speech outlining the reform package continued to roll in. It received an assist from Beckerman, the New York public-relations firm that the Moroccan government retains to encourage upbeat stories about the country, but the basis for the positive ink was something deeper than standard-issue PR flackery and story placement. One might call this something the "relativity effect." Since the beginning of the year, all the news from the Arab world had been about revolutions, strife in the streets, and bloody police or military onslaughts against peaceful protesters. By contrast, Morocco's comparatively mild (albeit not quite nonviolent) management of its own protests seemed a model of reasonableness. Refusing to gun down demonstrators hardly makes a government democratic, but the media—perhaps eager for something different from the usual "autocratic Arab regimes behaving badly" stories—was nonetheless willing to run with the "Arab world's shining democratic exception" narrative.

In truth, the official Moroccan reaction to the upheavals that began in Tunisia in December 2010 was not only fairly restrained (though there were beatings and three protesters were killed), but also remarkably well managed. On 9 March 2011, not long after Ben Ali and Mubarak went down and less than three weeks after the first protesters appeared on Moroccan streets, King Mohammed gave a rare televised address. In it, he dramatically promised "comprehensive constitutional change" featuring "the rule of law," an "independent judiciary," and an "elected government that reflects the will of the people, through the ballot box." This was in truth a clever preemptive move, designed more to break the protests' momentum than to bring genuine change. The composition of the constitutional-reform commission that the king appointed the next day spoke volumes. It consisted of eighteen civil servants and was headed by a constitutional-law professor with a history of condoning autocracy.[2]

Still, the draft that this body produced might have featured bolder reforms if the protest movement (known as Feb20 after the day on which demonstrations began) had mustered enough savvy to keep the pressure on. Instead, the young Facebook activists who were calling the shots continued to rely solely on popular fervor, as if that would last forever. Crippled by inexperience as well as internal conflicts between Islamists and leftists, Feb20 failed to produce key leaders, central structures, or much of an agenda beyond "Down with absolutism!" sloganeering. With nothing but a single unstable asset—mass enthusiasm—the protest movement lost momentum and petered out even as the regime was maneuvering effectively to counter it.

The monarchy, meanwhile, played skillfully for time. It allowed street demonstrations to go unchallenged (and collected favorable Western media notices for its tolerance) from their inception in late February until the activists' numbers began to dwindle in May—at which point the police became more active with their truncheons. By the end of May, dozens of protesters had been injured and one had died. Then the Interior Ministry began to mobilize counterdemonstrators. Unlike the nonviolent Feb20 people, these proregime toughs showed up armed with stones and clubs, openly spoiling for fights while the police looked the other way.

On June 17, as tension was peaking, the king spoke again on television to introduce the draft constitution and announce the July 1 referendum. The rush to a vote was obviously meant to take full advantage of the monarchy's new momentum by leaving opponents almost no time to organize. The campaign period was outrageously dominated by the regime and its mouthpieces. State-controlled television stations and mosques sang the new constitution's praises. On election day itself, reports of fraud came from virtually every corner of the Kingdom. As videos posted online showed officials rummaging in open ballot boxes, scores of voters testified that no identity checks had been performed at polling stations, thus enabling widespread ballot-stuffing. To veteran observers of Moroccan politics, the lopsided official results announced that night came as no surprise.

Yet in spite of all this, it is fair to acknowledge that Moroccan officials worked hard to back up their case for the new basic law. Despite the hasty referendum and its embarrassingly hard-to-credit result, the constitution does appear to offer some support to those who would like to see it as a silver lining to these unseemly events. Yet closer scrutiny dims the luster.

Deception: State of the Art, and an Art of the State

From the outset of the reform movement's demonstrations, its top demand had been the creation of a "parliamentary monarchy." The crowds had also called for the "separation of powers" and "accountability by those in charge." All three of these can be found in the new basic law's first article, which defines the very foundations of the Kingdom's regime. As for the king himself, he made a pair of highly regarded moves by abandoning his constitutional "sacredness" and binding himself to choose a prime minister exclusively from the ranks of the party that wins legislative elections. The prime minister, in turn, enjoys new constitutional powers. Finally, the new constitution severs all ties between judges and the Justice Ministry, and solemnly declares that judicial power is independent of executive power.

At first glance, these look like major concessions. The king may not have abandoned all his powers, but he seems to have curtailed a significant part of them. More decisively, the new constitution seems to subject executive authority to the broad standards of human rights and, if not democracy, at least fairly balanced power sharing. Hence, Morocco may well be, after all, the "Arab exception" that the international media are so eager to commend.

Or maybe not.

Let us be clear: All the foregoing provisions are indeed found in the new constitution, and Morocco is a place where the constitution matters and is taken seriously by all. But here is the tricky—and yes, possibly the exceptional—thing about Morocco: Nothing is quite what it seems. Whoever does a closer reading of the new document, or takes the trouble to consider its articles in relation with one another, or views the whole text in light of other legal texts and the larger political, economic, and social context of the country will understand how misleading appearances are. Morocco's monarchy has made some concessions, but they are less than meets the eye, and autocratic features remain.

The current king's father, Hassan II, ruled for 38 years (1961–99), and during that time made deception an art of the state. In a freshly decolonized Third World where one-party systems were the norm, he made sure that Morocco's 1962 Constitution enshrined multipartism. Yet his concern was less to foster democracy than to set up a divide-and-rule dynamic. He created puppet parties (complete with election results rigged in their favor) to counter those who might dare to dispute royal supremacy, and secured the election of charismatic oppositionists for their public-relations value as members of parliament. Even while engaging in such stratagems, he always insisted that he was a neutral arbiter above the political fray. Anyone who complained too long or too loudly about his Machiavellian duplicity risked jail, torture, or—in rare cases—assassination.

Like many of his counterparts in the Third World—and all his Arab peers—King Hassan could have skipped the illusion game altogether and held himself up as an enlightened despot from whom almost everything proceeded. But he was a despot of another kind—the kind who enjoys praise and recognition abroad as much as absolute power at home. Consequently, he devoted as much time and energy to burnishing his image as a wise, democracy-friendly statesman as he did to maintaining his iron grip on Morocco. To that end, the country's key institutions and laws (and above all its constitution) were carefully engineered to give the appearance of relative openness while remaining flawed enough in substance to leave plenty of room for corruption and autocratic *dirigisme*.

Thus when it comes to marketing itself, however spuriously, as a poster child for democratic aspirations, the Moroccan monarchy has longstanding expertise—certainly more than any other regime in the Arab world has ever developed. It comes as no surprise, then, to find that the Kingdom's new constitution may look generally liberal but in fact maintains and even strengthens the forces of absolutism and oligarchy.

"A Tongue Has No Bone"

The first of the regime's marketing techniques is a universal classic: lip service. If we compare the new constitution to the former one, we see that the Preamble has grown five times longer, with a section of "General Dispositions and Fundamental Principles" that is more than eight times the length of its predecessor. The new text's introductory sections flood the reader with good intentions, beginning with this:

> Faithful to its irreversible choice to build a democratic State based on the rule of law, the Kingdom of Morocco resolutely continues the process of consolidating and reinforcing the institutions of a modern State, the fundamentals of which are the principles of participation, pluralism and good governance.[3]

It goes on like that for pages, with little that is concrete but much that is glowing and high-sounding, as if the goal were to please everyone (liberals, Muslim conservatives, Western opinion leaders) by name-checking every possible reference (human rights, Islamic law, international conventions, and the like). As a Moroccan proverb goes, "A tongue has no bone," meaning roughly, "You can twist it as much as you want" (or in other words: talk is cheap, and words can be used with little regard for their real implications).

Another proverb, this one in English, says that one cannot have one's cake and eat it too. Yet Morocco's monarchy is trying hard. Whether out of conviction or a desire to look good in the concert of nations, the government has over the years ratified scores of international human-rights accords. As it happens, some of these (including the International Covenant on Civil and Political Rights, or ICCPR) grant freedoms (such as those of thought, conscience, religious opinion, and religious practice) that are intrinsically denied by certain pieces of national legislation (such as the Penal Code, which basically subjects the spiritual, social, and sexual lives of Moroccans to Islam).[4] By affirming in the constitution's Preamble that "duly ratified international conventions" will be accorded "primacy over the internal law of the country," the monarchy seems courageously to bind itself to respect human rights, to the detriment of its Islamic power base.

Regime apologists have made much of this, but wait: The same passage puts matters in a different light by also declaring that this primacy is to be accorded only "within the framework of the dispositions of the Constitution and laws of the Kingdom, in respect of its immutable national identity" (namely, Islam). If you think it through, having "primacy" over a thing (Moroccan law) only "within the framework" set by this same thing makes no sense. As if the constitution's authors had a feeling that not everyone would be fooled, they closed by stating the Kingdom's commitment "to harmonize in consequence the pertinent dispositions of its national legislation." Who shall decide which laws are "pertinent" when it comes to meeting international human-rights standards? The constitution does not say. And at any rate, Morocco ratified the ICCPR way back in 1979, but has yet to "harmonize" anything.

Perhaps the first thing to come in for harmonization should be the constitution's Arabic and French versions. On at least one crucial matter, they differ. This is the question of the king's "sacredness." The official line is that this antiquated feature has been abandoned for the sake of modernization. Yet that is far from clear, and may depend on whether you read the constitution from the standpoint of a cosmopolitan, French-speaking opinion leader, or from that of the average, Arabic-speaking Moroccan. The article that previously stated (in both languages) "The person of the King is inviolable and sacred" now states two different things depending on the language used. In French, Article 46 of the new basic law reads: "La personne du Roi est inviolable, et respect Lui est dû (The King's person is inviolable, and respect is owed to Him).

But in Arabic, it reads: "The King's person is inviolable, and *ihtiram* [respect] and *tawqeer* are owed to him."[5] *Ihtiram wa tawqeer* is an ancient expression used to signify the privileged status of those who claim descent from Muhammad himself—a group that includes the members of Morocco's 350-year-old Alaouite dynasty. Though dictionary definitions of *tawqeer* vary, the most commonly found are "reverence," "veneration," "adoration," and "obeisance." Some thesauruses also propose "augustness," "exaltation," and "glorification." To be fair, "respect" can be found among the alternate translations, but if *tawqeer* is simply meant as another word for *ihtiram,* one wonders what they are doing in the same sentence. More important, why would one of them—the bolder and more dramatic—be quietly left out when the Western public is watching? Has Morocco's king really renounced his "sacred" character—no trivial thing in a country where many superstitiously worship "saints" and "descendants of the Prophet"—or has he merely rephrased it, resorting to an ancient formula that stems from deeply archaic roots? What then of "modernization"?

As if to underline the relevance of these questions, on 30 July 2011, a month after the purportedly sacredness-free constitution was adopted, the annual allegiance ceremony went forward as it has for many years.[6] The king sat mounted on a thoroughbred before the royal palace in the city of Tétouan. Thousands of white-clad local officials bowed to him, as servants wearing red *shashia* caps (the traditional headgear of slaves) shouted "Our Lord bestows his blessing on you!" Then the entire cabinet and general staff lined up to kiss His Majesty's hand as television cameras beamed the scene live to every corner of the Kingdom. Versions of this pharaonic performance are repeated regularly throughout the year at various royal reviews and ribbon-cuttings, complete with adoring crowds, bowing servants, and hand-kissing officials, all united in devotion to a monarch blessed with divine potency. Who shall tell the average Moroccan that his sovereign is not sacred anymore?

Looking beyond the palace to other institutions is no more encouraging. Morocco has a Parliament elected by the people, but the king can still block any law he dislikes. He alone convenes, presides over, and sets the agenda for the Council of Ministers—a body whose approval is needed before Parliament can even consider a bill. Also, he alone appoints and dismisses the secretary-general of the government, an official who can block laws at any stage (including after Parliament approves them) by subjecting them to a "review" process that many bills have entered but never left. Add to this that Article 42 gives the king the personal privilege of issuing laws by royal decree—which is in fact how most laws get made.[7] To see free and fair legislative elections (which Morocco indeed has) as the most important element in this picture would be misleading, to say the least. Competitive elections for Parliament are doubtless a fine thing, but if the legislature thus chosen

cannot do its job, what is the point of such voting except perhaps to provide democratic window dressing?

To grasp the futility of elections, one needs only to note how Moroccan politicians behave. In a nepotistic system where the king hires and
fires cabinet ministers at will regardless of electoral outcomes, the key
to a successful career is not democratic electioneering, but forelock-
tugging courtiership. Most politicians have long known that "reaching
consensus with" (that is, knuckling under to) the palace is the only way.[8]
This attitude came close to the point of absurdity when top elected politicians, provided by the seismic events of 2011 with an opportunity to
constitutionally empower themselves in relation to the monarchy, let
the chance slip through their fingers for fear that they might offend the
king.[9] And yet perhaps this cautious attitude was not such an absurdity:
Morocco's fragmented partisan landscape (34 parties) and biased redis-
tricting and eligibility thresholds combine in such a way that no party
can end up with more than about a fourth of the seats in Parliament—not
enough to challenge the palace. Freedom at the polls coexists with a
structurally rigged electoral system.

When we take that rigging into account, we can see that there is no
point in making much of the new constitution's Article 47, which com-
pels the king to pick the prime minister from the party that "ranks first"
in legislative elections. As long as the electoral law encourages partisan
balkanization, ranking first will mean little. The premier going into the
25 November 2011 elections, Abbas el Fassi, came from the "first-rank-
ing" party (Istiqlal, which held just 16 percent of Parliament) when the
king appointed him after the 2007 elections. His government was a coalition of seven parties whose only common value was a shared subser-
vience to the royal palace—and consequently, a readiness to flip against
the prime minister whenever the king snapped his fingers. Under such
a system, the political parties (including the one "ranked first") have no
choice but to do what the palace wants or be shoved aside.

Constitutional Doubletalk

In the 2011 elections, as it turned out, the Islamist formation known as
the Party for Justice and Development (PJD) won an unprecedented 27
percent of the seats—nearly double the number that the Istiqlal incumbents were able to garner. This outcome seems all the more remarkable
given the palace's enduring wariness toward Islamists. Although PJD
leader Abdelilah Benkirane may enjoy more popular legitimacy than his
predecessor could claim, it will not make the new premier any less a constitutional hostage of the monarchy. Although much remains uncertain
so soon after the elections, it seems likely that significant parts of the
remaining 73 percent of Parliament will refuse to cooperate smoothly
with the PJD. Indeed, in all probability the Benkirane cabinet will have

to wage an exhausting, never-ending guerrilla-style battle on all institutional fronts against both the royal palace and its political minions.

Benkirane holds a fresh title ("Chief of Government" or CoG) under the new constitution but has no real additional room for maneuver. Indeed, whatever his office is now called, he remains bound hand and foot to the royal palace. The king continues to appoint and dismiss ministers at will. The CoG is allowed to "propose" ministers for nomination or, in a new wrinkle, to "require" that a minister be dismissed—but the king is not bound to go along, and retains the last word in both cases. Moreover, the king can still reshuffle the cabinet whenever he pleases. The constitution now says that he is to "consult" the CoG, but again, that official's opinion is not binding on the palace.

As regards the CoG's powers, the new constitution offers striking examples of doubletalk. Article 92, for instance, brands the Council of Government, a cabinet meeting over which the CoG presides, as an important tool for managing public affairs. Yet nothing discussed there can be settled without a green light from the Council of Ministers, which is also a meeting of the cabinet, but this time called at the king's initiative and with him in the presider's chair. Moreover, the Council of Ministers has prerogatives under Article 49 that far outweigh those of the Council of Government, including the right to appoint governors, ambassadors, the central-bank chairman, high security officials, and "executives of strategic public enterprises and establishments." Article 91 states that the CoG has appointment powers as regards the civil service and senior public-enterprise positions, but then qualifies this by saying that these powers are "without prejudice to the stipulations of article 49 of the present Consitution"—an article that of course leaves the CoG nothing serious.

Likewise, Article 98 says that the government exerts executive power "under the authority of the Chief of Government," but what can this mean given that executive power is also exerted—and more decisively—under the authority of the king? This kind of verbiage is merely a smokescreen, intended to give regime apologists a basis for hyping the CoG's supposed importance. In reality, the only powers that the CoG has are those which the palace chooses to bestow upon him, period.

Many in the Western media brought up the CoG's new privilege of dissolving Parliament under Article 104. This article is probably the strangest of all. It reads: "The Chief of Government can dissolve the Chamber of Representatives, by decree taken in the Council of Ministers, after having consulted the King." What on earth does that mean? Can anything be issued in a council over which the king presides merely by *consulting* him (that is, without needing his consent)? Even assuming the question makes sense, it is at present technically impossible to answer it since none of the Council of Ministers' procedural rules has ever been made public. The overwhelming likelihood, of course, is that no such rule—one that would let the ministers issue decrees without royal consent—exists or ever has existed. Thus what Article 104 really means is that the king, who already has the power to dissolve Parliament by direct decree under Article 51, can also (if he finds it convenient, as well he might in some cases) do so indirectly by making the Chief of Government take responsibility for this grave act. Here we see the new constitution in all its devious, two-faced brilliance. It offers a handy hook ("The elected Chief of Government has a major new power!") for purposes of pushing the "Morocco as aspiring democracy" narrative. Yet in fact this new power is actually a liability for the CoG and another asset potentially of use in the fine-tuning of royal supremacy.

In truth, the only "new power" of the CoG pertains not to any constitutional innovation, but to Benkirane's personality. If the king bullies him by leaning too heavily on his constitutional privileges, the new CoG could well decide to resign in protest—a move that none of his predecessors would have ever considered. By all accounts, political suicide is the only option left for a Morrocan premier to demonstrate his independence vis-à-vis the palace.

Who Will Guarantee the Guarantor?

No less than Morocco's political class, its judiciary is at the palace's beck and call. From the time of the first constitution's adoption in 1962, the Superior Council of Magistrates (CSM), an official body with exclusive powers to appoint, transfer, promote, and sanction judges, was effectively presided over by the justice minister. Targeting this blatant subordination of the judiciary to the executive, the 2011 protesters called loudly and often for "Free justice!" Well aware of the discontent, and eager to cleanse Morocco's image, the framers of the new constitution took pains to remove the justice minister from the supervisory body for magistrates, and even declared (in Article 107) that "[t]he judicial power is independent of the legislative power and the executive power."

What needs to be noted here is that the justice minister, while he may have exercised day-to-day control over the CSM, was in fact only its *vice*-president. Its president was—and still is—the king. Moreover, Article 115 of the new constitution gives the king power to name half the CSM's members, a bump up from the previous figure of 40 percent. Article 107 adds that "[t]he king is the guarantor of the judicial power's independence." And yet, one wonders: *Quis custodiet ipsos custodes?*

The constitution contains many other embedded loopholes, including some that will allow corruption to continue corroding every sector of public life—not least the economy. Article 36, probably the most widely noticed by the Kingdom's businessmen, strikes another brave note with this stern proclamation:

The traffic in influence and privileges, the abuse of dominant position and monopoly, and all other practices contrary to the principles of free competition and fair dealing in economic relations, are punished by the law.

This sounds wonderful until one asks what law is supposed to do the punishing, and discovers that no such law exists. For a clue as to the reason behind its absence, one should consider that King Mohammed is Morocco's biggest banker, farmer, grocer, and landowner, and controls the country's markets for such staples as milk, sugar, and yogurt. Through Copropar, a mutual fund that includes nine dummy companies (the best-known of which is called Siger—"regis" or king spelled backward), the royal family owns Morocco's largest conglomerate, the SNI group, whose revenues have at times totaled as much as 8 percent of annual GDP.

King Hassan acquired the SNI group, but it is fair to say that when it comes to business, the son surpasses the father. King Mohammed's right hand and wheel horse is Mounir Majidi, who is both his private secretary and Siger's CEO. Between 1999 and 2009, the royal group's profits skyrocketed, and dividends paid to the royal family increased sevenfold. This much is known because the royal companies had to keep transparent financial records in order to comply with the rules of the Casablanca Stock Exchange. But such transparency is over now. Ending transparency (and the distasteful press coverage that it spawned) might have been a core reason behind Morocco's biggest ever buyout: In 2010, Siger and its eight sister companies bought around US$1 billion of their own group's shares in order to exit the stock market. What will happen next is shrouded in mystery, though such a heavy investment in opacity seems unlikely to presage an era of fair and ethical business practices.

As if all this was not enough, a U.S. diplomatic cable that became public via WikiLeaks in 2010 highlighted the "appalling greed" of King Mohammed's entourage. "Major institutions and processes of the Moroccan state are being used by the Palace to coerce and solicit bribes in the country's real estate sector," read the cable, quoting a businessman who himself had been a victim of such solicitations. The same person once heard a top SNI manager tell a foreign investor:

> Morocco's major investment decisions are effectively made by 3 individuals: Fouad Ali El Himma [a former interior minister and schoolmate of the king's], Mounir Majidi [Siger's CEO], and the King himself. To have discussions with anyone else would be a waste of time.

The Royal Smokescreen and the Winds of Discontent

Seen from afar, Morocco's constitution looks fairly democratic and compares favorably to others around the Arab world. But those who take a closer look can see that behind the elaborate democratic veneer lies an archaic and corrupt absolute monarchy. It is a regime under which the three fundamental powers of government—executive, legislative, and judicial—are subjected to the will of one man; where this man's cronies act as puppetmasters of the political system and ransack the economy; and where those who dare to speak out against abuses are promptly crushed.

During the early 2000s, Morocco had a press that was free enough and felt confident enough to act like a real fourth estate. Media coverage shined a light into some of the royal regime's less seemly corners, offering among other things detailed reports (complete with hard numbers) on the king's business dealings. The palace struck back with police seizures and crooked trials of journalists. Yet there was always a backlash from Western watchdog groups that could and did mount widely publicized protests. So the monarchy switched tactics and began bleeding troublesome press outlets dry through comprehensive commercial embargos. The royal secretariat's economic leverage within Morocco is immense, and its quiet campaign to deny advertising revenue to independent newspapers was a success. Within a few years, critical papers had either toned themselves down or gone bankrupt—and it was all perfectly legal.

So here Morocco stands today: The monarchy enjoys renewed legitimacy after a massive popular vote in favor of a cleverly packaged and sold but still resolutely absolutist constitution; the royal regime's relative handful of critics have been either silenced or marginalized; and Western governments and media organs are applauding or even (in the case of France) tossing bouquets.[10] The legislative elections of November 2011 changed nothing—the king and his entourage retain absolute dominance in every field of public life.

Some would argue that the new constitution, though biased and tricky, provides at least some breathing room for democracy advocates, who can try to take its more liberal stipulations at face value and leverage them to demand deeper reforms. Yet exerting leverage requires not only a lever, but a solid place on which to stand and rest a fulcrum. Morocco today, sadly, offers no such firm ground. Since the Parliament, the judiciary, and the press are toothless, street protests are the only method left for pressuring the monarchy from inside the country. If a moment like the one that gave rise to the Feb20 movement ever comes around again, its leaders will have to show greater acuity and presence of mind than their predecessors did, and keep the momentum going with better organization and better strategic choices.

The sources of discontent are still present. Corruption is growing worse: Morocco's position on Transparency International's Corruption Perceptions Index has been decaying for years, going from 52nd in 2002 to 85th in 2010. (Tunisia was 59th in that latter year.) More important still, the "youth bulge" remains prominent.[11] Using numbers from multiple sources, a European think tank notes:

> The Moroccan population is as young as in the other countries in the region, with one-third of the population between 15 and 29 years old and

higher levels of youth unemployment than in Tunisia or Egypt. According to a government report published in 2006, Morocco needed to double the number of new jobs it created each year from 200,000 to 400,000 in order to deal with the country's deficit in terms of human development. With almost three times as many people entering the job market each year as there are jobs created, the pressures. . . are huge: one in four graduates does not have a job.[12]

It is no coincidence that the strongest nonideological pressure group in Morocco is the "unemployed graduates" who often stage dramatic protests (including attempted self-immolations) in front of Parliament.

The palace sees the dangers of popular anger, and rushes to head it off when it flares—not only with promises of political reform but also with huge spending. Recently, the minimum salary has been hiked 15 percent; more than 3,400 "unemployed graduates" have received civil-service jobs; and public employees have raked in the highest raise in Moroccan history (up to 35 percent in some cases). The state's Equalization Fund, whose mission is to hold down the prices of consumer staples (and with them, political discontent), has seen its budget nearly triple. According to Moroccan economist Fouad Abdelmoumni, such gigantic spending is unsustainable in the medium term, because of the country's structural lack of competitiveness.[13] Morocco is not oil-rich, and its economy still heavily relies on volatile sources such as money transfers from emigrés, foreign investment, and tourism—all of which have been in deep recession since the global financial crisis of 2008. Today, the Kingdom can still finance its deficit by recourse to international lenders, but the latters' conditions are growing ever more stringent. Soon they will require budget cuts that may be drastic enough to touch off another round of popular fury.

By laying down an elaborate constitutional smokescreen, the monarchy may have outfoxed its opponents. Yet its victory is likely to prove short-lived. A strong-enough wind will disperse any smokescreen. In 2011, a high wind blowing in from elsewhere in the region swept the country before turning into a soft breeze. The next time, the wind may come from within Morocco's borders, and a struggling economy plus a lack of democratic political outlets may intensify its effects. From whatever quarter this wind arises, moreover, it will likely find embers still hot enough to be stirred again to flame. The upheavals of 2011, whatever may have been their problems and however uncertain may be their effects, have shown that time is not on the side of the Arab world's autocracies. However smart its leaders may be, Morocco's autocracy is no exception.

NOTES

1. In the 2007 general election, official turnout was 37 percent.

2. Professor Abdeltif Menouni once explained, in a periodical published by Mohammed V University in Rabat, that "royal prerogative" means "the monarch's discretionary privi-

lege to act for the good of the country in the absence of constitutional provisions or by his personal interpretation of any." See his essay "Le recours à l'article 19, une nouvelle lecture de la Constitution?" *Revue juridique, politique et économique du Maroc,* January 1984, 42.

3. As of this writing in December 2011, the government has not yet released the official English-language version of the new constitution. My discussion relates to the Arabic and French versions, the latter of which is available at *www.sgg.gov.ma/BO/bulletin/ FR/2011/BO_5964-Bis_Fr.pdf.* All translations are my own.

4. To cite only the boldest, Articles 220, 222, 489, and 490 of the Penal Code prohibit anyone from even affirming—much less preaching or acting in accord with—any religious beliefs (including agnosticism and atheism) other than those of Islam. The Code also forbids homosexual relations, as well as sexual relations between individuals of opposite sexes who are not religiously married. All the above offenses are punishable by imprisonment.

5. In transliterated form, the Arabic text of Article 46 reads: "Chakhs al malik la tuntahaku hurmatuh, wa lil malik wajib al ihtiram wa tawqeer."

6. The ceremony of *tajdid al walae* (renewal of loyalty) is an annual reminder that the king's legitimacy stems first and foremost from the *bey'a*—the traditional pledge of allegiance that deems him the "lieutenant of God on his land." Hassan II realized that straightforward absolutism would not work in the modern age, so he nominally "constitutionalized" royal authority by writing extremely broad royal powers into the 1962 Constitution's Article 19. When the February 20 demonstrations broke out in 2011, one of their main demands called for this article's repeal. This has not really happened: The powers are still there, reinforced, expanded, and reorganized into Articles 41 and 42 of the new basic law.

7. This is documented through the late 1980s by Mohamed Achergui, cited in Rachida Cherifi's book *Le Makhzen politique au Maroc* (Casablanca: Afrique Orient, 1988). No more recent study is available, but it stands to reason that most laws still come from royal decrees since both the king's privileges and the organic law covering Parliament have remained materially unchanged since the 1980s.

8. This way comes complete with a "rent system" that spreads corruption throughout the whole length and breadth of the political world. In Morocco, many lucrative activities (transportation, the commercial exploitation of sandpits or stone pits, big-game fishing, and the like) can be carried out only with state permits, which the royal palace hands out on a discretionary basis in order to reward its clients. King Hassan took particular pains to involve all the politicians he could with this rent system, so that he could retain permanent leverage over them. This continues today on an even wider scale.

9. In March 2011, the constitutional-reform commission asked all parties to submit their views. Most of these submissions barely differed from the status quo, and in some respects were less bold even than those proposed by the king himself.

10. After the July 1 referendum, French president Nicolas Sarkozy saluted Morocco's "exemplary process," while Foreign Minister Alain Juppé hailed the "clear and historic decision of the people of Morocco."

11. Fareed Zakaria, "Why There's No Turning Back in the Middle East," *Time,* 17 February 2011.

12. Susi Dennison, Nicu Popescu, and José Ignacio Torreblanca, "A Chance to Reform: How the EU Can Support Democratic Evolution in Morocco," European Council on Foreign Relations, May 2011, 3. Available at *www.ecfr.eu/page/-/ECFR33_MOROC-CO_BRIEF(1).pdf.*

13. Personal e-mail communication to author, September 2011.

28

JORDAN: THE RUSE OF REFORM

Sean L. Yom

Sean L. Yom *is assistant professor of political science at Temple University. His essay "Resilient Royals: How Arab Monarchies Hang On" (coauthored with F. Gregory Gause III) appeared in the October 2012 issue of the* Journal of Democracy.

Jordan is a geographic absurdity burdened by natural-resource scarcity and demographic uncertainty. Haphazardly drawn by British cartographers in 1921, this arid hinterland east of the River Jordan has little water and no oil. Ever reliant on foreign aid, the ruling monarchy reigns over a fractious society split between its traditional base of support, mostly tribal East Bankers, and an urban Palestinian majority that has long been excluded from power. Yet unlike the rulers of its more powerful Arab neighbors, the monarchy of the Hashemites—a clan from the Hejaz region of the Arabian Peninsula whom the British made rulers of what was then called Transjordan—has never been toppled.

The palace's confidence in this record of stability did not serve it well during the Arab Spring, however. Instead of grasping the historic character of this upsurge of popular unrest and acting accordingly, the regime contented itself with making only the shallowest of political reforms. Despite facing unprecedented opposition, the forces gathered around the throne of King Abdullah II appear to believe that they can retain power as in the past. Yet as political discontent and economic difficulties deepen, this has become a shaky assumption. Since ascending to the throne in 1999, the king has never faced such doubt about his future.

The January 2013 parliamentary election was supposed to induce the opposite conclusion. One of the cleanest on record, the election bookended a two-year royal campaign of democratic reforms, which began after weekly protests demanding popular representation and an end to corruption broke out in January 2011.[1] After thousands of demonstrations and a raft of constitutional amendments, however, the political scene of early 2013 looks much like it did before the Arab Spring. The parliament remains a toothless body, created by an electoral law so tilted to favor conservatives that it triggered a boycott by Islamists and other opposition figures. The kingship and its government still dictate all major policy stances, and the security apparatus continues to loom over civic life with overarching authority.

If Jordan's polity remains mired in stasis, its society does not: Never before have so many Jordanians been willing to express so much hostility toward the monarchy. In a rare moment, opposition has mobilized across deep social cleavages—Islamist and secular, Palestinian and East Banker, urban and tribal, brick-and-mortar parties and Facebook networks, old-line dissidents and former regime officials, military veterans and regular civilians. A decade ago, burning the king's picture would have been an unthinkable crime; this year, the palace did not publicly celebrate his birthday for fear that official portraits of him would be defaced.[2]

While in the past the Hashemite crown has managed to overcome inherent structural and geopolitical disadvantages, surviving this latest test may strain its resources to the limit. Nothing short of bold internal transformation will suffice. For more than two decades, the regime has responded to protests and petitions for democracy with bouts of controlled liberalization. The palace has tried that again this time, but opposition mobilization has not abated. Worse, the rising unemployment and living costs associated with the anemic economy, which needed an IMF bailout worth US$2 billion in August 2012, will ensure continued frustration on the street.

Controlled liberalization has failed, yet in the wake of the Arab Spring and the higher expectations of openness that it brought, imposing a clampdown like the one that marked the martial-law period of the 1980s is out of the question. Moving forward, the monarchy has two options. It can play for time and hope that the opposition will demobilize, or it can take meaningful steps toward delivering on the singular promise that it made at the onset of the Arab Spring. The latter course would mean becoming a constitutional monarchy by divesting itself of absolute power and recognizing the authority to rule of a democratically elected government. At a minimum this would require a complete overhaul of the electoral law and the reconstruction of the legislature as a meaningful institution of governance rather than a ceremonial theater for bickering yes-men. As unappetizing as that prospect may be to the palace, the first tactic—stalling in hopes that the opposition will fall apart amid infighting or otherwise lose steam—has so far not proven successful for any Middle Eastern autocracy without vast oil wealth to spread around.

Before discussing Jordan's reform efforts during the Arab Spring, it is important to understand *why* authoritarianism in this kingdom remains so stubborn. The Hashemite monarchy is far from exceptional in its reluctance to surrender its executive prerogatives to popular sovereignty. Nor is it a trailblazer in substituting hollow liberalization for real democratic change—though decades of experience have made it highly adept at operating as a liberalized autocracy, relaxing the reins of repression while still maintaining ironclad control of the state. What makes it exceptional is that virtually no constituency apart from domestic oppositionists and international human-rights organizations puts consistent pressure on the kingdom to democratize. Why? Western policy makers and Jordanian officials have successfully cultivated the kingdom's image as a "moderate" Arab state, an oasis of stability and key ally in the world's most strategic and turbulent region. Jordan is the Goldilocks of the Arab world—not as repressive as Syria, not as democratic as Tunisia, not as religious as Saudi Arabia, not as fractious as Iraq, and not as poor as Egypt. The potential uncertainty and instability bred by democratization would upend it.

At the heart of this presentation is Jordan's high degree of "linkage" with the West, and especially the United States.[3] King Abdullah has been on more U.S. visits than any other Arab head of state, and his son, Crown Prince Hussein, now attends Georgetown University. Abdullah's consultants intersperse popular appearances for the American public (he has chatted with Jon Stewart on *The Daily Show*, for instance) with high-level White House and Congressional meetings. He has cultivated the reputation of a benevolent leader, one who regularly grants media interviews and even comments on Jordanian blogs. Early in his tenure, impressed journalists described him as the Arab world's "can-do guy," a monarch who could safeguard the U.S.-Jordanian alliance while gradually enlightening his backward Arab nation with democratic reform.[4]

At the institutional level, examples of Jordan's openness include its dispatch of numerous exchange students to Western universities, its welcoming of Pope Benedict's visit in 2009, and the decision to orient its tourism industry toward Christian and Jewish visitors. At the policy level, the regime burnishes not only its 1994 peace accord with Israel but also the fruits of U.S.-Jordanian cooperation, such as liberalized investment and trade agreements, intelligence collaboration regarding the War on Terror, and diplomatic coordination regarding regional issues such as the Iraq War and dealings with Iran. Not least because of such support, the regime has reaped tremendous economic rewards. Since the 1990s, the United States has become one of Jordan's largest trade partners as well as its biggest aid donor. Most recently, from 2008 to 2012, Jordan netted almost $4 billion in military and economic assistance, with annual aid ranging from $650 to $800 million.

The Islamist Bogeyman

From the standpoint of *Realpolitik,* backing the autocratic status quo makes sense only if the uncertainty entailed by democratization would result in extremist forces taking control of the kingdom. Indeed, alarm-ists in Washington and Amman like to portray Jordan as constantly on the brink of collapse, besieged from within by Islamic fundamentalism and ethnic conflict. Only a centralized and powerful monarchy, the argument goes, can keep the country together. Yet upon closer scrutiny, these threats are bogeymen. The greatest peril to Jordan's political stability is neither religion nor identity, but rather the regime's own deafness to the popular roar for democracy.

Jordan does have a large Islamist sector. Dominated by the Muslim Brotherhood and its party, the Islamic Action Front (IAF), this sector is no stranger to politics. The Brotherhood was among the few organizations that remained legal throughout the martial-law era, and remains the best-organized opposition today. Its stance is a moderate one: Brotherhood leaders say that they aim for a negotiated transition to constitutional monarchism, not a revolutionary Islamic state.[5] During 2011 and 2012, Islamist-organized weekly protests in Amman regularly drew hundreds of supporters and were given a wide berth by the police. Virtually all these protests were peaceful, with the largest drawing thousands, including members of professional syndicates and parties on the secular left. Yet the Brotherhood's decision to boycott the January 2013 elections undercut the voting's legitimacy enough to arouse renewed hostility from the palace. Thinly veiled threats of dissolution have become commonplace.[6]

The regime hesitates before the prospect of any democratic reform that could end up empowering Islamists. Exploiting Western consternation over Egyptian president Mohamed Morsi's failed late-2012 power grab, King Abdullah recently reminded observers (including Jordan's small Christian minority) that the monarchy would defend religious tolerance, whereas an Islamist regime would impose theocratic tyranny.[7] The geopolitical ramifications would also be dire, for an Islamist regime could end both the peace treaty with Israel and the U.S.-Jordanian alliance. Another scaremongering tactic is emphasizing Jordan's vulnerability to radicalism and violence. The War on Terror uncovered local ties to al-Qaeda and other radical networks, and for every successful attack, such as the November 2005 Amman hotel bombings, there are numerous foiled plots, such as a jihadist bombing plot uncovered in October 2012. Officials also warn that Islamist militants could be operating among the nearly 400,000 Syrian refugees already in the kingdom.

It is highly unlikely, however, that democratization would give rise to religious dictatorship in Jordan, and even an Islamist-oriented government would not turn its back on the West. For one thing, much as the Muslim Brotherhood did in Egypt under Mubarak, the Jordanian Muslim Brotherhood relies on a modest number of middle-class supporters whose willingness to turn out for public demonstrations fools observers into inflating the Brothers' numbers.[8] This is not to say that Jordanian Islamists resemble their Egyptian counterparts in all respects. On the contrary, the Islamists of Jordan have never suffered the kind of repressive onslaughts that often produce radical militancy, and historically have focused as much on the Israeli-Palestinian conflict as on domestic politics. Moreover, their claim to religious authenticity must concede the Hashemite dynasty's ancestral relationship to Muhammad himself.

Free and fair elections would allow the IAF to become part of a ruling parliamentary coalition, but the Front would have to cooperate with secular forces as well as honor its electoral promises, as Ennahdha has discovered in Tunisia. Nor is it clear that Islamist successes at the ballot box will result in blowback for the West. For instance, Turkey wishes to *enter* the European Union, not snub it, while Egypt—so far—is maintaining its peace treaty with Israel and its alliance with the United States, its most important foreign donor.

Jordan does live in one of the world's toughest neighborhoods, of course, and has always been heavily affected by neighboring conflicts. After the armed destruction of Saddam Hussein's regime in Iraq in 2003, nearly 700,000 Iraqis fled west to Jordan. The flow of refugees from the internal war that is now raging in Syria, just to Jordan's north, may well surpass that number. There were draconian crackdowns on civil liberties during the Iraq War, but they did little to convince the public that safety could substitute for freedom. The Jordanian regime likes to portray itself as beleaguered and insecure, but in fact its powerful General Intelligence Directorate (GID), which is responsible for identifying and suppressing all perceived threats, is highly effective and does an admirable job of tracking down genuine terrorist activity. It is not credible, however, to pretend that monitoring and squashing peaceful domestic political opposition is a legitimate antiterrorist mission.

Identity and Youth Politics

The second justification for postponing Jordanian democracy is the potential for social conflict between the country's ethnic-Palestinian majority and tribal East Bankers. Following the Black September civil war of 1970—in which King Abdullah's father Hussein and the army drove the Palestine Liberation Organization out of Jordan and into Lebanon, killing perhaps as many as ten-thousand people along the way—identity came to structure not just social relationships but also the national political economy. Palestinian Jordanians dominated the private sector, but prejudice and xenophobia barred their access to political power. Tribal Jordanians filled the bloated public sector, including the military and security forces, and enjoyed far closer relations with the monarchy and its institutions. State officials treat this fragile imbalance as permanent, implying that democratization will result in a worst-case scenario in which Palestinians use their numbers to gain control of the state, touching off a violent conflict with tribal Jordanians and East Bank nationalists.

Yet there are reasons to believe that identity issues are not quite the flashpoint that the regime claims they are. To begin with, Palestinian Jordanians are not a cohesive social force. They range from the urban poor and wage workers to educated professionals and even top regime figures: Queen Rania is from a Palestinian family, as are some of her husband's senior advisors. Some Palestinians entered before or during the 1948 Arab-Israeli War, some came after the 1967 Arab-Israeli War, which saw the West Bank revert back to Israeli control, and still others came during the mass expulsion of Palestinians from the Gulf after the First Gulf War in the early 1990s.[9] Some would depart for an independent Palestinian state, while others would not uproot their lives for a land that they have never seen. Others have disengaged from politics altogether due to long-running discrimination, and have little desire to "Palestinize" Jordan.[10] In sum, the Palestinian majority is more mosaic than monolith, and there is no reason to think that it harbors some primordial fealty which would transform a democratic Jordan into an ethnocracy.

Second, over the past decade many tribal Jordanians have begun to see the *monarchy,* not Palestinians, as the greatest threat to their livelihood. Neoliberal economic policies implemented since the early 2000s, such as privatization and trade liberalization, have dislocated many East Bankers who depended on work in public bureaucracies and state-owned enterprises. Though the economy has barely grown since 2009, even during the boom years of the mid-2000s Jordan suffered the phenomenon of "growth without jobs."[11] Leading industries such as real estate, banking, and retailing attracted foreign capital but generated little new employment for the country's growing labor force, least of all in tribal-dominated rural areas.

At the same time, weak regulations allowed labor-intensive sectors like tourism, construction, and textiles to continue hiring cheaper foreign workers from places such as Egypt and the Philippines. The privatization of state assets such as phosphate and potash factories caused the loss of guaranteed jobs in tribal towns like Tafileh, which already suffered from poor infrastructure and services. The military and security services remain amply funded, but can only absorb so many more East Bankers; as it stands, a quarter of the entire national labor force already carries a gun on the job.[12] Subsistence-level informal employment is rampant, and real joblessness is at least double the official rate of 12.5 percent. That the November 2012 riots, sparked by an IMF-mandated cut to fuel subsidies, were most violent in tribal areas signals the danger that may flow from ignoring the losers of economic modernization.

While in the long run the monarchy envisages shifting its base of support from the countryside to the city, in the short run it has paid a high price. "We watered the soil of Jordan with our blood," goes one typical tribal complaint, "only to see the king sell it off to the highest bidder."[13] Years before the Arab Spring, East Banker tribal sheikhs, military veterans, and intellectuals began publicly criticizing the monarchy for its clumsiness in dealing with its tribal bedrock. Former regime officials have also stepped into the limelight. In May 2011, Ahmad Obeidat, who was prime minister in 1984–85, set up the National Front for Reform, an opposition coalition that has attracted many urban East Bankers.

In poorer rural areas, tribal youths created their own popular opposition through the *hirak* movement, a grassroots phenomenon that organized hundreds of rallies. Though sparsely covered by Western journalists, these were the most regime-unfriendly demonstrations yet. Shattering stereotypes, tribal activists mobilized not for jobs and patronage but to demand that autocratic abuses end and that the king stick to his reform promises.[14] By mid-2011, young protesters were defying arrest threats by calling for the regime's downfall and comparing King Abdullah to the recently deposed Egyptian dictator Hosni Mubarak.

The rise of bold resistance among the young is something that Jordan has in common with the Arab Spring countries, where youth activists rather than formal organizations (including the Muslim Brotherhood) led the charge against dictatorship. In addition to tribal dissenters, tech-savvy youth networks in Amman have also made their voices heard. New groups such as the 24 March Movement have been using Facebook and the blogosphere to call for constitutional monarchy, ignoring as they do so old taboos surrounding such topics as political corruption and the GID's sweeping powers. Their activism suggests that opposition to the regime as currently constituted may be less religious or ethnic than *generational.*

Parliament Redux

As its favorite social and political pretexts for shelving democracy have lost credibility, the regime has fallen back on claims that, given their Islamic heritage and cultural values, Jordanians *need* a king who rules and does not merely reign.[15] Noxious ethnocentrism aside, such last-gasp reasoning runs into several problems. It is true that the Arab Spring toppled uncrowned despots but no monarch, yet Bahrain's Sunni ruling family survived a revolutionary uprising that involved fully a fifth of the citizenry only by dint of armed Saudi intervention and Western complicity. Oil wealth may be enough to shield Saudi Arabia and the other Gulf kingdoms from social unrest, but Morocco and Jordan have no black gold. In each country, moreover, the awe-inspiring character of absolute monarchy was not enough to keep tens of thousands of protesters off the streets. No timeless affinity binds Jordanians (or other Arabs) to royal absolutism. The Hashemites had no tribal ties to the area that would later become Jordan prior to being granted this British-concocted kingdom. Middle Eastern history is rife with fallen monarchies whose cultural essence failed to save them from coups or revolutions, whether in Egypt (1952), Tunisia (1957), Iraq (1958), North Yemen (1962), Libya (1969), or Iran (1979).[16] It should be recalled that the last king of Iraq—shot by soldiers during the July 1958 putsch in Baghdad—was also a member of the Hashemite family.

Bereft of excuses, Jordanian officials nonetheless treated the January 2013 elections for the House of Representatives (the lower chamber of the National Assembly) as the inauguration of a new democratic era.[17] The previous two years had seen increased political volatility, with King Abdullah naming five successive cabinets in a losing effort to appease popular protests. The product of a revamped electoral law, the contest was deemed competitive by an independent electoral committee and international monitors. Turnout reached almost 57 percent of registered voters (or about 40 percent of all those eligible to vote), eclipsing the 53 percent seen in the 2010 elections. More than 1,500 candidates contested 150 seats, with 15 set aside for women, the largest such allocation yet. A new national-list system introduced proportional representation (PR) in order to satisfy proponents of political parties.

The resulting parliament enjoys an unprecedented responsibility. Whereas in the past the king alone appointed the prime minister and cabinet, a new constitutional arrangement adopted in 2012 requires the palace to consult with the legislature before selecting a new government. Additional reforms include the creation of a constitutional court and some prosecution of high-level corruption.[18] The official narrative paints the election as a milestone on the road to constitutional monarchy, which the king had promised in a televised June 2011 speech. King Abdullah calls it a "White Revolution" that will peacefully enfranchise the marginalized and create a new model of free government for the region.[19]

Students of Middle Eastern history may recall that the Shah of Iran also declared a White Revolution in 1963, a decade and a half before a revolution of another sort swept him from his throne. In Jordan, the White Revolution rhetoric is a rebranding of the familiar controlled-liberalization game, in which there is some tinkering at the edges of authoritarianism but no change at its coercive core. The new parliament cooperated with the king to reappoint the same premier as before, though perhaps in the future the net will be cast wider when new cabinet members are being named. Political parties remain weak, as most seats are still filled through the Single Non-Transferable Vote (SNTV) system, which encourages Jordanians to spend their one vote on independent deputies on the basis of tribal, kinship, or patronage ties. The tentacles of royal power still reach far, and the GID regularly bribes deputies in order to influence their public positions.

Public mistrust about this "transition" remains deep, so much so that the idea of enthroning a new king—perhaps 33-year-old Prince Hamzah, the 51-year-old Abdullah's half-brother—has become a matter of public

discussion. *Hirak* activists, youth networks, and the Islamists continue
to mobilize new protests that still draw hundreds, with fiscal austerity
and the rising cost of living serving as triggers. Tribal towns such as
Tafileh and Karak, long touted by academic researchers as bastions of
support for the monarchy, are now sites of cyclic contentions in which
arrests of young protesters touch off more demonstrations and, to complete the circle, more police clampdowns.

An Autopsy of Reform

The January 2013 balloting saw the conduct of elections improve,
but the underlying electoral ecology maintained by the regime was as
flawed as ever. Despite advice from civic leaders, political scientists,
and even its own appointed reform committee, the palace heeded GID
warnings that the electoral system needed to systematically disadvantage opposition by preventing the formation of new opposition parties
and stymieing Islamist predominance. One GID assessment predicted
that with 108 lower-house seats still beholden to SNTV, the IAF could
win no more than 30 seats, whereas discarding the system in favor of a
two-vote formula—a proposal fronted by the king's own reform committee—would double that figure.[20] Because so many seats are decided
in advance through informal primaries that allow citizens to promise
their single vote to favored candidates in exchange for gifts and favors,
many races are more "selection" than election.[21] Further, the new PR-
style national-list system encompasses just 27 seats, far short of public
expectations.

Confusion and limited financing resulted in a crowded field of more
than 60 weak blocs, with 23 lists winning seats and only one managing
to take three. That compares dismally to tribal results: The powerful
Bani Hasan confederation alone won ten seats. Finally, grossly malap-
portioned districts continue to leave urban Palestinian areas underrep-
resented, as the palace worries about how actively the IAF and other
opposition groups campaign in these neighborhoods. The tribal-dominated rural governorates continue to send disproportionate numbers
of deputies to the legislature, and together with progovernment independents control over 110 of the 150 lower-house seats. Political disil-
lusionment remains pervasive among urban Palestinians, who equate
the act of voting to legitimating a rigged system. For instance, whereas
many rural districts reported over 80 percent turnout, some far larger
urban districts in Amman reported less than 15 percent turnout.[22]

Apart from its paradoxical success at conducting competitive elections on the basis of uncompetitive laws, the regime has made little
progress. The biggest problem concerns parliament itself. Since this
institution would receive many of the powers conceded by the monarchy in a hypothetical democratic transition, the regime has every rea-

son to encage it in suffocating restrictions. Jordan's national legislature thus lacks basic lawmaking authority: It cannot initiate laws, change the budget, or form oversight committees to look into the doings of the military and the GID. If oppositionists ever manage to achieve lower-house dominance, the royal appointees in the Senate will easily check them. Yet even that situation would be an improvement over the current predominance of independent deputies such as businessmen and tribal elders who are disconnected from the street and do nothing but fight over reputation and patronage. The circus that the Jordanian public sees in the parliament plays right into the palace's strategy, of course.[23] How could anyone want power to devolve from the monarchy into the hands of such petty squabblers?

Other royal initiatives framed as concessions to democratic demands contain built-in safeguards. For instance, constitutional amendments unveiled in September 2011 authorized the creation of a national constitutional court, which satisfies an old complaint from human-rights activists. It enjoys sweeping jurisdiction over all state institutions—except the monarchy and the GID, which like the military answer only to the king. The GID's budget, like that of the king's court, remains off-limits to internal watchdogs such as the Audit Bureau and the Ombudsman Bureau. The secretive State Security Courts still prosecute journalists and activists who run afoul of the state without affording them full legal rights. Prosecutions aimed at elite businesspeople and political figures accused of embezzling millions from privatization deals have netted a few big fish, including a former GID director. Yet the targeting of these efforts remains narrow and has been calculated to avoid implicating the palace or anyone close to it.

On other fronts, civic freedoms continue to erode under a steady drip of new regulations.[24] Two of five Jordanians are regular Internet users and the regime has committed itself to universal access, but only on its own terms. A September 2012 law allows the government to censor online writings, thereby taking away the country's last source of unregulated independent journalism. The printed daily newspapers are semi-official organs whose reporters have long needed to heed impossibly vague rules about how they cover anything that the government deems related to national security, including palace affairs, foreign relations, tribal politics, and military issues.

The Oliver Twist Method

In the first half of 2013, two factors stemmed (for a time at least) the rising tides of protest and opposition in Jordan. The first was the blood-bath next door in Syria, where deepening violence forced Jordanians to think hard about the worst possible consequences that might flow from state-society struggle. As the movement of Syrian refugees grows, so too will trepidation about anything that might stir up internal unrest in Jordan. The second is the sheer prevalence of cynicism and apathy among the many Jordanians, Palestinians and East Bankers alike, who no longer credit any of the palace's vows about democratic reform. This is the more significant variable. The Syrian fighting will die down before King Abdullah regains Jordanians' faith in his leadership. In order to have any hope of that, he would have to lay out a concrete timeline for institutional changes leading to a real constitutional monarchy. As a first step, he would have to fully overhaul the electoral law by getting rid of SNTV and enlarging the national list to encompass at least half of all lower-house seats. And he would have to rein in the security apparatus that causes both fear and fury among civic activists.

These are heroic expectations, to be sure, but the palace has also failed to make even symbolic gestures to engage its new waves of opposition. Few agents of the state understand urban youth and *hirak* movements, activists who reject the conservativism of their elders and dare to talk about long-forbidden topics, such as the viability of King Abdullah's suddenly rocky tenure. At the same time, the regime's assumption that controlled liberalization can pacify the public has become shaky as well. Jordanians have seen too many false promises of reform to be fooled any longer. Yet King Abdullah continues to portray his reign as a liberal one, casting blame for Jordan's authoritarian doldrums on everyone—Islamists, businessmen, tribes, the GID, even his own family—except himself.[25]

International actors are not without democracy-promotion leverage here. The economy is the place to start. Jordan is the Oliver Twist of the Middle East, as it needs aid money and cannot survive without continually asking for "more." Bereft of natural resources, stuck with a weak tax-collection system, and trapped by the need to maintain its huge military-security establishment and bureaucratic payrolls, the state is perennially broke. In good years, Jordan receives enough Western and Gulf money to scrape by; in bad years, it racks up billions in public debt (which now measures $20 billion, or two-thirds of GDP) and tries to contain social spending. Conditioning economic gifts on achieving democratic benchmarks remains the only foreseeable way that the autocratic regime will heed any advice to quicken the pace of reform. While Jordan also receives financial assistance from Saudi Arabia, such support is sporadic and has its own conditionality, such as pressure to harbor the Syrian opposition. Foreign aid from the United States and its allies remains the kingdom's economic lifeline, and the best way to encourage the regime to actually take popular demands into account in its next reform gambit. With stability on the line, the next five years will prove to be the crucible for the Jordanian crown.

NOTES

1. "Popular Protest in North Africa and the Middle East (IX): Dallying with Reform in a Divided Jordan," *ICG Middle East/North Africa Report,* No. 118., Brussels, 12 March 2012.

2. Author's confidential interview with Prime Ministry official, Amman, Jordan, June 2012.

3. For more on linkage, see Steven Levitsky and Lucan Way, *Competitive Authoritarianism: Hybrid Regimes After the Cold War* (New York: Cambridge University Press, 2010), 37–83.

4. Lee Smith, "The Arab World's Can-Do Guy: Abdullah II's Jordan Is a Model for the Middle East," *Slate,* 7 May 2004.

5. For more on Jordan's Muslim Brotherhood, see Jillian Schwedler, *Faith in Moderation: Islamist Parties in Jordan and Yemen* (New York: Cambridge University Press, 2007).

6. Muhammad al-Najjar, "Rasaa'il saakhinah baina al-qasr wa ikhwan al-urdun" [Heated messages between the palace and the Jordanian Brotherhood], *Al-Jazeera.net,* 21 January 2013.

7. Tamer al-Samadi, "Abdullah al-thani yuhadhir min diktatoriyat diniyyah" [King Abdullah warns of religious dictatorships], *Al-Hayat,* 13 January 2013.

8. Tarek Masoud, "Why Islam Wins: Electoral Ecologies and Economies of Political Islam in Contemporary Egypt," PhD diss., Yale University, 2009.

9. For a full genealogical catalogue, see Abdulraouf al-Rawabdeh, *Mu'jam al-'asha'ir al-urduniyyah* [Compendium of Jordanian families and tribes] (Amman: Dar al-shuruq lil-nashr wa al-tazwi, 2010).

10. Sarah Tobin, "Jordan's Arab Spring: The Middle Class and Anti-Revolution," *Middle East Policy* 19 (Spring 2012): 96–109.

11. Luis Abugattas-Majluf, "Jordan: Model Reformer Without Upgrading?" *Studies in Comparative International Development* 47 (June 2012): 231–53.

12. I am indebted to Dr. Riad Khouri for providing this striking insight in Amman in May 2012.

13. Author's confidential interview with tribal representative, Irbid, Jordan, June 2012.

14. Sean Yom and Wael al-Khatib, "Jordan's New Politics of Tribal Dissent," *Foreign Policy.com,* 7 August 2012, available at *http://mideast.foreignpolicy.com/posts/2012/08/07/jordans_new_politics_of_tribal_dissent.*

15. Such sentiment flavored several confidential interviews that I conducted with officials from the Foreign Ministry and Hashemite Royal Court in Amman during June 2011 and July 2012. Ironically, this resonates with Orientalist thinking as represented, for example, by Bernard Lewis, "Monarchy in the Middle East," in Joseph Kostiner, ed., *Middle East Monarchies: The Challenge of Modernity* (Boulder, Colo.: Lynne Rienner, 2000).

16. Sean Yom and F. Gregory Gause, III, "Resilient Royals: How Arab Monarchies Hang On," *Journal of Democracy* 23 (October 2012): 74–88.

17. Nicholas Seeley, "The Jordanian State Buys Itself Time," *Middle East Report Online*, 12 February 2013, available at *www.merip.org/mero/mero021213*.

18. Hassan Barari and Christina Satkowski, "The Arab Spring: The Case of Jordan," *Middle Eastern Studies: Journal of Politics and International Relations* 3 (July 2012): 41–57.

19. Jumana Ghunaimat, "Thawra baydha" [The White Revolution], *Al-Ghad*, 12 February 2013.

20. Muhammad al-Najjar, "Mas'a urduni lil-intikhabaat dun aghlabiyyah lil-ikhwan" [Jordanian efforts for elections without Islamist majority], *Al-Jazeera.net*, 4 June 2012.

21. Ellen Lust, Sami Hourani, and Mohammad El-Momani, "Jordan Votes: Election or Selection?" *Journal of Democracy* 22 (April 2011): 119–29.

22. *Al-taqrir Al-nihaa' Lil-mukhrajat Muraaqabat Al-intikhabaat Al-barlamaaniyyah Al-urduniyyah 2013* [Final report on the monitoring of the 2013 Jordanian parliamentary elections] (Amman, Jordan: Al-Hayat Center for Civil Society Development, 2013).

23. Public surveys consistently report that the vast majority is dissatisfied with parliamentary performance. See the quarterly polls done by the Center for Strategic Studies of the University of Jordan, available at *www.jcss.org/ShowAllNewsar.aspx?catid=12*.

24. For a discussion of previous restrictions on civil liberty, see Sean Yom, "Jordan: Ten More Years of Autocracy," *Journal of Democracy* 20 (October 2009): 151–66.

25. Jeffrey Goldberg, "The Modern King in the Arab Spring," *The Atlantic,* 18 March 2013.

29

IS SAUDI ARABIA IMMUNE?

Stéphane Lacroix

Stéphane Lacroix *is associate professor of political science at Sciences Po in Paris, and author of* Awakening Islam: The Politics of Religious Dissent in Contemporary Saudi Arabia *(2011). This essay originally appeared in the October 2011 issue of the* Journal of Democracy.

When protests started spreading throughout the Arab world in January 2011, numerous observers predicted that Saudi Arabia's turn would soon come. The same factors that caused uprisings elsewhere exist in the Kingdom: Unemployment among young people is extremely high (probably above 25 percent), corruption is pervasive, repression is widespread, and there is a growing gap between an aging ruling elite and the populace—generally estimated to number between 26 and 28 million, 75 percent of whom are under 30.

There was some truth to those expectations, as February and early March 2011 witnessed an unusual degree of political activism by the Kingdom's standards. And yet, by mid-March the regime had regained complete control of the situation. Who were these Saudi activists who challenged the regime and what did they want? And how did the regime manage to silence their protests? Does this episode mean that change is impossible in Saudi Arabia?

There have been episodes of political dissent in Saudi Arabia since the 1950s. Most notably, on 20 November 1979, a few hundred armed militants seized the Grand Mosque in Mecca with the aim of consecrating one of their leaders as the *mahdi,* the Islamic Messiah. The mosque was retaken two weeks later at a cost of more than two-hundred people killed, including militants, security personnel, and bystanders. During the siege, which occurred not long after the Iranian Revolution, a Shia uprising broke out in the Eastern Province, but government forces violently crushed it within a week.

The most significant protest, however, happened in the early 1990s in the wake of the First Gulf War. It was spearheaded by sheikhs (or religious scholars) and intellectuals belonging to the Sahwa (or Islamic Awakening), the Kingdom's largest Islamist movement, which blends the political ideology of the Muslim Brotherhood with local Wahhabi religious ideas. Petitions asking for radical reforms were made public, and demonstrations occurred. In 1994 and 1995, hundreds, if not thousands, of protesters were arrested, putting an end to what became known as the "Sahwa insurrection."

Starting in the late 1990s, new forms of political activism emerged. The most visible—and violent—was the terror campaign launched by "al-Qaeda in the Arabian Peninsula," which carried out domestic attacks from 2003 until 2006, by which point the state's response had reduced it to an insignificant threat.[1] But peaceful forms of activism also gained momentum. In particular, former figures of the Sahwa insurrection such as Abdullah al-Hamid and Abd al-Aziz al-Qasim decided to join hands with representatives of other political forces, including liberals and Shias, in order to call for the establishment of a constitutional monarchy.

Those demands, carefully framed in the language of Islam, were unprecedented in the Kingdom, as was the coalition of Islamists and non-Islamists behind them. Beginning in 2003, despite harassment and arrests, this group of "constitutional reformists" submitted a number of petitions and manifestos. In February 2007, the publication of a text entitled "Milestones on the Way to Constitutional Monarchy" led to the arrest of ten prominent members of the group, whom the government accused of supporting terrorism. Those men, it is rumored, were about to announce the creation of a political party. Most remain in jail at the time of this writing in early August 2011.

The lack of a major reaction by Saudi society to those arrests convinced the activists that they needed to change their approach. "We thought that speaking the language of Islam would be enough to connect with society," said one reformist. "But our discourse still remained too abstract in a society with very little political awareness."[2] A new priority emerged: the defense of human rights, especially for political prisoners—10,000 to 30,000 of whom have been held without trial since 2003, most on the charge of supporting terrorism.[3] The activists attacked this as a violation not only of Islamic principles but also of Saudi laws and decrees.

In October 2009, some of these activists announced the creation of the first truly independent human-rights association based in the Kingdom, the Saudi Civil and Political Rights Association (SCPRA). Despite the arrests of some of its members, the Association has continued issuing statements and has maintained a functioning website (*www.acpra.net*).

Not surprisingly, when the uprisings started in Tunisia and Egypt, the Saudi constitutional reformists were among the first to take advantage of the opening thus provided. On February 10, ten individuals—most of them previously linked to the constitutional movement—announced the establishment of the Kingdom's first political party, the Islamic Umma Party. They gave as their rationale the belief that an organized political life was a prerequisite for political reform. The founders of the party were particularly influenced by the writings of Hakim al-Mutairi, a Kuwaiti religious scholar known for his attempts to justify democratic principles using salafist references. Al-Mutairi had previously played a key role in the establishment of Kuwait's Umma Party, which appears to be linked to its Saudi counterpart through an informal transnational structure called the Conference of the Umma. A particular feature of the Islamic Umma Party is its calls for the establishment of a "righteous government," a concept which aims to go beyond the idea of a constitutional monarchy by questioning the monarchical system of government itself. A few days after the party was announced, seven of its ten founding members were arrested. On February 11, in the wake of the ouster of Egyptian president Hosni Mubarak, the SCPRA increased the pressure on the government by publishing a provocative statement arguing that the only way for Saudi Arabia to avoid revolution would be to implement constitutional reform.

Seizing an Opportunity

On February 23, constitutional reformists were instrumental in the publication of two petitions asking for political change in the Kingdom, with explicit reference to the events underway in the rest of the Arab world. The two texts were posted online and received thousands of signatures. The first, signed by more liberal-leaning activists headed by former Arab nationalist Muhammad Sa'id Tayyib and former communist Najib al-Khunayzi, advocated a constitutional monarchy.[4] The second, "Toward a State of Rights and Institutions," was signed by more Islamist-leaning activists.[5] It stopped short of explicitly calling for a constitutional monarchy but did call for a fully elected Majlis al-Shura (the currently appointed Consultative Council of Saudi Arabia) and a government accountable to it.

Among the drafters of this second petition were a number of influential Islamist sheikhs and intellectuals with links to the Sahwa, including Salman al-'Awda, a key figure in the 1990s Sahwa insurrection who had, since his release from jail in 1999, maintained good relations with the regime. With the beginning of the Arab world's upheavals, however, al-'Awda started to adopt a more politically aggressive tone, praising the forced exits from office of Mubarak and Tunisian president Zine al-Abidine Ben Ali and openly criticizing the Saudi government for giving asylum to the latter. This position is said to have cost al-'Awda his weekly television show, which was canceled in early February. Worth mentioning as well is Muhammad al-Ahmari, who was a key figure in both petitions. A former leading Sahwa intellectual and the head of the Islamic Assembly of North America (IANA) in the 1990s, he has emerged in the last few years as one of the most influential Islamist prodemocracy activists in the Kingdom.

February also witnessed increased activism from a new generation of young prodemocracy activists, mainly present on Facebook and Twitter. Many of them had spent time in Sahwa circles, but had left because they disagreed with the dogmatism of the movement's leaders or their lack of a clear stance on political reform. In a way, these young Saudis share a profile with the "Muslim Brotherhood youth" of Egypt: Both groups are clearly postideological in the sense that they do not feel bound by their elders' political allegiances and are therefore keen to bridge the old Isla-mist-liberal divide. To this end, they state their primary identity merely as "youth." This is how 49 of these activists introduced themselves in a February 23 open letter to 88-year-old King Abdullah. Among their demands was that the average age of cabinet ministers and members of the Majlis be brought down to 40 and 45, respectively.[6]

To be sure, these young activists did not come out of nowhere. Their presence had been growing on Facebook since at least 2008, and they had already conducted a number of noticeable campaigns there, includ-ing one demanding accountability for the poor official response to the 2009 Jeddah floods, which killed more than a hundred people. Thus pressed, the king promised an investigation—though it came to little. More recently, the young activists, like the SCPRA, have concentrated their efforts on human-rights issues. Prominent members of this group include Walid Abu al-Khayr, founder of the Facebook-based "Monitor of Human Rights in Saudi"; Fuad al-Farhan, an influential blogger who was jailed in 2007; and Muhammad al-Bijadi, a proponent of peaceful "civil jihad" aimed at obtaining rights, who was arrested in March 2011. A few of the members have also managed to make a name for them-selves in intellectual circles, including Ibrahim al-Nawfal, who founded the online magazine *Vision* (*www.royaah.net*), and Muhammad al-Abd al-Karim, who was jailed in December 2010 for a few months after pub-lishing an article about the need for the state to rely on popular legiti-macy instead of depending on a royal family whose divisions threaten the country's future.

From early February on, anonymous pages purportedly created by young Saudis began showing up on Facebook. Several groups announced their existence, among which the "Free Youth Coalition" soon attracted the largest number of sympathizers. Pages calling for a Saudi "Day of Anger" in imitation of the Tunisian and Egyptian protests started ap-pearing around the same time. Several dates were discussed, with a con-sensus soon settling on March 11. The Free Youth Coalition voiced sup-port for the planned protest, followed by the recently founded Islamic Umma Party—the only nonanonymous entity to take that step. Without making any explicit reference to March 11, a number of Islamist sheikhs close to the constitutional reformists published works arguing that public demonstrations could be a legitimate means of calling for reform.[7]

Shortly thereafter, the Day of Anger was being touted on Facebook as the "Hunayn Revolution." This was an Islamic reference to the Battle of Hunayn (630 C.E.), a victory that the early Muslims won over a Bedouin tribe called the Hawazin. Before long, tens of thousands of Facebook users had registered as Hunayn "fans." On March 4, a young man named Muhammad al-Wad'ani was filmed calling for "the fall of the monarchy" in front of the al-Rajhi Mosque in Riyadh. Though he was immediately arrested, the video, which was uploaded on YouTube together with other recorded statements in which he encouraged people to come out in numbers on March 11, produced the impression that the event was gathering momentum.

Unrest in the East

By that time, a similar—albeit organizationally quite separate—mobilization had begun in the oil-rich Eastern Province, home to most of Saudi Arabia's Shias. At the forefront stood a new generation of young Shia activists, who—like their Sunni counterparts—had made themselves known through blogs and Facebook and were largely independent of the two main established Shia political groups, the Shiraziyya and the "Line of the Imam." The leaders of these groups had long preferred quiet negotiations over open confrontations with the state. Many young activists disagreed, however. They wondered what good a low-key approach had done for a Shia community—widely thought to make up 10 to 15 percent of the country's population—that still faced social, economic, and religious discrimination.

In February, Facebook pages started calling for demonstrations. Some of those pages were focused exclusively on the defense of Shia rights, while others supported the broader project of pressing for constitutional monarchy. The activists had two main causes to promote. First, they demanded the release of the "forgotten prisoners" who had been detained without trial since the 1996 Khobar Towers bombing that killed 19 U.S. servicemen and a Saudi, and which the government had blamed on Saudi Hezbollah. Second, they proclaimed solidarity with the protests that had erupted in Bahrain on February 14. These appeals won the backing of a few Shia clerics, including the controversial Nimr al-Nimr, who had made headlines in 2009 for a sermon threatening the secession of the Eastern Province.

The first demonstration took place on February 17 in 'Awamiyya—Nimr al-Nimr's hometown, where protests had erupted in 2009. Protests continued on a weekly or even daily basis. They gained particular momentum after March 14, when Saudi troops, under the umbrella of the Gulf Cooperation Council's Peninsula Shield intervention force, entered Bahrain to quell the "revolution" there. According to Shia activists, there were as many as ten-thousand protesters in the streets of Saudi Arabia's main Shia cities on March 18 and 19.[8]

As editor-in-chef Tariq al-Humayyid of the London-based newspaper *Asharq Al-Awsat* has argued, however, "Saudi Arabia is not Egypt or Tunisia."[9] The Saudi state wields unique and massive resources, both material and symbolic. It produces around nine-million barrels of oil per day, which—with a barrel at around US$100—provides colossal revenue. This is in addition to the state's current cash reserves, which are known to be around $400 billion. These extraordinary means not only serve to buy and keep society's allegiance, but also to pay for a comprehensive security and intelligence apparatus as well as a vast empire of both international and domestic media outlets.

At the symbolic level, the state can rely on two intertwined discourses of legitimization, each of which has a corresponding apparatus. Saudi Arabia is the "land of the two holy places" (that is, the sacred cities of Mecca and Medina) and the protector of Wahhabi salafism, a purist brand of Islam whose origins go back to Muhammad Abd al-Wahhab (1703–92), cofounder of the first Saudi polity. An official religious establishment, headed by the grand mufti (the country's chief Sunni religious scholar), exists to legitimize the state's political decisions.

In addition, the state has recently striven to promote a complementary legitimating discourse: It presents itself as the provider of development and modernity and, especially since the late 1990s, as the guarantor of the unity of a "Saudi nation" that is bound at its core to the leadership of the royal family. This more secular discourse has become the trademark of a group of regime-friendly intellectuals who are active in the Saudi media and certain local institutions. It is noteworthy that the boundaries of this incipient Saudi nationalism have shifted over time: While King Abdullah, through his sponsorship of the first "national dialogues" in 2003 and 2004, once appeared favorable to a trans-sectarian definition of the nation that would make room for the Shia minority, Saudi-nationalist discourse has recently taken more pronounced sectarian overtones, with the stigmatization of Iran—and by extension, Shia Islam—as the enemy.

From early February on, the Saudi state started deploying its resources. The official clerical establishment proved instrumental in delegitimizing any attempt to protest. In early March, the mufti—who had already been critical of the revolutions in Egypt and Tunisia—joined his senior colleagues in issuing a *fatwa* (an opinion on the interpretation or application of Islamic law) against petitions and demonstrations.[10] A petition of ninety official sheikhs expressed the same position. On the planned Day of Anger, the Ministry of Religious Endowments ordered all imams in the Kingdom to read a prewritten sermon denouncing the protests.

The official or quasi-official media also played a key role: In the days preceding March 11, numerous articles and editorials denounced a conspiracy against the country, using strong nationalist rhetoric.

On February 24, as he returned from medical treatment abroad, King Abdullah announced the adoption of a domestic-aid program worth $37 billion. A more comprehensive $97 billion aid package was subsequently announced on March 18. Most of the measures included in both packages were meant to target the groups that had been at the forefront of the revolutions in Egypt and Tunisia—that is, young people and the poor. The packages included unemployment benefits and housing subsidies as well as public-sector jobs, including sixty-thousand new security positions in the Interior Ministry. Government employees were also offered extra pay and a minimum monthly wage of 3,000 riyals (approximately $800). Significant amounts of new funding went to religious institutions, including the religious police. To further secure the loyalty of the religious establishment, a new press law was adopted on April 29 forbidding, among other things, any criticism of senior Saudi clerics.

The intelligence apparatus was used extensively against the calls for demonstrations on March 11. In particular, activists assert that government hackers managed to access the Facebook pages calling for protests and added content that was meant to create confusion among potential sympathizers.[11] One particular action consisted of posting content associating the March 11 call with the protests that were taking place at the same moment in the Eastern Province, suggesting that the activists calling for demonstrations in Riyadh were Shias backed by Iran. Some activists even argued that the name Hunayn Revolution had first appeared on a page created by Saudi intelligence, making it subsequently easy for government loyalists to point to Shia responsibility for the Day of Anger since the Battle of Hunayn, considered above all a victory engineered by Ali, is an especially popular reference with Shias.

The Interior Ministry explicitly denounced the calls for demonstrations and warned that the authorities would not hesitate to use force. On the days of the protests, the security apparatus was out in large numbers. In Riyadh on March 11, the security presence made it impossible for anyone to reach the square where demonstrations were to take place. In the Eastern Province, protests were repressed, and a number of protesters were wounded. Hundreds of activists were arrested before, during, and after protests. The military intervention in Bahrain was also, in a way, meant to deliver to Saudi Shias the message that Saudi authorities were ready to use wider repression if unrest continued.

As a result of all this, the Day of Anger was a complete failure. Although the Shia protests continued until mid-May, they gradually lost momentum. At no point, therefore, did the Saudi regime feel the need to respond to protests and petitions by announcing political reforms. Its only political response, on March 22, was to finally set the date of the next municipal elections for September 2011—after they had been postponed for the last two years. As had been the case with the 2005 elections, moreover, authorities announced that only half of all munici-pal-council members would be elected and that, contrary to widespread expectations, women would not have the right to vote. This last decision was understood by many to be a reward to the religious establishment for its unwavering loyalty during the crisis.

The Opposition That Wasn't

What surprised some observers was the Sahwa's attitude during these events. While a few isolated figures signed the petition "Toward a State of Rights and Institutions," most Sahwa sheikhs refused to back the re-formist agenda. On February 28, as a response to the petitions published a few days earlier, some of the most prominent Sahwa clerics issued a statement outlining their vision of what had to be done for the country. Although it did mention the need to fight corruption, respect the legal rights of detainees, and find solutions to socioeconomic problems, the text stopped short of calling for any change in the political system. It also explicitly attacked liberals and Shias and warned against any form of Westernization.[12] In the days that followed, most major Sahwa fig-ures, including Nasir al-'Umar and the elderly Sheikh Abd al-Rahman al-Barrak, vocally denounced the calls for demonstrations.[13]

This was a significant blow to reformists. The Sahwa is the largest organized nonstate group in Saudi Arabia. Although some argue that its power has slightly decreased since the 1990s, it still commands a huge following, with arguably hundreds of thousands of members. The 2005 municipal elections demonstrated the extent of its mobilizing capacity: In most districts of all cities, Sahwa-backed candidates won with very high percentages. This makes the Sahwa the only force capable of dura-bly and effectively challenging the state. Just as in Egypt various young activists could launch protests, but without hope of success unless the Muslim Brotherhood supported them, so in Saudi Arabia no movement of dissent was going to get off the ground and take hold without the Sahwa's backing.

The comparison with Egypt ends there, however. Whereas Egyptian Islamism grew up on the margins of the state and in opposition to it, the Sahwa was the result of the cooptation of Muslim Brotherhood exiles into official Saudi institutions in the 1960s and 1970s. Since its incep-tion, therefore, the Sahwa has largely been embedded within the Saudi state, and has heavily benefited from the use of state structures and re-sources to spread its influence. Although some of the Sahwa's ideas are fundamentally critical of the policies favored by the Saudi state, the movement has generally been reluctant to confront it. The experi-ences of the early 1990s, when a number of Sahwa leaders spearheaded a failed "insurrection," have reinforced this reluctance. That explains why the Sahwa has largely proven unwilling to transform itself into a genuine opposition movement.

Just as the regime has effectively coopted Sunni Islamists, it also has been able to earn the silence, if not the support, of most major Shia leaders. When the recent protests started gaining momentum, some of the most influential Saudi Shias spoke out against them. On March 23 and April 21, two statements signed by dozens of sheikhs—including Abdullah al-Khunaizi, the former head of the Ja'fari (Shia) Islamic-law court in Qatif, and Hasan al-Saffar, the former leader of the Organization of the Islamic Revolution in the Arabian Peninsula—asked the youth to end their protests.[14] In the wake of these statements, the unrest among the Shia dwindled.

New Themes for Mobilization

By mid-March, most activists were ready to acknowledge that they had missed the opportunity to push a comprehensive reform agenda. Calls for structural change were replaced by more narrowly focused themes of mobilization. In particular, the issue of political prisoners— one of the few on which a consensus of all political forces could be reached—became central again. Despite their reluctance to confront the state, Sahwa sheikhs had proven much more responsive to this topic because many of the political prisoners were Sahwa youth who had been arrested on suspicions of harboring jihadist sympathies. On February 28, leading Sahwa figures, including Nasir al-'Umar, had even issued a statement demanding the release of, or fair trials for, those held without charge.[15] Later, Ibrahim al-Sikran and Yusuf al-Ahmad, two rising stars in the Sahwa, released videos in support of political prisoners. Young reformists, along with relatives of the detained and in coordination with the SCPRA, held monthly protests in front of the Interior Ministry in Riyadh. By Saudi standards, they were a success: YouTube videos show dozens of protesters, including many women, holding signs. A petition signed by 2,600 relatives of the detainees was also made public.[16]

The announcement of municipal elections for September 2011 also prompted activists to launch a boycott campaign. Calls were issued via Facebook and, on May 1, a boycott statement signed by 67 activists— many of them young—was posted online.[17] The reasons given by supporters of the boycott varied. Although most denounced the elections because municipal councils are only half-elected and have no real power, the more liberal-leaning activists also criticized the fact that women were denied the right to vote. Other young activists, rejecting the boycott altogether, argued that the elections would provide a welcome opportunity to promote political participation and to push for the election of youth representatives to the councils. To that end, groups such as the "Jeddah Youth to Municipal Council" appeared on Facebook and later moved to their own websites (such as *www.intekhab.at*).

Although the issue of women's rights had arisen during the boycott debate, it only gained steam in mid-May when pages calling for an end to the ban on driving by women started appearing on Facebook. Behind one of those pages was Manal al-Sharif, an employee of the state-owned oil company ARAMCO, who uploaded a video of herself defying the ban. Her May 21 arrest prompted liberal activists to start a nationwide campaign in her defense. They created a website (*www.freemanal.com*) and a petition that received more than a thousand signatures. After al-Sharif's May 30 release, she contributed to the launch of a Twitter campaign with the hashtag "#Women2drive," calling on women to defy the ban on June 17. According to reports, at least fifty women drove cars that day, some posting videos of themselves driving on YouTube. The move, hailed by liberals, provoked outrage in Islamist circles. Five of the women were subsequently arrested.[18]

On the face of it, the reemergence of the female-driving issue was good news for the regime. The placing of so much focus on a question of social reform made the more threatening debate on political reform even more marginal. At the same time, this episode brought to light interesting developments on the Saudi political scene. On previous occasions, the issue of women's right to drive had represented a clear dividing line between Islamists and liberals and a subject of heated disputes between them that the government knew how to use to its own advantage. This time, however, the fault lines were less clear-cut. Many of the young activists, including those with Islamist backgrounds, supported al-Sharif, even signing the petition in her favor. A few Islamist figures did the same, including Muhammad al-Ahmari, while some Sahwa sheikhs expressed support behind closed doors. Finally, a few official religious figures—including Qays al-Mubarak, a member of the Council of Senior Ulama since 2009—declared there was nothing in Islam to prohibit women from driving. It seems therefore that, on this issue at least, lines have started to move in Saudi Arabia.

The Saudi regime has largely been able to keep the domestic political situation under control. The momentum for political reform has been lost. This, however, does not mean that change will not happen in the future.

The state's resources, both material and symbolic, have limits. Because the state is so dependent on oil revenues, a prolonged drop in oil prices—not likely anytime soon, admittedly—would hamper its ability to buy social peace and coopt its opponents. Its monopoly on Islam is increasingly contested by independent clerics, despite the widely criticized September 2010 decree forbidding the issuance of *fatwas* by anyone but the official religious establishment. In addition, there is now a

growing community of young prodemocracy activists who are politically aware and know how to use new media to avoid official censorship.
Equally important, change is occurring within the Sahwa, as evidenced
by the participation of a few of its figures, such as Salman al-'Awda,
in reformist petitions. Despite the organic relationship that ties it to the
regime, the Sahwa remains a strategic actor. It threw its weight behind
protests against the regime once (in the early 1990s) and, in principle,
could do so again were it to become convinced that enough could be
gained by such a step. The issue of political prisoners—which has become central to the discourse of all oppositional political forces—could
serve as a trigger.

A defining moment for the Saudi regime will be the transition of
power to the second generation of royal princes. King Abdullah is 88,
his brother Crown Prince Sultan is 84, and the youngest first-generation
prince holding a government post is 66-year-old Prince Muqrin, who
heads the intelligence service. Until now, succession has been horizontal among the sons of the founding King Abdulaziz, from brother
to brother in order of seniority. Despite Abdullah's attempt to include
the whole family in the succession process by creating in 2006 an "allegiance committee" responsible for determining future succession to
the throne, many believe that the current horizontal system can hardly
be maintained within the second generation (which includes hundreds
of princes belonging to different branches), and that one of the family
branches will eventually try to impose its lineage as a basis for vertical
succession, possibly turning the monarchy into a more "classic" patri-
lineal system.

The potential for such a change in succession rules will make the
competition among the different branches much more acute during the
next few years. This could create opportunities for reformists, as one of
the branches may decide to seek their support in order to stand out from
the competition. This scenario, suggested by a young activist, would
be the smoothest way to effect change. "Otherwise," the same activist
added, "we are going to have thirty more years of dictatorship until the
situation simply explodes, and God help us when that happens."[19]

NOTES

1. Thomas Hegghammer, *Jihad in Saudi Arabia: Violence and Pan-Islamism since
1979* (Cambridge: Cambridge University Press, 2010).

2. Author's phone interview with a Saudi reformist, May 2010.

3. Sue Lloyd Roberts, "Saudi Arabia Show of Force Stifles 'Day of Rage' Protests,"
BBC News, 11 March 2011.

4. "I'lan watani li-l-islah" [National declaration of reform], *www.saudireform.com*.

5. "Nahwa dawlat al-huquq wa-l-mu'assasat" [Toward a state of rights and institutions], *www.dawlaty.info*.

6. "Risalat shabab 23 Febrayir ila-l-malik" [February 23 letter of the youth to the king], *www.alwahabi.com/?p=553*.

7. Abd al-Karim al-Khadar, "Al-adilla wa-l-bayyinat 'ala hukm al-muzaharat wa-l-i'tisamat" [Proof and evidence regarding the ruling on demonstrations and sit-ins], *http://acpra.net/news_view_113.html*; Sa'ud al-Funaysan, "Nazarat shar'iyya . . . fi wasa'il al-taghyir al-'asriyya" [Views of *shari'a* . . . on the modern ways to effect change], *http://taseel.com/display/pub/default.aspx?id=881&mot=1*.

8. "'Ashrat alaf mutazahir fi-l-Qatif yatadamanun ma' du'at al-dimuqratiyya fi-l-Bahrain" [Ten-thousand demonstrators in Qatif in solidarity with prodemocracy activists in Bahrain], *http://rasid.com/artc.php?id=43452*.

9. *Asharq Al-Awsat*, 15 March 2011.

10. "Saudi Clerics Slam Protest Calls," AFP, 6 March 2011.

11. "Li-madha fashalat da'awa al-tazahur yawm 11 mars?" [Why did the calls for March 11 demonstrations fail?], *www.saudiwave.com/ar/2010-11-09-15-55-47/706------11--.html*.

12. "Bayan da'wa li-l-islah" [Statement calling for reform], *www.islamlight.net/index.php?option=content&task=view&id=21468&Itemid=33*.

13. For al-Barrak, *www.muslm.net/vb/showthread.php?t=426493*; for al-'Umar, *www.YouTube.com/watch?v=BKAA-u8DxiU*.

14. "Al-shaykh al-Khunaizi yad'u ila waqf al-tazahurat fi-l-Qatif" [Sheikh al-Khunaizi calls for an end to demonstrations in Qatif], *www.rasid.com/artc.php?id=43553*; "rijal al-din fi-l-Qatif yad'un li waqf al-tazaharut al-ihtijajiyya" [Religious scholars in Qatif call for an end to protests], *www.rasid.com/artc.php?id=44029*.

15. For the statement, see *www.alhabdan.net/index.php?option=content&task=view&id=21467&Itemid=33*.

16. "'A'ilat al-mu'taqalin al-siyasiyyin mundhu sanawat bidun muhakama yab'athuna bikhitab ila khadim al-haramayn al-sharifayn" [The families of the political detainees held for many years without trial send a letter to the Custodian of the Holy Places], *http://royaah.net/detail.php?id=1141*.

17. "I'lan muqata'at al-intikhabat al-baladiyya al-sa'udiyya" [Announcement of boycott of the Saudi municipal elections], *http://baladi-sa.net/index.php?act=artc&id=85&show=news&newsname=default*.

18. For background from a participant, see Eman Al Nafjan, "Saudi Women Driving Movement," 29 June 2011, Saudiwoman's Weblog, *http://saudiwoman.wordpress.com/2011/06/29/saudi-women-driving-movement*.

19. Author's phone interview with a young Saudi activist, March 2011.

INDEX

Note:
n refers to a citation
f refers to a figure
t refers to a table

Abdullah (King of Jordan), xxxi, 117, 351, 353–55, 361
Abdullah (King of Saudi Arabia), 367, 374
Abul Futuh, Abdel Moneim, 19, 21, 101, 242, 257–258
Afghanistan, 24, 52, 115, 167, 279, 297
Ahmar clan, 278, 280–82, 286
AKP, 23, 26–27, 40, 51–52, 224
al-Ahmar, Ali Mohsen, 137, 167, 278, 280
al-Asala, 318–23
al-Assad, Bashar, ix, xix, 43, 93, 97, 112, 116, 127, 132, 136, 138, 146, 155, 163, 169–70, 194, 296, 300–312
al-Assad, Hafiz, 132, 137–38, 170
al-'Awda, Salman, 366, 374
Alawites, xix, 26, 93, 97, 137–38, 155, 170, 173n20, 303, 305–7, 311
Al-Azhar, 41, 102, 259
Albania, 82, 157, 160n7
Algeria: Arab Spring in, ix, xxx, 118t, 128, 188, 190–91, 290, 302, 328–29, 331–32; army, role of, in, 329, 333; authoritarian resilience in, xi, 326–27, 335; civil society in, 331; civil war in, xxx, 17; electoral system in, 183, 184t, 328; Green Algeria Alliance, 334–35; Islamism in, 40, 63t, 229, 329–30, 334–36; military spending in, 131, 333; minorities in, xix; 1991 elections in, 86, 191, 275, 327; oil rents in, 133t, 139–40, 328; patronage in, 327–28, 331–36; religious tolerance in, 60, 62; salafism in, 328; secularism in, 17, 76, 328, 331; strikes in, 191, 328, 330, 332; social media in, 191, 198; Sunnis in, 98; support for democracy in, 56f, 58, 64
al-Haq, 318–19, 322, 325n13
Al-Jazeera, 7, 71, 188, 191, 193–94, 196, 209
al-Khalifa, xxix, 112, 116, 120, 122–23, 125, 138, 169, 315–17, 320, 322–24
al-Minbar, 319–22
al-Qaeda, 19, 22–23, 25, 46, 169, 206, 278–79, 283, 288n13, 305, 309, 328, 354, 365
al-Wifaq, xxix, 315–16, 318–22, 324, 325nn13–14

April 6ᵗʰ Movement, xxvi, 101, 234, 252–54, 261

army, role of: in Algeria, xxx, 329, 333; in Arab Spring, 128, 162–64, 170–71; in Bahrain, xxiii, 169–70; in Egypt, 16, 23–24, 32–33, 41, 93, 136, 165–66, 194, 224, 238–39; Islamists and, 24, 31, 52; in Libya, 92, 155, 168, 291; in Syria, xxiii, 129, 132, 138, 148, 170, 307; in Tunisia, 94, 129, 136, 164–66, 211–12, 214–15, 225; in Yemen, xxiii, 149, 162, 164, 168, 172

authoritarian-democratic hybrid, xix, 85, 87

Ayatollah Khomeini, xv–xvi, 21, 35, 38–39, 41, 308

Baath party (Ba'ath), 11, 25; in Syria, 12, 170, 301, 305, 309

Bahrain, xiii*t*; Arab Spring in, xx, xxix–xxx, 26, 97, 112–14, 118*t*, 118–19, 126*n14*, 134–35, 137, 146, 187, 193, 315, 317, 321, 368; army in, xxiii, 169–70; autocracy in, 98–99, 109–110, 114–15, 117, 120, 127, 138, 148, 152, 171, 183, 302, 312, 318, 323; BICI, 316; constitutional reform in, xi; digital media in, 191, 195–96; electoral system in, 184*t*, 185; foreign patrons and, 121–23, 125, 140; Islamism in, xii; Jordan and, 319; Khalifa in, xxix, 110, 112, 116, 120, 122–23, 125, 138, 312, 315–17, 320, 322–24; Kuwait and, 138; military in, 131, 155, 164, 169–172; Muslim Brotherhood in, 318–319; oil rents in, xxi; protests in, xi; salafism in, 318–19, 325n13; Saudi Arabia and, 323, 368, 370; Shias in, xxiii, xxix, 110, 118, 120, 138, 155, 169–70, 191, 315–21; social media in, 190–92, 194–96, 198; Sunni Muslims in, xii, xx, xxiii, xxix, 99, 109, 119–120, 124*t*, 138, 148, 155, 169–70, 191, 196, 315–16, 318–23, 357; Sunni-Shia tensions within, 319–20, 322, 357. *See also* al-Asala; al-Minbar; al-Wifaq

Banna, Hassan al-, 30, 33–34, 47–48

Basij, 154, 308

Belaid, Chokri, 90, 107

Belhadj, Ali, 329–331

Ben Ali, Zine al-Abidine: fall of, ix, xxii, xxiv, 21, 55, 85, 88–90, 104, 112, 122, 131, 137, 148, 153, 165, 177, 186, 188–89, 203–16, 219, 221, 339, 366; military and, xxiii, 129, 136, 155, 164–65, 225; patronage and, 120; social media and, 191; sultanism of, 93–94, 132, 136, 162–63, 232*n25*

Benkirane, Abdelilah, xxx, 344–46

Berbers, 294, 328, 330–31

blasphemy laws: in Egypt, 259; in Pakistan, 45, 49–51, 53*n7*; in Tunisia, 106–7

Bouazizi, Mohamed, xxiv, 55, 144, 151–52, 187–88, 193–94, 205, 208; social media and, 188–89, 209, 216*n10*

Bourguiba, Habib, xxv, 88, 90, 133; coup against, 204, 229; military and, 165, 225; secularization and, 228–230, 231*n11*; women and, 210

Bouteflika, Abdelaziz, 328, 331–32, 334, 336

Bulgaria, 147, 295

Catholic, 17, 81–82, 84

Chile, 81, 91, 236

China, xxix, 42, 143–44, 148–49, 153–54, 159, 304, 308

Christians: in Algeria, 28n5; democratization and, 36–37, 40; in Egypt, 87, 98, 103, 146, 175, 241, 244, 259; electoral systems and, 177, 180, 184t; in Europe, 42; in Indonesia, 84; in Jordan, 119, 353–54; in Morocco, 28n5; Nahda and, 6; in Pakistan, 51, 53n7; in Syria, 98, 305. *See also* Coptic Christians

civil society, xvii; in Algeria, 331; Arab Spring and, 7, 210; army and, 163; in Egypt, 88, 223, 260; in Kuwait, 117; liberalism and, 249–50; in Libya, 159, 289, 294, 296, 298; oil rents and, 130; religion and, 82, 220; in Russia, 156; social media and, xxiv, 187, 189–90, 195–96, 198–99, 203; threats to, 60; in Tunisia, xxiv, 88, 104, 213, 221, 223

civil state, 84; in Egypt, 258; in Tunisia, 107

civil war: in Algeria, xxx, 17; in Bahrain, 193; in Iraq, xi; in Jordan, 355; in Libya, xix, xxviii, 92, 149, 168, 172, 193; in Syria, ix, xii, xviii–xxix, 26, 43, 93, 97, 112, 127, 134–45, 138, 140, 146, 193, 277, 300–309, 312–13, 322, 355, 360–61; in Tunisia, 229, 281; in Yemen, 149, 168–69, 172, 182, 184, 193, 287

communism, 11, 35, 37, 39; fall of, 86, 151, 153–54, 156. *See also* postcommunism

communist parties, 52–53; in China, 153; in Cuba, 153; in France, 39; in North Korea, 153; in Poland, 157; in Portugal, 16–17; in Spain, 16–17; in the Soviet Union, 37

constitutions: in Algeria, 328, 334; in Bahrain, 318–19, 321, 324;

democratization and, 156–57, 185; in Egypt, xiii–xiv, xx, 31–32, 65, 86–87, 100–103, 111n10, 136, 174–76, 238, 240–43, 245, 251, 255–60, 264–74, 276–77; in EU, 18; in Jordan, 351–52, 354, 357–58, 360–61; in Libya, xxviii, 109, 134, 167, 292–94, 297; monarchies and, 114, 117, 128, 186; in Morocco, xxx, 338–49, 349–50n2, 350nn3,4; in Pakistan, 50; in Saudi Arabia, 365–66, 368; *shari'a* and, 9, 11, 26–27, 95n13; in Syria, 311; in Tunisia, xi, xiii, xxiv, 89–90, 105–7, 179, 213–14, 219, 221–22, 226–28; Turkish model of, 23; the "twin tolerations" and, 82; in Yemen, 182, 277–78, 281–82, 284–86, 288n17

Coptic Christians, 21; in Egypt, 86, 98, 103, 175, 177, 244, 259; in Tunisia, 146

corruption: in Algeria, 333; Arab Spring and, xxii, 54, 57; in Bahrain, 321–22; in Egypt, 65, 93, 156, 183, 233, 235, 237, 244, 252; in Jordan, 351, 357–58; in Kuwait, 118; monarchies and, 121, 140; in Saudi Arabia, xxxi, 364, 371; social media and, 187, 189, 212; in Tunisia, 66, 156, 165, 187, 207, 212; in Yemen, xxvii, 167, 278, 280–81, 283

Cuba, 42, 148, 153–54, 159

culture: Arab Spring and, xxxii; Islam and, xiv, xviii, 4, 10, 18–20, 24, 27, 43, 69–72, 74–75, 77, 123, 210, 226; monarchism and, 113–14, 125; secularism and, 26, 73, 78–80

Czech Republic, 151, 157

Day of Anger, xxxii, 368–70

democracy, support for, xii, xvii,
54–56, 56f, 58; in Algeria, 56f,
58, 64; in Egypt, 63t, 64–65,
237, 239–40, 245; in Jordan,
56–59, 64, 68n12; in Lebanon,
56f, 56–59, 58t, 64; in Russia,
156; in Tunisia, 66
democratization: in Algeria, xxx,
326–27; Arab Spring and,
ix, xv, xvii 144, 152, 158; in
Bahrain, 353–55; civil war and,
300–301; culture and, 4, 80;
digital media and, 187, 191–92,
197–98; in Egypt, 147, 156,
158, 177, 223–24, 239–40,
246–47, 254, 263–64, 268–73,
276; Islam and, xviii, 16–18,
20–21, 28–31, 37, 43–44, 60,
63, 82–83; in Jordan, xxxi,
353–55; in Libya, 290, 292,
296, 298; pact-making and, 97;
in Saudi Arabia, 312, 353–55;
sultanism and, xix, 91; in Syria,
xxii, xxix, 171–72, 312–13; in
Tunisia, xxv, xxxii, 103–4, 134,
156, 223; *Weltanschauung* politics and, 10, 13
Denmark, 82, 84
digital media: Arab Spring and, xiv,
xxiv, 186–87, 192–93, 197–99;
in Bahrain, 191, 195–96; democratization and, 187, 191–92,
197–98; in Egypt, 189–90,
195–96; in Libya, 196; in Morocco, 195; in Saudi Arabia, 196;
in Syria, 190, 192–95, 198; in
Tunisia, 187–88. *See also* Facebook; Internet; social media;
Twitter; YouTube
Dominican Republic, 91–92, 142n15

Eastern Europe, xxii, 147, 153;
democratization in, 157–58, 250;
fall of Communism in, 151–152.
See also country names

Egypt, xiiit, 118t, 133t, 144, 171,
233–76, 280, 290, 302–3, 330,
354–55, 357–58, 365–67,
369–71; civil society in, 88, 223,
260; constitutions in, 31–32, 65,
86–87, 100–103, 111n10, 136,
174–76, 238, 240–43, 245, 251,
255–60, 264–74, 276–77; Coptic
Christians in, 21, 146, 175; corruption in, 65, 93, 156, 183, 233,
235, 237, 244, 252; culture in,
78, 263; democratization in, 147,
156, 158, 177, 223–24, 239–40,
246–47, 254, 263–64, 268–73,
276; digital media in, 189–90,
195–96; economy in, xxvi, 65,
120, 238–39, 245–47, 349, 353,
356; electoral systems in, xxi,
174, 176, 181, 183, 184t, 184,
237, 240, 242, 253, 263, 265–66,
268; Facebook in, 77, 189–90,
254; Islamism in, xxvi, xxvii,
16, 22, 24, 26, 44–45, 64, 146,
159, 241–43, 258–59, 273–75,
297, 334, 354; Israel and, 25, 42,
236, 239; January 25 Revolution
in, xi, 186, 254–55; Kifaya in,
xi, xxvi, 234, 251–53, 256, 261;
liberalism in, xxvi, 21–22, 41,
86, 102, 223, 227, 238, 249–51,
254–58, 260–61; military in,
xxvi–xxvii, 24, 31, 64, 66,
86–87, 99–100, 112, 129, 136,
146, 155, 165–66, 170, 184, 198,
222, 225, 236, 238–40, 258–59,
264–65, 267–68, 269–70, 274,
334; Muslim Brotherhood in,
xii, xv–xvii, xix, xxvi–xxvii, 17,
21, 25, 27, 30–43, 52, 65, 66,
86–88, 97, 100–102, 109, 111n9,
146, 159, 176–77, 189, 224–25,
237, 239–243, 248–49, 251–61,
266–69, 273–76, 367; NDC in,
103, 111n10; patrons and, 122,
195; salafism in, 16–17, 19, 21,

65, 100–101, 159, 176–77, 243, 248, 255–59; secularism in, xix–xx, xxvi, 22, 86–87, 98, 100, 103, 158–59, 176–77, 237, 239, 241–43, 249, 253, 255–59, 261, 262n12; *shari'a* in, 88, 241, 256, 258–60; social media in, xxiv, 77, 188–90, 194–96, 254; sultanism in, 92–93, 132, 162–63, 233; Sunnis in, 98; support for democracy in, 56*t*, 63*t*, 64–65, 239–40, 245. *See also* ElBaradei; Morsi; Mubarak; SCAF

ElBaradei, Mohamed, 234, 240, 253–54, 257–59, 261

electoral systems, xii, xxi, 184*t*; in Algeria, 183, 184*t*, 328; in Bahrain, 183, 184*t*; in Egypt, xxi, 174, 176, 181, 183, 184*t*, 184, 237, 240, 242, 253, 263, 265–66, 268; goals of, 175; in Jordan, 181, 183, 184*t*, 359; in Lebanon, 183, 184*t*; in liberalized autocracies, 98; in Libya, 293; in Morocco, 183, 184*t*, 344; in Palestine, 182, 183, 184*t*; in Syria, 183, 184*t*; in Tunisia, xxiii, 177, 183, 184*t*, 185, 215, 222; in Yemen, 183, 184*t*, 284

Ennahda, 13, 16–17, 21, 23–24, 39, 52, 66–67, 83–84, 88–89, 105–7, 159, 213, 215, 219–20, 222, 224–25, 229, 231n4, 334

Essebsi, Béji Caïd, 90, 106, 213, 215

EU (European Union), 18, 26, 82, 157–58

Facebook, xxx, 149, 187, 197, 199; in Algeria, 188; in China, 144; in Egypt, 77, 189–90, 254; in Jordan, 352, 357; in Morocco, 339; in Saudi Arabia, 367–68, 370, 372–73; in Syria 194; in Tunisia, 203, 209. *See also* social media

Feb20 (Moroccan protest), 339, 348

festivalization, 72, 78–79

FIRC (Foreign-Imposed Regime Change), 133, 134, 140; in Iraq, 135, 140; in Libya, 135, 137, 139–40

FIS (Islamic Salvation Front), 327, 329–30, 334

FJP (Freedom and Justice Party), 101, 109, 255–57

FLN (National Liberation Front), 327, 334–36

foreign patrons, monarchies and, 114, 122–23

France, 17, 32, 39, 124*t*, 137, 150n4, 165, 204, 211–12, 219, 225, 227–28, 231n5, 327, 348, 350n10; secularism of, xxv, 12, 51, 82, 84, 218–19, 228

fundamentalism, Islamic, xxxi, 6, 20, 354. *See also* salafism; Wahhabi

Gaza, 22, 181

GCC (Gulf Cooperation Council), xxix, 133; in Bahrain, 112, 117, 119, 121, 123, 124*t*, 140, 312; in Jordan, 121–23, 124*t*, 312; in Morocco, 312; in Oman, 121–22, 124*t*; in Yemen, 137, 277, 281, 283

Germany, 82, 84, 131, 151

Ghannouchi, Mohamed, 213, 220

Ghannouchi, Rachid, 13, 23, 52, 83–84, 89, 104–106, 213, 224–25, 229, 231n8

Ghonim, Wael, 189–90, 195

GNC (General National Congress), 289–93, 295, 297

GPC (General People's Congress), 182, 278, 280, 282, 284, 286, 290

Green Algeria Alliance, 334–35

Hadi, Abdu Rabu Mansour, 137, 277, 281–84

Hamas, xii, 22, 25–26, 40, 60, 63, 68n17, 181, 275
Hezbollah, xxix, 26, 138, 303–5, 308, 311, 368
Hinduism, 82–84
human rights: Arab Spring and, 15, 29; democratization and, 14, 42; in Egypt, 21, 65, 244, 259, 261, 263; in language, xv, 6–7; in Morocco, 340–42; in Saudi Arabia, 365, 367; in Syria, 306; in Tunisia, 66, 107, 210
Hungary, 147, 151, 156–57
Huntington, Samuel P., 43, 82, 114, 143, 154, 238
hydrocarbon rents, 114, 121, 123–24, 130. *See also* oil rents

IAF (Islamic Action Front), 354–55, 359
Ibn Khaldun, 13, 226
India, xix, 48–49, 82–84, 131, 218, 222
Indonesia, xix, 82–85, 87, 120, 171, 198, 218
Internet: in Algeria, 188; Arab Spring and, 8, 187, 192–93, 195, 198; civil society and, xxiv, 78, 199; culture and, xviii, 71–73, 77; in Egypt, xi, xxiv, 189–90, 251; in Jordan, 360; in Libya, 294; religiosity and, 20; in Saudi Arabia, 196; social change and, 19; in Syria, 303; in Tunisia, xxiv, 188, 209; in Yemen, 283. *See also* digital media; Facebook; social media; Twitter; YouTube
Iran: Algeria and, 229; Arab Spring and, 151; authoritarian resilience in, 148, 153–55, 159; Bahrain and, 169, 321, 323; culture in, 78; Egypt and, xvi, 16, 21, 24, 32; Internet in, 77, 189; Iraq and, 154, 308; Isla-

mism in, 22, 35, 41–42, 52; Israel, and 26; Jordan and, 353; monarchy in, 115, 121, 358; Muslim Brotherhood and, 43; Saudi Arabia and, 323, 364, 369–70; secularism in, 20; *shari‘a* in, 20; Shia in, 26, 147, 169, 287n1, 370; Syria and, xxi, 138, 303–305, 308, 311; Tunisia and, 16, 21, 24
Iraq: al-Qaeda in, 19, 279, 309; Arab Spring and, 118t, 145, 174; Bahrain and, 320; civil war in, xi, xxix, 98, 109, 320; democracy in, xi–xii, xiv, 19, 24; FIRC in, 135, 140; and Iran, 154, 308; Islamism in, xii, 98; Jordan and, 353, 355; Kurds in, 310; Libya and, 297; regime in, xiiit, xviii, xxix, 115, 120, 133, 358; Shias in, 26, 98, 109, 287n1, 320; Sunnis in, xii, xix, 98, 109, 320
Islah, 182, 277–86, 334
Islamic exceptionalism, 73–74
Islamic law, xv, xvii, 8–9, 48–49, 106–7, 224, 241, 253, 258, 262n5, 297, 210, 342, 369. See also *shari‘a*
Islamic revival, 6, 46–48
Islamic revolution, 16, 38, 41, 254, 321, 372, in Afghanistan, 52; in Algeria, xxx, 76, 327–31, 334–36; Arab culture and, 5–8, 10, 25–26, 35–37, 43, 70, 74–76; authoritarian resilience and, xii, xix, 75–76, 97–98; in Bahrain, xii, xxix, 109, 316, 318–23; democratization and, x, xv–xvi, 13, 16–17, 20, 22–24, 26, 30–31, 35, 38, 40, 42, 48–49, 52–53, 63, 83, 97, 108, 145, 147–48, 158; in Egypt, xi, xvi, xx, xxvi–xxvii, 15–17, 24, 29, 44, 47, 64–65, 67, 76, 86, 95n13, 98, 100–103, 109, 127, 146, 159, 176, 190, 235,

240–43, 247–48, 250–61, 262*n5*, 265–70, 272–76, 371; in Iraq, xii, 98; in Iran, 22, 35, 41–42, 52; in Jordan, xxxi, 25, 44, 63*t*, 64, 98, 352–55, 359, 361; in Kuwait, xii; in Lebanon, 61*t*, 62, 63*t*; in Libya, xxviii, 295–98; in Morocco, 98, 339, 344; in Pakistan, xvii, 44–46, 49–51; in Palestine, xii; in Saudi Arabia, 26, 365–68, 372–73; secularism and, 22–23, 26–27, 31, 33, 45–46, 51–53, 98; in Sudan, 52; in Syria, xxix, 97, 109, 303, 305, 309–11; in Tunisia, xix, 15–17, 24–25, 64, 66–67, 83, 88, 90, 98, 104–9, 159, 206, 211, 213, 215–16, 219–20, 224, 229–30, 231*n10*; in Turkey, 51–52; in Yemen, 98, 182, 277, 287. *See also* Muslim Brotherhood

Israel: Arab-Israeli conflict, 15, 25, 43, 152, 355; digital media and, 190, 195; Egypt and, 25, 42, 236, 239; Hamas and, 40; Iran and, 26; Jordan and, 353–54; Lebanon and, 22; Saudi Arabia and, 26; Syria and, 137, 302

Jamaat-e-Islami, 46, 48, 52
Jebali, Hamadi, 84, 90, 219, 224–25
Jews, 6; in Jordan, 353; in Tunisia, 227
jihadists, 19, 23, 46, 51, 77, 105, 108, 297, 354, 372
JMP (Joint Meeting Parties), 182, 277, 280–82
Jordan, xiii*t*, 56*f*, 133*t*; Arab Spring and, xxxi, 188, 198; authoritarian resilience in, xi–xii, 44, 112–19, 122–24, 135, 140, 186, 302, 312, 351–61; Bahrain and, 319; electoral system in, 179–81, 183–84, 184*t*, 185n3; GCC and, 121–23, 124*t*, 133; GID in,

355, 357–61; Islamism in, 25, 44, 63*t*, 64, 98; Muslim Brotherhood in, 25, 354, 357; NDC in, 180; religious tolerance in, 60–62; secularism in, 352, 354–55; support for democracy in, 56–59, 64, 68*n12*

Khalifa, xxix, 110, 112, 116, 120, 122–23, 125, 138, 312, 315–17, 320, 322–24
Kifaya, xi, xxvi, 234, 251–53, 256, 261
Kurds: in Iraq, 310; in Syria, 305–6
Kuwait, xiii*t*, 118*t*, 133*t*; Arab Spring in, 112, 117–118; authoritarian resilience in, 114–16, 119–21, 131, 135, 302; Bahrain and, 138; elections in, 117; Islamism in, xii; Muslim Brotherhood in, 25; oil rents and, 121, 124*t*, 126*n20*, 130; patrons and, 122; Saudi Arabia and, 366; Sunnis in, xii, 119–20, 124*t*

laïcité, xxv, 12, 51–52, 82, 84, 228
Lebanon, xiii*t*; Arab Spring and, 118*t*, 174, 183, 188; Cedar Revolution in, xi; culture in, 77, 79; electoral system in, 184*t*; Hezbollah in, 22, 305; Islamism in, 61*t*, 62, 63*t*; sectarianism in, xiv, 14*n9*; *shari'a* in, 60; support for democracy in, 56*f*, 56–59, 58*t*, 64; Syria and, xi, 137, 305
Libya, xiii*t*; Arab Spring in, ix, 112, 118*t*, 133*t*, 133–34; army in, xxiii, 162, 164, 167–68, 171; civil war in, xix, xxviii, 92, 149, 168, 172, 193; constitutional reform in, xxviii, 109, 134, 167, 292–94, 297; economy in, 121; FIRC in, 135, 137, 139–40; Islamism in, xxviii, 295–98; militias in, xxviii, 92, 109, 127,

Libya *(cont'd)*
155, 291–92, 295–98; Muslim
Brotherhood in, 296–97; oil rents
in, 130, 137; patrons in, 123–24;
populism in, 139, 297; regime in,
xiv, xix, xxi–xxii, xxvi, xxxiii*in5*,
85, 159, 167, 172, 183, 184*t*,
185–86, 292–93, 296; salafism
in, 296–97; secularism in, 297;
shari'a in, 297–98; social media
in, xxiv, 190–91, 193–94, 198,
294; sultanism in, 92–93, 155.
See also Qadhafi
LIFG (Libyan Islamic Fighting
Group), 295–96
Lipset, Seymour Martin, 3–5, 11,
13–14, 14*n2*

Majlis al Shura, 316–18, 323,
366–67
Marcos, Ferdinand, 92–93, 142*n15*
Marzouki, Moncef, 89, 105, 213,
219–20
Mawdudi, Sayyid Abu'l A'la, 48,
50, 52
militias, 134; in Libya, xxviii, 92,
109, 127, 155, 291–92, 295–98;
in Syria, 305, 308; in Yemen,
281
minority populations: in Bahrain,
119–20, 124*t*, 148, 155, 191;
democracy and, xix, xxix; in
Egypt, 98, 103, 146, 175, 239,
249–50, 257; in India, 84; in
Indonesia, 84; in Jordan, 119,
124*t*, 354; in Kuwait, 119, 124*t*;
in Morocco, 98; in Pakistan,
53*n7*; in Syria, xix, 93, 98, 137–
38, 148, 155, 170, 303, 305–7,
310–11; in Tunisia, 179; in
Yemen, 284. *See also* Alawites;
Coptic Christians; Kurds
monarchism, 115–17, 125, 128–30,
354
Morocco, xiii*t*, 124*t*, 133*t*; Arab

Spring in, ix, xxx–xxxi, 118*t*,
118–19, 122, 135, 151, 183,
184*t*, 186; authoritarian resilience in, xix, 112–17, 302, 338–
49; COG (Chief of Government)
in, 345–46; constitution in, xxx,
338–49, 349–50*n2*, 350*nn3,4*;
CSM (Superior Council of Magistrates) in, 346; festivalization
in, 79; GCC and, 121, 312; Islamism in, 23, 98, 334; minorities
in, 98; monarchy in, xiv, 133,
140, 357; patrons and, 122; salafism in, 71; social media in, 195,
198; Sunnis in, 98
Morsi, Mohamed, xxvi, 31, 39, 42,
47, 66, 87, 101–2, 248, 257–60,
263–64, 266–70, 273–76, 354
Moussa, Amr, 240, 257–59
MSP (Movement for a Peaceful
Society), 328, 334, 336
Mubarak, Gamal, xxiii, 93, 132,
166, 237, 250
Mubarak, Hosni, ix, xi, xvi, xx, xxii,
xxv–xxvii, 21, 32, 38, 47, 55,
85–89, 93, 99–100, 112, 115–16,
120–23, 132, 136, 144, 146, 148,
153, 155, 163, 166, 175–76,
185*n1*, 186, 189–91, 194–97,
221, 233–37, 240, 244–45,
248–60, 263–64, 270, 275–76,
280, 330, 339, 357, 366
mukhabarat (secret police), 60, 98;
Ben Ali's, 203–4, 208
Muslim Brotherhood: Arab Spring
and, 16, 19; in Bahrain, 318–19;
culture and, 18, 76; democratization and, 22, 24, 30–43, 46–48,
240; in Egypt, xii, xv–xvii,
xix, xxvi–xxvii, 17, 21, 25, 27,
30–43, 52, 65, 66, 86–88, 97,
100–102, 109, 111*n9*, 146, 159,
176–77, 189, 224–25, 237, 239–
43, 248–49, 251–61, 266–69,
273–76, 367; in Jordan, 25, 354,

357; in Kuwait, 25; in Libya, 296–97; in Pakistan, 50; re-Islamization and, 20–21, 49; in Saudi Arabia, 26, 365, 367, 371; in Syria, 25, 137, 170, 309

NAC (National Association for Change), 253–54
Nahda (Arab Renaissance), 6, 33, 258
Nasser, Gamel Abdel, xv, xxvii, 176, 245
NATO, ix, xxi, 92, 135, 139–40, 155, 168, 186
NCCD (National Coordination for Change and Democracy), 330–31
NDC (National Defense Council), in Egypt, 103, 111*n10*
NDC (National Dialogue Conference), in Jordan, 180; in Yemen, 277–78, 282–86
NDF (National Defense Force), 305, 308
NDP (National Democratic Party), xxv–xxvi, 175–76, 235–36, 240, 244, 249–51, 256
NGOs (nongovernmental organizations), 71, 99, 102, 210
North Korea, 154, 159
Nour party, 16, 19, 65, 101, 177, 255, 258
NTC (National Transitional Council), 291–97

oil rents, in Algeria, 328, 332–33; Arab Spring and, 28*n9*, 128, 130, 133*t*, 134; authoritarian resilience and, xx–xxi, 113, 119, 121–22, 125, 126*n20*, 135, 139–40; in Bahrain, 134, 137–38, 140, 169; democratization and, xiii, 97; in Libya, xxviii, 134–35, 137, 139, 289, 294; in Qatar, 121, 123–24, 124*t*, 131, 133*t*;

in Saudi Arabia, xxxi, 124*t*, 130–31, 357, 369; in Syria, xxi, 133*t*, 134; in UAE, 121, 124*t*; in Yemen, xxvii, 280. *See also* hydrocarbon rents
Oman, xiii*t*; Arab Spring and, 112, 118*t*, 118, 133*t*; GCC and, 123, 124*t*; liberalization in, 191; rebellions in, 116

pacts (for democratic transition), xix, 97, 100, 103
Pakistan, xvii, 44–53; Bahrain and, 138; blasphemy laws in, 51, 53*n7*; Islamism in, 45–46, 49–51; secularism in, 45, 49–50; *shari'a* in, 45, 49–50
Palestine, xii, 22, 174, 181–83, 184*t*, 185, 275
Palestinian Jordanians, 119, 124*t*, 180–81, 183, 351–52, 355–56, 359
PDP (Progressive Democratic Party), 220, 225
Philippines, 92, 142n15
Poland, 94, 147, 151, 156–57
postcommunism, 147, 152, 156–57

Qadhafi, Muammar, 95*n10*, 121, 123, 183; digital media and, 191, 194, 196, 294; fall of, ix, xxviii, 112, 135, 139, 146, 289, 298; hereditary succession plans of, 92, 116, 167; Islamism and, 296–97; military and, 168–69, 291; NATO and, 123, 135, 139, 155, 186; populism of, 139; reforms of, 294–96; sultanism of, 92, 155, 290
Qatar, xiii*t*; Arab Spring in, 112, 118*t*, 118; monarchy in, 114–15; oil rents and, 121, 123–24, 124*t*, 131, 133*t*

racial tolerance, 54, 60, 63*t*, 64

Rawls, John, 85, 230*n1*
RCD (Democratic Constitutional Assembly: Tunisia), 206, 213–15
RCD (Rally for Culture and Democracy: Algeria), 330
religiosity, 13, 20–21, 36, 43, 51, 70, 72–73
RND (National Democratic Rally), 328, 334–35
Romania, 147, 151–52, 157–58
Russia, xxii, xxix, 42, 138, 156–57, 304; and Syria, 308, 311. *See also* Soviet Union

Sabahi, Hamdeen, 239, 257, 259
Sadat, Anwar, xxvii, 25, 39, 235
Sahwa (Islamic Awakening), xxxii, 365–67, 370–74
salafism, xv, xviii, 18, 20, 22–23, 25–27, 30, 37, 39–40, 70–77, 79–80; in Algeria, 328; in Bahrain, 318–19, 325*n13*; in Egypt, 16–17, 19, 21, 65, 100–101, 159, 176–77, 243, 248, 255–59; in Libya, 296–97; in Morocco, 71; in Saudi Arabia, 26, 366, 369; in Syria, 310; in Tunisia, 21, 67, 90, 105–7, 146; in Yemen, 279–80, 283, 287*n5*
Saleh, Ali Abdallah, ix, xxii, xxvii–xxviii, 112, 116, 136–37, 146, 163, 167–69, 182–84, 277–83, 286–87
Saudi Arabia, xiii*t*; Arab Spring in, ix, xxxii, 16, 112, 114, 118*t*, 118, 128, 186, 364, 370; authoritarian resilience in, 302, 312; Bahrain and, xxix, 109, 114, 117, 119, 123, 138, 140, 146, 315, 317, 322–23, 357, 370; constitutional reforms in, 366; corruption in, xxxi, 364, 371; digital media in, 190, 192, 196, 198, 367–68; GCC and, 112, 119, 123, 137; human rights in, 365; Israel and,
26; Jordan and, 122, 124, 361; monarchy in, 114–15, 119, 121, 133*t*, 135, 140, 316, 374; Muslim Brotherhood in, 26; oil rents in, xxxi, 124*t*, 130–31, 357, 369; salafism in, 26; secularism in, 369; *shari'a* in, 20, 63; Shia in, xxxii, 118, 123, 364–65, 368–72; Sunnis in, 123, 368–69, 372; Syria and, 138; United States and, 122; women's rights in, 373
SCAF (Supreme Council of the Armed Forces), 31, 64, 86–87, 89, 99–102, 136, 146, 156, 166, 176, 221–22, 238–43, 245, 255, 257–58
SCPRA (Saudi Civil and Political Rights Assoc.), 265–67, 372
secularism, xv, xviii, 6, 10, 12, 16, 27–28, 44, 70, 75; in Algeria, 17, 76, 328, 331; in culture, 71–73, 78–79; democracy and, 17–18, 20, 29, 45–48, 63–64, 78, 80, 82, 218–19; in Egypt, xix–xx, xxvi, 22, 86–87, 98, 100, 103, 158–59, 176–77, 237, 239, 241–43, 249, 253, 255–59, 261, 262*n12*; in Iran, 20; Islamism and, 22–23, 26–27, 31, 33, 45–46, 51–53, 98; in Jordan, 352, 354–55; in Libya, 297; in Morocco, 71; in Pakistan, 45, 49–50; in Saudi Arabia, 369; in Syria, 305, 310; in Tunisia, xix, xxv, 17, 22, 88–90, 104–8, 158–59, 203, 211, 215–16, 220, 223–30, 232*n25*; in Turkey, 171
Senegal, xix, 82–85, 218
Serbia, 147, 157–58
shabiha militias, 304, 307
Shafiq, Ahmed, 65, 101, 243, 257–58
shari'a, xv, xvii, 6, 8–12, 14–15, 22–23, 27, 39–40, 49, 70, 75, 83; culture and, 71; in Egypt, 88, 241, 256, 258–60; in Indonesia,

83; in Libya, 297–98; in Pakistan, 45, 49–50; in Palestine, 63; in Saudi Arabia, 20, 63; support for, 60, 61*t*, 61–62; in Tunisia, 13, 21, 216, 224

Shater, Khairat al-, 31, 33–35, 41, 92, 266

Shia Islam, 26, 99, 109, 147, 173*n20*, 287*n1*; in Bahrain, xxiii, xxix, 110, 118, 120, 138, 155, 169–70, 191, 315–21; in Iran, 41; in Iraq, xii, 98; in Kuwait, 119; in Lebanon, 22; in Saudi Arabia, xxxii, 118, 123, 364–65, 368–72; in Yemen, 278

Slovakia, 147, 157–58

SMC (Supreme Military Council), 309–10

social media, xxiv, xxxii, 8, 187, 196, 199, 203, 210. *See also* digital media; Facebook; Internet; Twitter; YouTube

Solidarity, 94, 157

Soviet Union, xxii, 25, 37, 144, 147–48, 152, 254, 160, 250. *See also* Russia

Sudan, 52, 55, 118*t*, 188, 191, 239, 245

Sufis, 20, 40, 226

sultanism, xix, 81, 85, 91–92, 115, 131, 140, 142*n15*, 162; in Egypt, 93, 132, 162–63, 233; in Libya, 92–93, 155, 162–63; in Oman, 116, 191; in Syria, xix, 92–93, 116, 132, 135, 137, 139, 162–63; in Tunisia, 93–94, 132, 162–63, 165; in Yemen, 162–63

Sunni Muslims, 26, 40–41, 147, 287*n5*; in Algeria, 98; in Bahrain, xii, xx, xxiii, xxix, 99, 109, 119–20, 124*t*, 138, 148, 155, 169–70, 191, 196, 315–16, 318–23, 357; in Egypt, 98; in Iraq, xii, xix, 98, 109, 320; in Kuwait, xii, 119–20, 124*t*; in Morocco, 98; in Saudi Arabia,

123, 368–69, 372; in Syria, 99, 109, 170, 305–7, 310; in Tunisia, 98, 104, 218; in Yemen, 283

Supreme Constitutional Court, 257, 266–68

Sweden, 82, 84

Switzerland, 82, 84

Syria: Arab Spring in, 164; army in, xxiii, 129, 132, 138, 148, 170, 307; authoritarian resilience in, 97, 99, 109, 148, 152, 169, 181; Baath party in, 12, 170, 301, 305, 309; Christians in, 98, 305; civil war in, ix, xii, xviii–xxix, 26, 43, 93, 97, 112, 127, 134–45, 138, 140, 146, 193, 277, 300–309, 312–13, 322, 355, 360–61; constitution in, 311; culture in, 78; democratization in, xxii, 171–72, 312–13; digital media in, 190, 192–95, 198; economy in, 121; electoral system in, 118*t*, 133, 183, 184*t*; Facebook in, 194; human rights in, 306; Internet in, xxiv, 303; Iran and, xxi, 138, 303–305, 308, 311; Islamism in, xxix, 97, 109, 303, 305, 309–11; Israel and, 137, 302; Kurds in, 305–6; Lebanon and, xi, 137; militias in, 305, 308; minority populations in, xix, 93, 98, 137–38, 148, 155, 170, 303, 305–7, 310–11; Muslim Brotherhood in, 25, 137, 170, 309; oil rents and, xxi, 133*t*, 134; Russia and, 308, 311; salafism in, 310; Saudi Arabia and, 138; secularism in, 305, 310; sultanism in, xix, 92–93, 116, 132, 135, 137, 139, 162–63; Sunnis in, 99, 109, 170, 305–7, 310; traditional media in, 196. *See also* al-Assad

Tunisia: Arab Spring in, ix, xiii*t*,
xxiv; army in, xxiii, 94, 129, 136,
164–66, 211–12, 214–15, 225;
civil society in, xxiv; constitutional reform in, xi, xiii, xxiv,
89–90, 105–7, 179, 213–14, 219,
221–22, 226–28; democratization in, xxv, xxxii, 103–4, 134,
156, 223; digital media in, xxiv,
187–88; electoral system in, xxiii,
177, 183, 184*t*, 185, 215, 222;
Facebook in, 203, 209; Internet
in, xxiv, 188, 209; Islamism in,
xvii, xix, xx, 15–17, 24–25, 64,
66–67, 83, 88, 90, 98, 104–9,
159, 206, 211, 213, 215–16, 219–
20, 224, 229–30, 231*n10*; minorities in, 179; salafism in, 21, 67,
90, 105–7, 146; secularism in,
xix, xxv, 17, 22, 88–90, 104–8,
158–59, 203, 211, 215–16, 220,
223–30, 232*n25*; *shari'a* in, 13,
21, 216, 224; social media in,
xxiv; sultanism in, 93–94, 132,
162–63, 165; Sunnis in, 98, 104,
218; the "twin tolerations" in,
xxv, 45, 218, 223–26, 228, 230.
See also Ben Ali
"twin tolerations," the, xviii, xxv,
45, 82–84, 218–19, 223–26,
228, 230
Twitter, xxxii, 129, 149, 187–88,
193–94, 197; in Bahrain, 195;
in Morocco, 195; in Saudi Arabia, 367, 373; in Syria, 195; in
Tunisia, 196, 203, 209. *See also*
digital media; social media

Ukraine, 147, 158
ulama, 20, 38, 69, 74–75, 373
umma ("Arab nation," "community
of believers"), 15, 25, 33, 40, 43,
74, 80
Umma party (Saudi Arabia), 365–66
United Arab Emirates (UAE): Arab

Spring and, 112, 118; Bahrain
and, 138; oil rents and, 121,
124*t*; monarchy and, 114, 125*n2*,
133*t*; United States and, 122
United States: Bahrain and, 316;
democratization in, 17; Egypt
and, 166, 239, 251; Jordan and,
353, 361; Libya and, 139–40,
168; patronage of, 114, 122;
Syria and, 304; Tunisia and,
211–12; Yemen and, 278

Wahhabi, xxxi, 26, 119, 364, 369
We Are All Khaled Said, 189, 254,
261
Weltanschauung politics (WP), xv,
10–12

Yemen, xiii*t*; al Qaeda in, 19, 169,
278–79, 283, 288*n13*; Arab
Spring and, xvii–xviii, 133–35,
140; army in, xxiii, 149, 162,
164, 168, 172; authoritarian resilience in, xi–xii, xvii, xxi, 118*t*,
137, 148, 152, 192; civil war
in, 149, 168–69, 172, 182, 184,
193, 287; corruption in, xxvii,
167, 278, 280–81, 283; democratization in, xiv, xxii, 127, 137,
172; economy in, 121; electoral
system in, 183, 184*t*, 284; fragmentation of, 109, 146, 277–78;
Islamism in, 60–64, 98; support
for democracy in, 55, 56*f*, 57–59,
58*t*; tribalism in, 137, 167
YouTube, 129, 187–88, 197; in
Saudi Arabia, 368, 373; in Syria,
194; in Tunisia, 209. *See also*
digital media; social media
YSP (Yemeni Socialist Party), 277,
279, 284

Zia ul-Haq, Muhammed, xvii, 45,
49–50
Zionism, 19, 252